Sweet Blue Flowers

Part Five

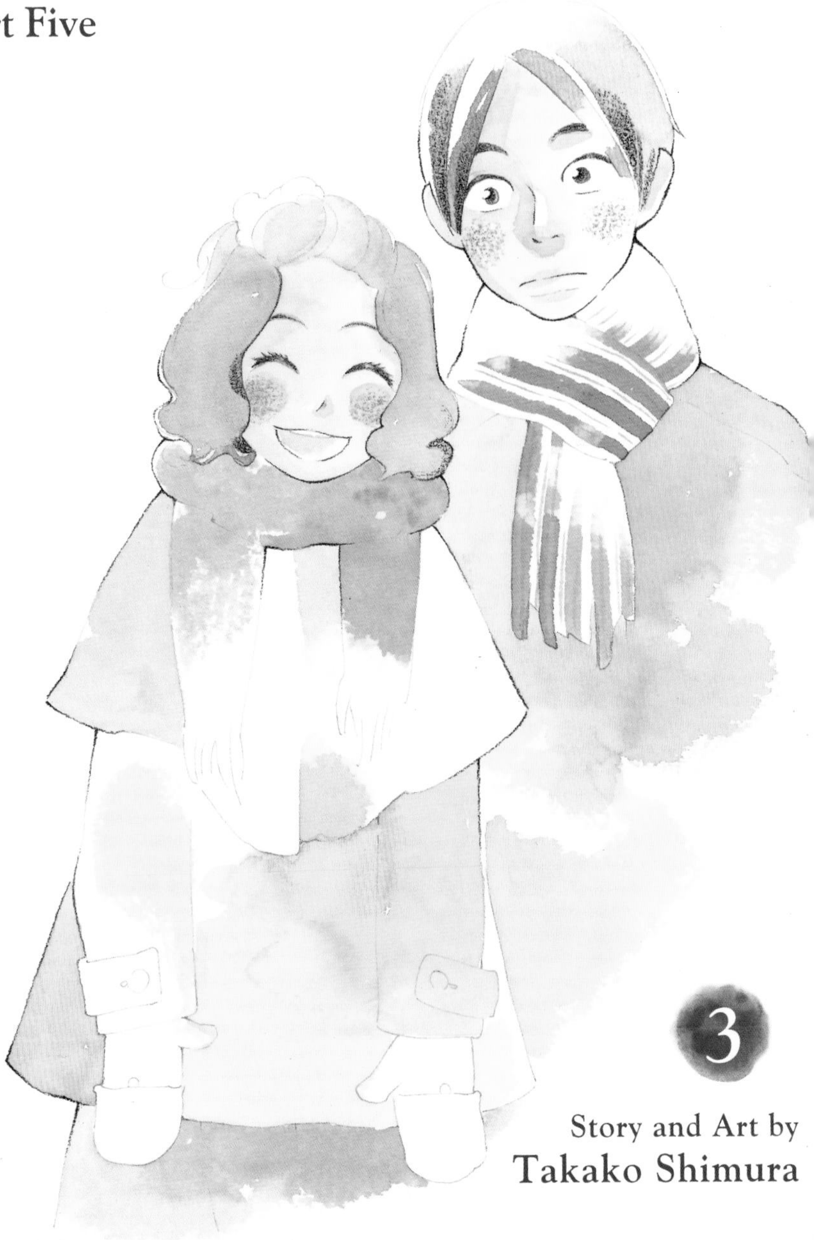

3

Story and Art by
Takako Shimura

Sweet Blue Flowers

Part Five

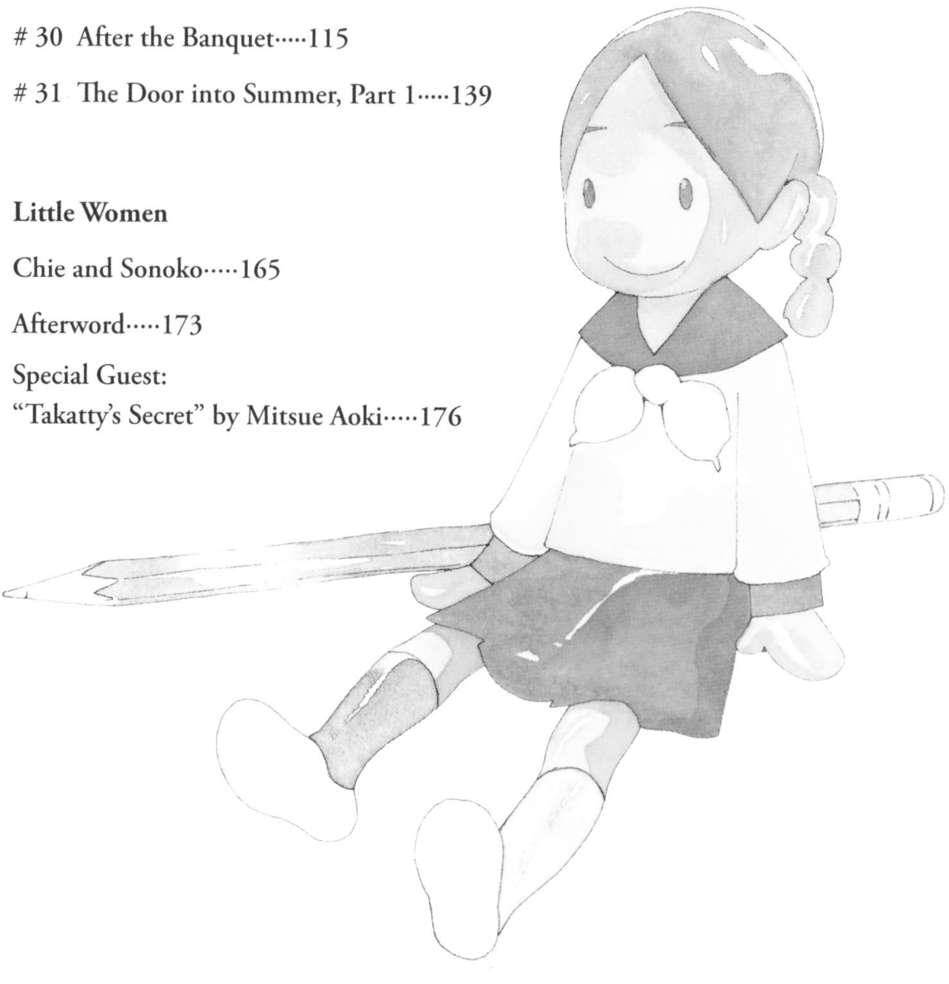

Sweet Blue Flowers

Characters

Fujigaya Women's Academy High School

Kyoko Ikumi

Year 2. Like Akira, she's a member of the Drama Club. The other girls admire her for her maturity. Despite her engagement to Ko Sawanoi, she's had a one-sided crush on Yasuko Sugimoto since junior high.

Akira Okudaira

Year 2. She's small, innocent and honest, and has yet to experience love. Akira has felt uncomfortable ever since her childhood friend Fumi told her she likes her.

Hinako Yamashina

Science teacher. She is Akira's homeroom teacher and a graduate of Fujigaya. Her girlfriend is Haruka Ono's older sister Orie.

Haruka Ono

Year 1. She's an energetic girl who joined the Drama Club because she admires theater, and now she's becoming good friends with a lot of older students.

Ryoko Ueda

Year 2. She's in the same class as Akira. She's a member of the Library Club but plans to make a guest appearance onstage at the Fujigaya Theater Festival.

Matsuoka Girls' High School

Fumi Manjome

Year 2. She's tall and pretty—and a worrywart crybaby. She recently realized that Akira was her first love, but they're close friends, so she's trying to suppress her feelings even as they deepen.

Yasuko Sugimoto

She dated Fumi while she was a student at Matsuoka, but the relationship fell apart after a few months. Currently she's studying in England. At Matsuoka, she was seen as the popular princely type, but inside she was clinging to childish feelings for her first love.

Miwa Motegi

Year 2. Nickname: Mogi. She's a quiet girl who is a member of the Drama Club. She's dating Akira's older brother Shinobu.

Misako Yasuda

Year 2. Nickname: Yassan. She's the head of the school's very small and informal Drama Club. She has a boyish personality.

Yoko Honatsugi

Year 2. Nickname: Pon. She's a member of the Drama Club. She has a bright personality and isn't afraid of anything.

Chizu Hanashiro

Fumi's cousin on her mother's side. She was Fumi's first girlfriend, but she surprised Fumi by getting married.

Ko Sawanoi

Kyoko Ikumi's fiancé. He's in his second year at university. He has a gentle and considerate personality, and he's serious about Kyoko.

Shinobu Okudaira

Akira's brother. He's in his third year at university. He has a serious sister complex, but maybe he's beginning to change now that he's dating Miwa Motegi?

Sweet *Blue* *Flowers*

#26 Rokumeikan, Part 5

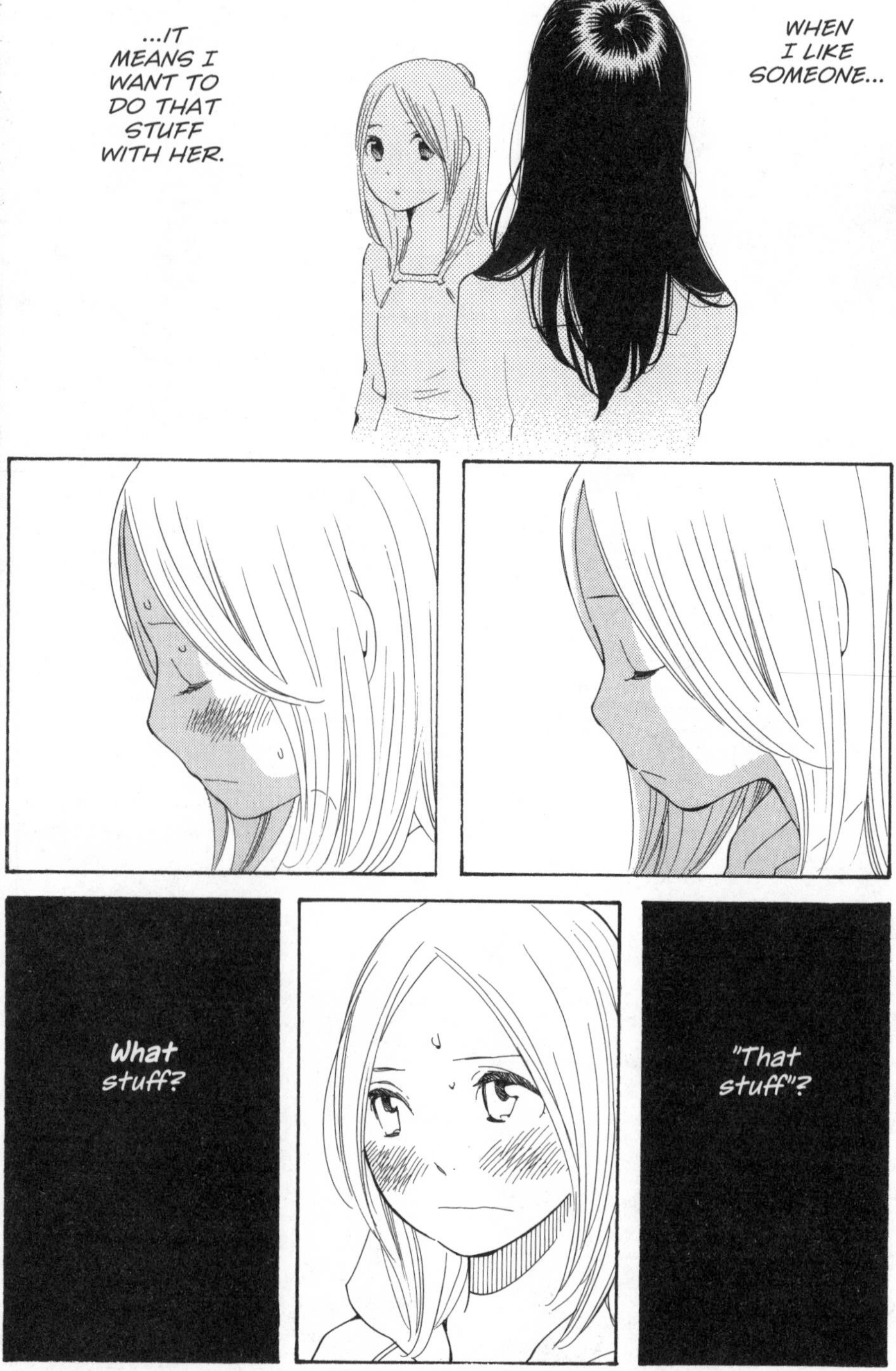
WHEN I LIKE SOMEONE...
...IT MEANS I WANT TO DO THAT STUFF WITH HER.
"That stuff"?
What stuff?

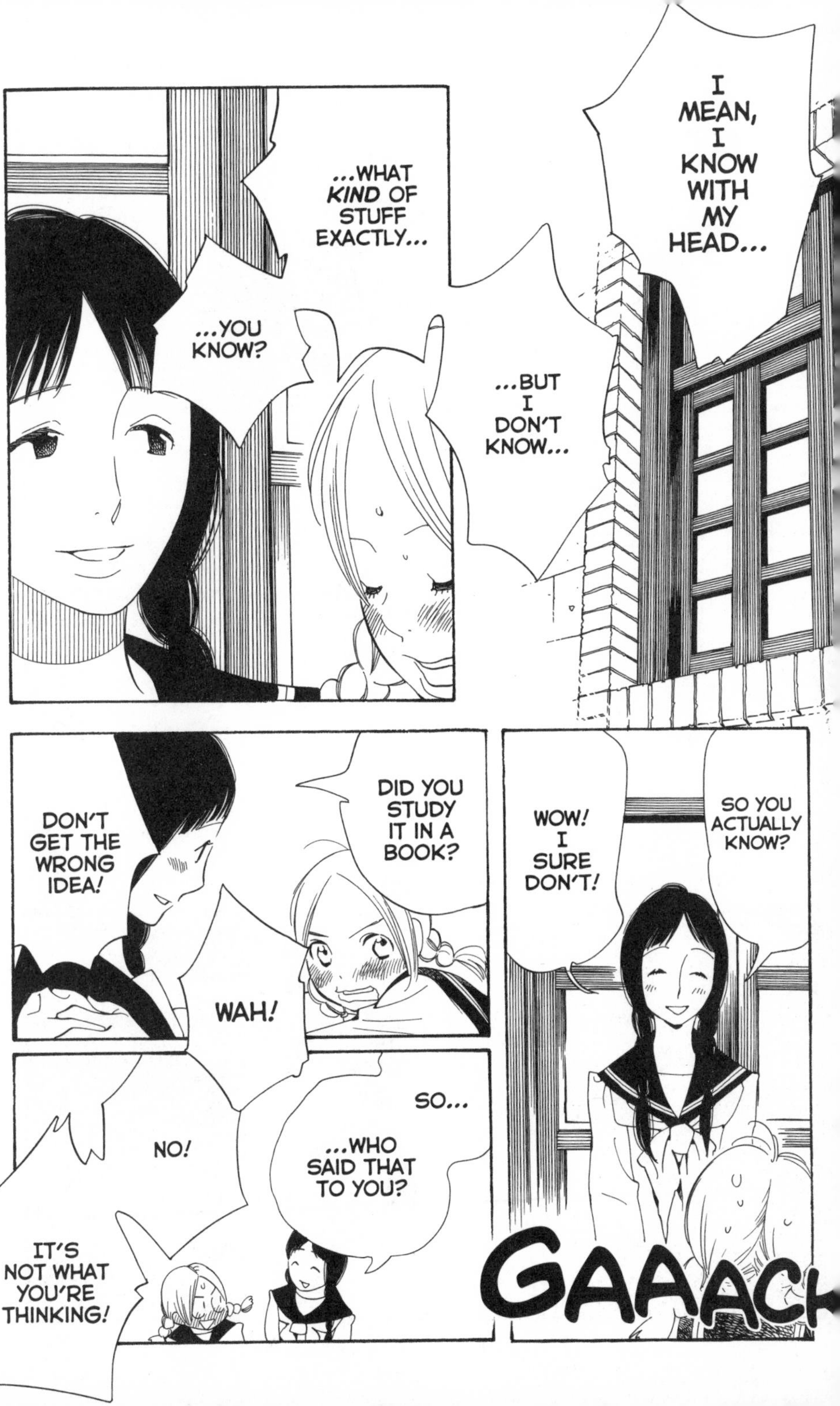
I MEAN, I KNOW WITH MY HEAD...
...BUT I DON'T KNOW...
...WHAT KIND OF STUFF EXACTLY...
...YOU KNOW?
SO YOU ACTUALLY KNOW?
WOW! I SURE DON'T!
GAAACK
DID YOU STUDY IT IN A BOOK?
DON'T GET THE WRONG IDEA!
WAH!
SO...
...WHO SAID THAT TO YOU?
NO!
IT'S NOT WHAT YOU'RE THINKING!

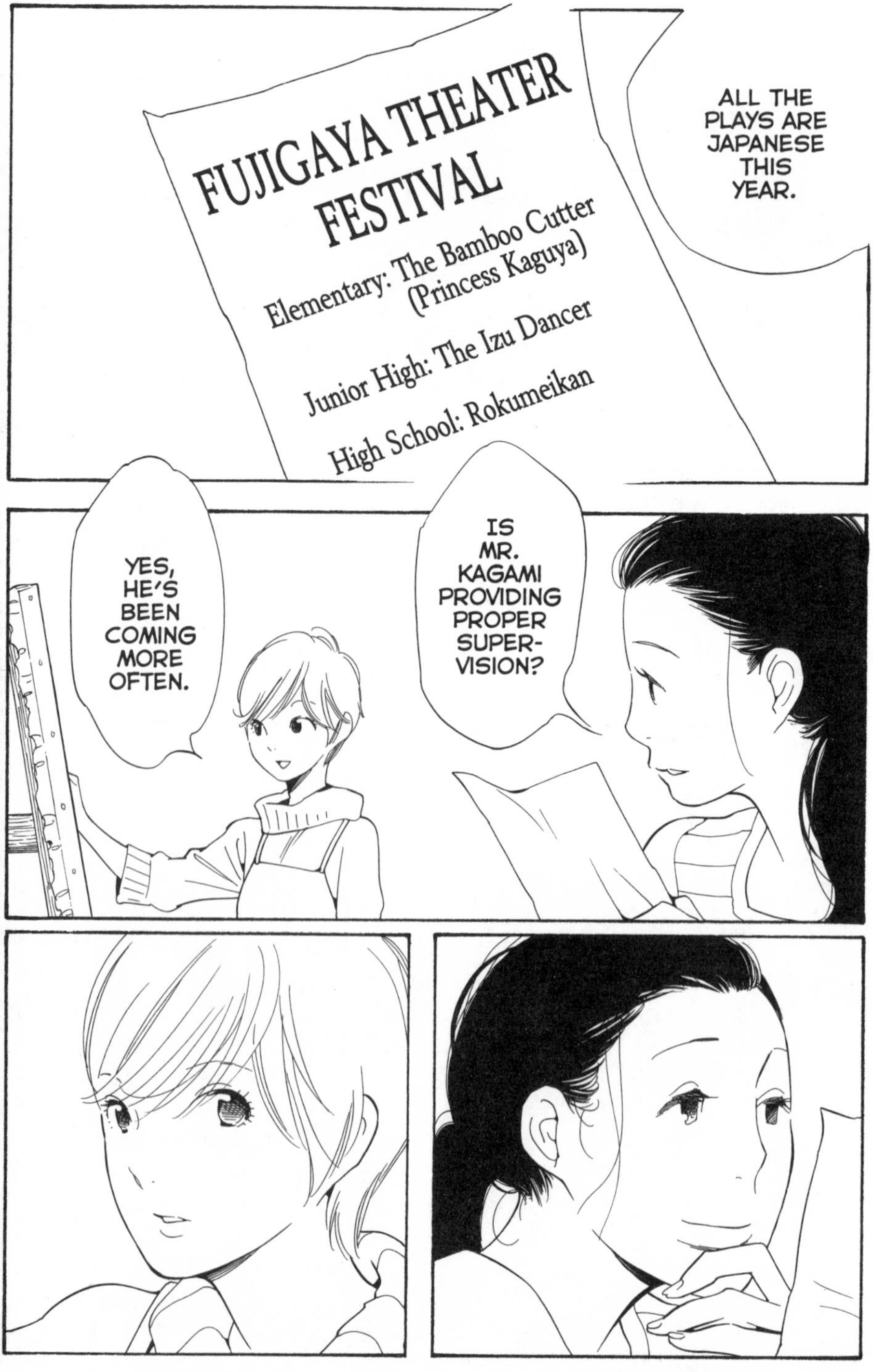
ALL THE PLAYS ARE JAPANESE THIS YEAR.
FUJIGAYA THEATER FESTIVAL
Elementary: The Bamboo Cutter (Princess Kaguya)
Junior High: The Izu Dancer
High School: Rokumeikan
IS MR. KAGAMI PROVIDING PROPER SUPER-VISION?
YES, HE'S BEEN COMING MORE OFTEN.

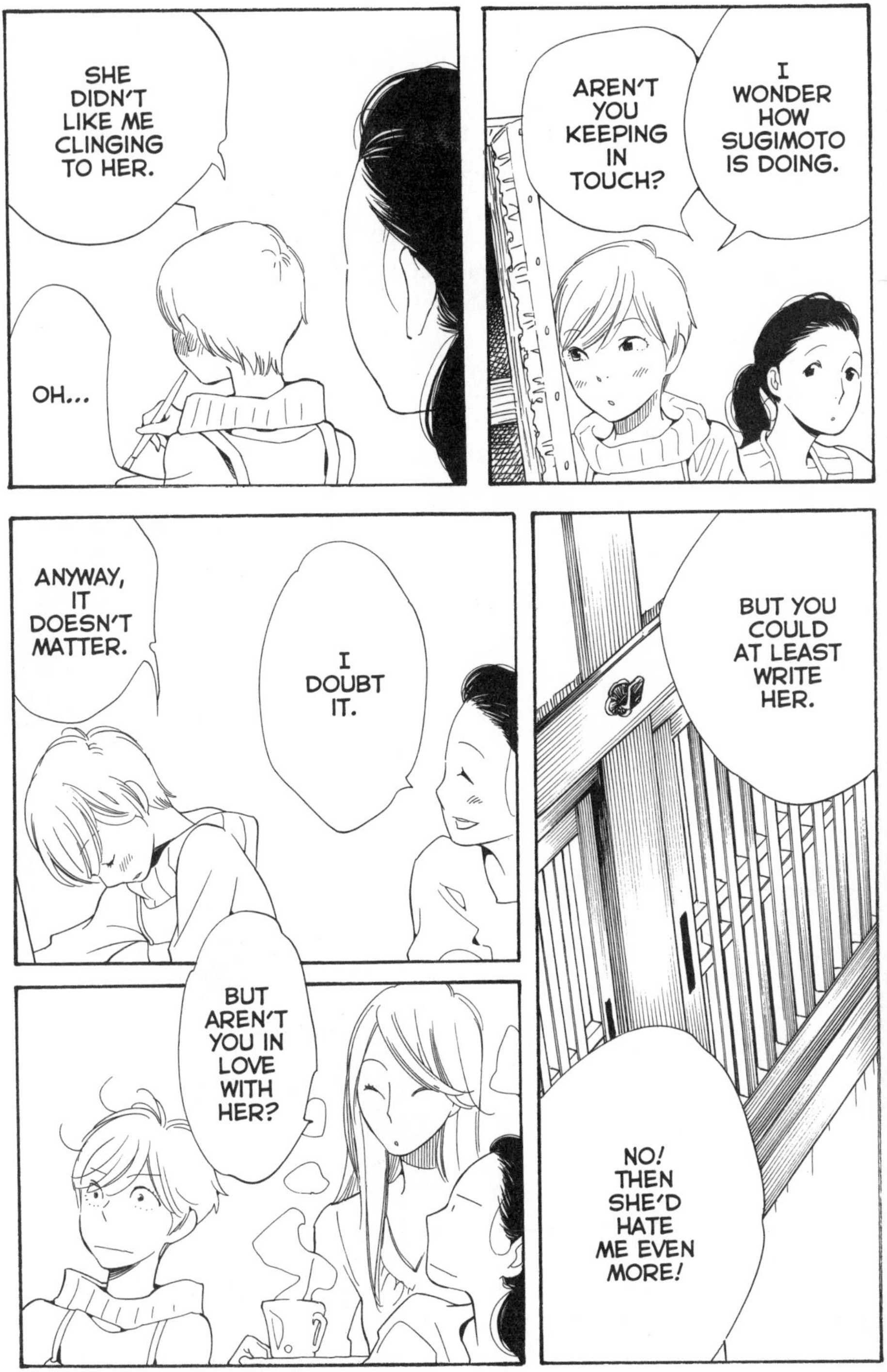
I WONDER HOW SUGIMOTO IS DOING.
AREN'T YOU KEEPING IN TOUCH?
SHE DIDN'T LIKE ME CLINGING TO HER.
OH...
BUT YOU COULD AT LEAST WRITE HER.
NO! THEN SHE'D HATE ME EVEN MORE!
ANYWAY, IT DOESN'T MATTER.
I DOUBT IT.
BUT AREN'T YOU IN LOVE WITH HER?

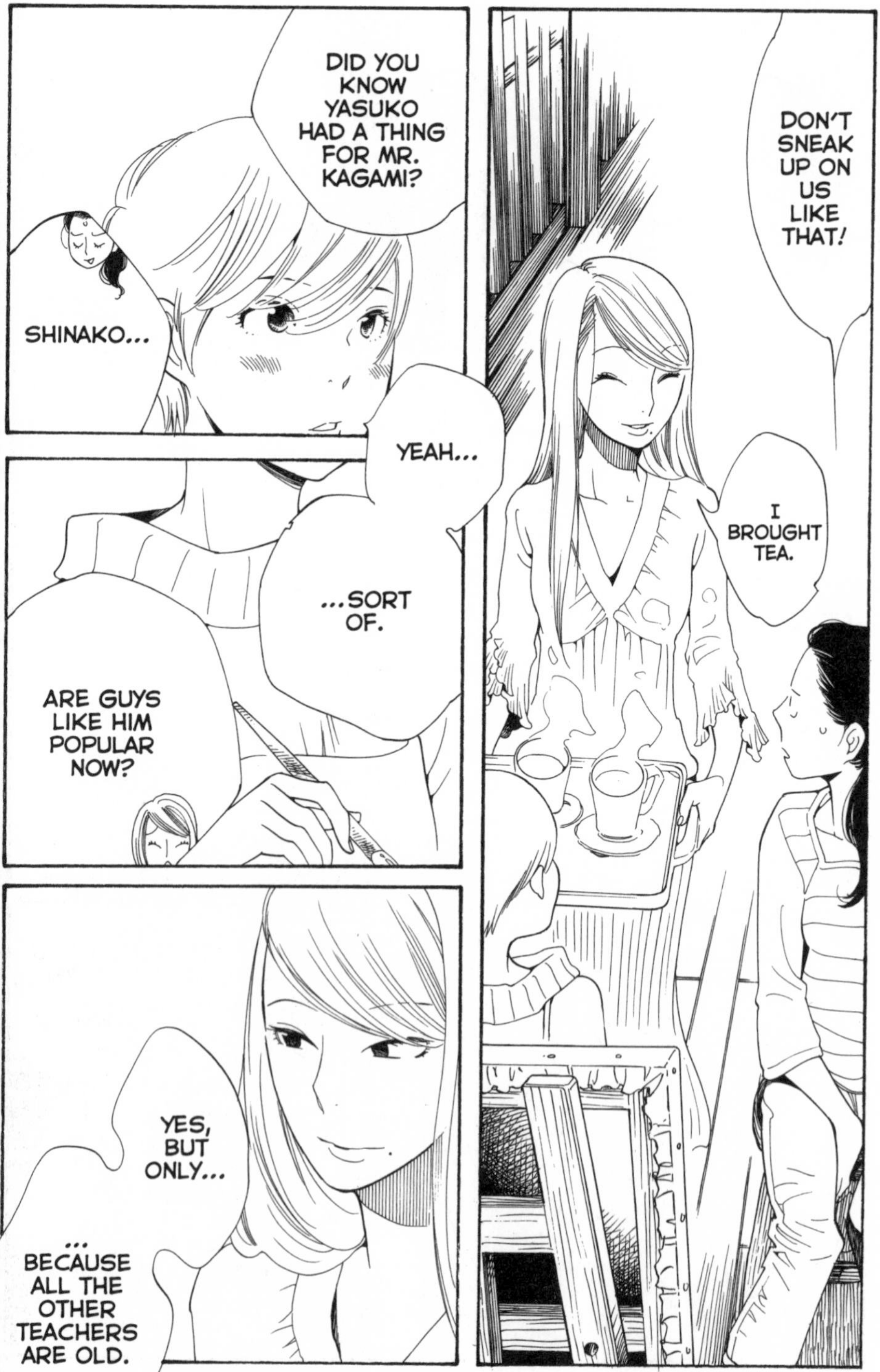
DON'T SNEAK UP ON US LIKE THAT!
I BROUGHT TEA.
DID YOU KNOW YASUKO HAD A THING FOR MR. KAGAMI?
SHINAKO...
YEAH...
...SORT OF.
ARE GUYS LIKE HIM POPULAR NOW?
YES, BUT ONLY...
... BECAUSE ALL THE OTHER TEACHERS ARE OLD.

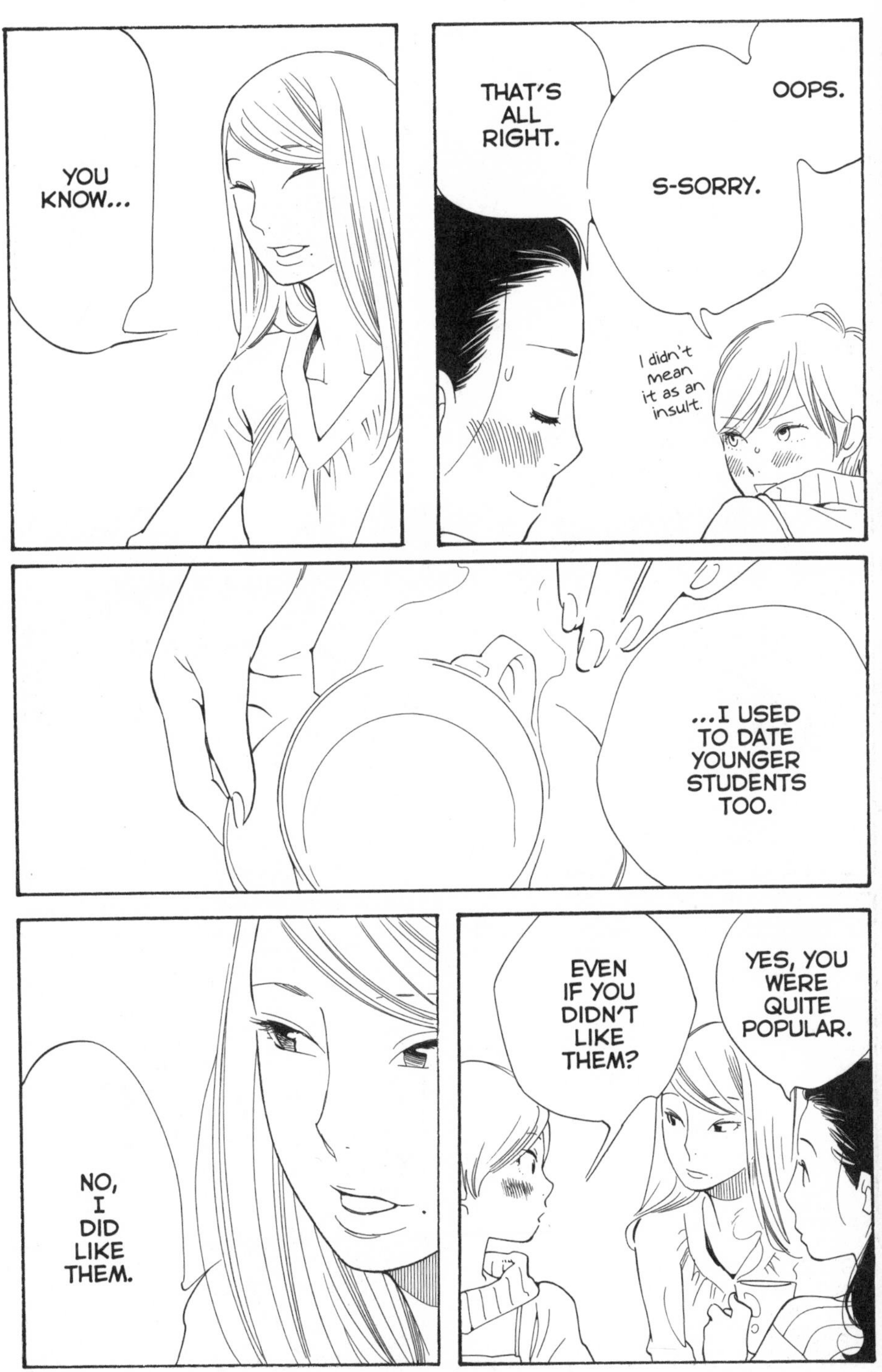
OOPS.
S-SORRY.
THAT'S ALL RIGHT.
I didn't mean it as an insult.
YOU KNOW...
...I USED TO DATE YOUNGER STUDENTS TOO.
YES, YOU WERE QUITE POPULAR.
EVEN IF YOU DIDN'T LIKE THEM?
NO, I DID LIKE THEM.

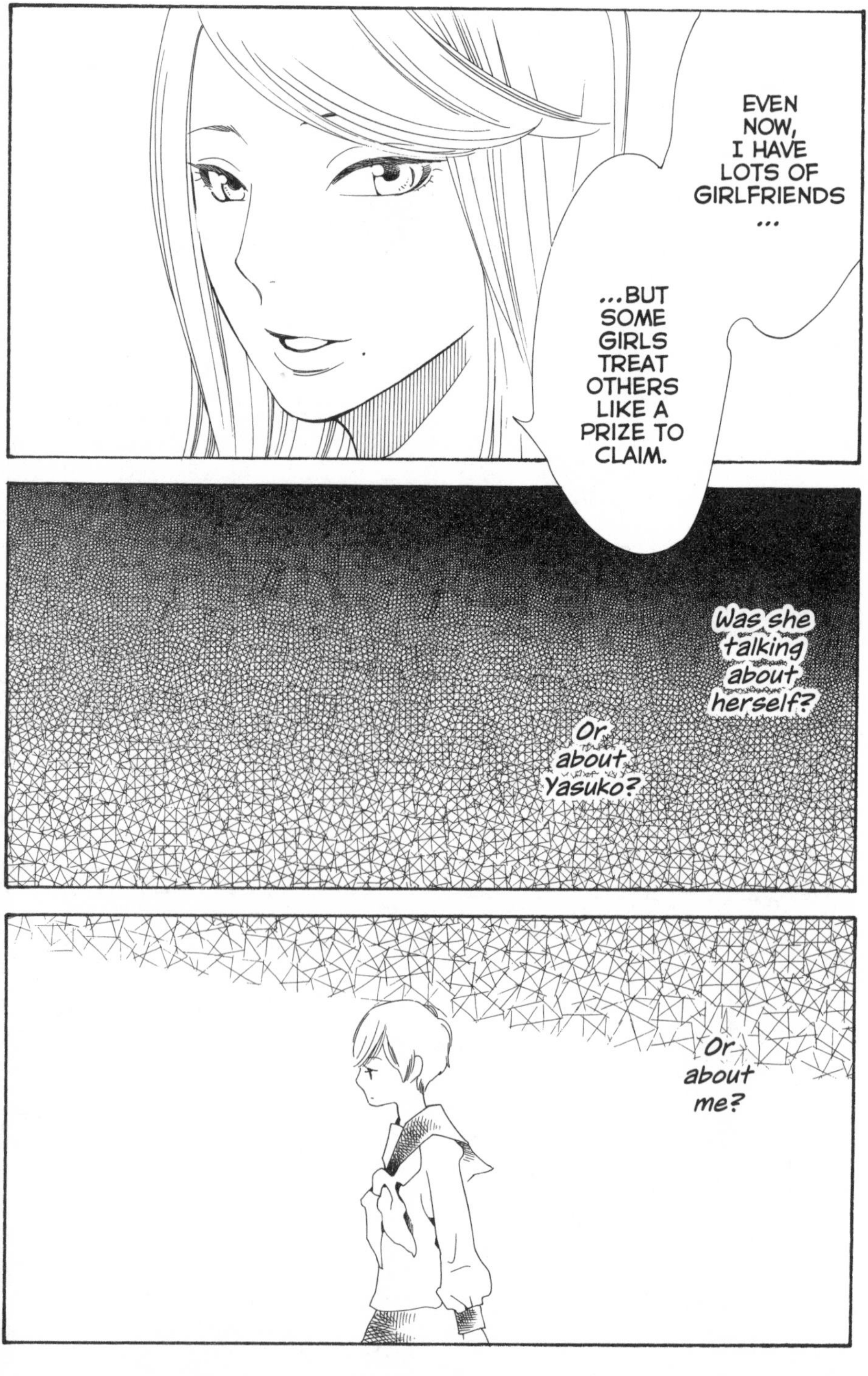
EVEN NOW, I HAVE LOTS OF GIRLFRIENDS ...
...BUT SOME GIRLS TREAT OTHERS LIKE A PRIZE TO CLAIM.
Was she talking about herself?
Or about Yasuko?
Or about me?

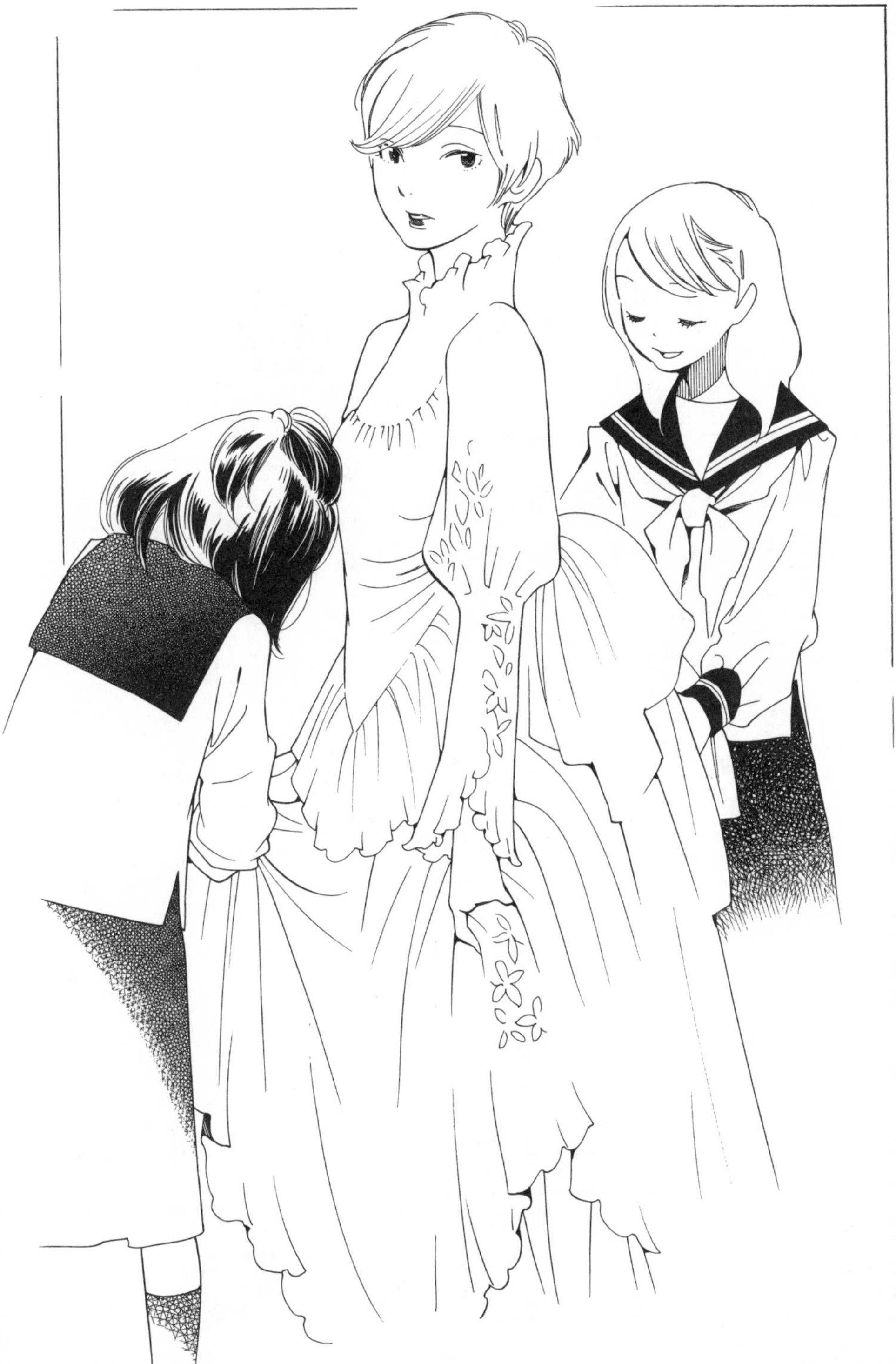

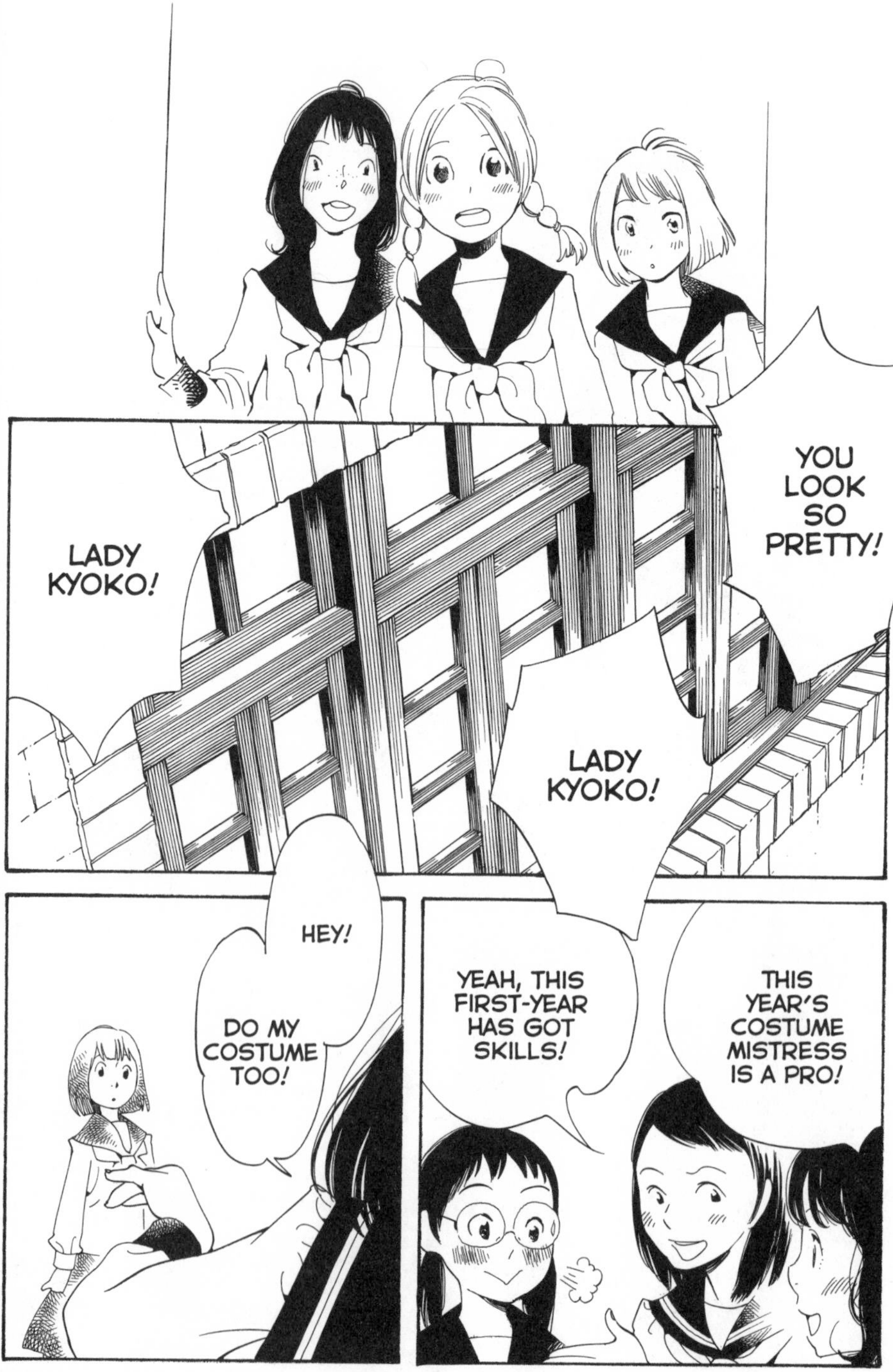
YOU LOOK SO PRETTY!
LADY KYOKO!
LADY KYOKO!
THIS YEAR'S COSTUME MISTRESS IS A PRO!
YEAH, THIS FIRST-YEAR HAS GOT SKILLS!
HEY!
DO MY COSTUME TOO!

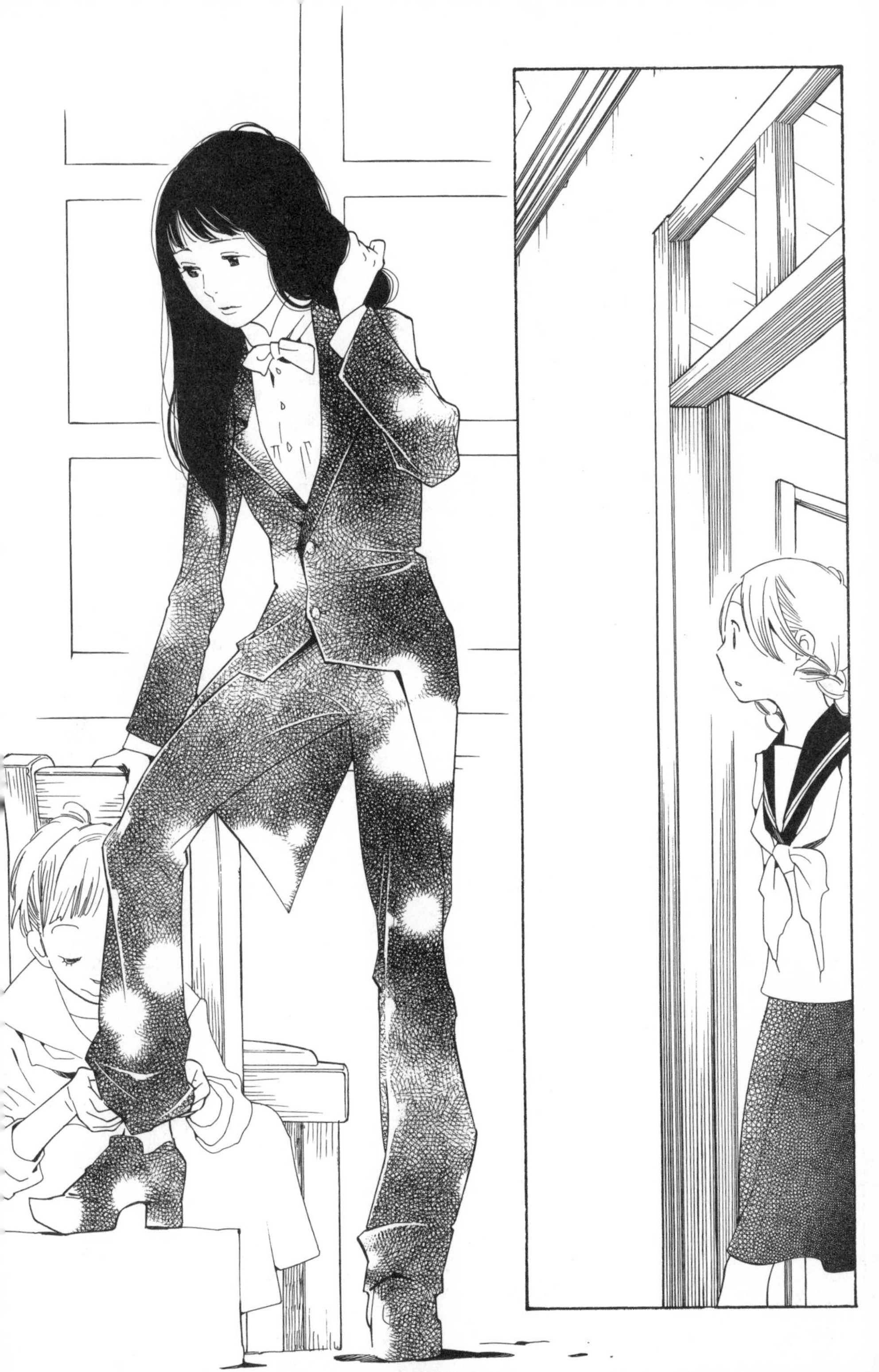

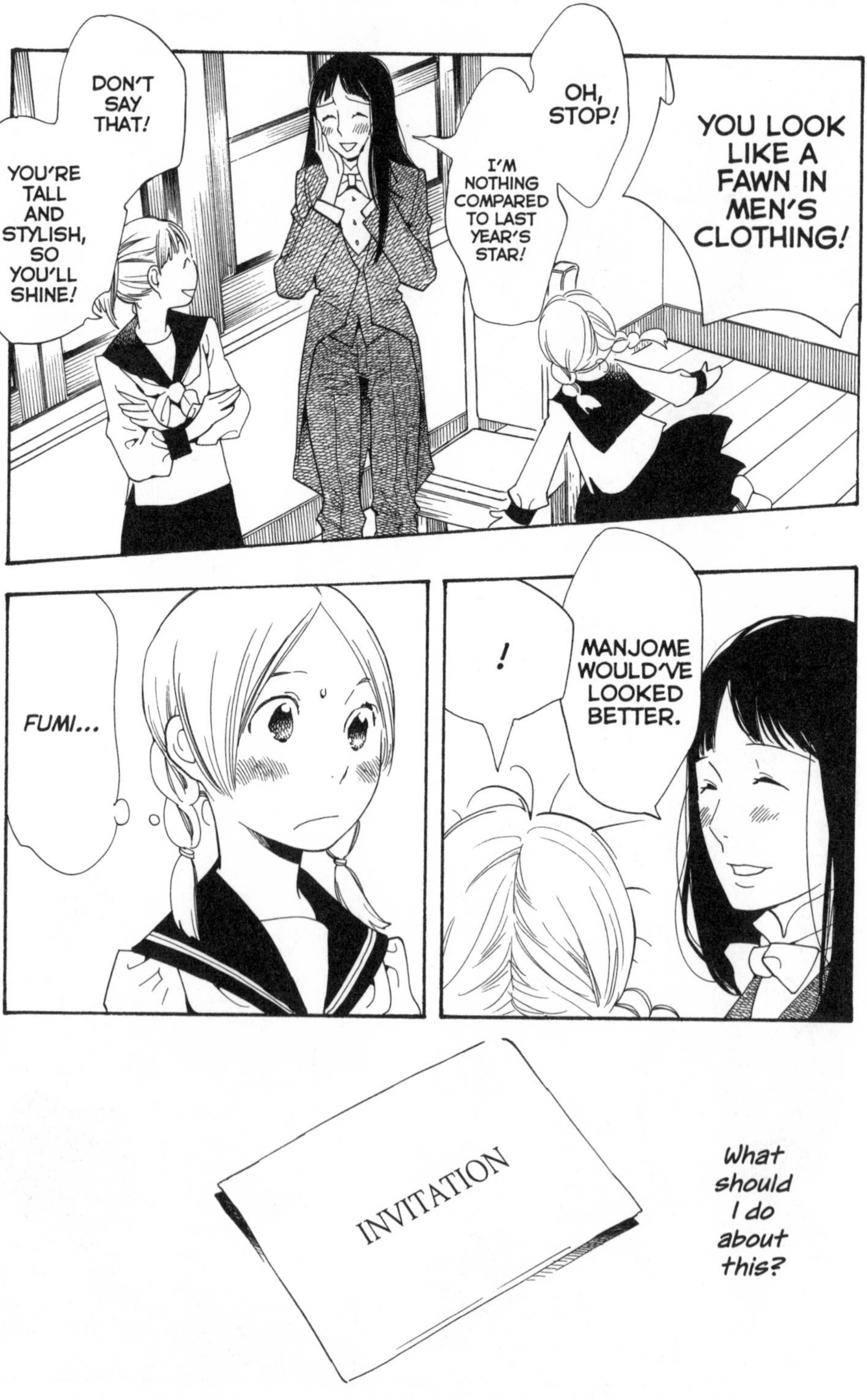
YOU LOOK LIKE A FAWN IN MEN'S CLOTHING!
OH, STOP!
I'M NOTHING COMPARED TO LAST YEAR'S STAR!
DON'T SAY THAT!
YOU'RE TALL AND STYLISH, SO YOU'LL SHINE!
MANJOME WOULD'VE LOOKED BETTER.
!
FUMI...
What should I do about this?
INVITATION

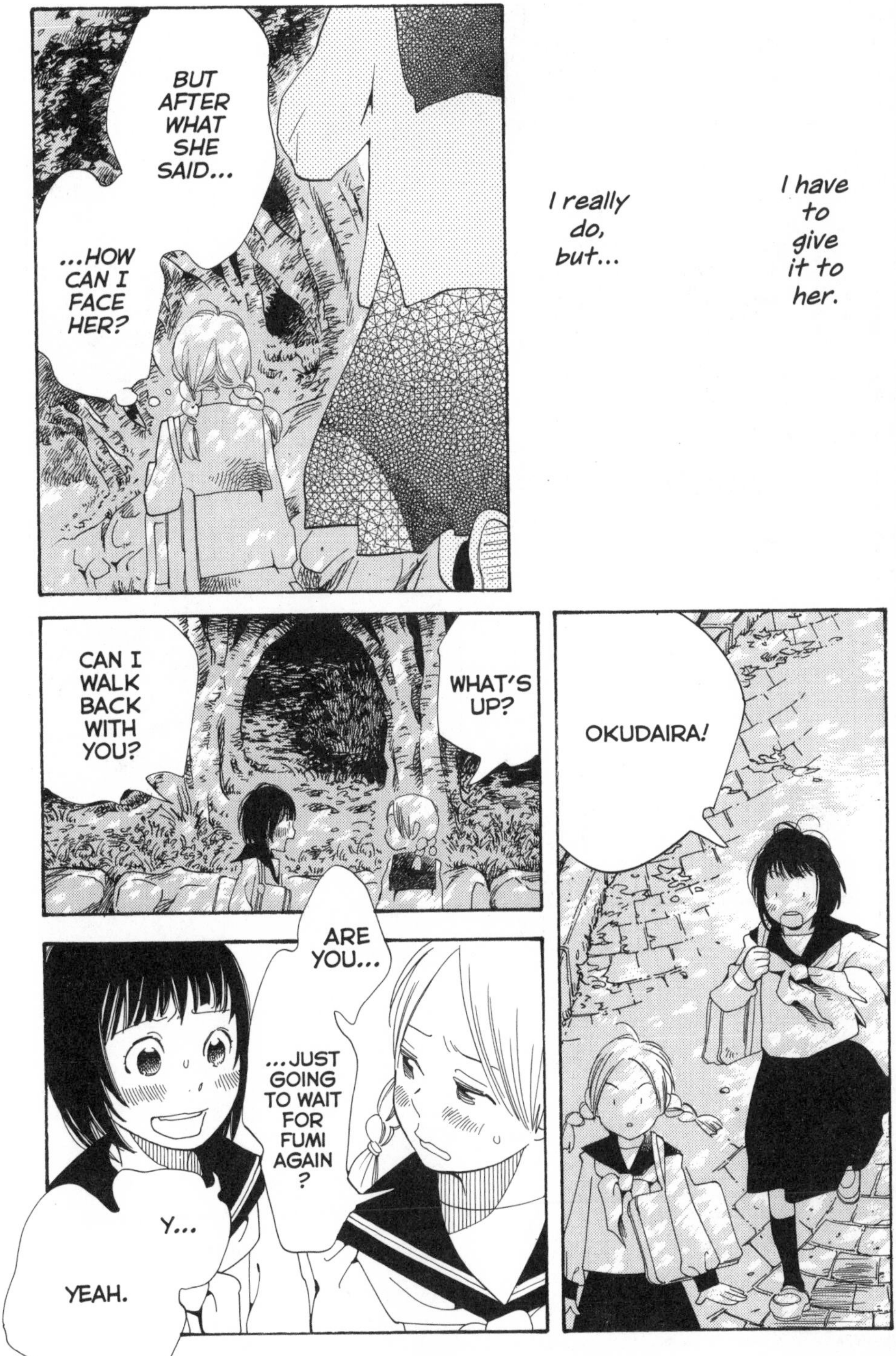
I have to give it to her.
I really do, but...
BUT AFTER WHAT SHE SAID...
...HOW CAN I FACE HER?
OKUDAIRA!
WHAT'S UP?
CAN I WALK BACK WITH YOU?
ARE YOU...
...JUST GOING TO WAIT FOR FUMI AGAIN?
Y...
YEAH.

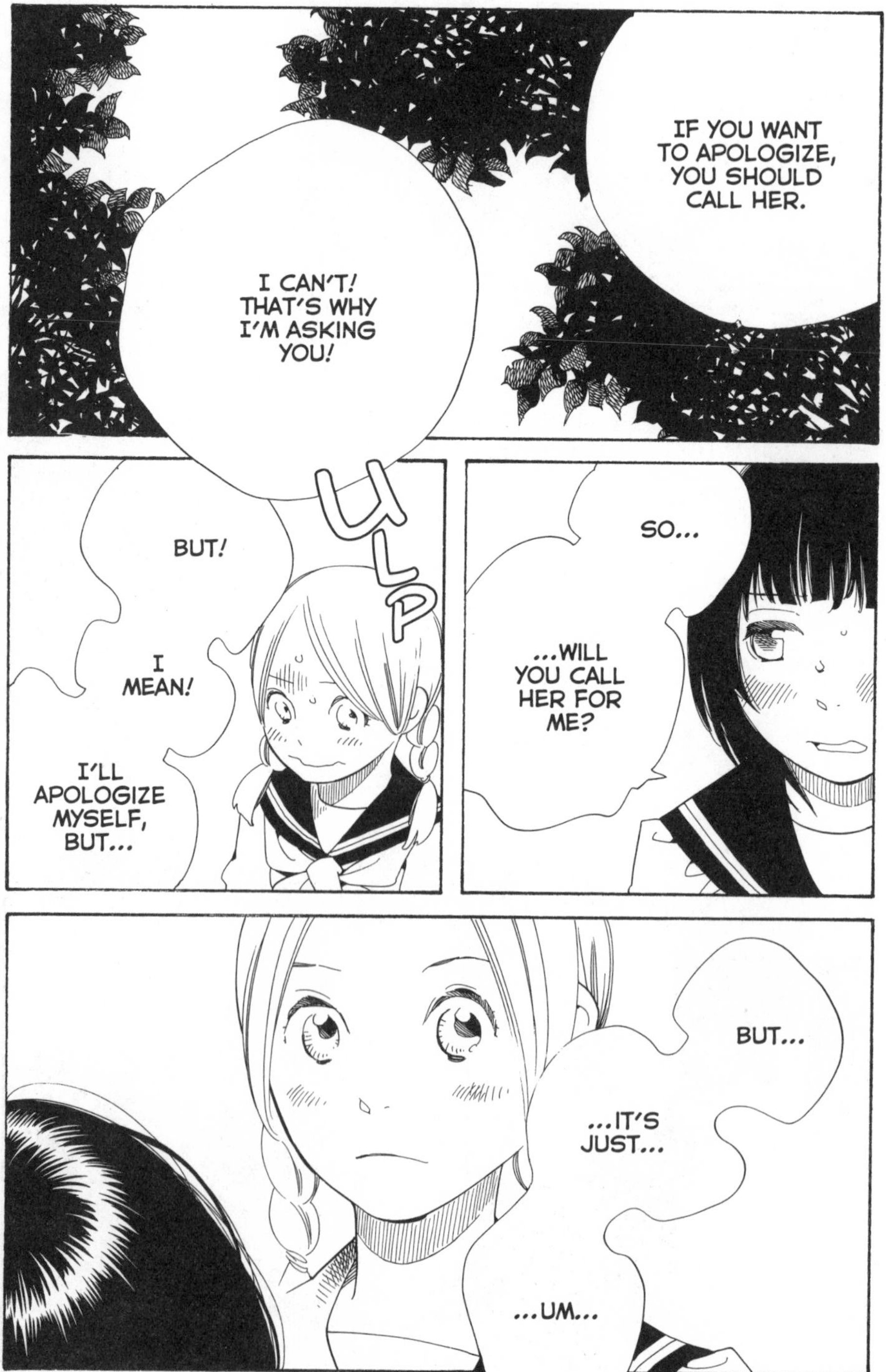
IF YOU WANT TO APOLOGIZE, YOU SHOULD CALL HER.
I CAN'T! THAT'S WHY I'M ASKING YOU!
SO...
...WILL YOU CALL HER FOR ME?
ULP
BUT!
I MEAN!
I'LL APOLOGIZE MYSELF, BUT...
BUT...
...IT'S JUST...
...UM...

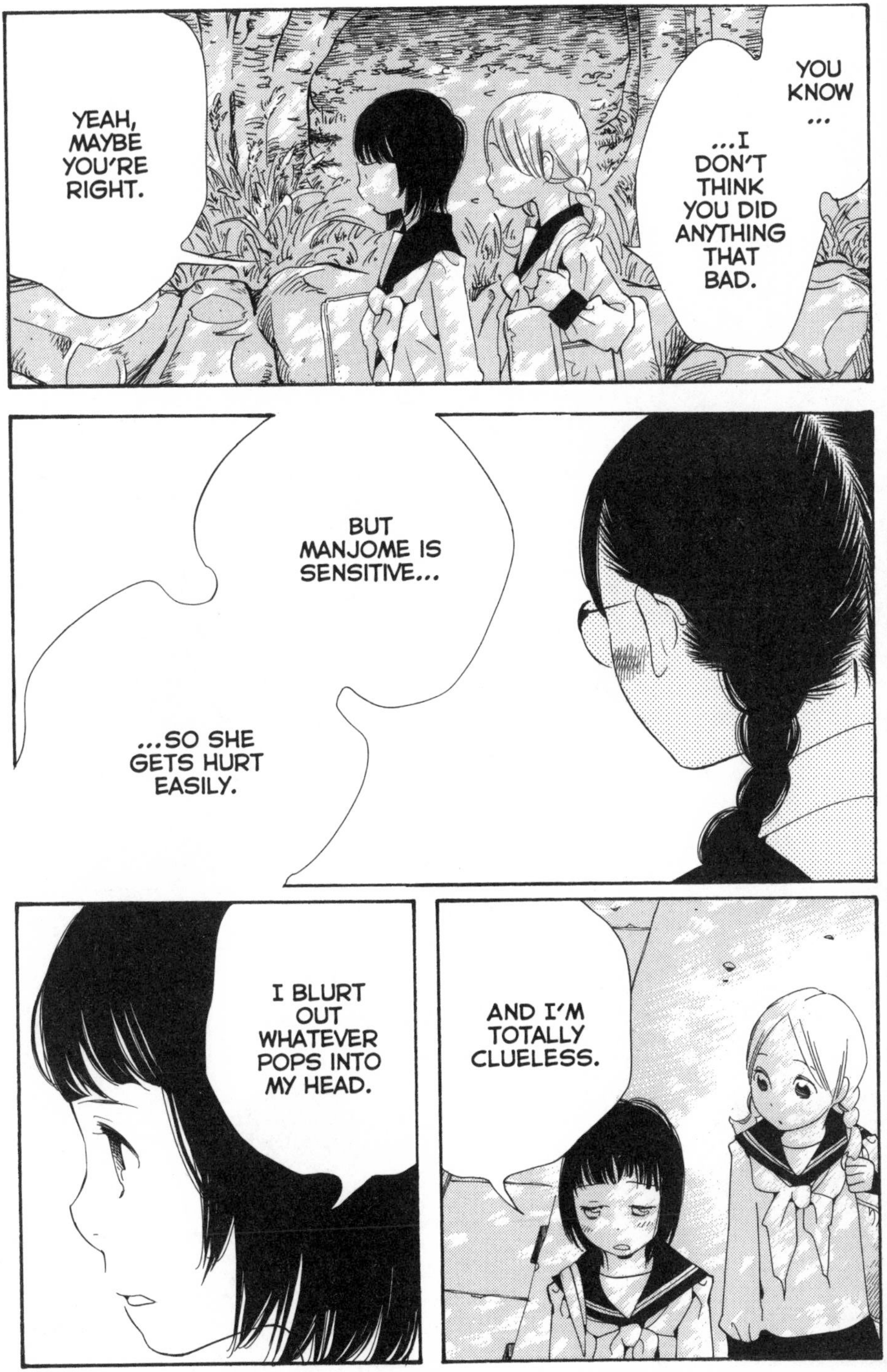
YOU KNOW ...
...I DON'T THINK YOU DID ANYTHING THAT BAD.
YEAH, MAYBE YOU'RE RIGHT.
BUT MANJOME IS SENSITIVE...
...SO SHE GETS HURT EASILY.
AND I'M TOTALLY CLUELESS.
I BLURT OUT WHATEVER POPS INTO MY HEAD.

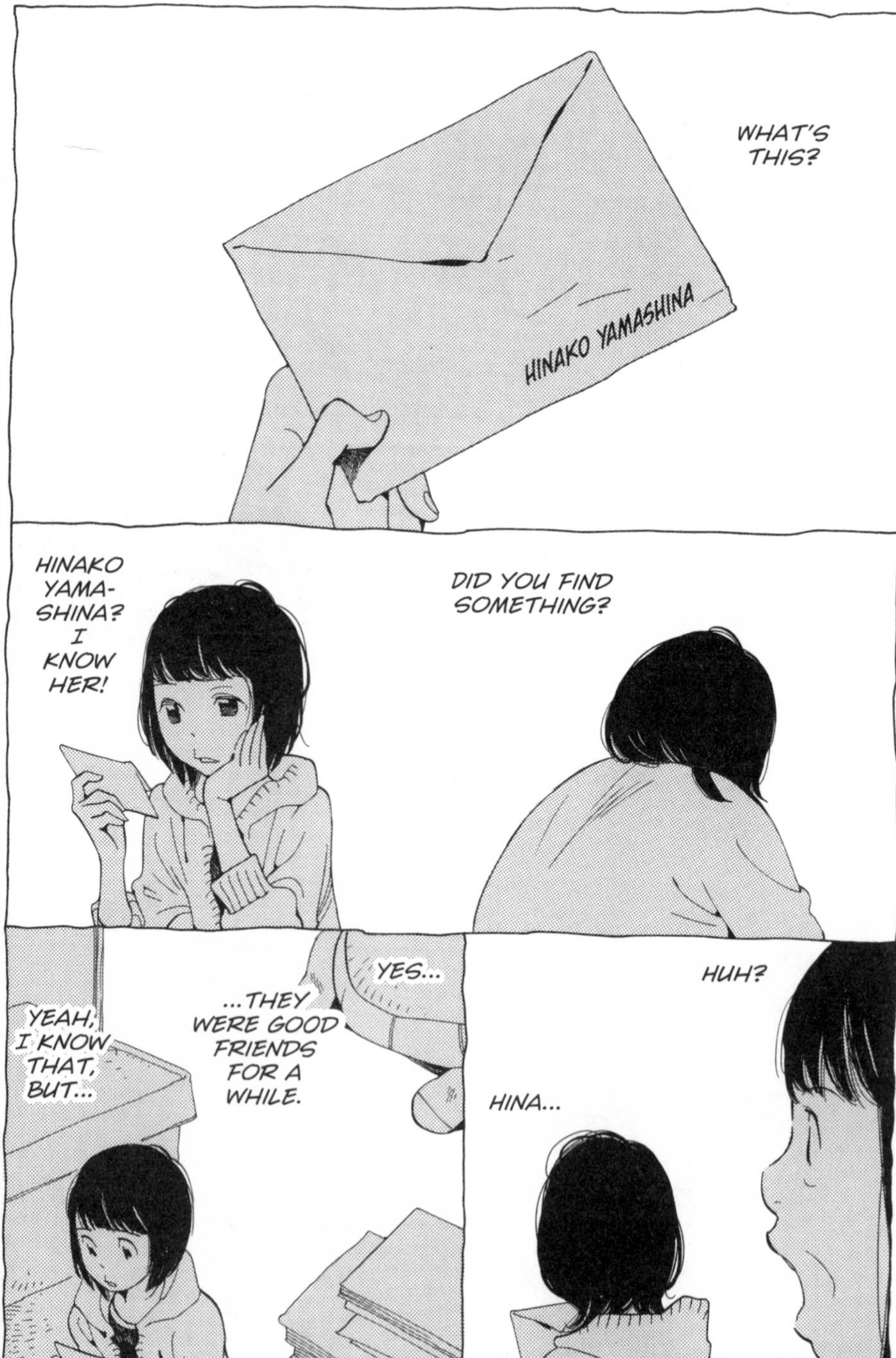
WHAT'S THIS?
HINAKO YAMASHINA
DID YOU FIND SOMETHING?
HINAKO YAMA-SHINA? I KNOW HER!
HUH?
HINA...
YES...
...THEY WERE GOOD FRIENDS FOR A WHILE.
YEAH, I KNOW THAT, BUT...

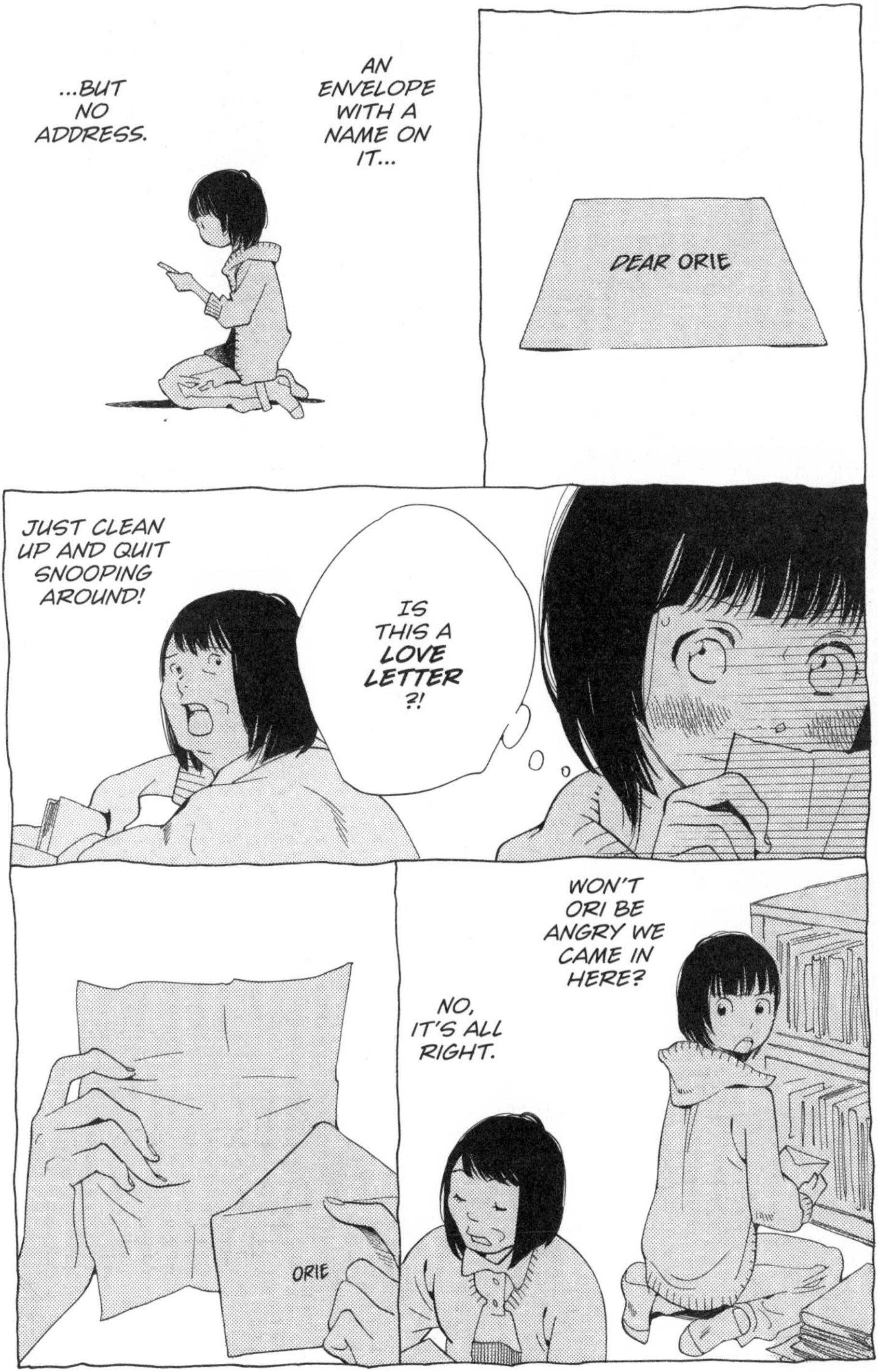
DEAR ORIE
AN ENVELOPE WITH A NAME ON IT...
...BUT NO ADDRESS.
IS THIS A LOVE LETTER ?!
JUST CLEAN UP AND QUIT SNOOPING AROUND!
WON'T ORI BE ANGRY WE CAME IN HERE?
NO, IT'S ALL RIGHT.
ORIE

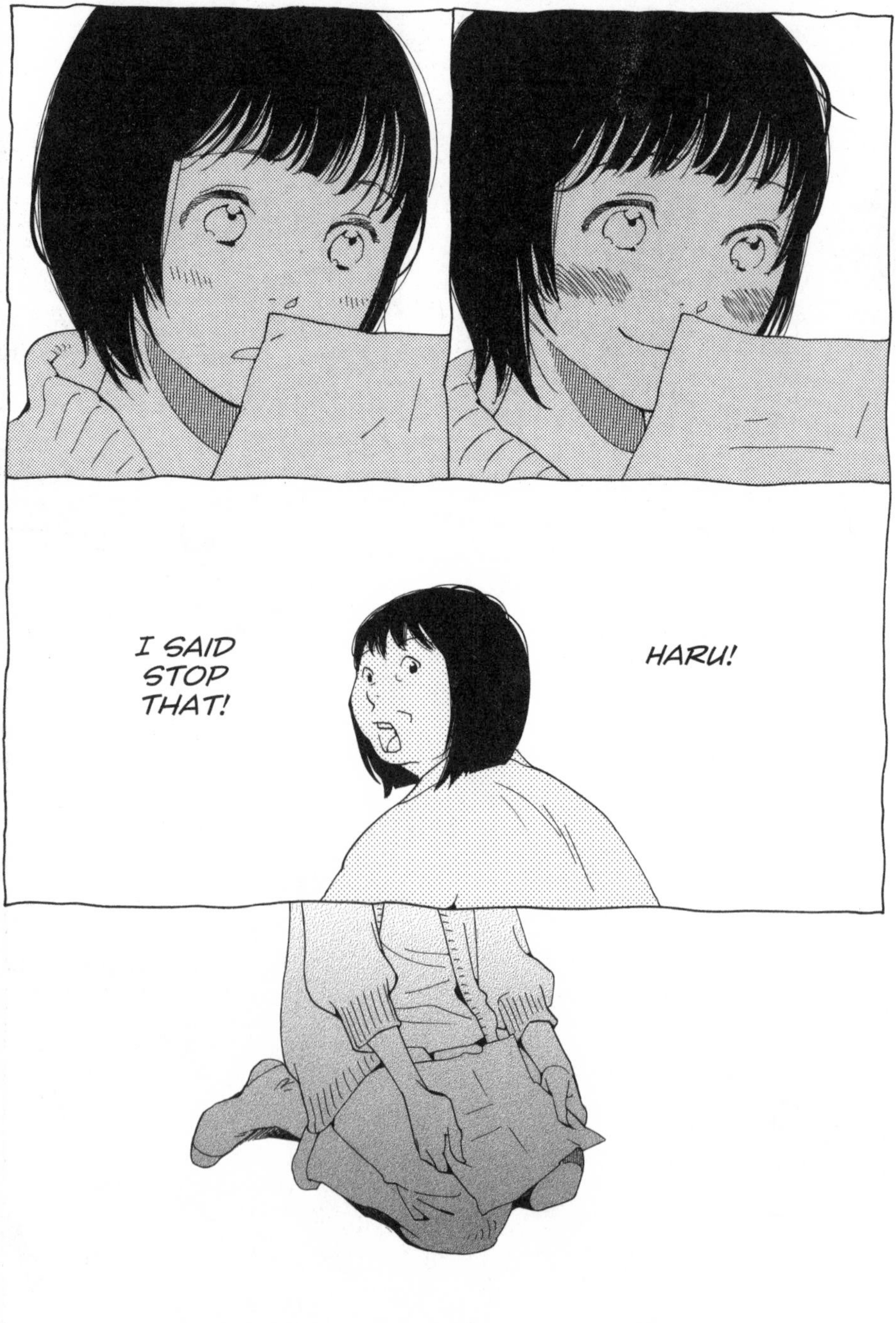
HARU!
I SAID STOP THAT!

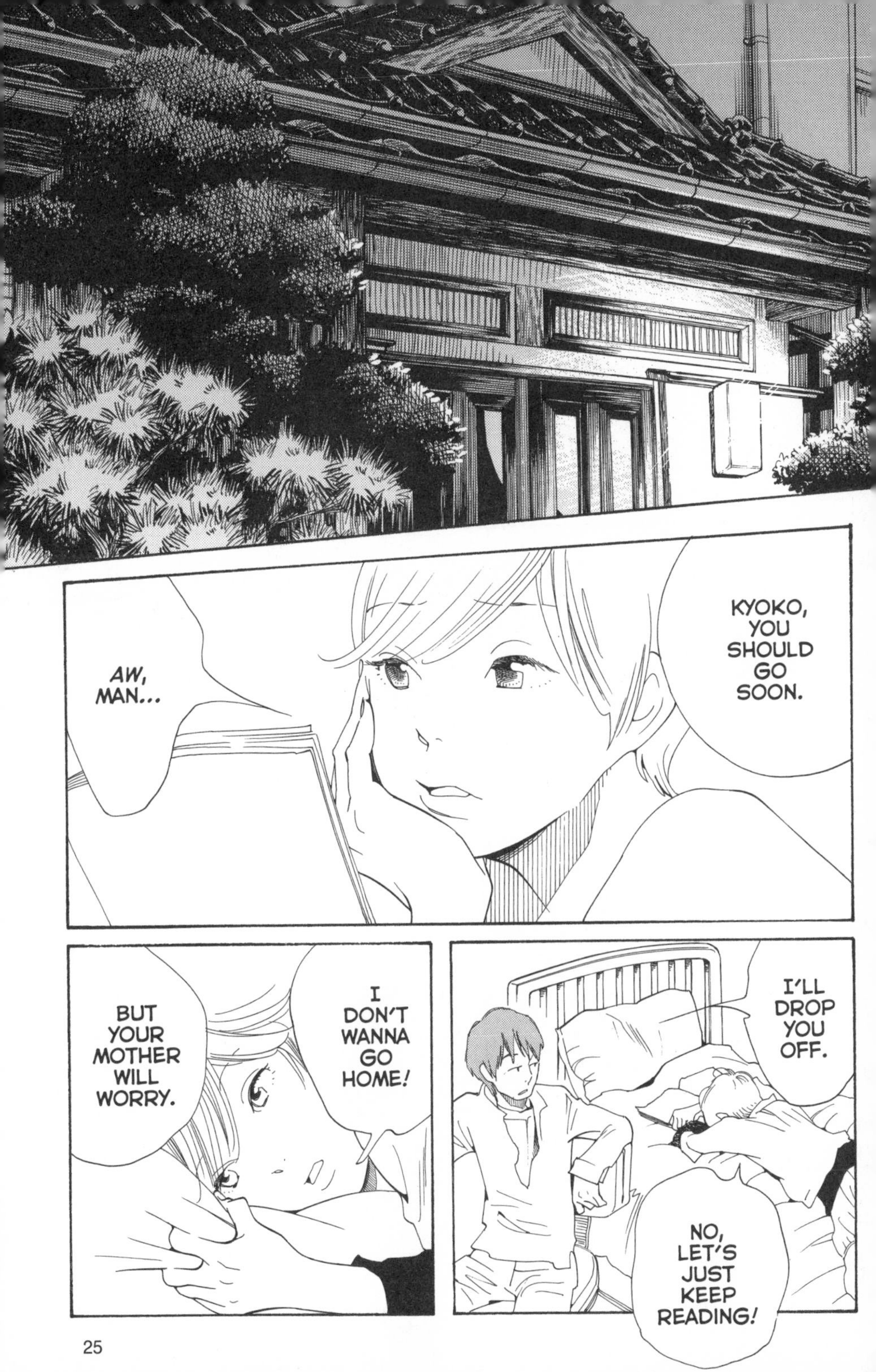
KYOKO, YOU SHOULD GO SOON.
AW, MAN...
I'LL DROP YOU OFF.
NO, LET'S JUST KEEP READING!
I DON'T WANNA GO HOME!
BUT YOUR MOTHER WILL WORRY.

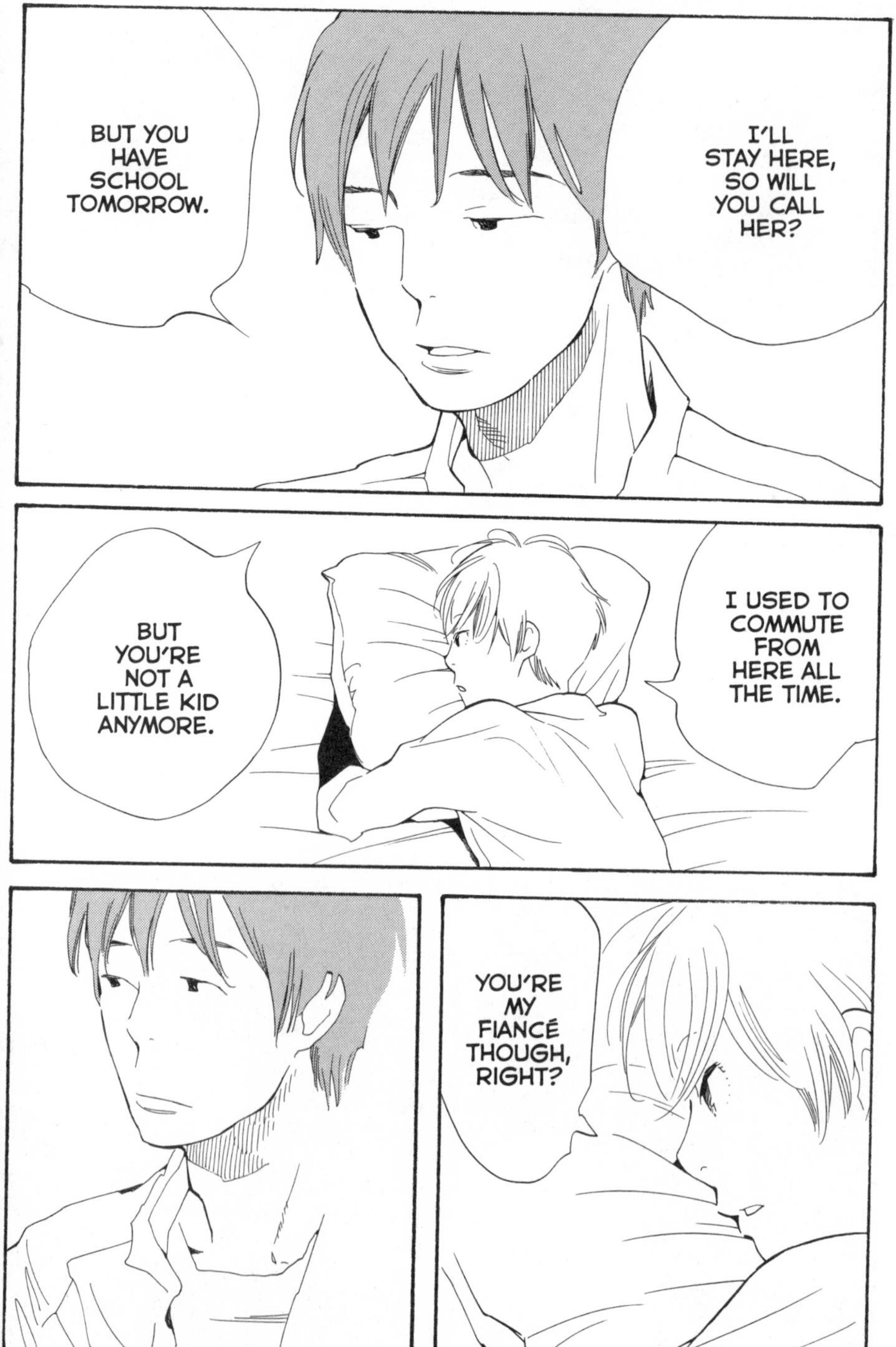
I'LL STAY HERE, SO WILL YOU CALL HER?
BUT YOU HAVE SCHOOL TOMORROW.
I USED TO COMMUTE FROM HERE ALL THE TIME.
BUT YOU'RE NOT A LITTLE KID ANYMORE.
YOU'RE MY FIANCÉ THOUGH, RIGHT?

ACTUALLY, LET'S CALL THAT OFF.

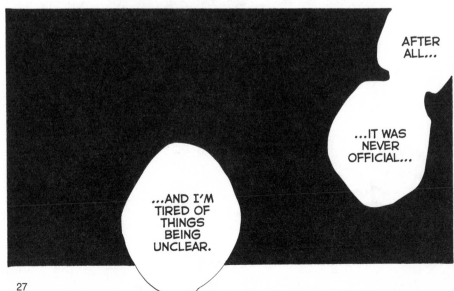

AFTER ALL...

...IT WAS NEVER OFFICIAL...

...AND I'M TIRED OF THINGS BEING UNCLEAR.

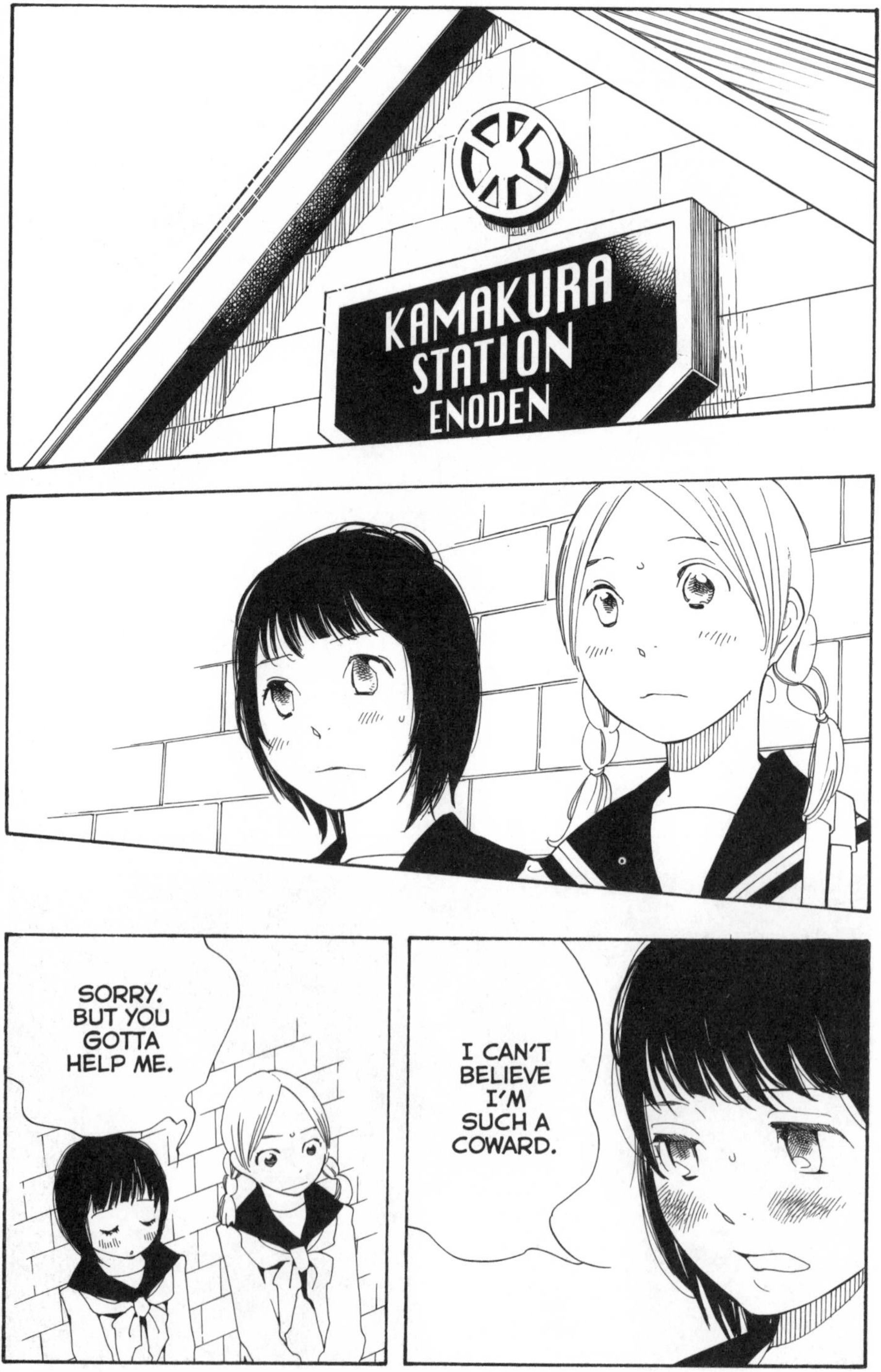
KAMAKURA
STATION
ENODEN
I CAN'T BELIEVE I'M SUCH A COWARD.
SORRY. BUT YOU GOTTA HELP ME.

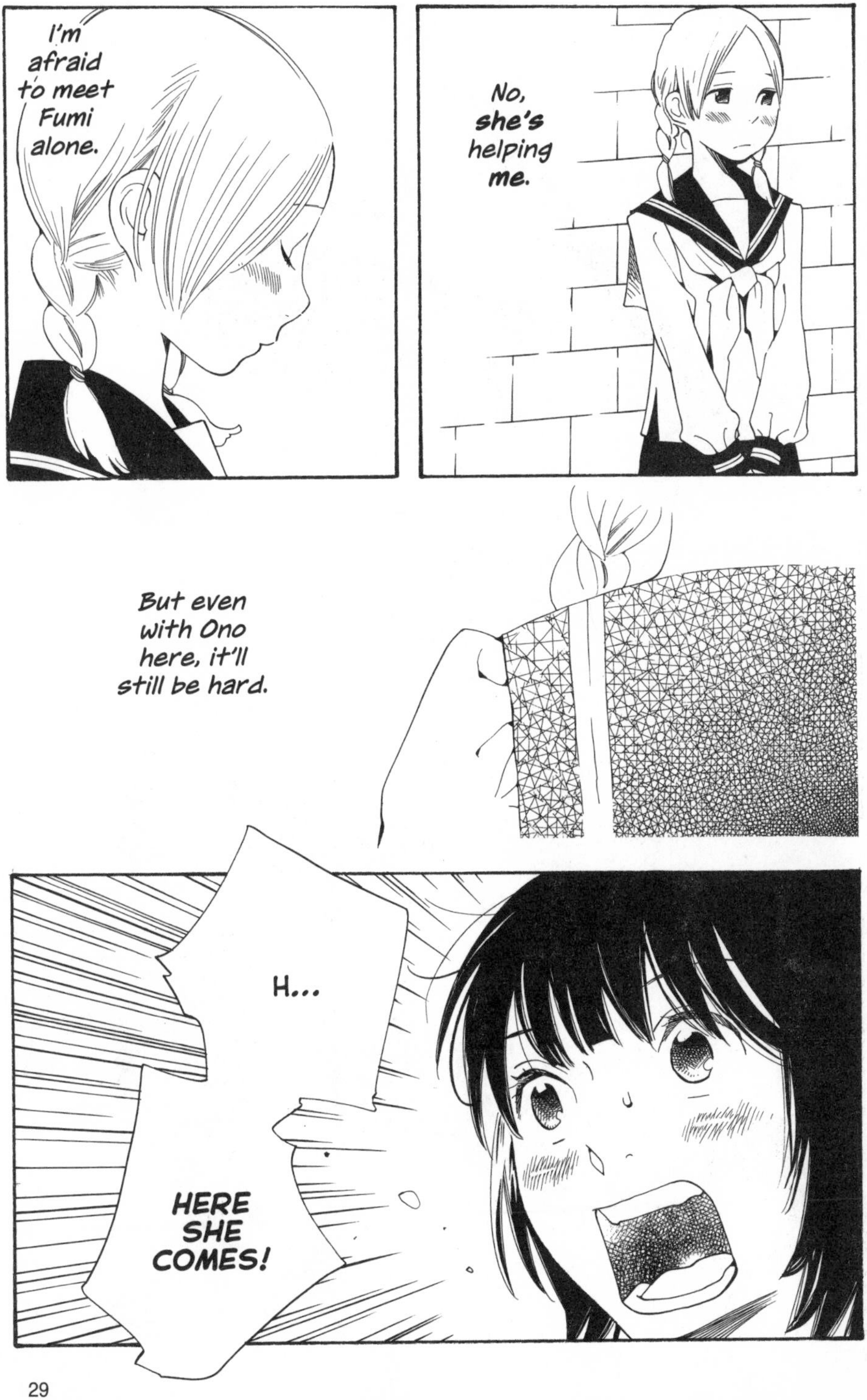
No, she's helping me.
I'm afraid to meet Fumi alone.
But even with Ono here, it'll still be hard.
H...
HERE SHE COMES!

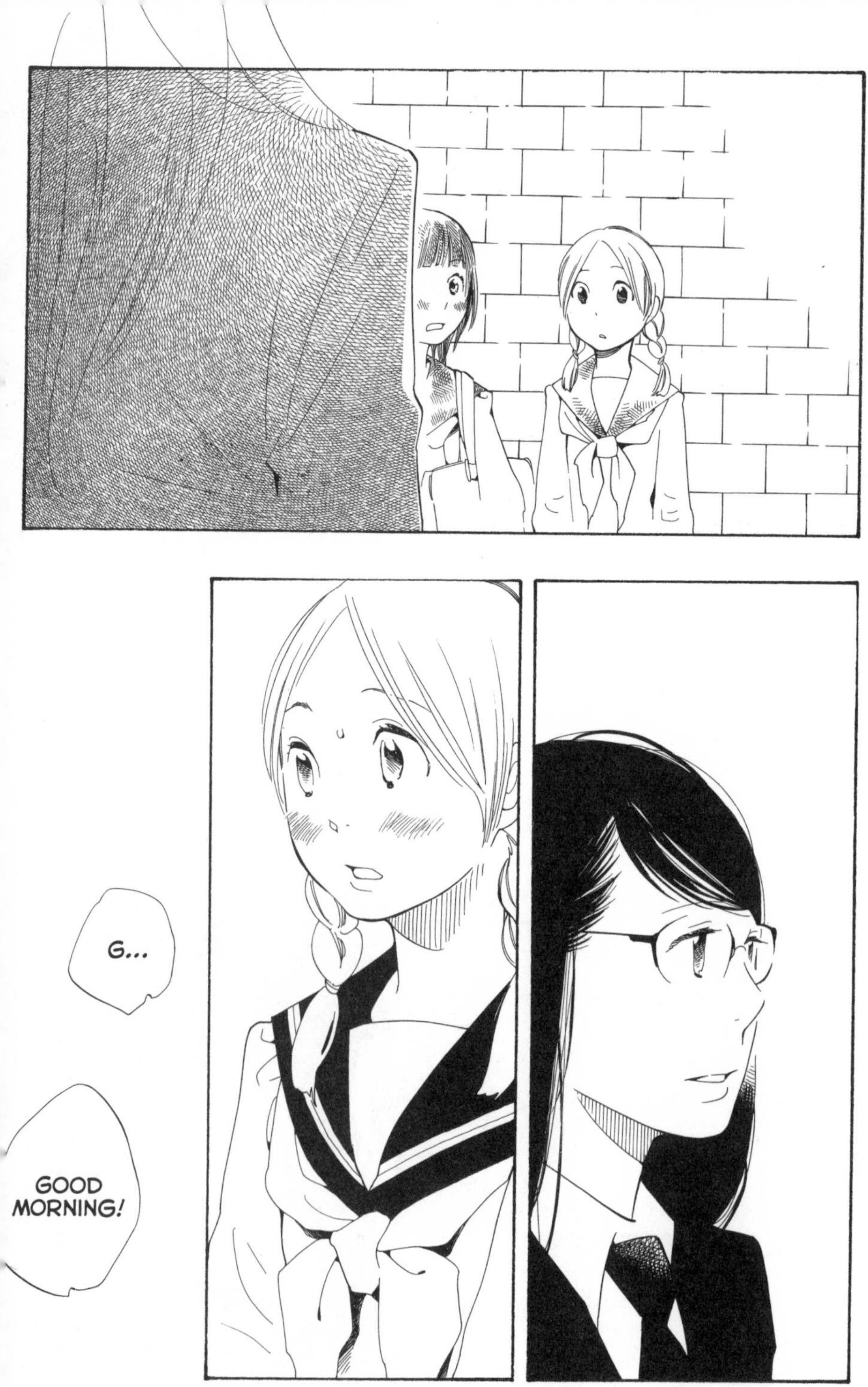
G...
GOOD MORNING!

Sweet Blue Flowers

#27 Rokumeikan, Part 6

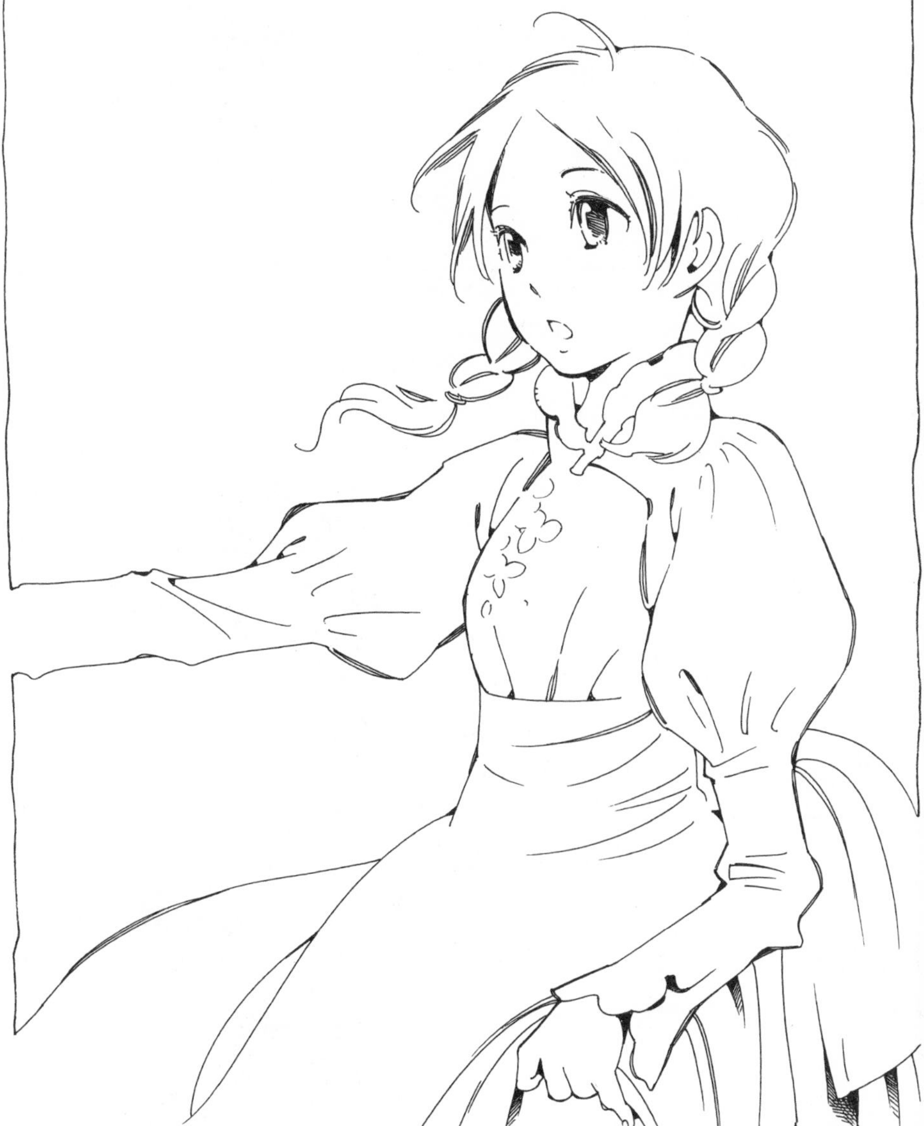

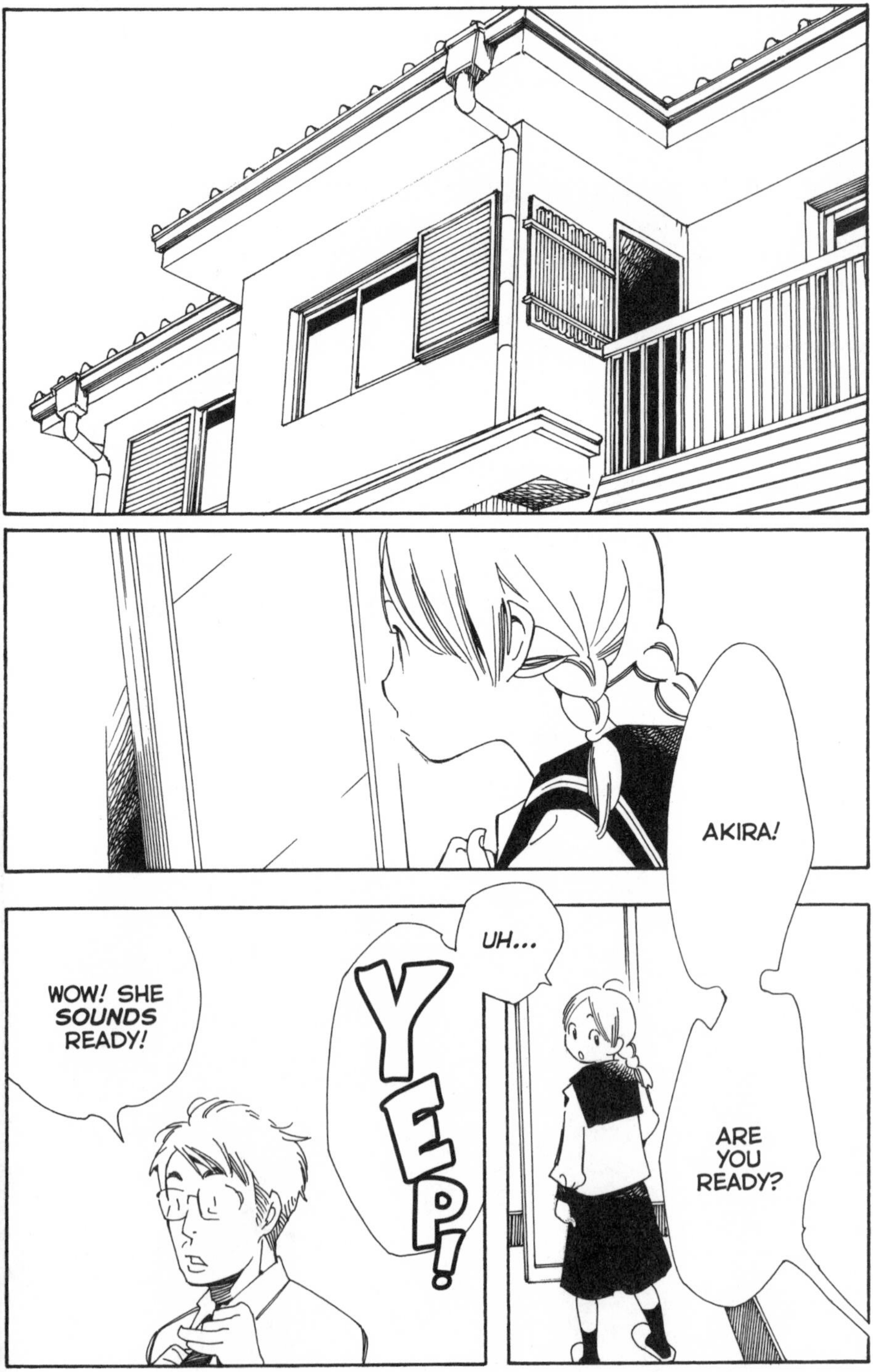
AKIRA!
ARE YOU READY?
UH...
YEP!
WOW! SHE SOUNDS READY!

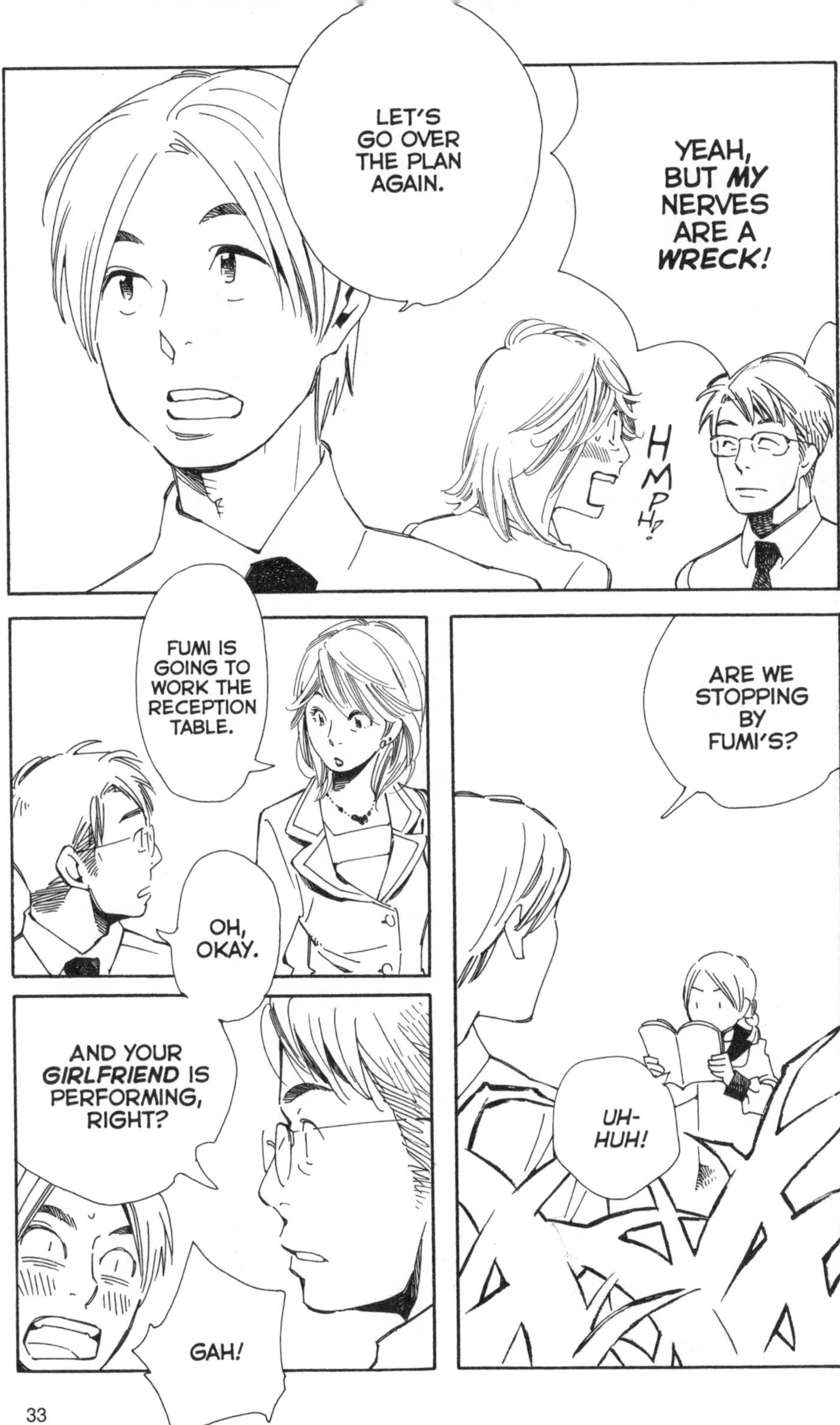
LET'S GO OVER THE PLAN AGAIN.
YEAH, BUT *MY* NERVES ARE A *WRECK*!
HMPH!
ARE WE STOPPING BY FUMI'S?
UH-HUH!
FUMI IS GOING TO WORK THE RECEPTION TABLE.
OH, OKAY.
AND YOUR *GIRLFRIEND* IS PERFORMING, RIGHT?
GAH!

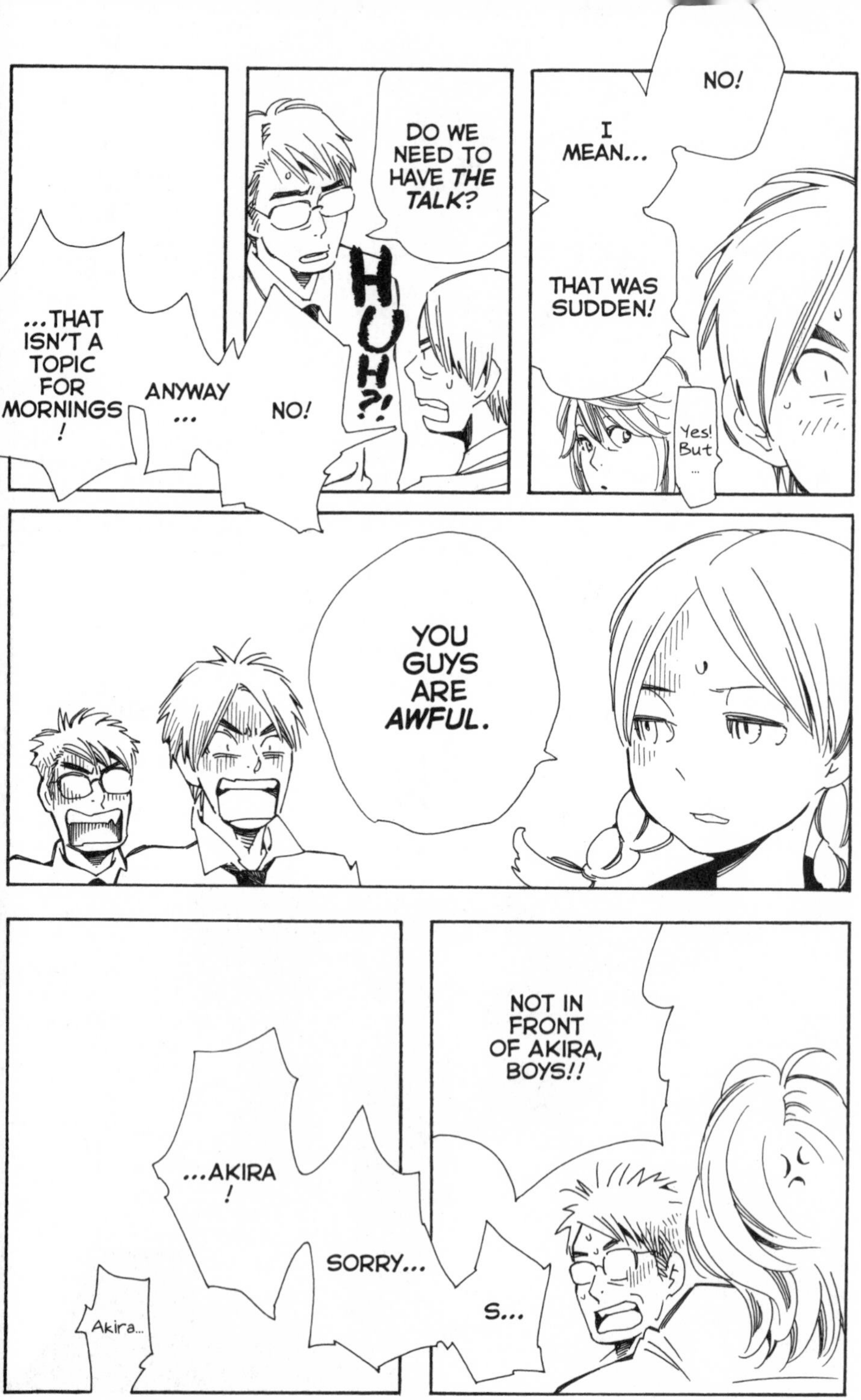
NO!
I MEAN...
THAT WAS SUDDEN!
Yes! But ...
DO WE NEED TO HAVE *THE TALK*?
HUH?!
NO!
ANYWAY ...
...THAT ISN'T A TOPIC FOR MORNINGS!
YOU GUYS ARE *AWFUL*.
NOT IN FRONT OF AKIRA, BOYS!!
S...
SORRY...
...AKIRA!
Akira...

I talked to Fumi...

...about things.

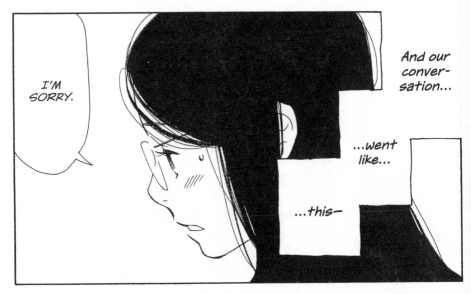

I'M SORRY.

And our conversation...

...went like...

...this—

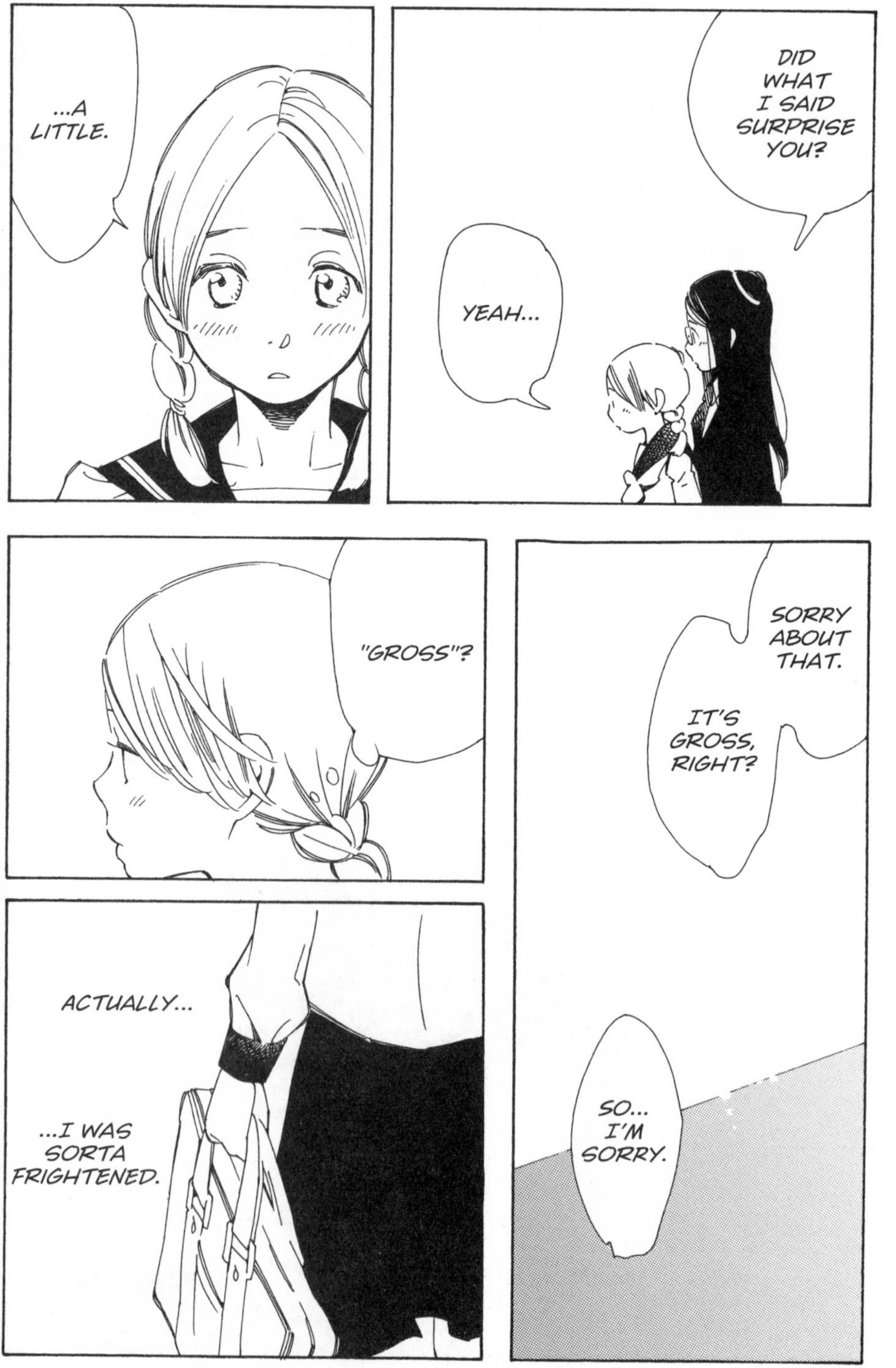
DID WHAT I SAID SURPRISE YOU?
YEAH...
...A LITTLE.
SORRY ABOUT THAT.
IT'S GROSS, RIGHT?
SO... I'M SORRY.
"GROSS"?
ACTUALLY...
...I WAS SORTA FRIGHTENED.

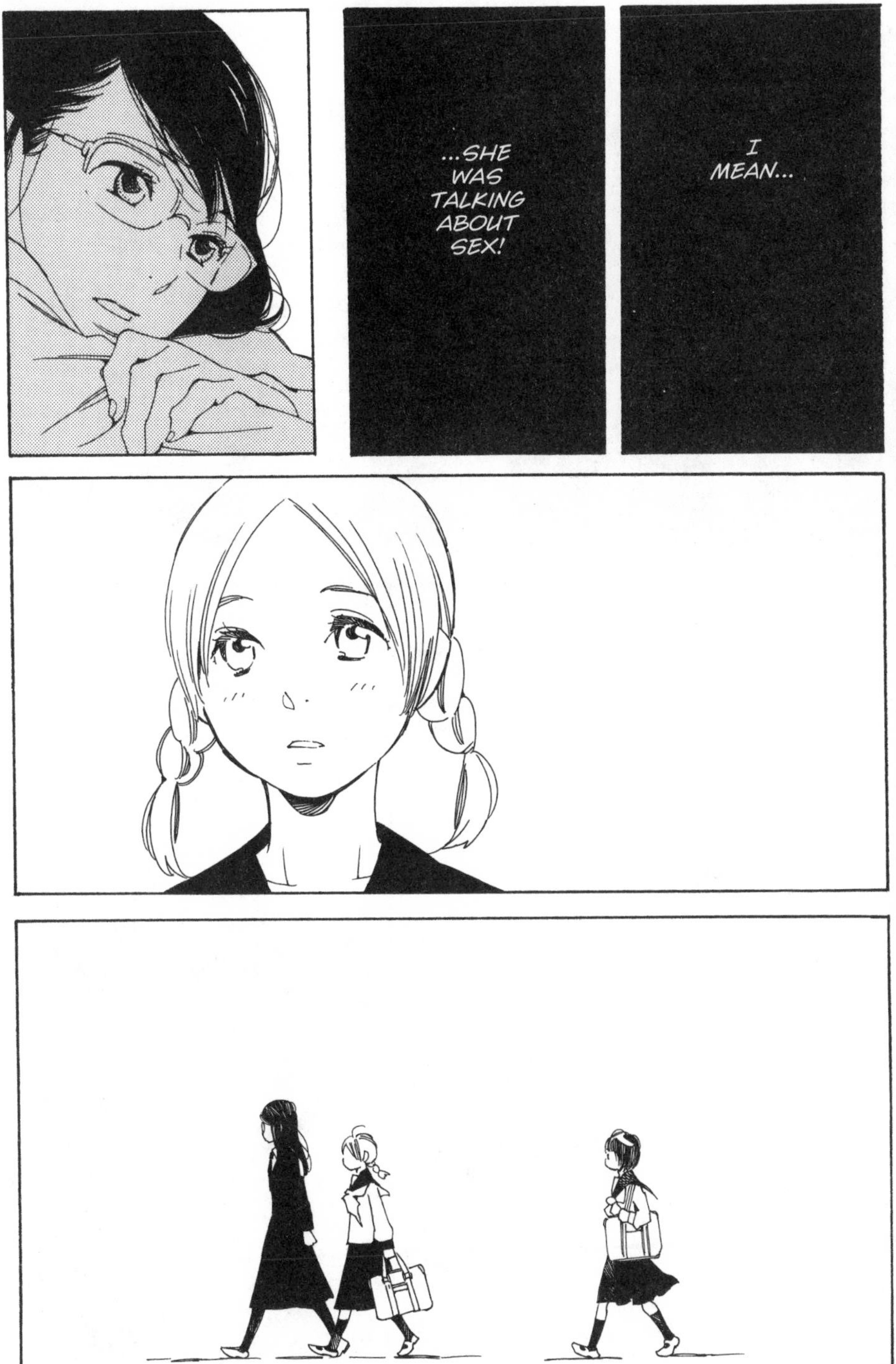
I MEAN...
...SHE WAS TALKING ABOUT SEX!

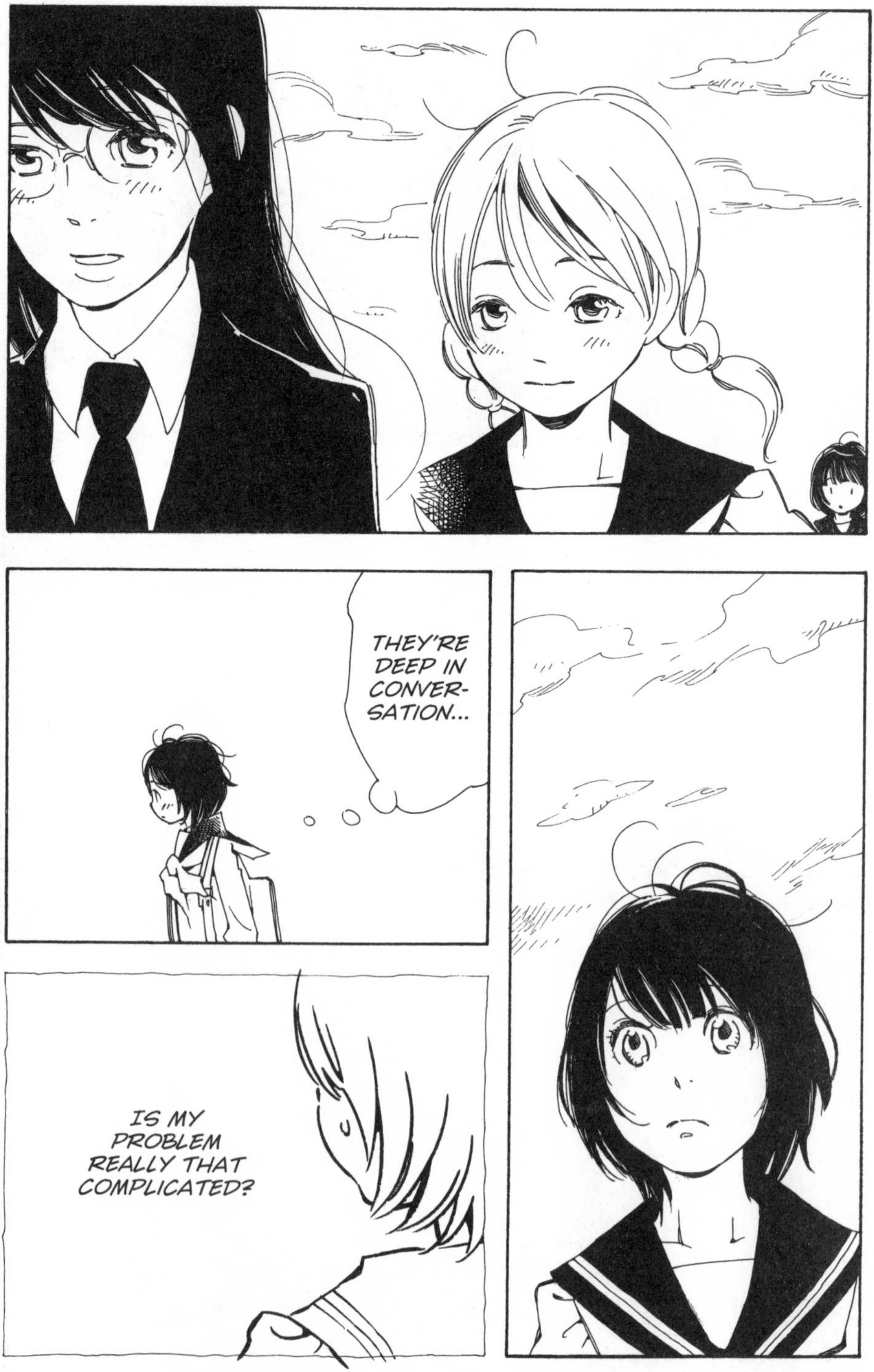
THEY'RE DEEP IN CONVER-SATION...
IS MY PROBLEM REALLY THAT COMPLICATED?

DON'T WORRY, AKIRA. I WON'T DO ANYTHING TO MAKE YOU UNCOMFORTABLE.

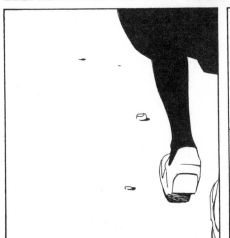

SO JUST...

...BE MY FRIEND.

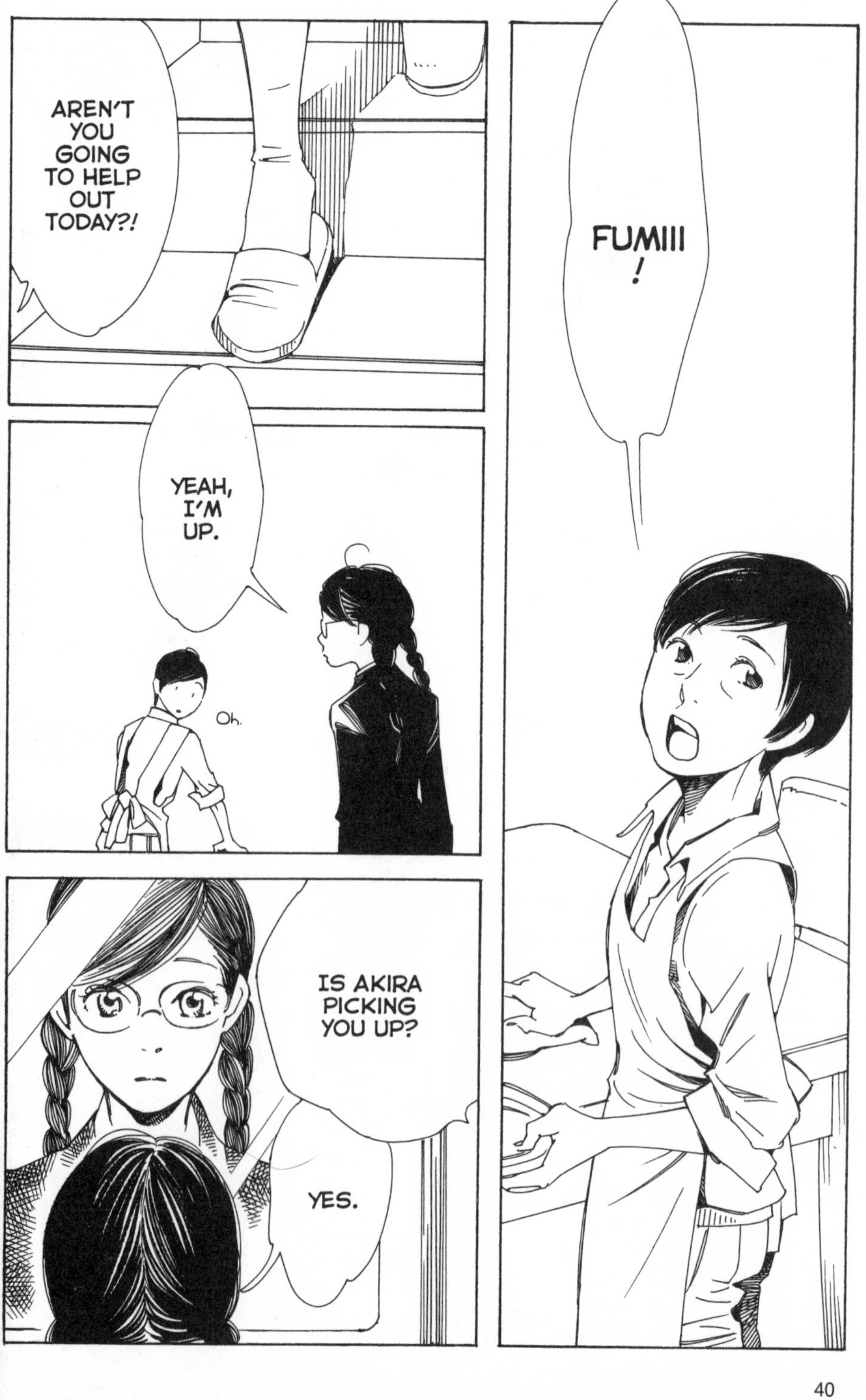
FUMIII!
....
AREN'T YOU GOING TO HELP OUT TODAY?!
YEAH, I'M UP.
Oh.
IS AKIRA PICKING YOU UP?
YES.

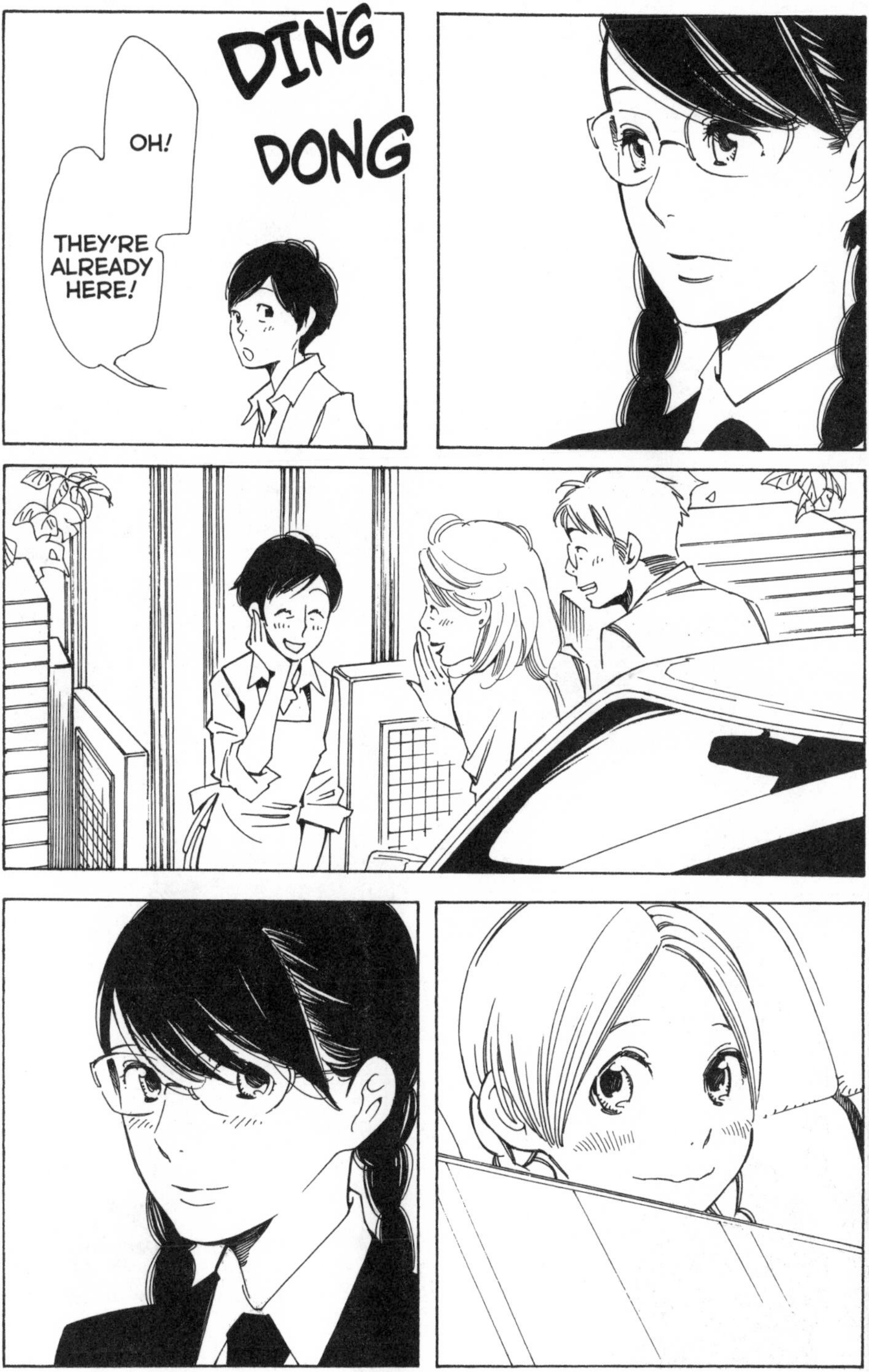
DING DONG
OH!
THEY'RE ALREADY HERE!

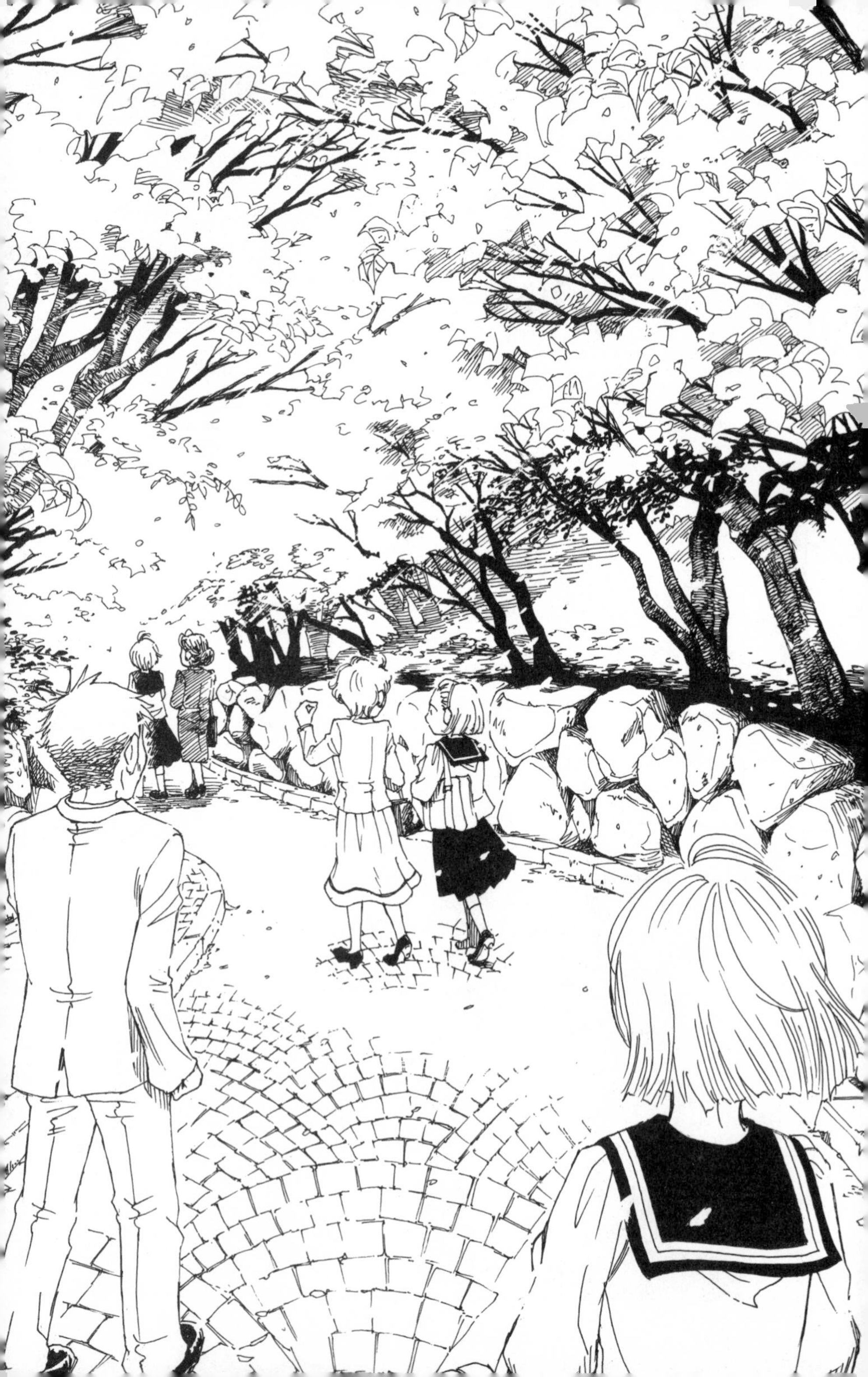

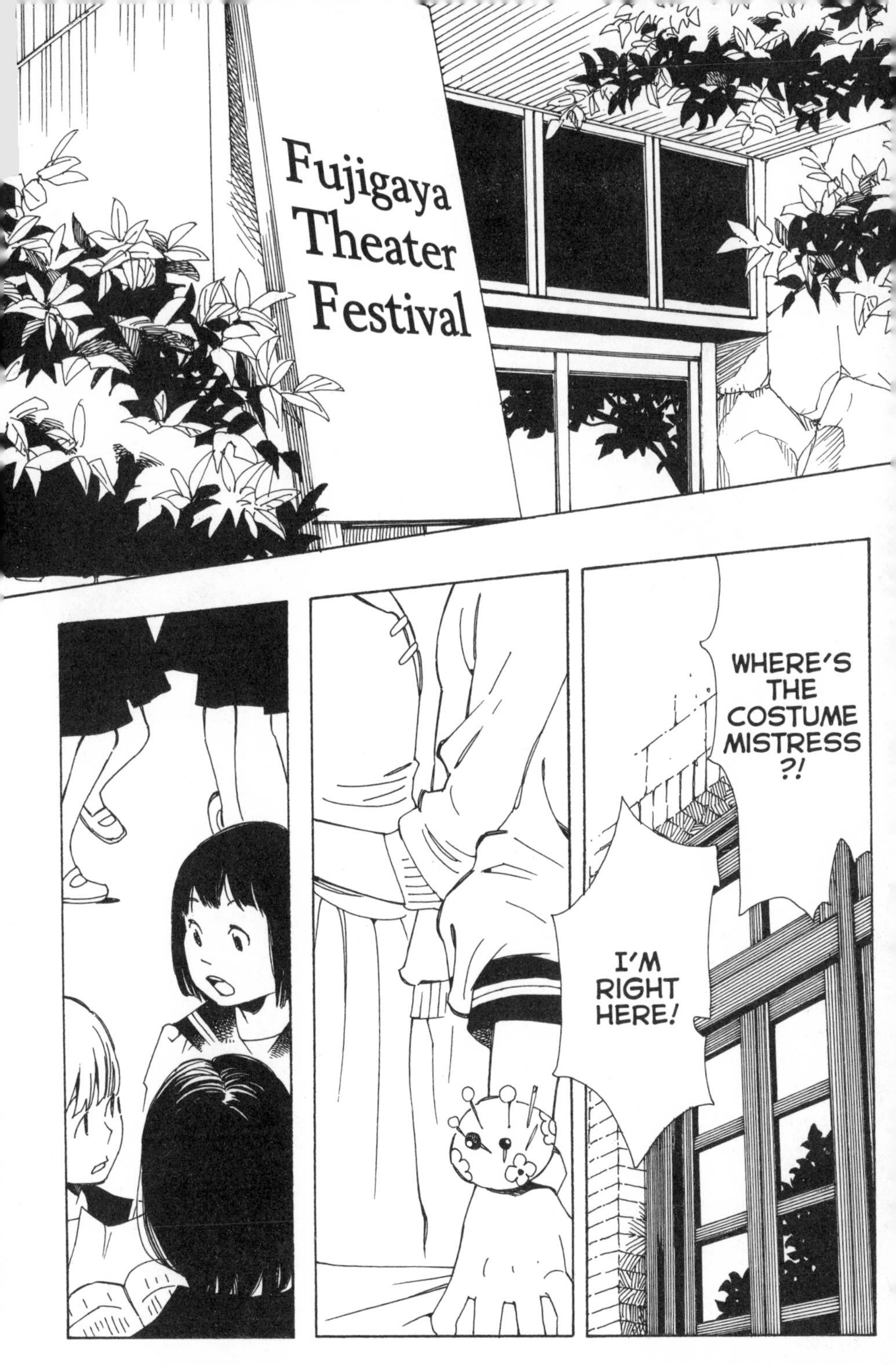
Fujigaya Theater Festival
WHERE'S THE COSTUME MISTRESS?!
I'M RIGHT HERE!

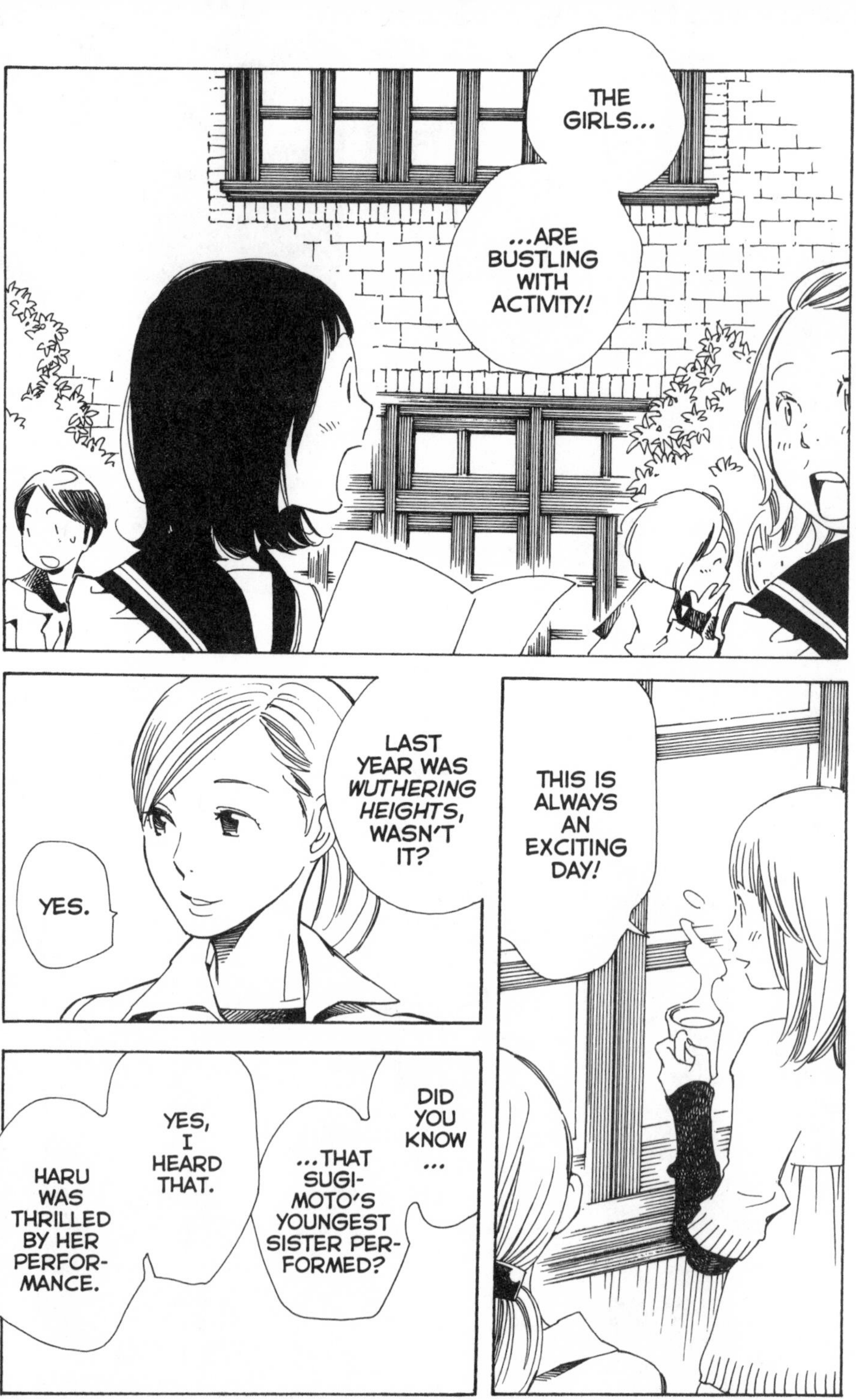
THE GIRLS...
...ARE BUSTLING WITH ACTIVITY!
THIS IS ALWAYS AN EXCITING DAY!
LAST YEAR WAS *WUTHERING HEIGHTS*, WASN'T IT?
YES.
DID YOU KNOW...
...THAT SUGIMOTO'S YOUNGEST SISTER PERFORMED?
YES, I HEARD THAT.
HARU WAS THRILLED BY HER PERFORMANCE.

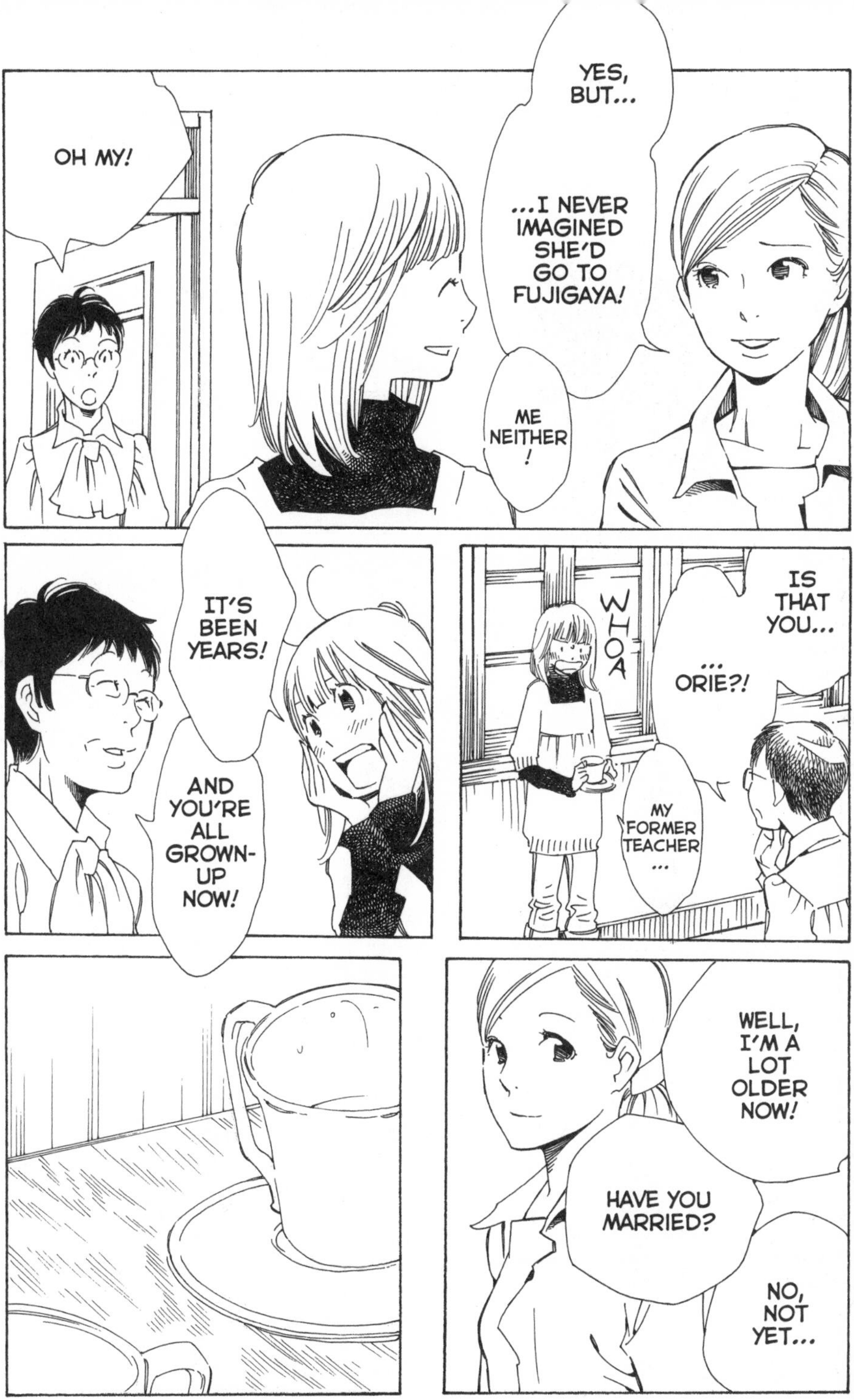
YES, BUT...
...I NEVER IMAGINED SHE'D GO TO FUJIGAYA!
ME NEITHER!
OH MY!
IS THAT YOU...
...ORIE?!
WHOA
MY FORMER TEACHER...
IT'S BEEN YEARS!
AND YOU'RE ALL GROWN-UP NOW!
WELL, I'M A LOT OLDER NOW!
HAVE YOU MARRIED?
NO, NOT YET...

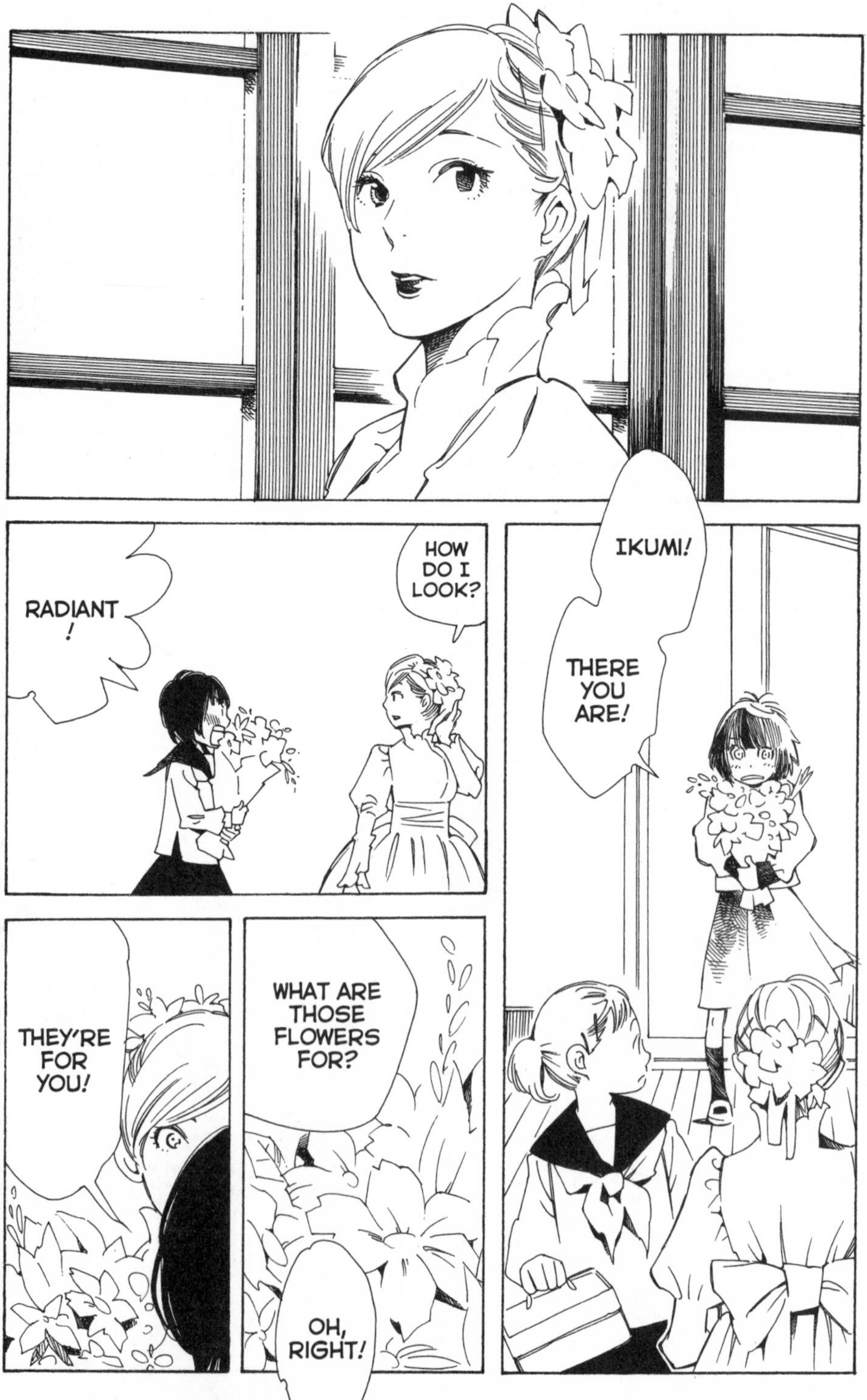
IKUMI!
THERE YOU ARE!
HOW DO I LOOK?
RADIANT!
WHAT ARE THOSE FLOWERS FOR?
OH, RIGHT!
THEY'RE FOR YOU!

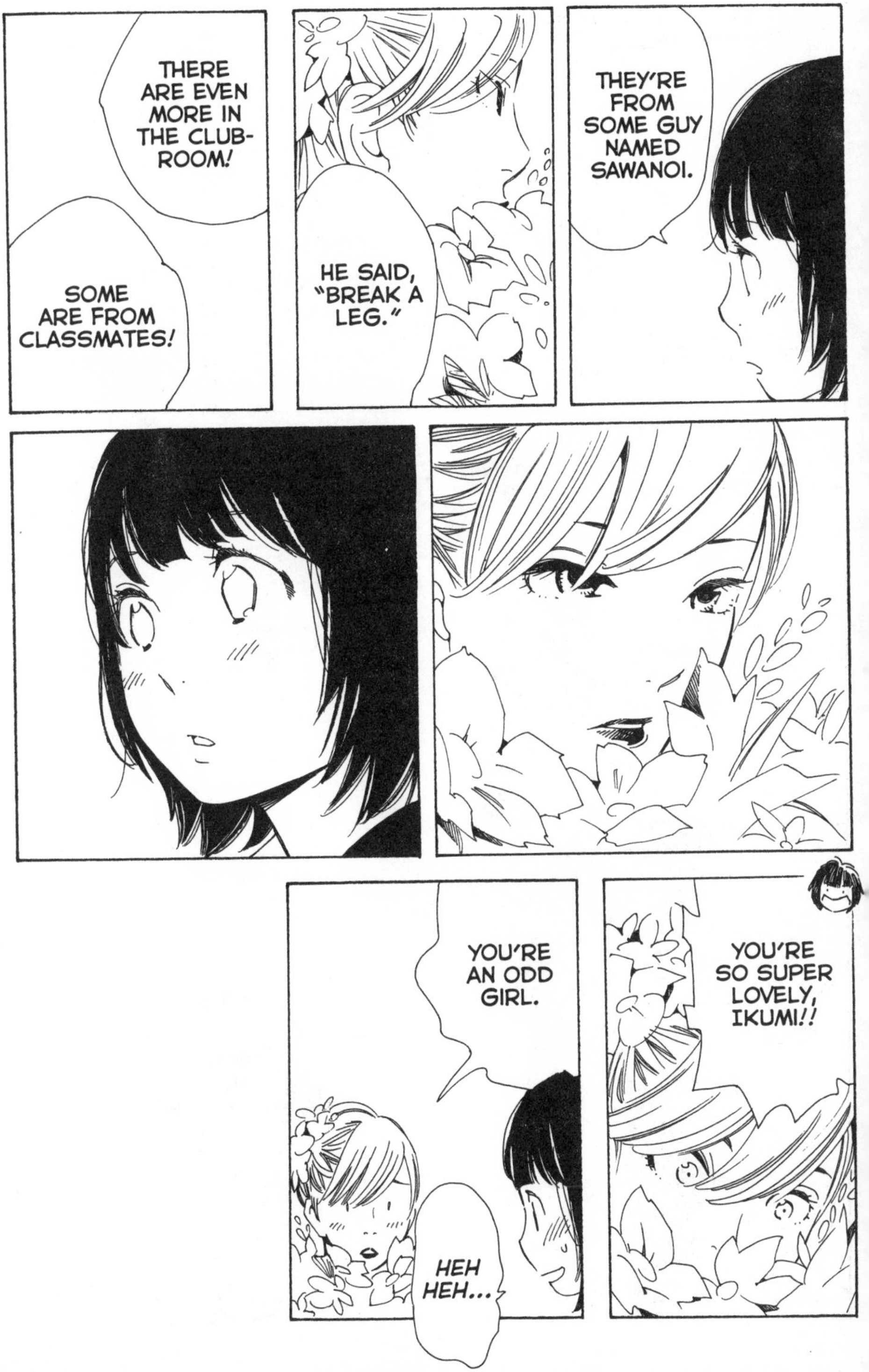
THEY'RE FROM SOME GUY NAMED SAWANOI.
HE SAID, "BREAK A LEG."
THERE ARE EVEN MORE IN THE CLUB-ROOM!
SOME ARE FROM CLASSMATES!
YOU'RE SO SUPER LOVELY, IKUMI!!
YOU'RE AN ODD GIRL.
HEH HEH...

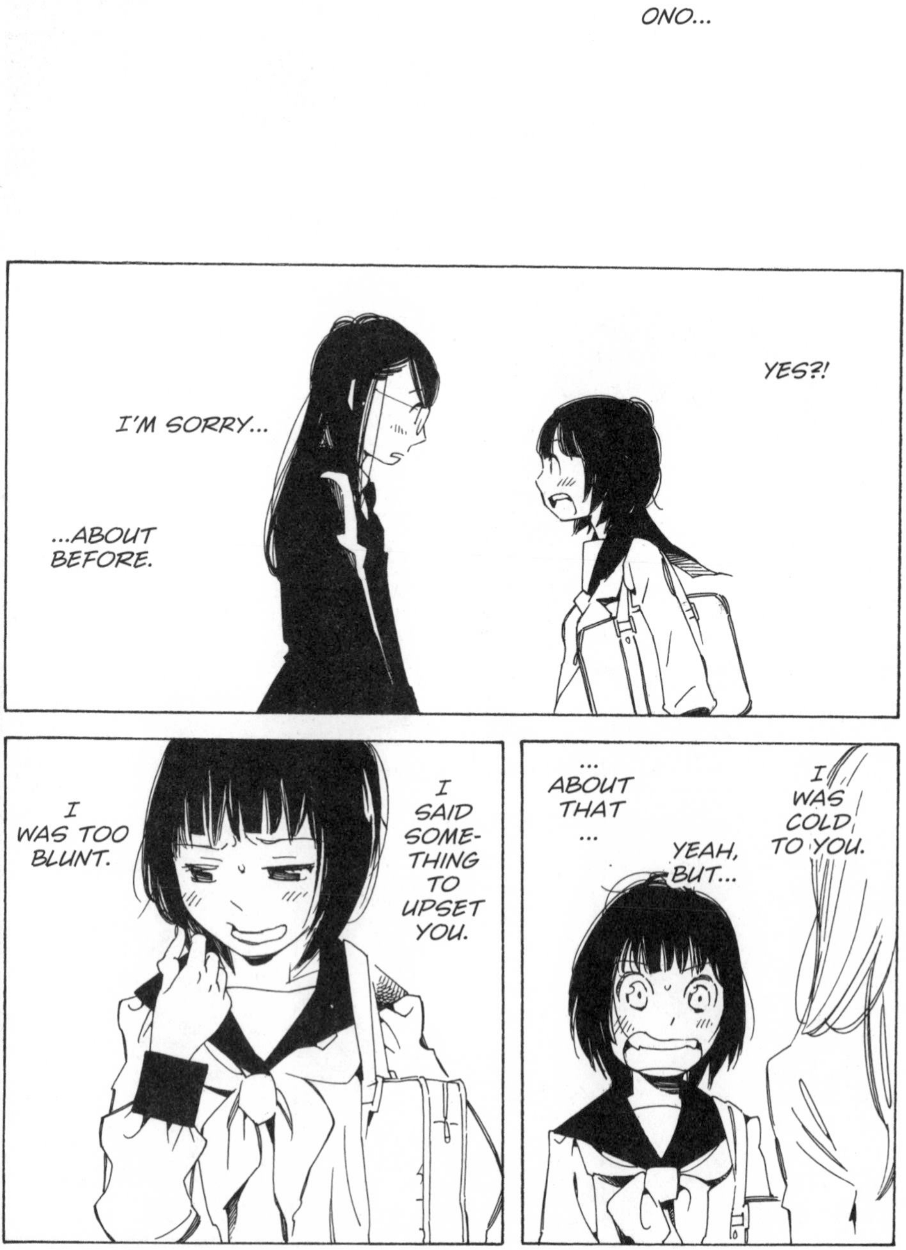
ONO...
YES?!
I'M SORRY...
...ABOUT BEFORE.
I WAS COLD TO YOU.
...ABOUT THAT...
YEAH, BUT...
I SAID SOMETHING TO UPSET YOU.
I WAS TOO BLUNT.

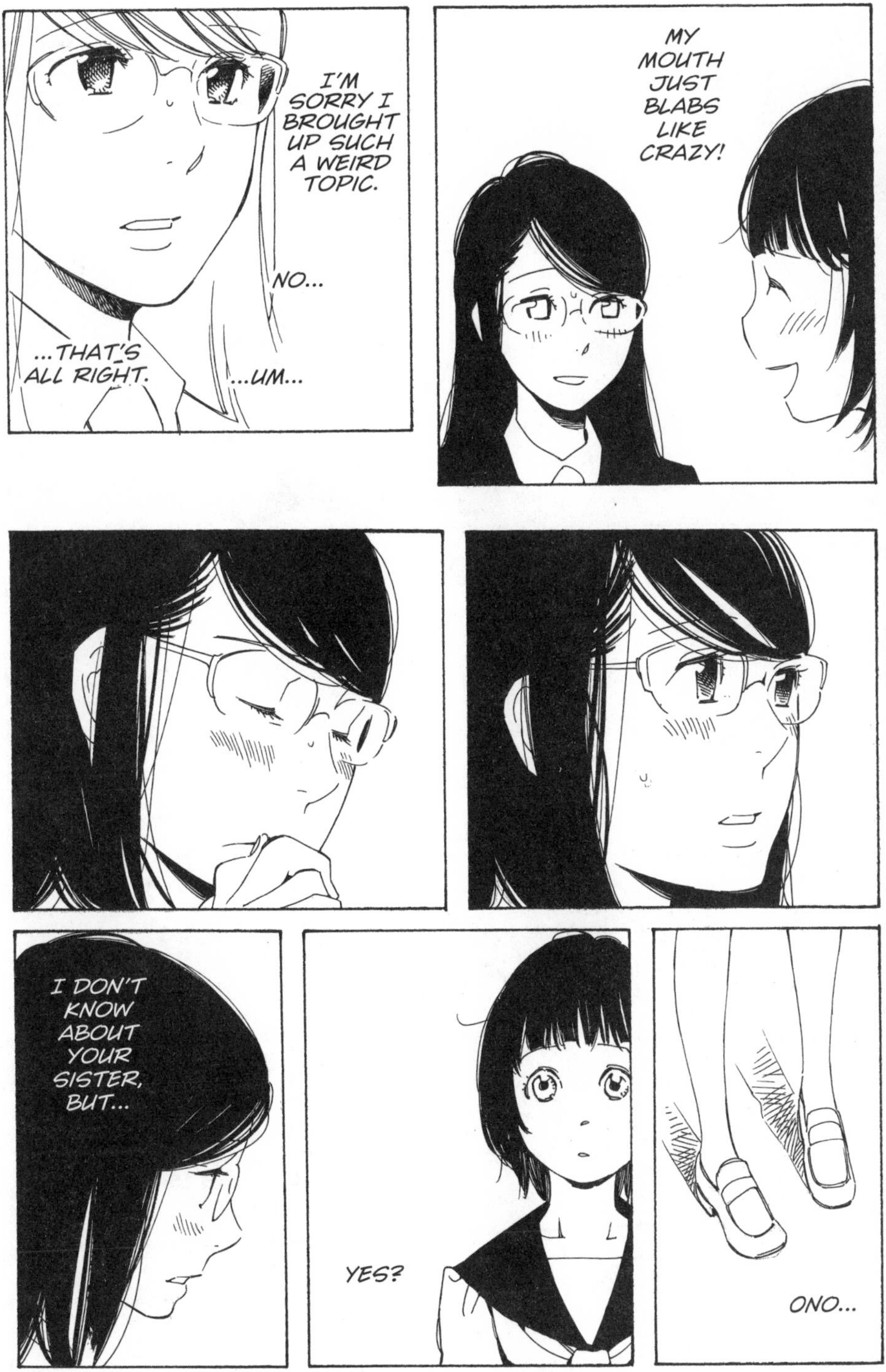
MY MOUTH JUST BLABS LIKE CRAZY!
I'M SORRY I BROUGHT UP SUCH A WEIRD TOPIC.
NO...
...UM...
...THAT'S ALL RIGHT.
ONO...
YES?
I DON'T KNOW ABOUT YOUR SISTER, BUT...

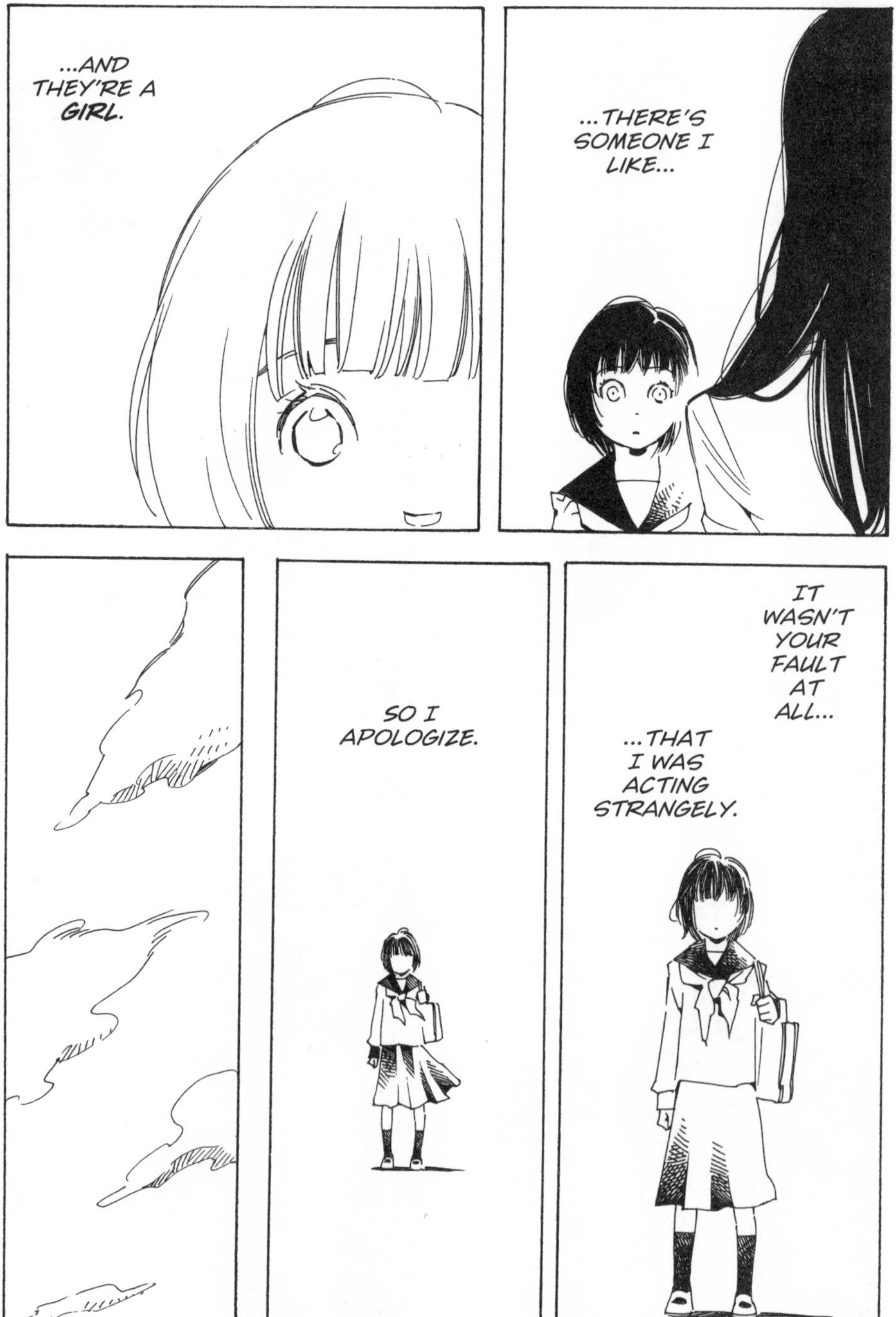
...THERE'S SOMEONE I LIKE...
...AND THEY'RE A **GIRL**.
IT WASN'T YOUR FAULT AT ALL...
...THAT I WAS ACTING STRANGELY.
SO I APOLOGIZE.

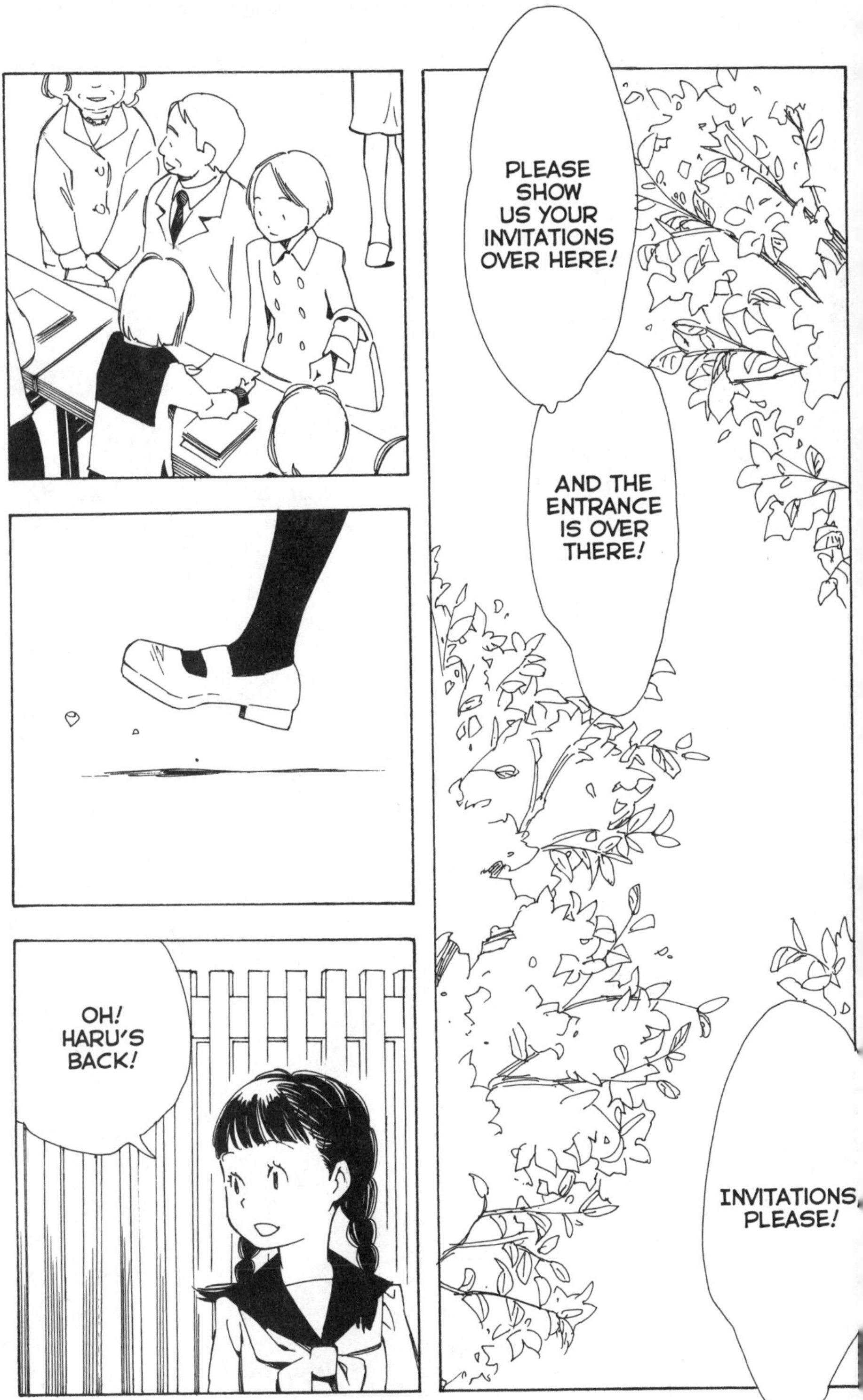
PLEASE SHOW US YOUR INVITATIONS OVER HERE!
AND THE ENTRANCE IS OVER THERE!
INVITATIONS, PLEASE!
OH! HARU'S BACK!

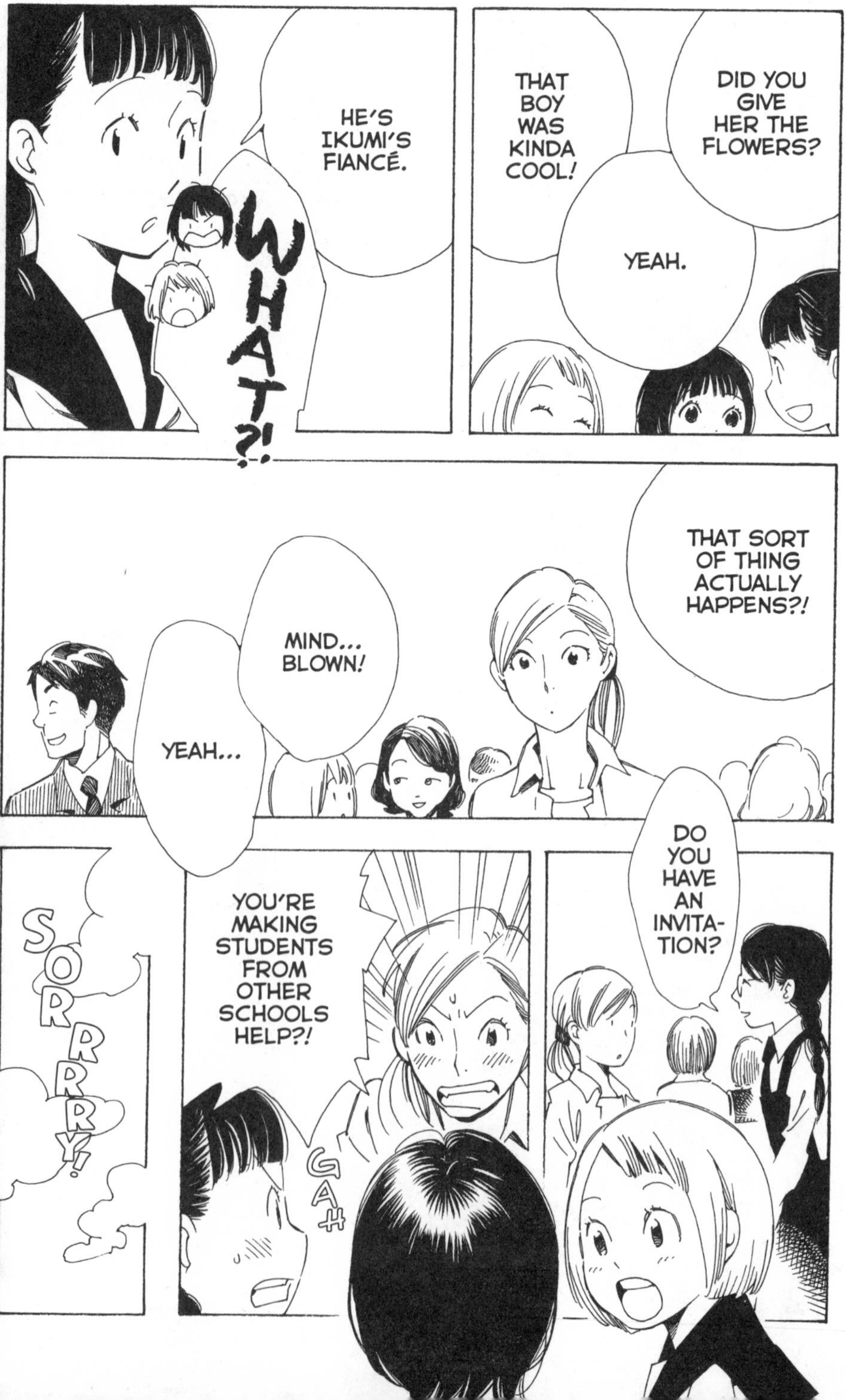
DID YOU GIVE HER THE FLOWERS?
THAT BOY WAS KINDA COOL!
YEAH.
HE'S IKUMI'S FIANCÉ.
WHAT?!
THAT SORT OF THING ACTUALLY HAPPENS?!
MIND... BLOWN!
YEAH...
DO YOU HAVE AN INVITATION?
YOU'RE MAKING STUDENTS FROM OTHER SCHOOLS HELP?!
GAH
SORRRRY!

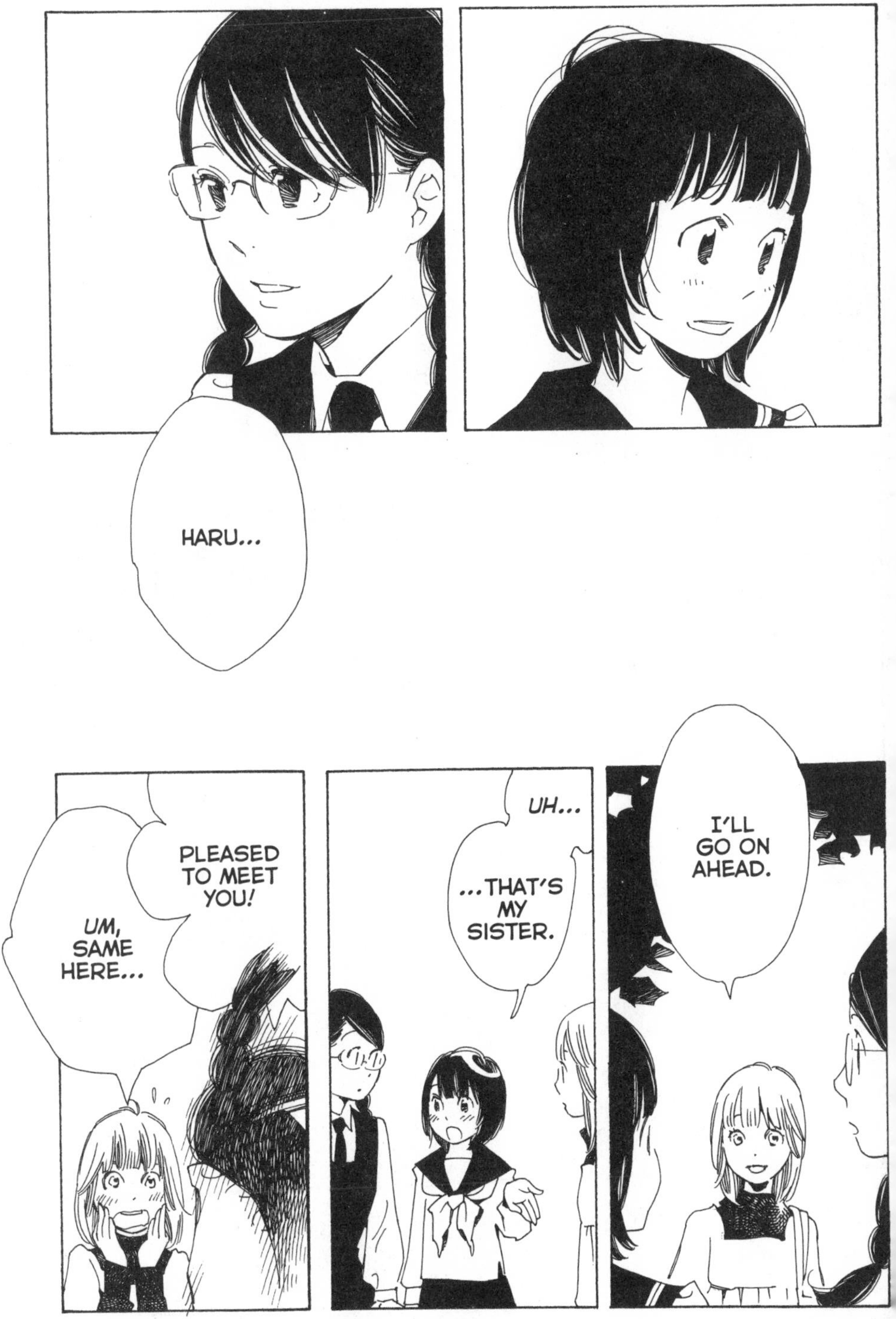
HARU...
I'LL GO ON AHEAD.
UH...
...THAT'S MY SISTER.
PLEASED TO MEET YOU!
UM, SAME HERE...

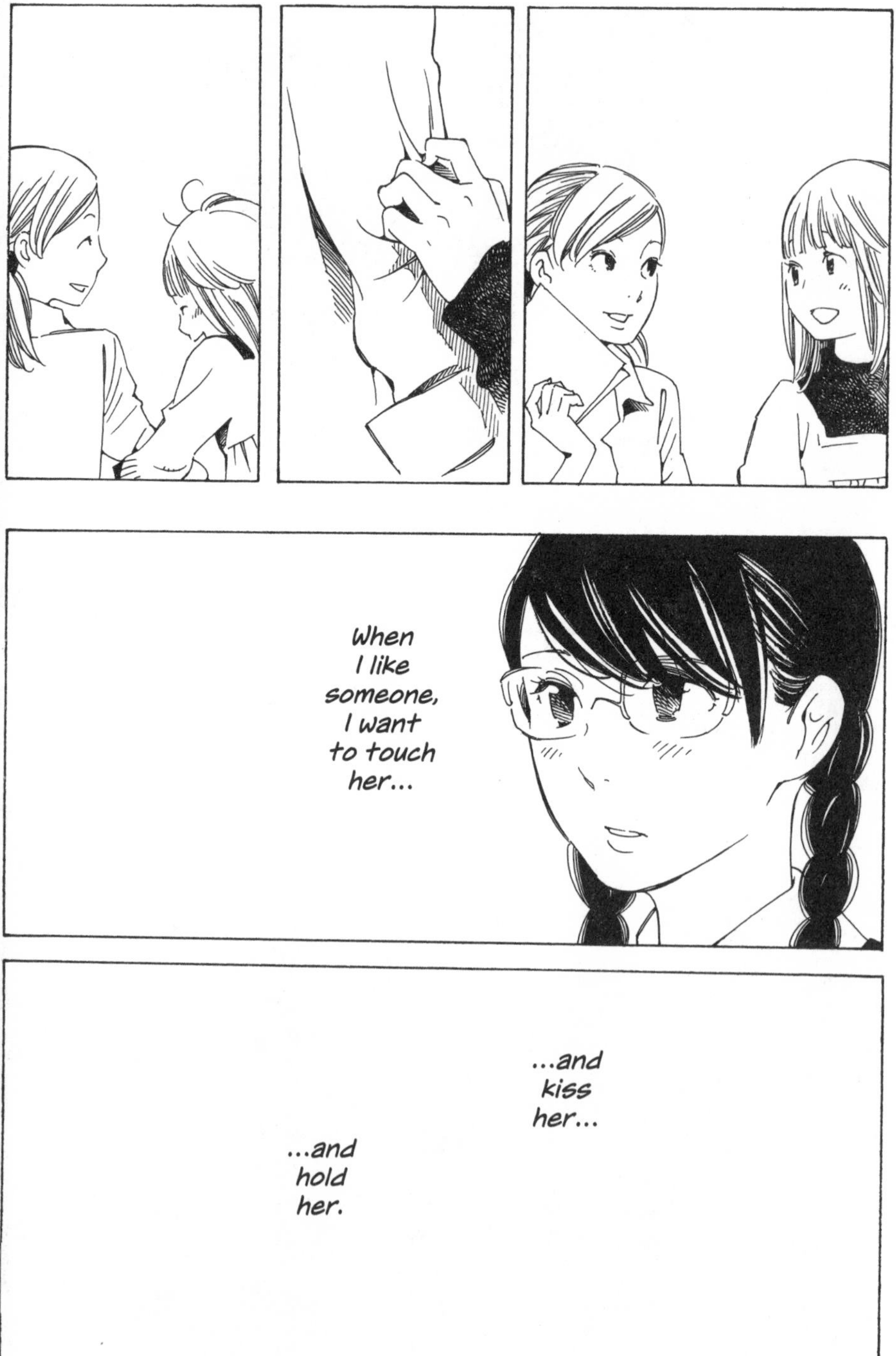
When I like someone, I want to touch her...
...and kiss her...
...and hold her.

Sweet **Blue**
Flowers

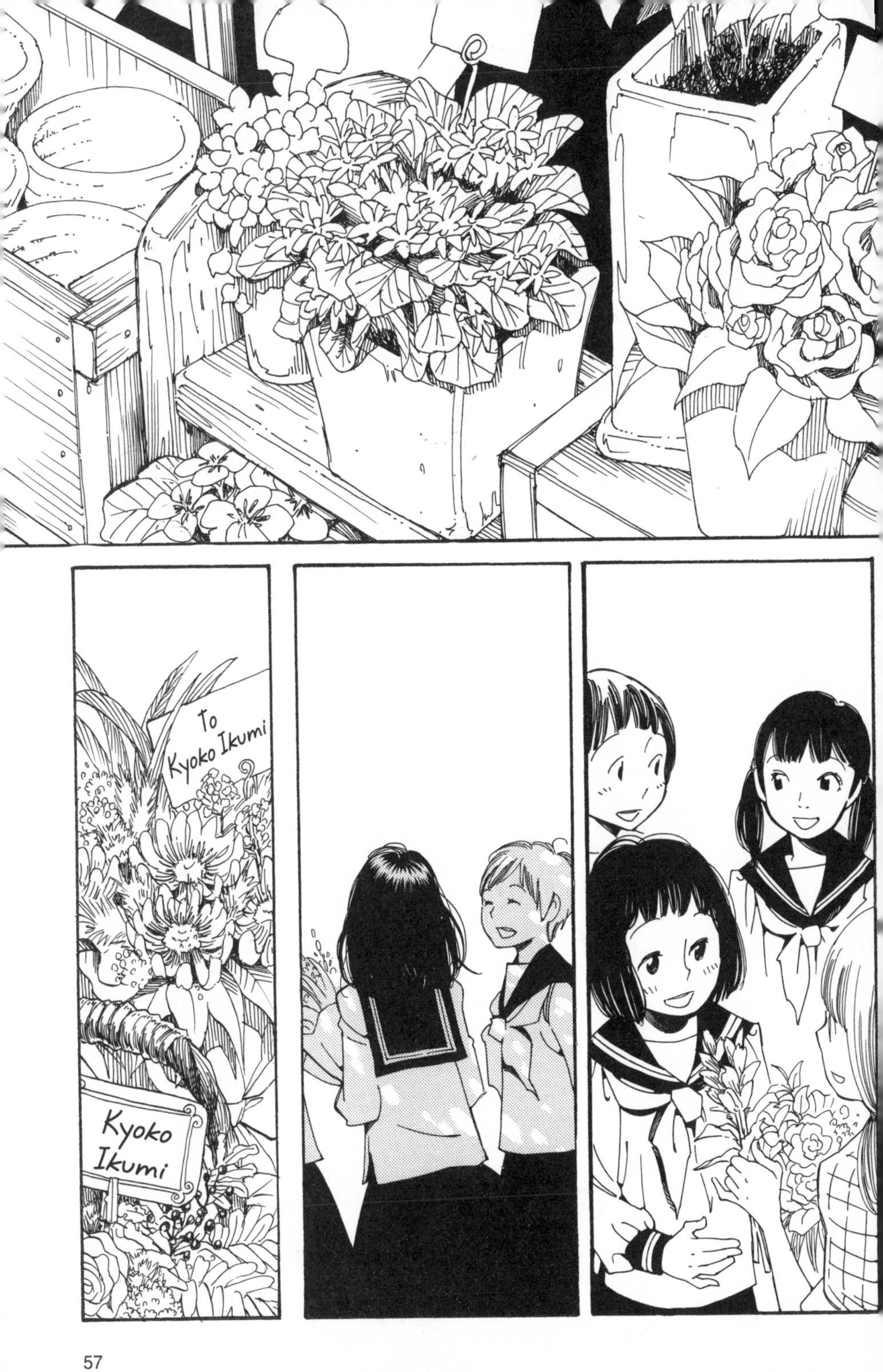
To Kyoko Ikumi
Kyoko Ikumi

Sweet Blue Flowers

#28 Rokumeikan, Part 7

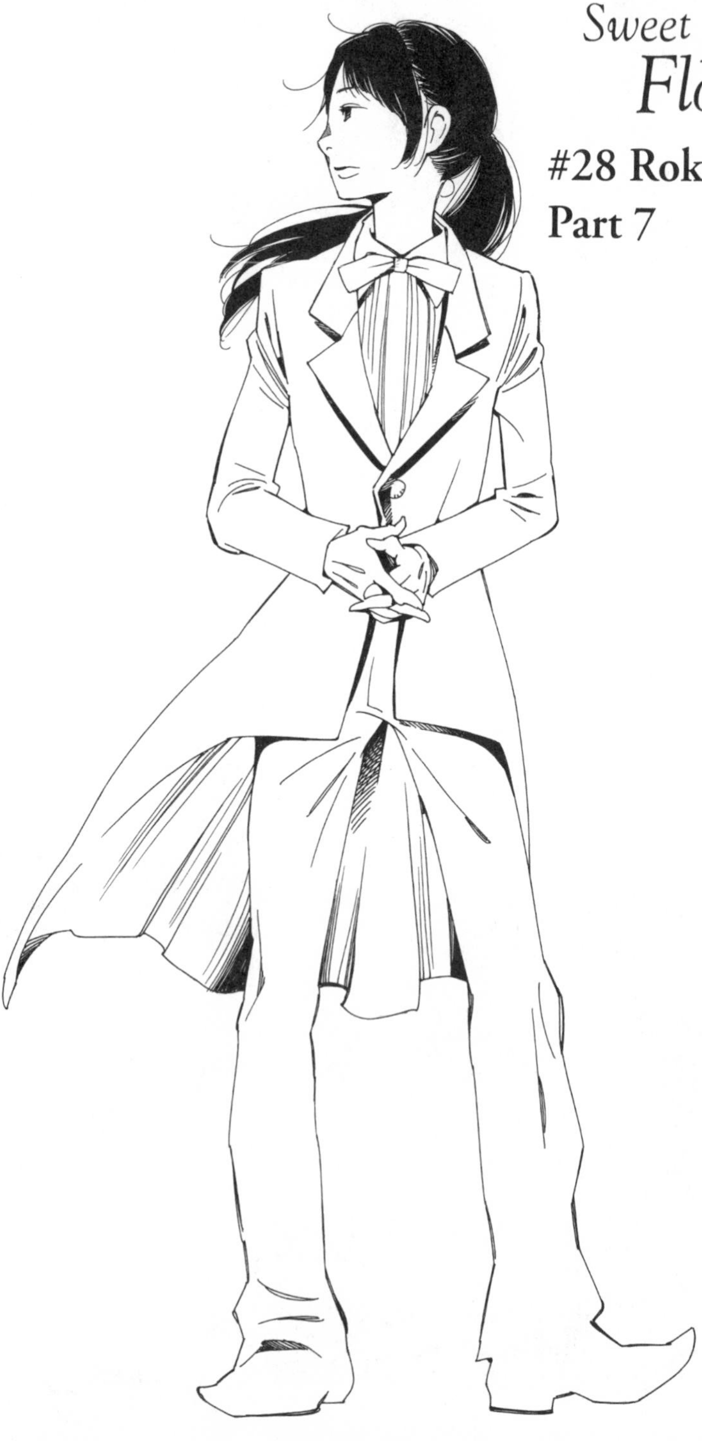

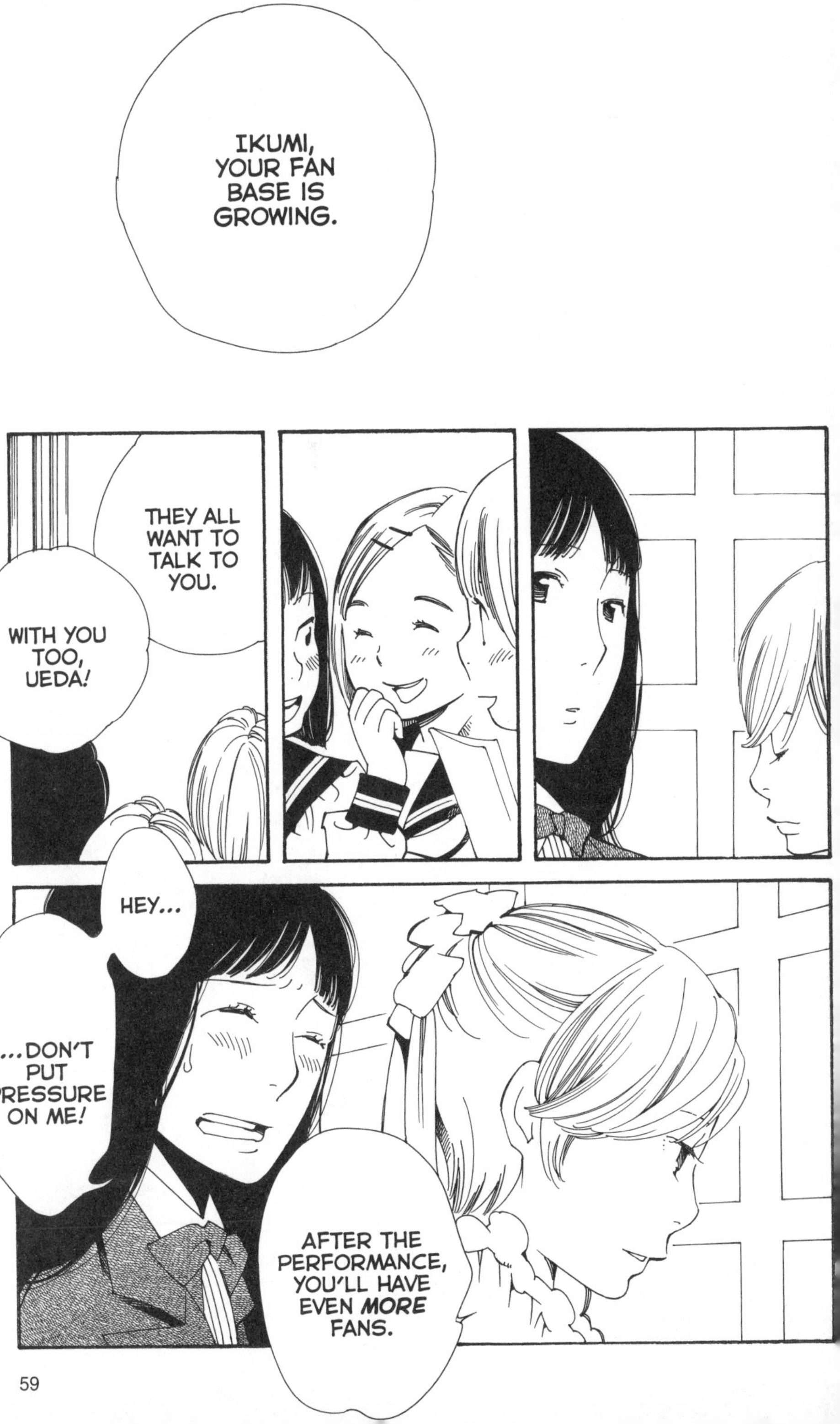
IKUMI, YOUR FAN BASE IS GROWING.
THEY ALL WANT TO TALK TO YOU.
WITH YOU TOO, UEDA!
AFTER THE PERFORMANCE, YOU'LL HAVE EVEN *MORE* FANS.
HEY...
...DON'T PUT PRESSURE ON ME!

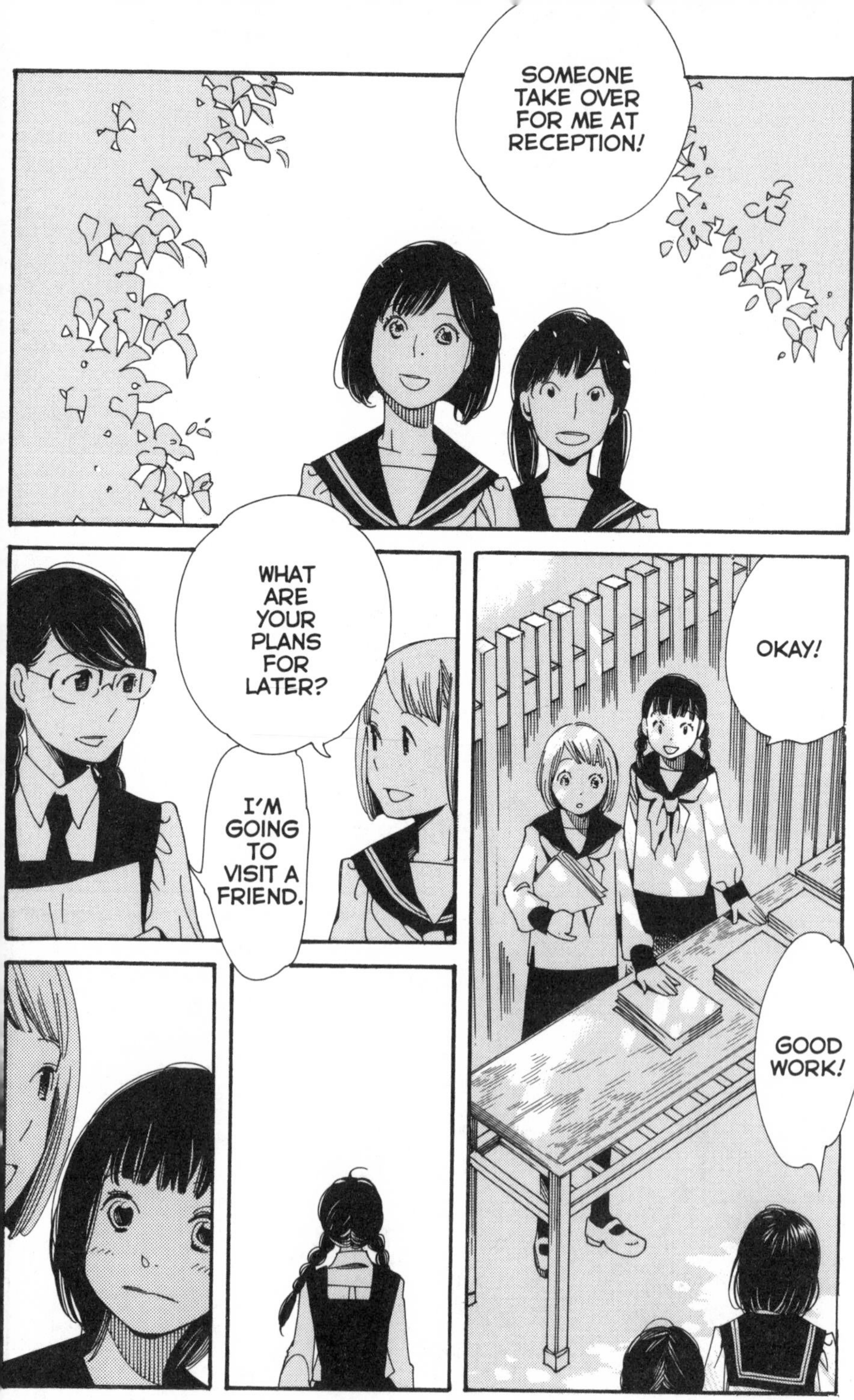
SOMEONE TAKE OVER FOR ME AT RECEPTION!
OKAY!
GOOD WORK!
WHAT ARE YOUR PLANS FOR LATER?
I'M GOING TO VISIT A FRIEND.

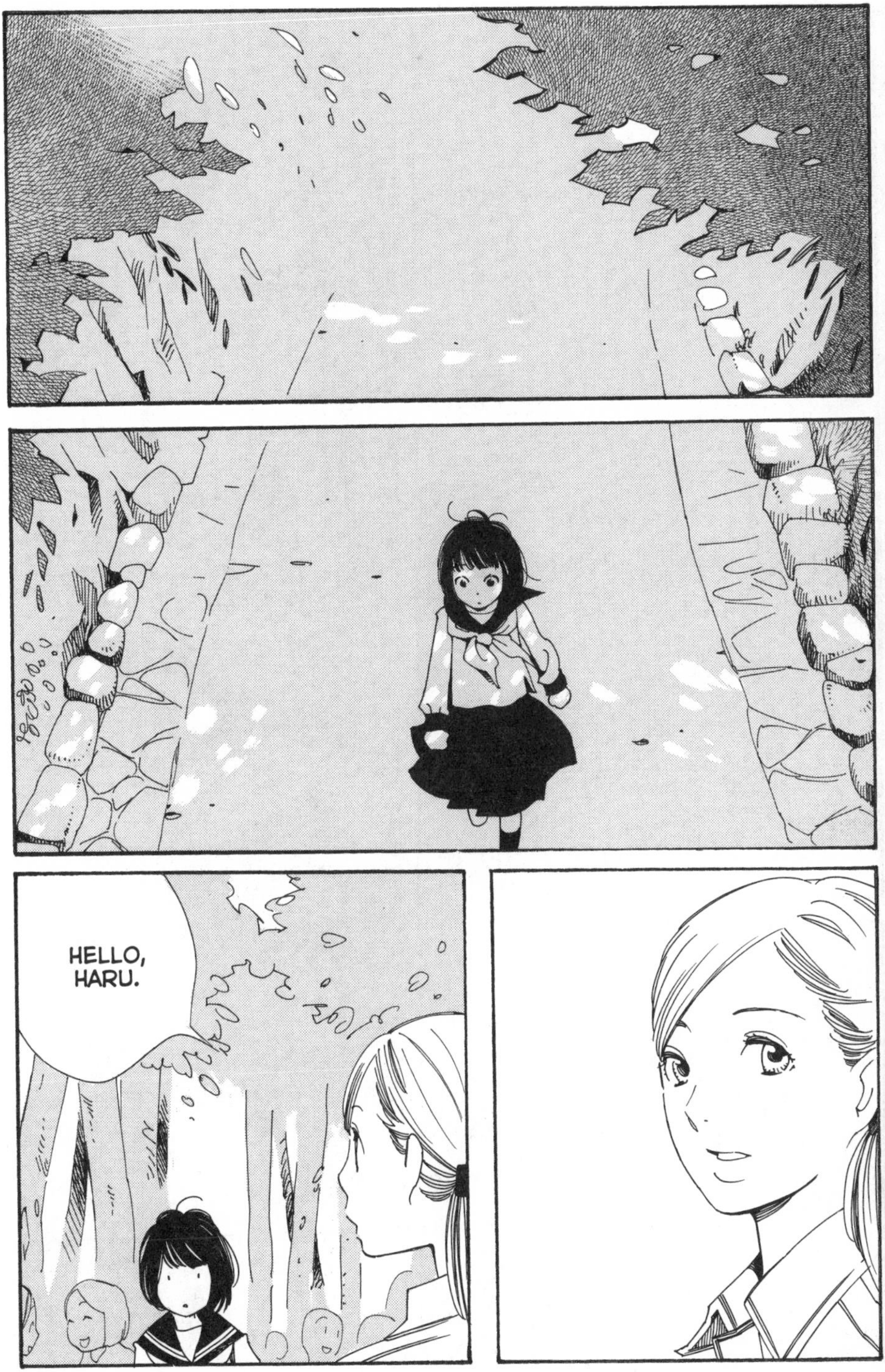
HELLO,
HARU.

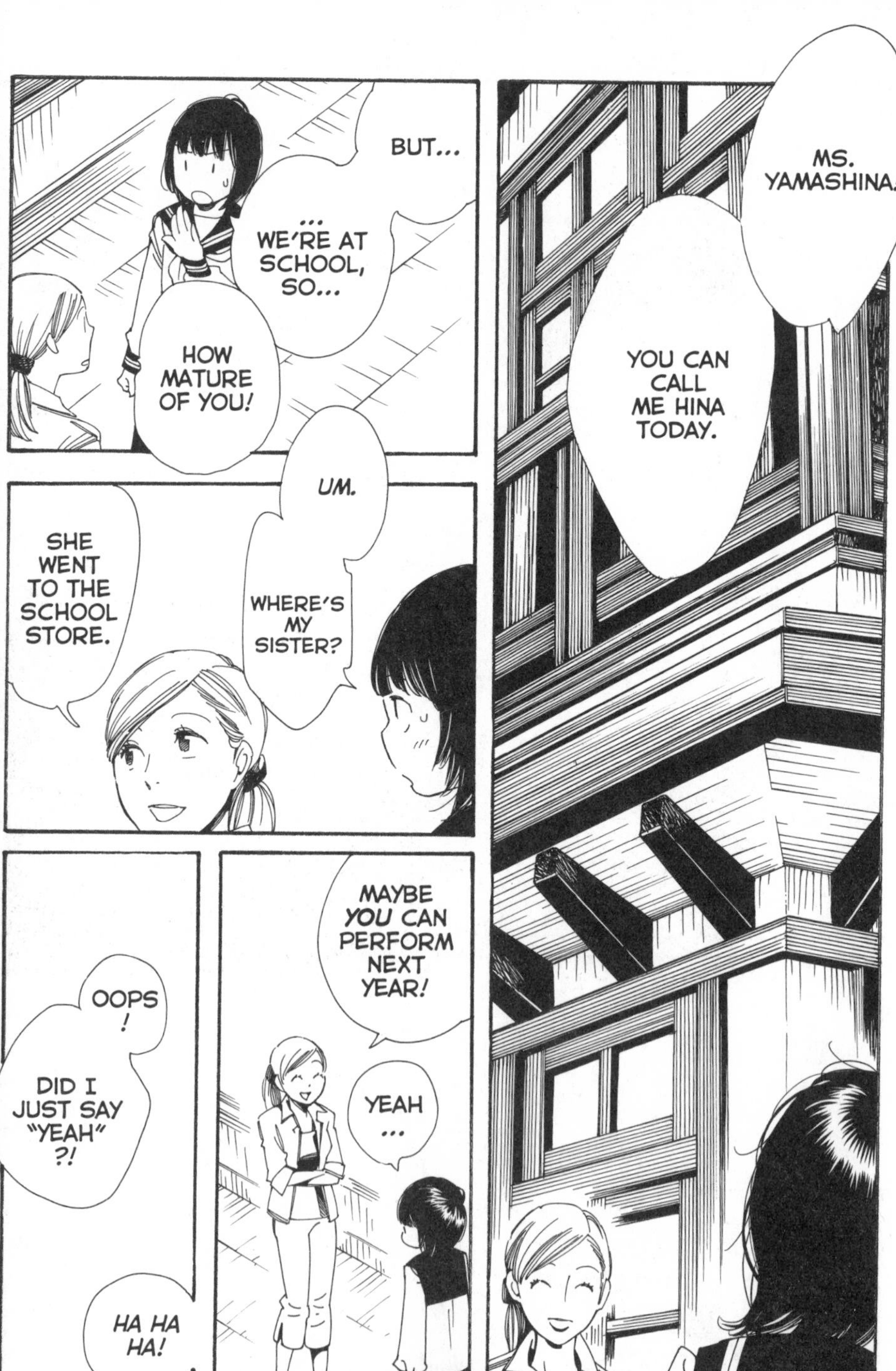
MS. YAMASHINA!
YOU CAN CALL ME HINA TODAY.
BUT...
...WE'RE AT SCHOOL, SO...
HOW MATURE OF YOU!
UM.
WHERE'S MY SISTER?
SHE WENT TO THE SCHOOL STORE.
MAYBE *YOU* CAN PERFORM NEXT YEAR!
YEAH...
OOPS!
DID I JUST SAY "YEAH"?!
HA HA HA!

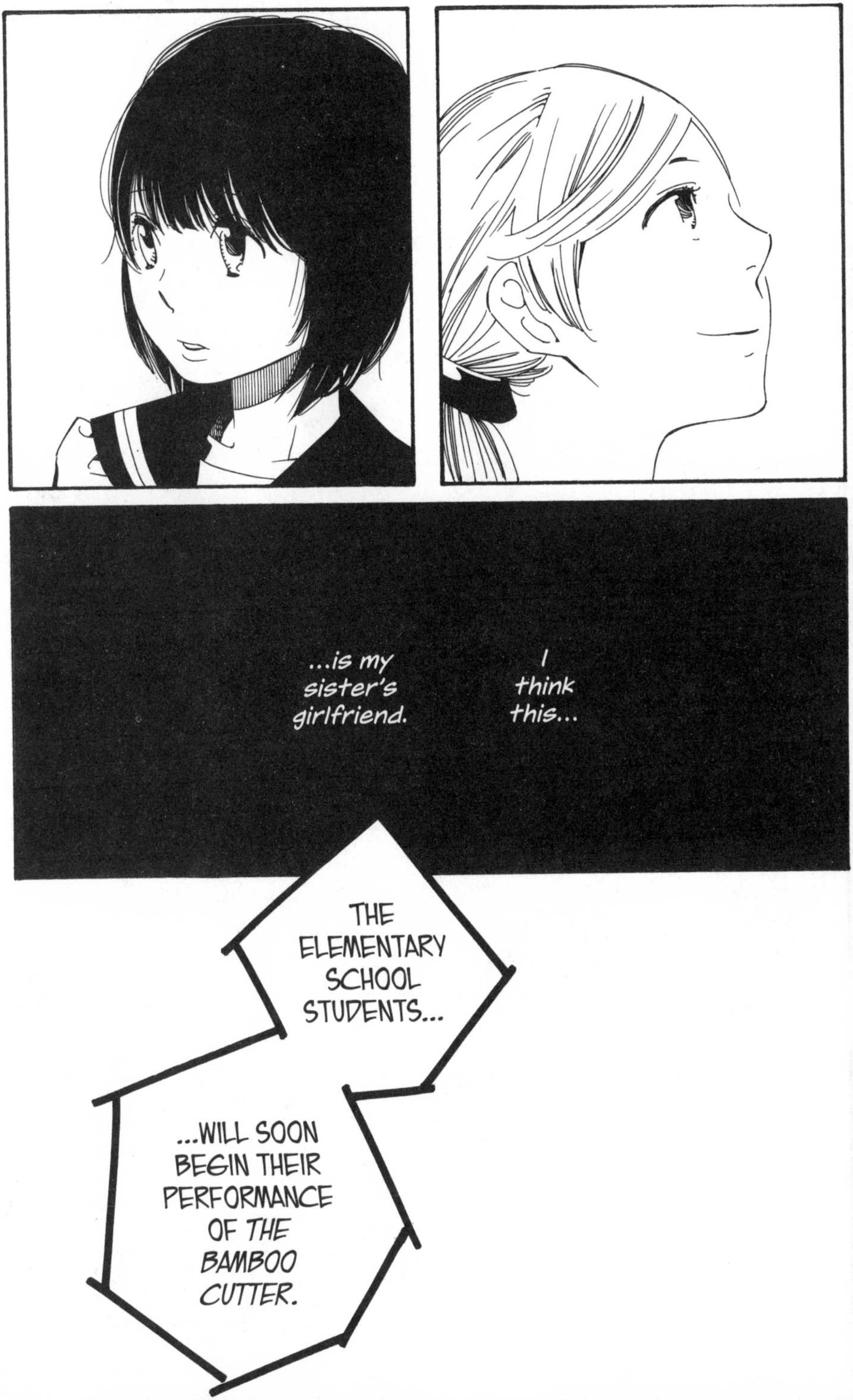
I think this...
...is my sister's girlfriend.
THE ELEMENTARY SCHOOL STUDENTS...
...WILL SOON BEGIN THEIR PERFORMANCE OF THE BAMBOO CUTTER.

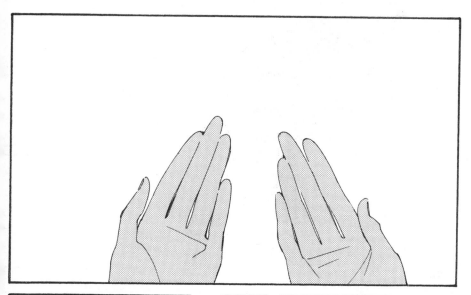

AKIRA...

...DO YOU HAVE A MINUTE?

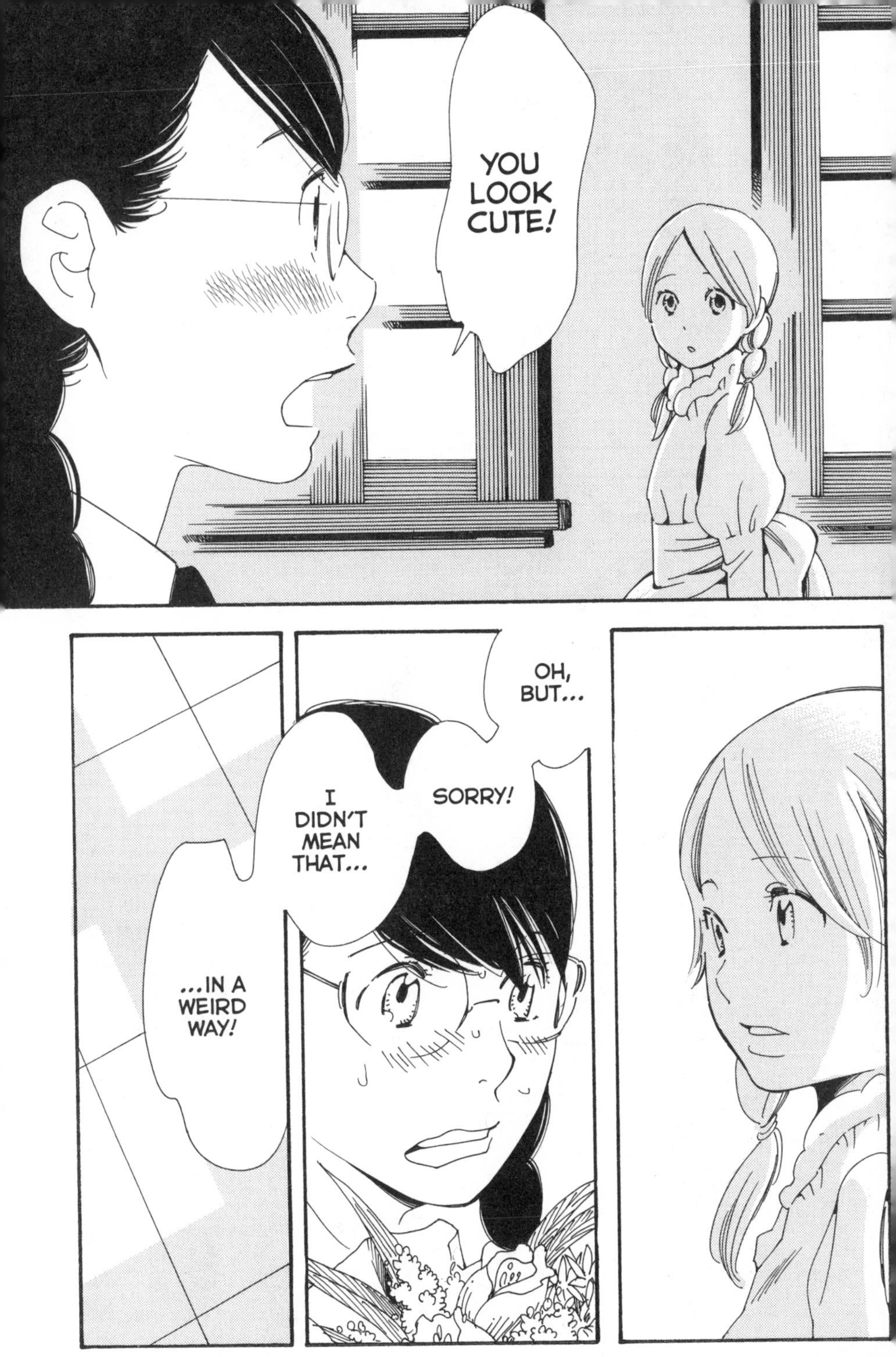
YOU LOOK CUTE!
OH, BUT...
SORRY!
I DIDN'T MEAN THAT...
...IN A WEIRD WAY!

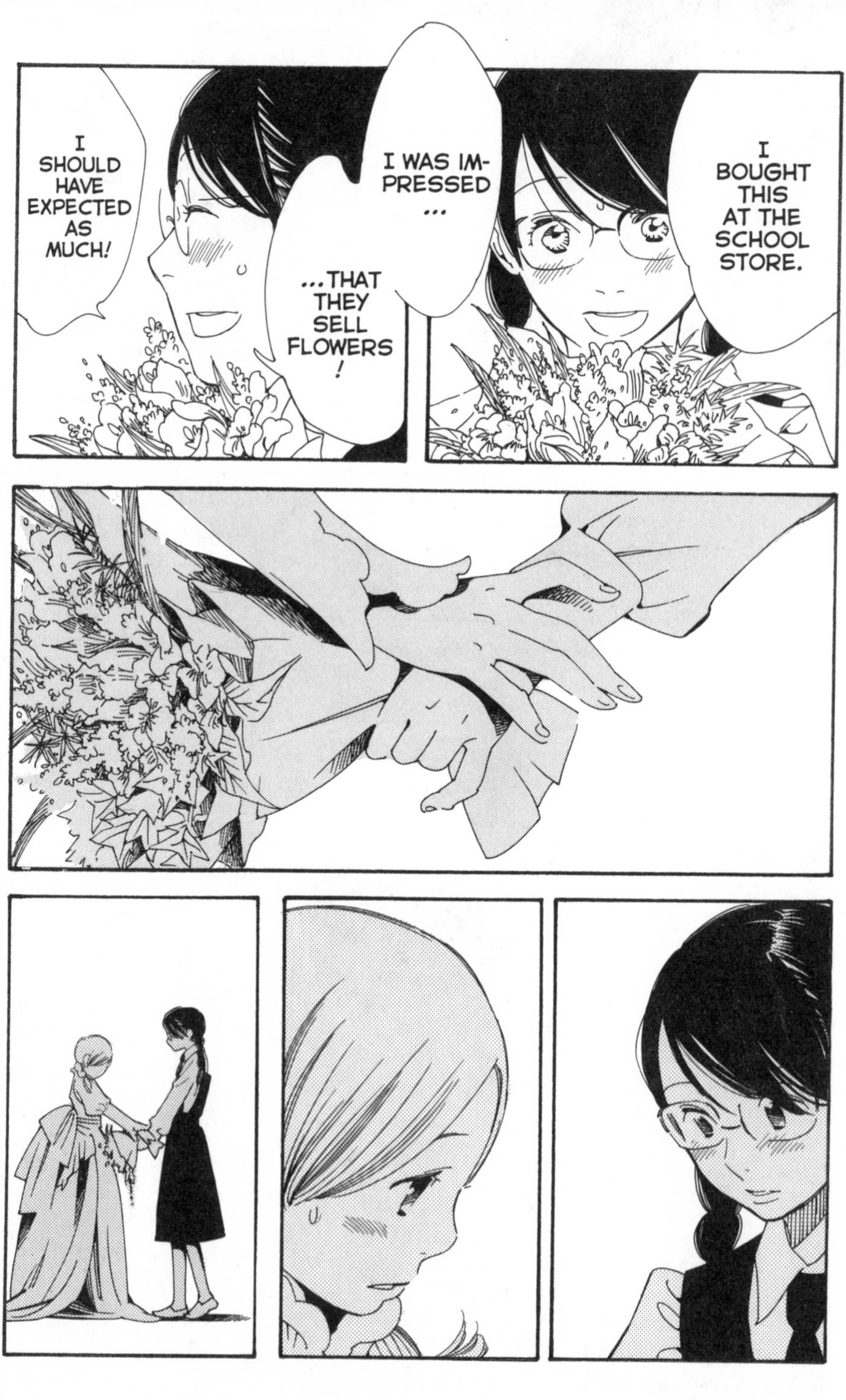
I BOUGHT THIS AT THE SCHOOL STORE.
I WAS IM-PRESSED...
...THAT THEY SELL FLOWERS!
I SHOULD HAVE EXPECTED AS MUCH!

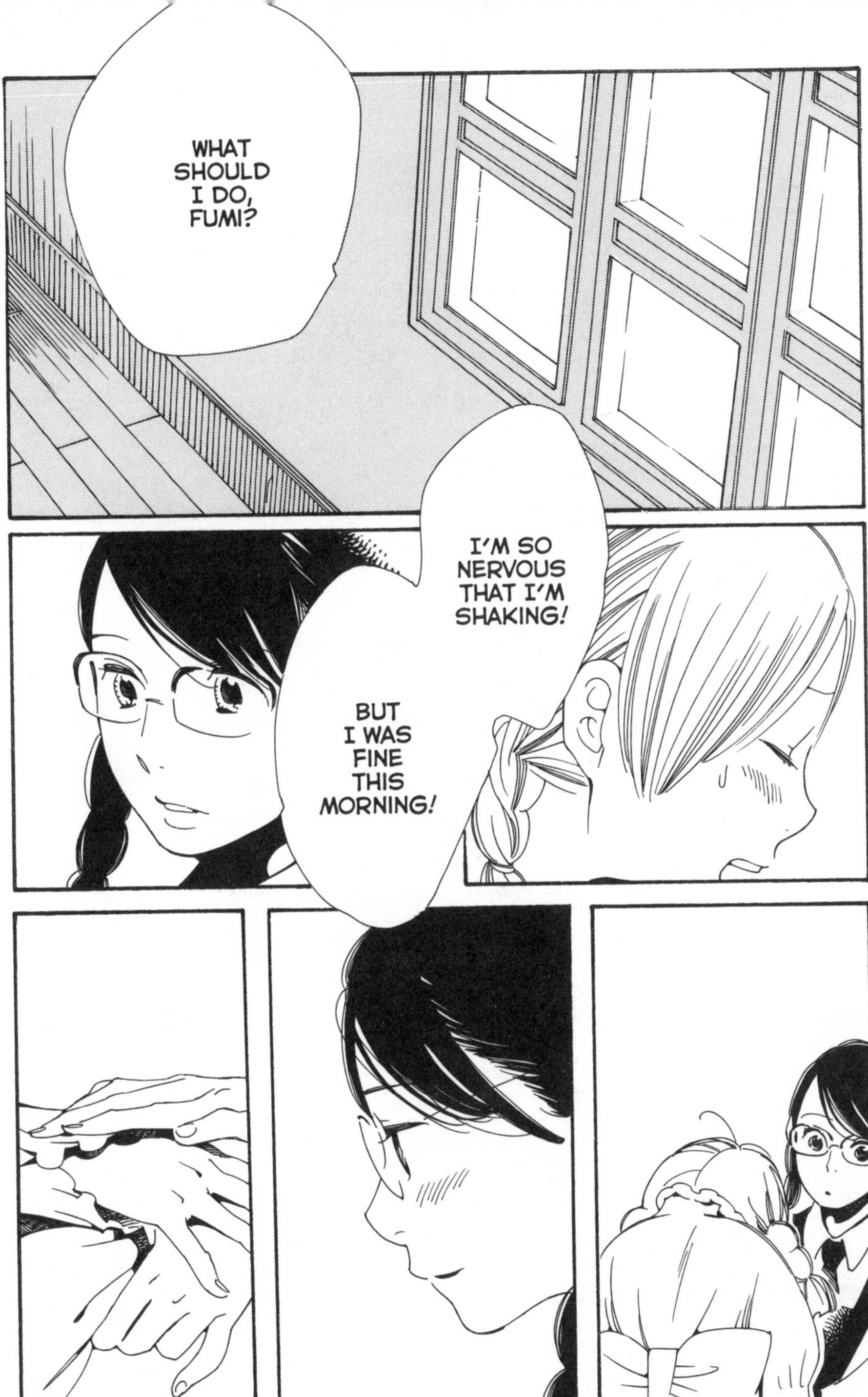
WHAT SHOULD I DO, FUMI?
I'M SO NERVOUS THAT I'M SHAKING!
BUT I WAS FINE THIS MORNING!

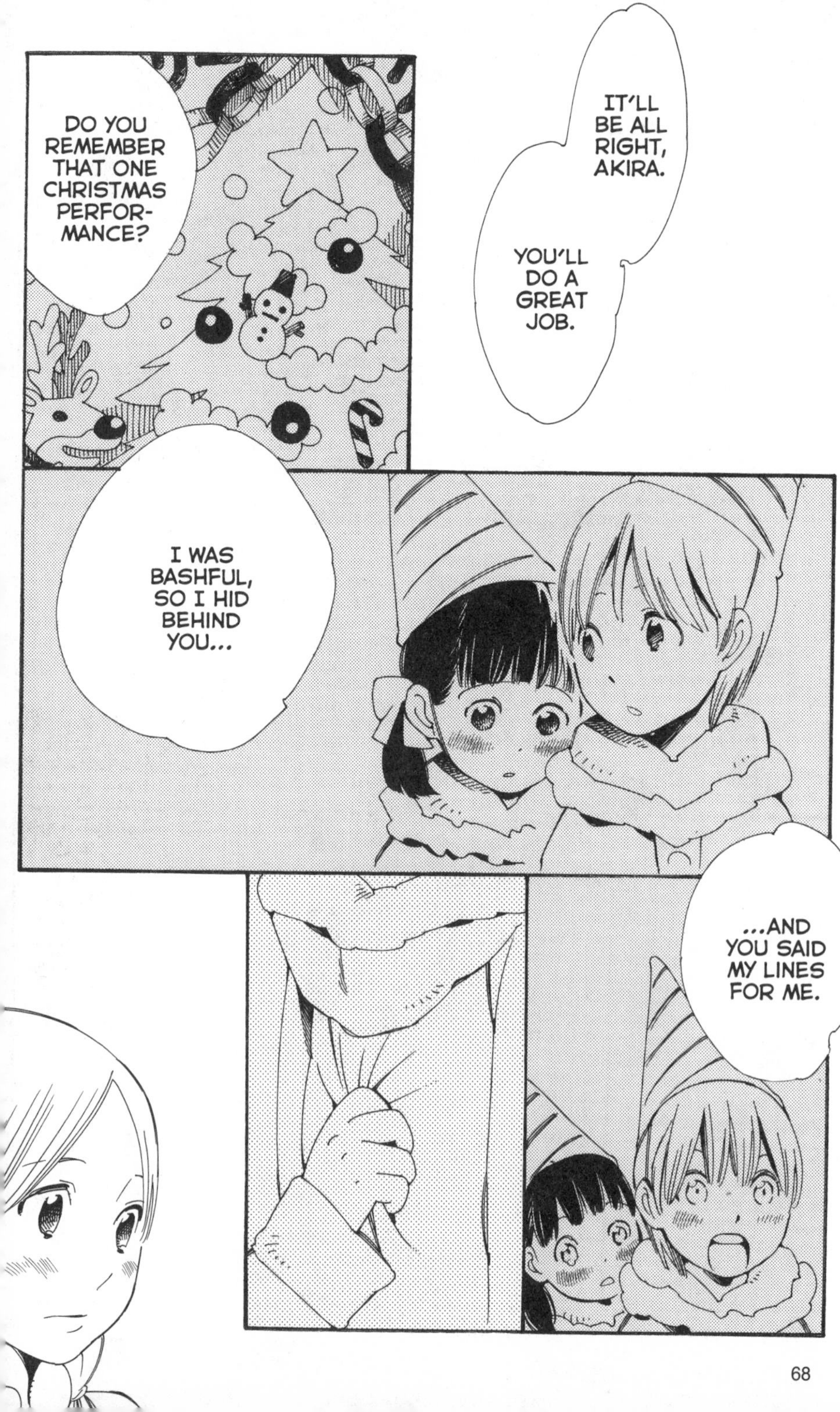
IT'LL BE ALL RIGHT, AKIRA.
YOU'LL DO A GREAT JOB.
DO YOU REMEMBER THAT ONE CHRISTMAS PERFOR-MANCE?
I WAS BASHFUL, SO I HID BEHIND YOU...
...AND YOU SAID MY LINES FOR ME.

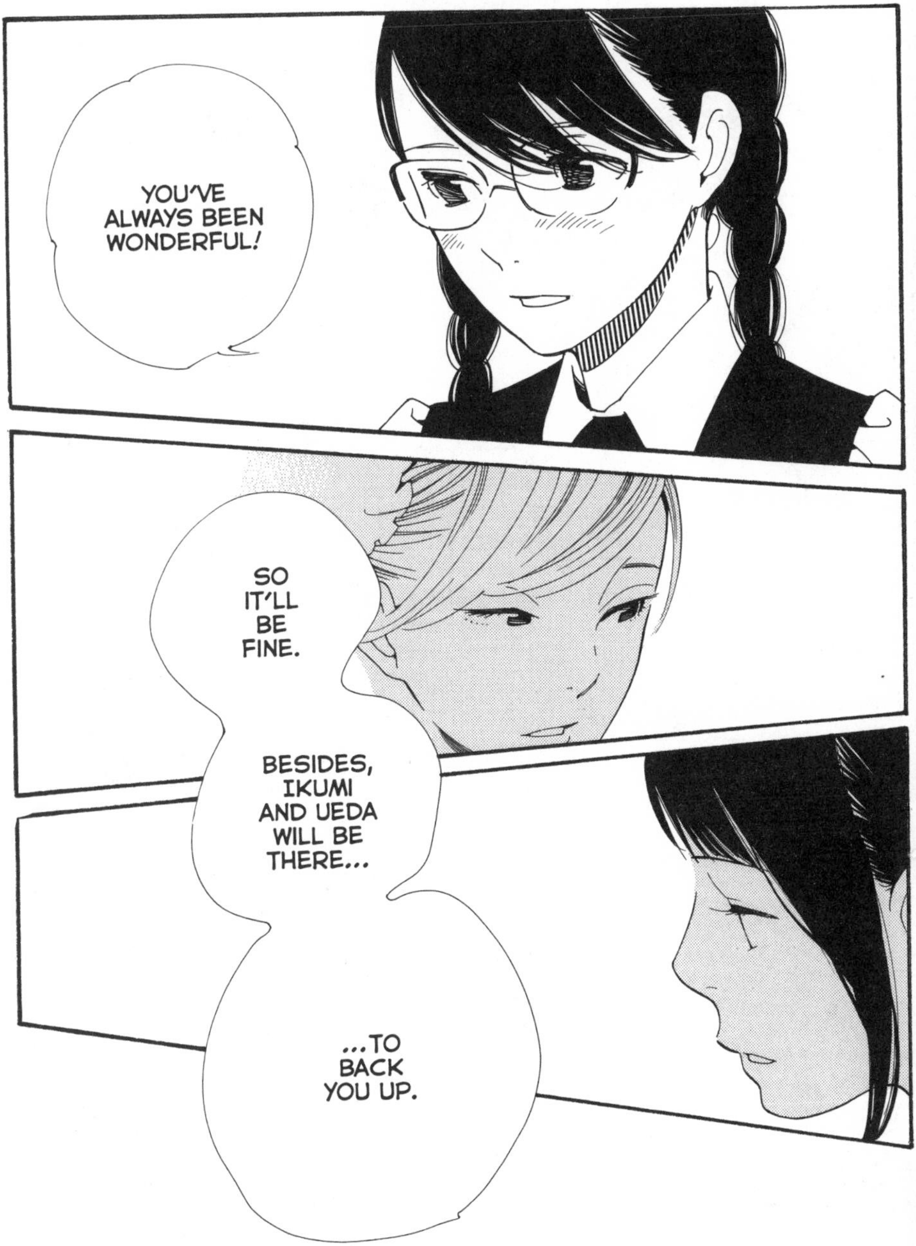
YOU'VE ALWAYS BEEN WONDERFUL!
SO IT'LL BE FINE.
BESIDES, IKUMI AND UEDA WILL BE THERE...
...TO BACK YOU UP.

AND I'LL STAY NEAR THE STAGE TO FEED YOU LINES, IF NECESSARY.

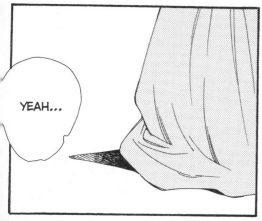

YEAH...

Elementary School Performance

The Bamboo Cutter

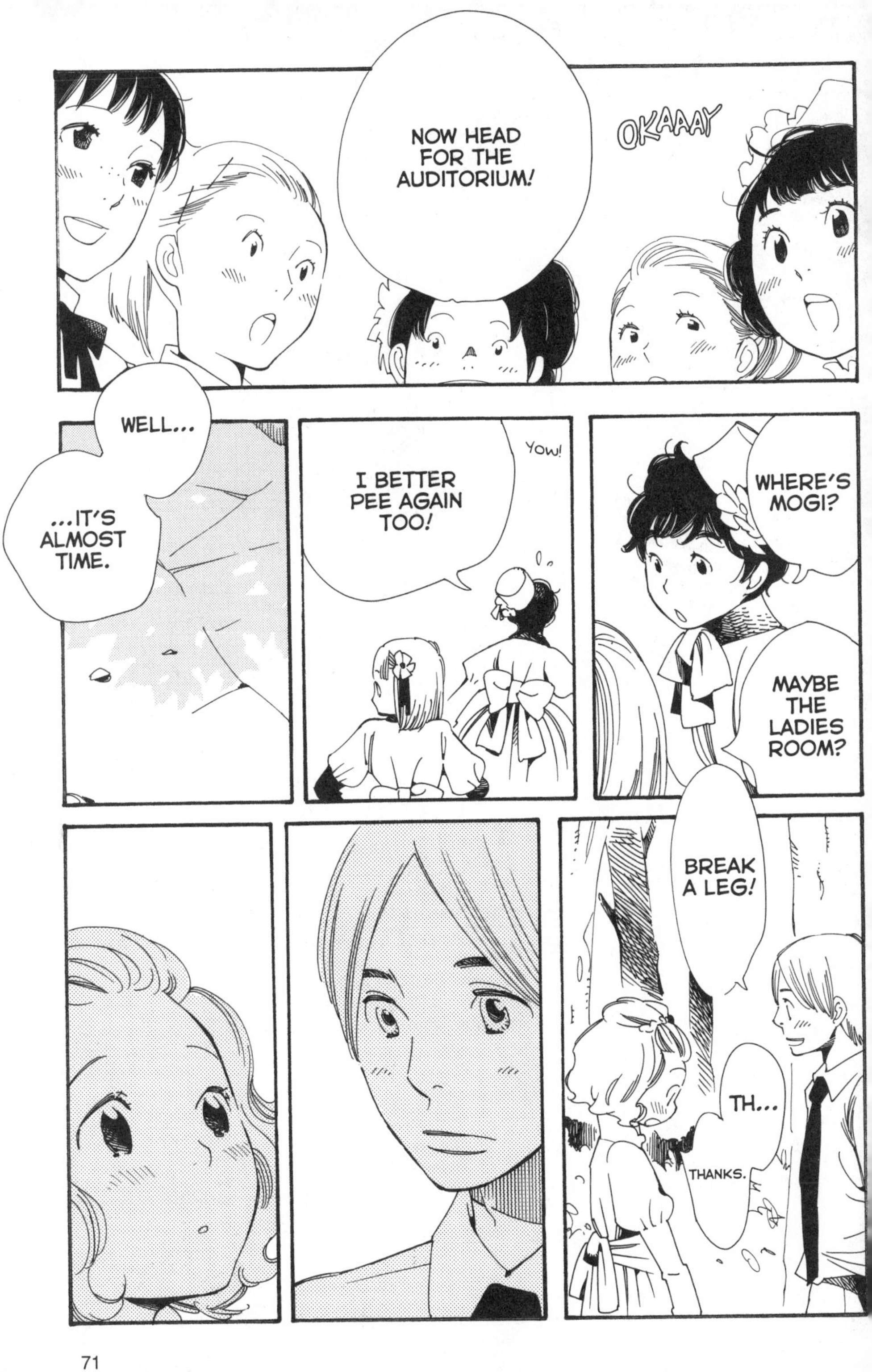
NOW HEAD FOR THE AUDITORIUM!
OKAAAY
WHERE'S MOGI?
MAYBE THE LADIES ROOM?
YOW!
I BETTER PEE AGAIN TOO!
WELL...
...IT'S ALMOST TIME.
BREAK A LEG!
TH...
THANKS.

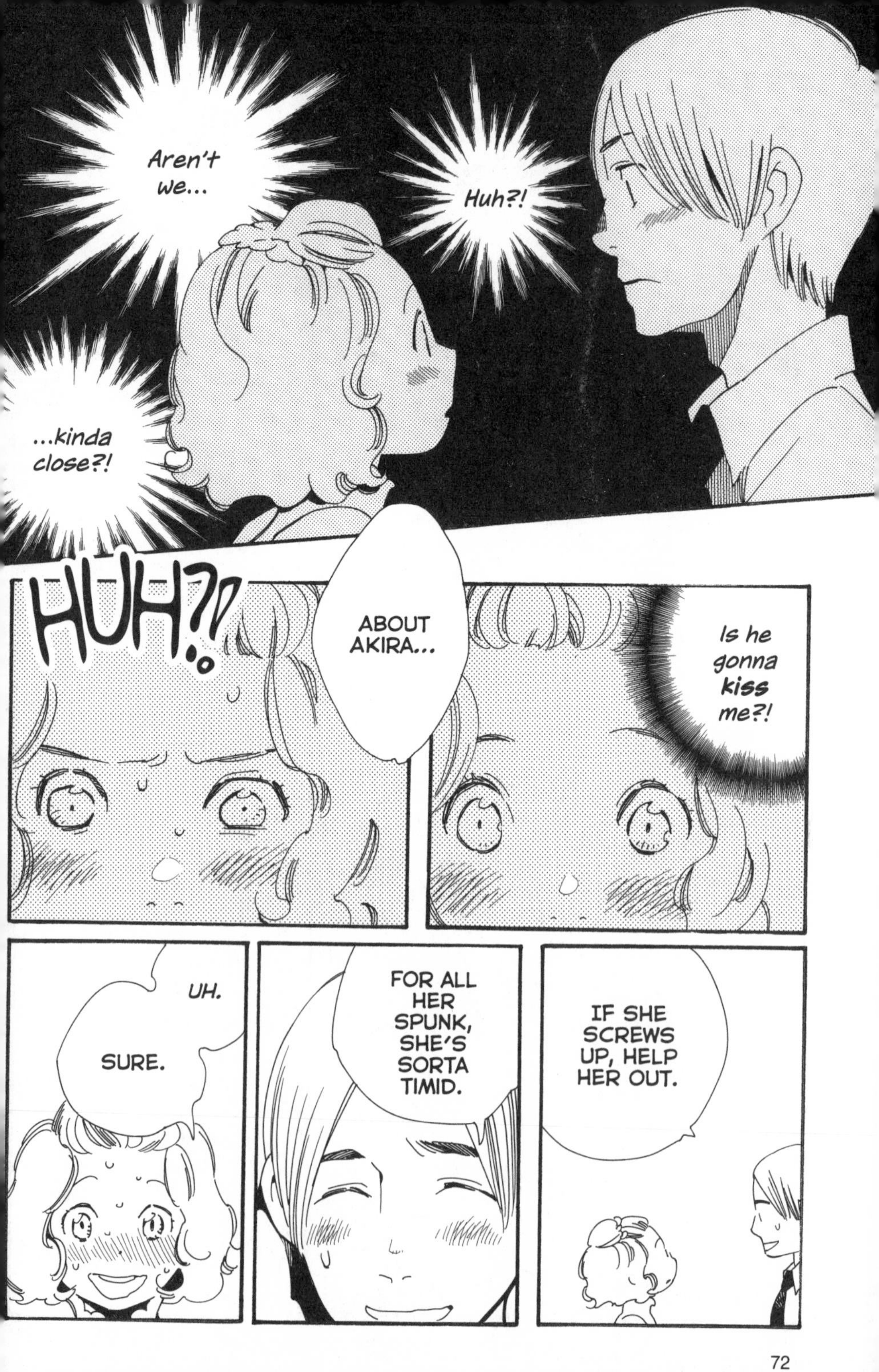

Huh?!
Aren't we...
...kinda close?!
Is he gonna **kiss** me?!
ABOUT AKIRA...
HUH?!
IF SHE SCREWS UP, HELP HER OUT.
FOR ALL HER SPUNK, SHE'S SORTA TIMID.
UH.
SURE.

OH!
THERE'S MOGI!
YEAH!
SHE'S WITH HER MAN.
SHE EVEN FOOLS AROUND AT SOMEONE ELSE'S SCHOOL!
WHOA!

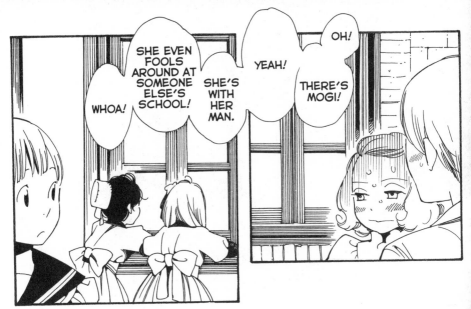

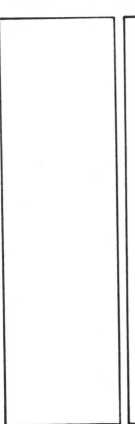

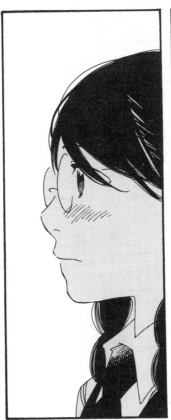

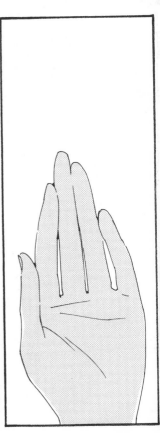

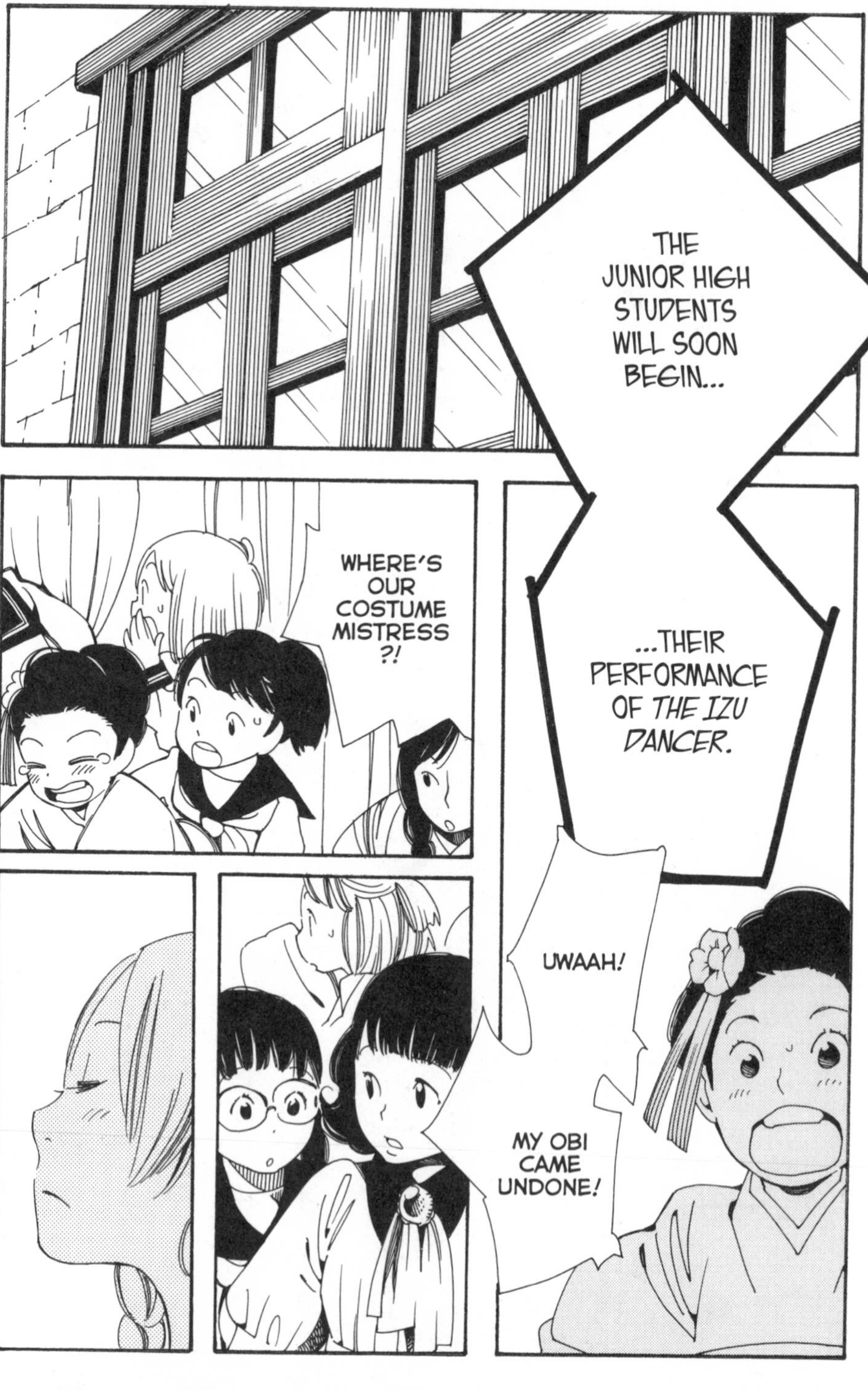
THE JUNIOR HIGH STUDENTS WILL SOON BEGIN...
...THEIR PERFORMANCE OF *THE IZU DANCER.*
UWAAH!
MY OBI CAME UNDONE!
WHERE'S OUR COSTUME MISTRESS?!

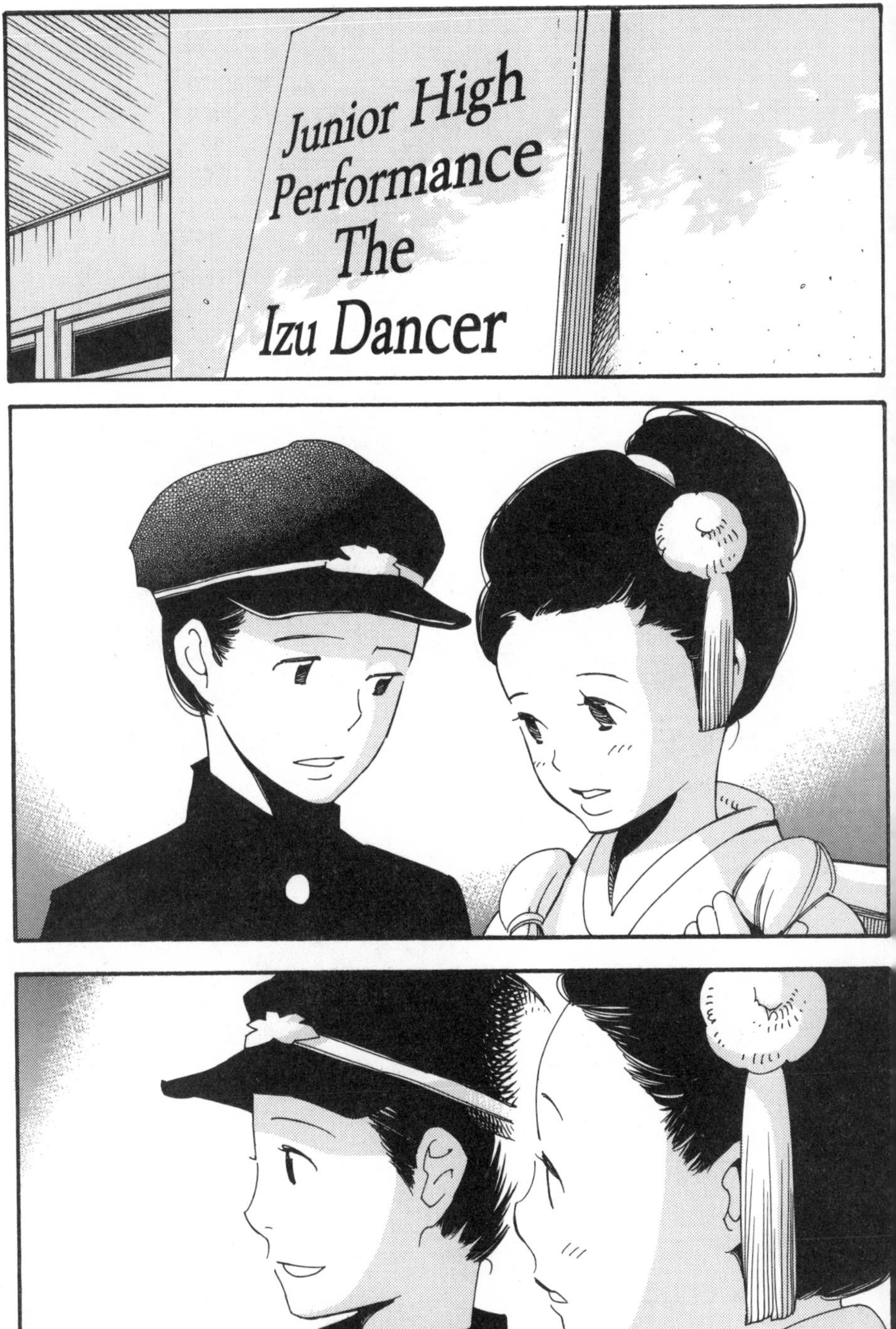
Junior High
Performance
The
Izu Dancer

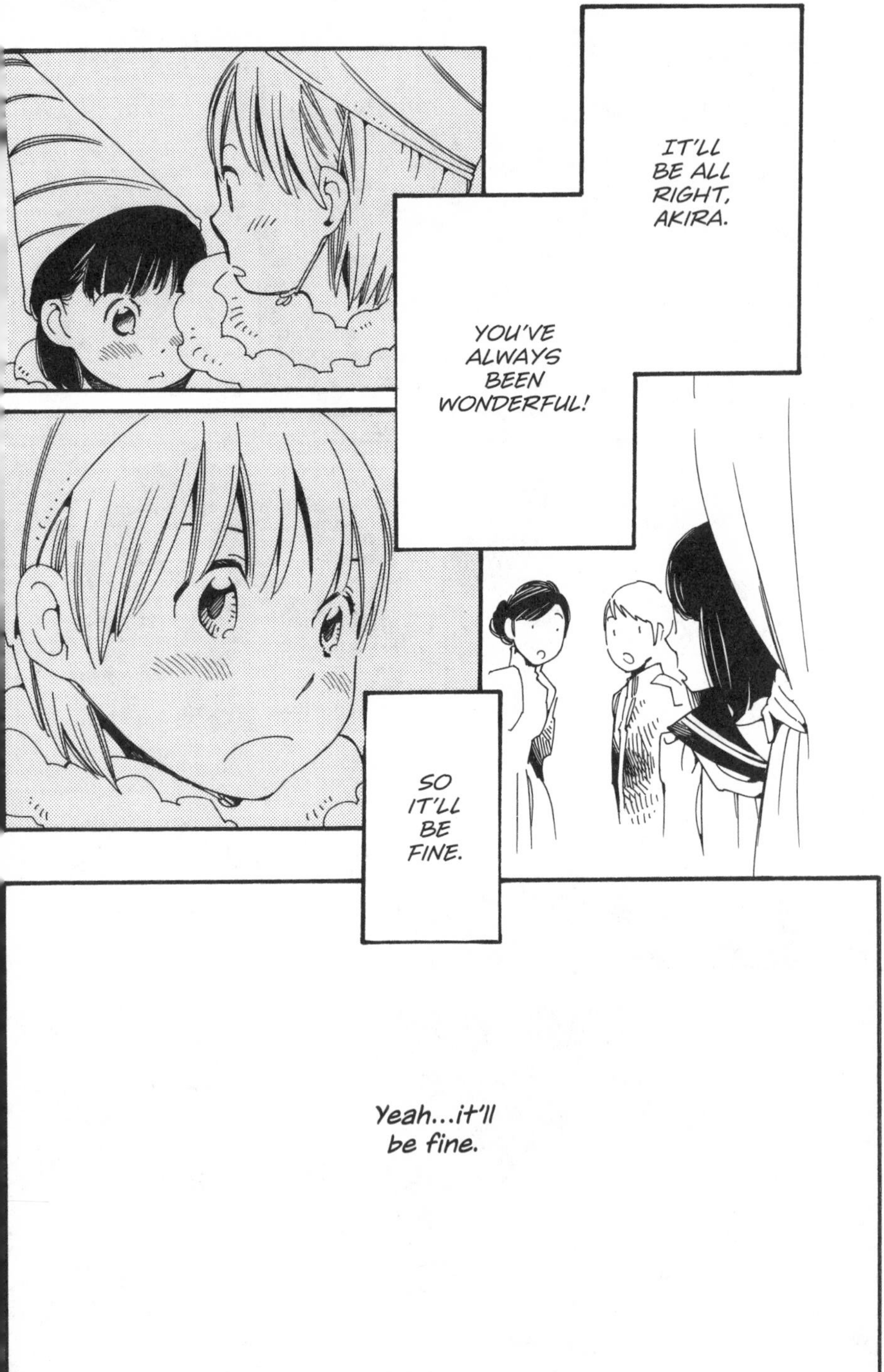
IT'LL BE ALL RIGHT, AKIRA.
YOU'VE ALWAYS BEEN WONDERFUL!
SO IT'LL BE FINE.
Yeah...it'll be fine.

Sweet **Blue**
Flowers

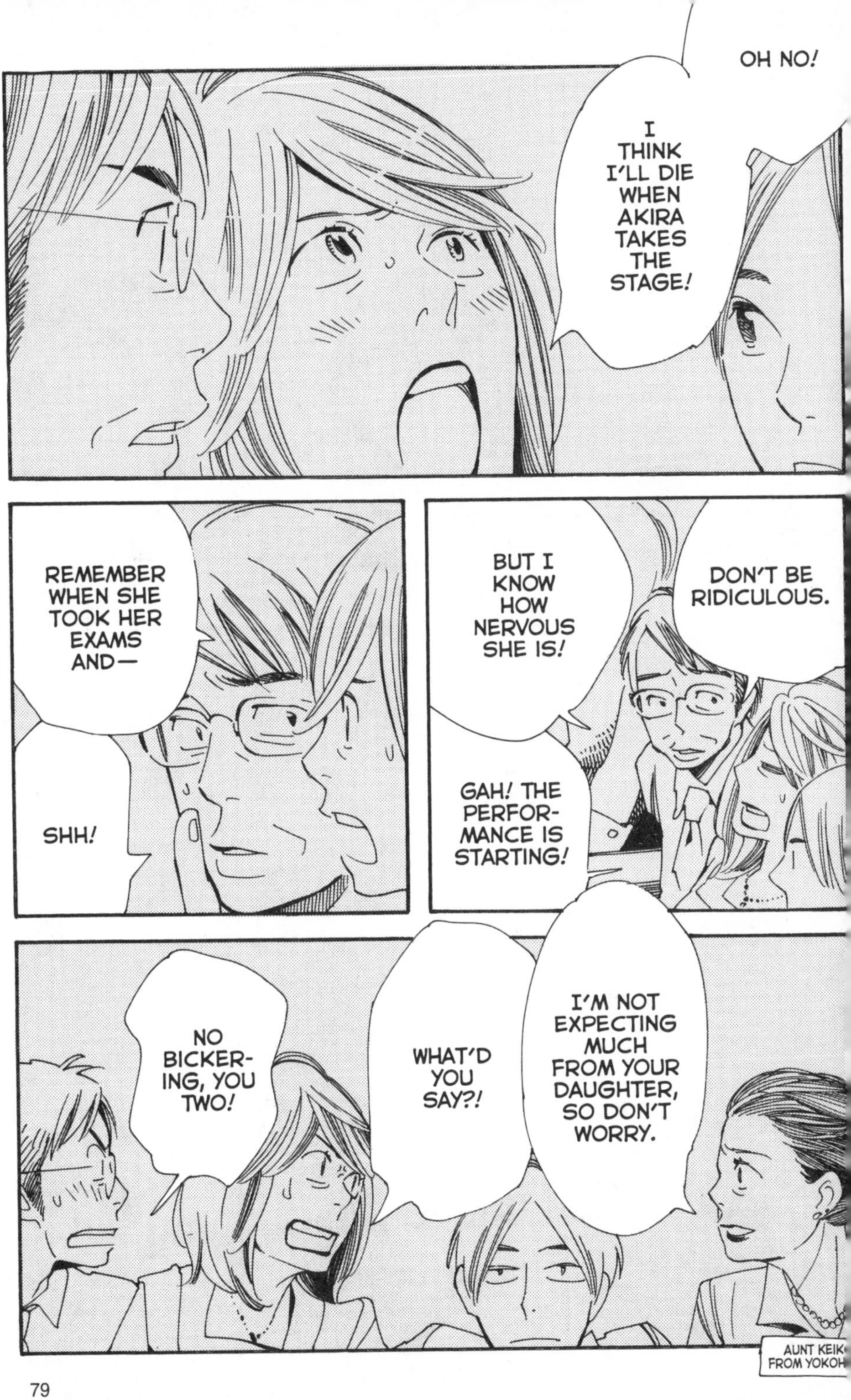
OH NO!
I THINK I'LL DIE WHEN AKIRA TAKES THE STAGE!
DON'T BE RIDICULOUS.
BUT I KNOW HOW NERVOUS SHE IS!
GAH! THE PERFORMANCE IS STARTING!
REMEMBER WHEN SHE TOOK HER EXAMS AND—
SHH!
I'M NOT EXPECTING MUCH FROM YOUR DAUGHTER, SO DON'T WORRY.
WHAT'D YOU SAY?!
NO BICKERING, YOU TWO!
AUNT KEIK
FROM YOKOH

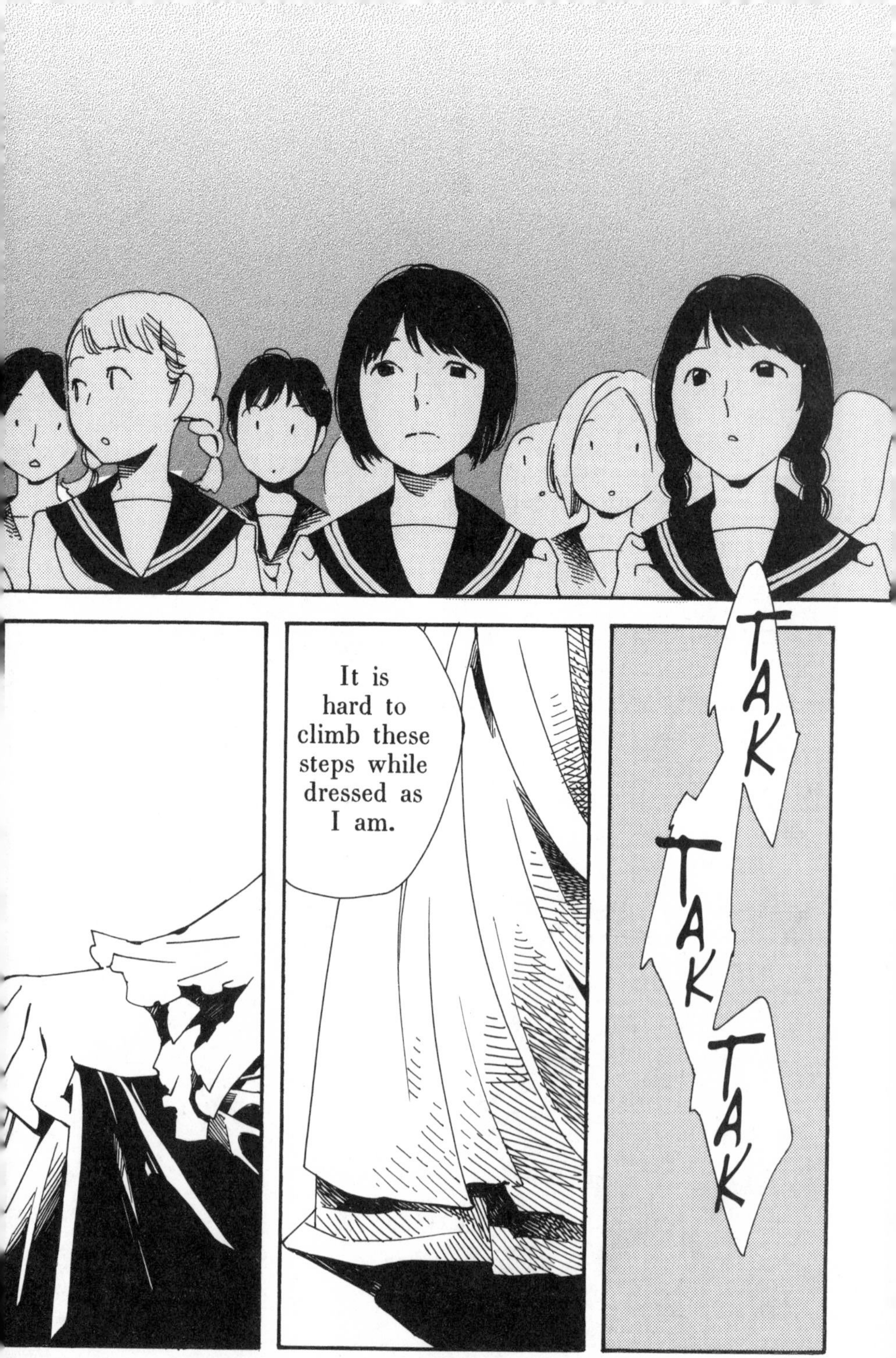
TAK
TAK
TAK
It is hard to climb these steps while dressed as I am.

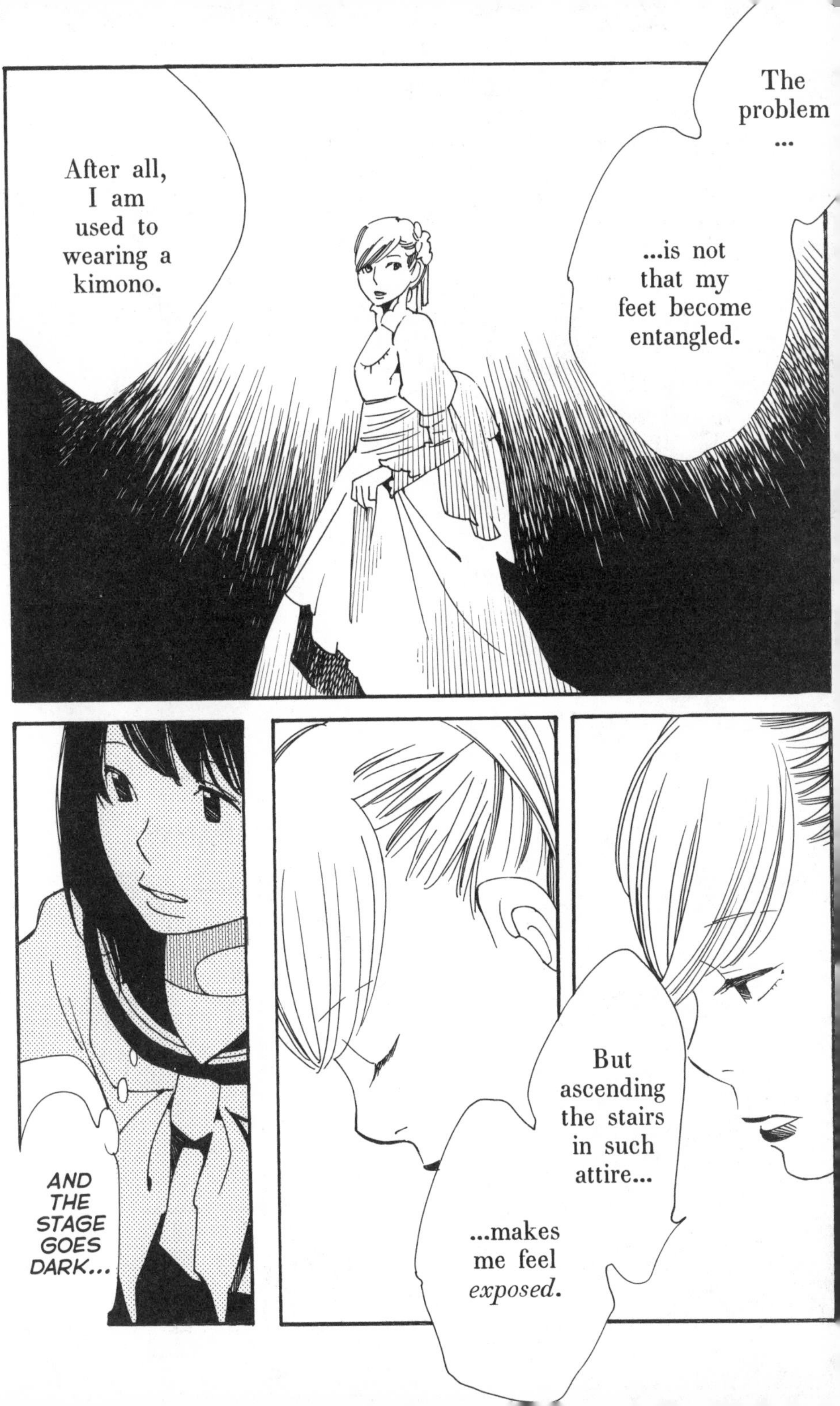
The problem ...
...is not that my feet become entangled.
After all, I am used to wearing a kimono.
But ascending the stairs in such attire...
...makes me feel *exposed*.
AND THE STAGE GOES DARK...

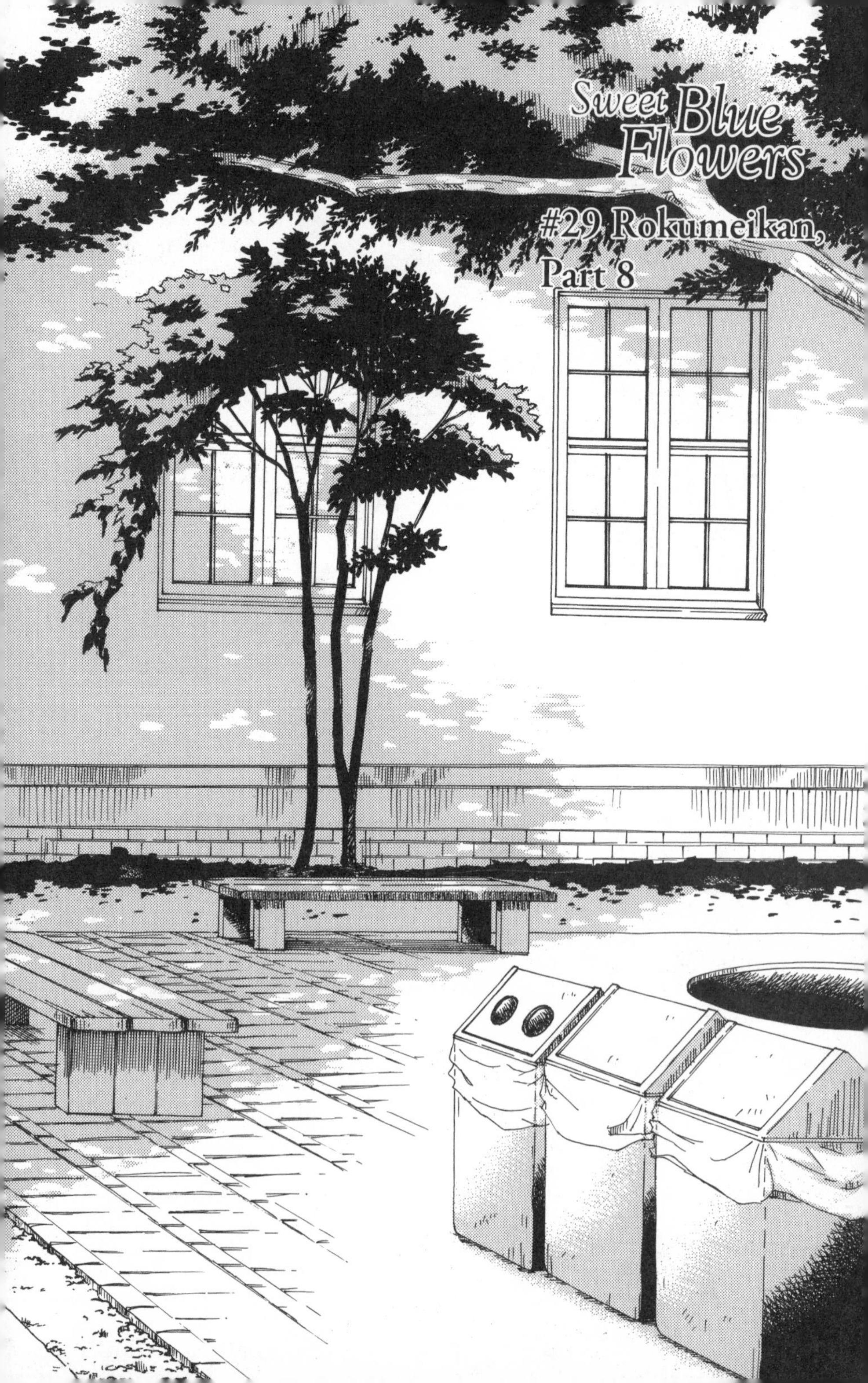
Sweet Blue Flowers
#29 Rokumeikan, Part 8

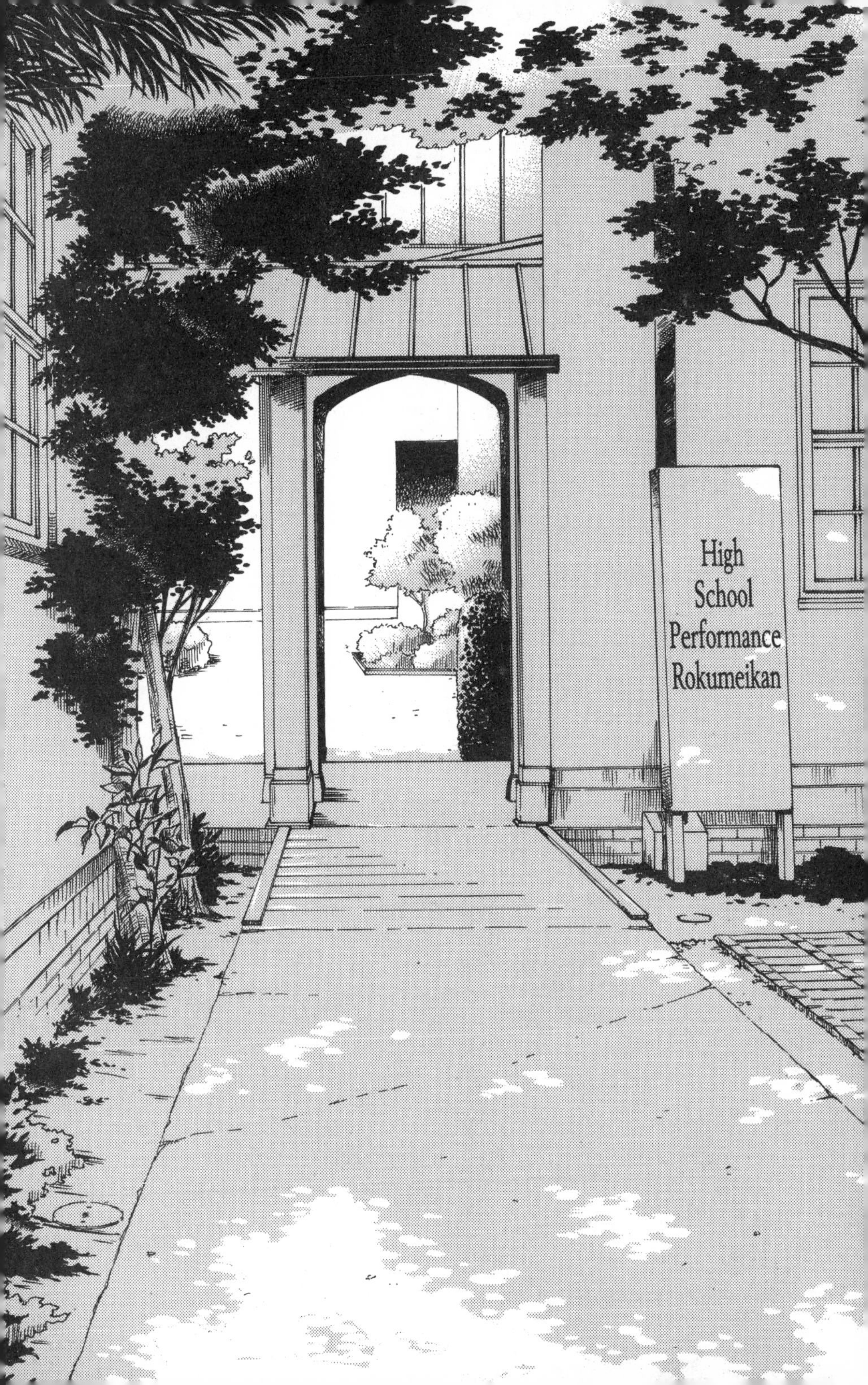
High
School
Performance
Rokumeikan

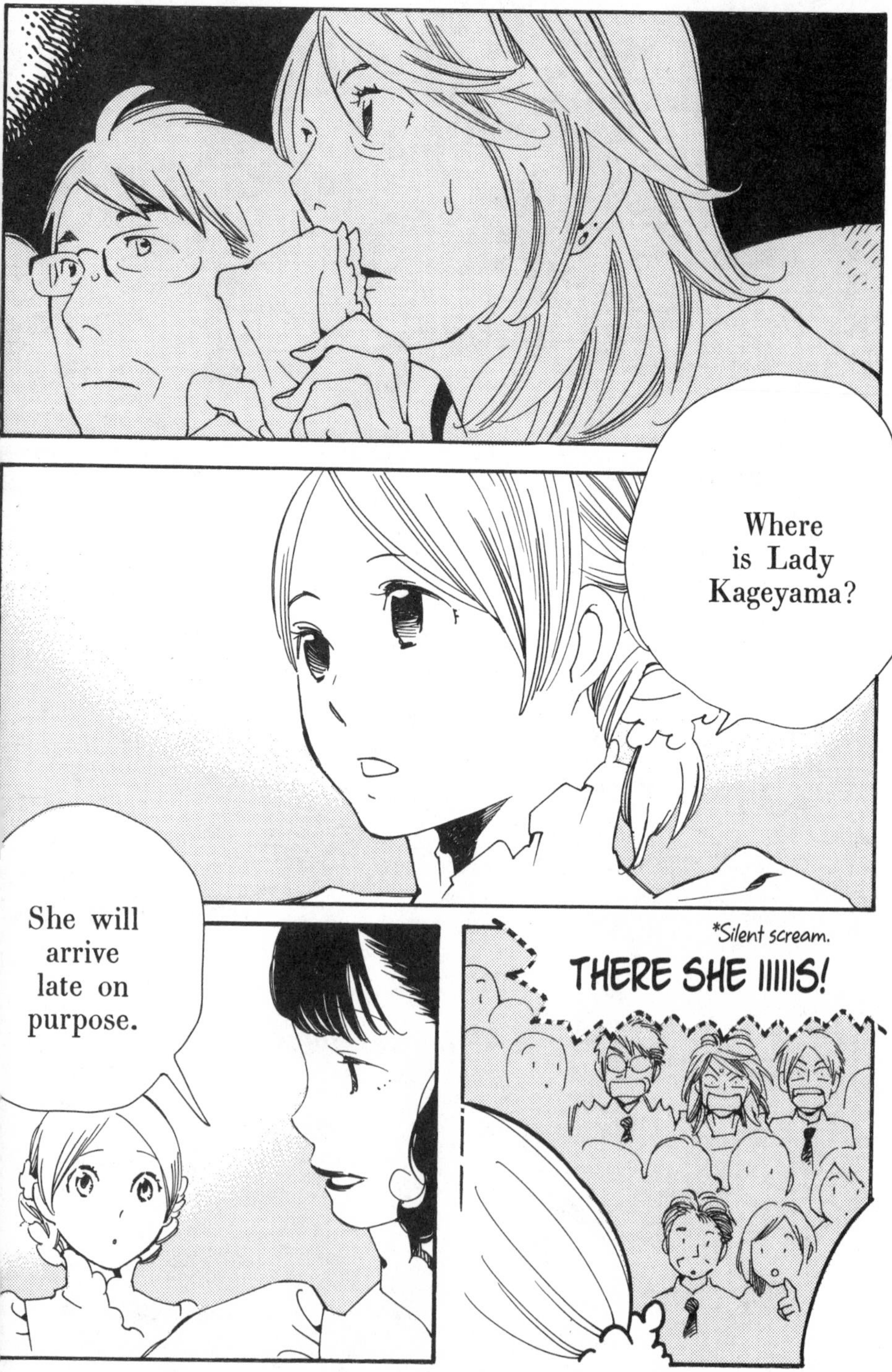
Where is Lady Kageyama?
*Silent scream.
THERE SHE IIIIIS!
She will arrive late on purpose.

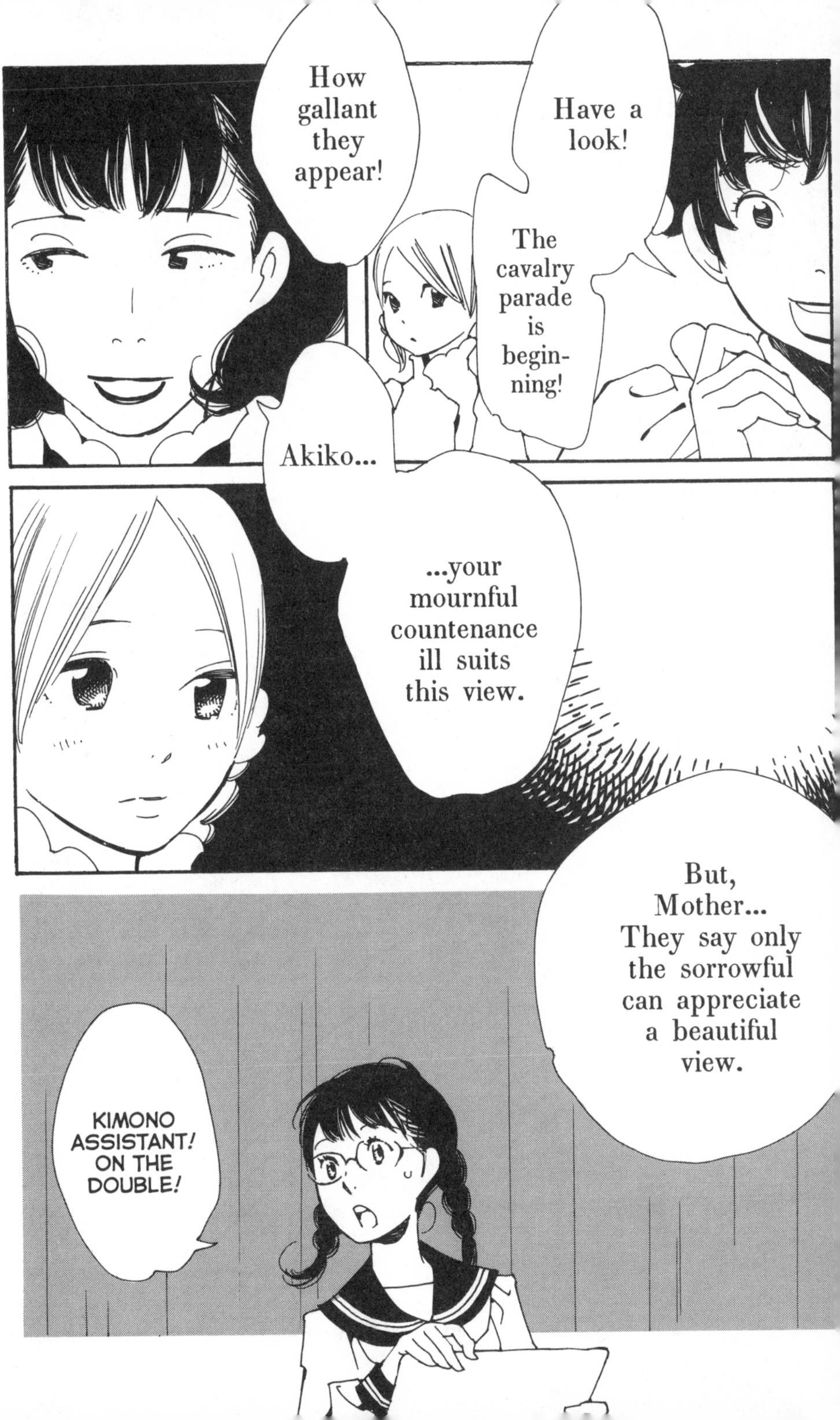

Have a look!
The cavalry parade is beginning!
How gallant they appear!
Akiko...
...your mournful countenance ill suits this view.
But, Mother... They say only the sorrowful can appreciate a beautiful view.
KIMONO ASSISTANT! ON THE DOUBLE!

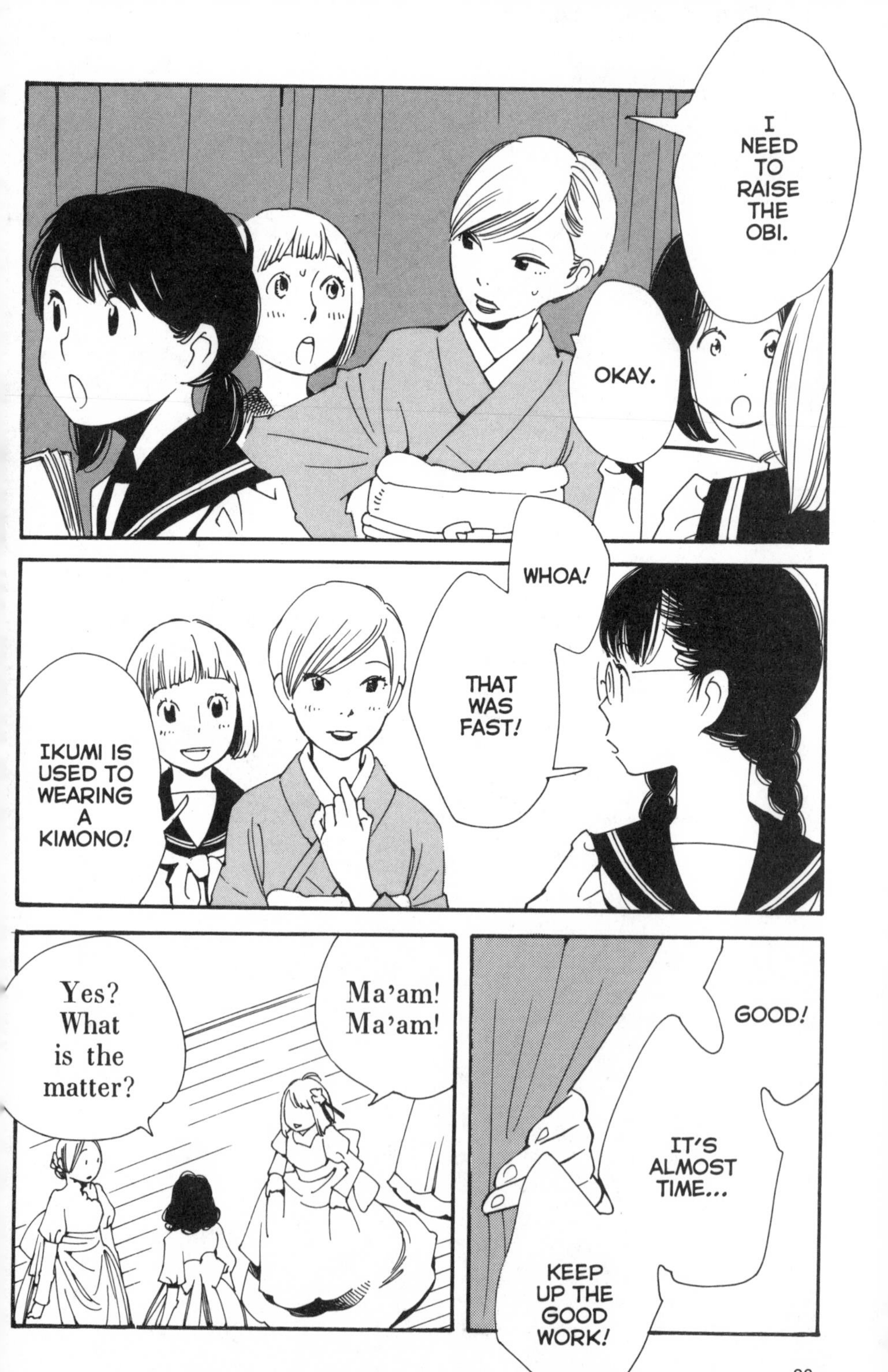
I NEED TO RAISE THE OBI.
OKAY.
WHOA!
THAT WAS FAST!
IKUMI IS USED TO WEARING A KIMONO!
GOOD!
IT'S ALMOST TIME...
KEEP UP THE GOOD WORK!
Ma'am! Ma'am!
Yes? What is the matter?

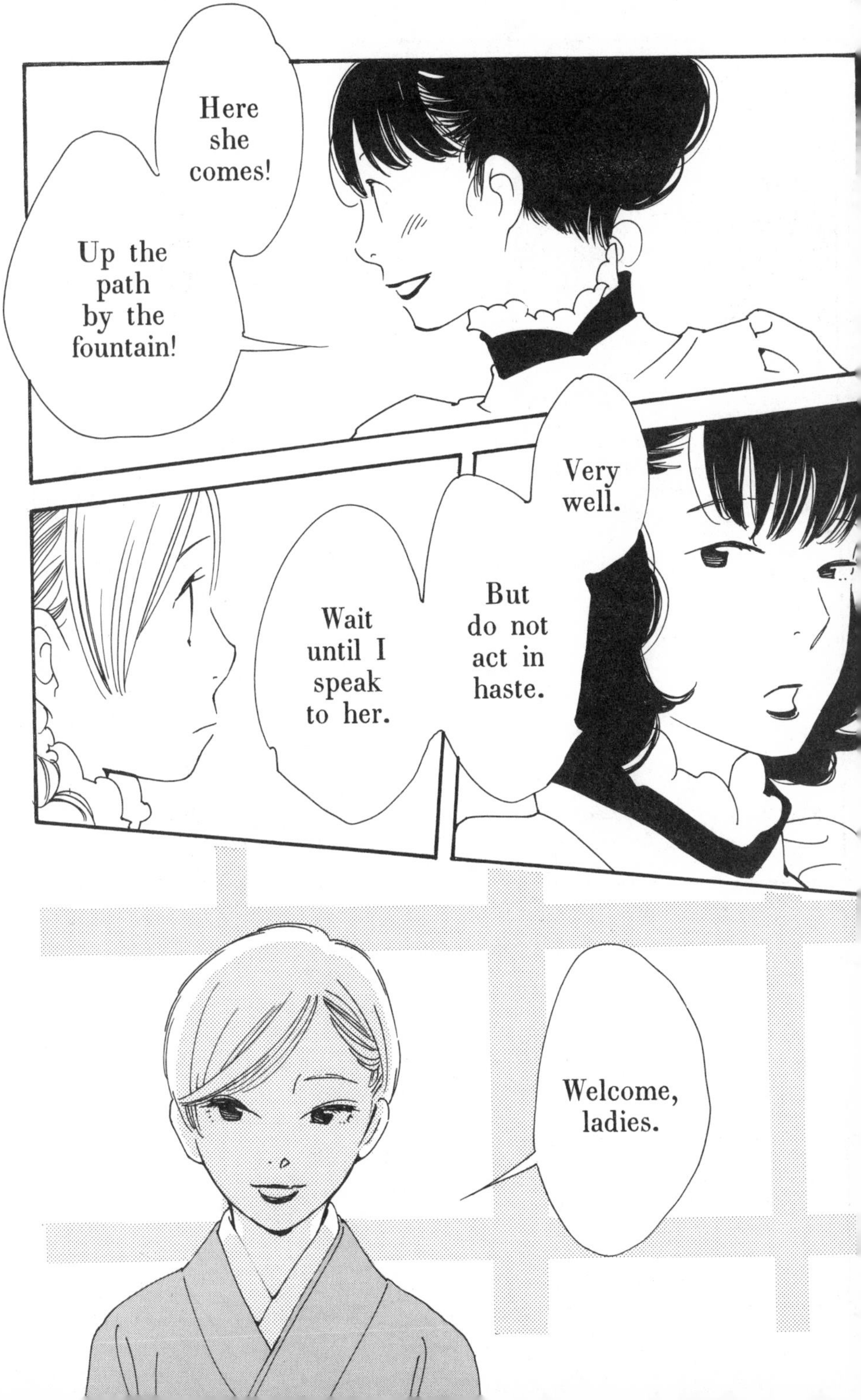
Here she comes!
Up the path by the fountain!
Very well.
But do not act in haste.
Wait until I speak to her.
Welcome, ladies.

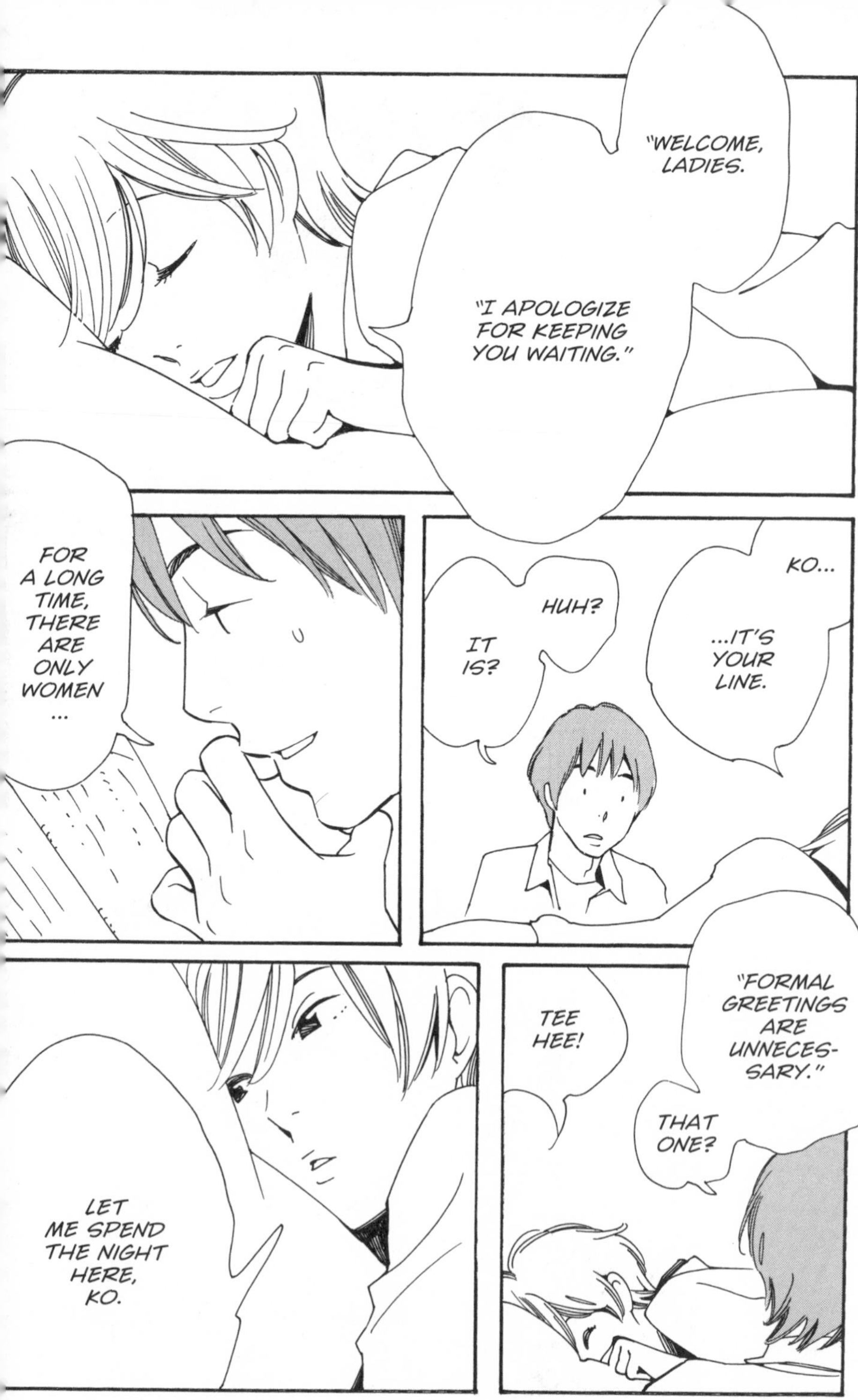
"WELCOME, LADIES.
"I APOLOGIZE FOR KEEPING YOU WAITING."
KO...
...IT'S YOUR LINE.
HUH?
IT IS?
FOR A LONG TIME, THERE ARE ONLY WOMEN ...
"FORMAL GREETINGS ARE UNNECES-SARY."
TEE HEE!
THAT ONE?
LET ME SPEND THE NIGHT HERE, KO.

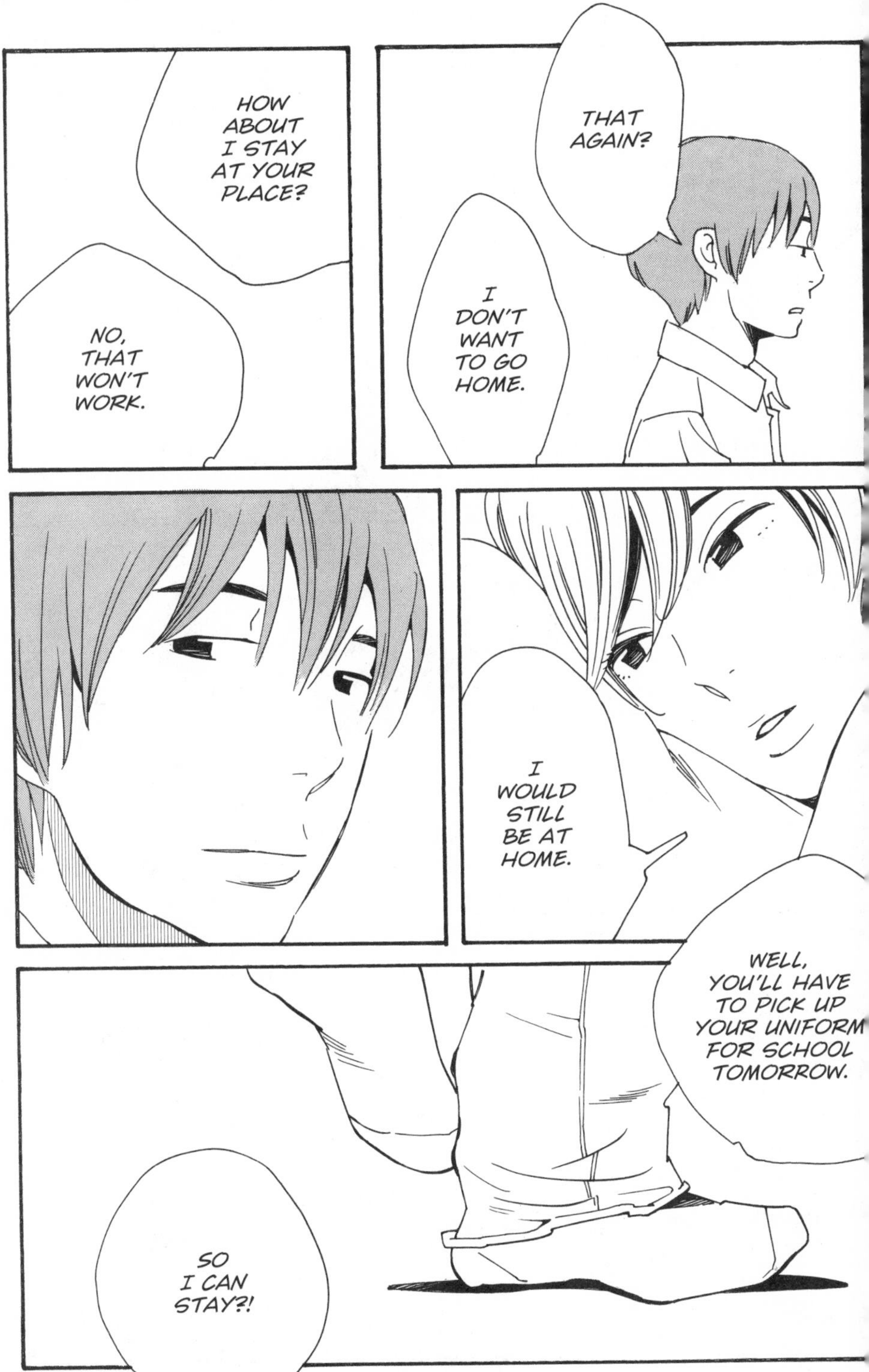
THAT AGAIN?
I DON'T WANT TO GO HOME.
HOW ABOUT I STAY AT YOUR PLACE?
NO, THAT WON'T WORK.
I WOULD STILL BE AT HOME.
WELL, YOU'LL HAVE TO PICK UP YOUR UNIFORM FOR SCHOOL TOMORROW.
SO I CAN STAY?!

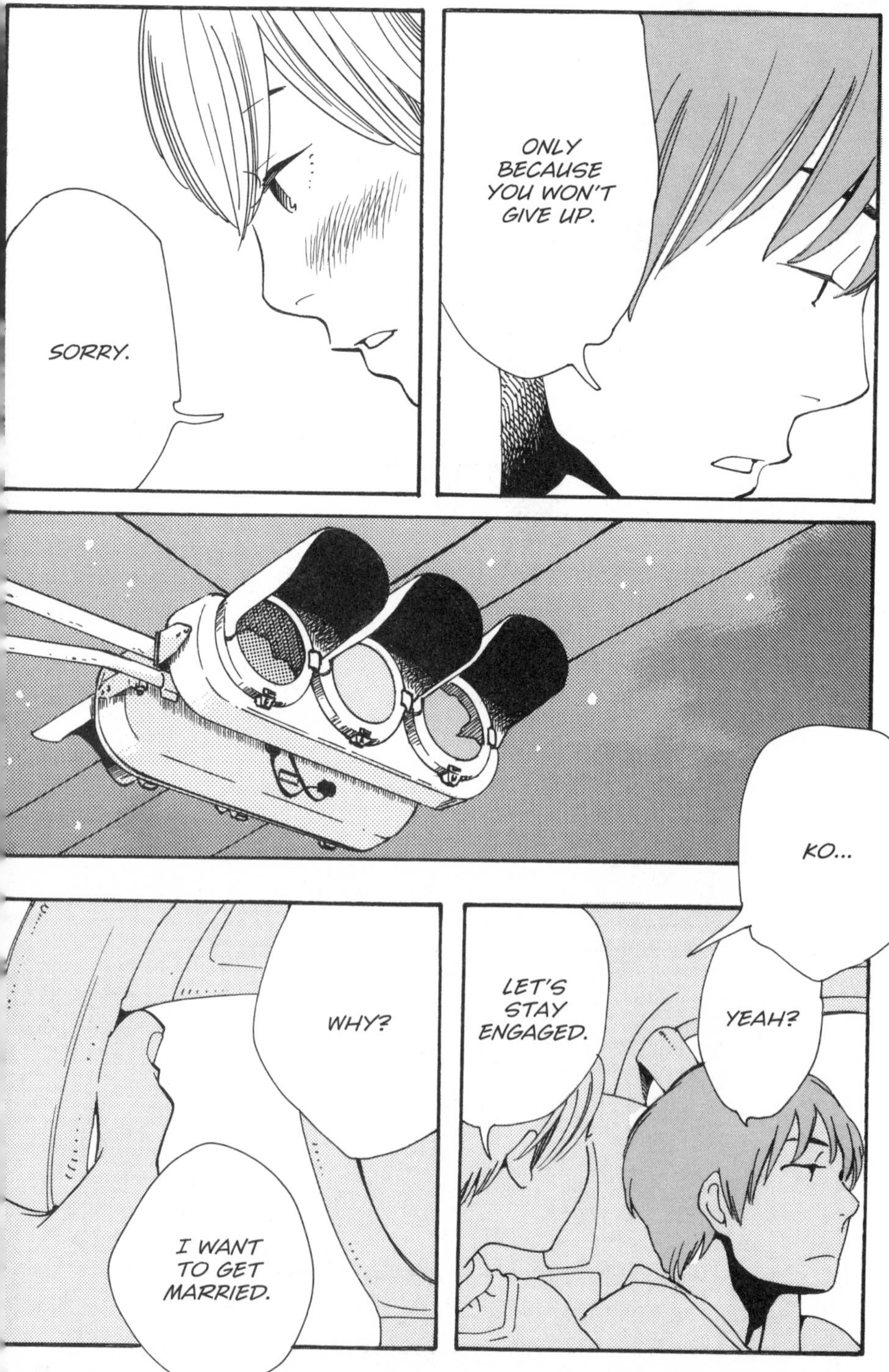
ONLY BECAUSE YOU WON'T GIVE UP.
SORRY.
KO...
YEAH?
LET'S STAY ENGAGED.
WHY?
I WANT TO GET MARRIED.

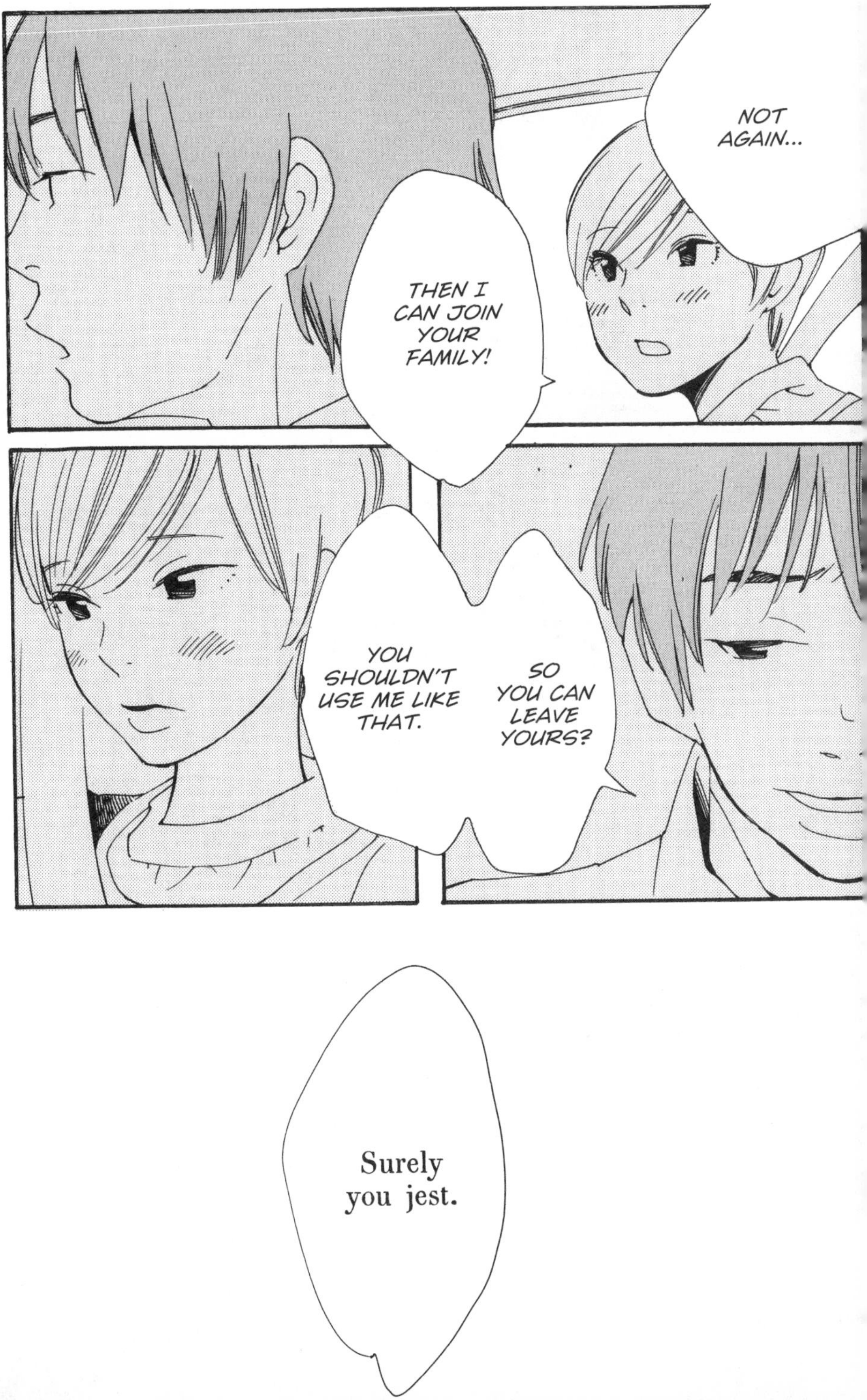
NOT AGAIN...
THEN I CAN JOIN YOUR FAMILY!
SO YOU CAN LEAVE YOURS?
YOU SHOULDN'T USE ME LIKE THAT.
Surely you jest.

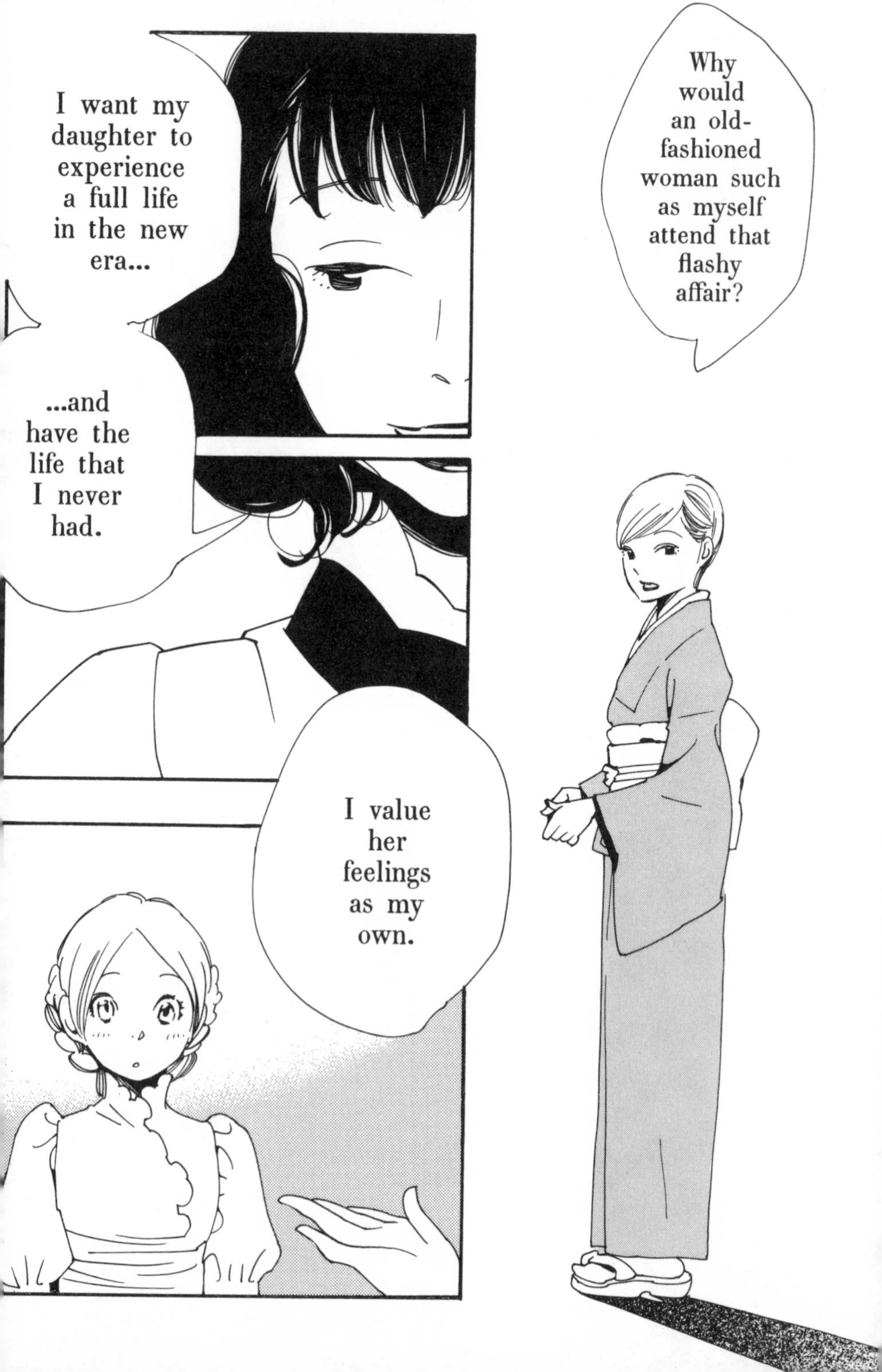
Why would an old-fashioned woman such as myself attend that flashy affair?
I want my daughter to experience a full life in the new era...
...and have the life that I never had.
I value her feelings as my own.

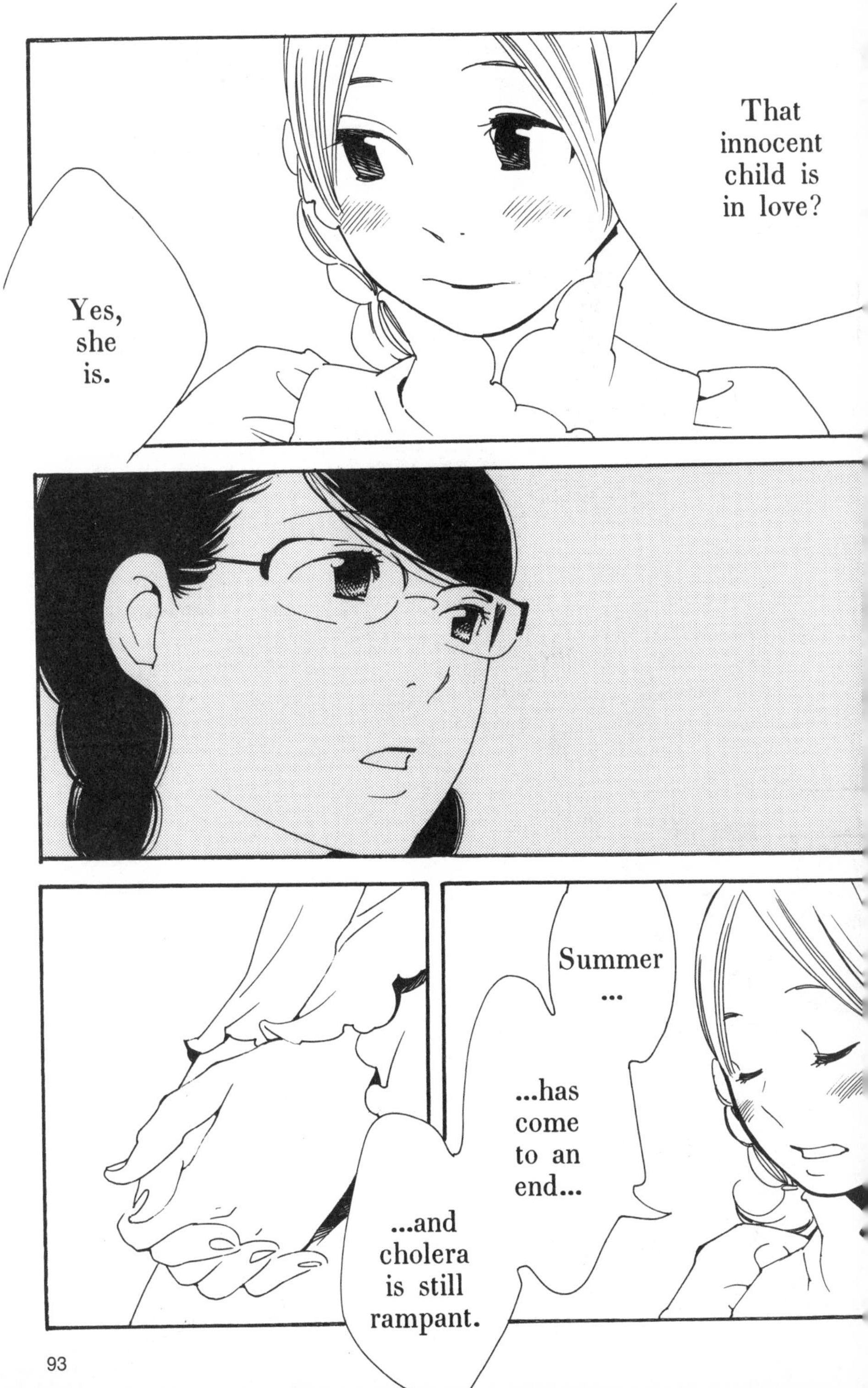
That innocent child is in love?
Yes, she is.
Summer ...
...has come to an end...
...and cholera is still rampant.

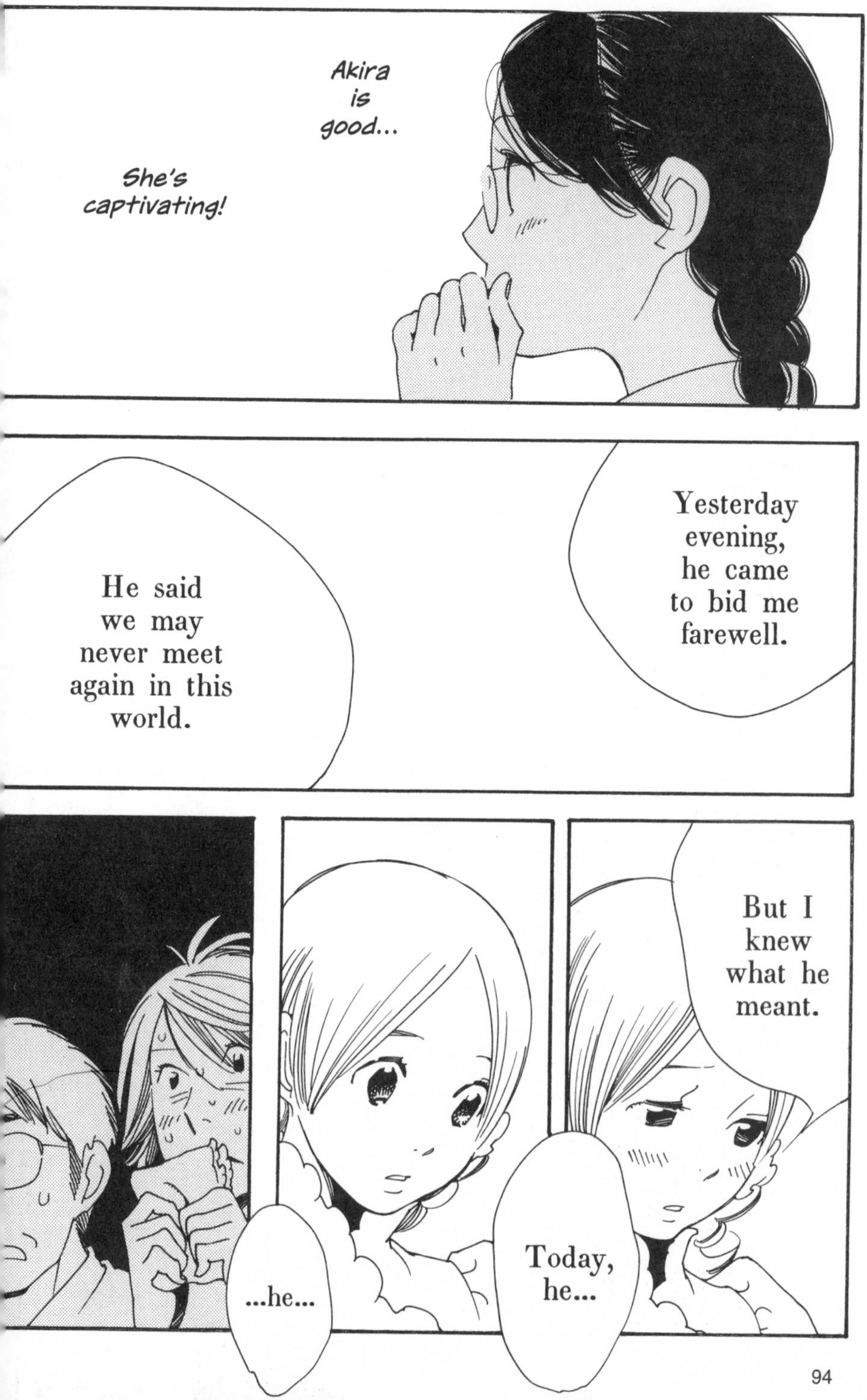
Akira is good...
She's captivating!
Yesterday evening, he came to bid me farewell.
He said we may never meet again in this world.
But I knew what he meant.
Today, he...
...he...

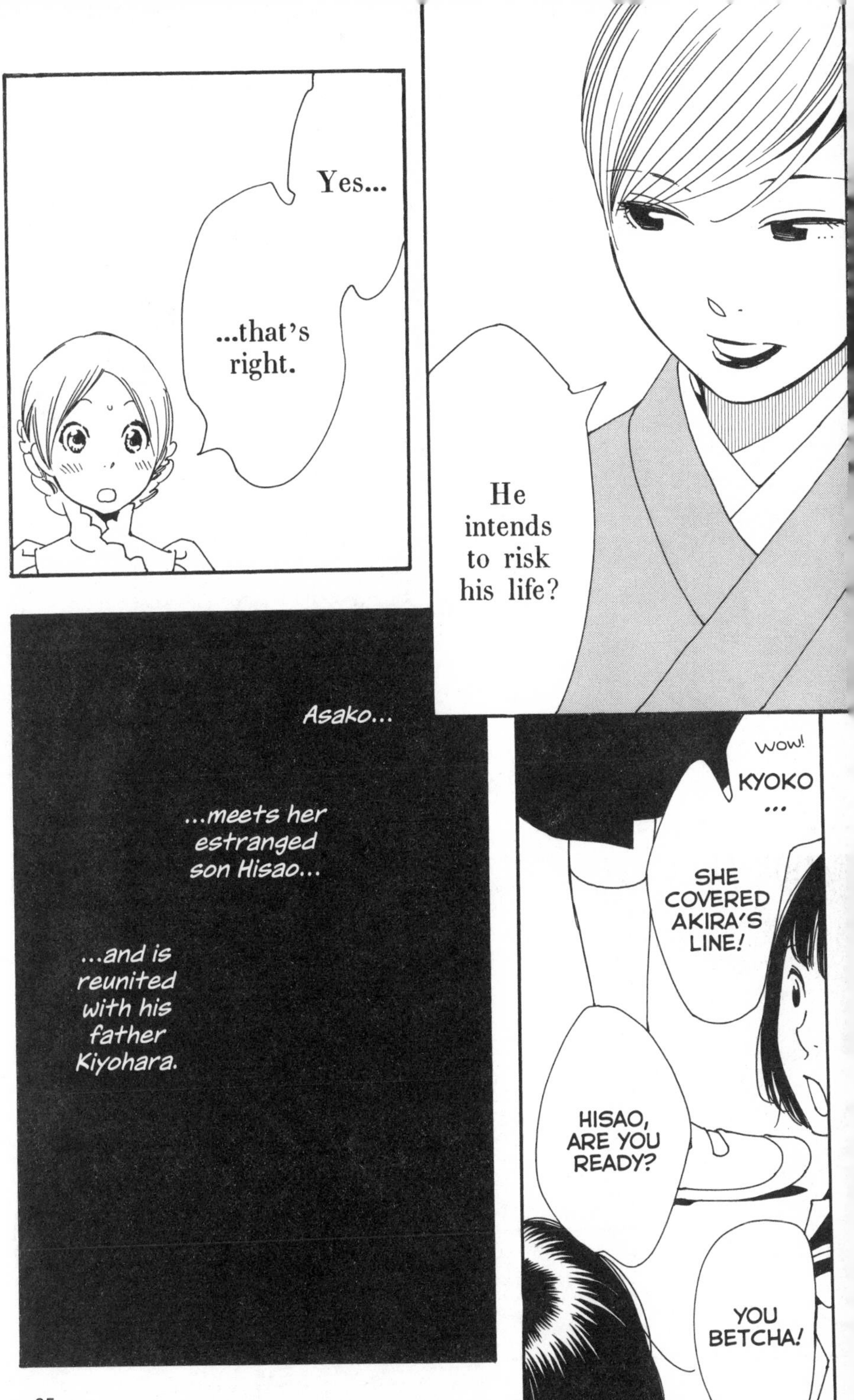
He intends to risk his life?
Yes...
...that's right.
Wow!
KYOKO...
SHE COVERED AKIRA'S LINE!
HISAO, ARE YOU READY?
YOU BETCHA!
Asako...
...meets her estranged son Hisao...
...and is reunited with his father Kiyohara.

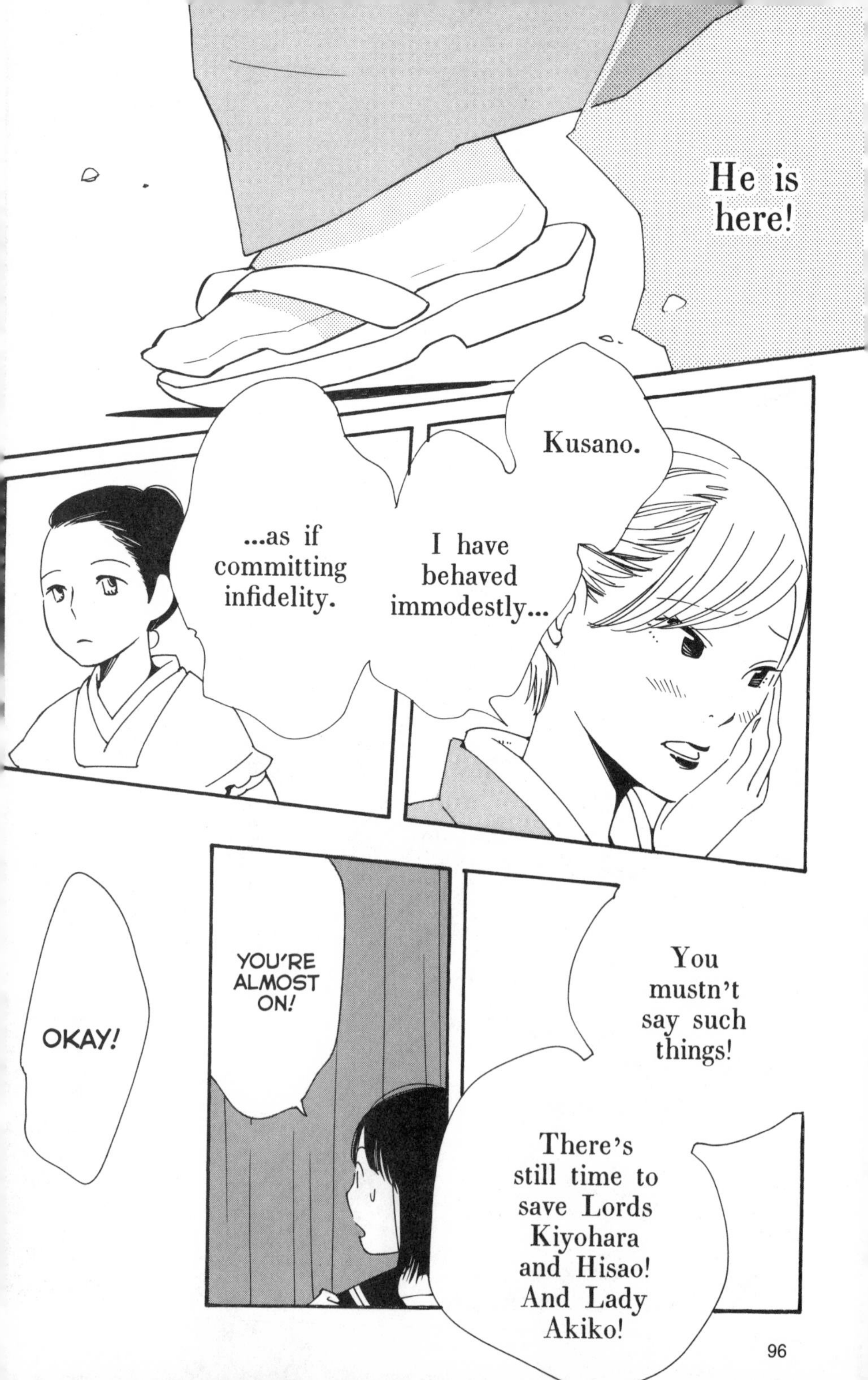
He is here!
Kusano.
I have behaved immodestly...
...as if committing infidelity.
You mustn't say such things!
There's still time to save Lords Kiyohara and Hisao! And Lady Akiko!
YOU'RE ALMOST ON!
OKAY!

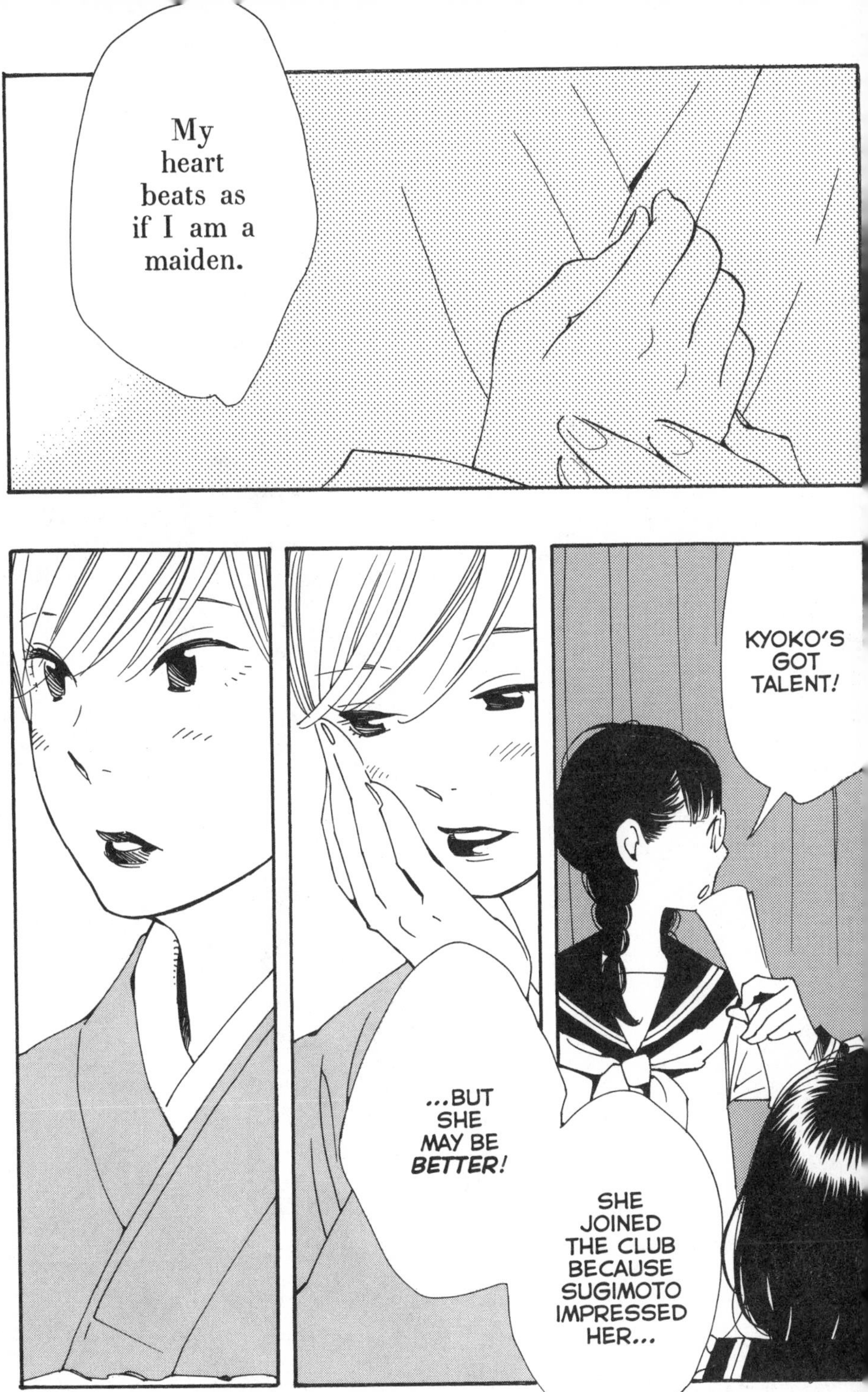
My heart beats as if I am a maiden.
KYOKO'S GOT TALENT!
SHE JOINED THE CLUB BECAUSE SUGIMOTO IMPRESSED HER...
...BUT SHE MAY BE *BETTER*!

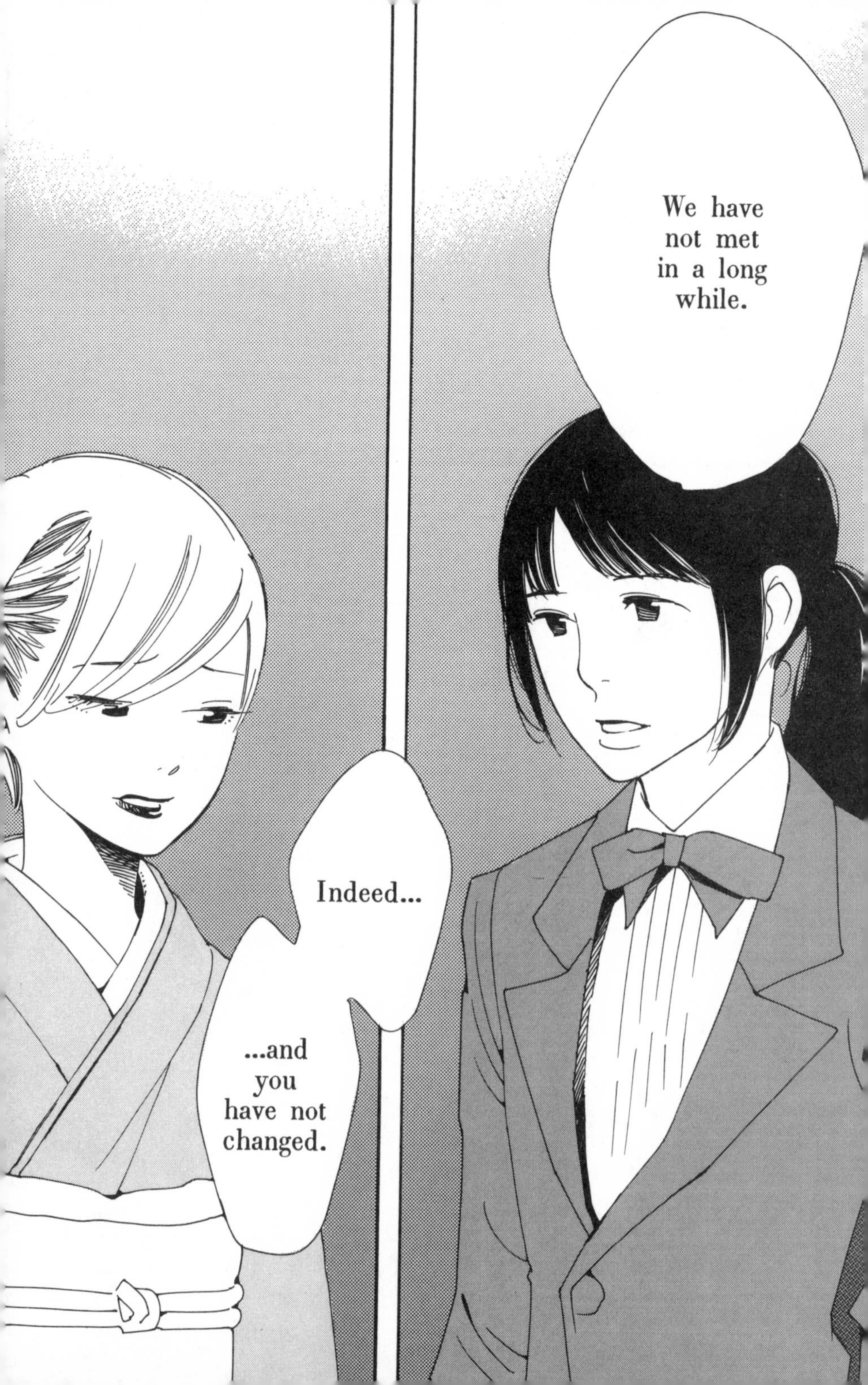
We have not met in a long while.
Indeed...
...and you have not changed.

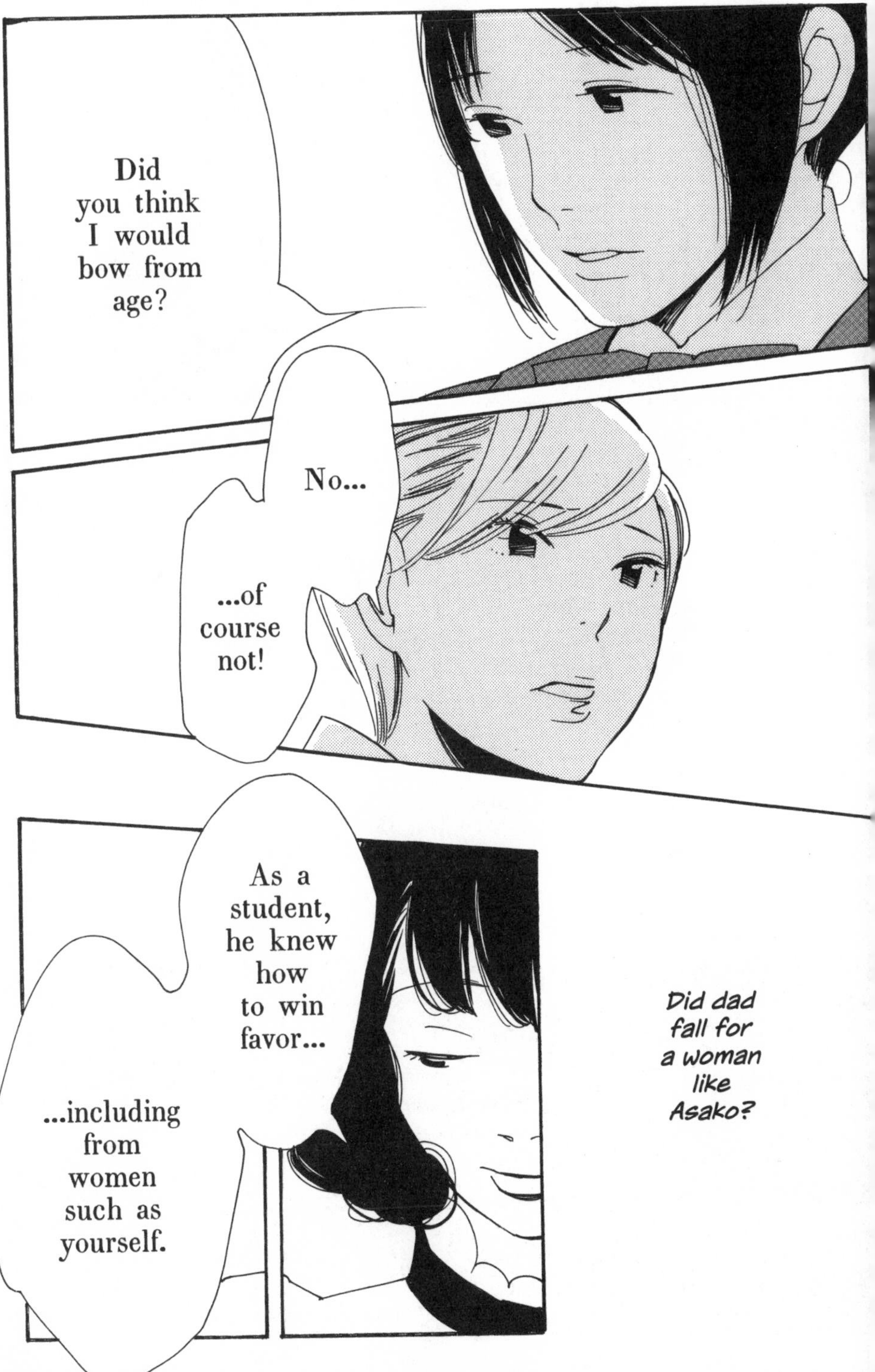
Did you think I would bow from age?
No...
...of course not!
Did dad fall for a woman like Asako?
As a student, he knew how to win favor...
...including from women such as yourself.

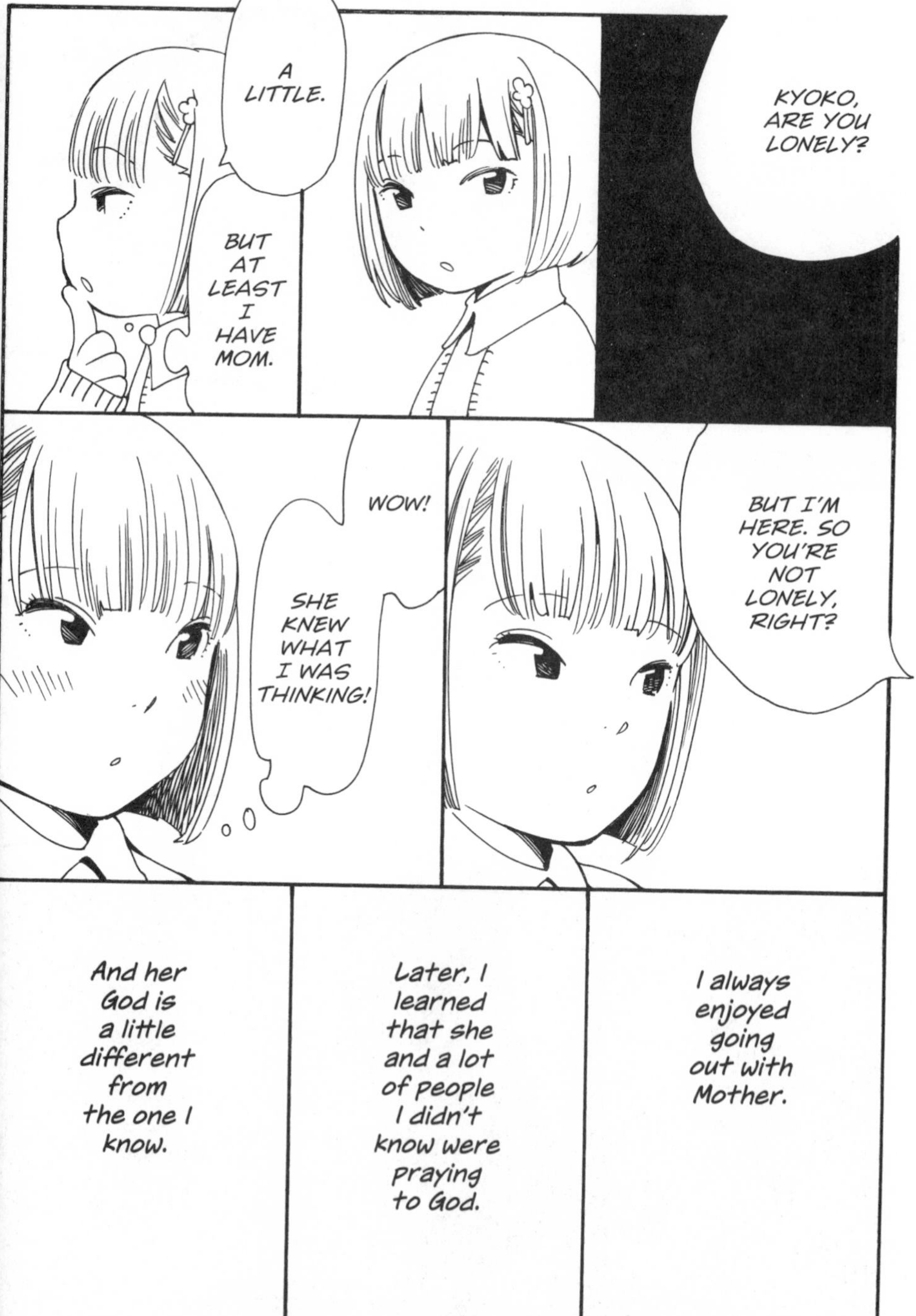
KYOKO, ARE YOU LONELY?
A LITTLE.
BUT AT LEAST I HAVE MOM.
BUT I'M HERE. SO YOU'RE NOT LONELY, RIGHT?
WOW!
SHE KNEW WHAT I WAS THINKING!
I always enjoyed going out with Mother.
Later, I learned that she and a lot of people I didn't know were praying to God.
And her God is a little different from the one I know.

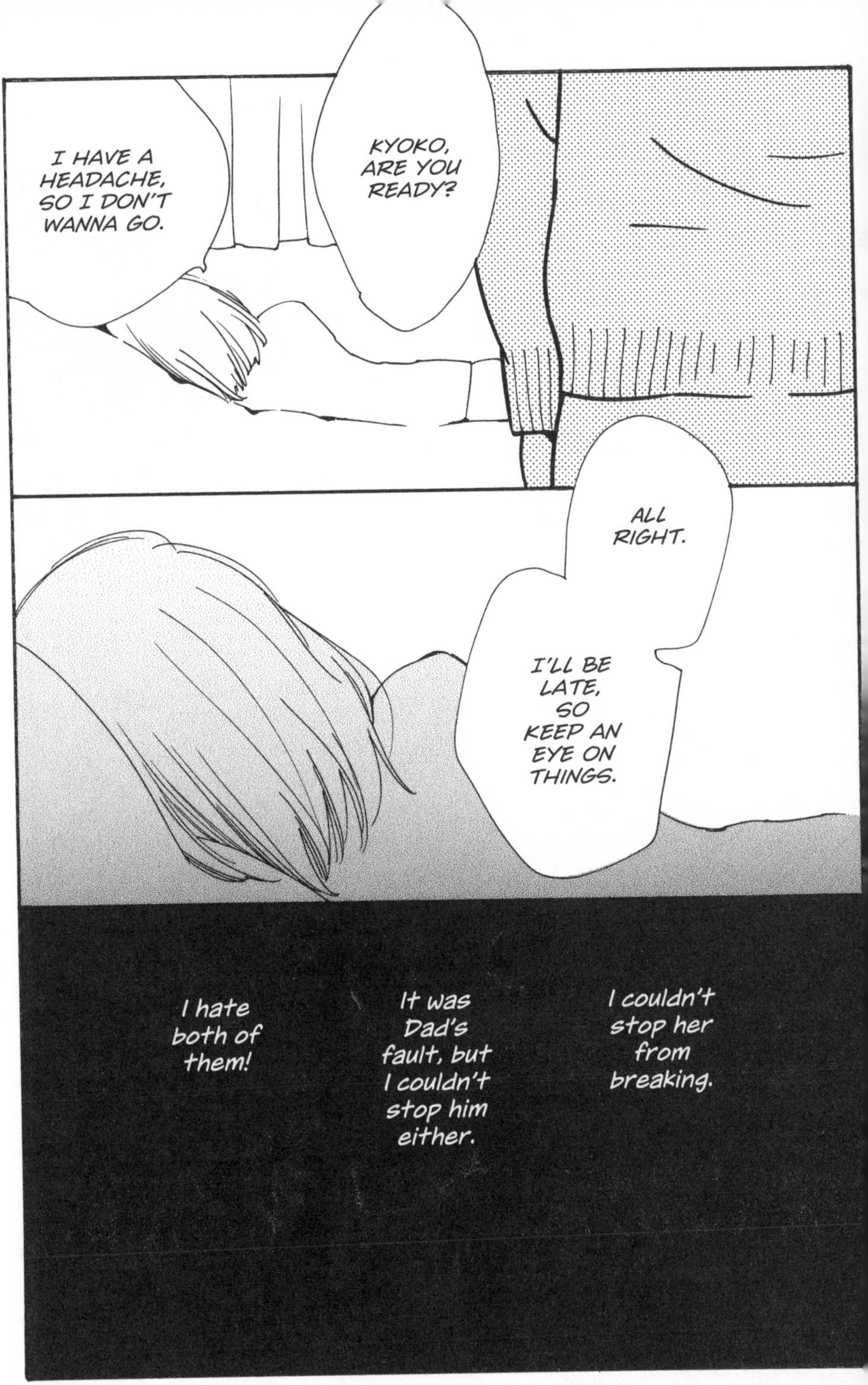
KYOKO, ARE YOU READY?
I HAVE A HEADACHE, SO I DON'T WANNA GO.
ALL RIGHT.
I'LL BE LATE, SO KEEP AN EYE ON THINGS.
I couldn't stop her from breaking.
It was Dad's fault, but I couldn't stop him either.
I hate both of them!

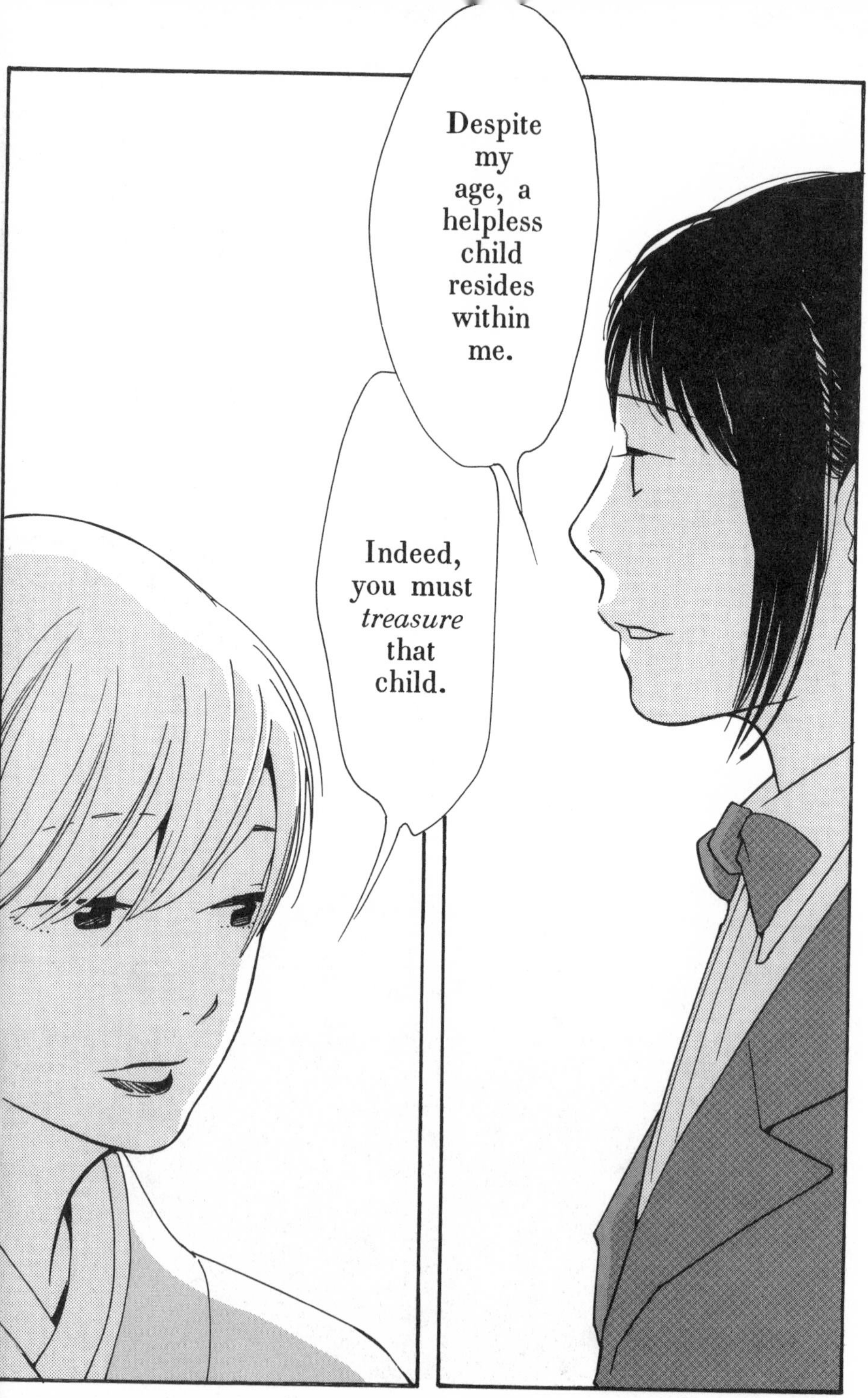
Despite my age, a helpless child resides within me.
Indeed, you must *treasure* that child.

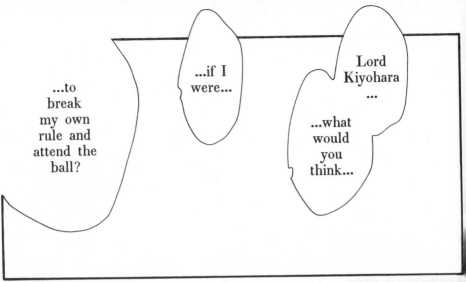

Lord Kiyohara...

...what would you think...

...if I were...

...to break my own rule and attend the ball?

Would you find me contemptible?

You?

Everyone in my family is worthless.

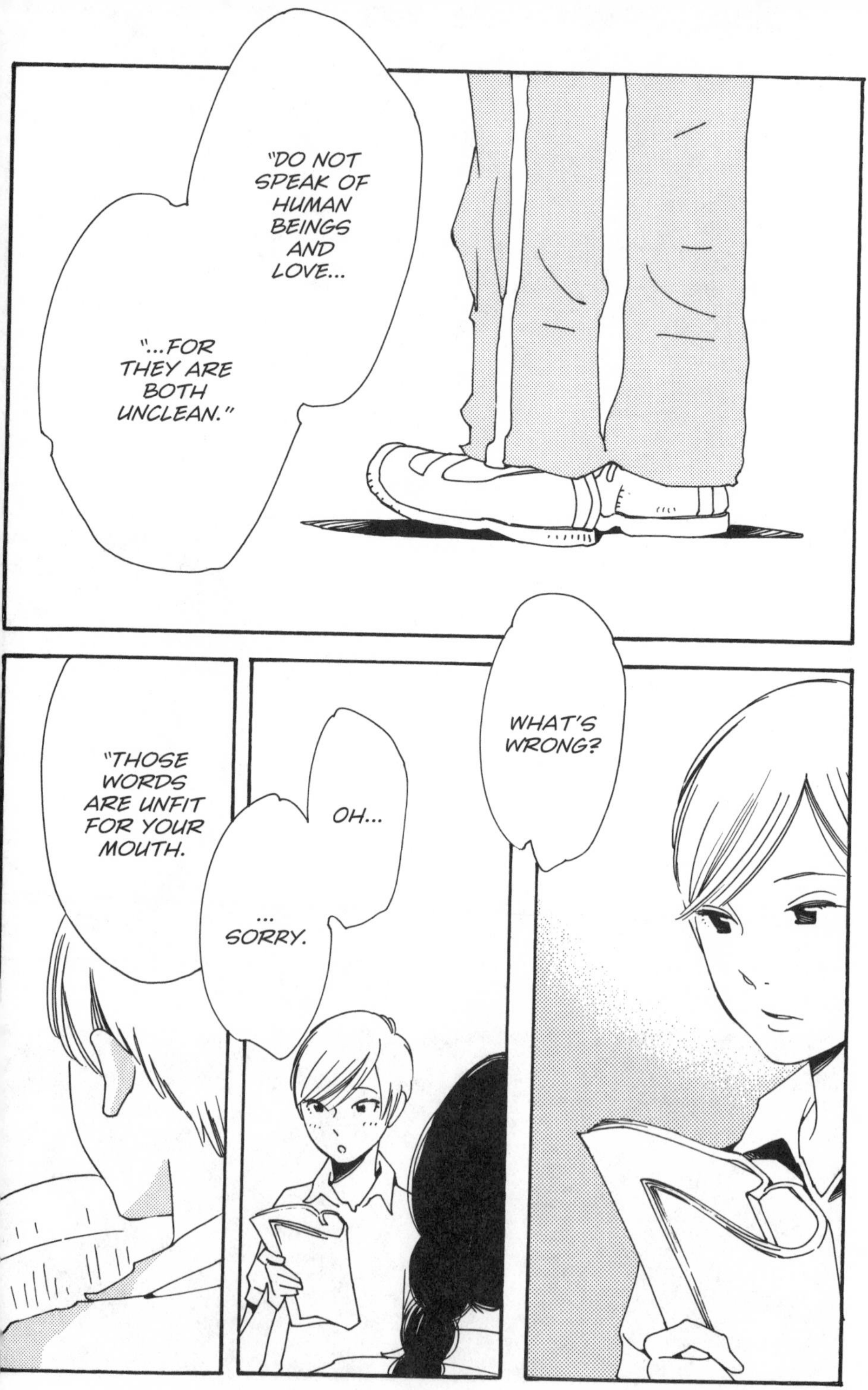
"DO NOT SPEAK OF HUMAN BEINGS AND LOVE...
"...FOR THEY ARE BOTH UNCLEAN."
WHAT'S WRONG?
OH...
... SORRY.
"THOSE WORDS ARE UNFIT FOR YOUR MOUTH.

"ONLY WHEN YOU ARE FAR REMOVED FROM HUMAN EMOTION...

"...MAY YOU REMAIN AS PURE AS ICE."

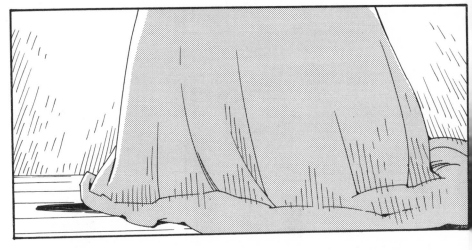

Oh dear!

I hear pistols!

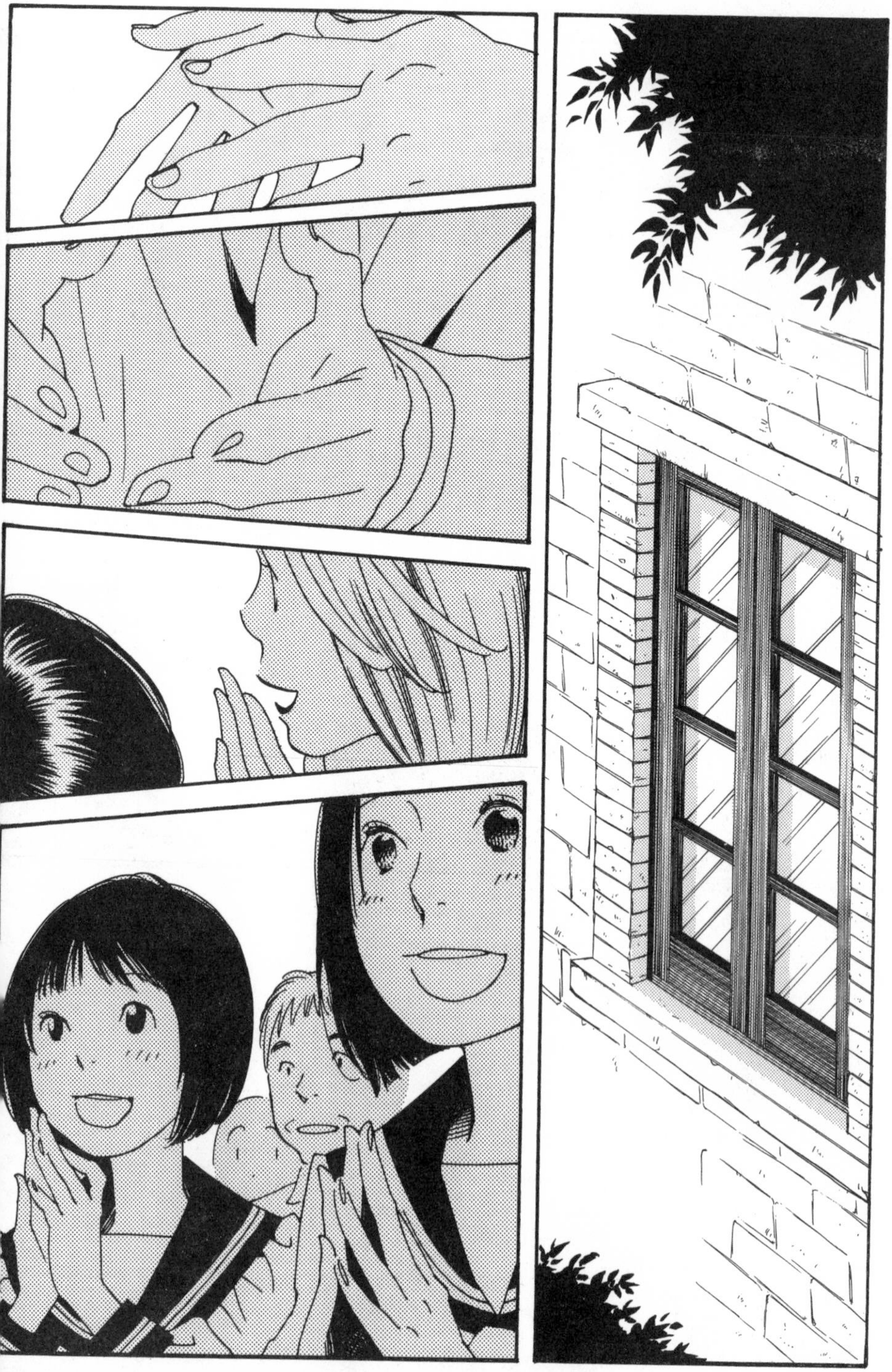

A HELPLESS CHILD INSIDE...

HMM...

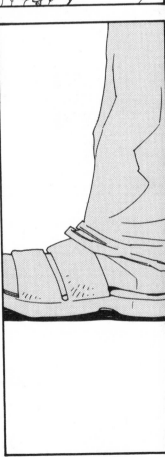

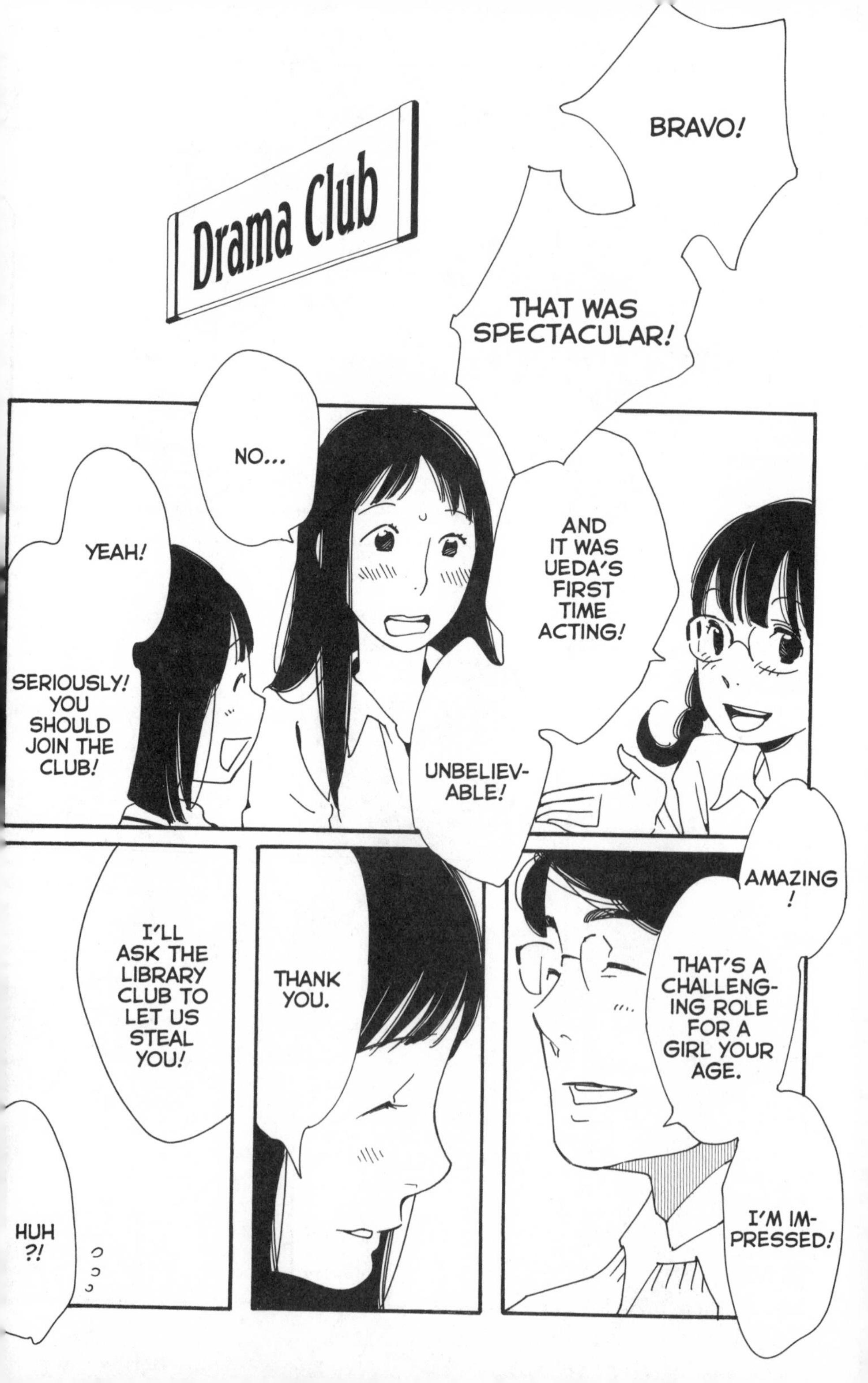
BRAVO!
Drama Club
THAT WAS SPECTACULAR!
AND IT WAS UEDA'S FIRST TIME ACTING!
NO...
UNBELIEV-ABLE!
YEAH!
SERIOUSLY! YOU SHOULD JOIN THE CLUB!
AMAZING!
THAT'S A CHALLENG-ING ROLE FOR A GIRL YOUR AGE.
I'M IM-PRESSED!
THANK YOU.
I'LL ASK THE LIBRARY CLUB TO LET US STEAL YOU!
HUH?!

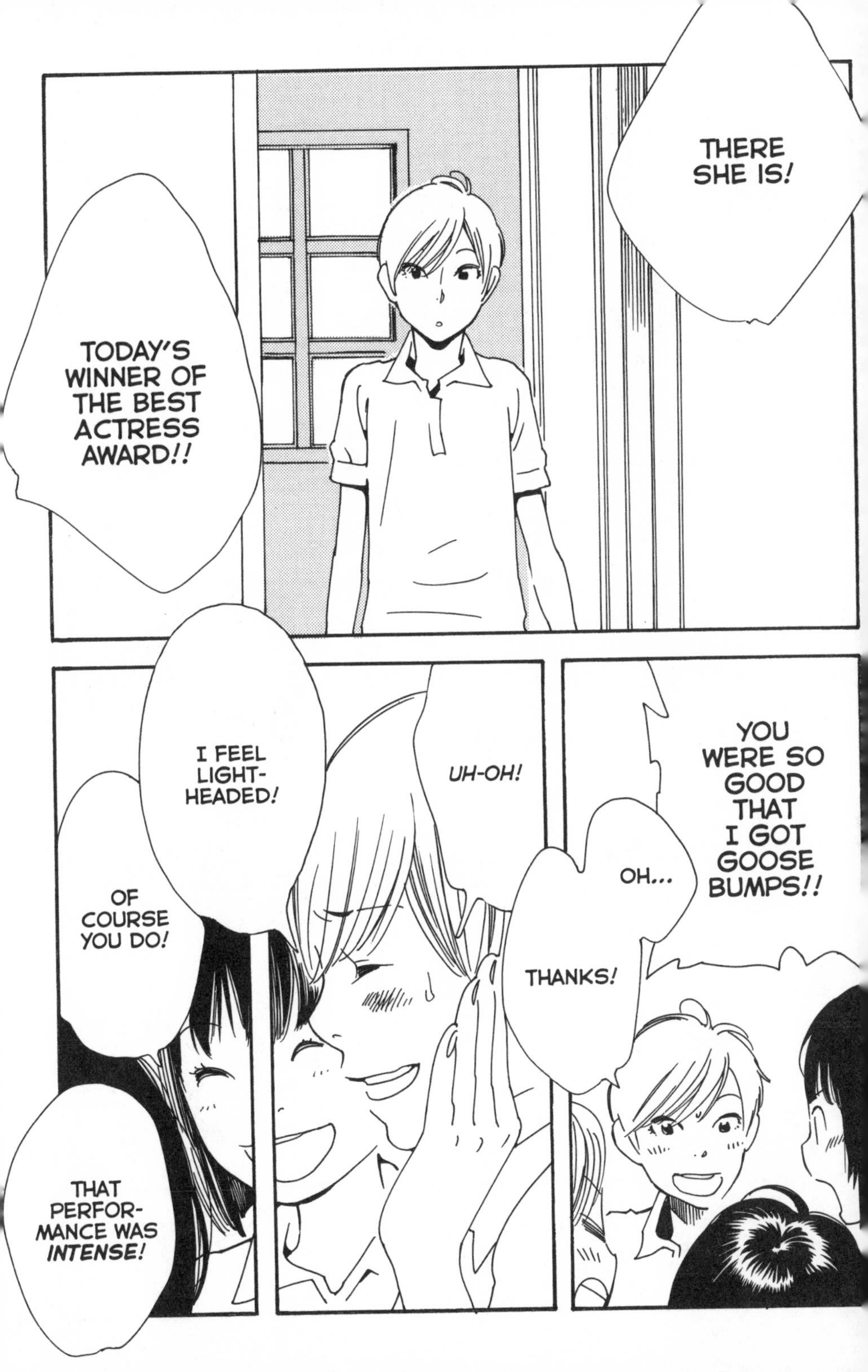

THERE SHE IS!
TODAY'S WINNER OF THE BEST ACTRESS AWARD!!
YOU WERE SO GOOD THAT I GOT GOOSE BUMPS!!
OH...
THANKS!
UH-OH!
I FEEL LIGHT-HEADED!
OF COURSE YOU DO!
THAT PERFORMANCE WAS *INTENSE!*

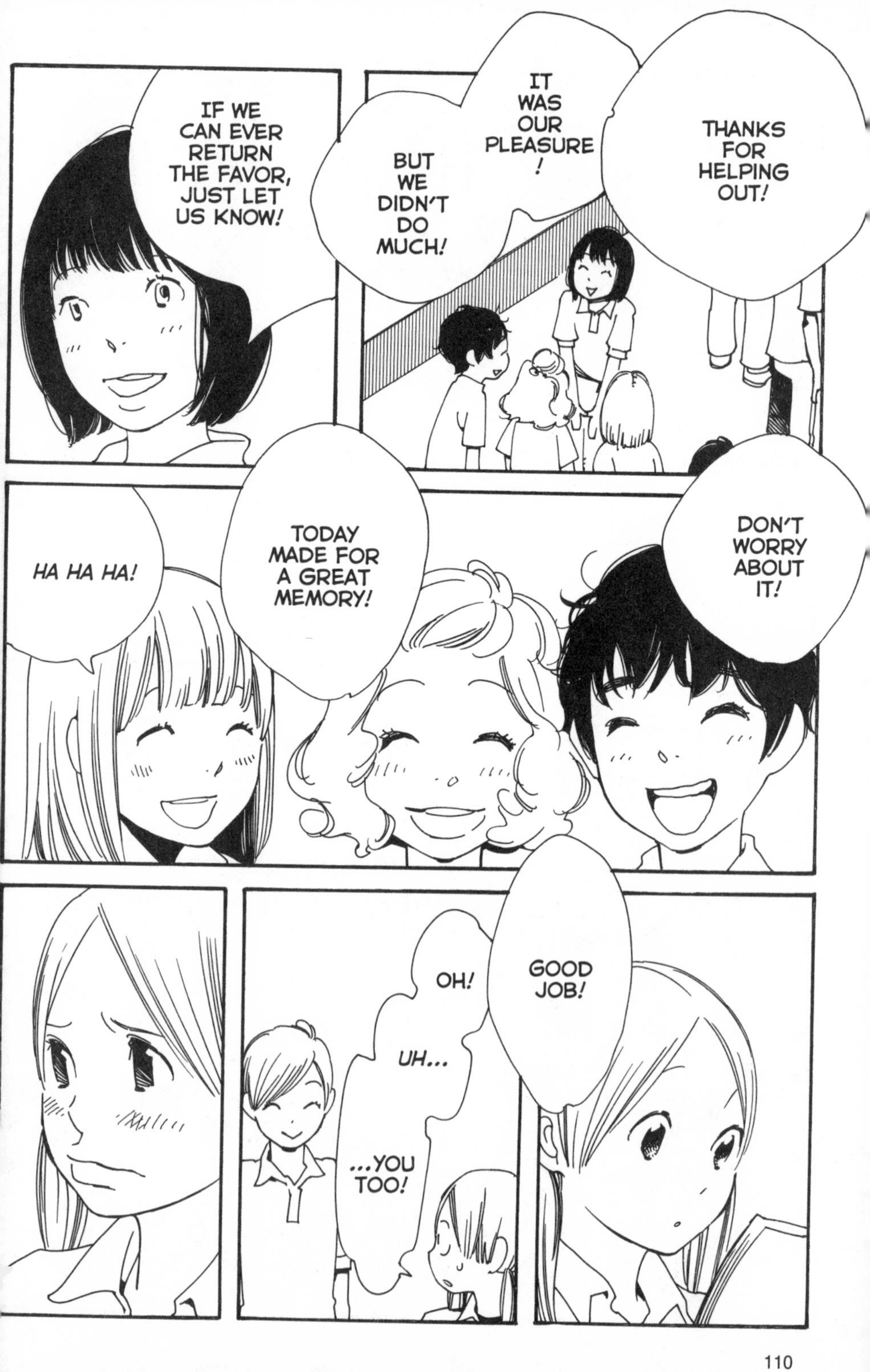
THANKS FOR HELPING OUT!
IT WAS OUR PLEASURE!
BUT WE DIDN'T DO MUCH!
IF WE CAN EVER RETURN THE FAVOR, JUST LET US KNOW!
DON'T WORRY ABOUT IT!
TODAY MADE FOR A GREAT MEMORY!
HA HA HA!
GOOD JOB!
OH!
UH...
...YOU TOO!

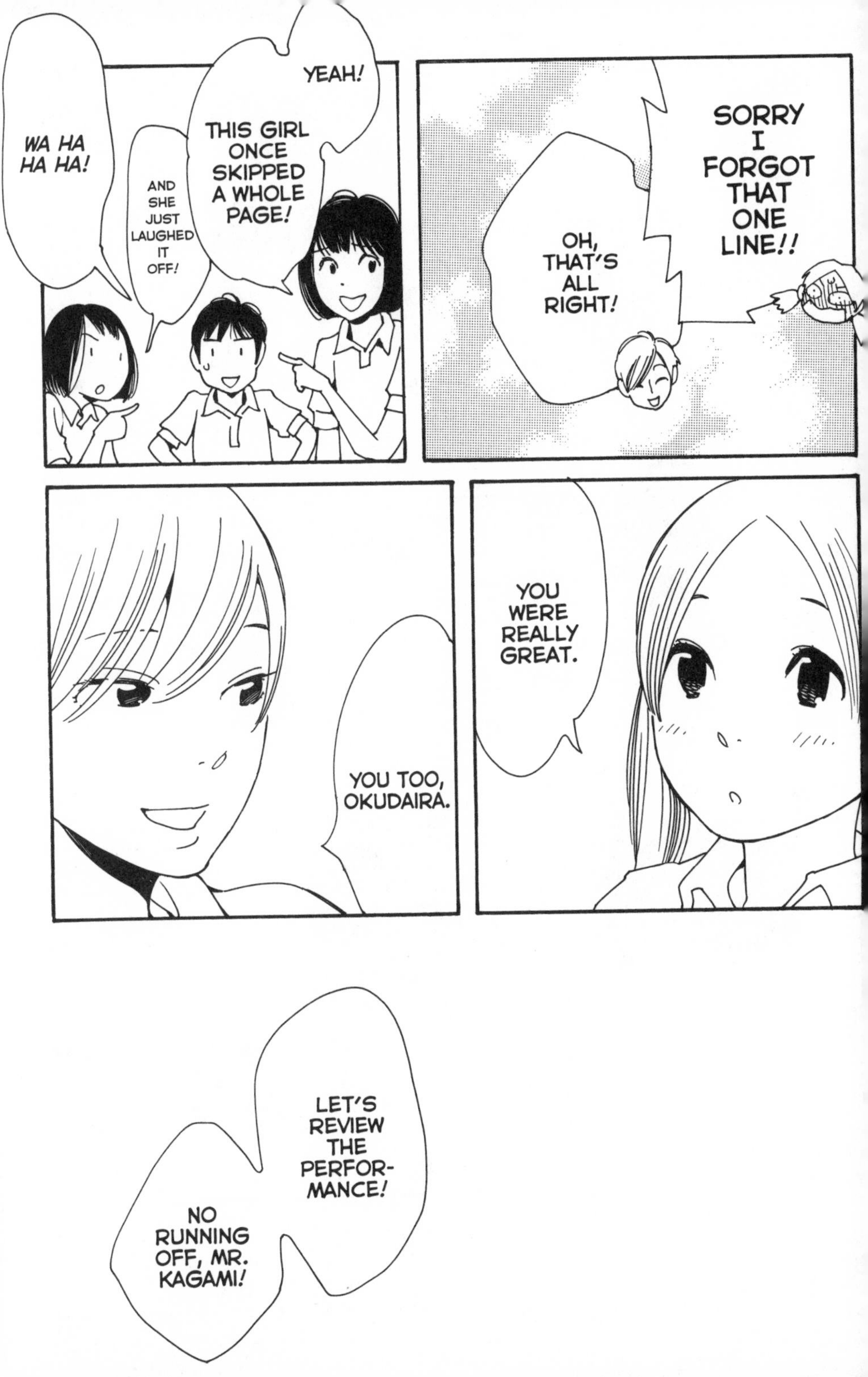
SORRY I FORGOT THAT ONE LINE!!
OH, THAT'S ALL RIGHT!
YEAH!
THIS GIRL ONCE SKIPPED A WHOLE PAGE!
AND SHE JUST LAUGHED IT OFF!
WA HA HA HA!
YOU WERE REALLY GREAT.
YOU TOO, OKUDAIRA.
LET'S REVIEW THE PERFORMANCE!
NO RUNNING OFF, MR. KAGAMI!

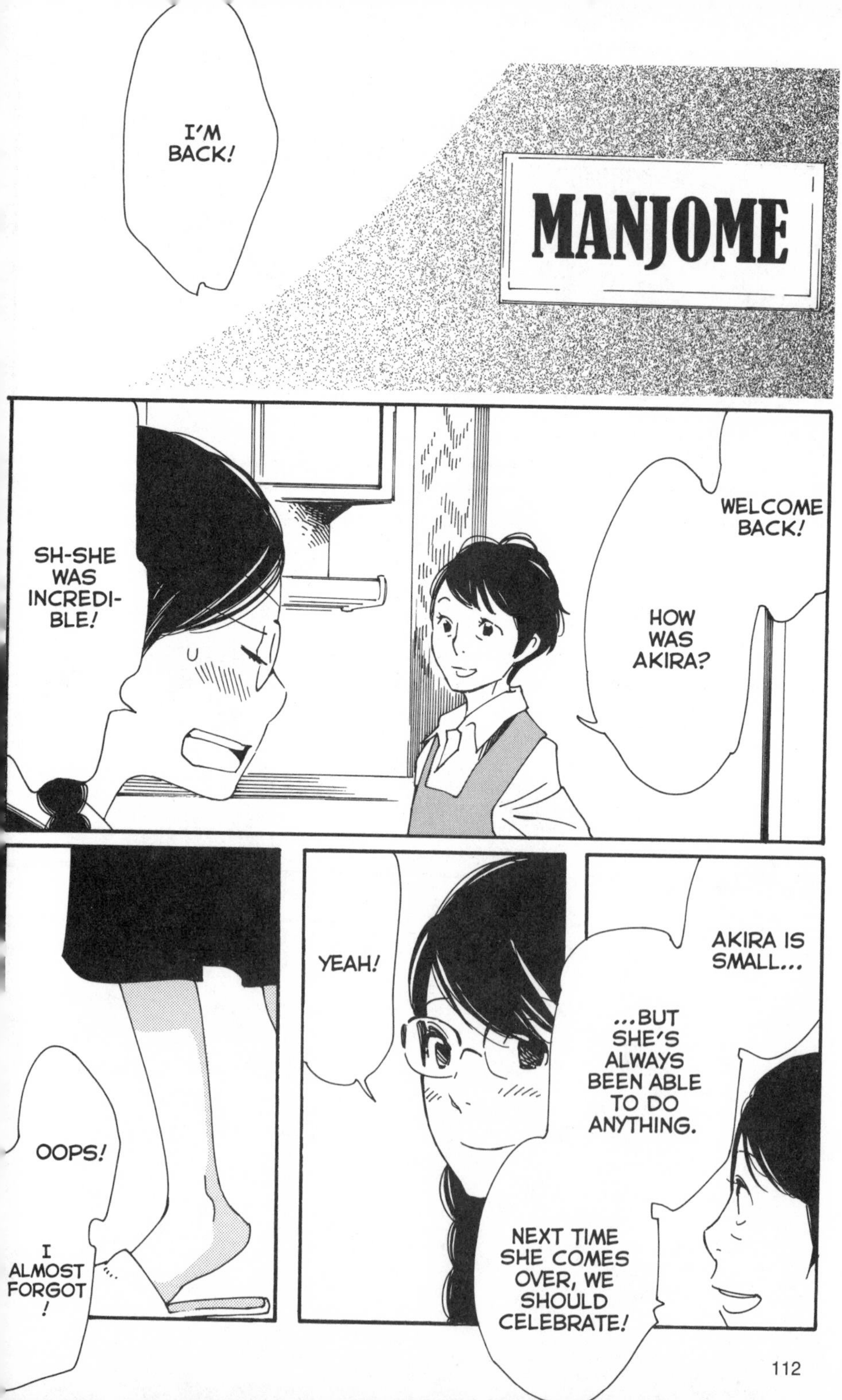
MANJOME
I'M BACK!
WELCOME BACK!
HOW WAS AKIRA?
SH-SHE WAS INCREDIBLE!
AKIRA IS SMALL...
...BUT SHE'S ALWAYS BEEN ABLE TO DO ANYTHING.
NEXT TIME SHE COMES OVER, WE SHOULD CELEBRATE!
YEAH!
OOPS!
I ALMOST FORGOT!

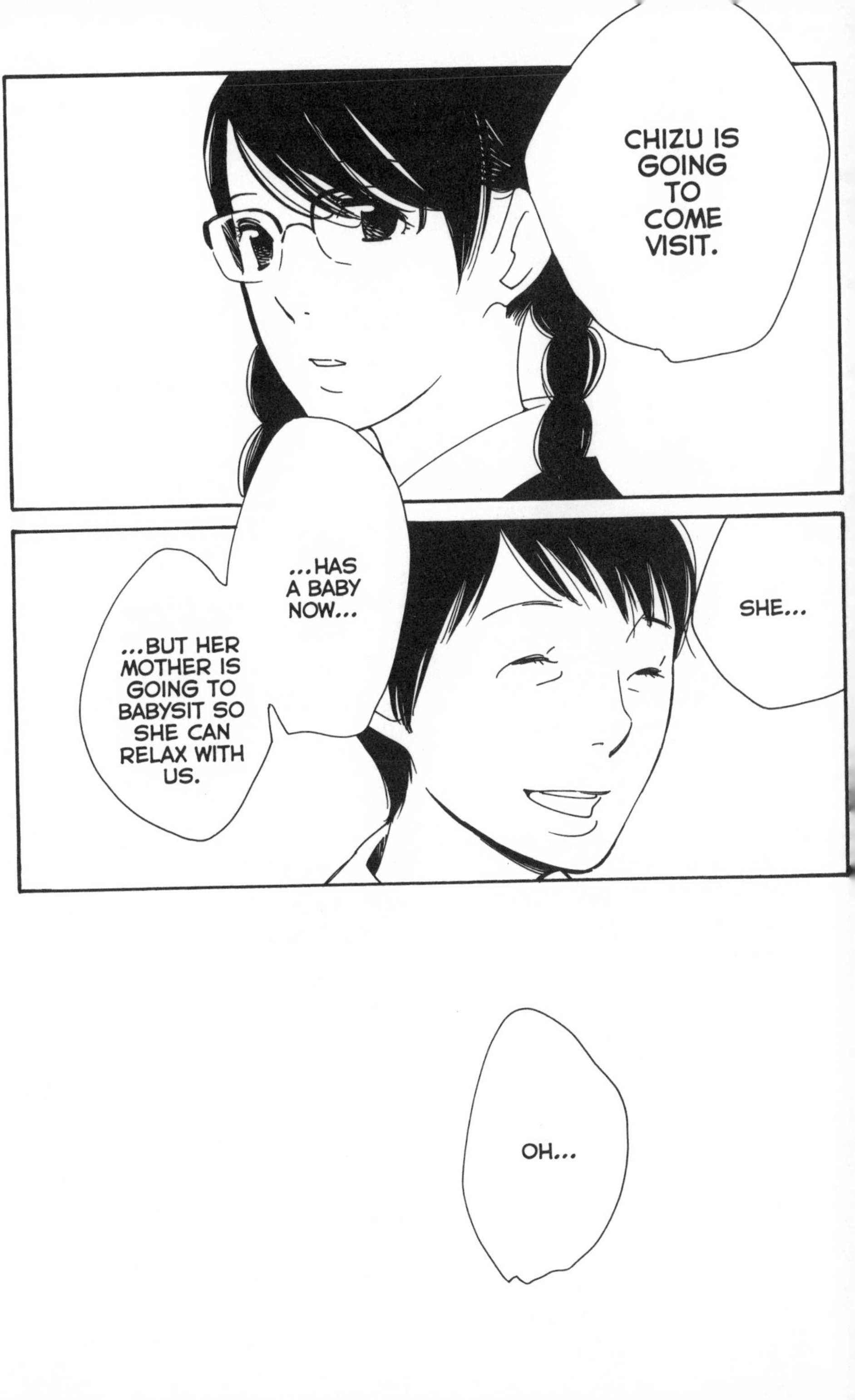
CHIZU IS GOING TO COME VISIT.
SHE...
...HAS A BABY NOW...
...BUT HER MOTHER IS GOING TO BABYSIT SO SHE CAN RELAX WITH US.
OH...

Sweet Blue Flowers

#30 After the Banquet

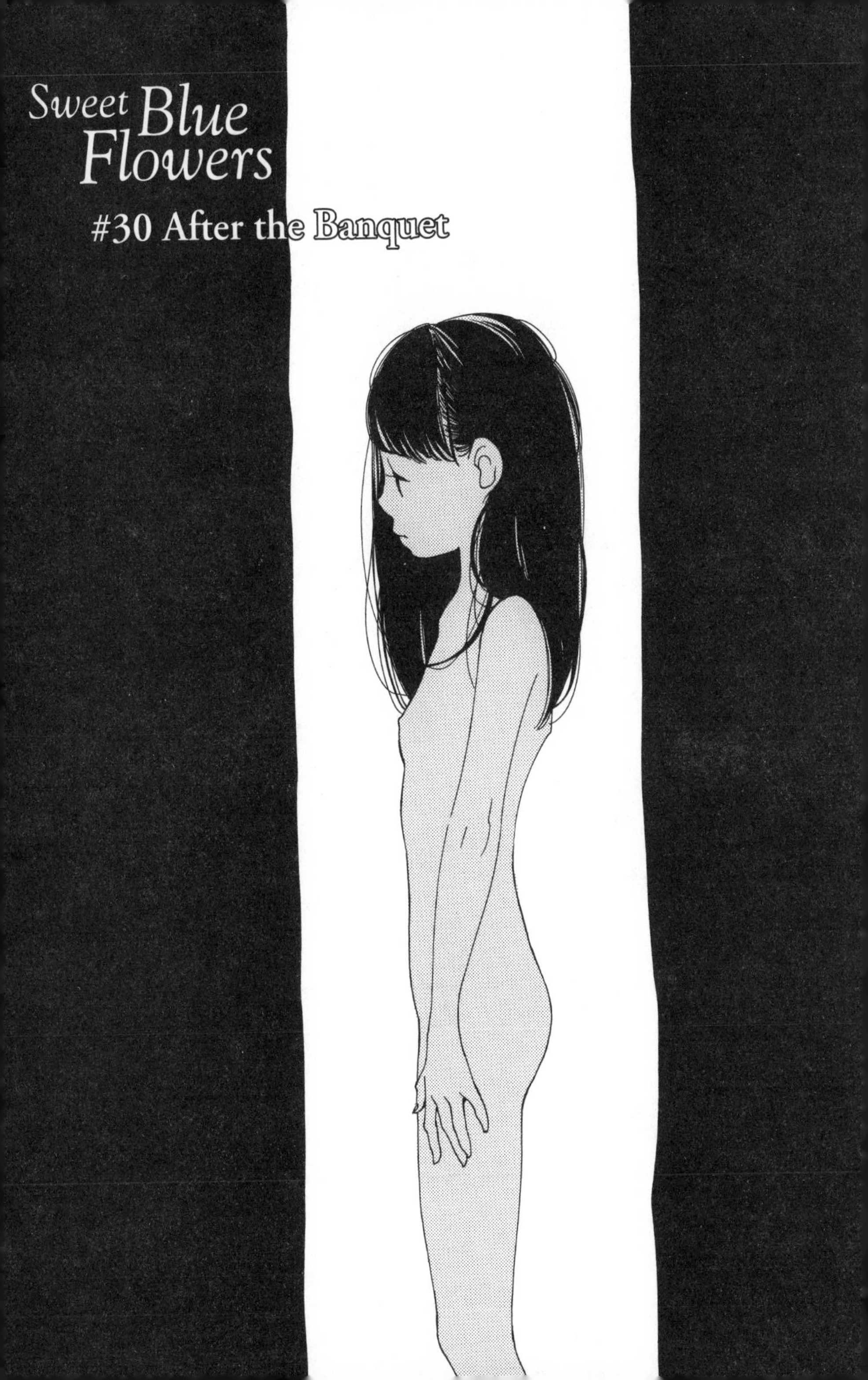

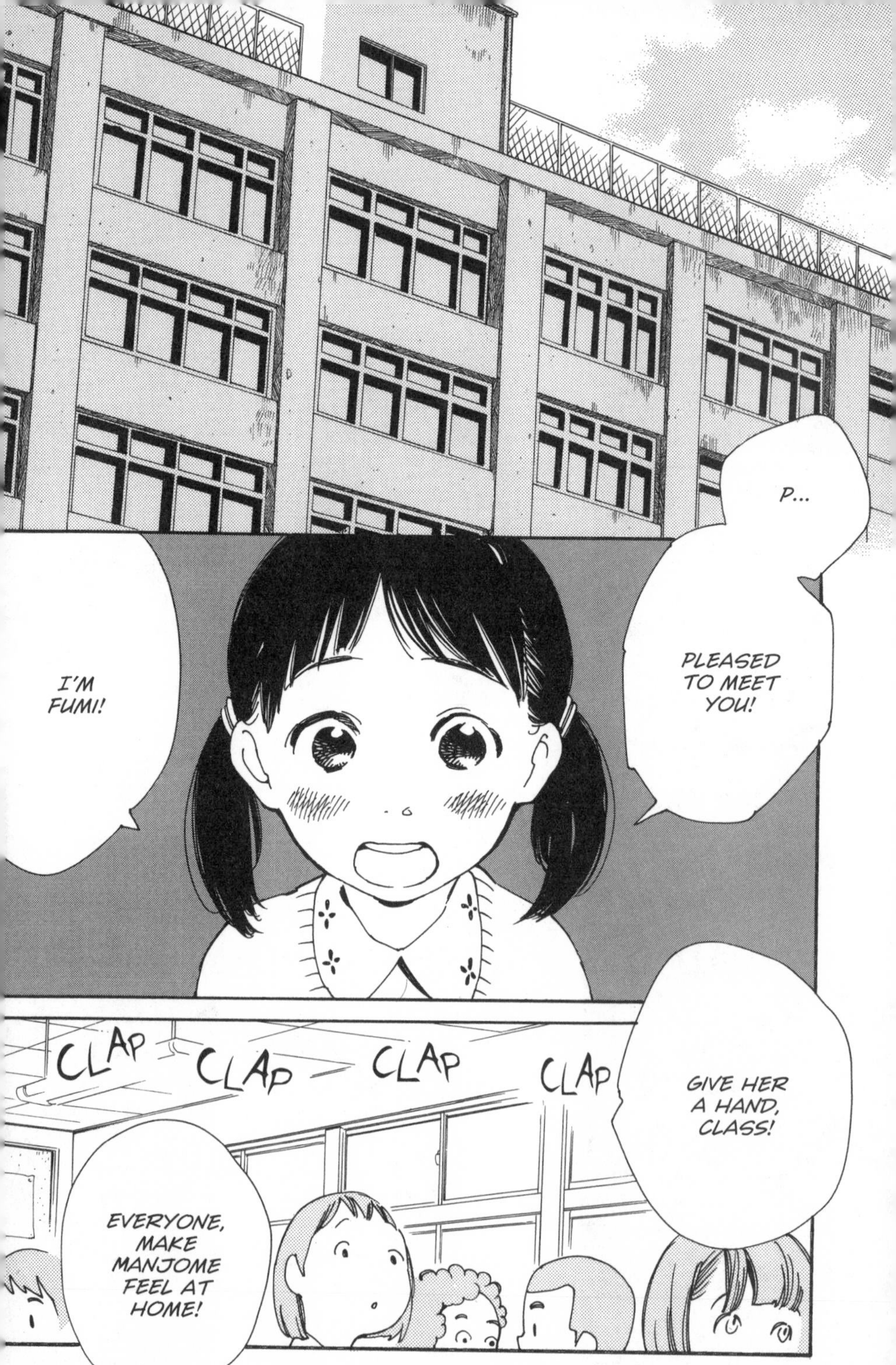
P...
PLEASED TO MEET YOU!
I'M FUMI!
GIVE HER A HAND, CLASS!
CLAP
CLAP
CLAP
CLAP
EVERYONE, MAKE MANJOME FEEL AT HOME!

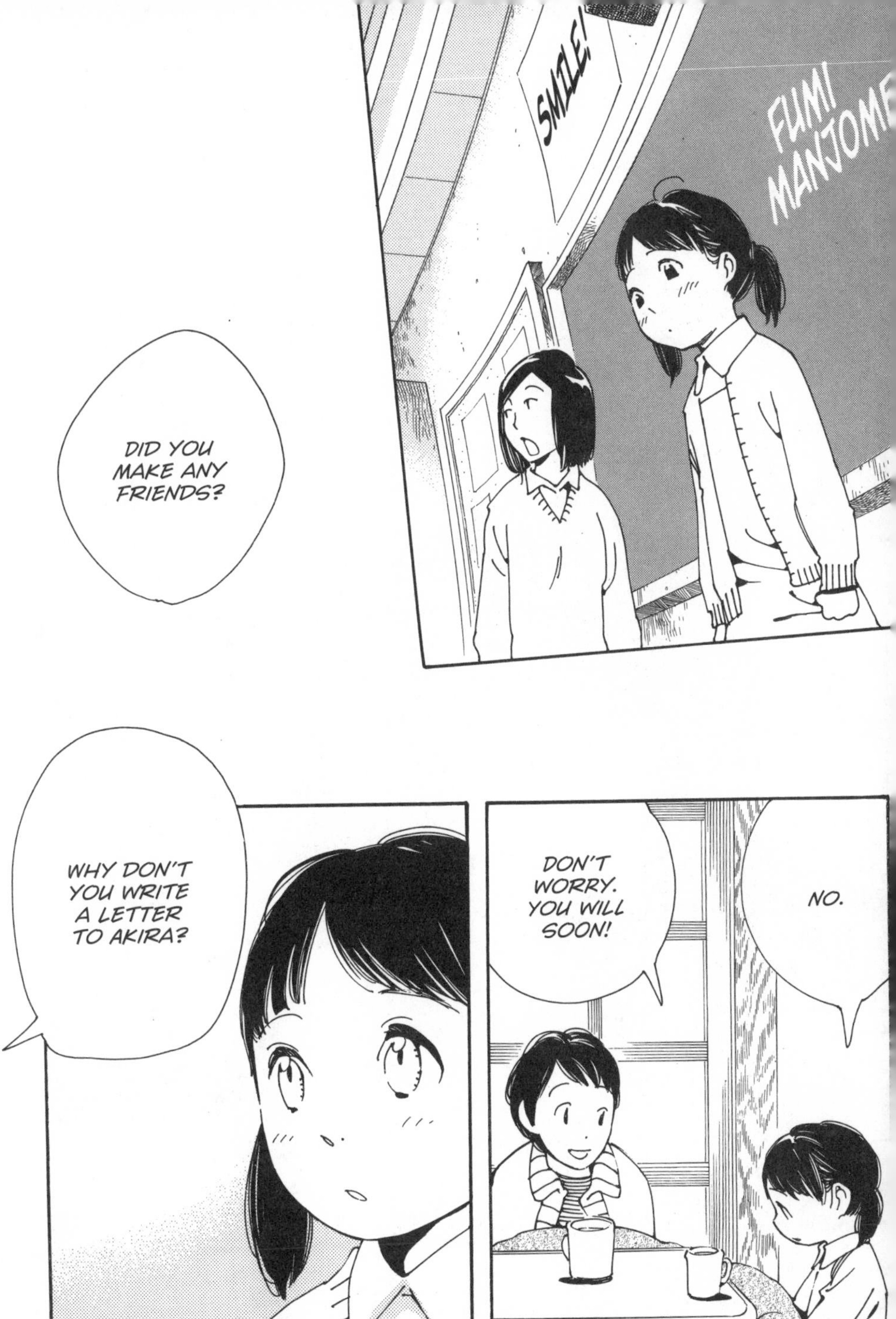
SMILE!
FUMI
DID YOU MAKE ANY FRIENDS?
NO.
DON'T WORRY. YOU WILL SOON!
WHY DON'T YOU WRITE A LETTER TO AKIRA?

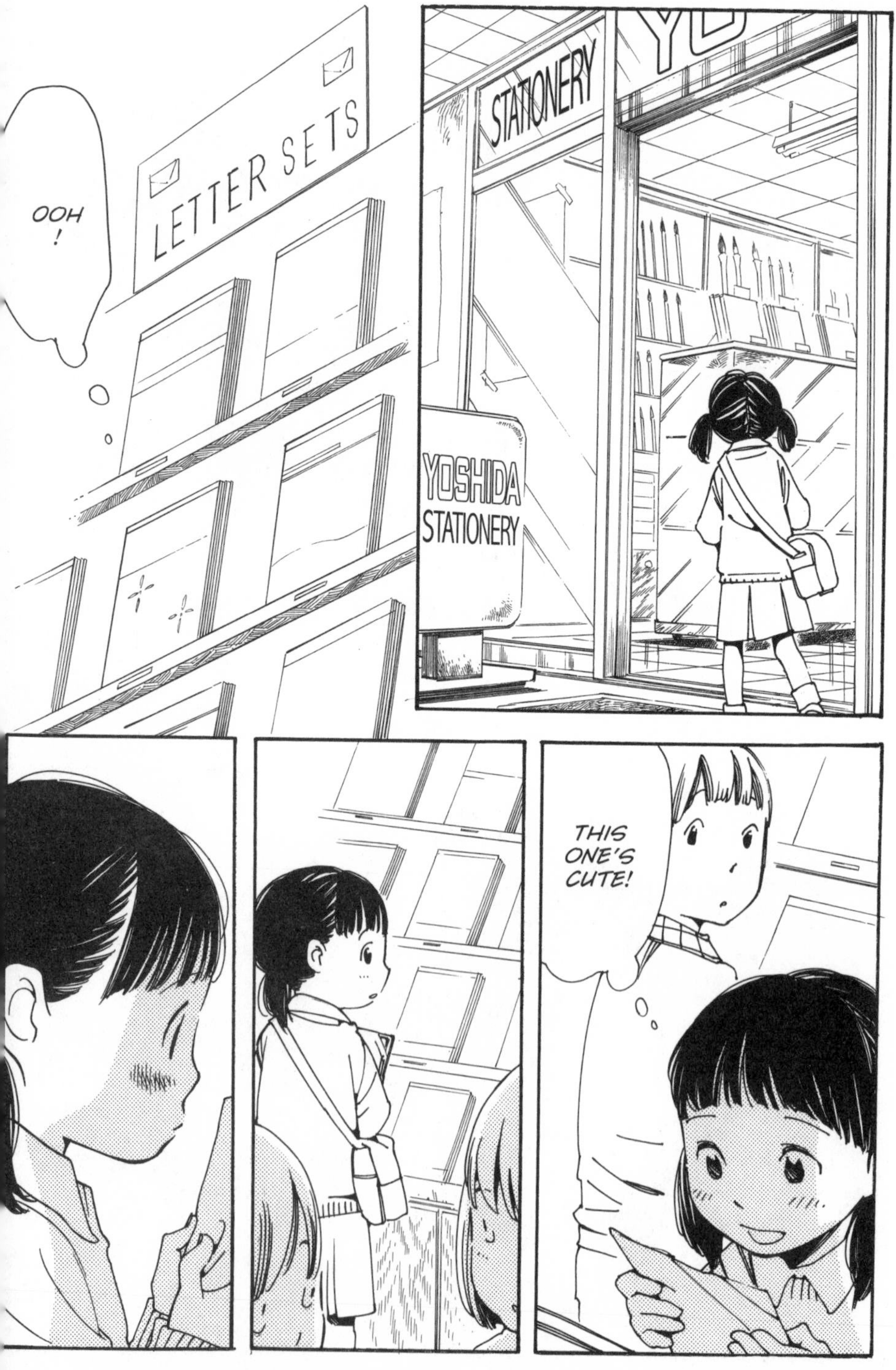
YD
STATIONERY
YOSHIDA STATIONERY
LETTER SETS
OOH!
THIS ONE'S CUTE!

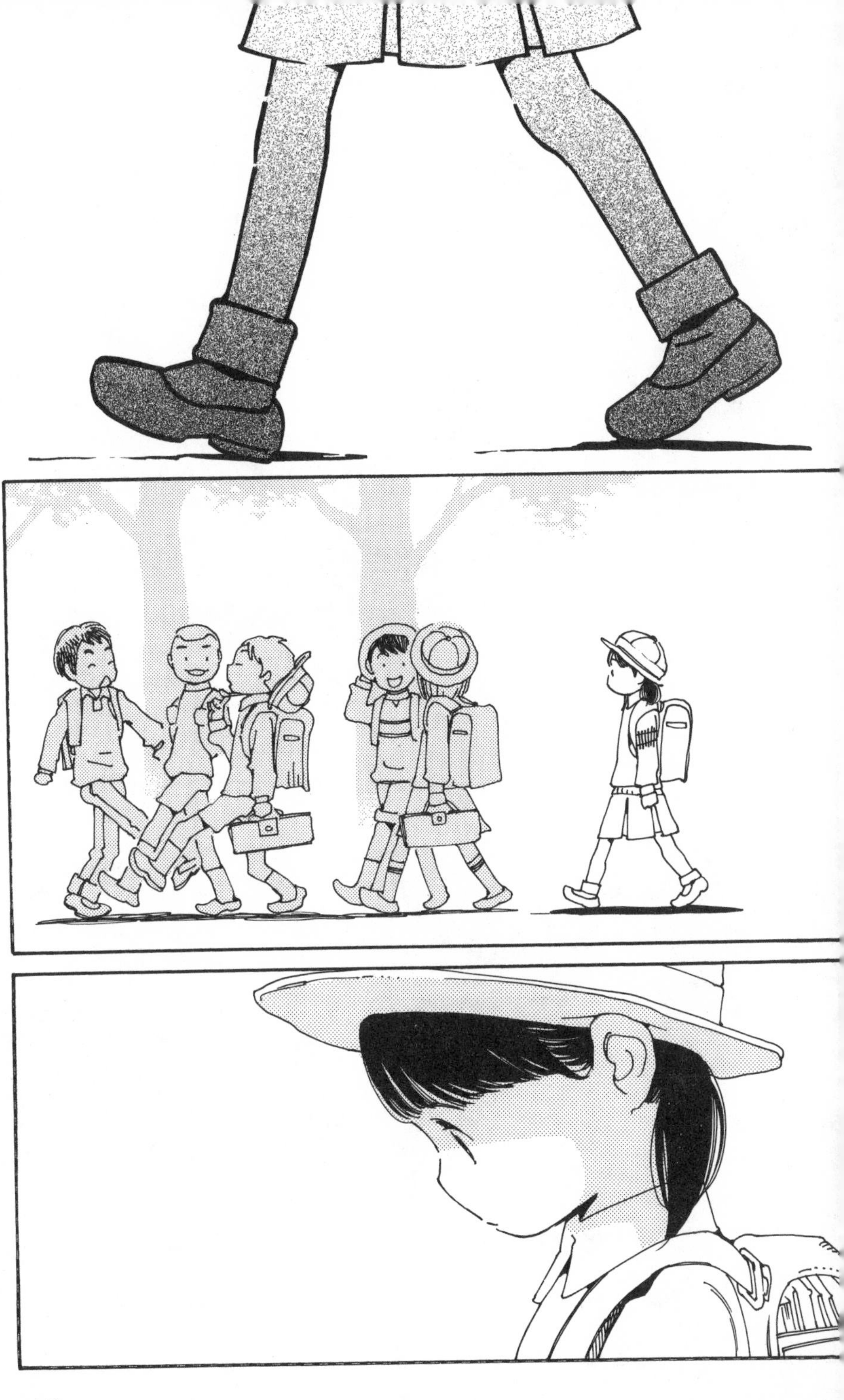

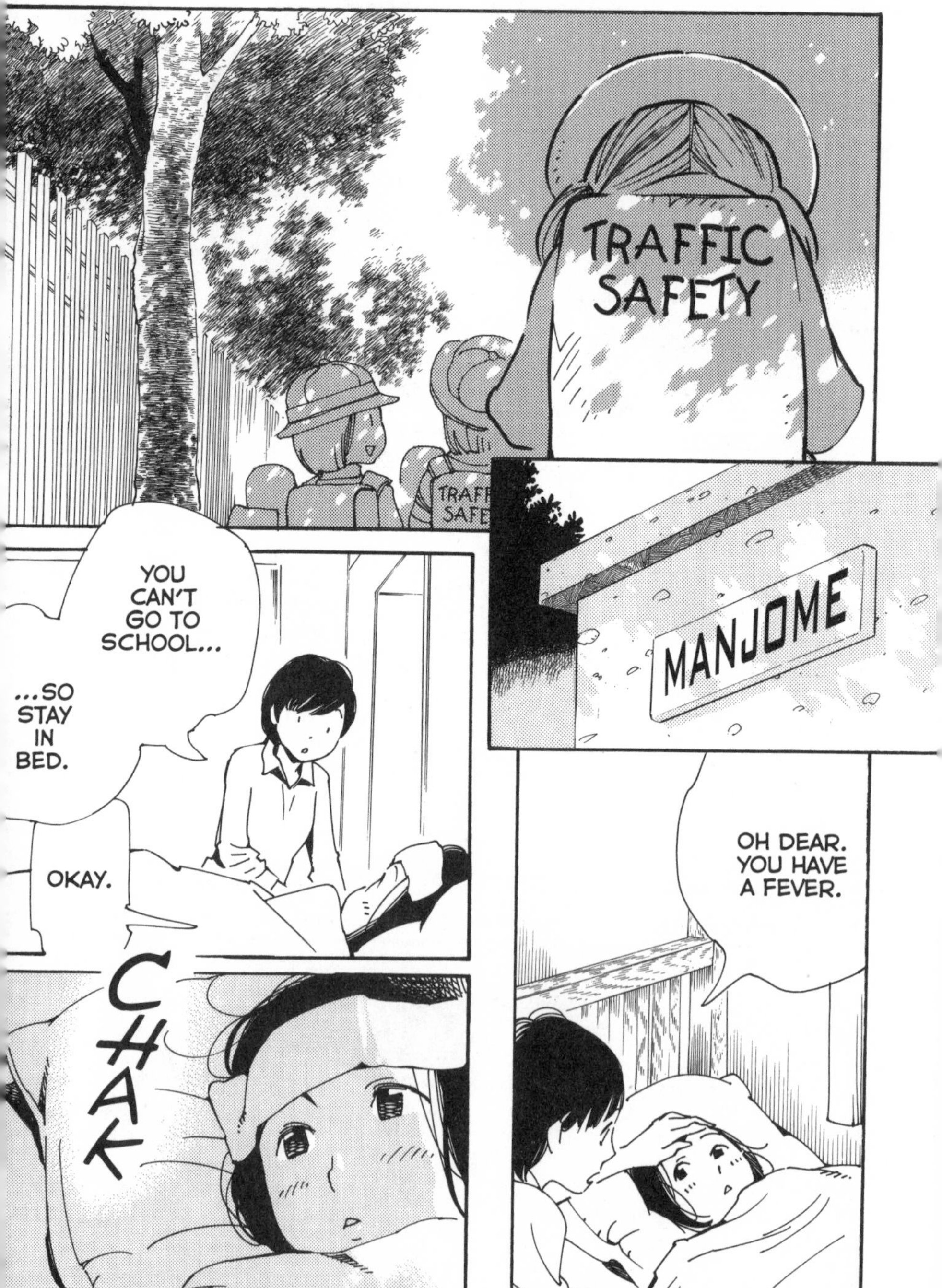

TRAFFIC SAFETY
MANJOME
OH DEAR. YOU HAVE A FEVER.
YOU CAN'T GO TO SCHOOL...
...SO STAY IN BED.
OKAY.
CHAK

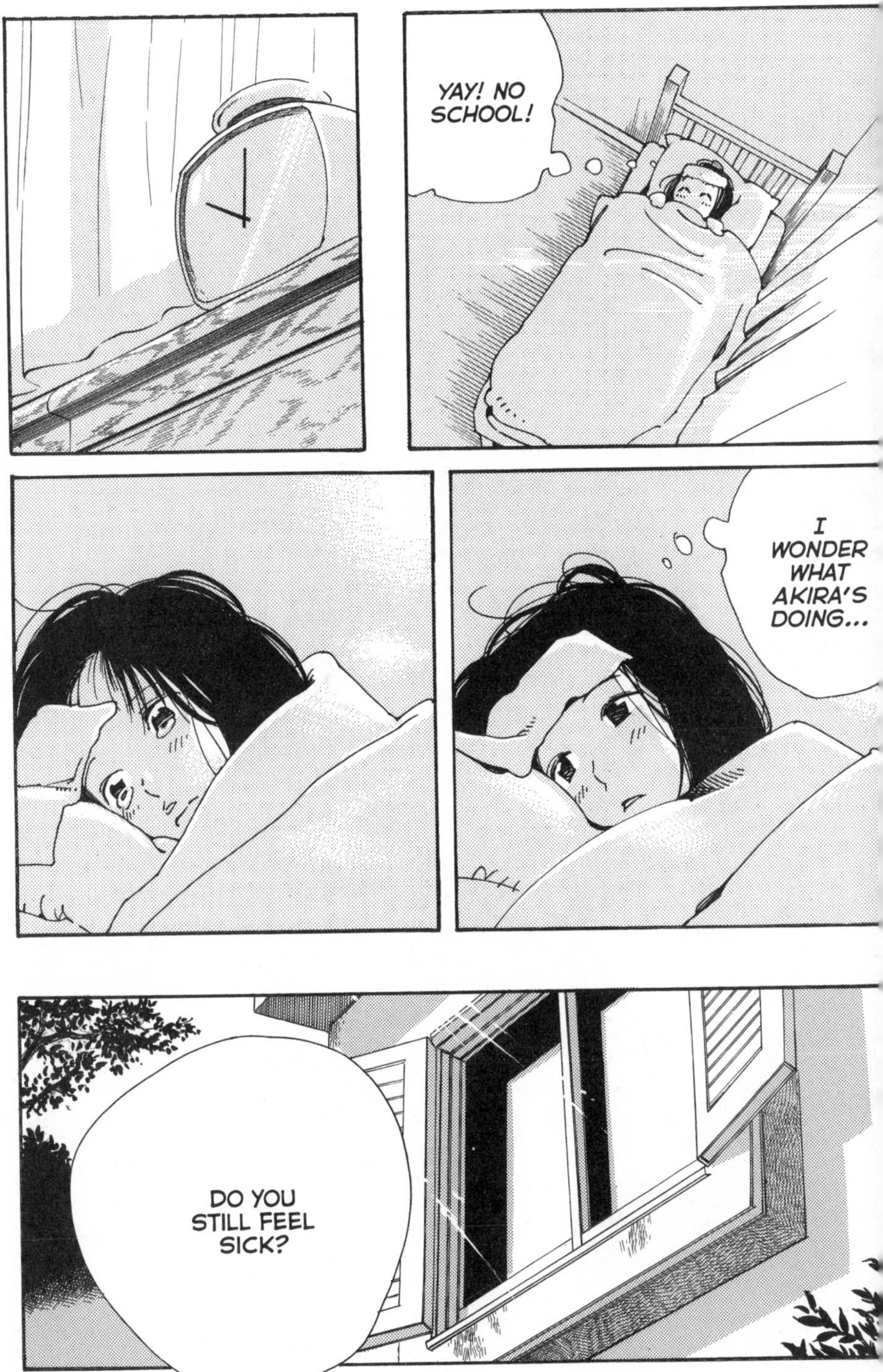
YAY! NO SCHOOL!
I WONDER WHAT AKIRA'S DOING...
DO YOU STILL FEEL SICK?

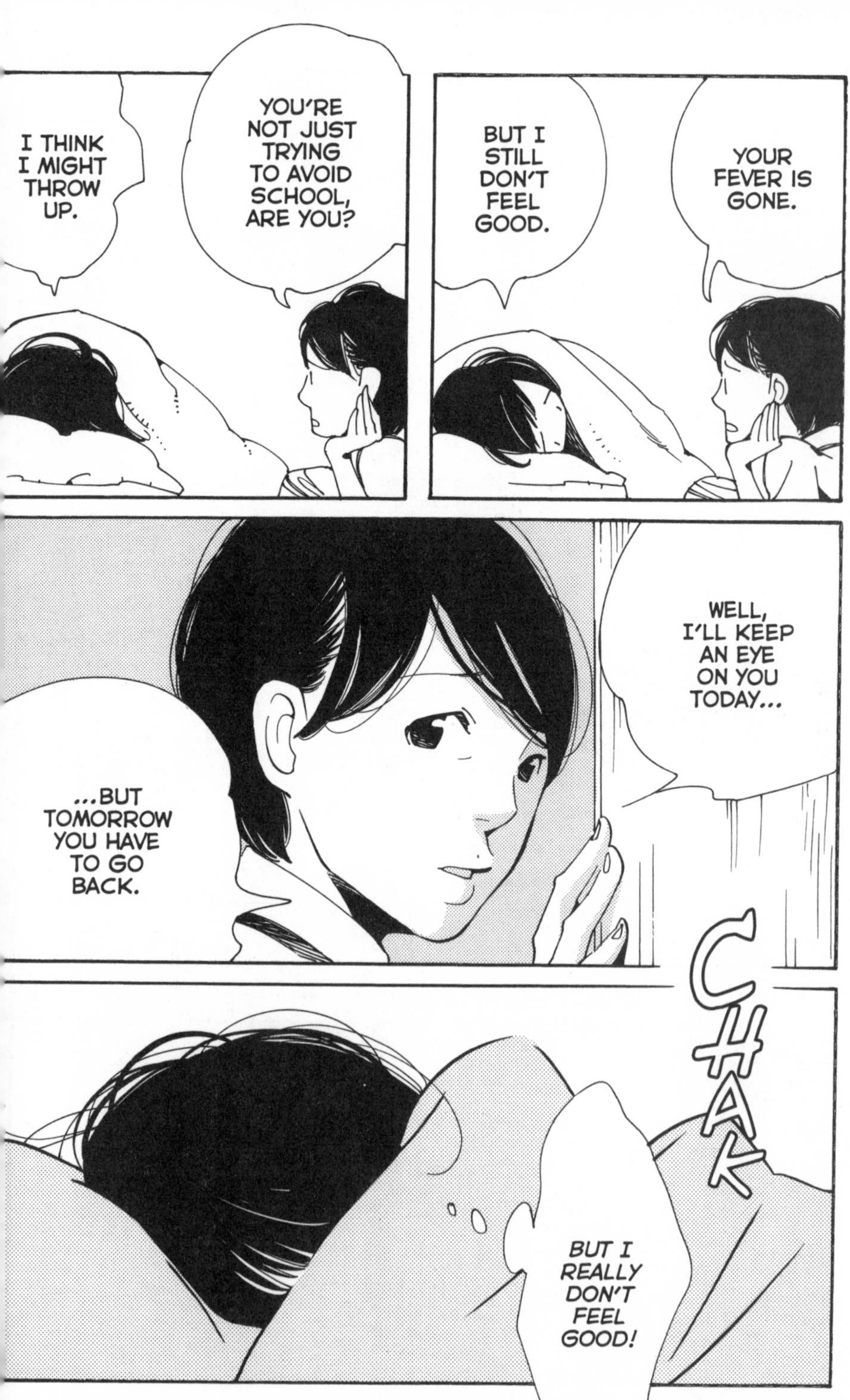
YOUR FEVER IS GONE.
BUT I STILL DON'T FEEL GOOD.
YOU'RE NOT JUST TRYING TO AVOID SCHOOL, ARE YOU?
I THINK I MIGHT THROW UP.
WELL, I'LL KEEP AN EYE ON YOU TODAY...
...BUT TOMORROW YOU HAVE TO GO BACK.
CHAK
BUT I REALLY DON'T FEEL GOOD!

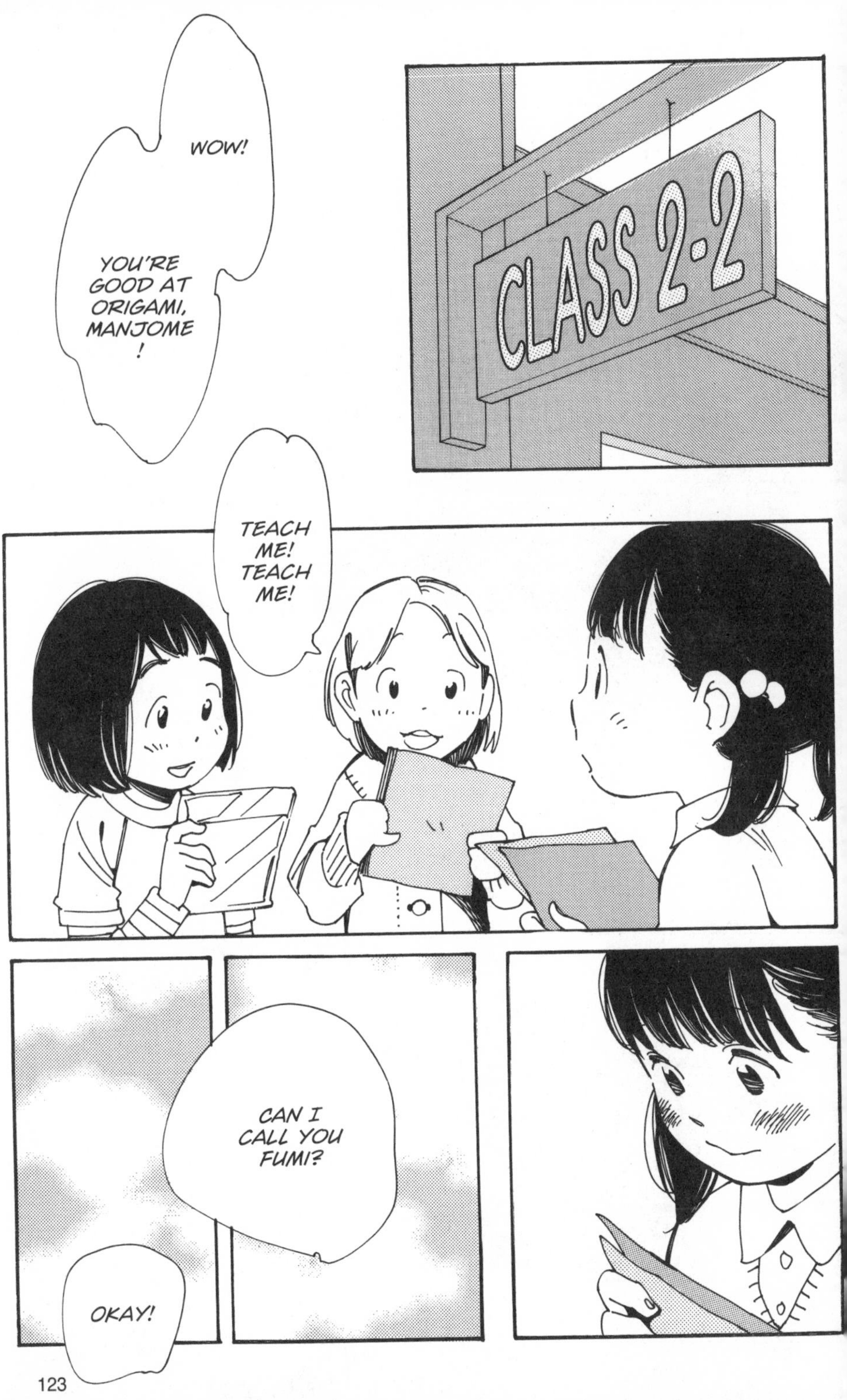
CLASS 2-2
WOW!
YOU'RE GOOD AT ORIGAMI, MANJOME!
TEACH ME! TEACH ME!
CAN I CALL YOU FUMI?
OKAY!

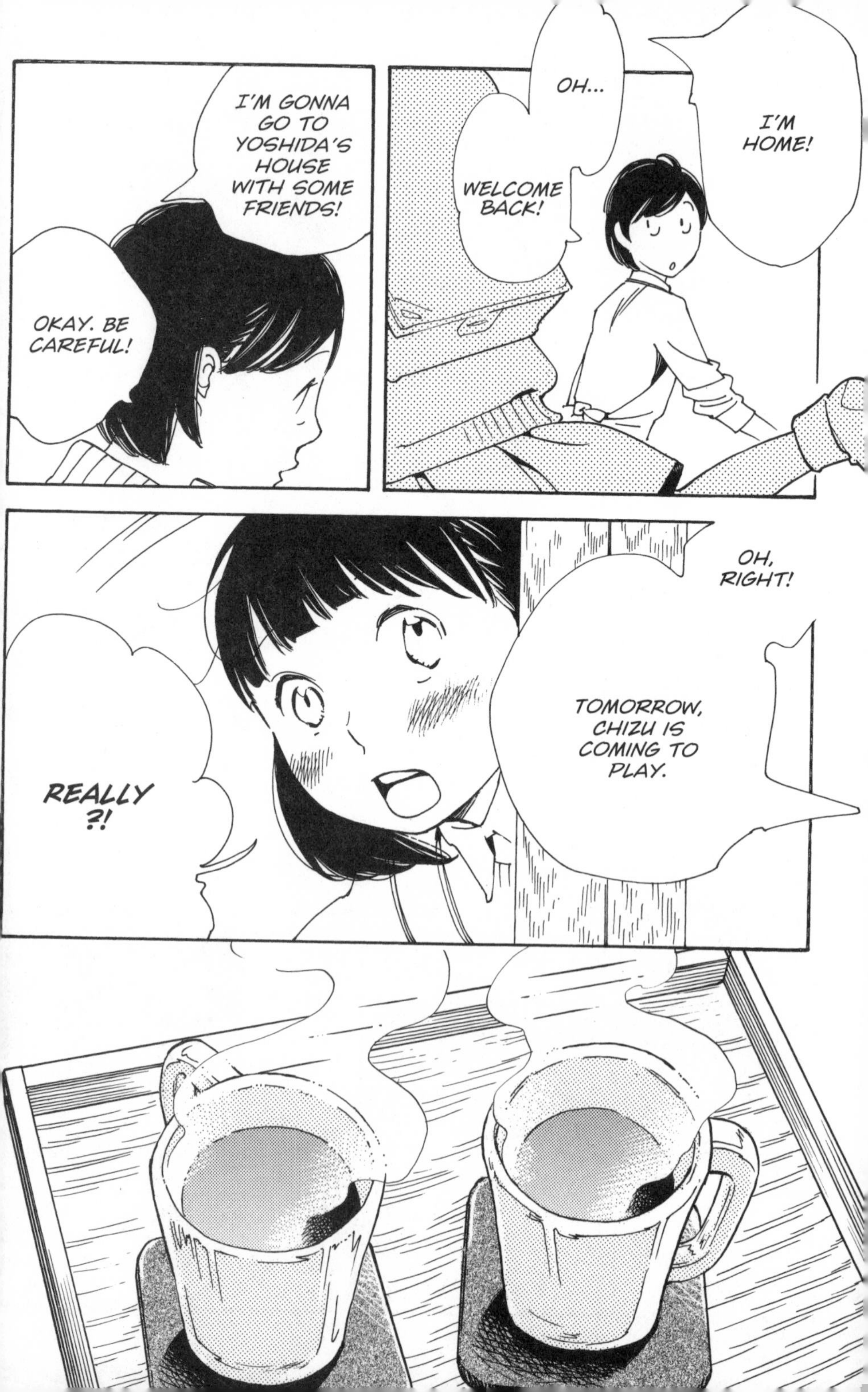
I'M HOME!
OH...
WELCOME BACK!
I'M GONNA GO TO YOSHIDA'S HOUSE WITH SOME FRIENDS!
OKAY. BE CAREFUL!
OH, RIGHT!
TOMORROW, CHIZU IS COMING TO PLAY.
REALLY?!

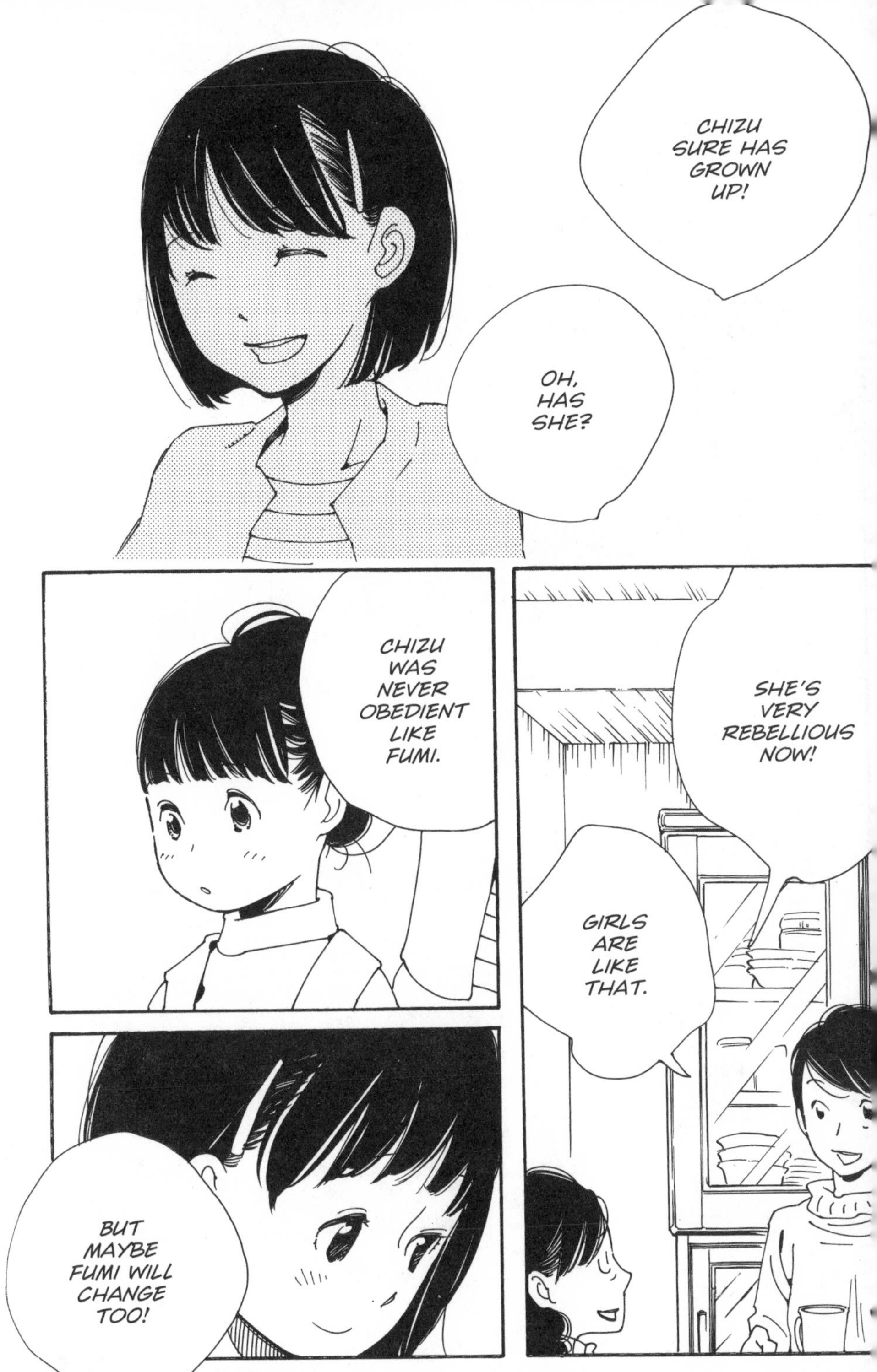
CHIZU SURE HAS GROWN UP!
OH, HAS SHE?
SHE'S VERY REBELLIOUS NOW!
GIRLS ARE LIKE THAT.
CHIZU WAS NEVER OBEDIENT LIKE FUMI.
BUT MAYBE FUMI WILL CHANGE TOO!
HA HA HA

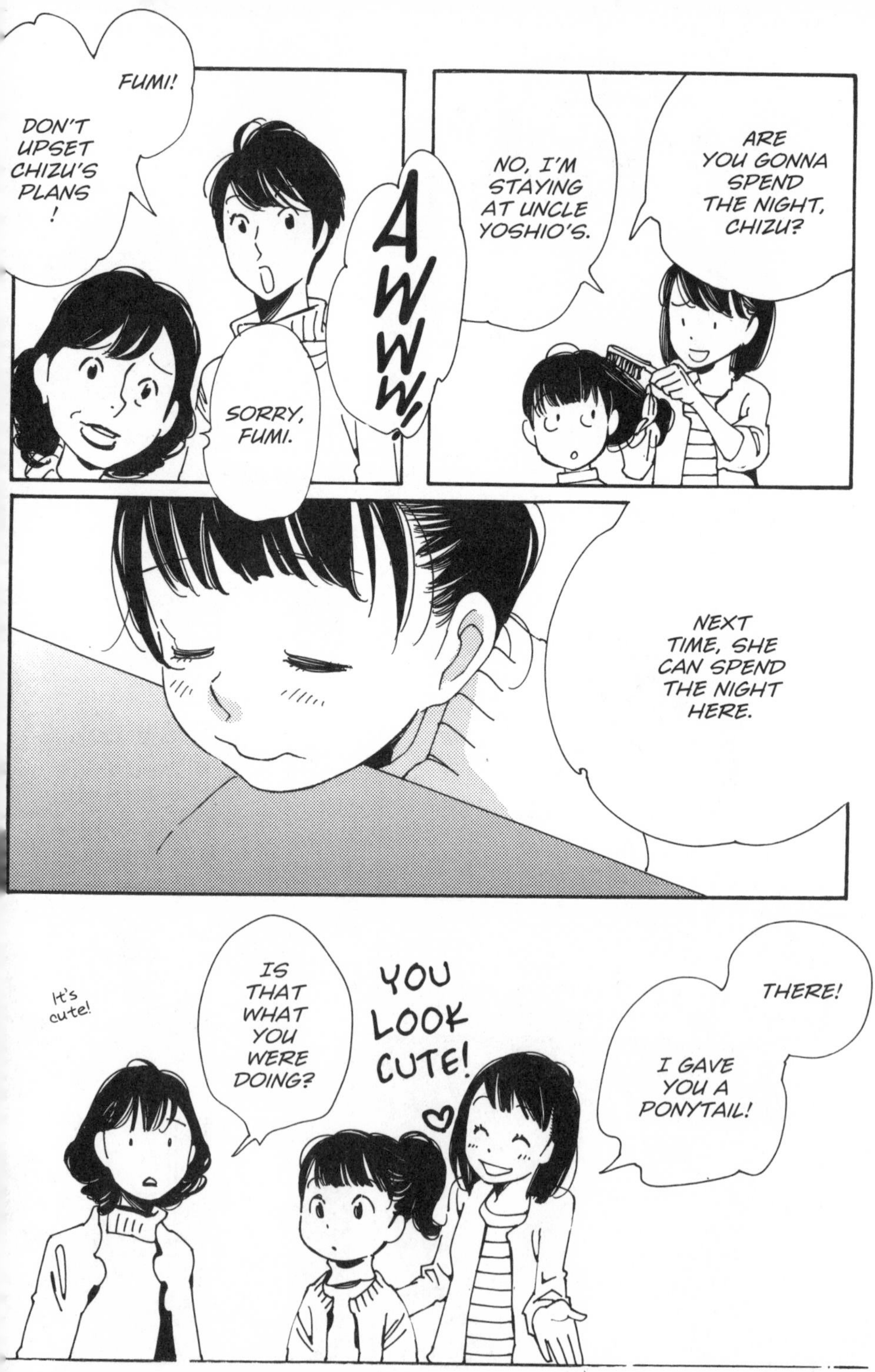
ARE YOU GONNA SPEND THE NIGHT, CHIZU?
NO, I'M STAYING AT UNCLE YOSHIO'S.
AWWW!
FUMI!
DON'T UPSET CHIZU'S PLANS!
SORRY, FUMI.
NEXT TIME, SHE CAN SPEND THE NIGHT HERE.
THERE!
I GAVE YOU A PONYTAIL!
YOU LOOK CUTE!
IS THAT WHAT YOU WERE DOING?
It's cute!

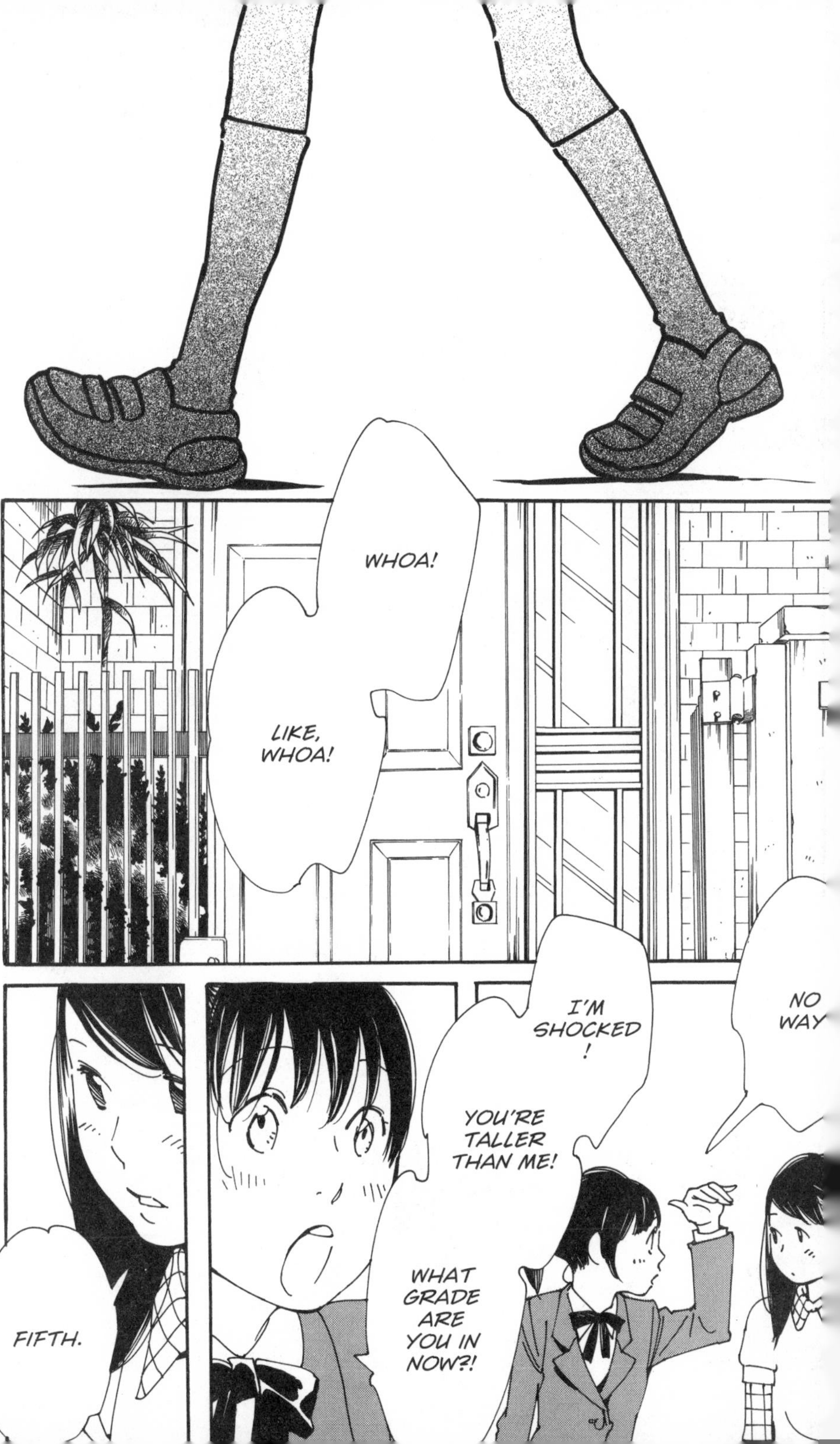
WHOA!
LIKE, WHOA!
NO WAY
I'M SHOCKED!
YOU'RE TALLER THAN ME!
WHAT GRADE ARE YOU IN NOW?!
FIFTH.

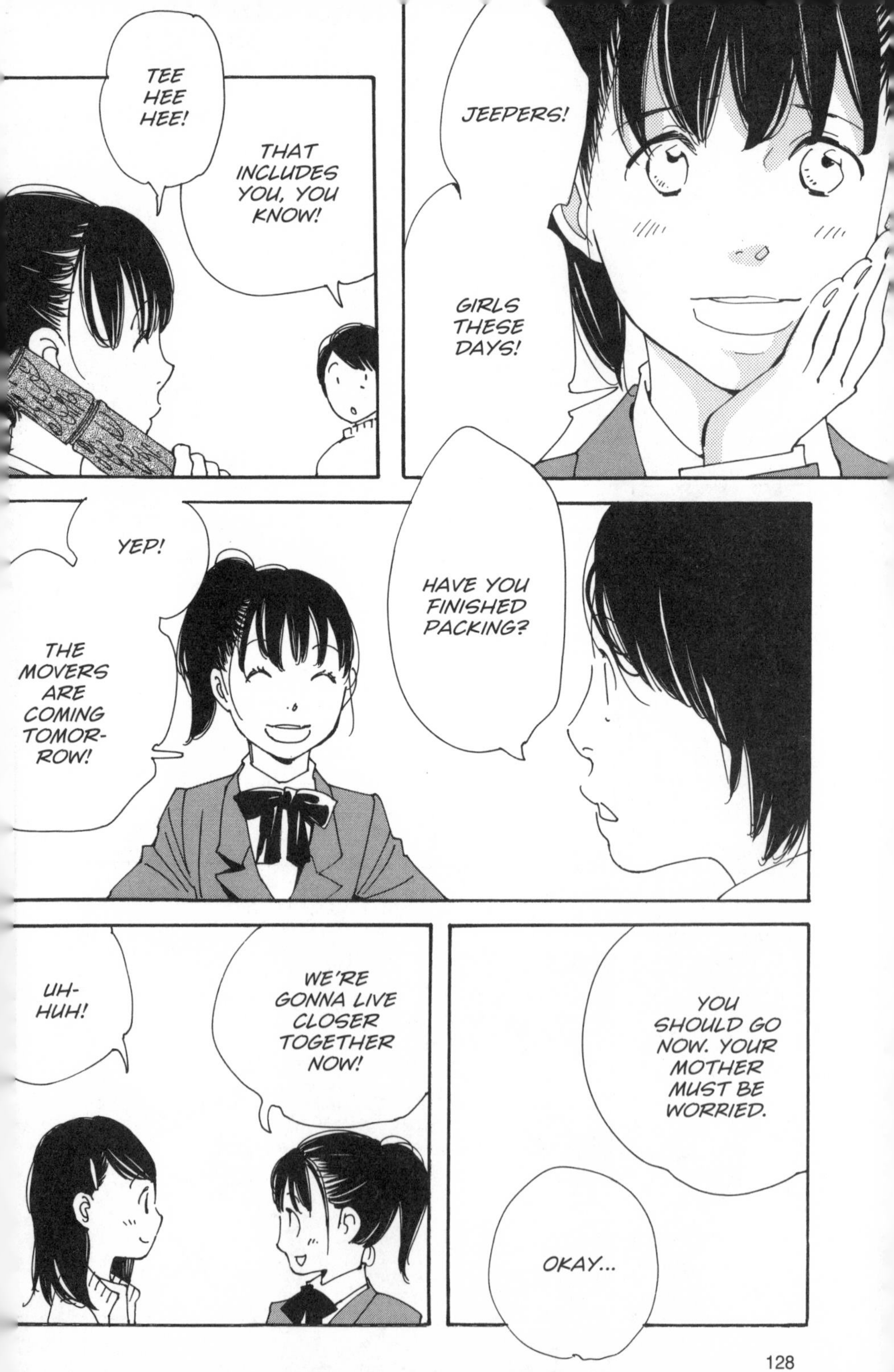
JEEPERS!
GIRLS THESE DAYS!
TEE HEE HEE!
THAT INCLUDES YOU, YOU KNOW!
HAVE YOU FINISHED PACKING?
YEP!
THE MOVERS ARE COMING TOMOR-ROW!
YOU SHOULD GO NOW. YOUR MOTHER MUST BE WORRIED.
OKAY...
WE'RE GONNA LIVE CLOSER TOGETHER NOW!
UH-HUH!

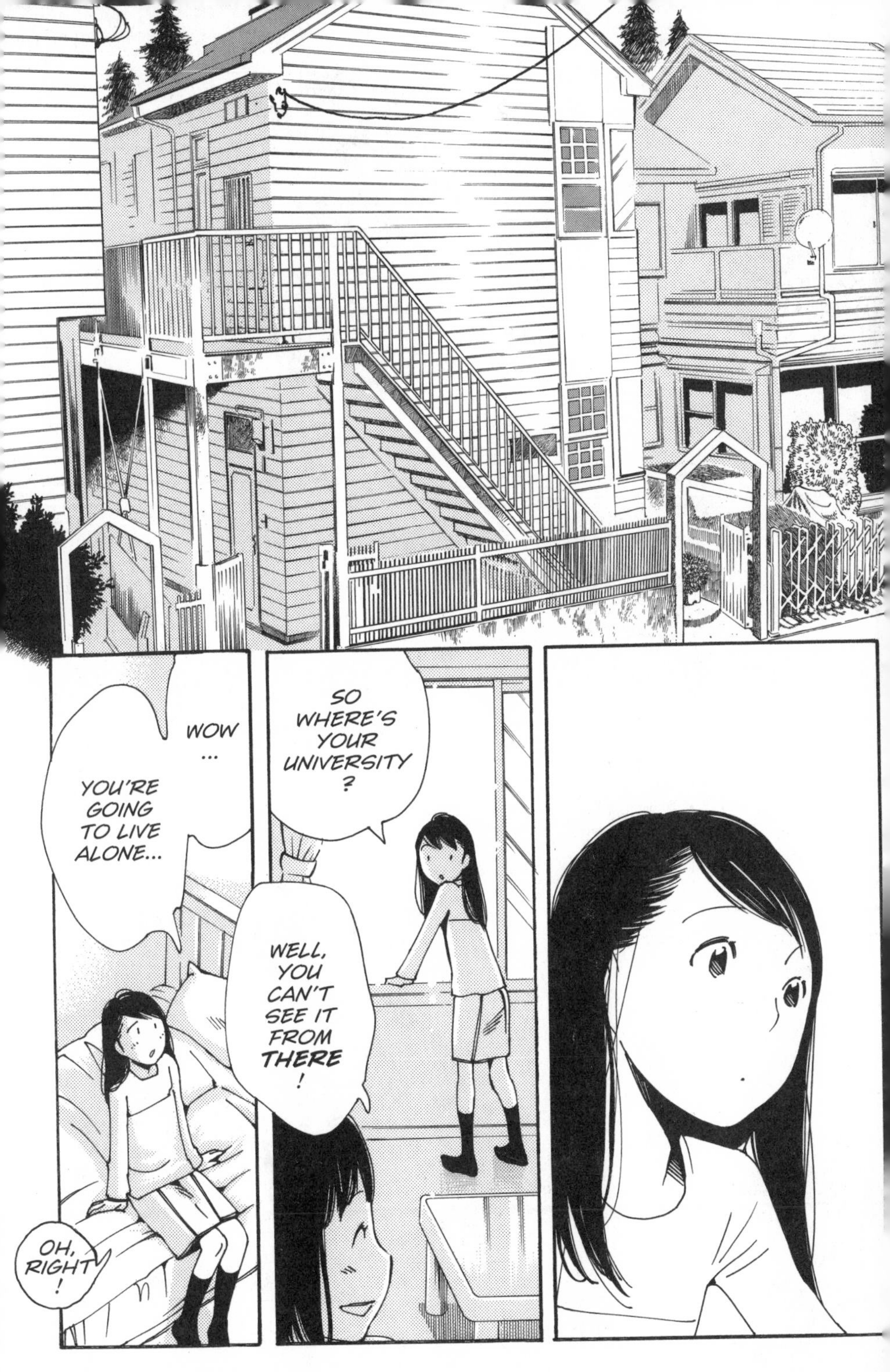
SO WHERE'S YOUR UNIVERSITY?
WELL, YOU CAN'T SEE IT FROM THERE!
WOW... YOU'RE GOING TO LIVE ALONE...
OH, RIGHT!

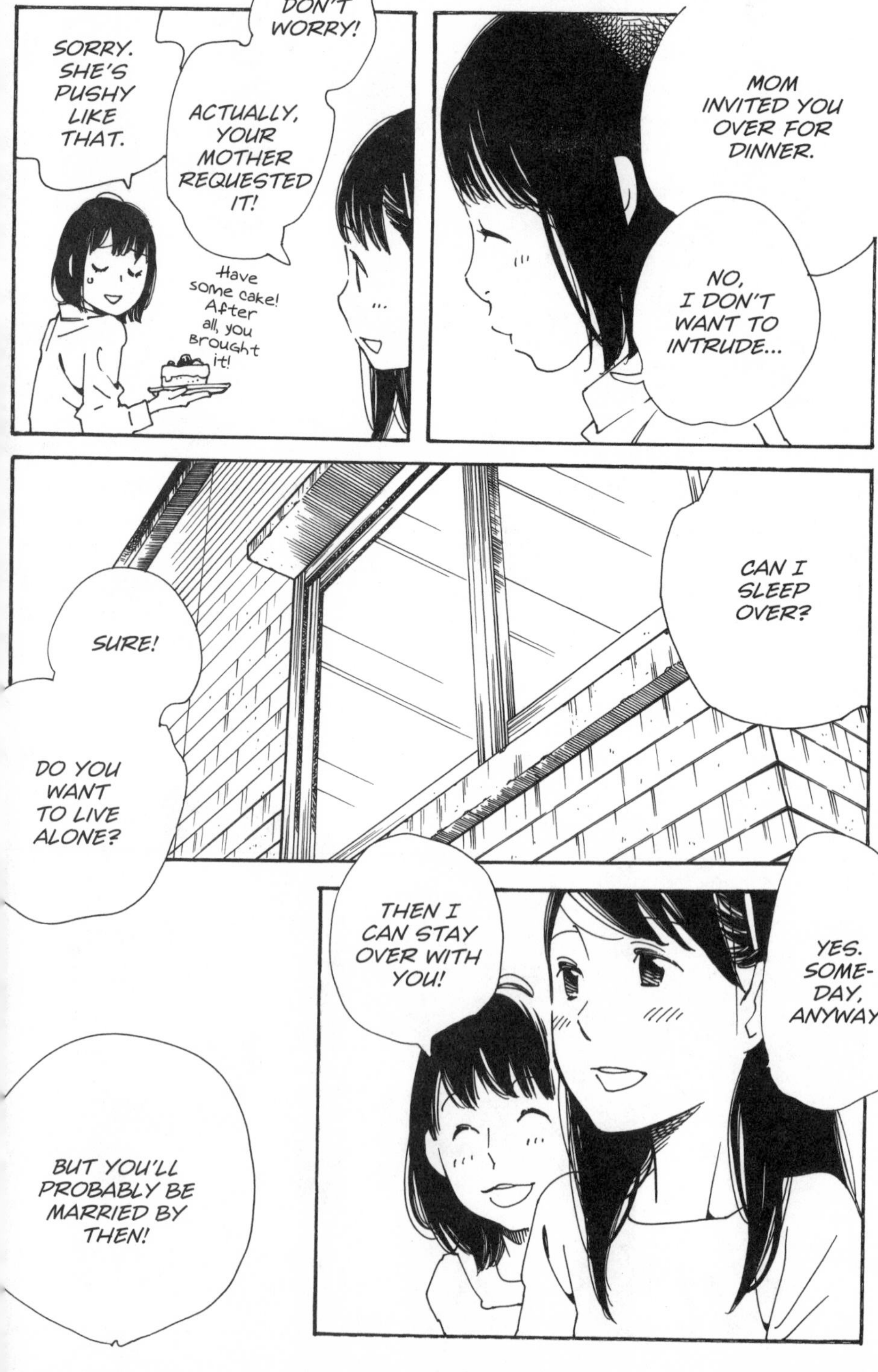
MOM INVITED YOU OVER FOR DINNER.
NO, I DON'T WANT TO INTRUDE...
DON'T WORRY!
ACTUALLY, YOUR MOTHER REQUESTED IT!
SORRY. SHE'S PUSHY LIKE THAT.
Have some cake! After all, you brought it!
...
CAN I SLEEP OVER?
SURE!
DO YOU WANT TO LIVE ALONE?
YES. SOMEDAY, ANYWAY.
THEN I CAN STAY OVER WITH YOU!
BUT YOU'LL PROBABLY BE MARRIED BY THEN!

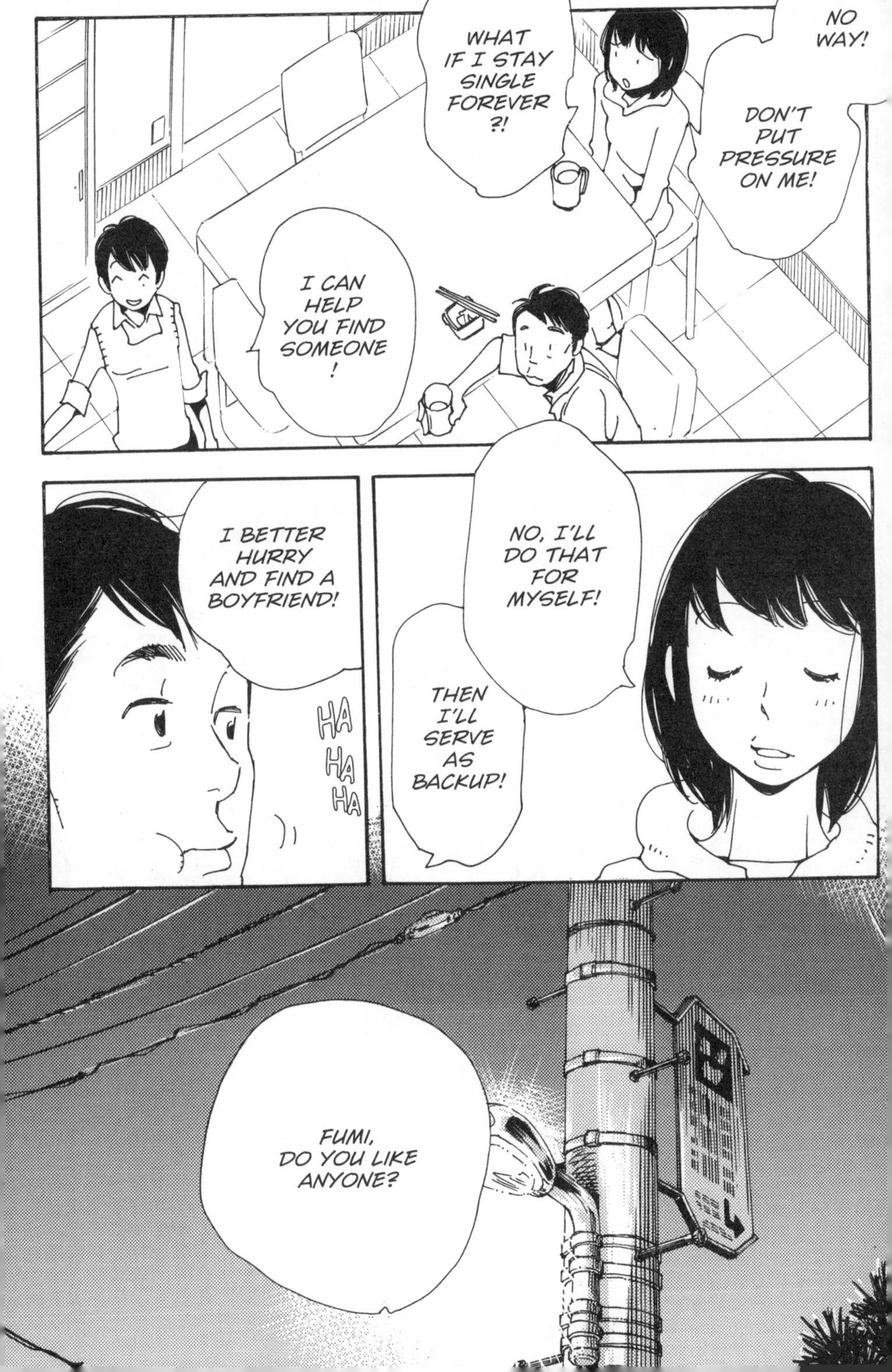
NO WAY!
DON'T PUT PRESSURE ON ME!
WHAT IF I STAY SINGLE FOREVER?!
I CAN HELP YOU FIND SOMEONE!
NO, I'LL DO THAT FOR MYSELF!
THEN I'LL SERVE AS BACKUP!
I BETTER HURRY AND FIND A BOYFRIEND!
HA HA HA
FUMI, DO YOU LIKE ANYONE?

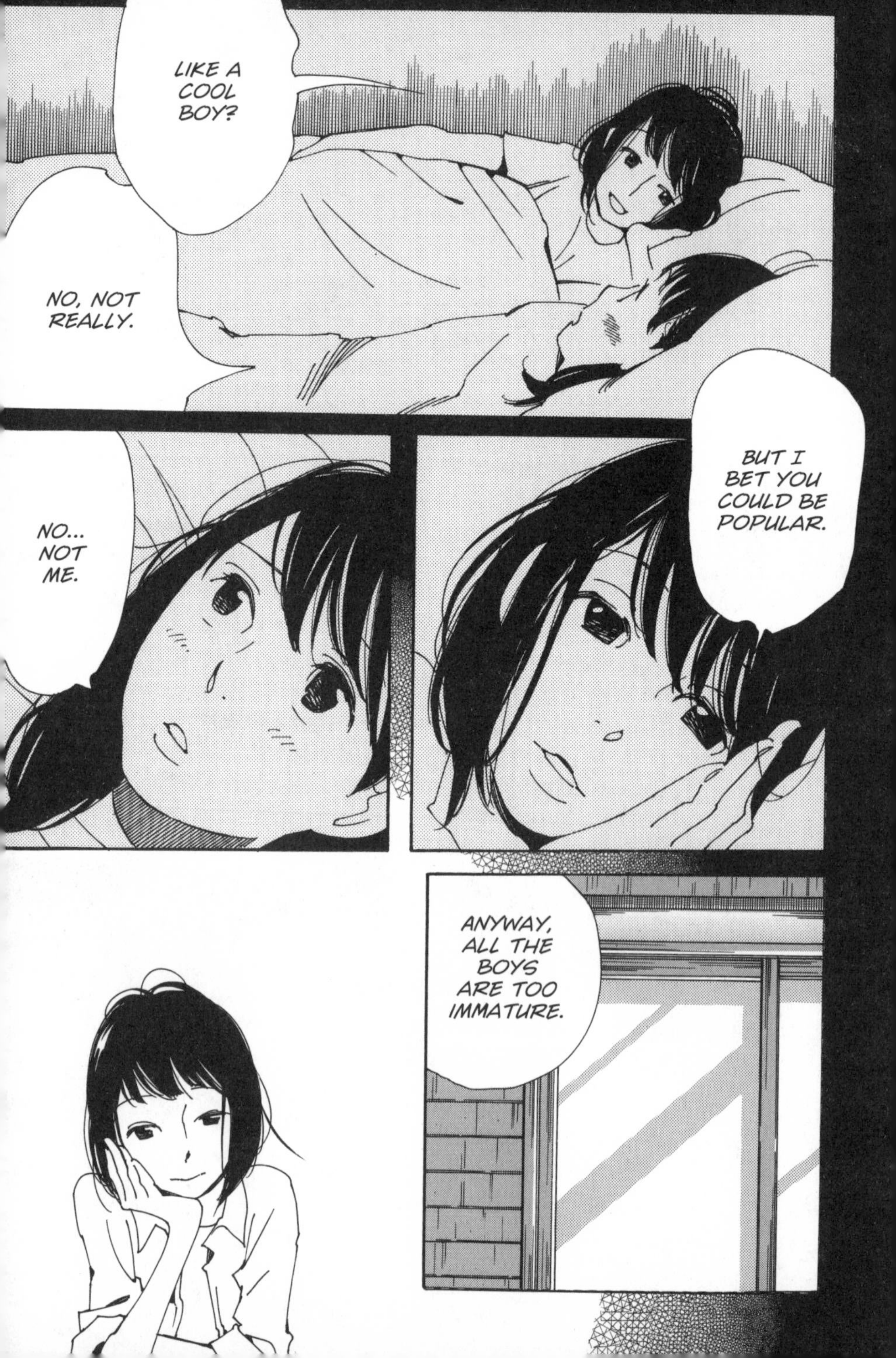
LIKE A COOL BOY?
NO, NOT REALLY.
BUT I BET YOU COULD BE POPULAR.
NO... NOT ME.
ANYWAY, ALL THE BOYS ARE TOO IMMATURE.

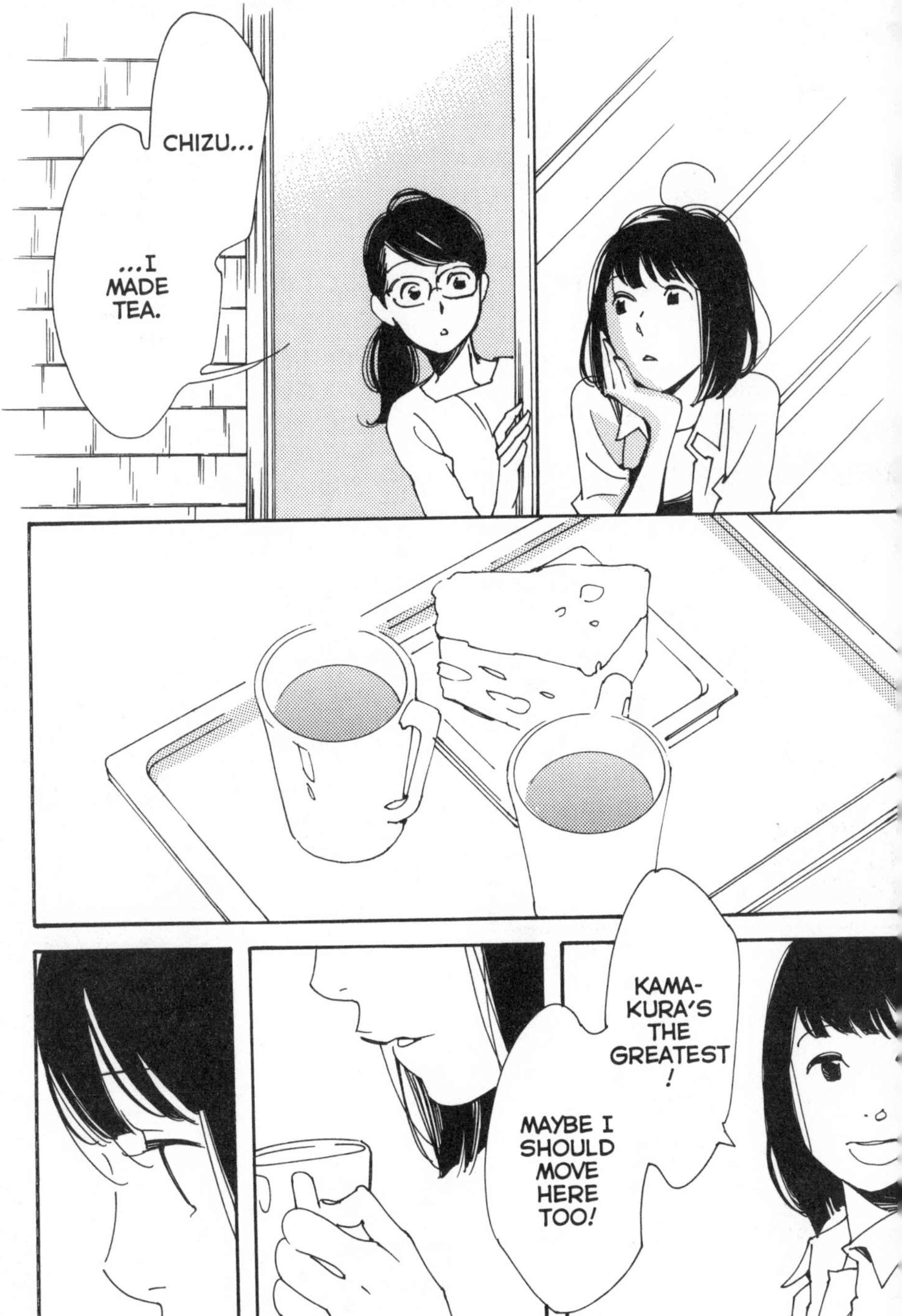
CHIZU...
...I MADE TEA.
KAMA-KURA'S THE GREATEST!
MAYBE I SHOULD MOVE HERE TOO!

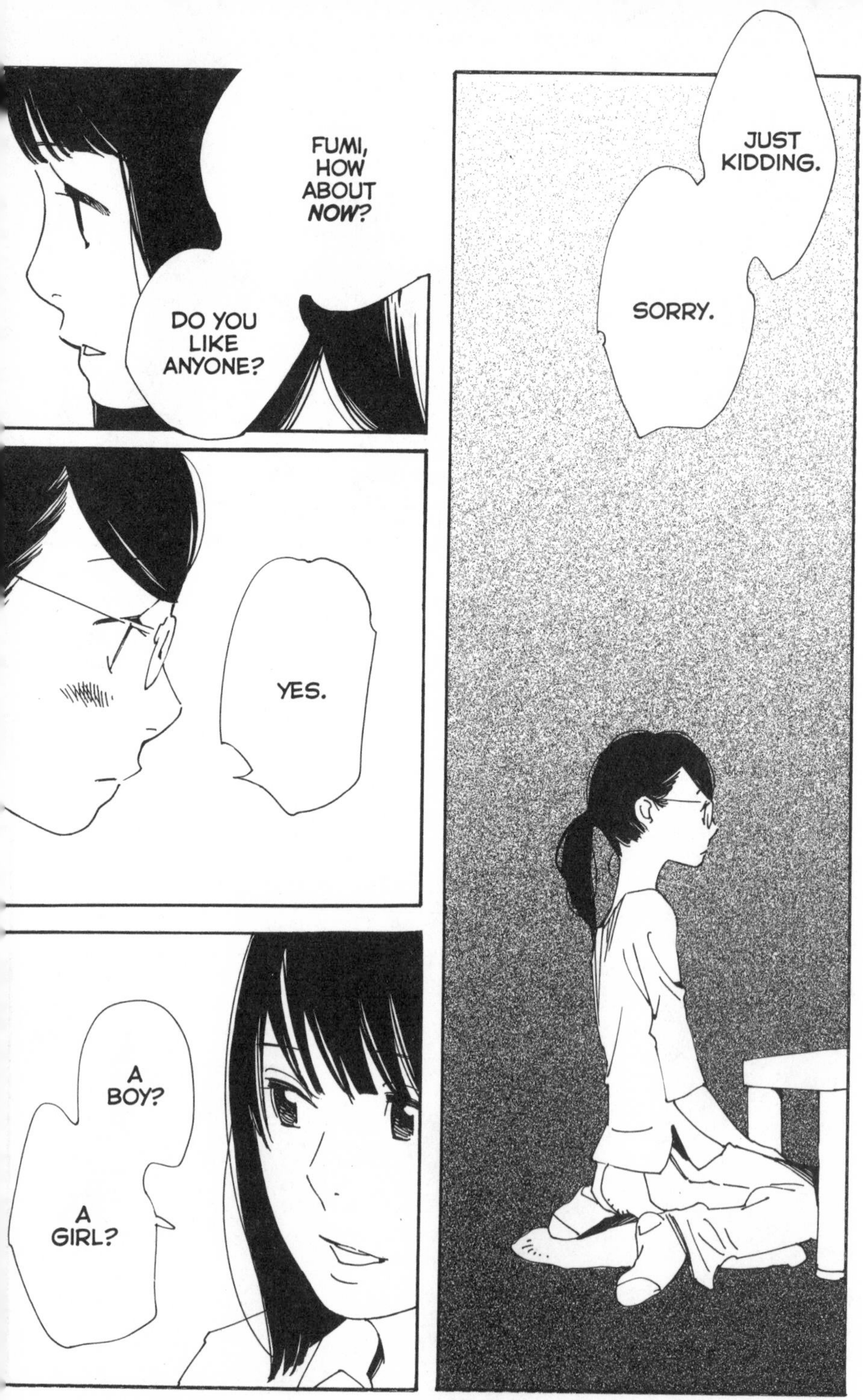
JUST KIDDING.
SORRY.
FUMI, HOW ABOUT *NOW?*
DO YOU LIKE ANYONE?
YES.
A BOY?
A GIRL?

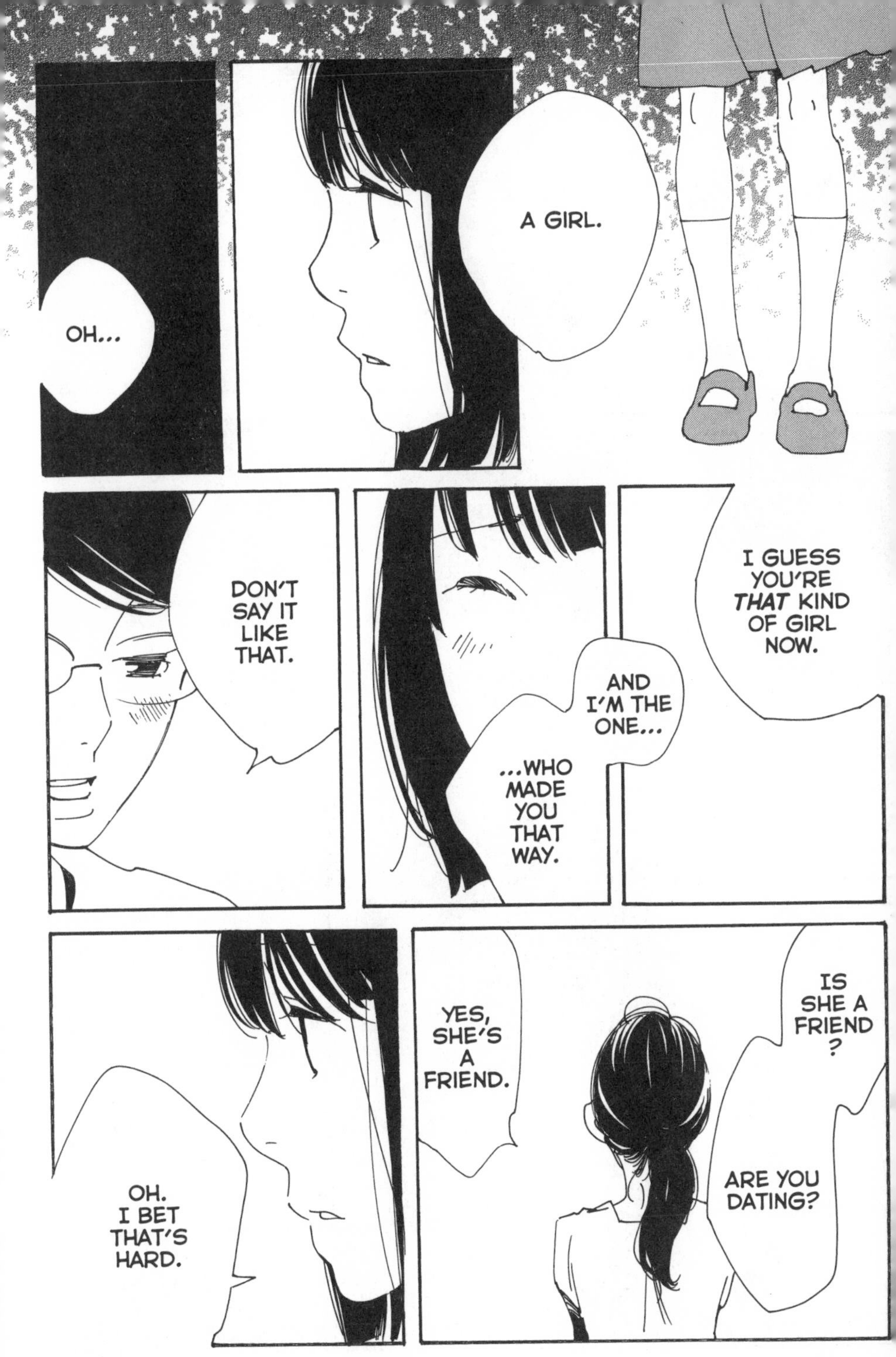
A GIRL.
OH...
I GUESS YOU'RE *THAT* KIND OF GIRL NOW.
AND I'M THE ONE...
...WHO MADE YOU THAT WAY.
DON'T SAY IT LIKE THAT.
IS SHE A FRIEND?
YES, SHE'S A FRIEND.
ARE YOU DATING?
OH. I BET THAT'S HARD.

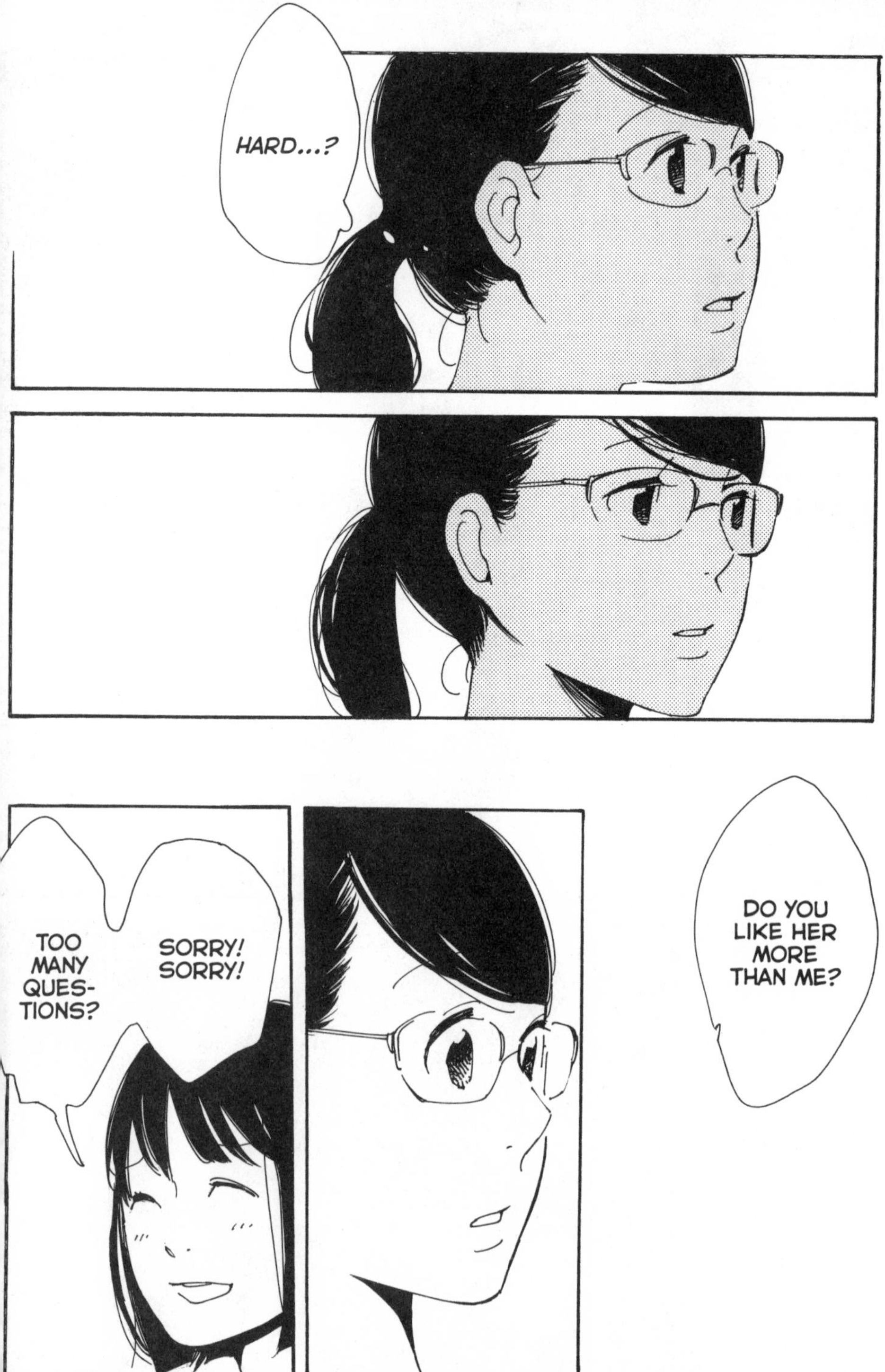
HARD...?
DO YOU LIKE HER MORE THAN ME?
SORRY! SORRY!
TOO MANY QUES-TIONS?

MY DAUGHTER LOOKS A LITTLE LIKE YOU.

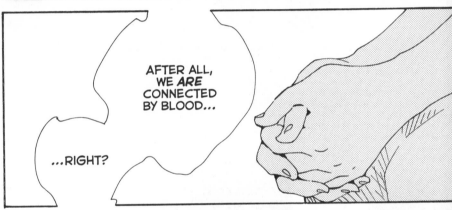

AFTER ALL, WE *ARE* CONNECTED BY BLOOD...

...RIGHT?

...SO I CAN'T BE *THAT* KIND OF GIRL.

...AND COUSINS...

WE'RE GIRLS...

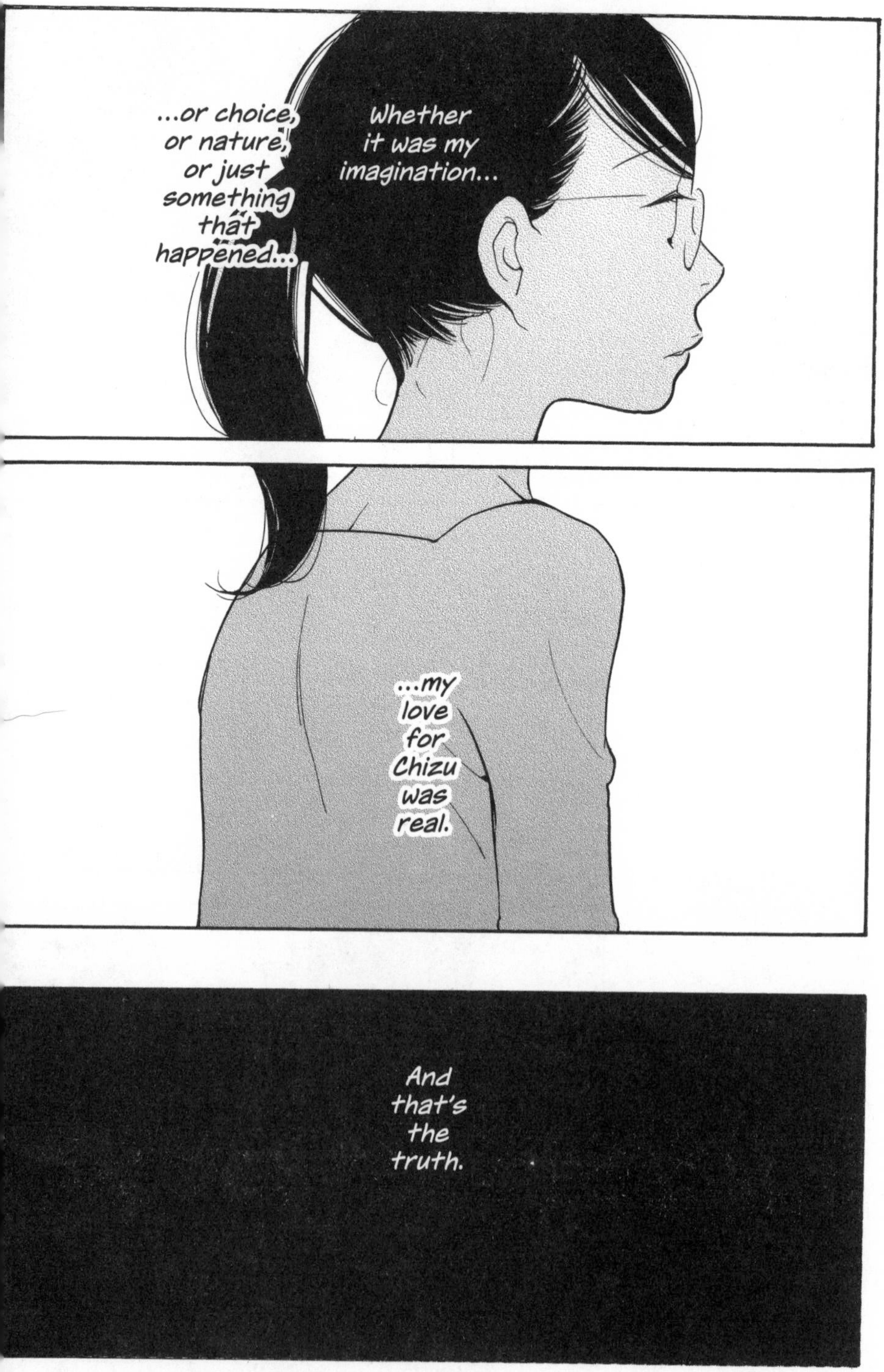
Whether it was my imagination...
...or choice, or nature, or just something that happened...
...my love for Chizu was real.
And that's the truth.

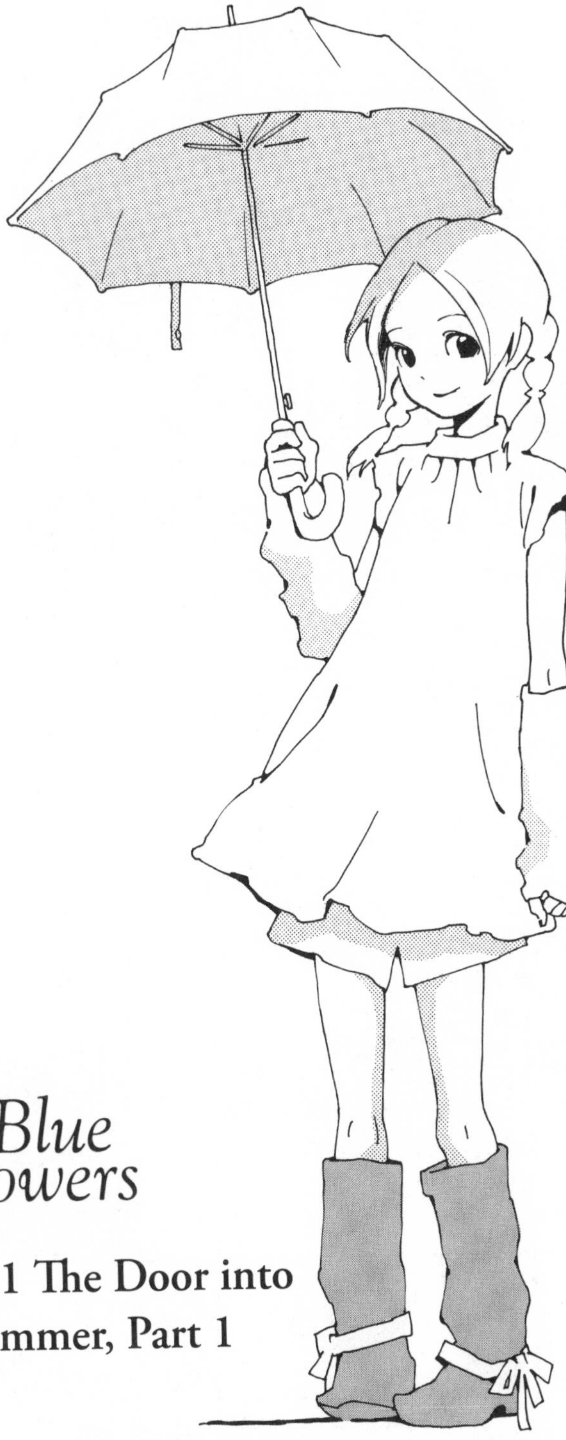

Sweet Blue Flowers

#31 The Door into Summer, Part 1

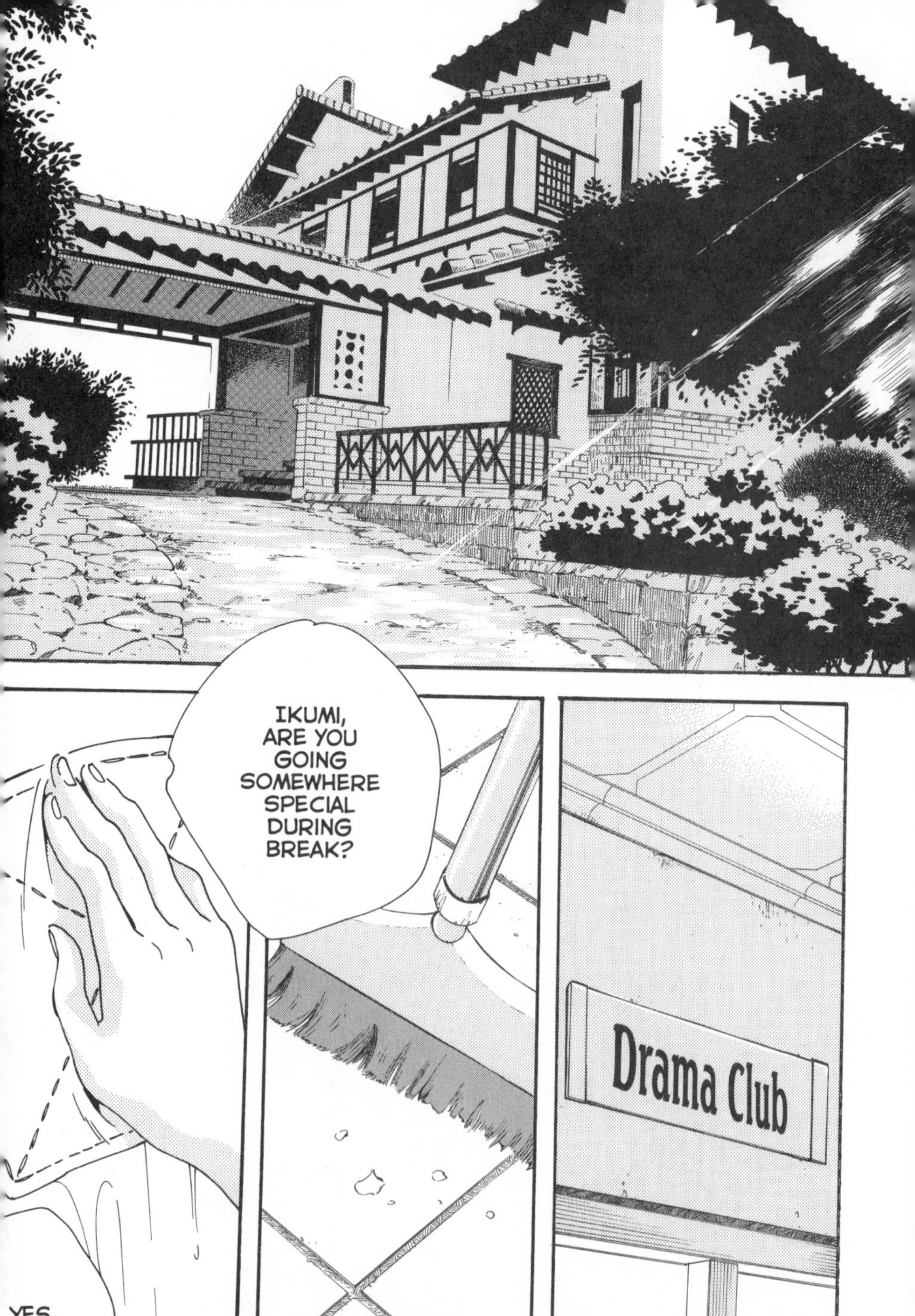
Drama Club
IKUMI, ARE YOU GOING SOMEWHERE SPECIAL DURING BREAK?
YES.

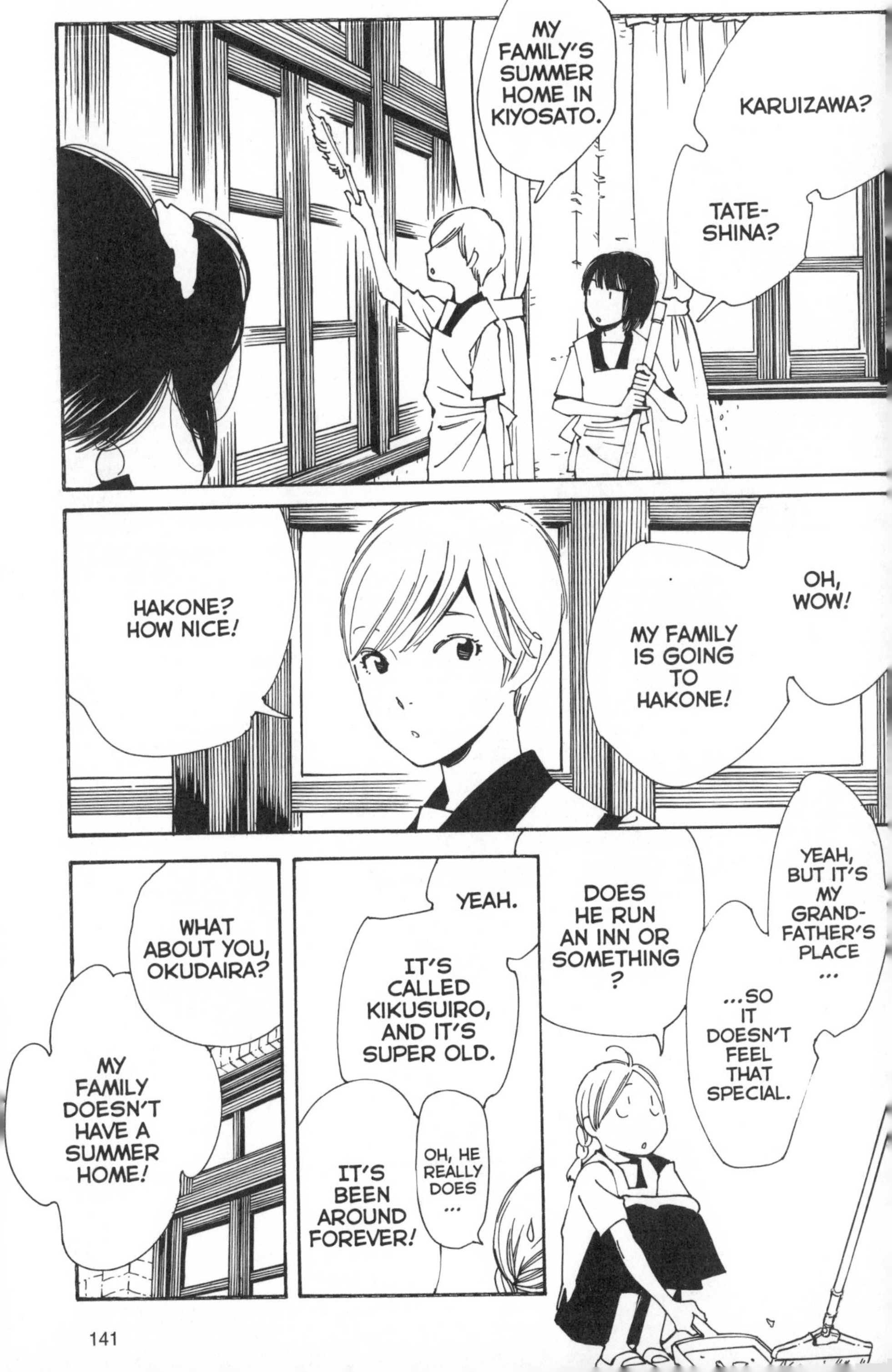
KARUIZAWA?
TATE-SHINA?
MY FAMILY'S SUMMER HOME IN KIYOSATO.
OH, WOW!
MY FAMILY IS GOING TO HAKONE!
HAKONE? HOW NICE!
YEAH, BUT IT'S MY GRAND-FATHER'S PLACE...
DOES HE RUN AN INN OR SOMETHING?
...SO IT DOESN'T FEEL THAT SPECIAL.
YEAH.
IT'S CALLED KIKUSUIRO, AND IT'S SUPER OLD.
OH, HE REALLY DOES...
IT'S BEEN AROUND FOREVER!
WHAT ABOUT YOU, OKUDAIRA?
MY FAMILY DOESN'T HAVE A SUMMER HOME!

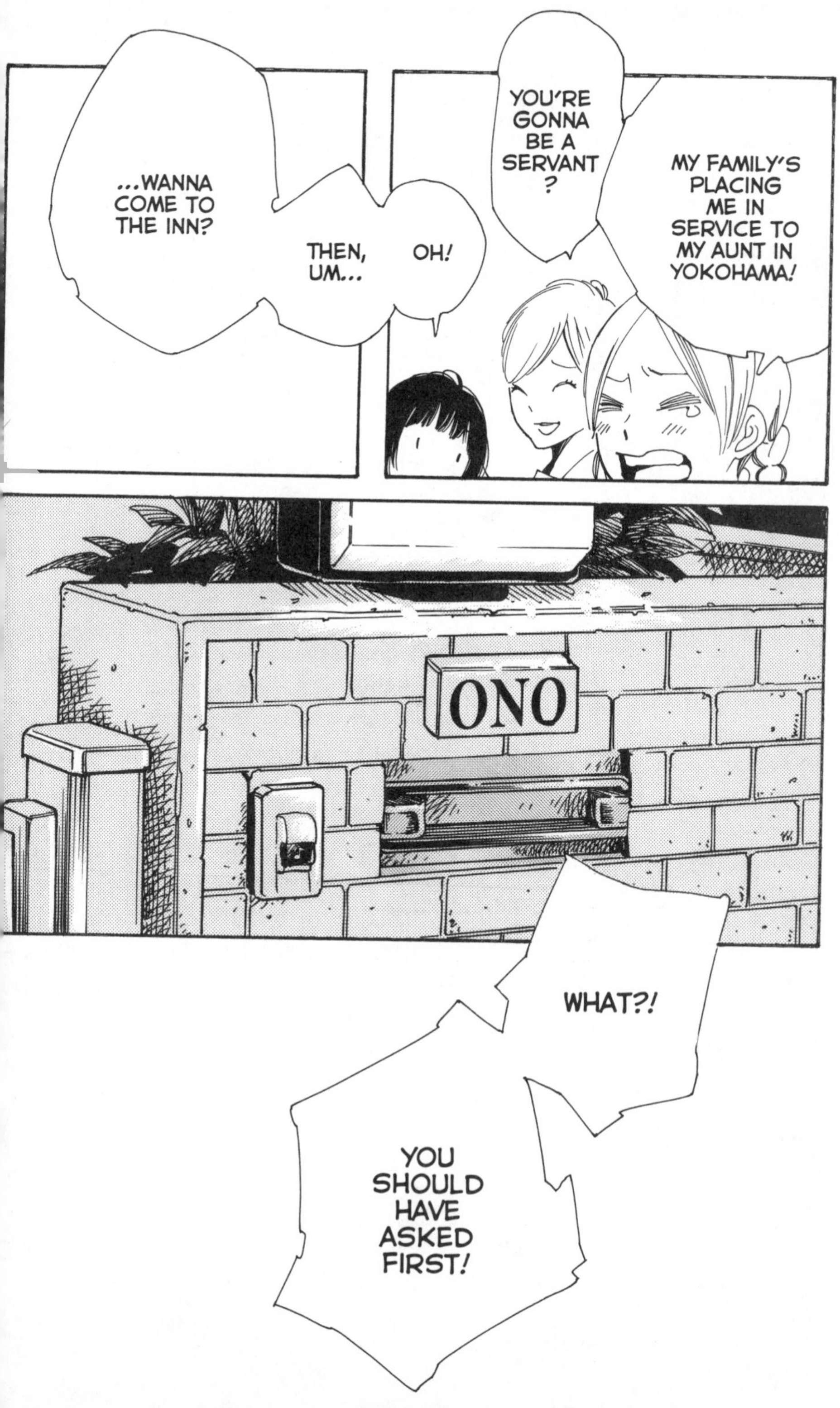
MY FAMILY'S PLACING ME IN SERVICE TO MY AUNT IN YOKOHAMA!
YOU'RE GONNA BE A SERVANT?
OH!
THEN, UM...
...WANNA COME TO THE INN?
ONO
WHAT?!
YOU SHOULD HAVE ASKED FIRST!

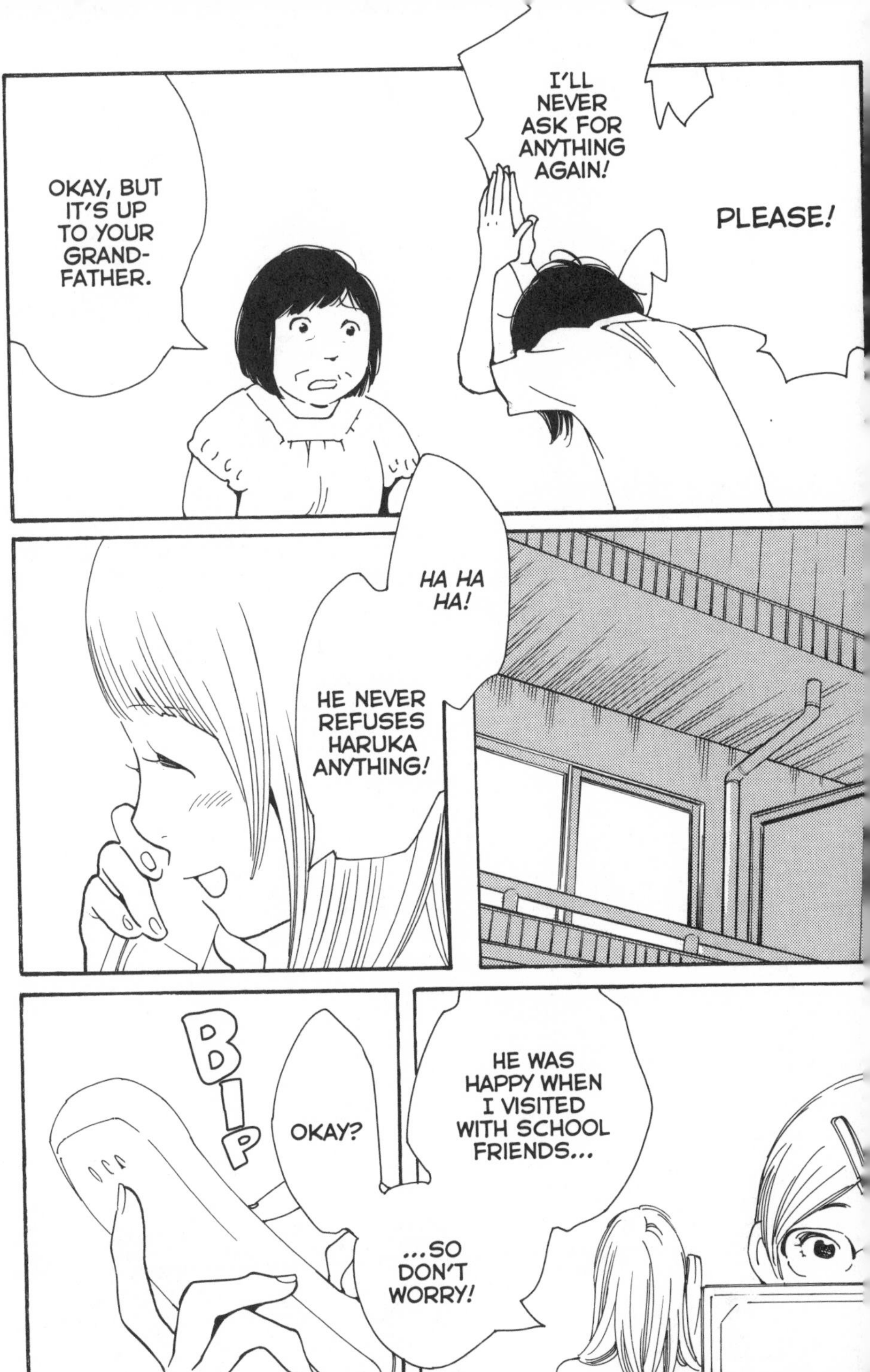

PLEASE!
I'LL NEVER ASK FOR ANYTHING AGAIN!
OKAY, BUT IT'S UP TO YOUR GRAND-FATHER.
HA HA HA!
HE NEVER REFUSES HARUKA ANYTHING!
HE WAS HAPPY WHEN I VISITED WITH SCHOOL FRIENDS...
...SO DON'T WORRY!
OKAY?
BIP

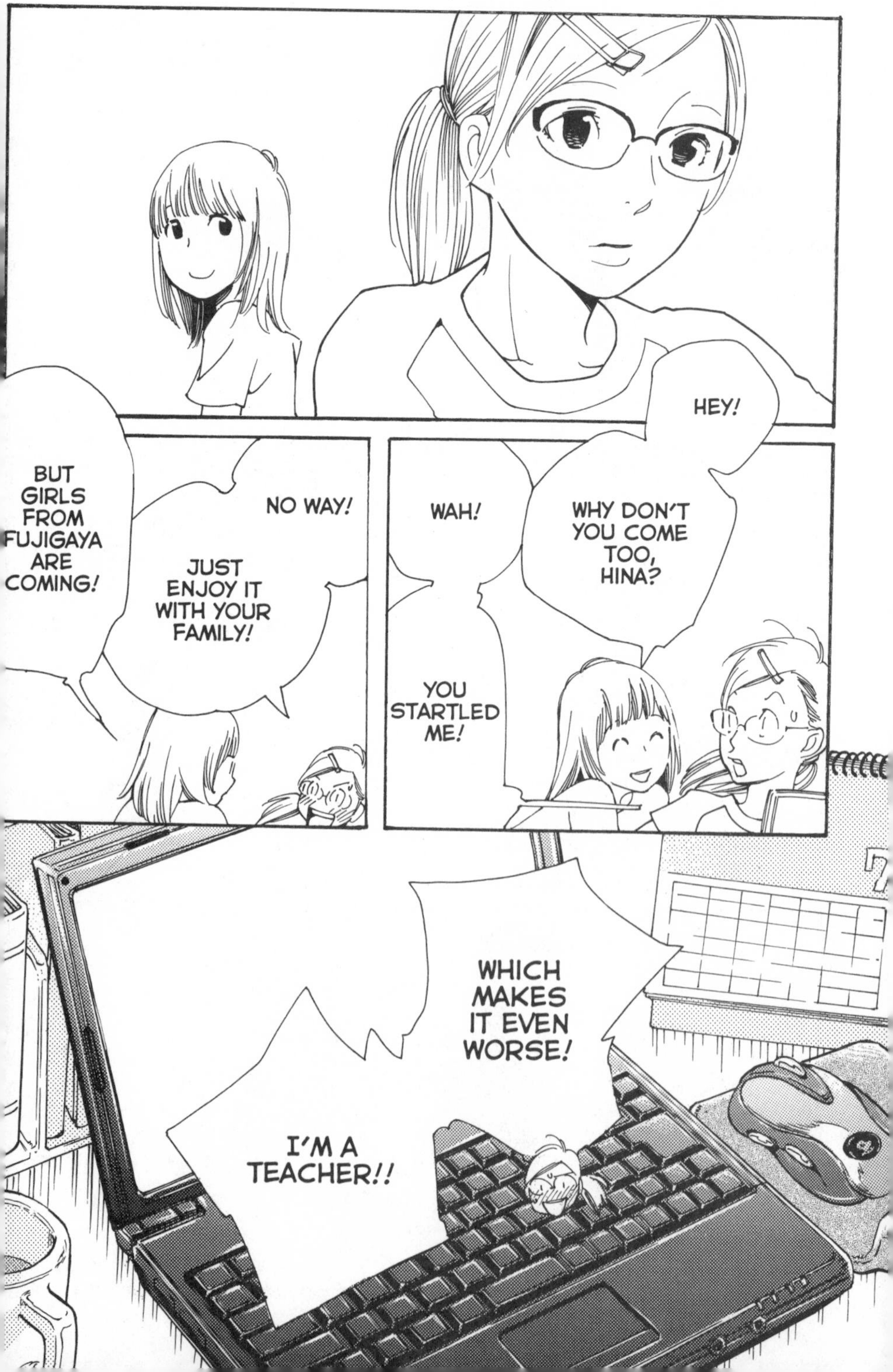
HEY!
WHY DON'T YOU COME TOO, HINA?
WAH!
YOU STARTLED ME!
NO WAY!
JUST ENJOY IT WITH YOUR FAMILY!
BUT GIRLS FROM FUJIGAYA ARE COMING!
WHICH MAKES IT EVEN WORSE!
I'M A TEACHER!!

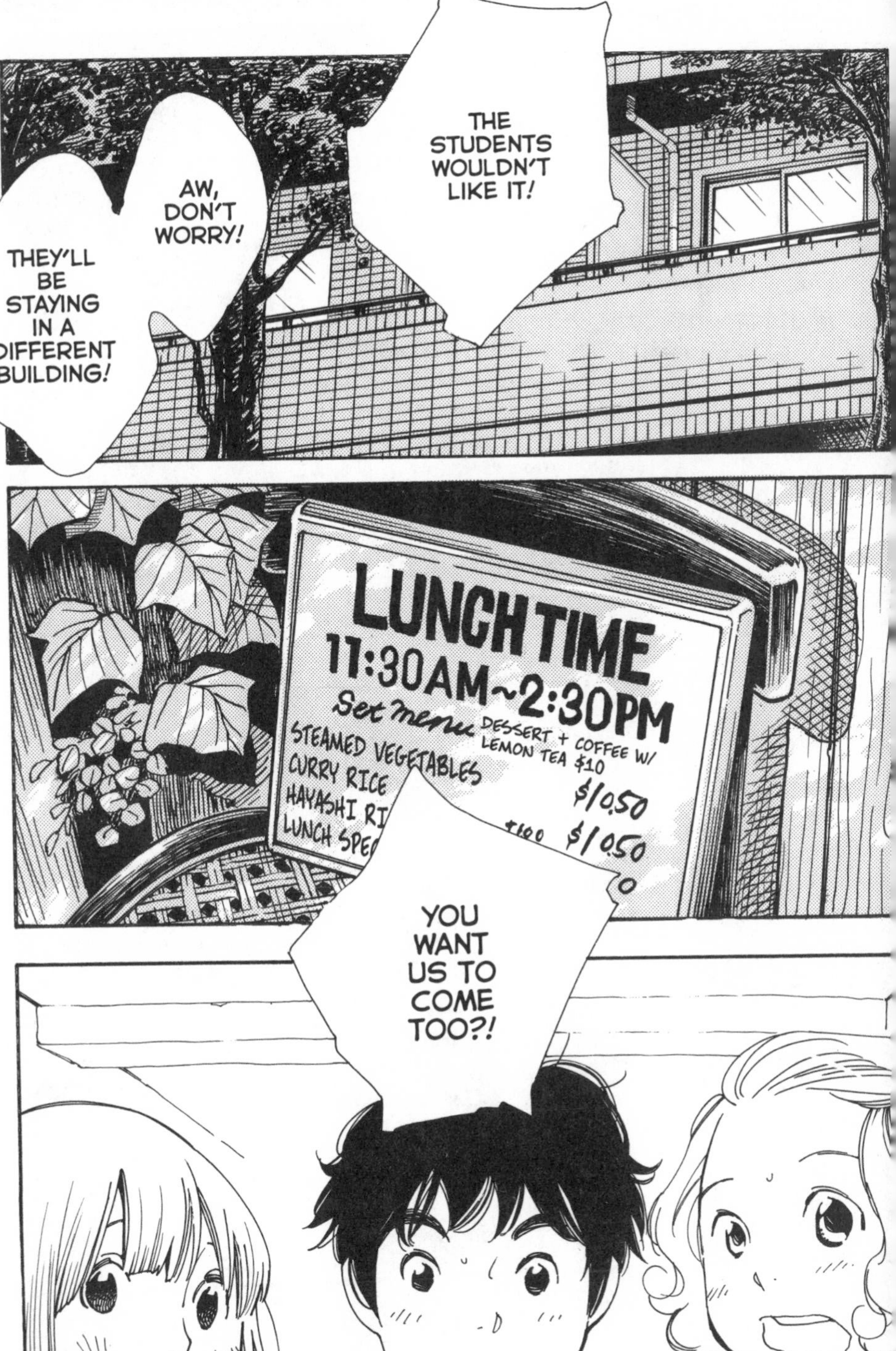
THE STUDENTS WOULDN'T LIKE IT!
AW, DON'T WORRY!
THEY'LL BE STAYING IN A DIFFERENT BUILDING!
LUNCH TIME
11:30AM~2:30PM
Set menu
DESSERT + COFFEE W/ LEMON TEA $10
STEAMED VEGETABLES
CURRY RICE
$10.50
$10.50
YOU WANT US TO COME TOO?!

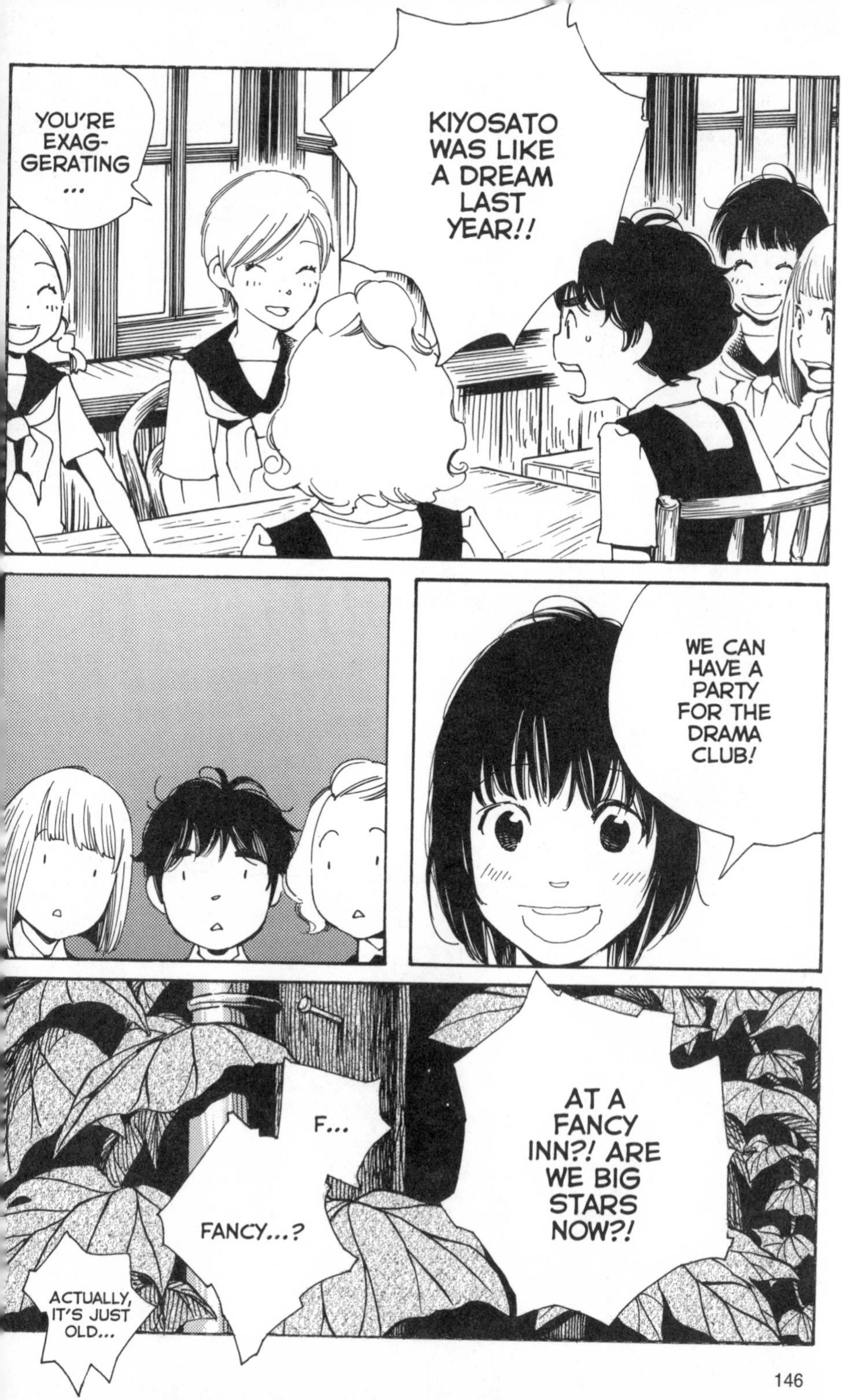
KIYOSATO WAS LIKE A DREAM LAST YEAR!!
YOU'RE EXAG-GERATING...
WE CAN HAVE A PARTY FOR THE DRAMA CLUB!
AT A FANCY INN?! ARE WE BIG STARS NOW?!
F...
FANCY...?
ACTUALLY, IT'S JUST OLD...

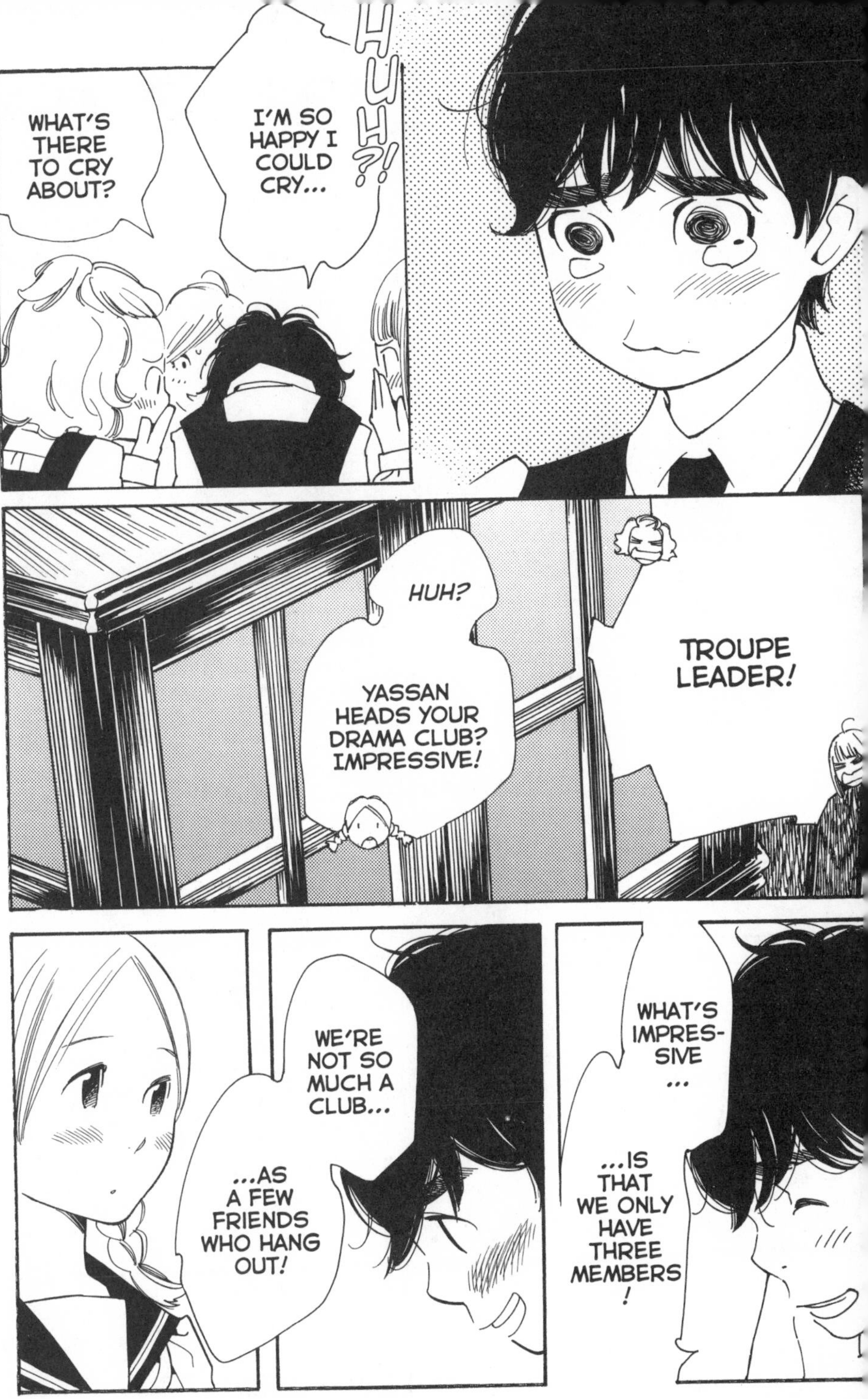
HUHH?!
I'M SO HAPPY I COULD CRY...
WHAT'S THERE TO CRY ABOUT?
TROUPE LEADER!
HUH?
YASSAN HEADS YOUR DRAMA CLUB? IMPRESSIVE!
WHAT'S IMPRES-SIVE...
...IS THAT WE ONLY HAVE THREE MEMBERS!
WE'RE NOT SO MUCH A CLUB...
...AS A FEW FRIENDS WHO HANG OUT!

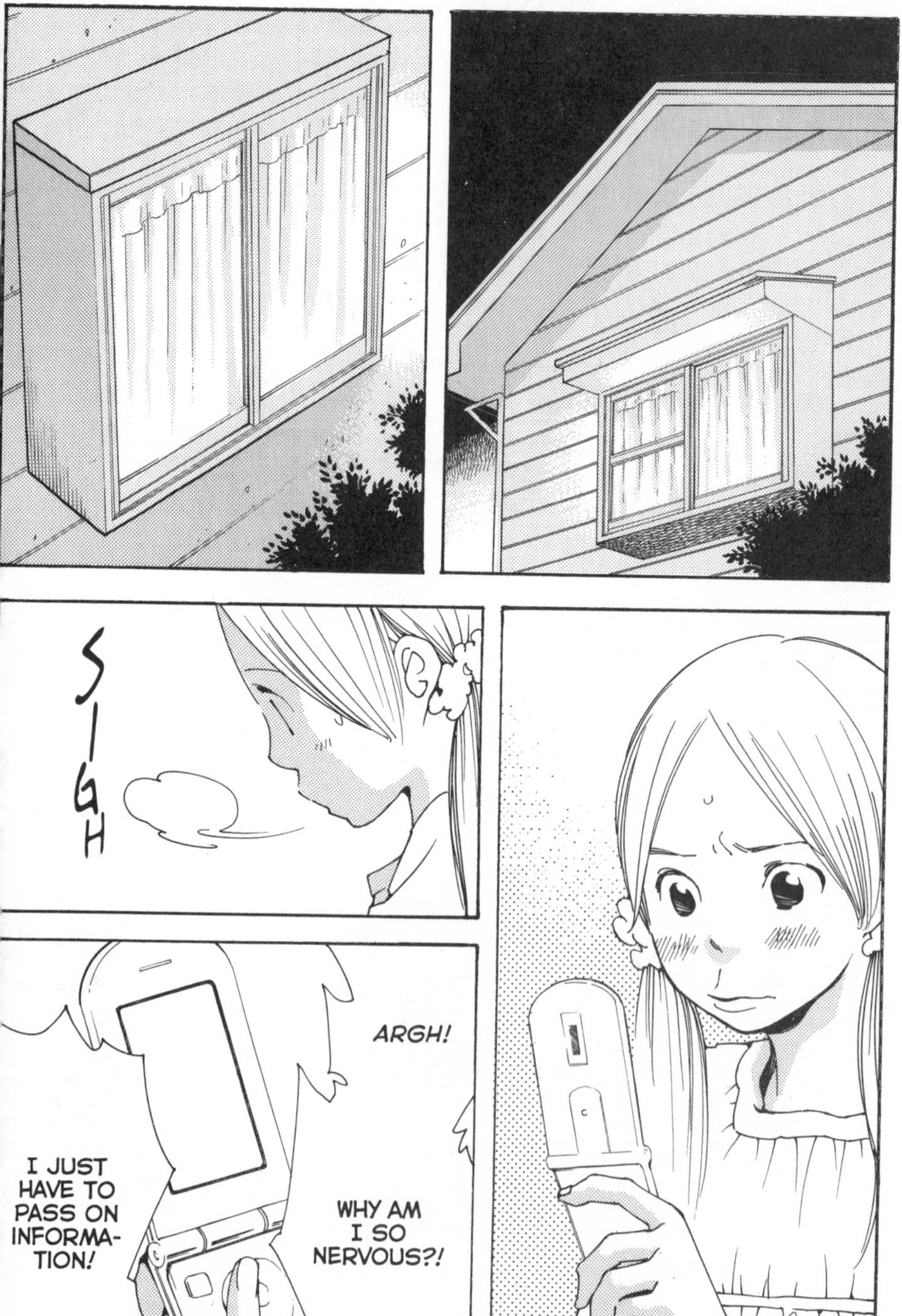
SIGH
ARGH!
WHY AM I SO NERVOUS?!
I JUST HAVE TO PASS ON INFORMATION!

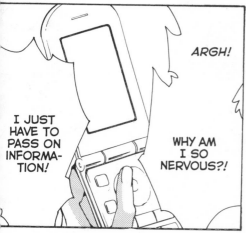

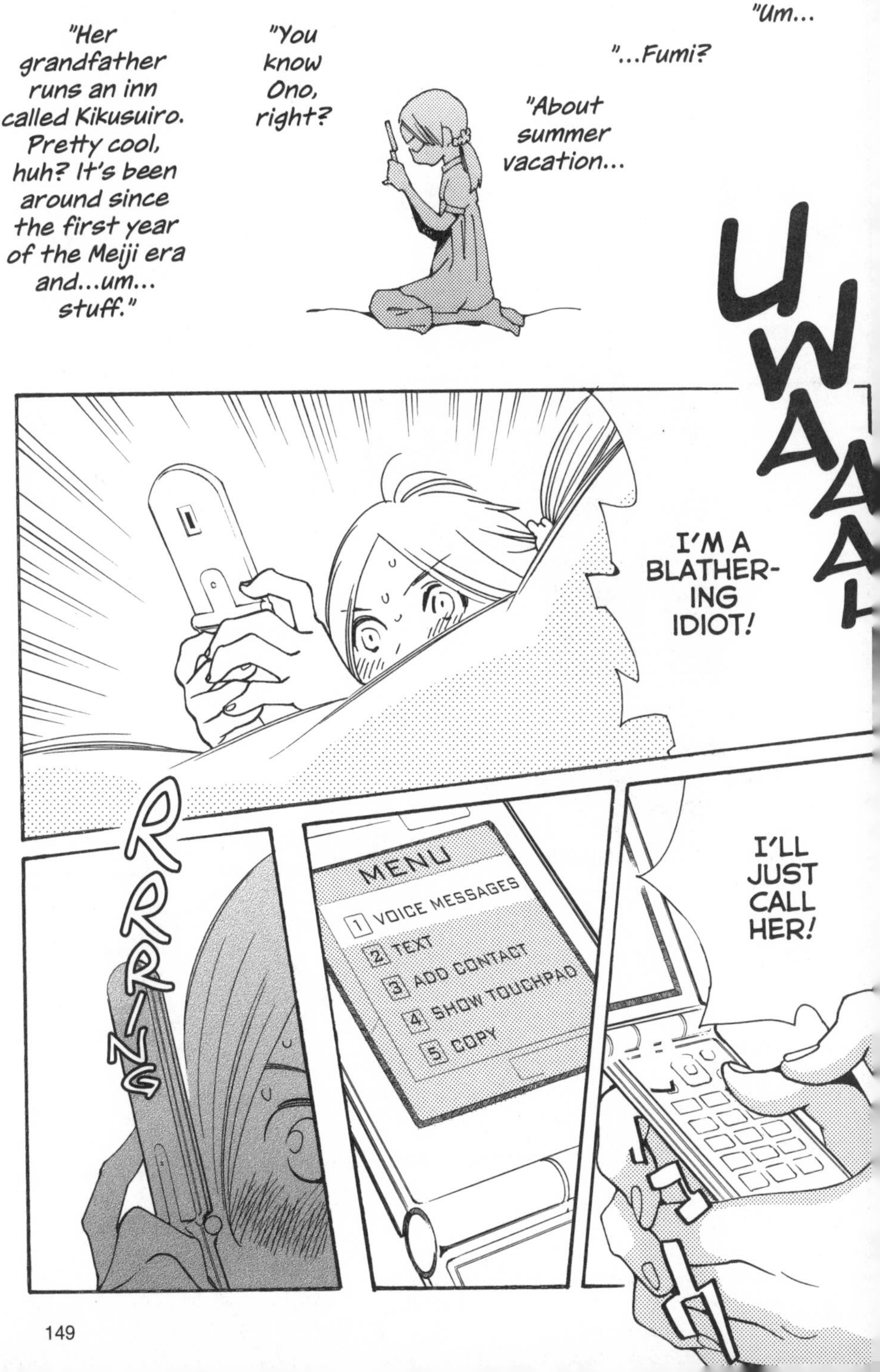
"Um...
"...Fumi?
"About summer vacation...
"You know Ono, right?
"Her grandfather runs an inn called Kikusuiro. Pretty cool, huh? It's been around since the first year of the Meiji era and...um... stuff."
UWAAA
I'M A BLATHER-ING IDIOT!
I'LL JUST CALL HER!
MENU
1 VOICE MESSAGES
2 TEXT
3 ADD CONTACT
4 SHOW TOUCHPAD
5 COPY
RRRRING

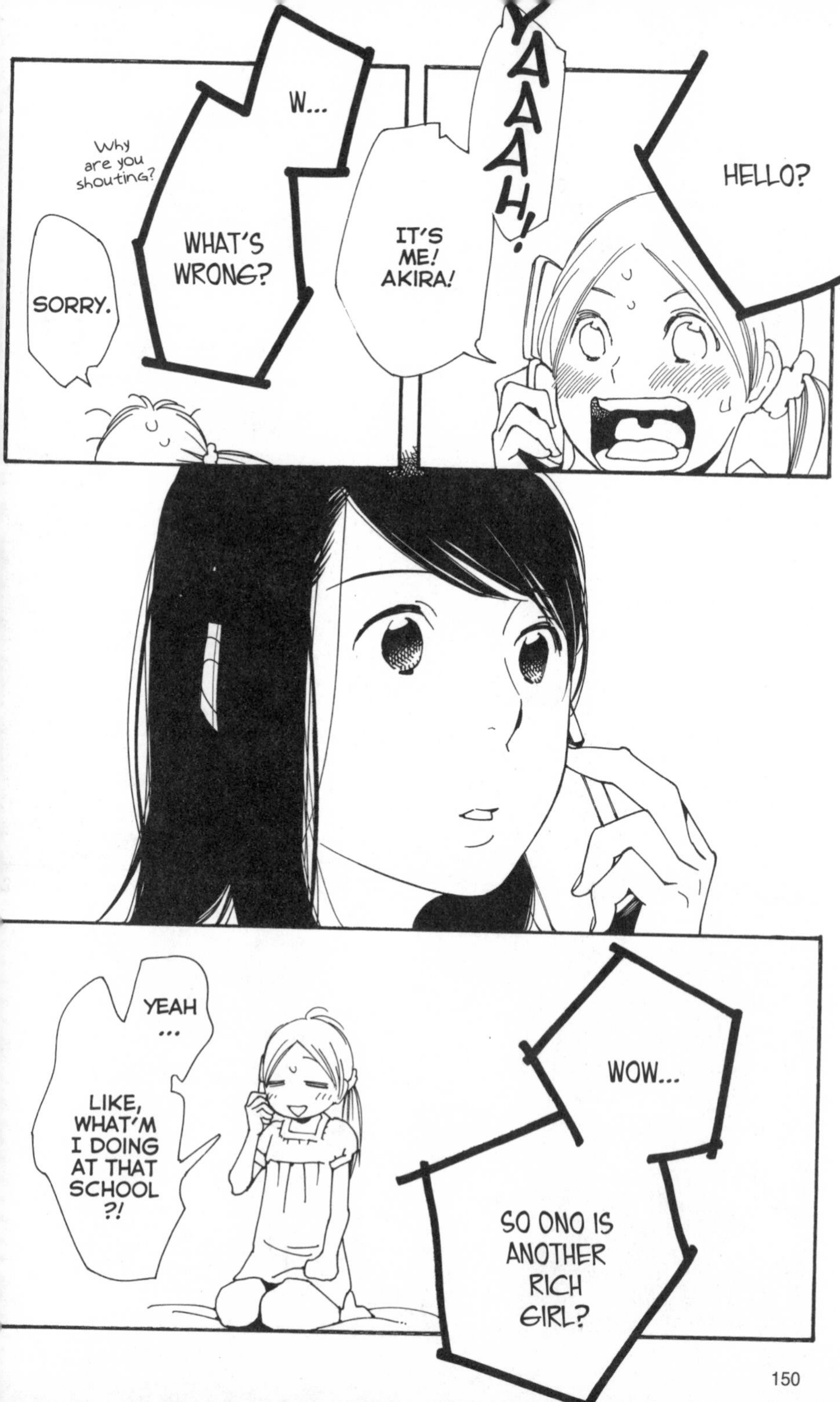
HELLO?
YAAAAH!
IT'S ME! AKIRA!
W...
WHAT'S WRONG?
Why are you shouting?
SORRY.
WOW...
SO ONO IS ANOTHER RICH GIRL?
YEAH ...
LIKE, WHAT'M I DOING AT THAT SCHOOL ?!

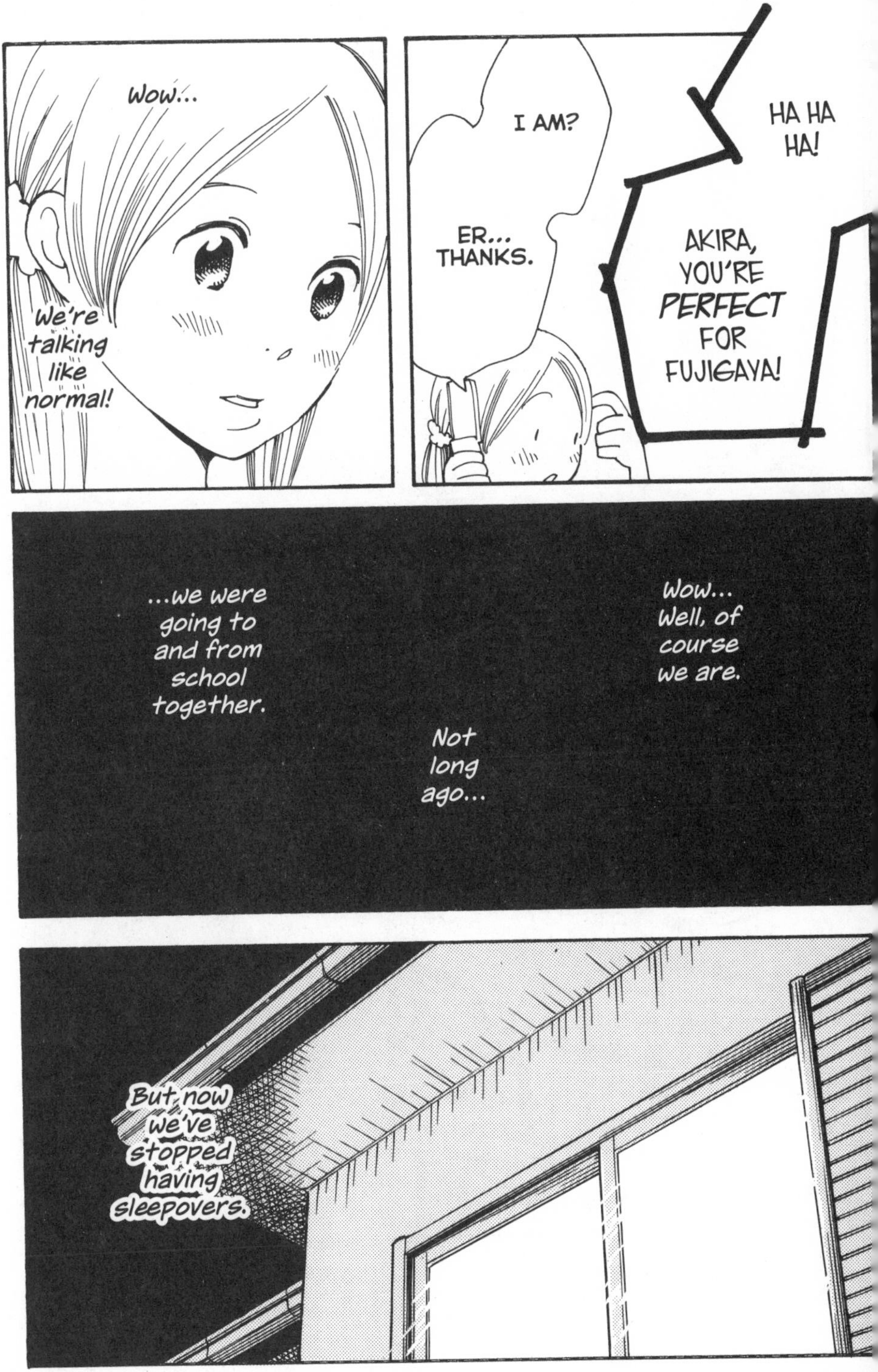
HA HA HA!
AKIRA, YOU'RE PERFECT FOR FUJIGAYA!
I AM?
ER... THANKS.
Wow...
We're talking like normal!
Wow... Well, of course we are.
Not long ago...
...we were going to and from school together.
But now we've stopped having sleepovers.

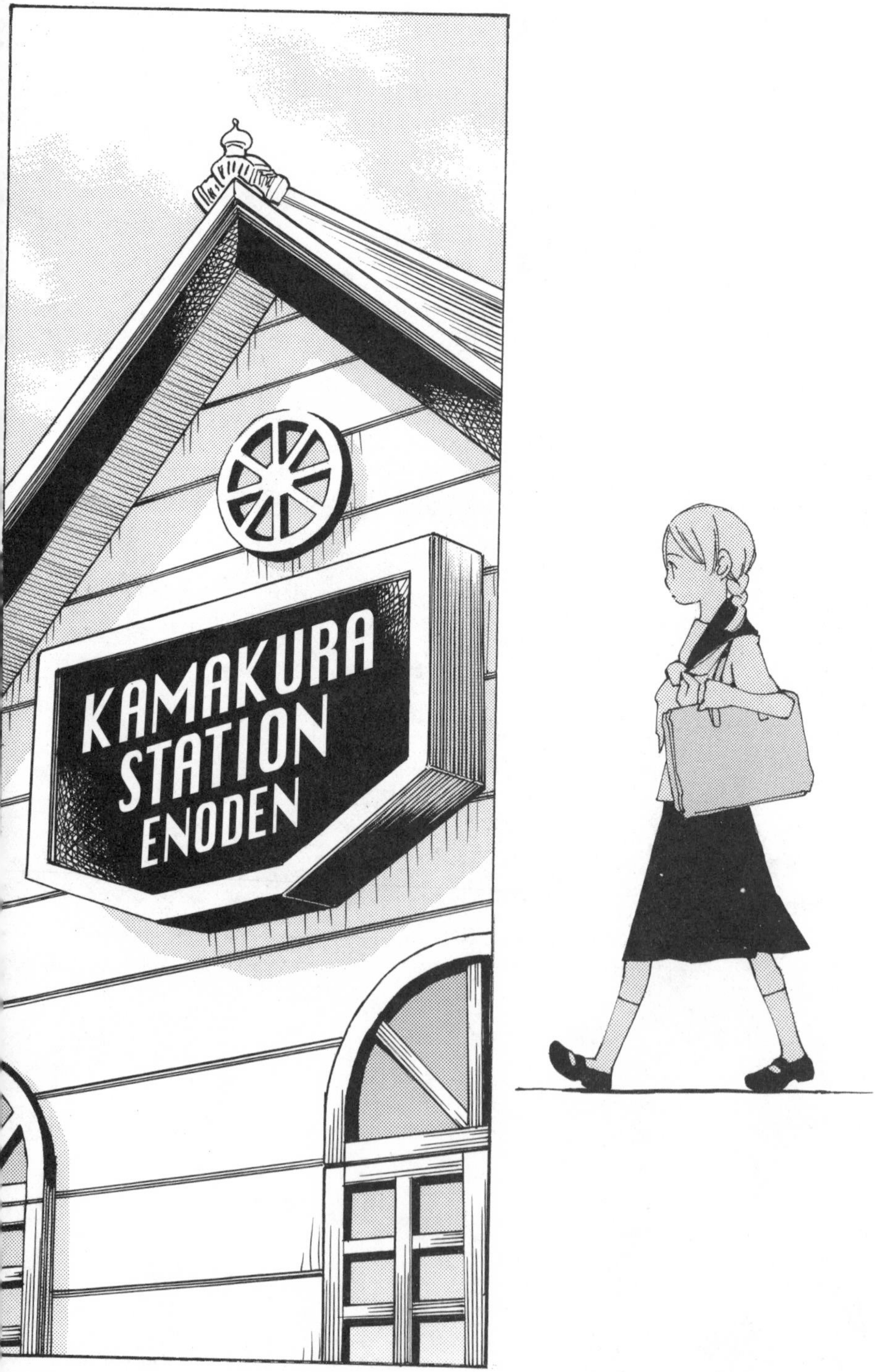
KAMAKURA
STATION
ENODEN

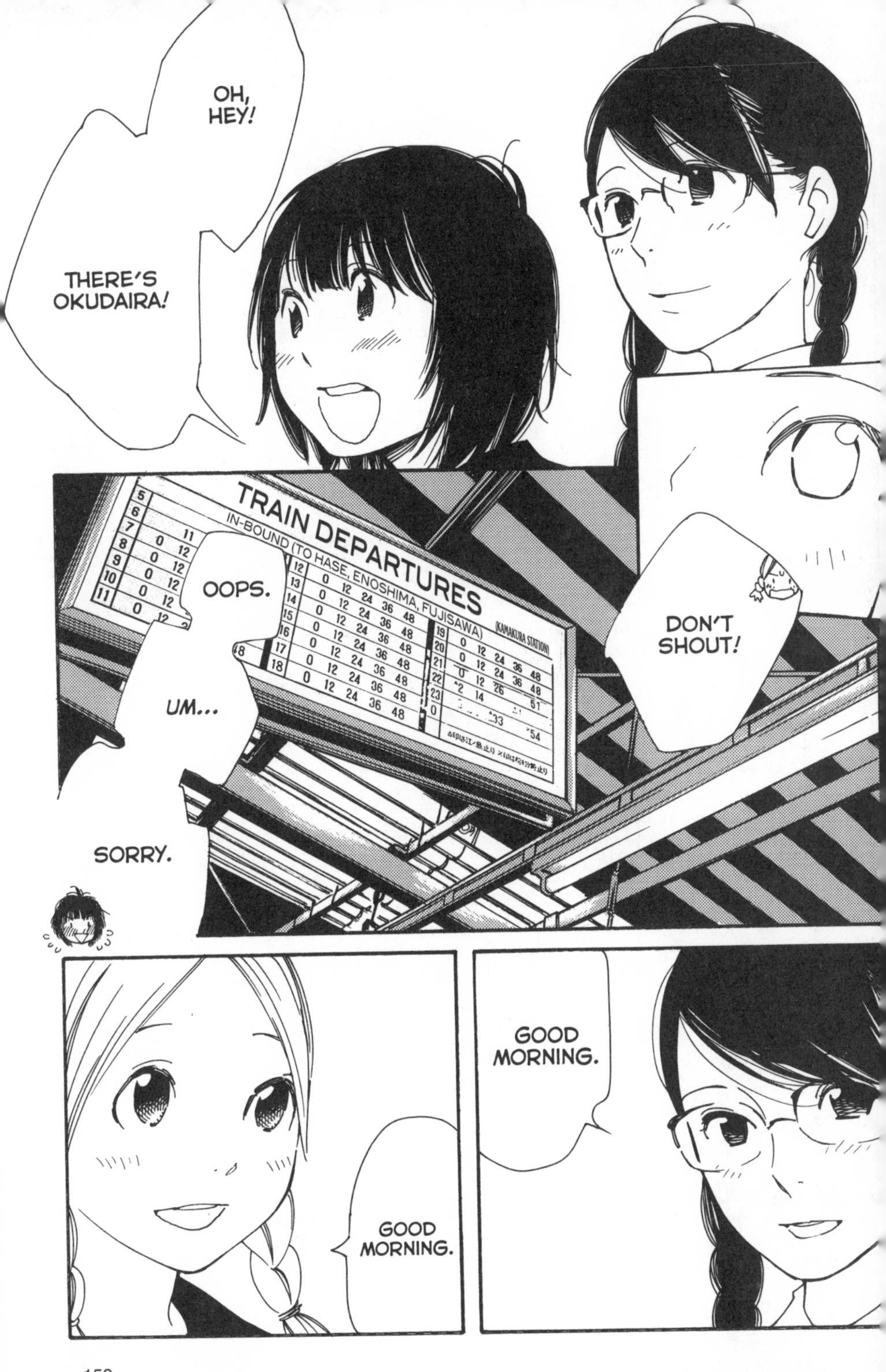
OH, HEY!
THERE'S OKUDAIRA!
DON'T SHOUT!
TRAIN DEPARTURES
IN-BOUND (TO HASE, ENOSHIMA, FUJISAWA)
(KAMAKURA STATION)
OOPS.
UM...
SORRY.
GOOD MORNING.
GOOD MORNING.

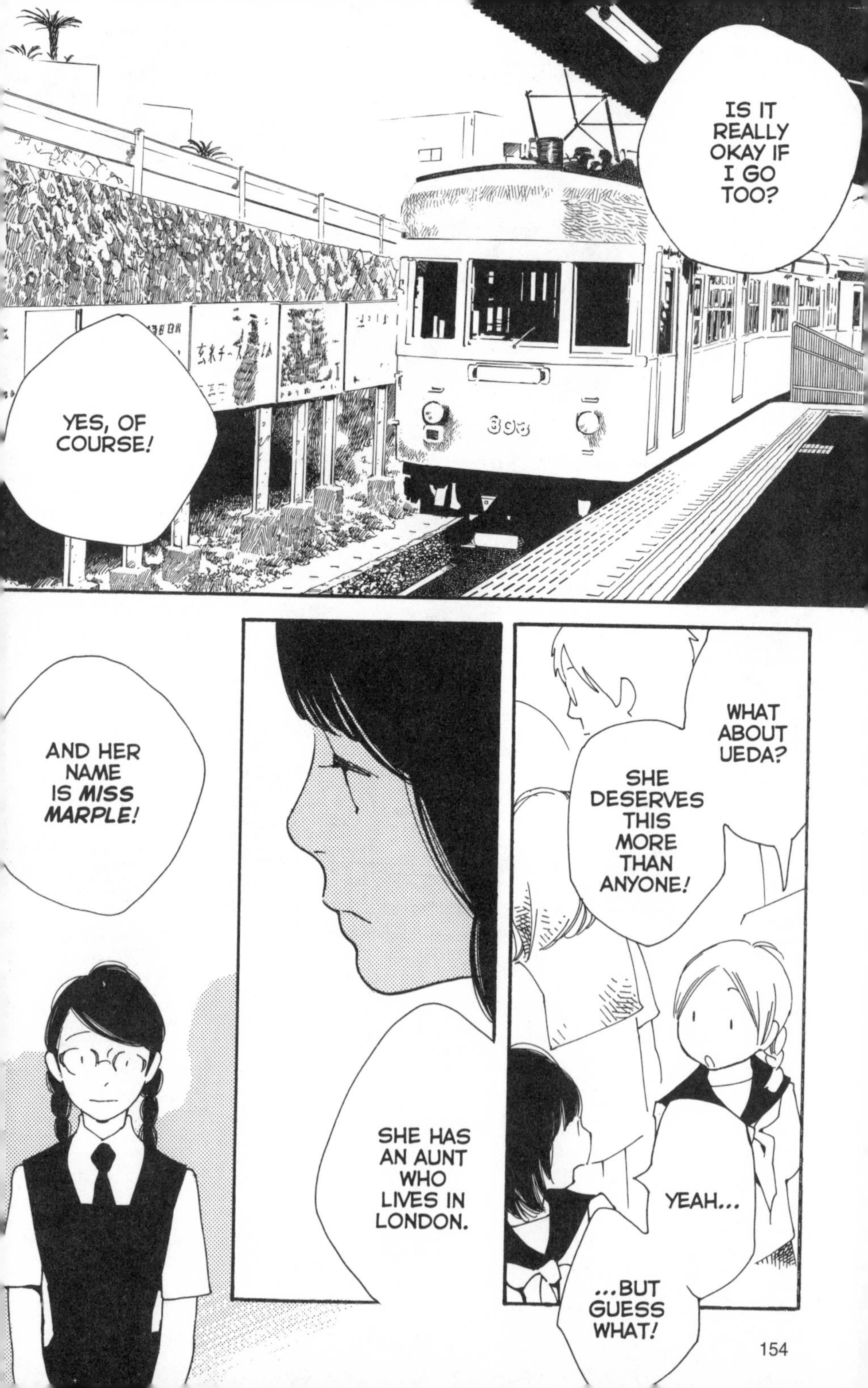
IS IT REALLY OKAY IF I GO TOO?
YES, OF COURSE!
WHAT ABOUT UEDA?
SHE DESERVES THIS MORE THAN ANYONE!
YEAH...
...BUT GUESS WHAT!
SHE HAS AN AUNT WHO LIVES IN LONDON.
AND HER NAME IS *MISS MARPLE!*

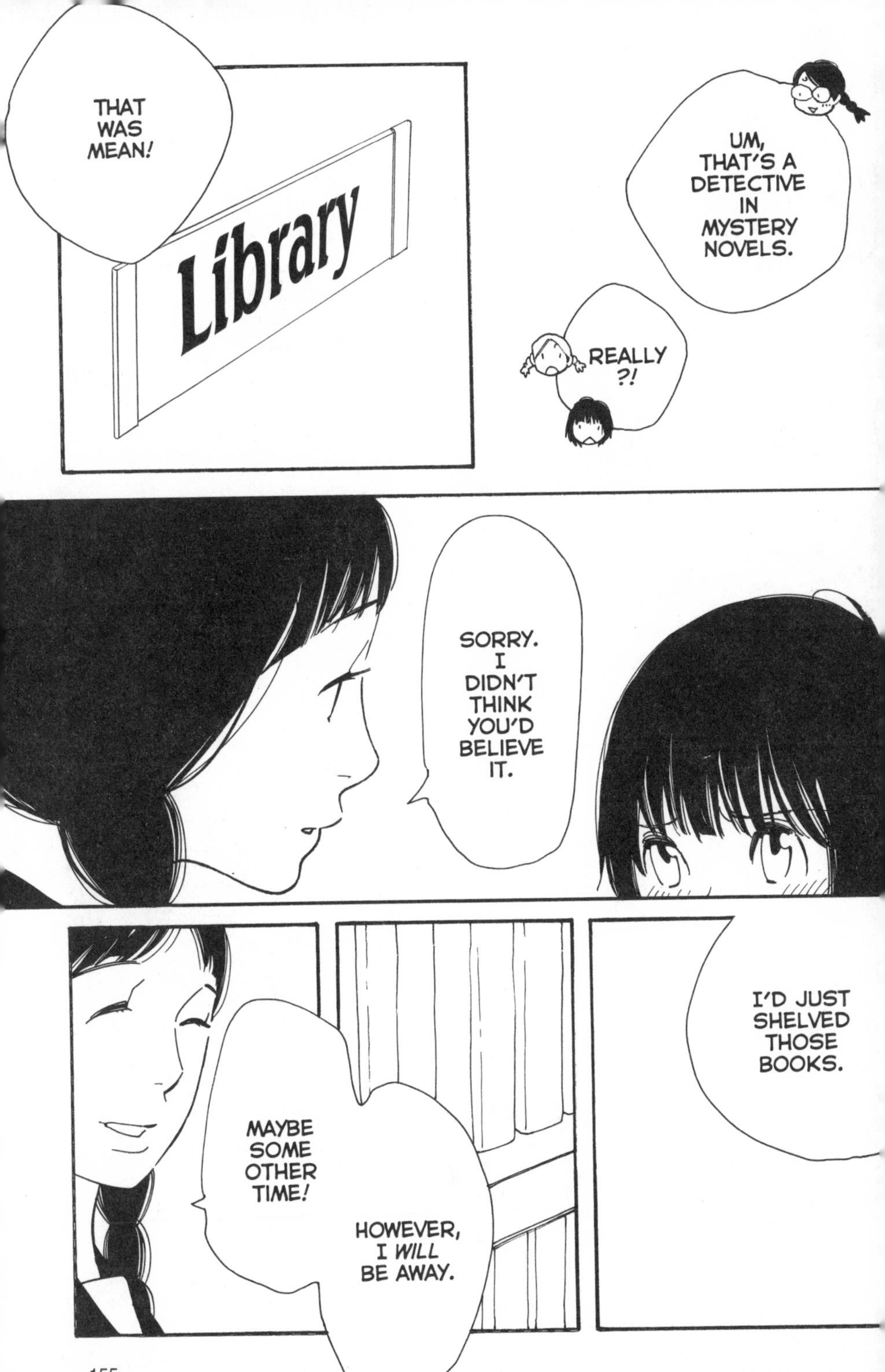
UM, THAT'S A DETECTIVE IN MYSTERY NOVELS.
REALLY ?!
THAT WAS MEAN!
Library
SORRY. I DIDN'T THINK YOU'D BELIEVE IT.
I'D JUST SHELVED THOSE BOOKS.
HOWEVER, I *WILL* BE AWAY.
MAYBE SOME OTHER TIME!

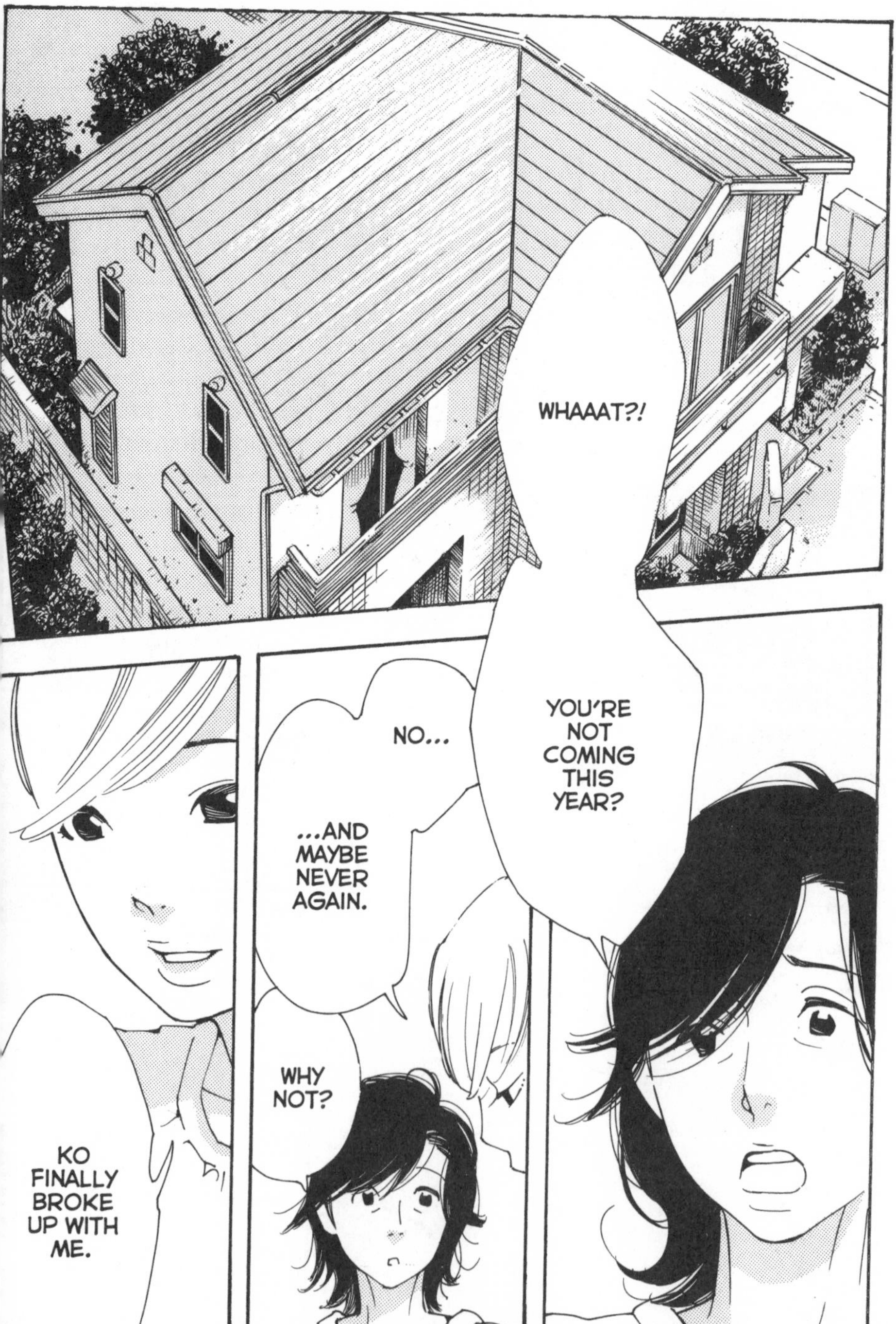
WHAAAT?!
YOU'RE NOT COMING THIS YEAR?
NO...
...AND MAYBE NEVER AGAIN.
WHY NOT?
KO FINALLY BROKE UP WITH ME.

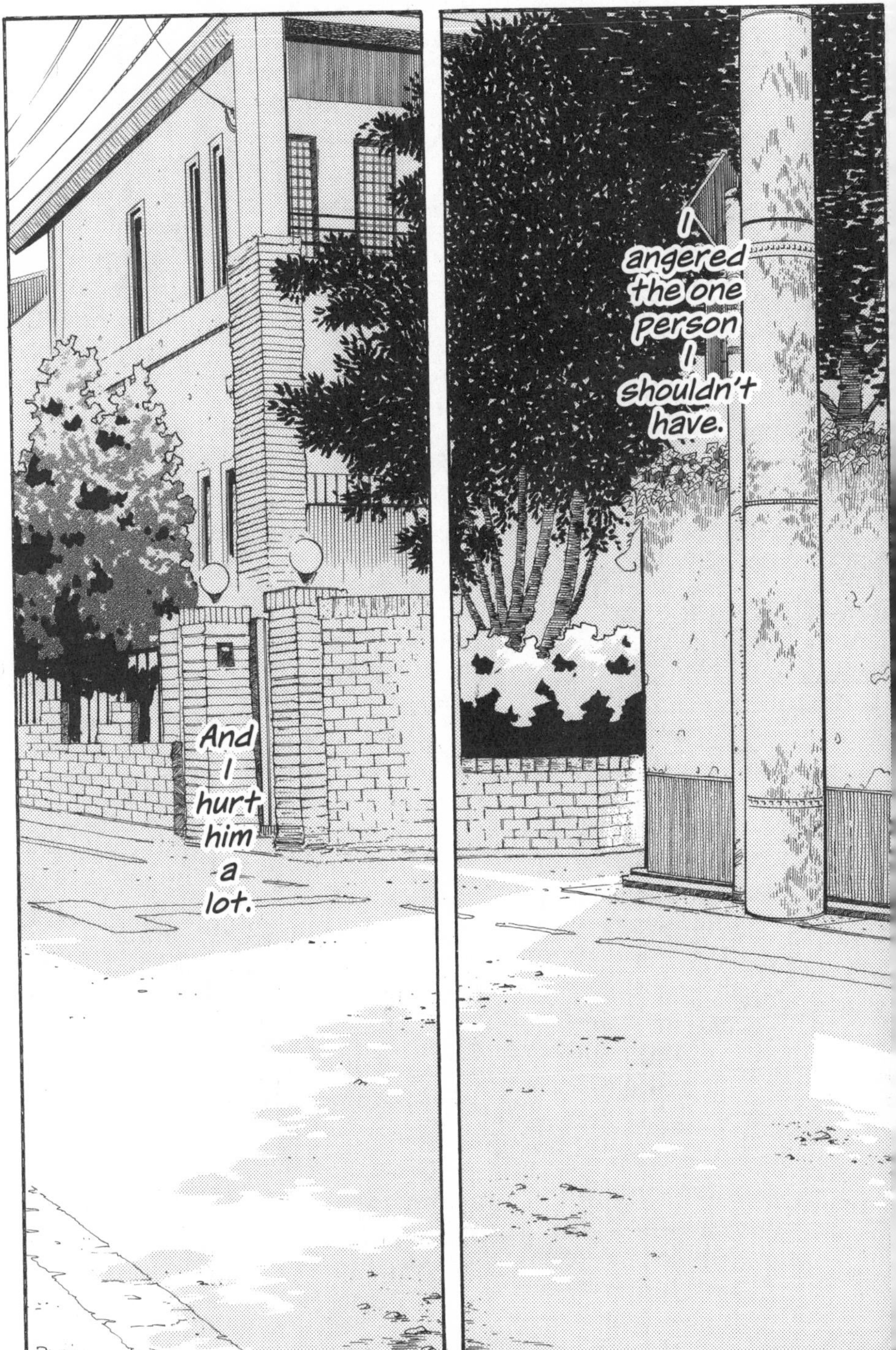
I angered the one person I shouldn't have.
And I hurt him a lot.

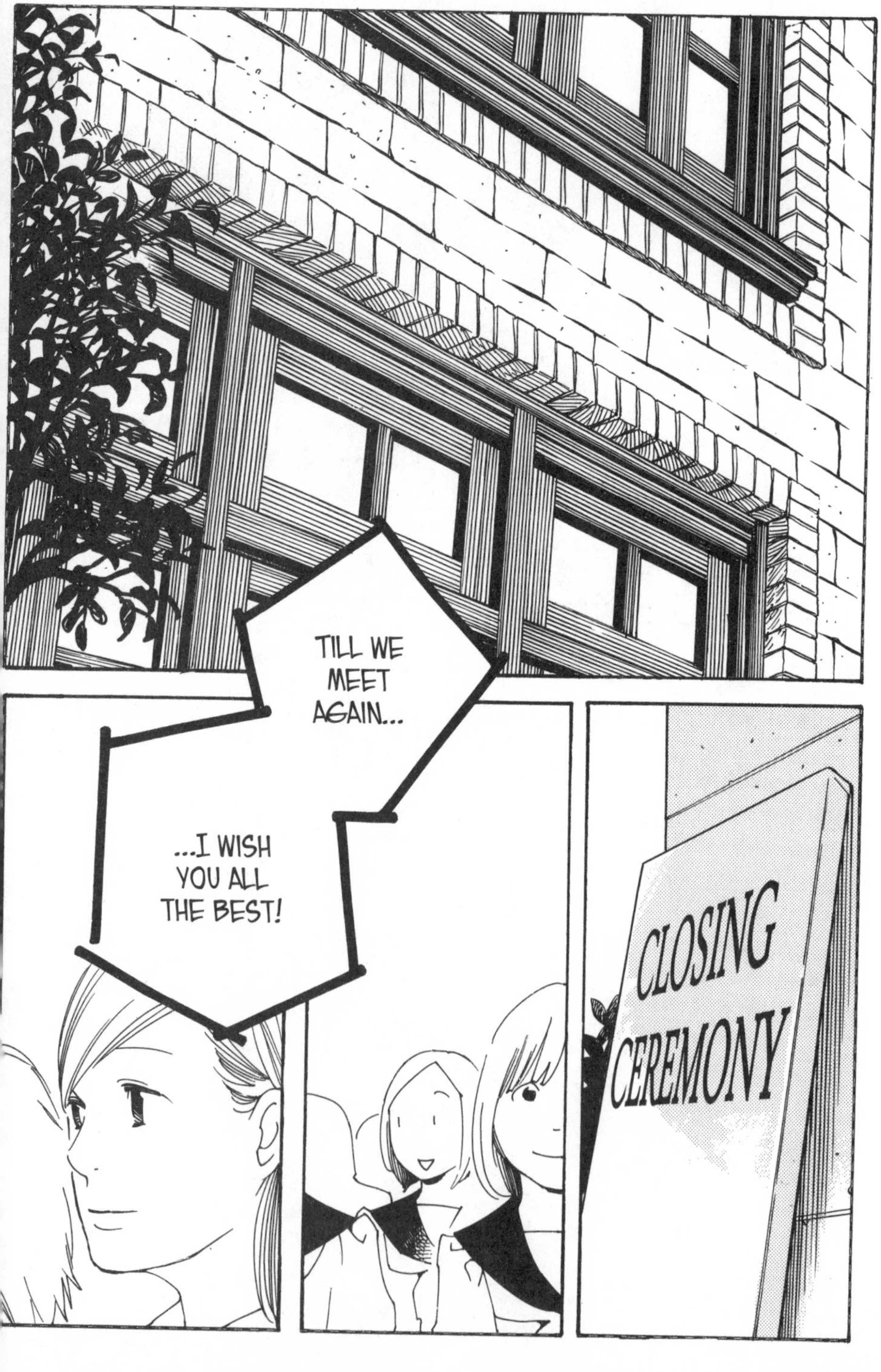
TILL WE MEET AGAIN... ...I WISH YOU ALL THE BEST!
CLOSING CEREMONY

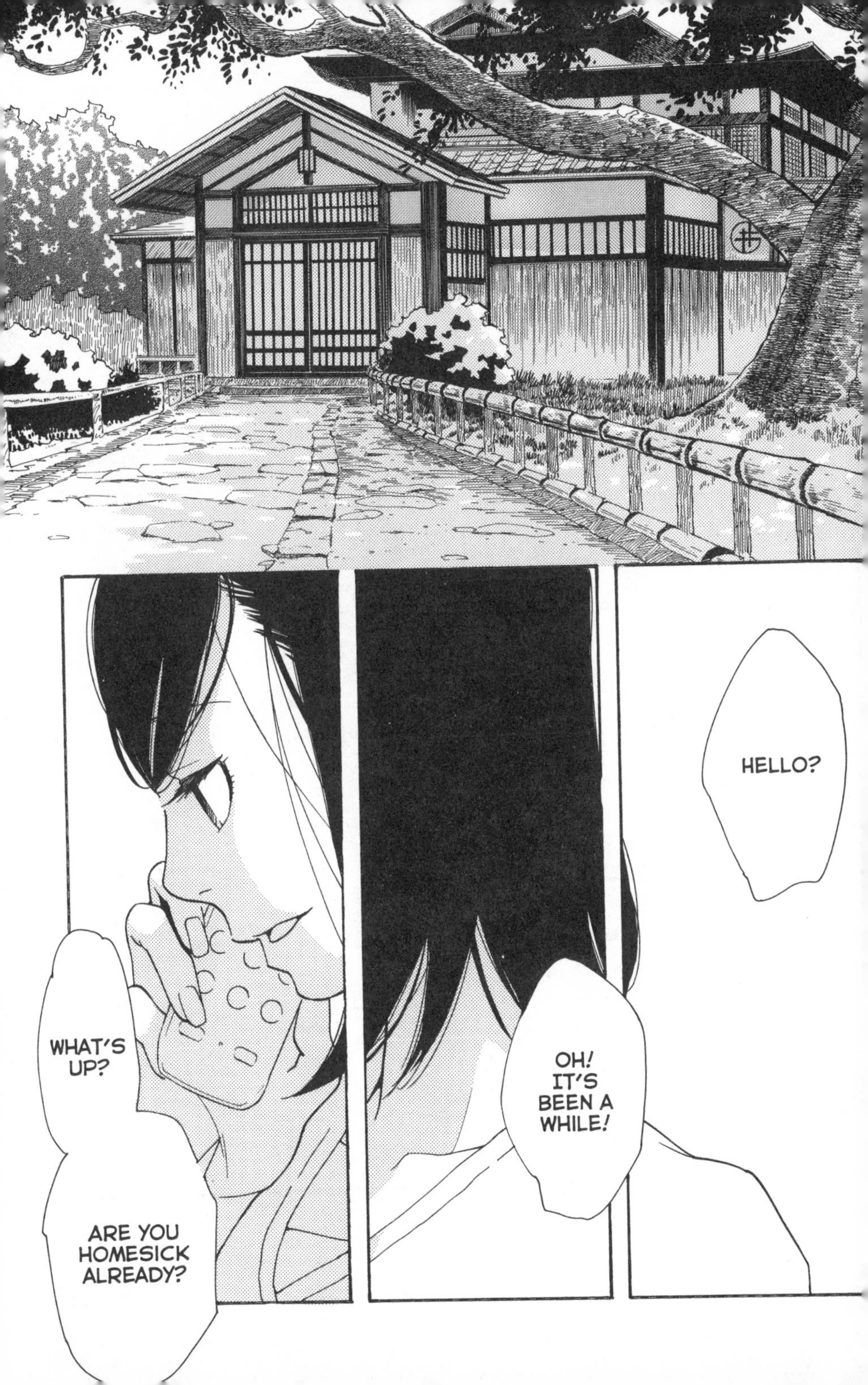
HELLO?
OH! IT'S BEEN A WHILE!
WHAT'S UP?
ARE YOU HOMESICK ALREADY?

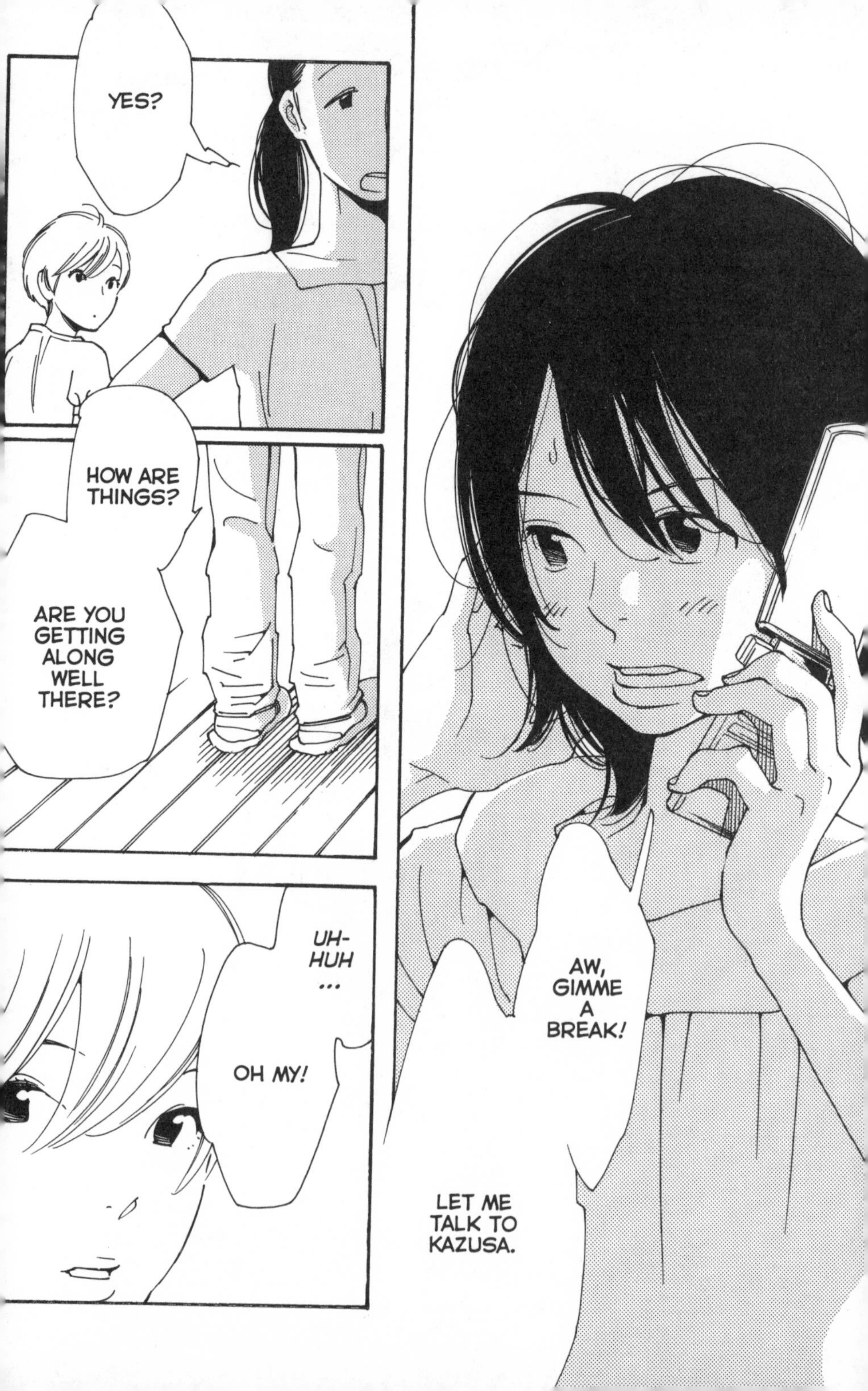
AW, GIMME A BREAK!
LET ME TALK TO KAZUSA.
YES?
HOW ARE THINGS?
ARE YOU GETTING ALONG WELL THERE?
UH-HUH...
OH MY!

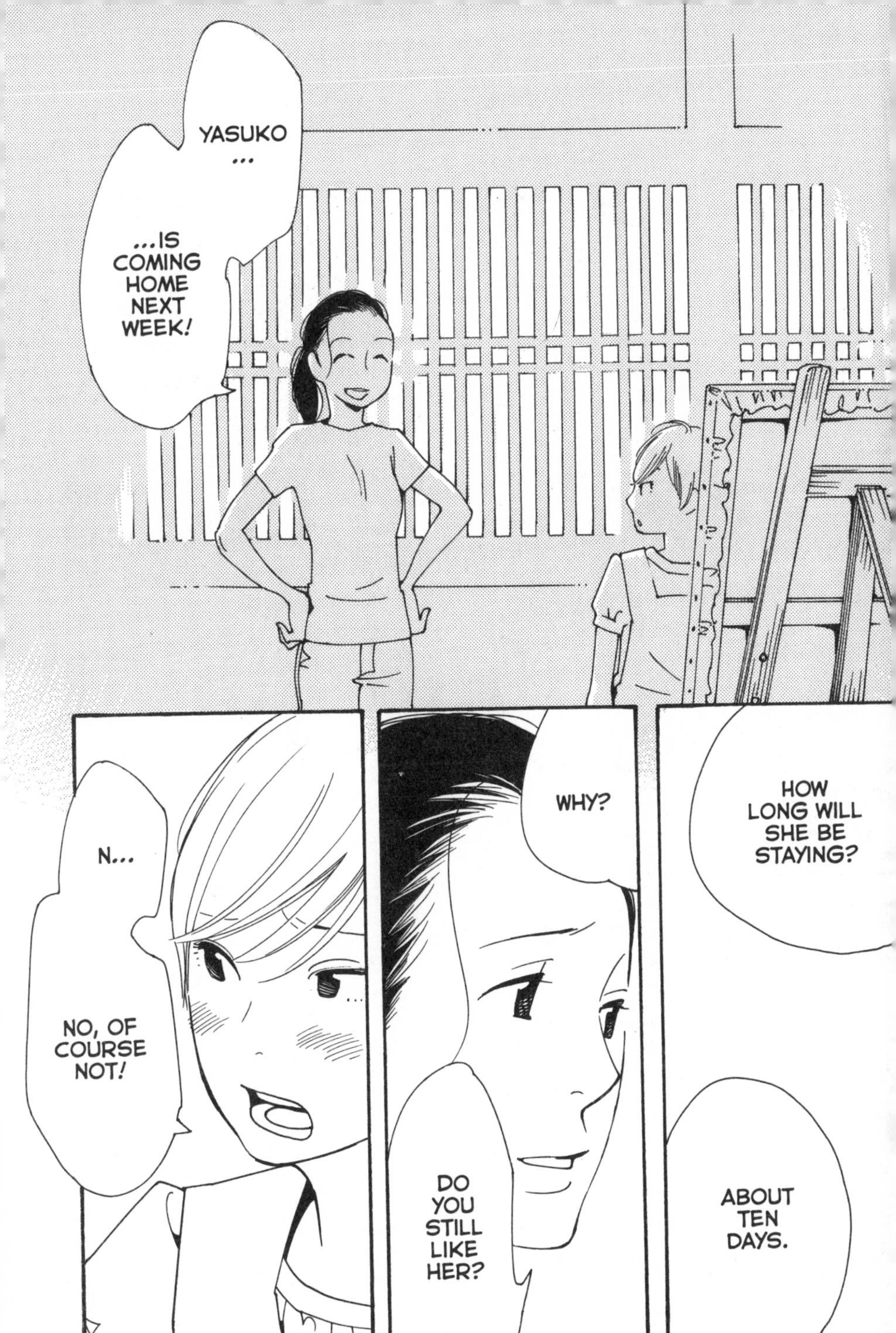

YASUKO...
...IS COMING HOME NEXT WEEK!
HOW LONG WILL SHE BE STAYING?
ABOUT TEN DAYS.
WHY?
DO YOU STILL LIKE HER?
N...
NO, OF COURSE NOT!

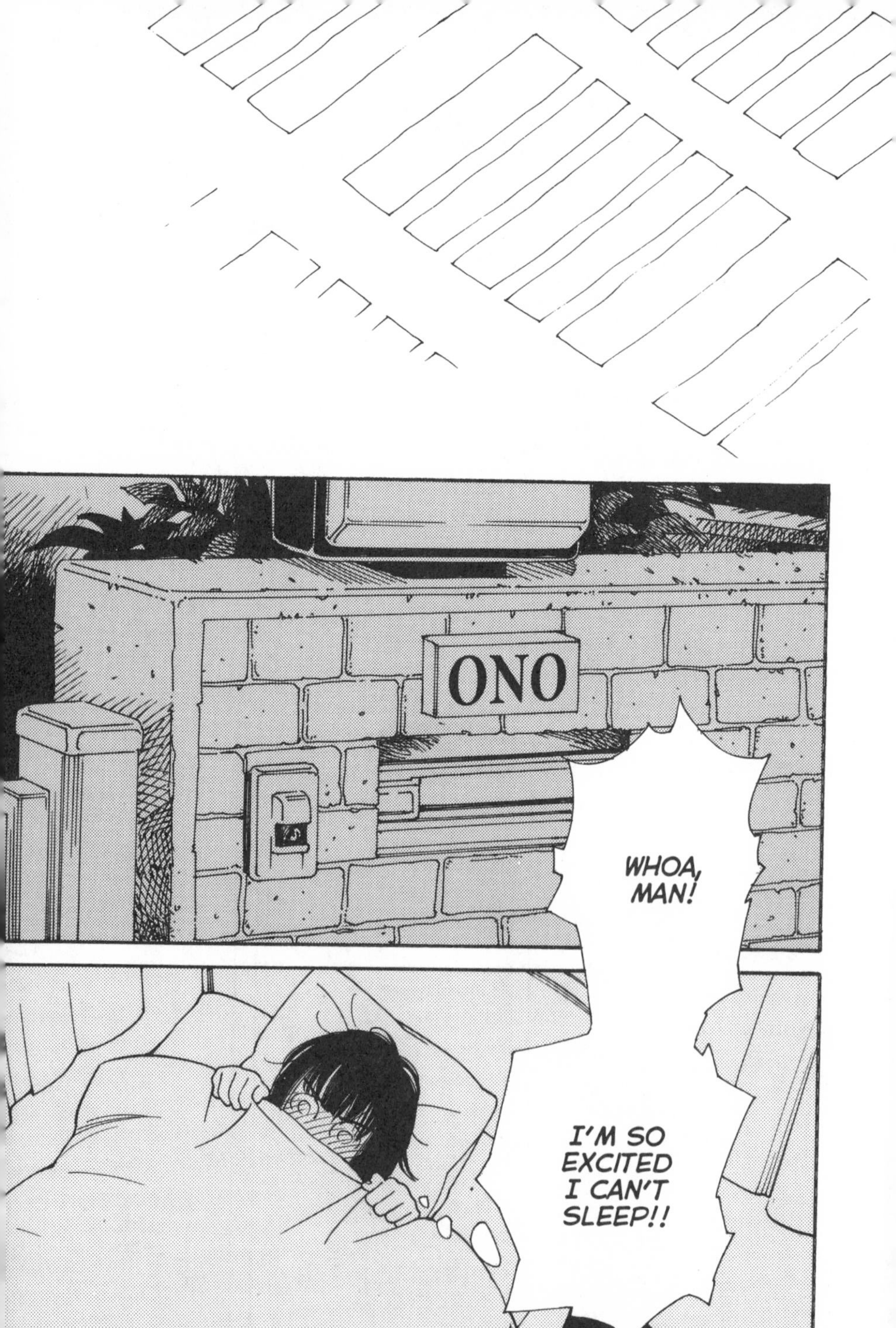
ONO
WHOA, MAN!
I'M SO EXCITED I CAN'T SLEEP!!

Sweet Blue
Flowers

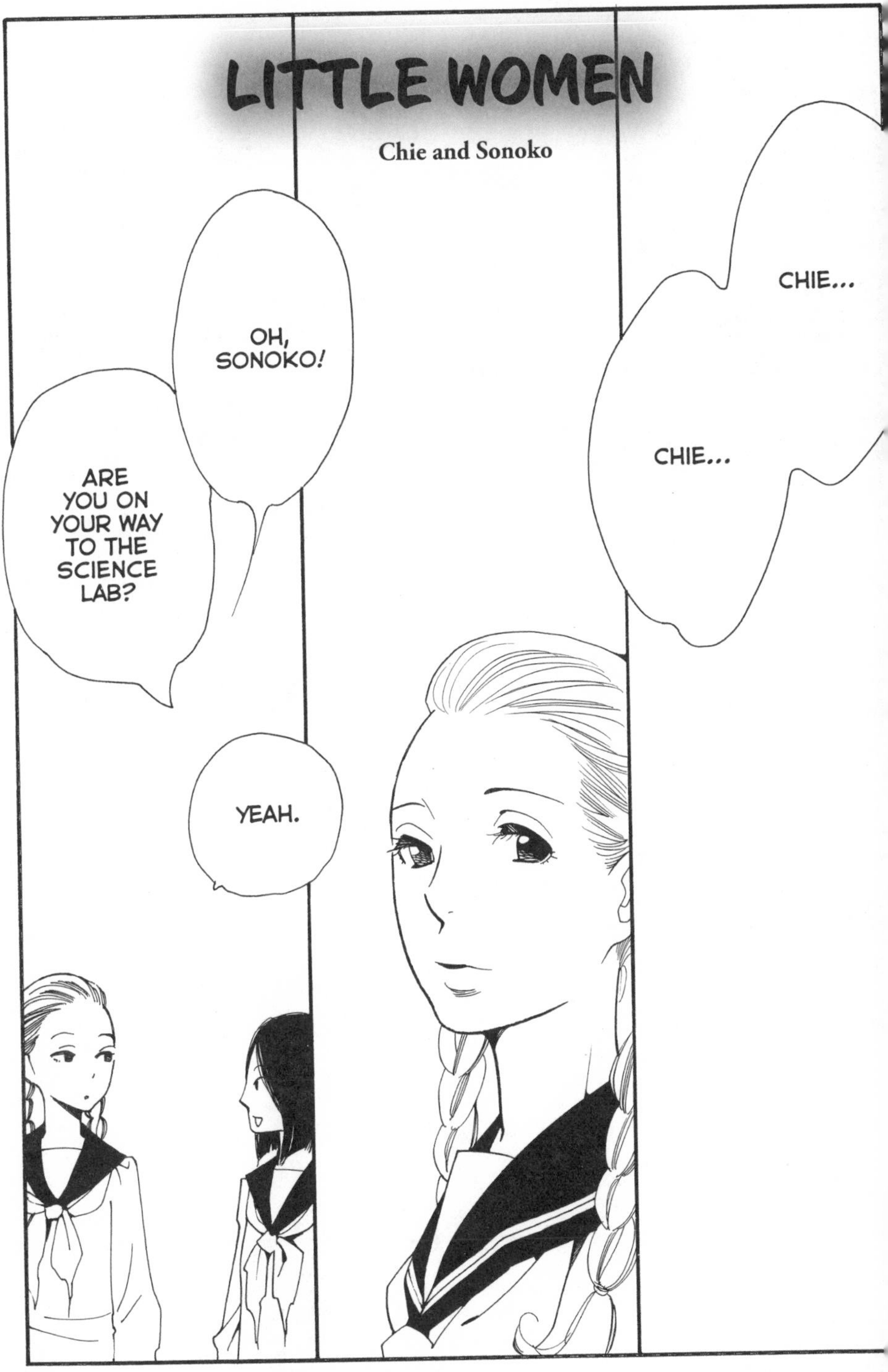
LITTLE WOMEN
Chie and Sonoko
CHIE...
CHIE...
OH, SONOKO!
ARE YOU ON YOUR WAY TO THE SCIENCE LAB?
YEAH.

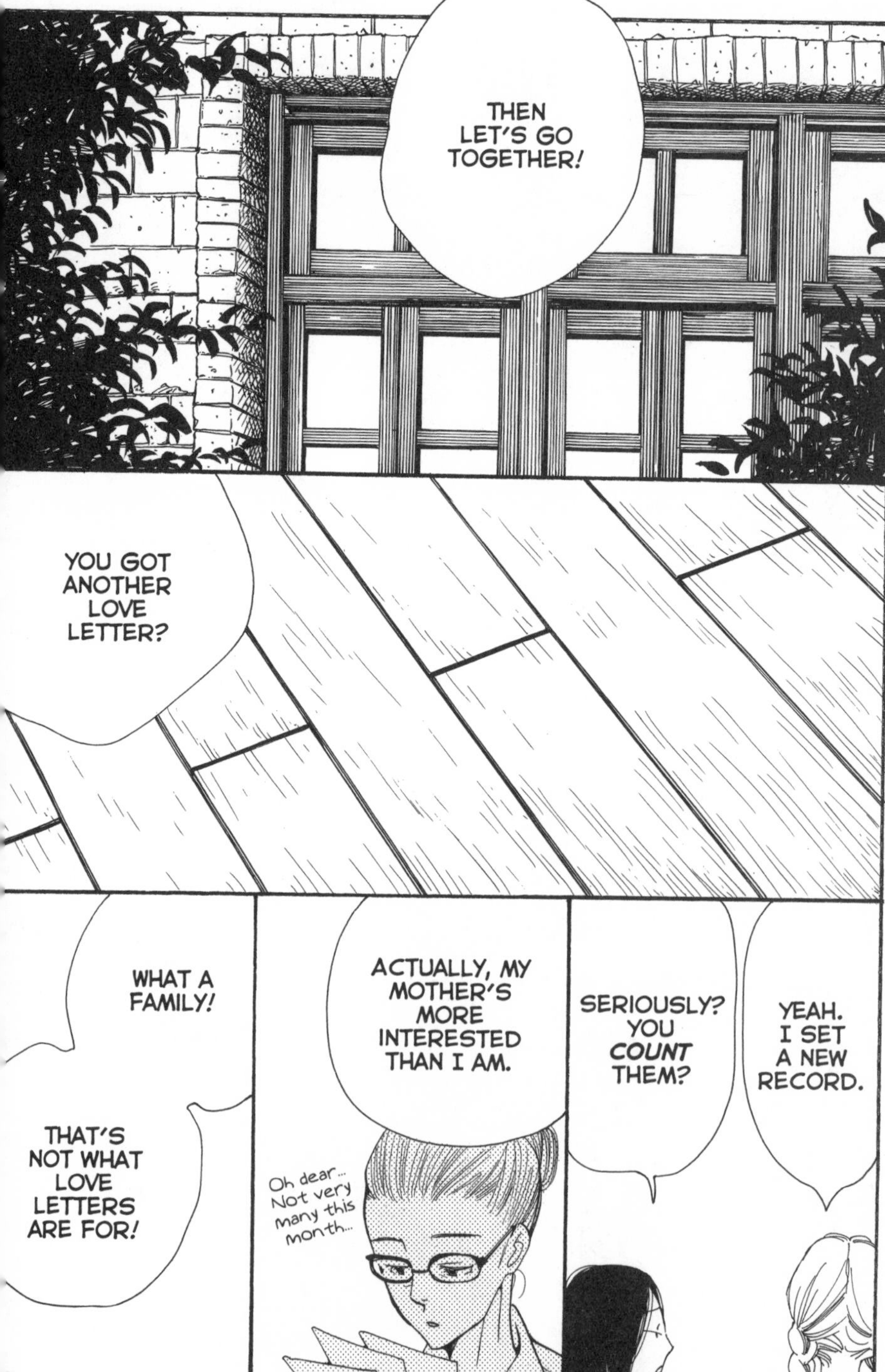
THEN LET'S GO TOGETHER!
YOU GOT ANOTHER LOVE LETTER?
YEAH. I SET A NEW RECORD.
SERIOUSLY? YOU *COUNT* THEM?
ACTUALLY, MY MOTHER'S MORE INTERESTED THAN I AM.
Oh dear... Not very many this month...
WHAT A FAMILY!
THAT'S NOT WHAT LOVE LETTERS ARE FOR!

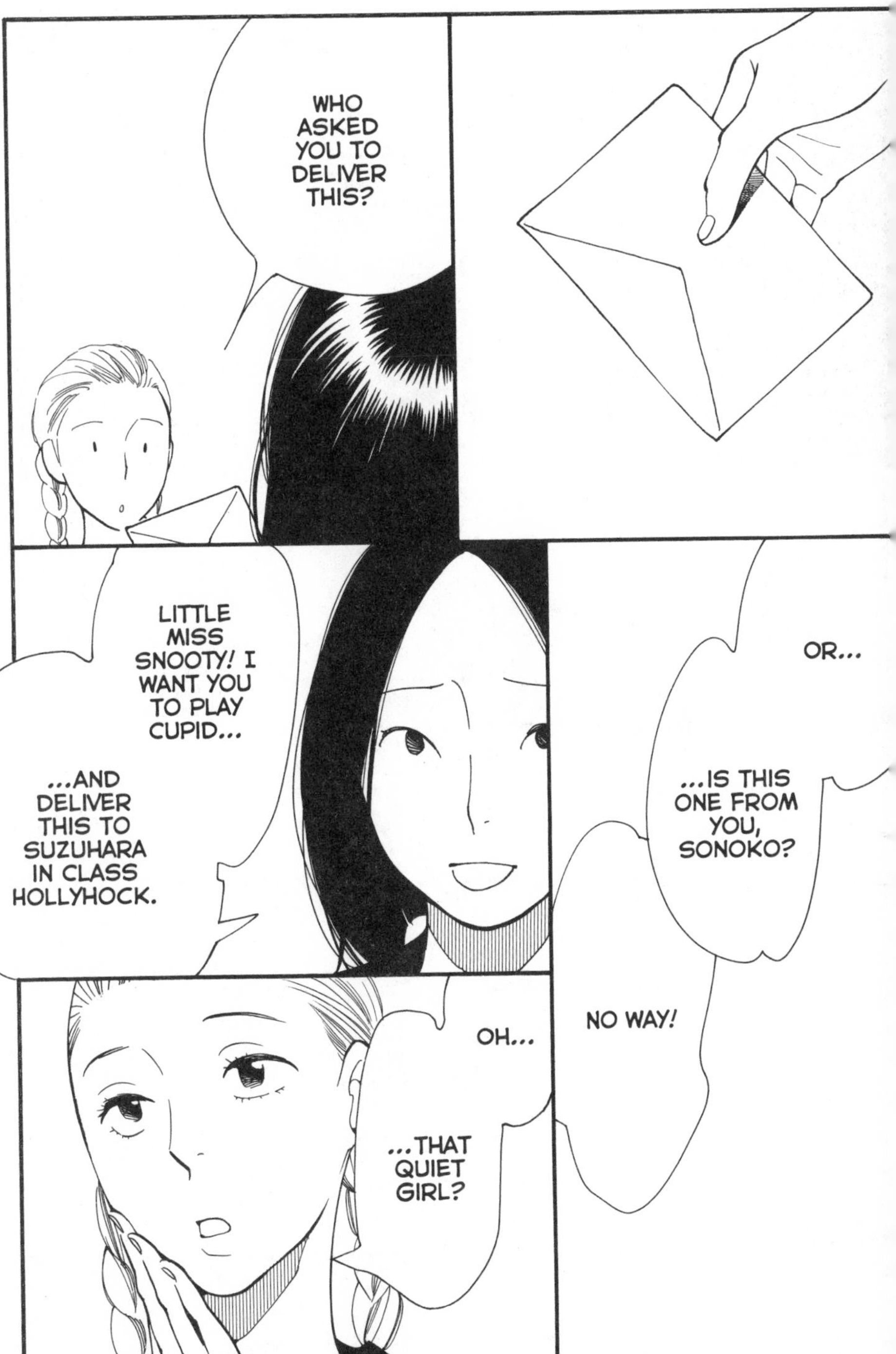
WHO ASKED YOU TO DELIVER THIS?
OR...
...IS THIS ONE FROM YOU, SONOKO?
NO WAY!
LITTLE MISS SNOOTY! I WANT YOU TO PLAY CUPID...
...AND DELIVER THIS TO SUZUHARA IN CLASS HOLLYHOCK.
OH...
...THAT QUIET GIRL?

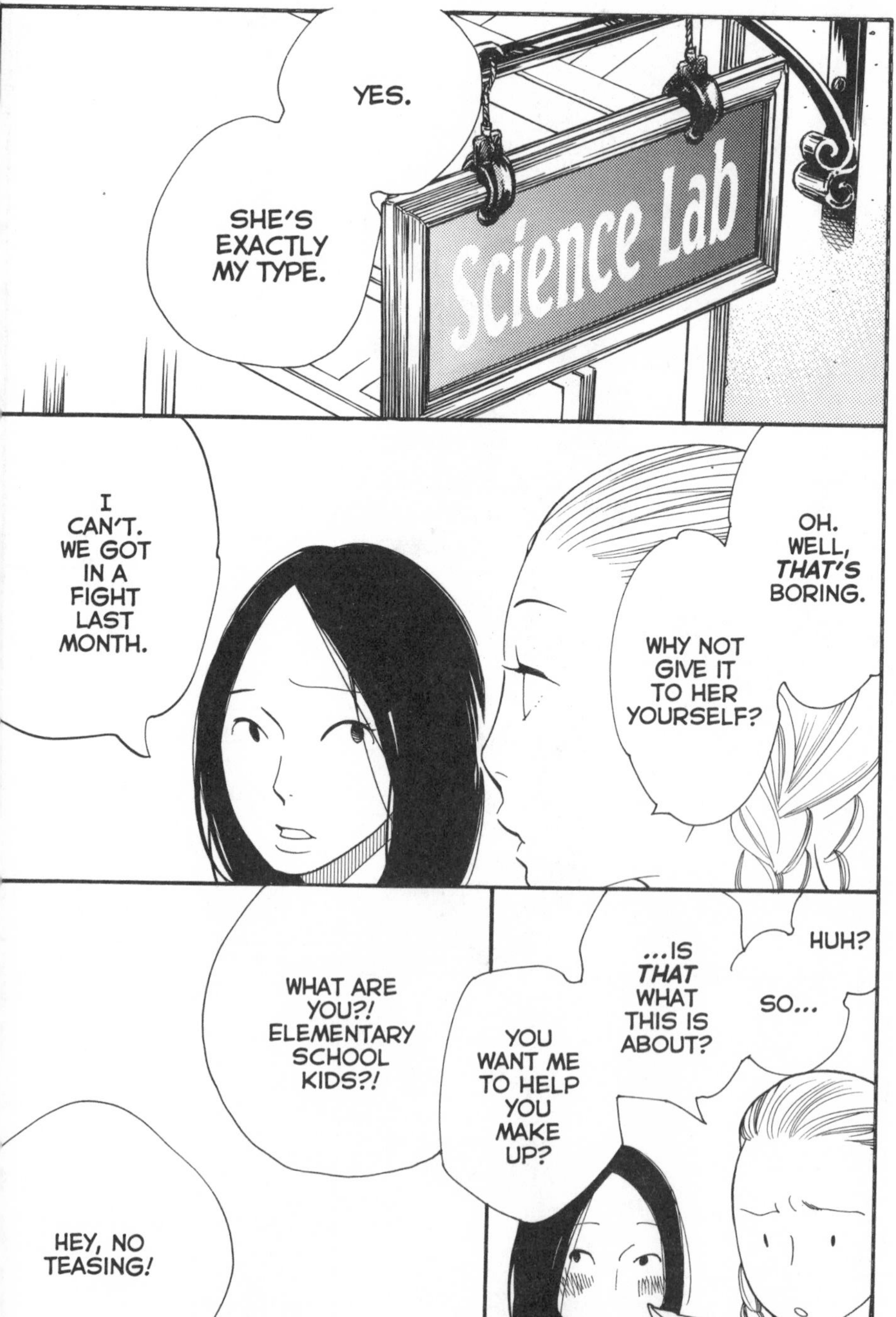
YES.
SHE'S EXACTLY MY TYPE.
Science Lab
OH. WELL, *THAT'S* BORING.
WHY NOT GIVE IT TO HER YOURSELF?
I CAN'T. WE GOT IN A FIGHT LAST MONTH.
HUH?
SO...
...IS *THAT* WHAT THIS IS ABOUT?
YOU WANT ME TO HELP YOU MAKE UP?
WHAT ARE YOU?! ELEMENTARY SCHOOL KIDS?!
HEY, NO TEASING!

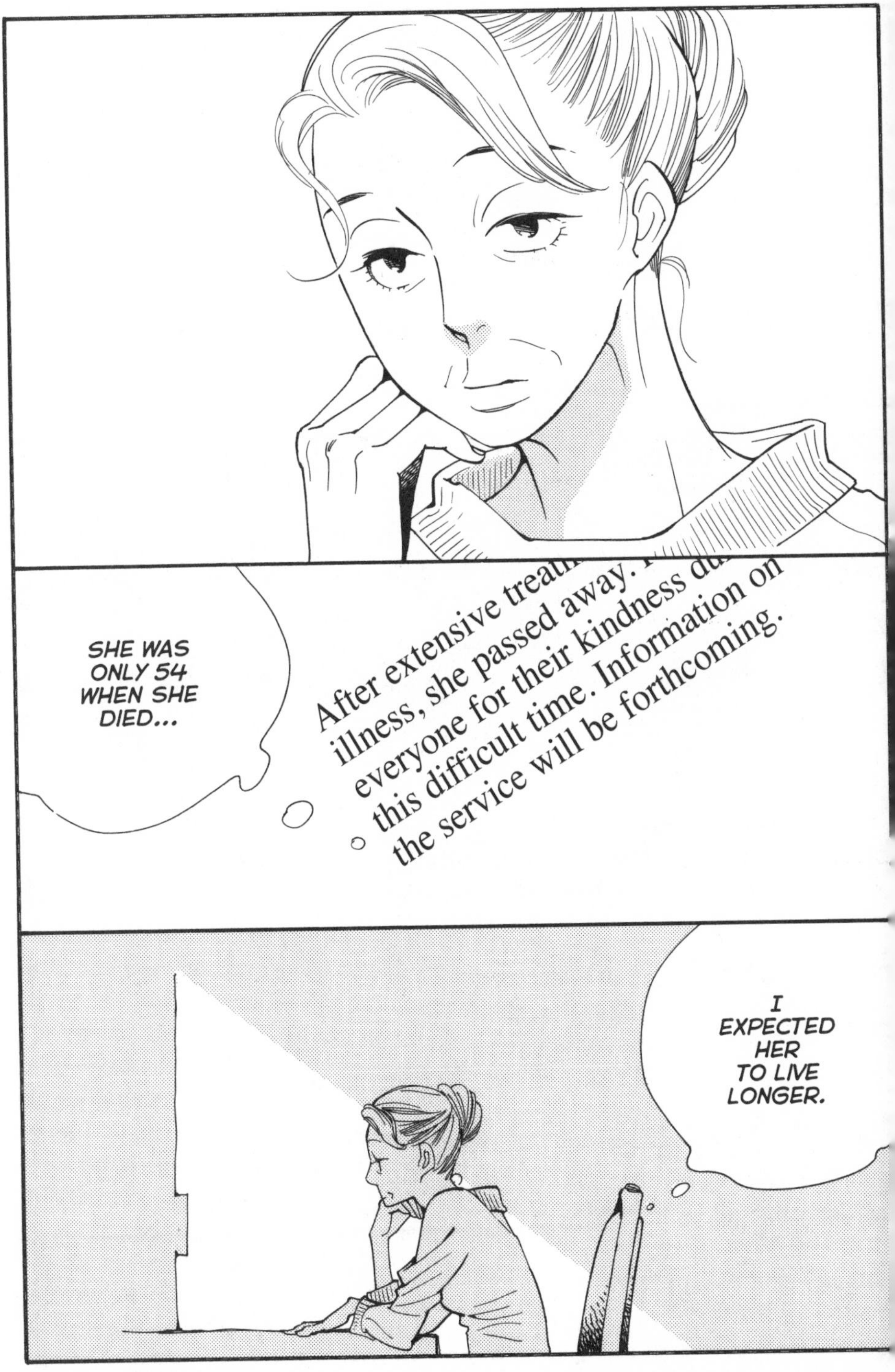
After extensive treat
illness, she passed away.
everyone for their kindness du
this difficult time. Information on
the service will be forthcoming.
SHE WAS ONLY 54 WHEN SHE DIED...
I EXPECTED HER TO LIVE LONGER.

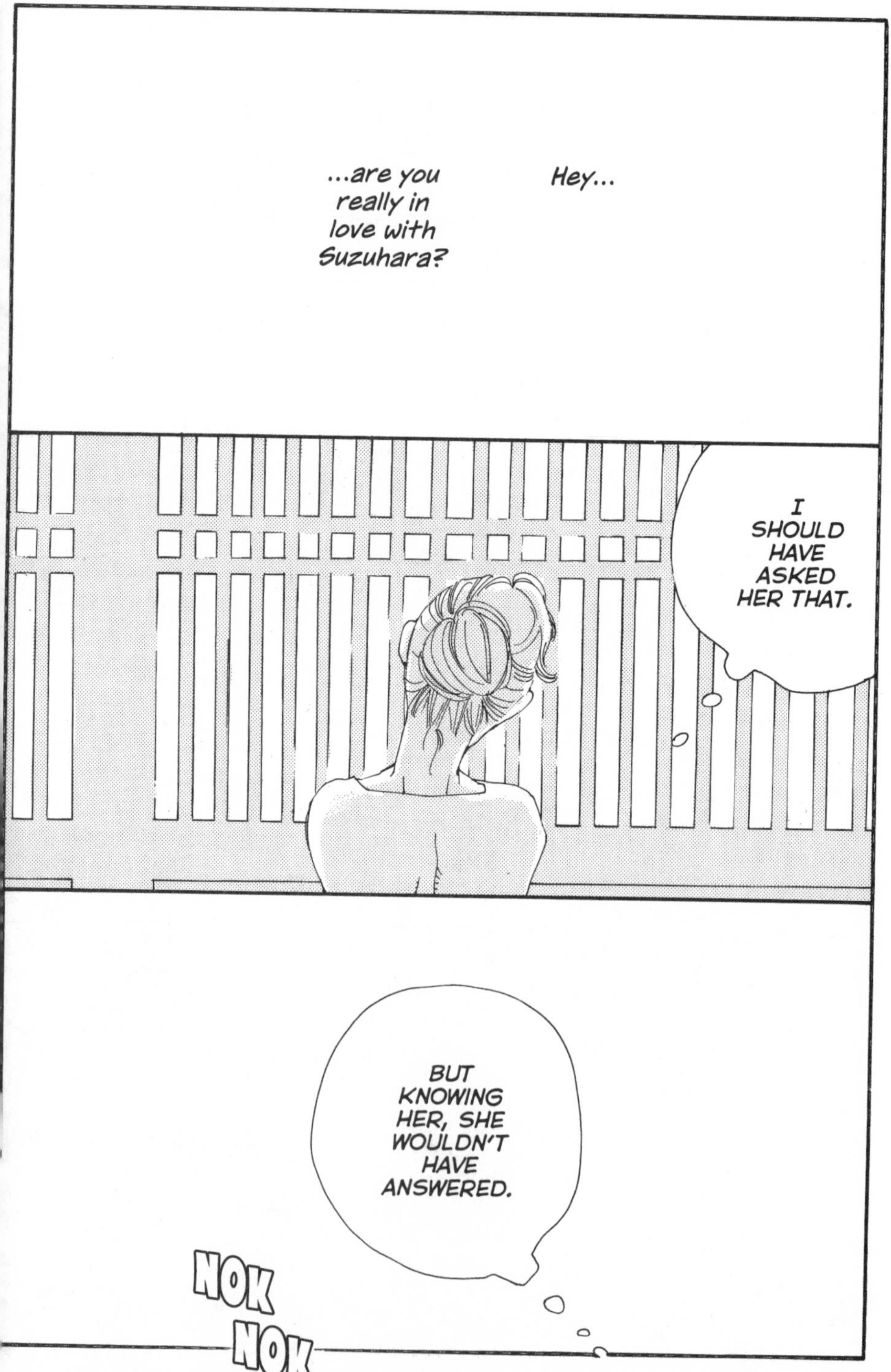
Hey...
...are you really in love with Suzuhara?
I SHOULD HAVE ASKED HER THAT.
BUT KNOWING HER, SHE WOULDN'T HAVE ANSWERED.
NOK NOK

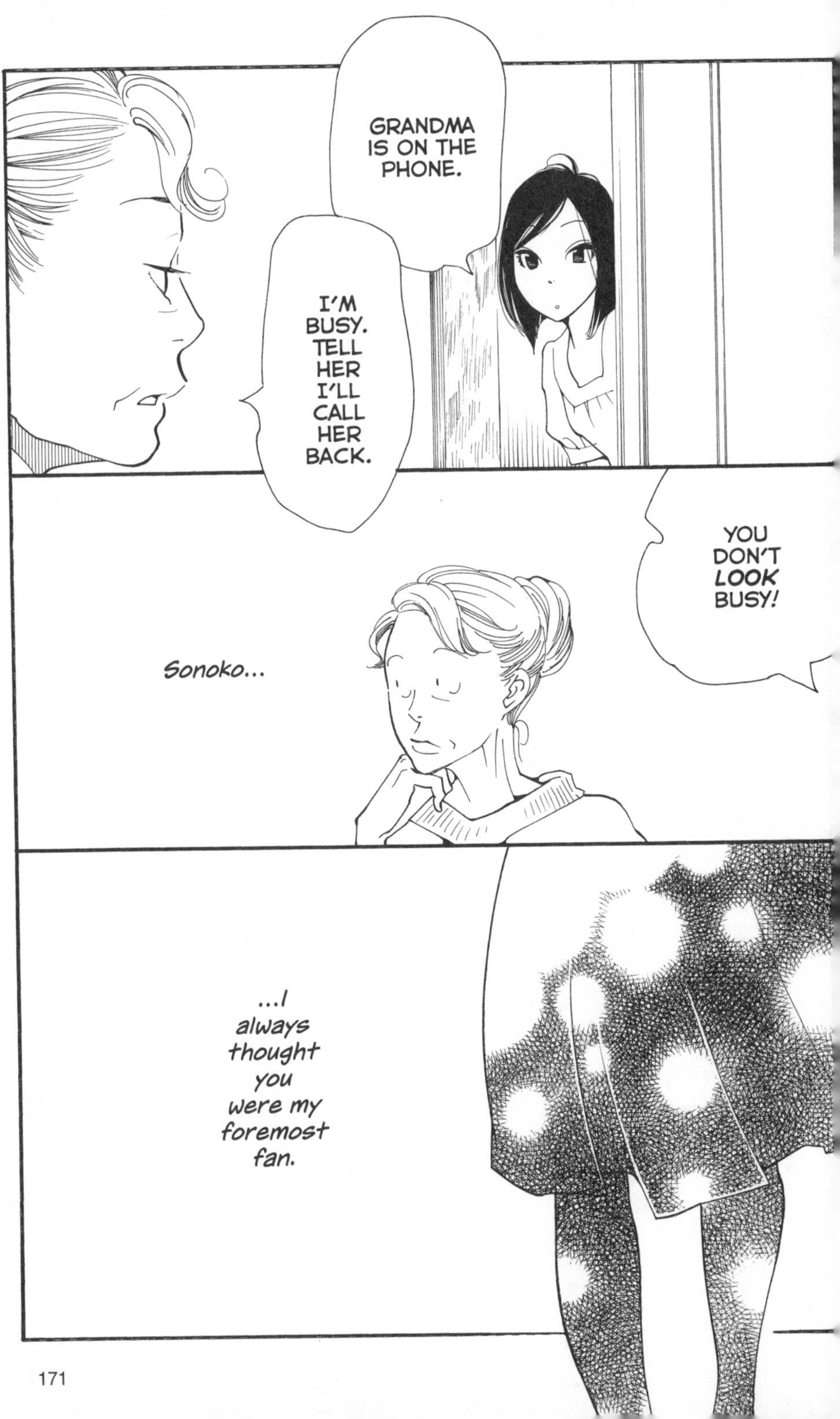
GRANDMA IS ON THE PHONE.
I'M BUSY. TELL HER I'LL CALL HER BACK.
YOU DON'T LOOK BUSY!
Sonoko...
...I always thought you were my foremost fan.

*Little Miss
Snooty!*

Afterword

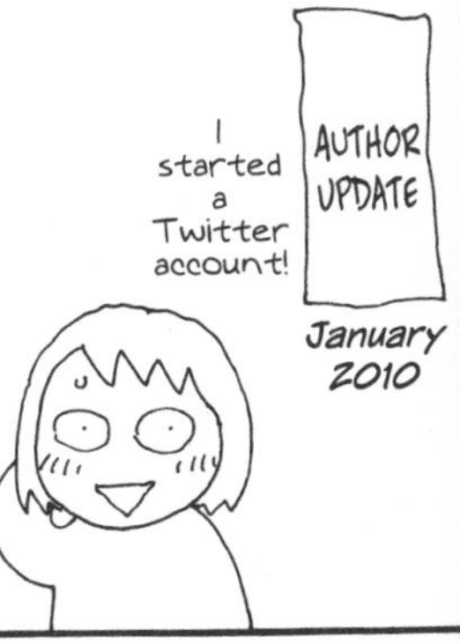
AUTHOR UPDATE
January 2010
I started a Twitter account!

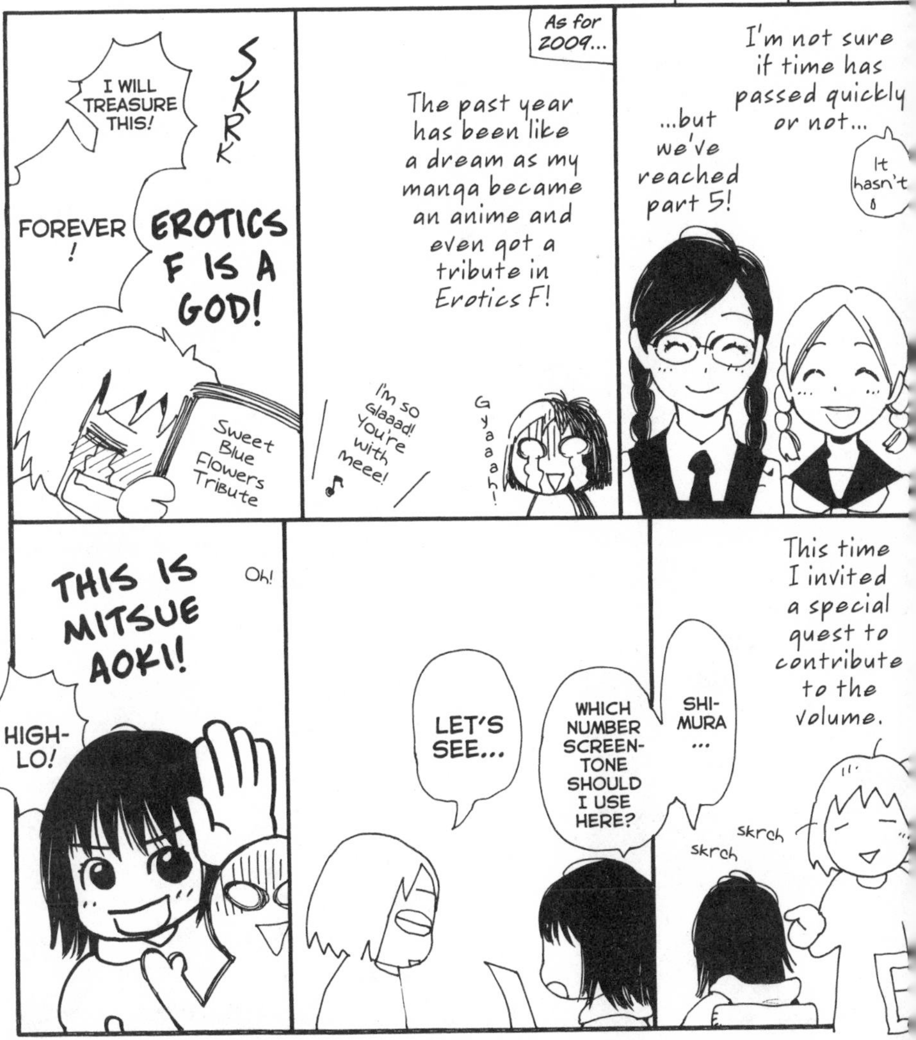
I'm not sure if time has passed quickly or not...
It hasn't
...but we've reached part 5!
As for 2009...
The past year has been like a dream as my manga became an anime and even got a tribute in Erotics F!
Gyaaaah!
I'm so Glaaad! You're with meee! ♪
SKRK
I WILL TREASURE THIS!
EROTICS F IS A GOD!
FOREVER!
Sweet Blue Flowers Tribute
This time I invited a special guest to contribute to the volume.
skrch
skrch
SHI-MURA...
WHICH NUMBER SCREEN-TONE SHOULD I USE HERE?
LET'S SEE...
Oh!
THIS IS MITSUE AOKI!
HIGH-LO!

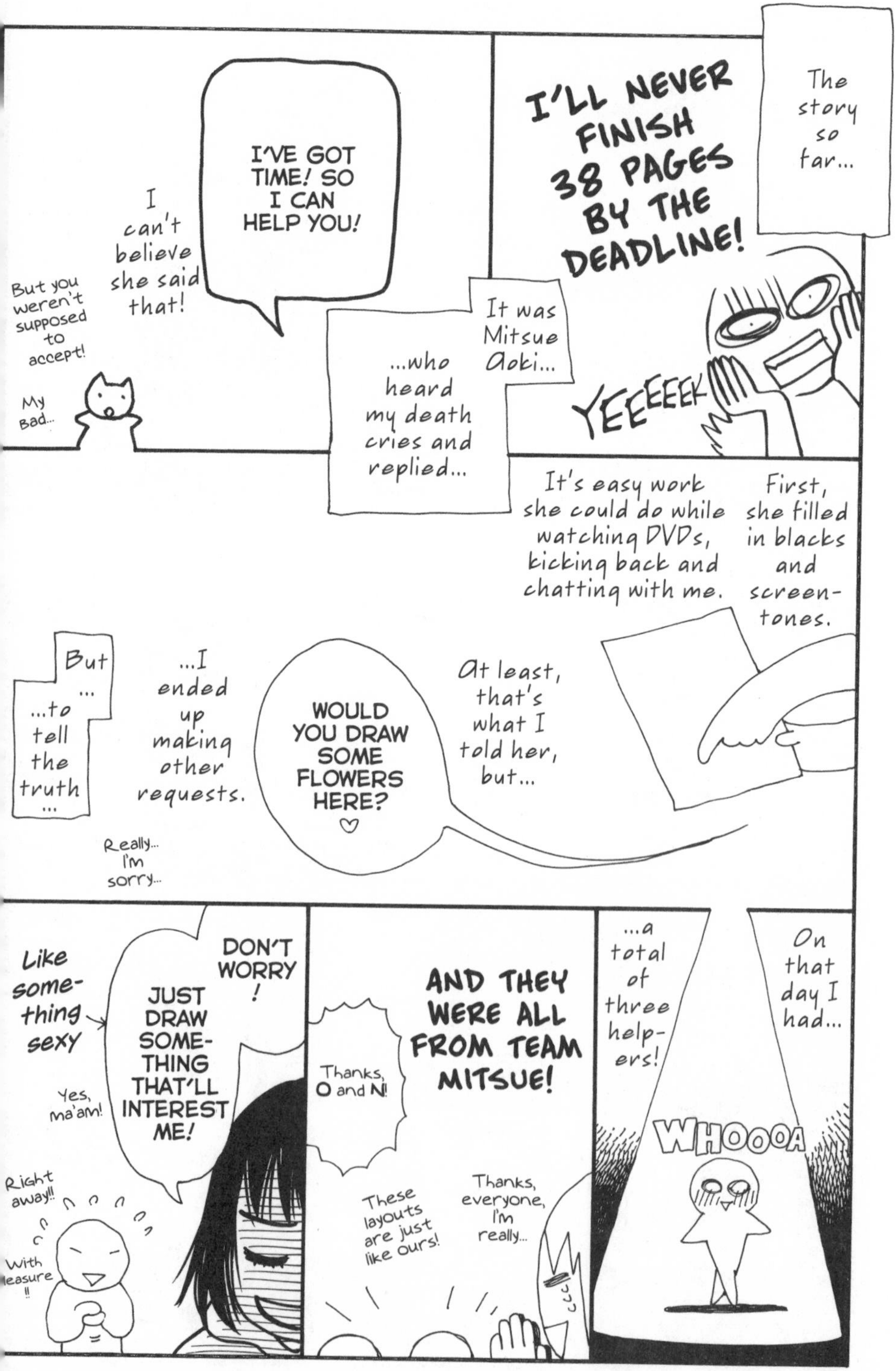
The story so far...
I'LL NEVER FINISH 38 PAGES BY THE DEADLINE!
YEEEEEK
It was Mitsue Aoki...
...who heard my death cries and replied...
I'VE GOT TIME! SO I CAN HELP YOU!
I can't believe she said that!
But you weren't supposed to accept!
My bad...
First, she filled in blacks and screentones.
It's easy work she could do while watching DVDs, kicking back and chatting with me.
At least, that's what I told her, but...
But...
...to tell the truth...
...I ended up making other requests.
WOULD YOU DRAW SOME FLOWERS HERE? ♡
Really... I'm sorry...
On that day I had...
...a total of three helpers!
WHOOOA
AND THEY WERE ALL FROM TEAM MITSUE!
Thanks, O and N!
Thanks, everyone, I'm really...
These layouts are just like ours!
DON'T WORRY!
JUST DRAW SOMETHING THAT'LL INTEREST ME!
Like something sexy
Yes, ma'am!
Right away!!
With leasure !!

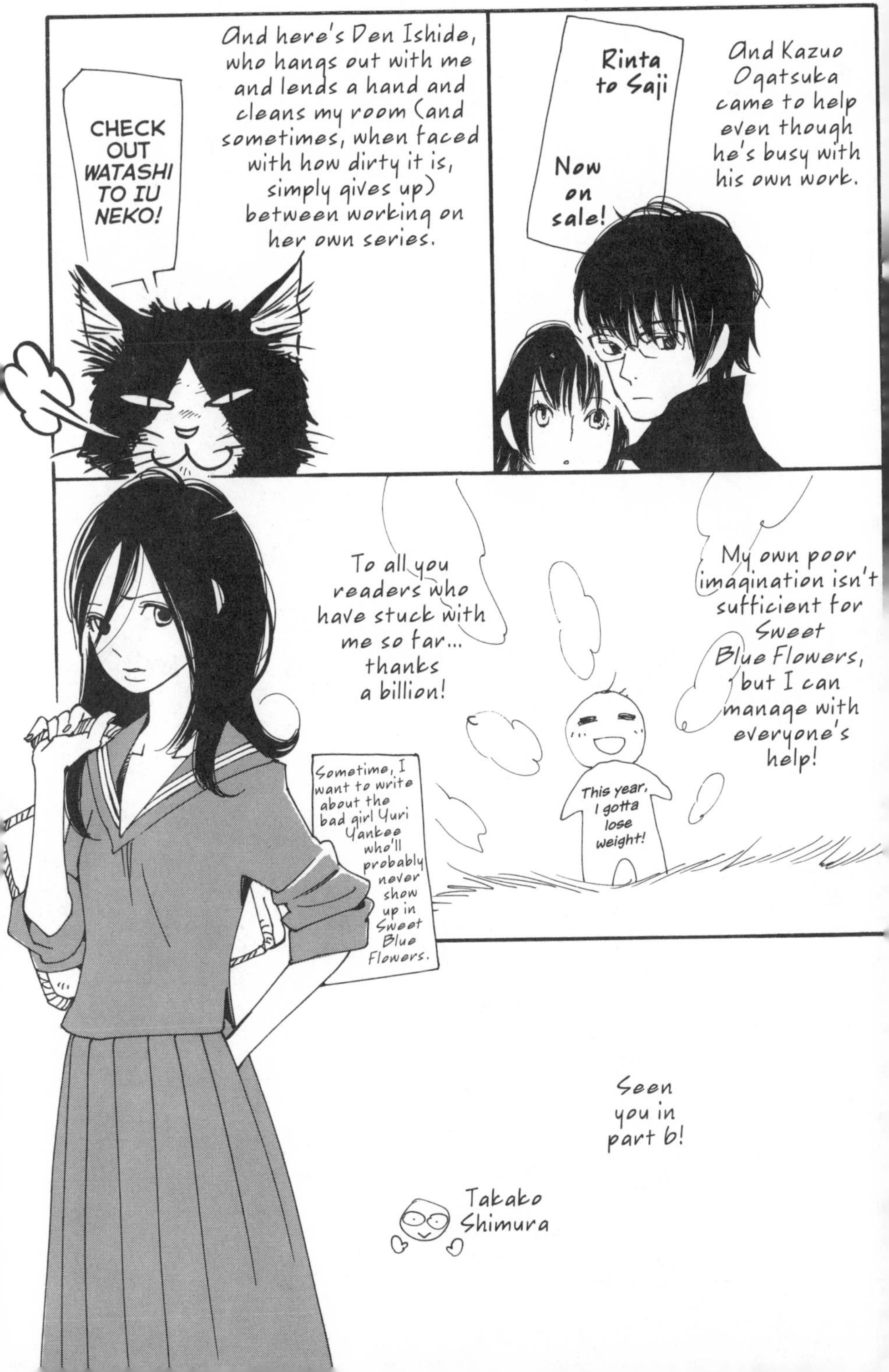
And Kazuo Ogatsuka came to help even though he's busy with his own work.
Rinta to Saji
Now on sale!
And here's Den Ishide, who hangs out with me and lends a hand and cleans my room (and sometimes, when faced with how dirty it is, simply gives up) between working on her own series.
CHECK OUT WATASHI TO IU NEKO!
My own poor imagination isn't sufficient for Sweet Blue Flowers, but I can manage with everyone's help!
This year, I gotta lose weight!
To all you readers who have stuck with me so far... thanks a billion!
Sometime, I want to write about the bad girl Yuri Yankee who'll probably never show up in Sweet Blue Flowers.
Seen you in part 6!
Takako Shimura

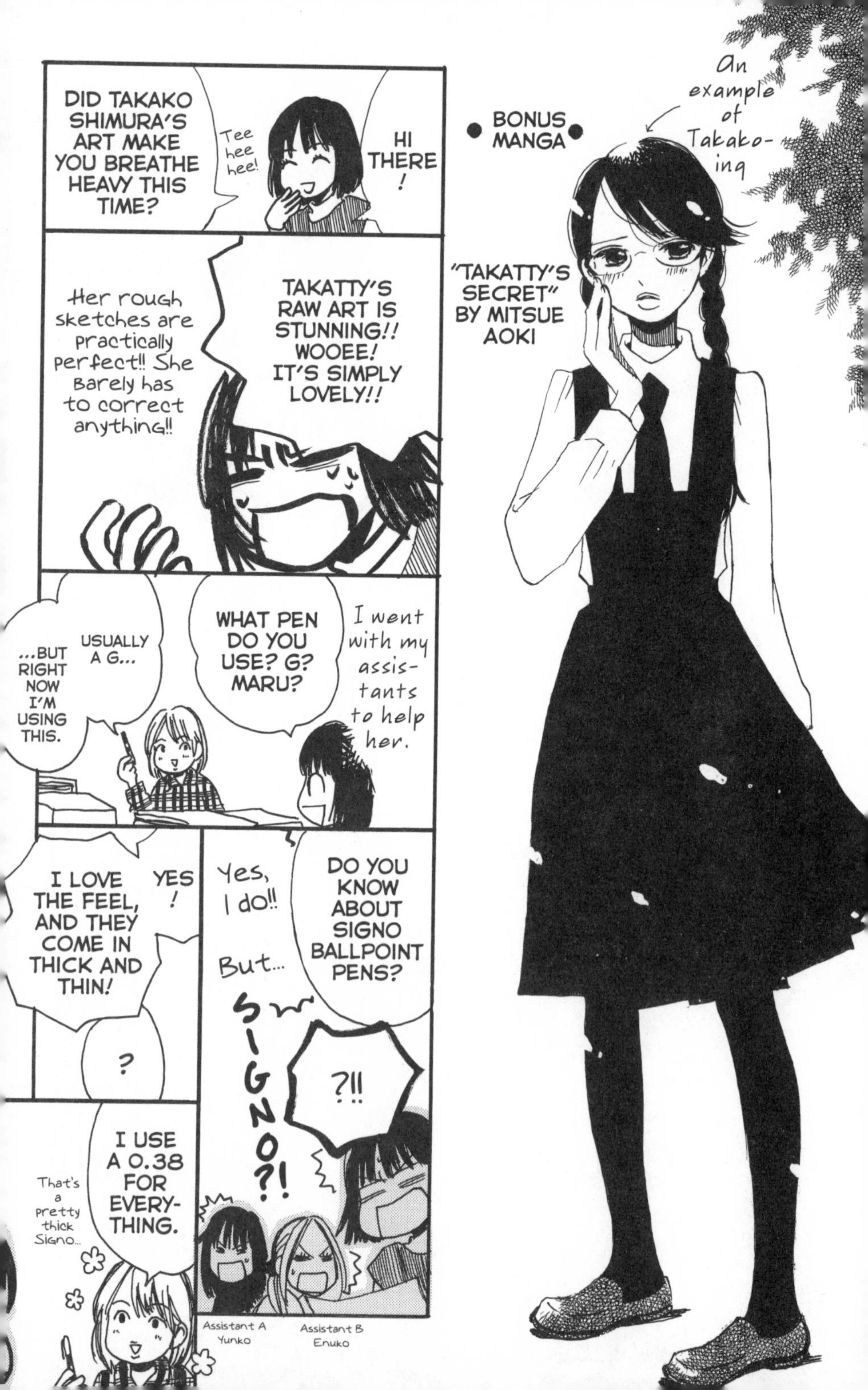

An example of Takako-ing
BONUS MANGA
"TAKATTY'S SECRET" BY MITSUE AOKI
HI THERE!
Tee hee hee!
DID TAKAKO SHIMURA'S ART MAKE YOU BREATHE HEAVY THIS TIME?
TAKATTY'S RAW ART IS STUNNING!! WOOEE! IT'S SIMPLY LOVELY!!
Her rough sketches are practically perfect!! She Barely has to correct anything!!
I went with my assistants to help her.
WHAT PEN DO YOU USE? G? MARU?
USUALLY A G...
...BUT RIGHT NOW I'M USING THIS.
DO YOU KNOW ABOUT SIGNO BALLPOINT PENS?
Yes, I do!!
But...
SIGNO?!
?!!
Assistant A Yunko
Assistant B Enuko
YES!
I LOVE THE FEEL, AND THEY COME IN THICK AND THIN!
?
I USE A 0.38 FOR EVERY-THING.
That's a pretty thick Signo...

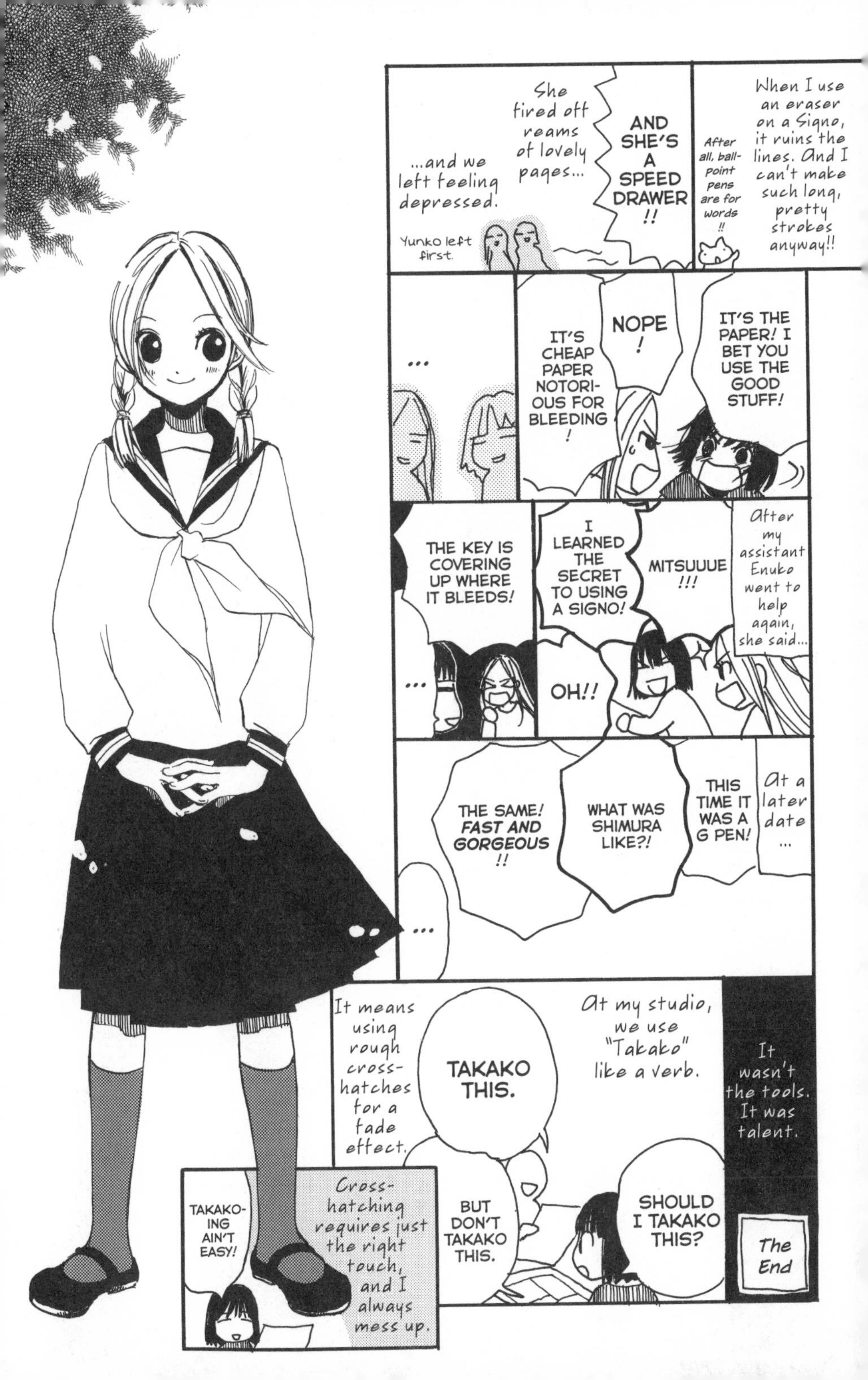
When I use an eraser on a Signo, it ruins the lines. And I can't make such long, pretty strokes anyway!!
After all, ball-point pens are for words!!
AND SHE'S A SPEED DRAWER!!
She fired off reams of lovely pages...
...and we left feeling depressed.
Yunko left first.
IT'S THE PAPER! I BET YOU USE THE GOOD STUFF!
NOPE!
IT'S CHEAP PAPER NOTORIOUS FOR BLEEDING!
...
After my assistant Enuko went to help again, she said...
MITSUUUE!!!
I LEARNED THE SECRET TO USING A SIGNO!
OH!!
THE KEY IS COVERING UP WHERE IT BLEEDS!
...
At a later date...
THIS TIME IT WAS A G PEN!
WHAT WAS SHIMURA LIKE?!
THE SAME! FAST AND GORGEOUS!!
...
It wasn't the tools. It was talent.
The End
At my studio, we use "Takako" like a verb.
TAKAKO THIS.
It means using rough cross-hatches for a fade effect.
SHOULD I TAKAKO THIS?
BUT DON'T TAKAKO THIS.
Cross-hatching requires just the right touch, and I always mess up.
TAKAKO-ING AIN'T EASY!

Sweet Blue Flowers

Part Six

Story and Art by
Takako Shimura

Sweet *Blue Flowers*
Part Six

Sweet *Blue*
Flowers

Characters

Fujigaya Women's Academy High School

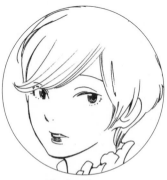

Kyoko Ikumi

Year 2. Like Akira, she's a member of the Drama Club. The other girls admire her for her maturity. Despite her engagement to Ko Sawanoi, she's had a one-sided crush on Yasuko Sugimoto since junior high.

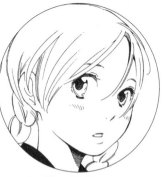

Akira Okudaira

Year 2. She's small, innocent and honest, and has yet to experience love. Akira has felt uncomfortable ever since her childhood friend Fumi told her she likes her.

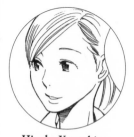

Hinako Yamashina

Science teacher. She is Akira's homeroom teacher and a graduate of Fujigaya. Her girlfriend is Haruka Ono's older sister Orie.

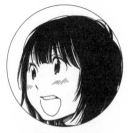

Haruka Ono

Year 1. She's an energetic girl who joined the Drama Club because she admires theater, and now she's becoming good friends with a lot of older students.

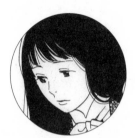

Ryoko Ueda

Year 2. She's in the same class as Akira. She's a member of the Library Club but plans to make a guest appearance onstage at the Fujigaya Theater Festival.

Matsuoka Girls' High School

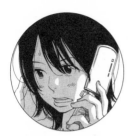

Yasuko Sugimoto

She dated Fumi while she was a student at Matsuoka, but the relationship fell apart after a few months. Currently she's studying in England. At Matsuoka, she was seen as the popular princely type, but inside she was clinging to childish feelings for her first love.

Fumi Manjome

Year 2. She's tall and pretty—and a worrywart crybaby. She recently realized that Akira was her first love, but they're close friends, so she's trying to suppress her feelings even as they deepen.

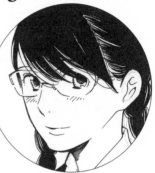

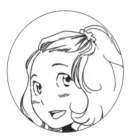

Miwa Motegi

Year 2. Nickname: Mogi. She's a quiet girl who is a member of the Drama Club. She's dating Akira's older brother Shinobu.

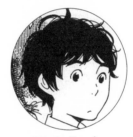

Misako Yasuda

Year 2. Nickname: Yassan. She's the head of the school's very small and informal Drama Club. She has a boyish personality.

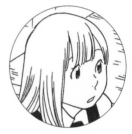

Yoko Honatsugi

Year 2. Nickname: Pon. She's a member of the Drama Club. She has a bright personality and isn't afraid of anything.

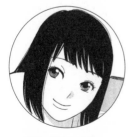

Chizu Hanashiro

Fumi's cousin on her mother's side. She was Fumi's first girlfriend, but she surprised Fumi by getting married.

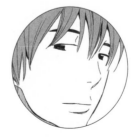

Ko Sawanoi

Kyoko Ikumi's fiancé. He's in his second year at university. He has a gentle and considerate personality, and he's serious about Kyoko.

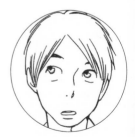

Shinobu Okudaira

Akira's brother. He's in his third year at university. He has a serious sister complex, but maybe he's beginning to change now that he's dating Miwa Motegi?

Sweet Blue Flowers

#32 The Door into Summer, Part 2

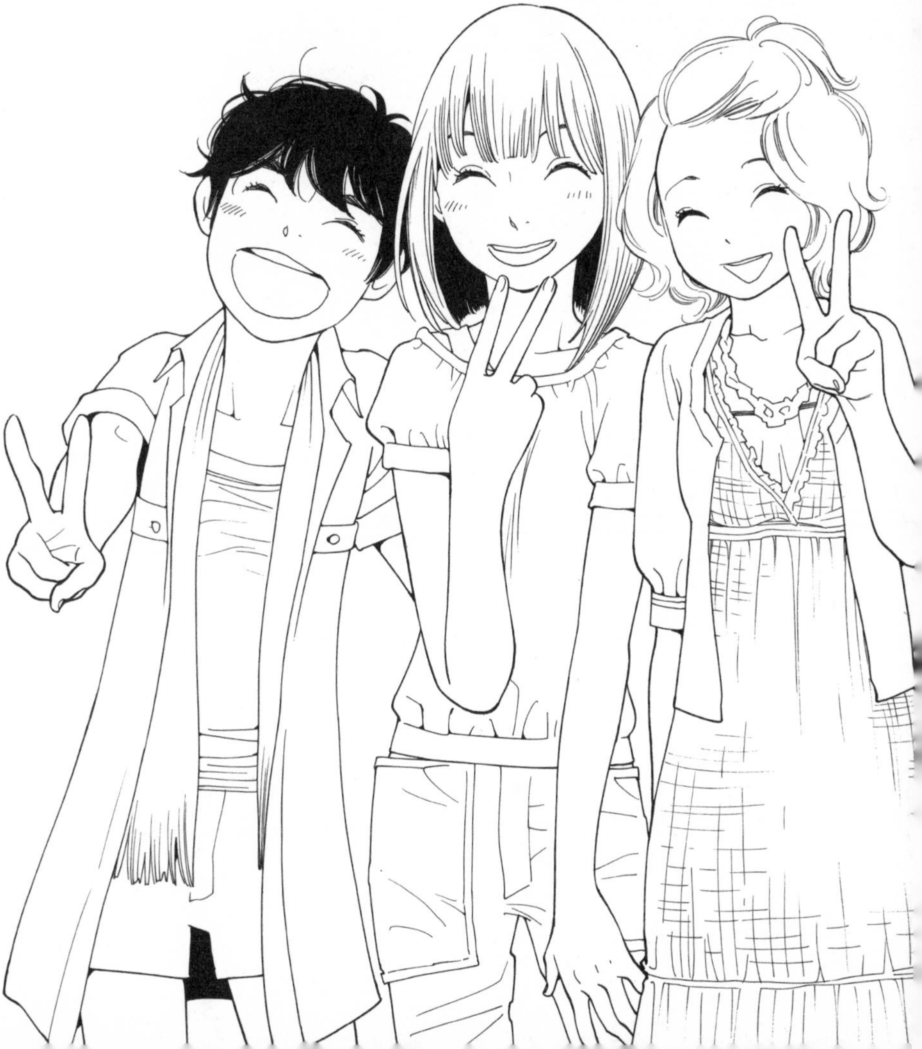

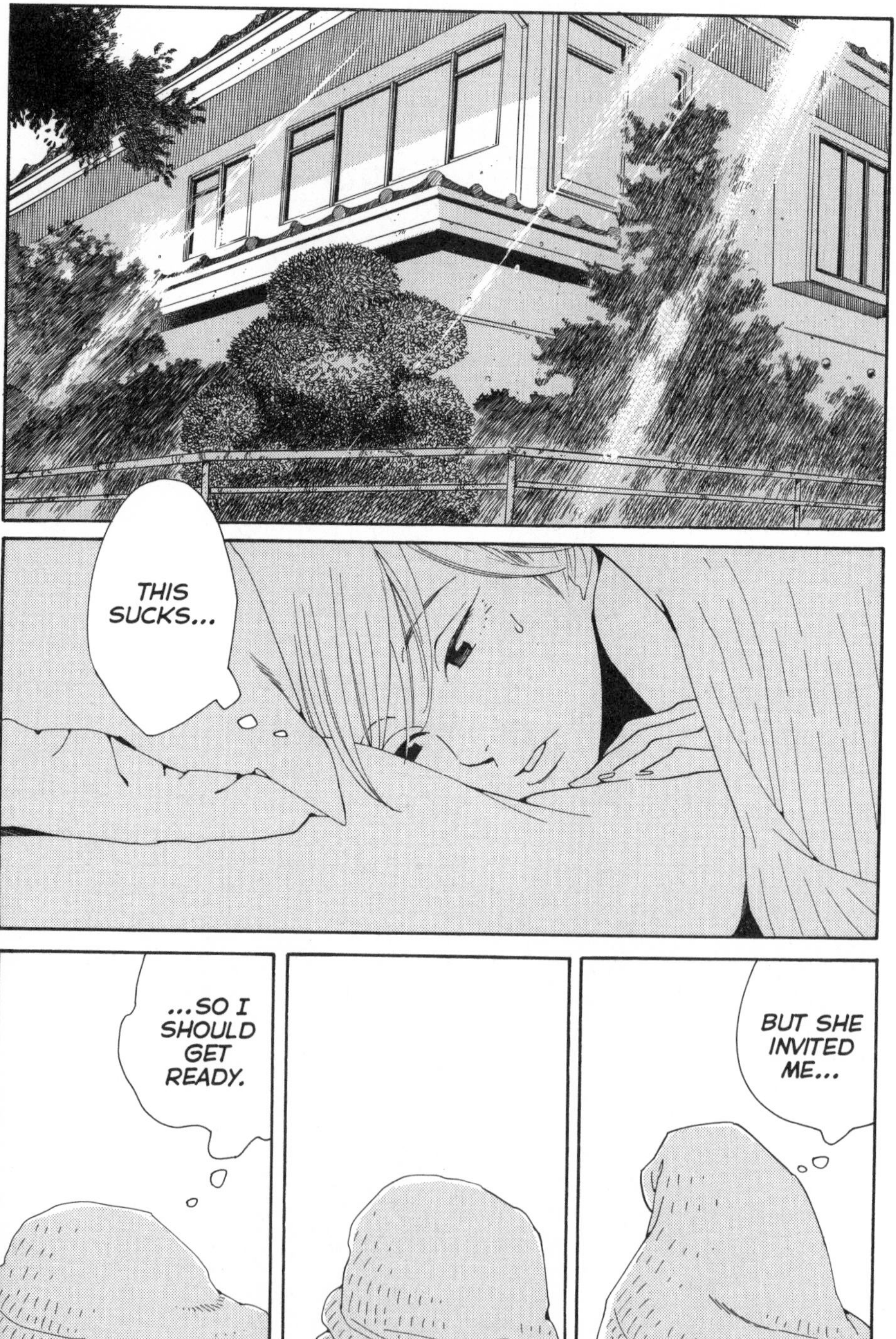
THIS SUCKS...
BUT SHE INVITED ME...
...SO I SHOULD GET READY.

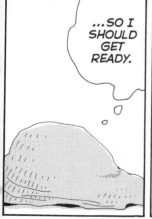

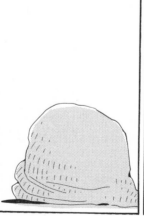

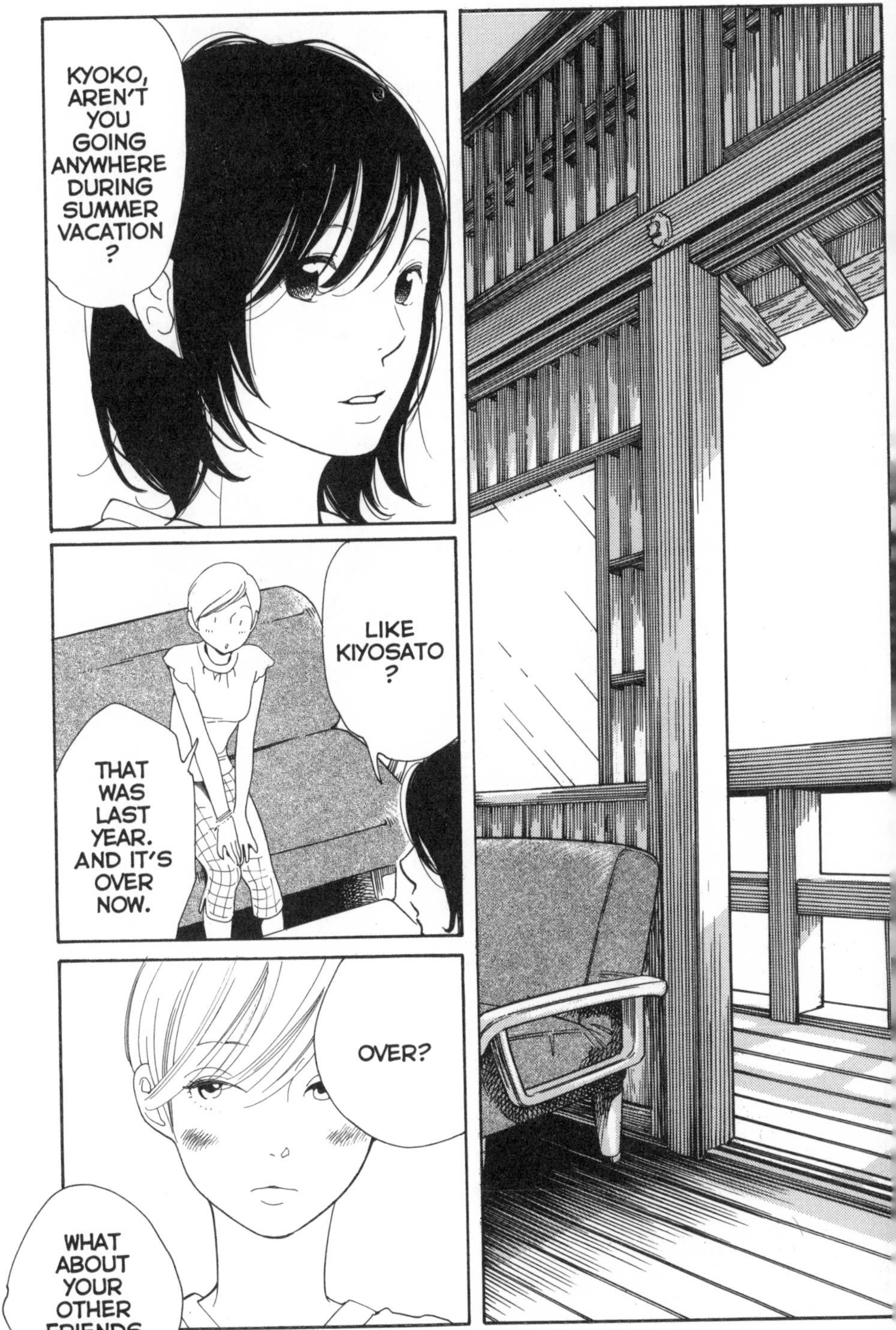
KYOKO, AREN'T YOU GOING ANYWHERE DURING SUMMER VACATION?
LIKE KIYOSATO?
THAT WAS LAST YEAR. AND IT'S OVER NOW.
OVER?
WHAT ABOUT YOUR OTHER FRIENDS?

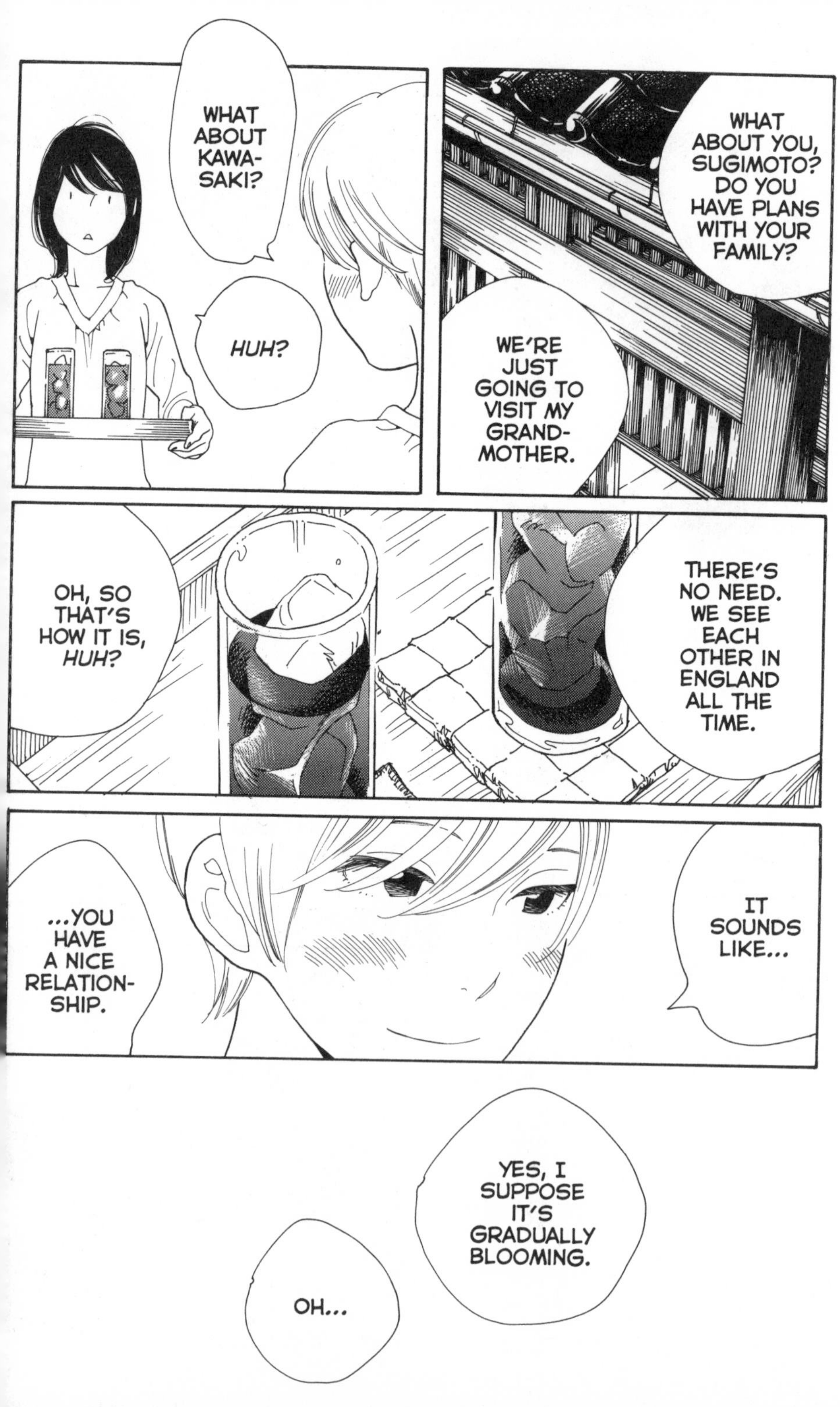
WHAT ABOUT YOU, SUGIMOTO? DO YOU HAVE PLANS WITH YOUR FAMILY?
WE'RE JUST GOING TO VISIT MY GRANDMOTHER.
WHAT ABOUT KAWASAKI?
HUH?
THERE'S NO NEED. WE SEE EACH OTHER IN ENGLAND ALL THE TIME.
OH, SO THAT'S HOW IT IS, *HUH?*
IT SOUNDS LIKE...
...YOU HAVE A NICE RELATIONSHIP.
YES, I SUPPOSE IT'S GRADUALLY BLOOMING.
OH...

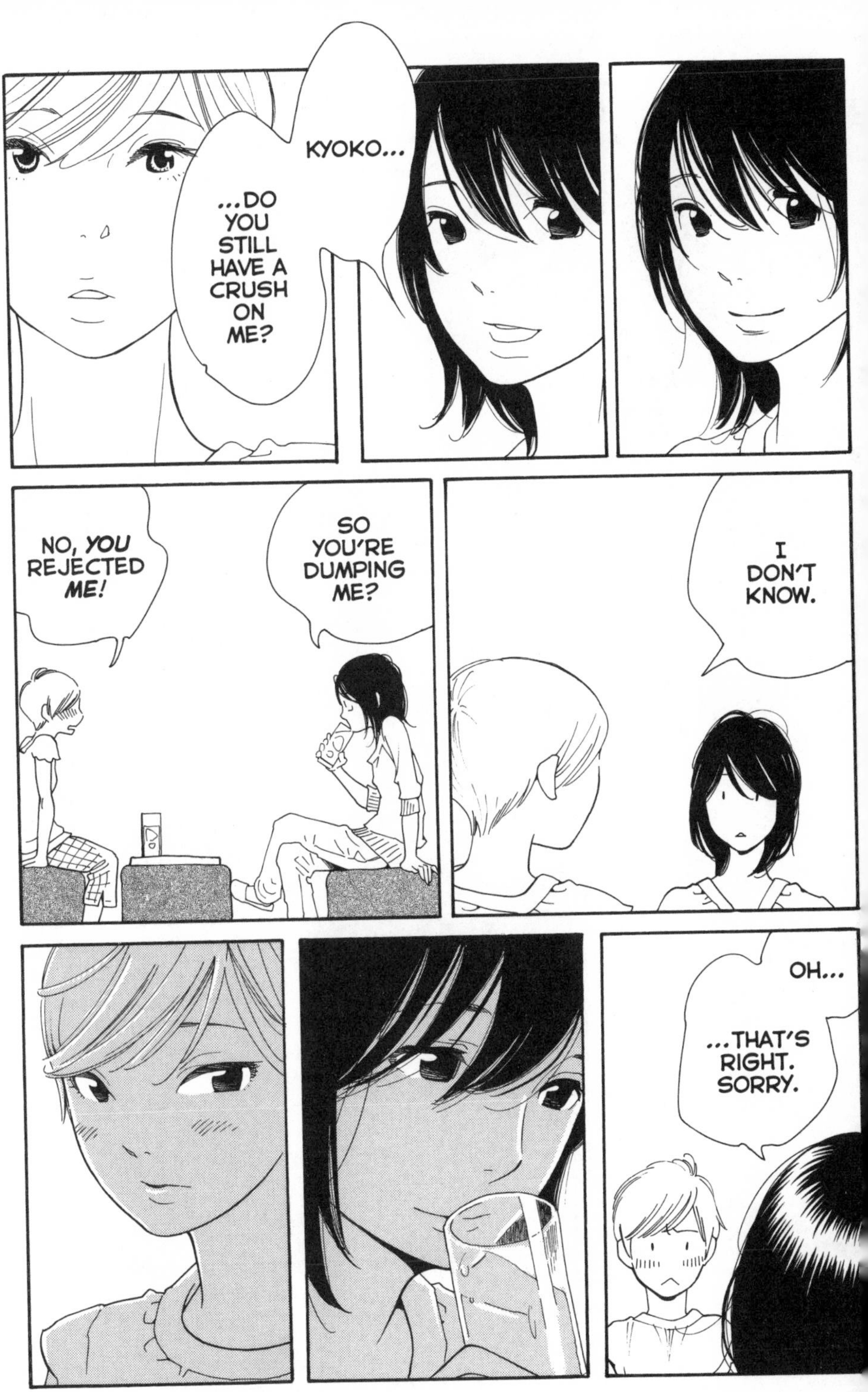
KYOKO...
...DO YOU STILL HAVE A CRUSH ON ME?
I DON'T KNOW.
SO YOU'RE DUMPING ME?
NO, *YOU* REJECTED *ME!*
OH...
...THAT'S RIGHT. SORRY.

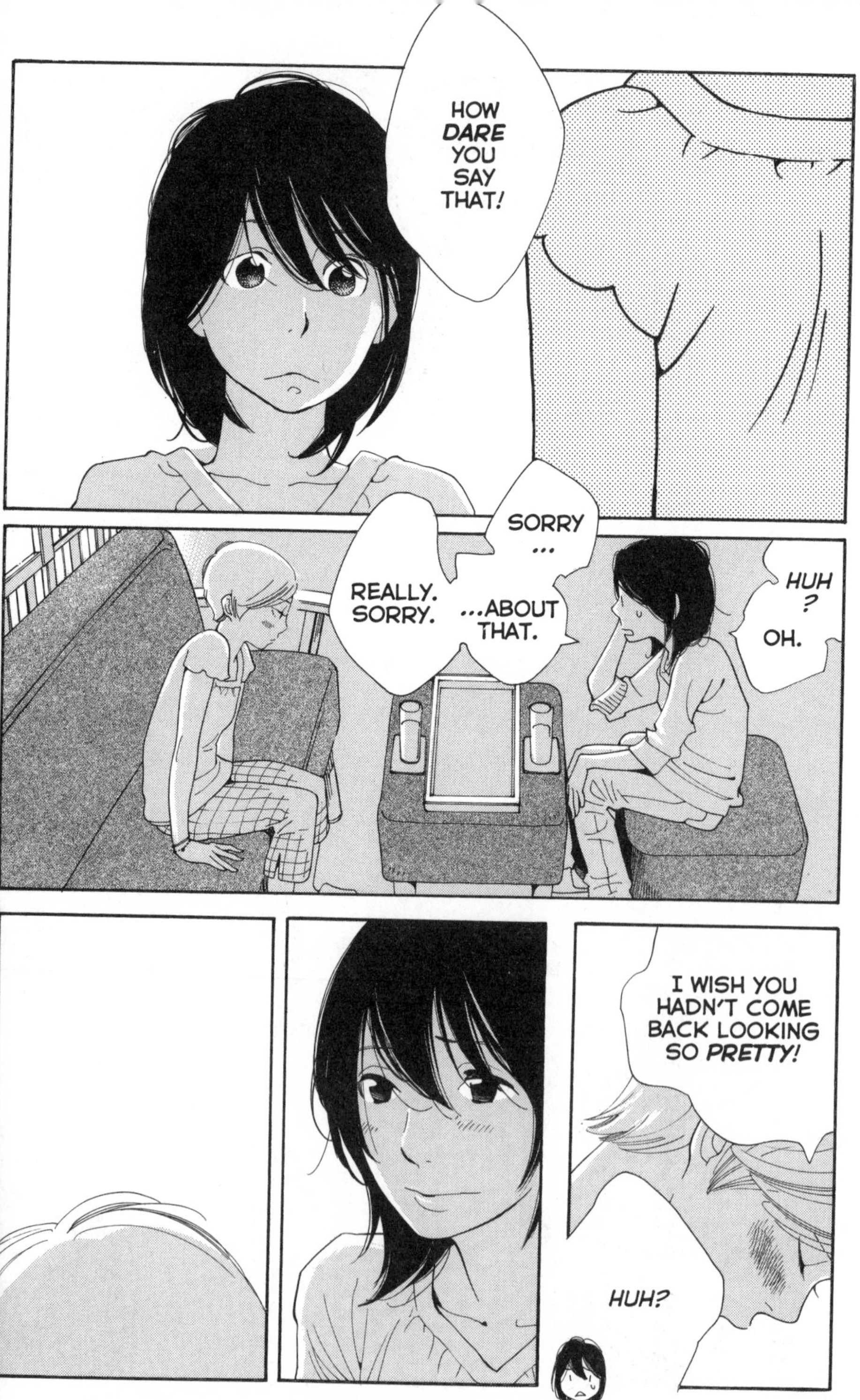
HOW *DARE* YOU SAY THAT!
HUH? OH.
SORRY... ...ABOUT THAT.
REALLY. SORRY.
I WISH YOU HADN'T COME BACK LOOKING SO *PRETTY!*
HUH?

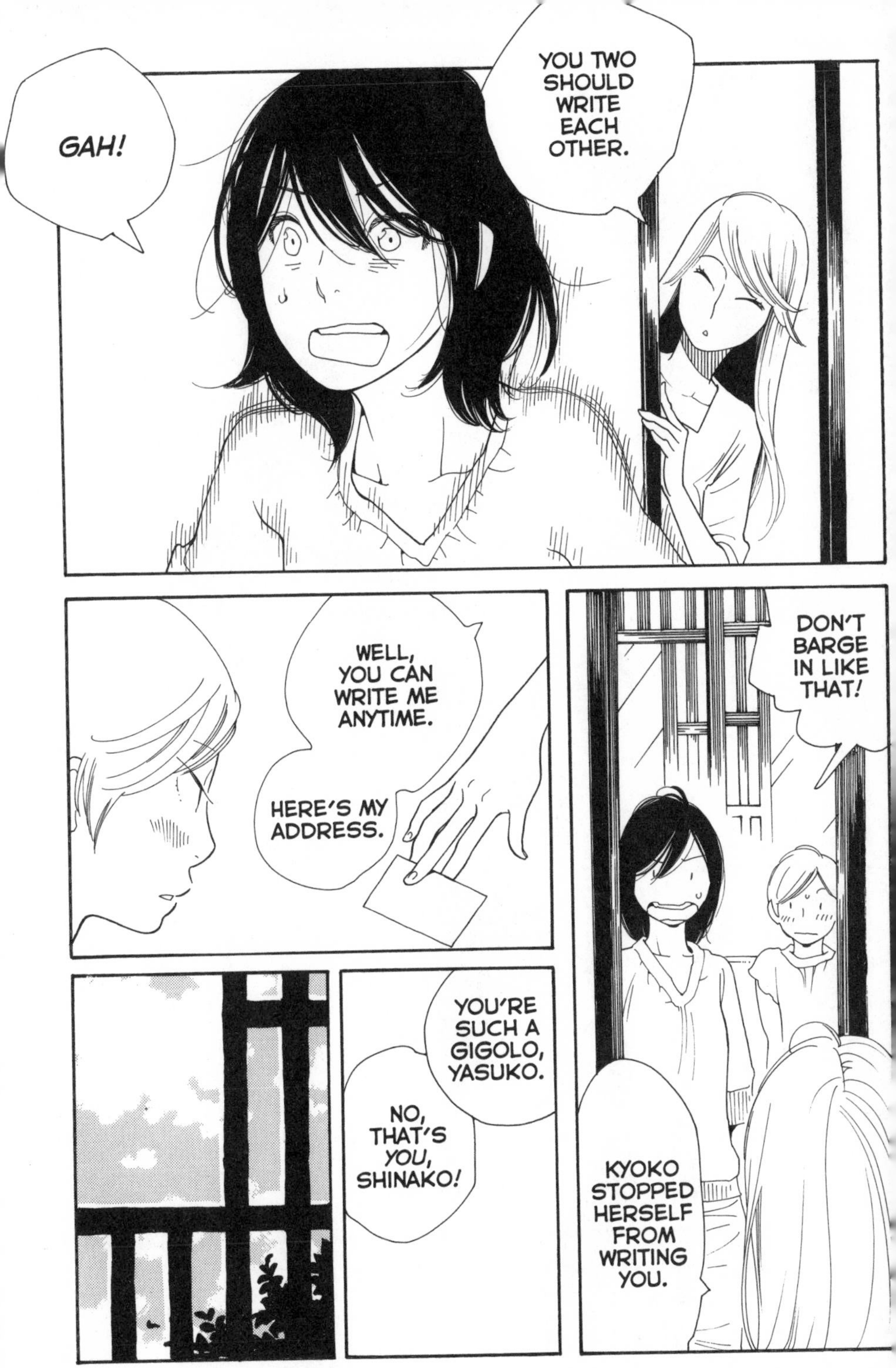
YOU TWO SHOULD WRITE EACH OTHER.
GAH!
DON'T BARGE IN LIKE THAT!
KYOKO STOPPED HERSELF FROM WRITING YOU.
WELL, YOU CAN WRITE ME ANYTIME.
HERE'S MY ADDRESS.
YOU'RE SUCH A GIGOLO, YASUKO.
NO, THAT'S *YOU*, SHINAKO!

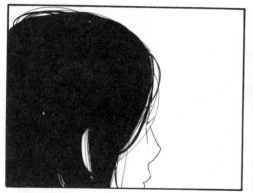

OH.

HERE COMES ASUKO !

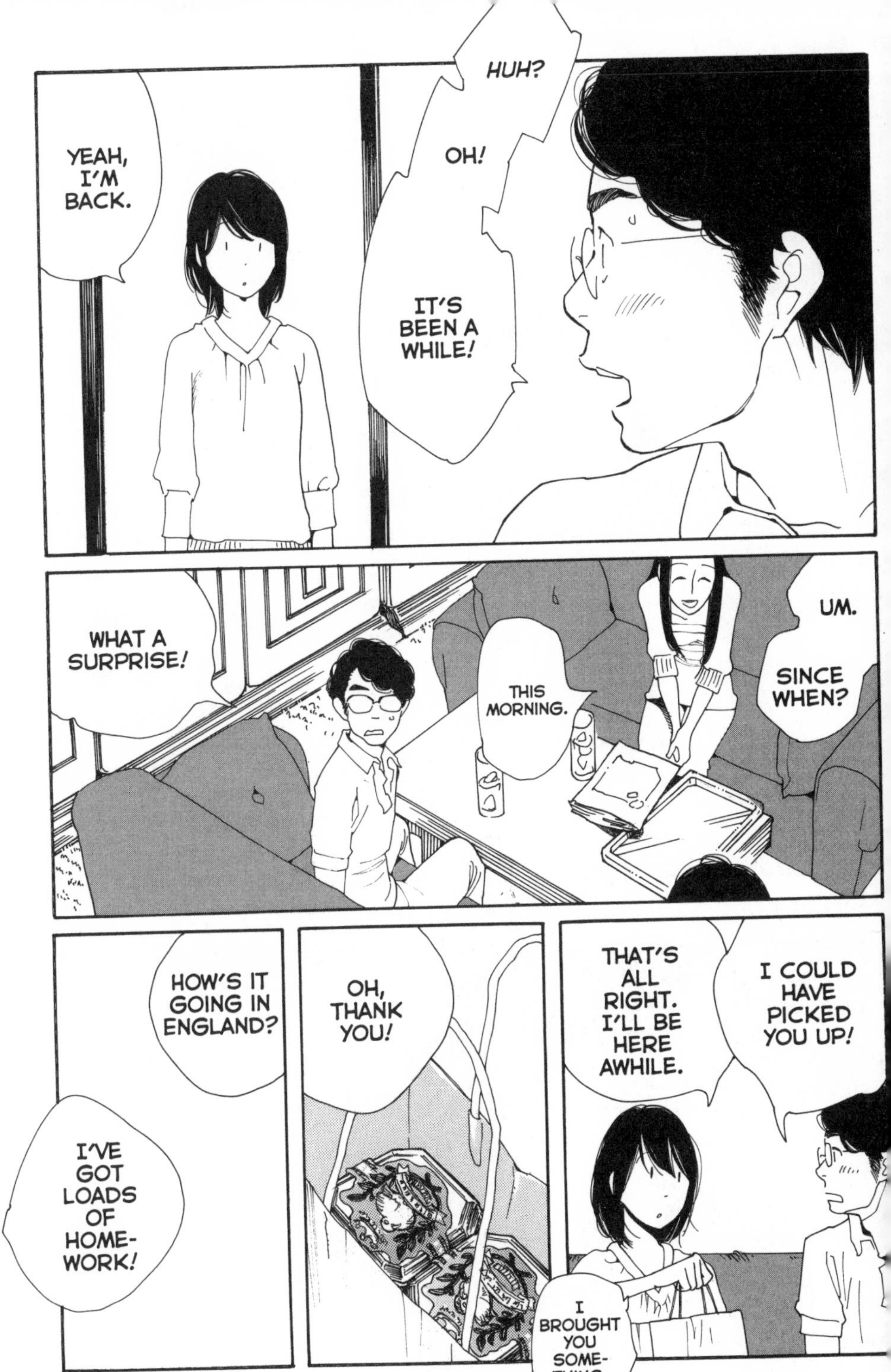
HUH?
OH!
IT'S BEEN A WHILE!
YEAH, I'M BACK.
UM.
SINCE WHEN?
THIS MORNING.
WHAT A SURPRISE!
I COULD HAVE PICKED YOU UP!
THAT'S ALL RIGHT. I'LL BE HERE AWHILE.
I BROUGHT YOU SOMETHING.
OH, THANK YOU!
HOW'S IT GOING IN ENGLAND?
I'VE GOT LOADS OF HOMEWORK!

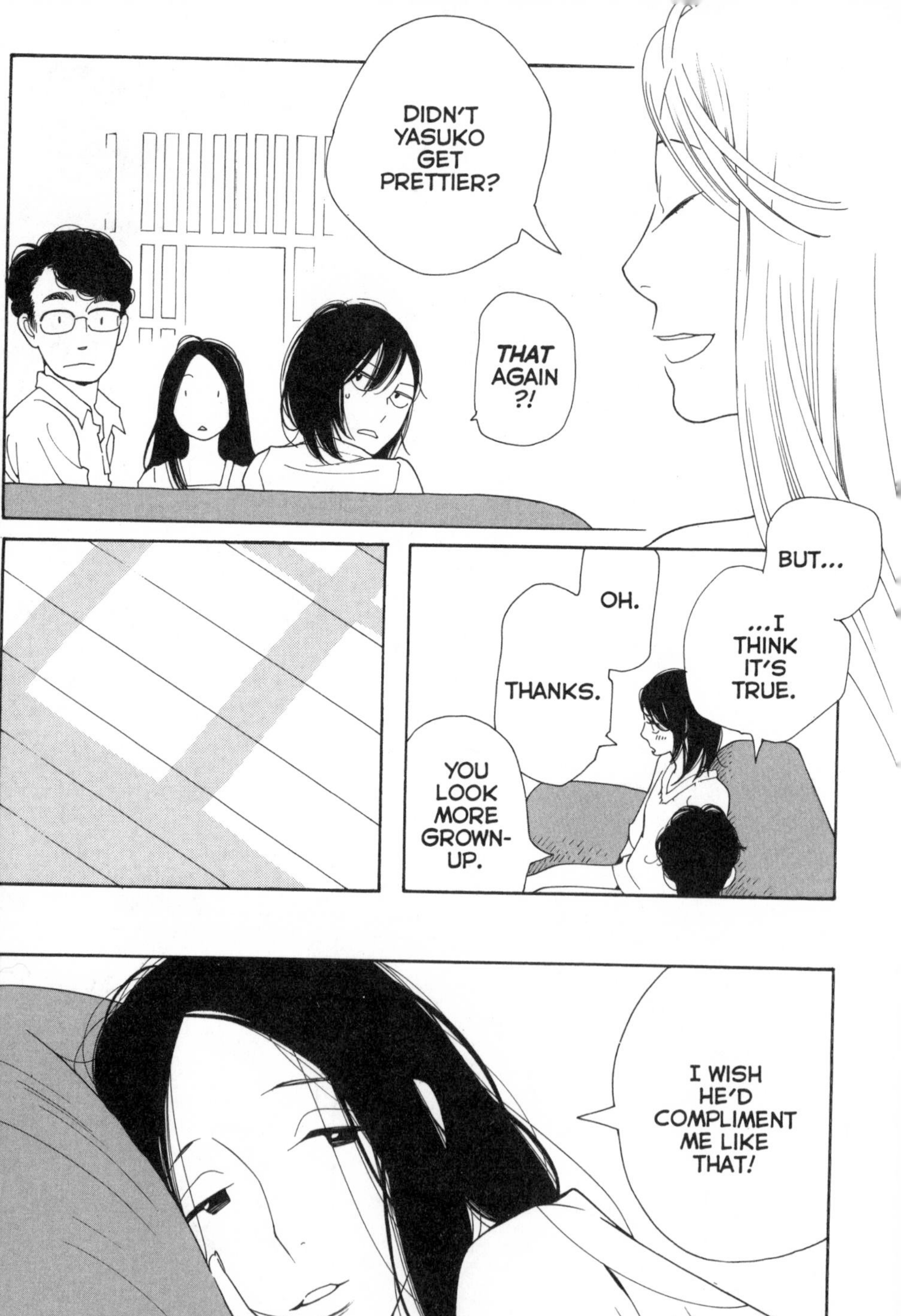
DIDN'T YASUKO GET PRETTIER?
THAT AGAIN?!
BUT...
...I THINK IT'S TRUE.
OH.
THANKS.
YOU LOOK MORE GROWN-UP.
I WISH HE'D COMPLIMENT ME LIKE THAT!

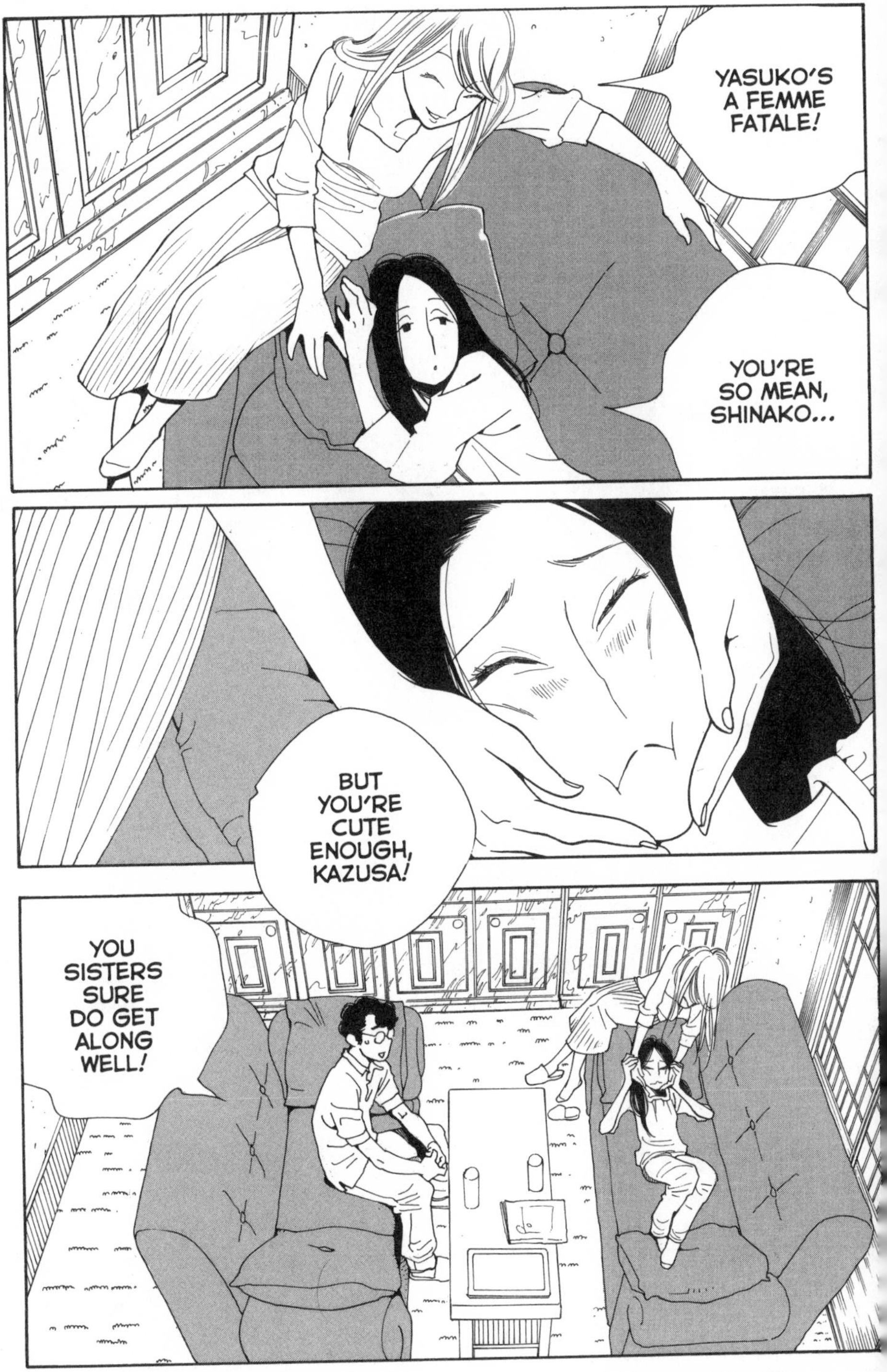
YASUKO'S A FEMME FATALE!
YOU'RE SO MEAN, SHINAKO...
BUT YOU'RE CUTE ENOUGH, KAZUSA!
YOU SISTERS SURE DO GET ALONG WELL!

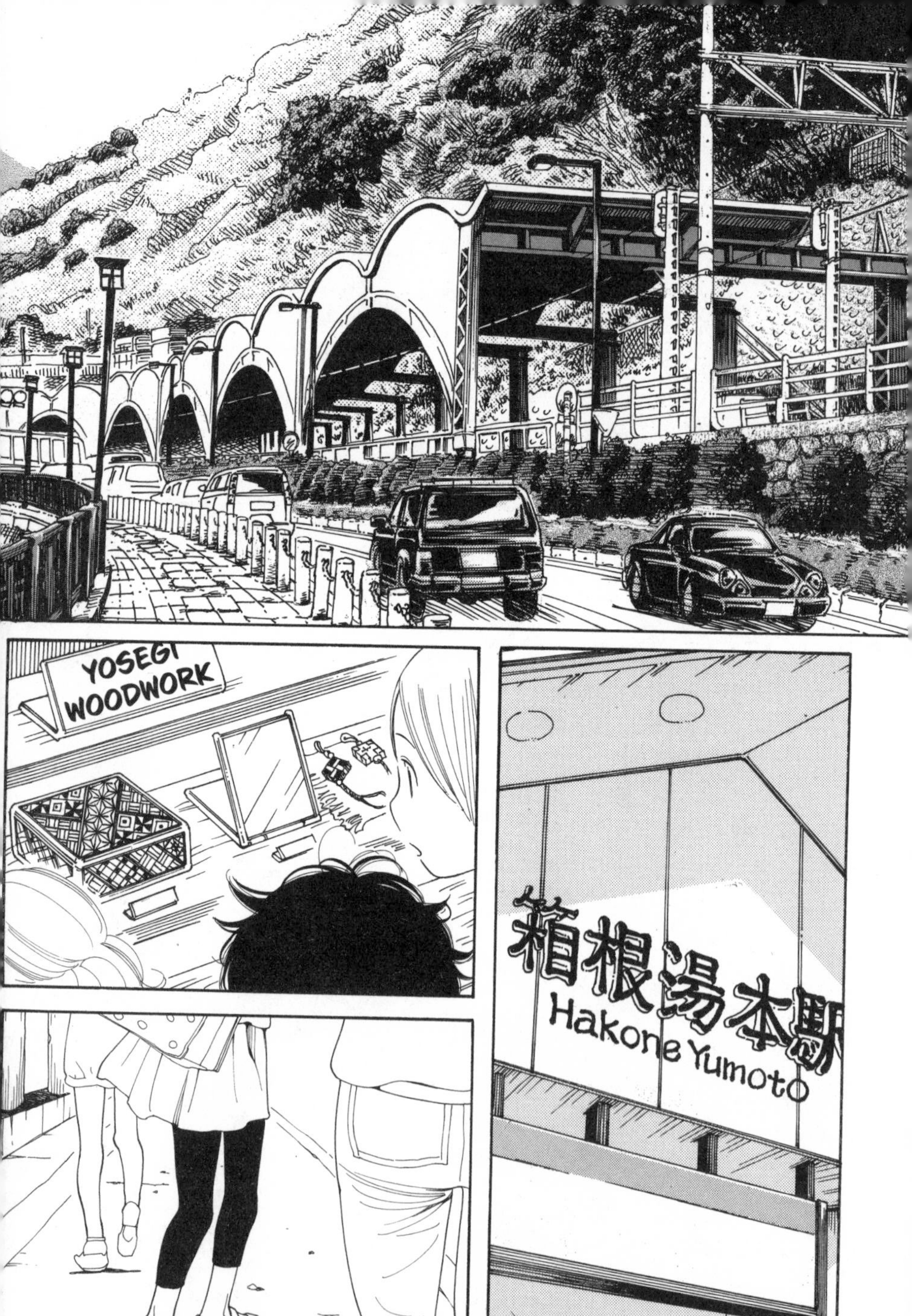
YOSEGI WOODWORK
箱根湯本駅
Hakone Yumoto

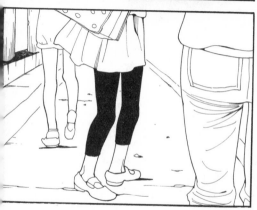

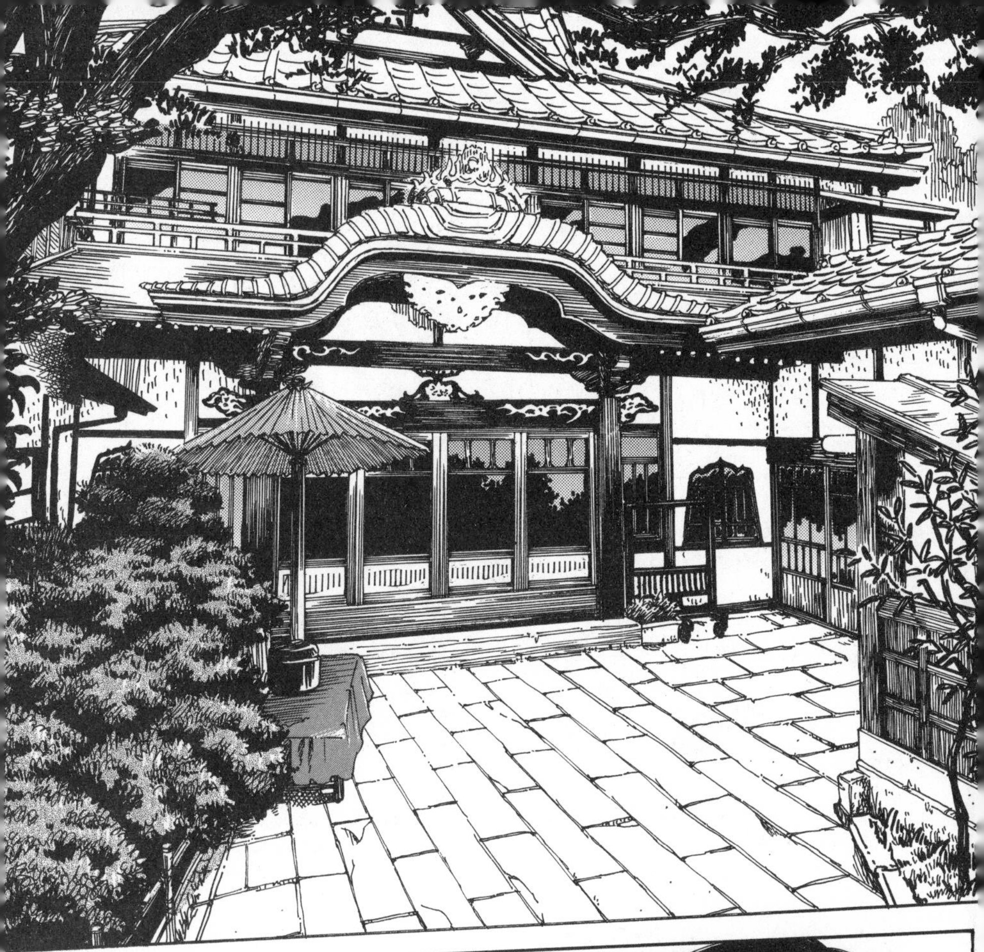

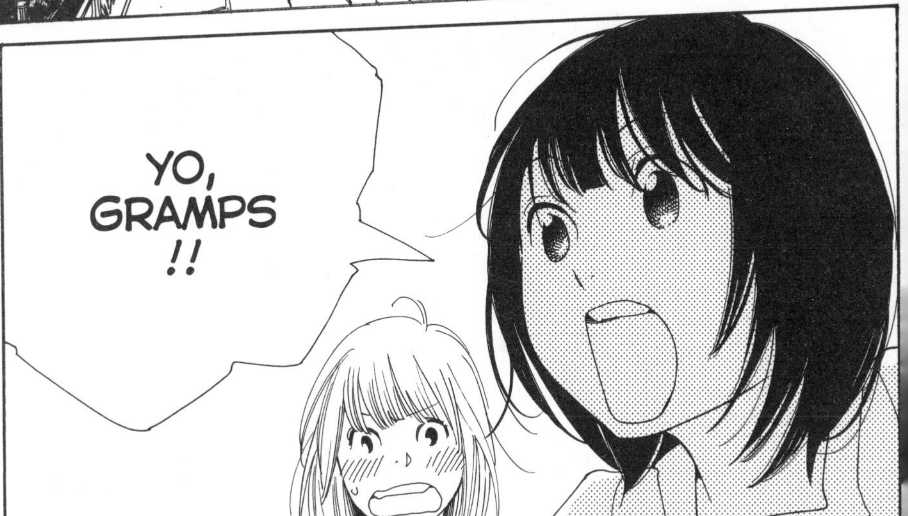
YO, GRAMPS !!

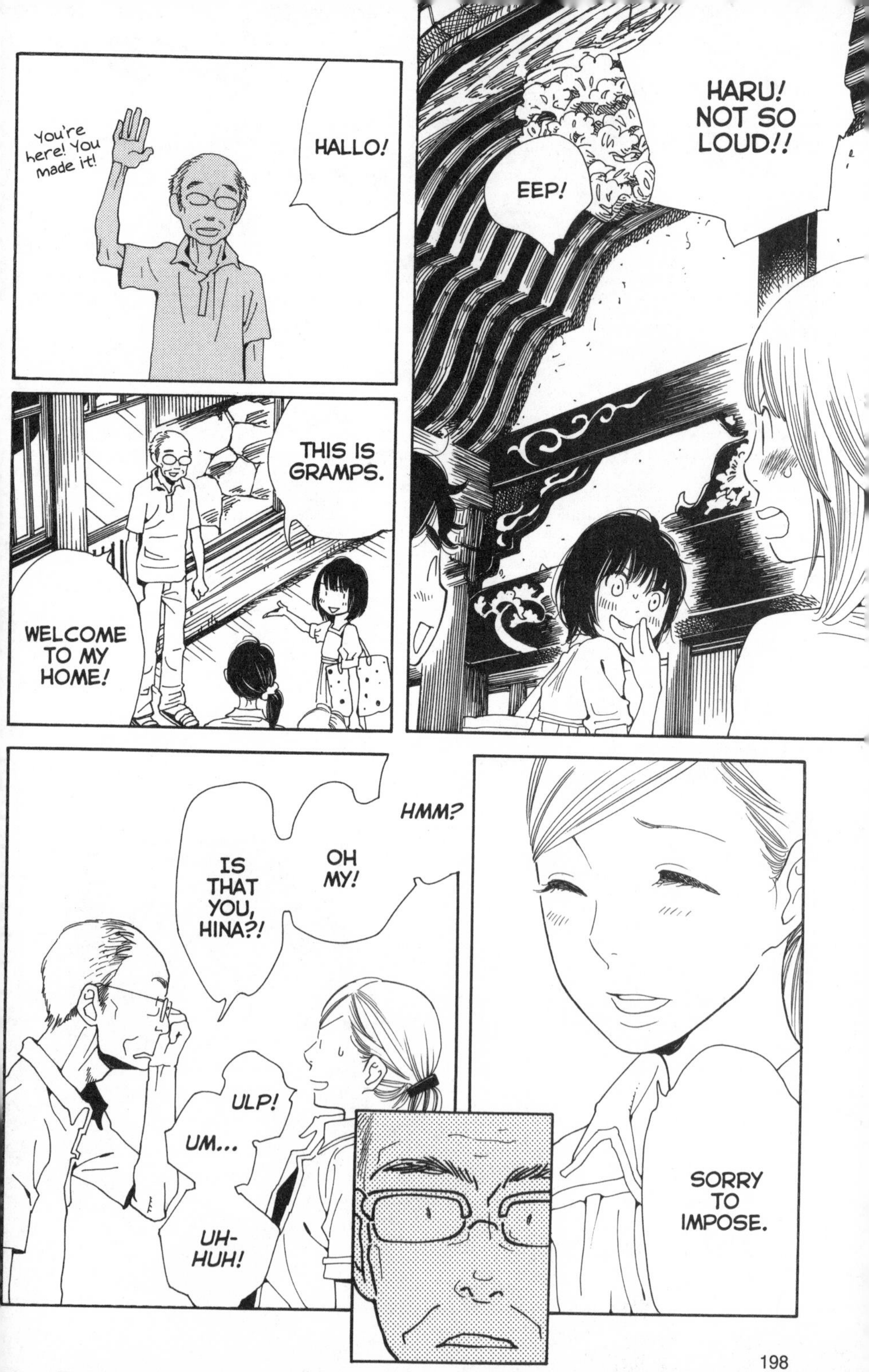
HARU! NOT SO LOUD!!
EEP!
HALLO!
You're here! You made it!
THIS IS GRAMPS.
WELCOME TO MY HOME!
SORRY TO IMPOSE.
HMM?
OH MY!
IS THAT YOU, HINA?!
ULP!
UM...
UH-HUH!

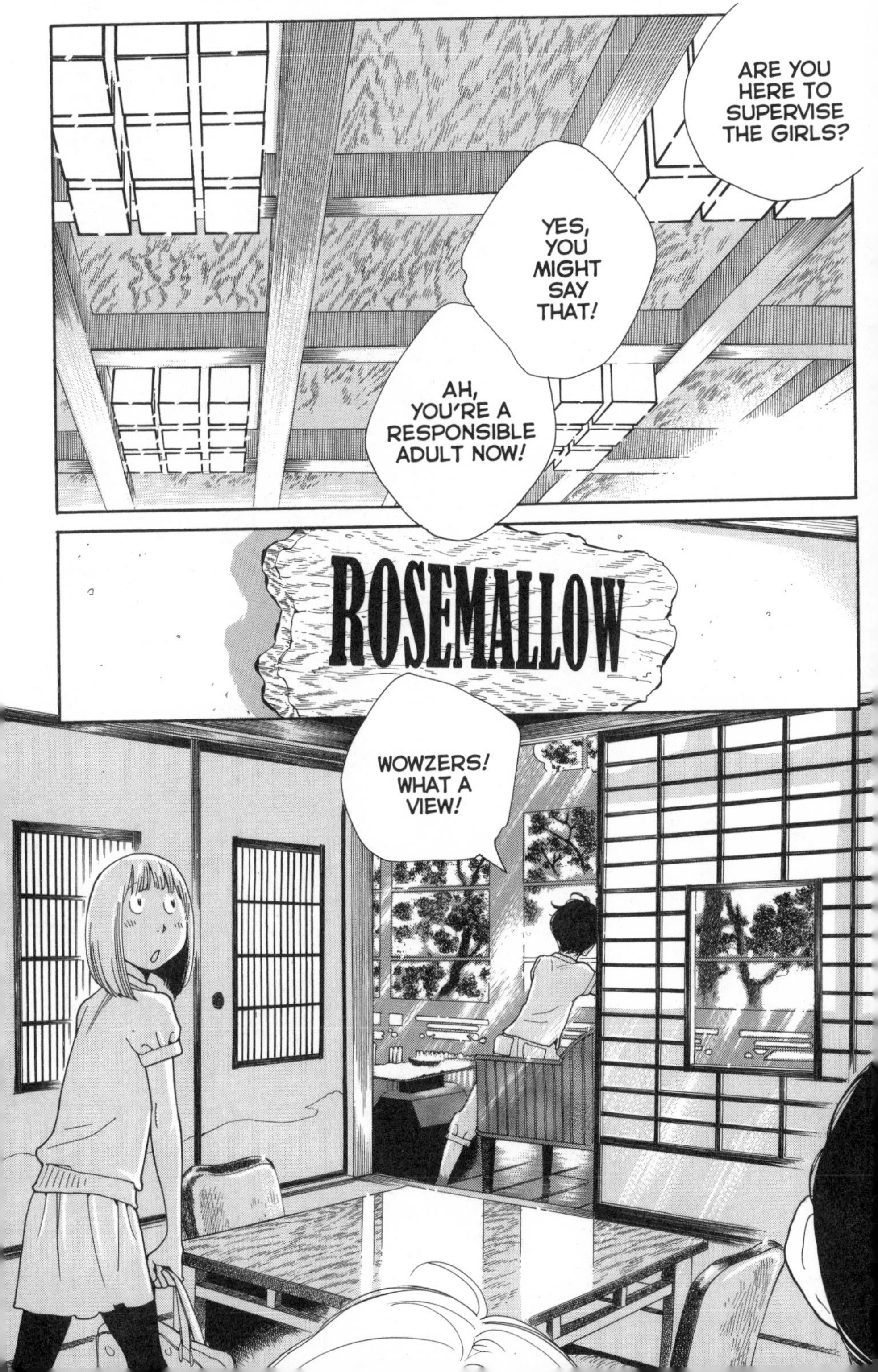
ARE YOU HERE TO SUPERVISE THE GIRLS?
YES, YOU MIGHT SAY THAT!
AH, YOU'RE A RESPONSIBLE ADULT NOW!
ROSEMALLOW
WOWZERS! WHAT A VIEW!

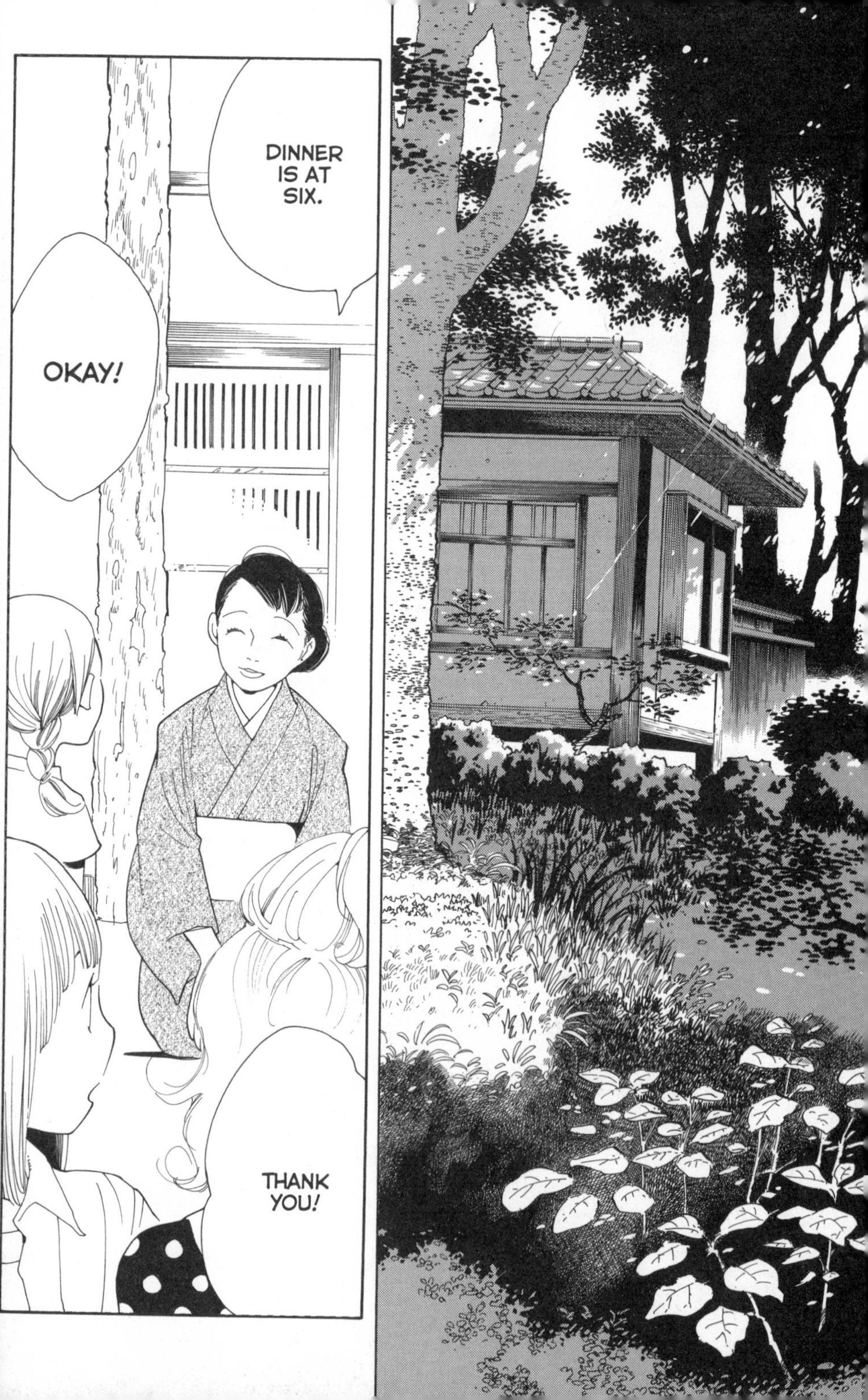
DINNER IS AT SIX.
OKAY!
THANK YOU!

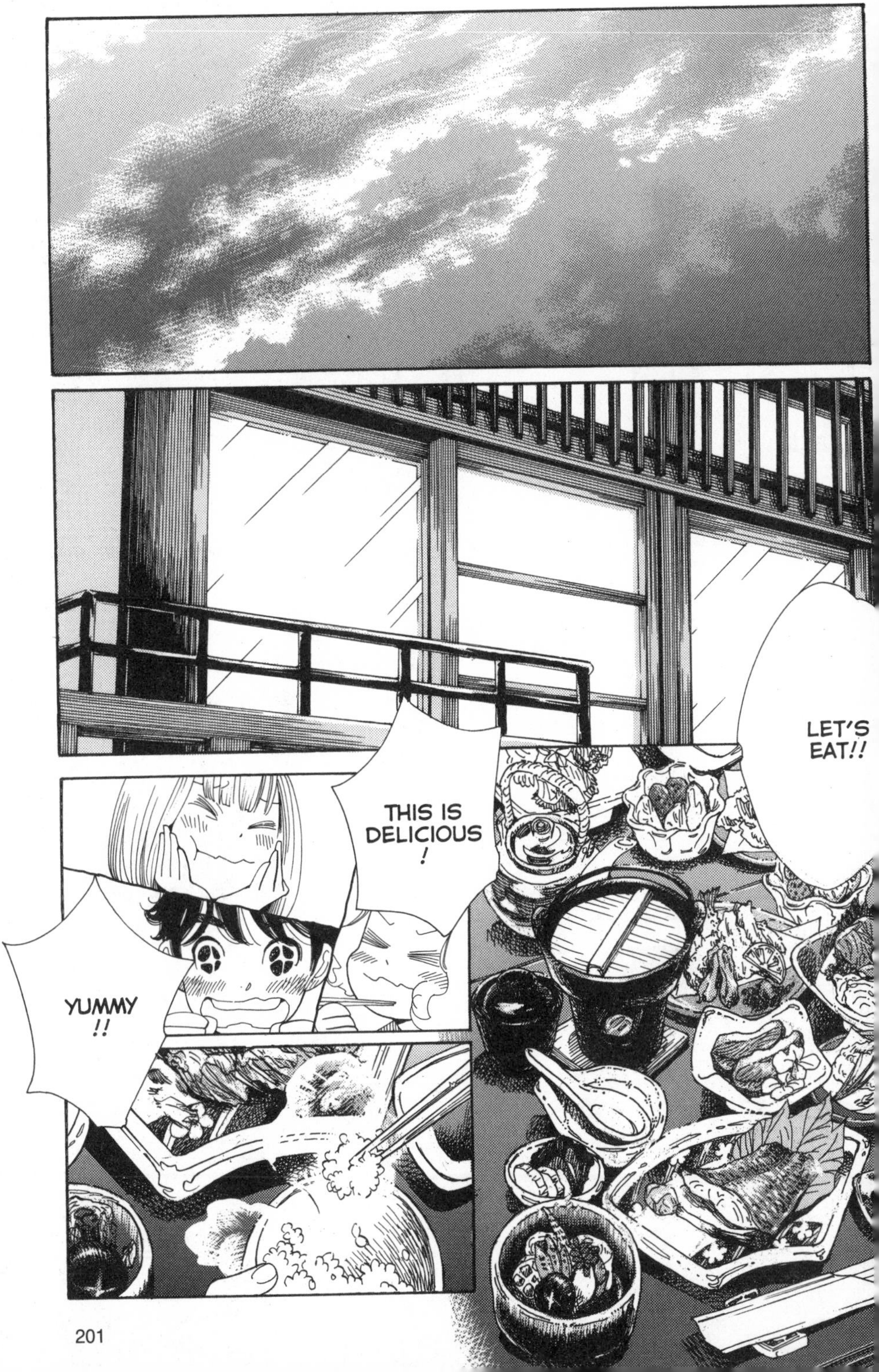
LET'S EAT!!
THIS IS DELICIOUS!
YUMMY!!

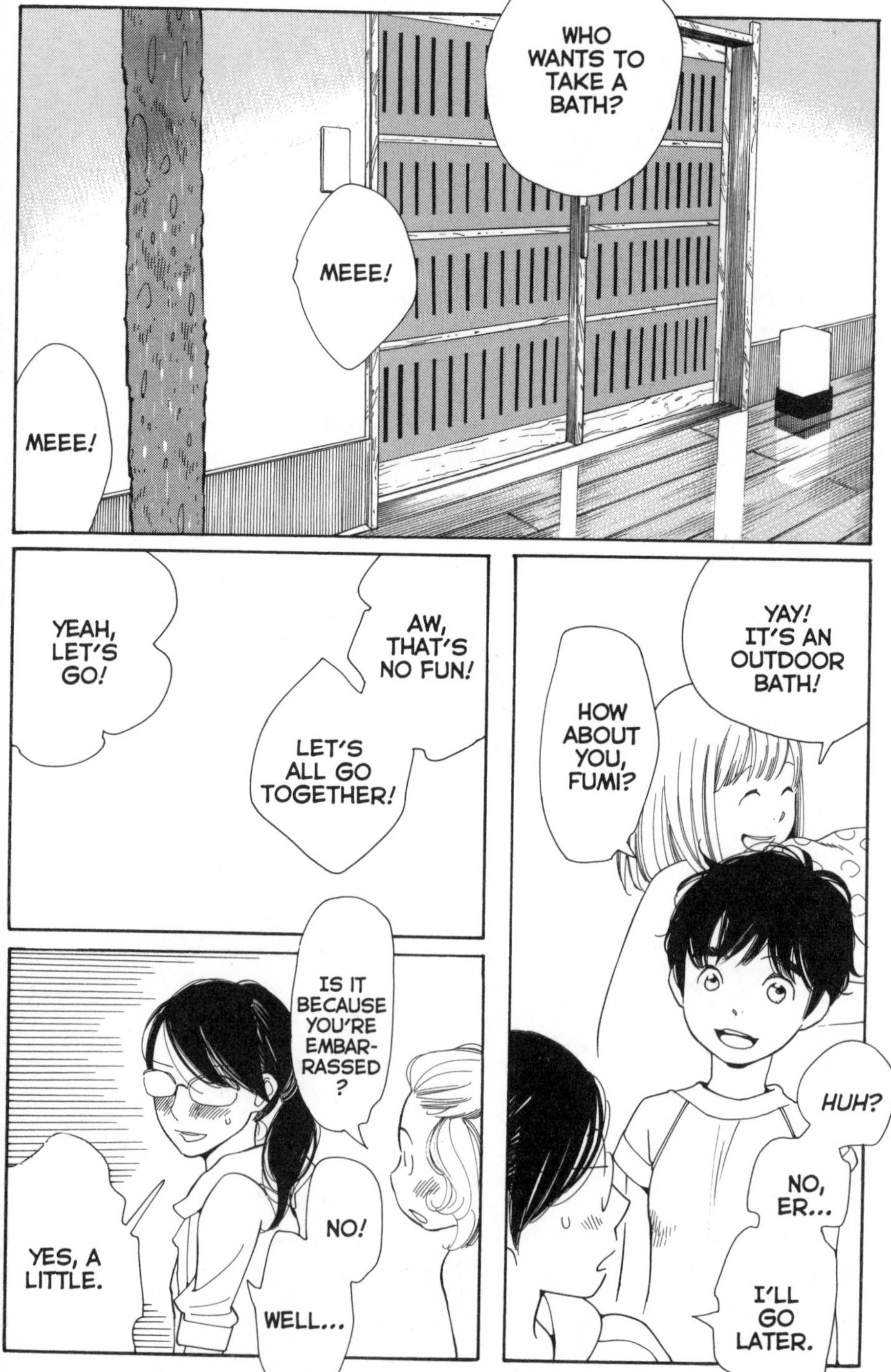
WHO WANTS TO TAKE A BATH?
MEEE!
MEEE!
YAY! IT'S AN OUTDOOR BATH!
HOW ABOUT YOU, FUMI?
HUH?
NO, ER...
I'LL GO LATER.
AW, THAT'S NO FUN!
LET'S ALL GO TOGETHER!
YEAH, LET'S GO!
IS IT BECAUSE YOU'RE EMBARRASSED?
NO!
WELL...
YES, A LITTLE.

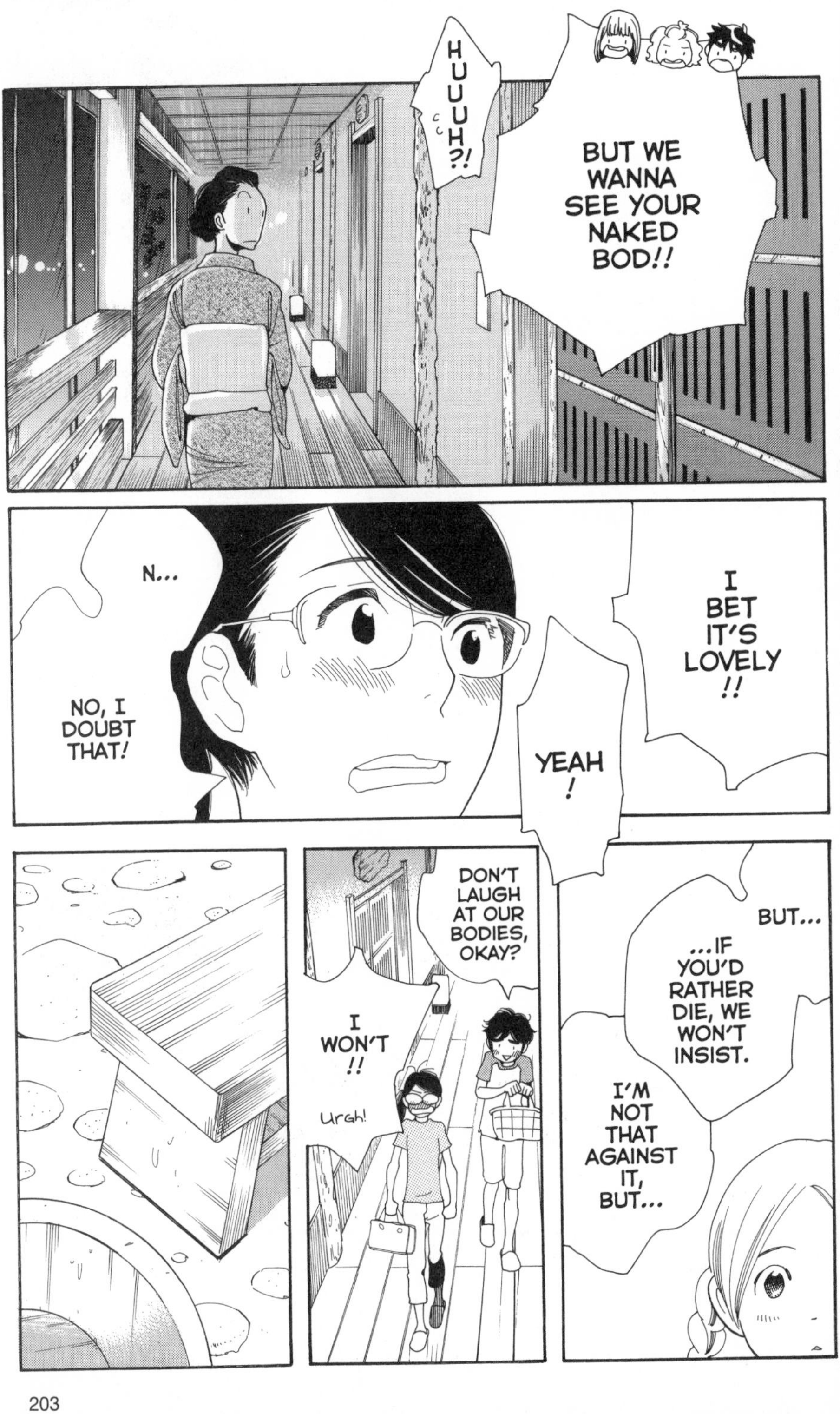

BUT WE WANNA SEE YOUR NAKED BOD!!
HUUUUH?!
I BET IT'S LOVELY!!
YEAH!
N...
NO, I DOUBT THAT!
BUT...
...IF YOU'D RATHER DIE, WE WON'T INSIST.
I'M NOT THAT AGAINST IT, BUT...
DON'T LAUGH AT OUR BODIES, OKAY?
I WON'T!!
Urgh!

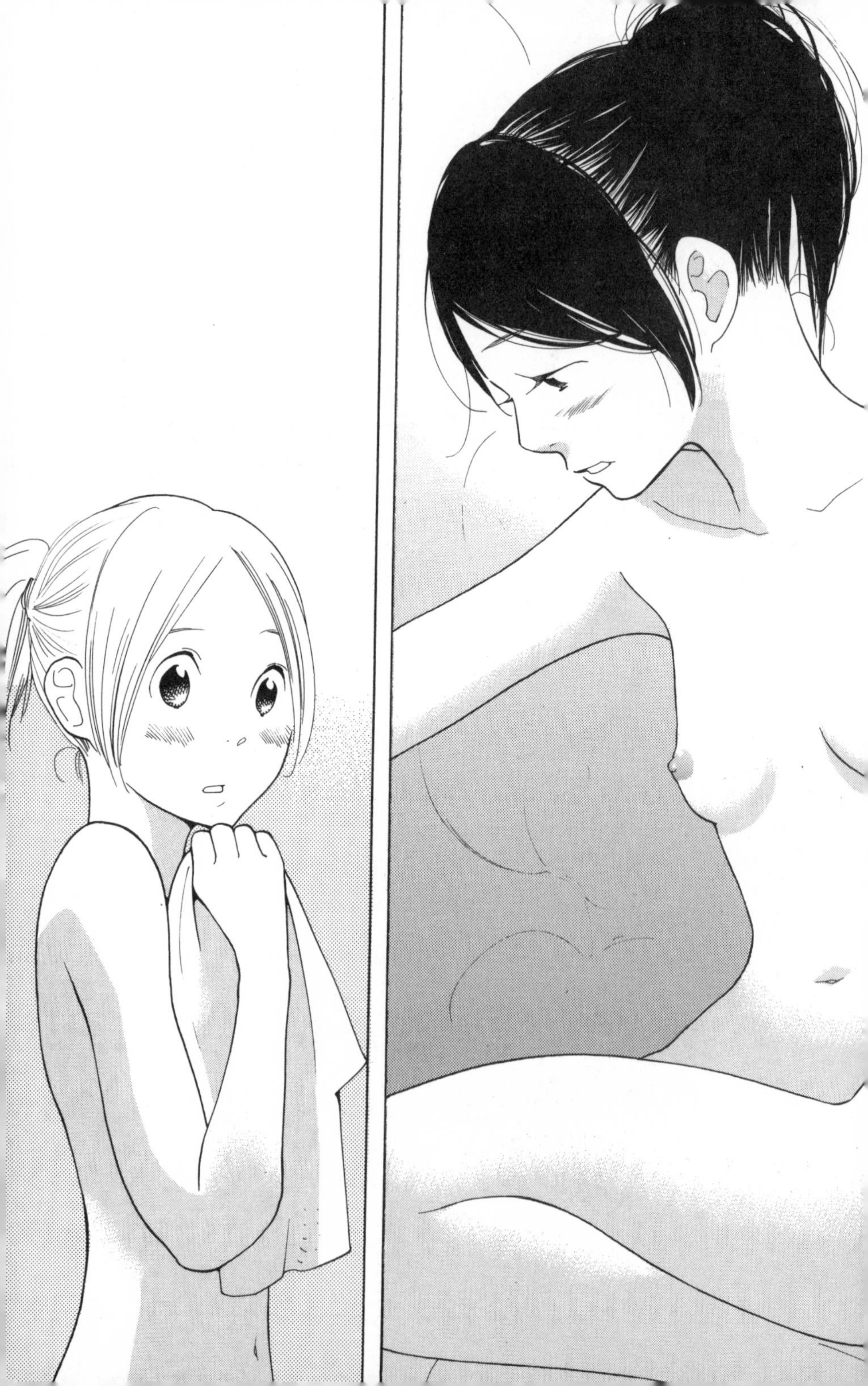

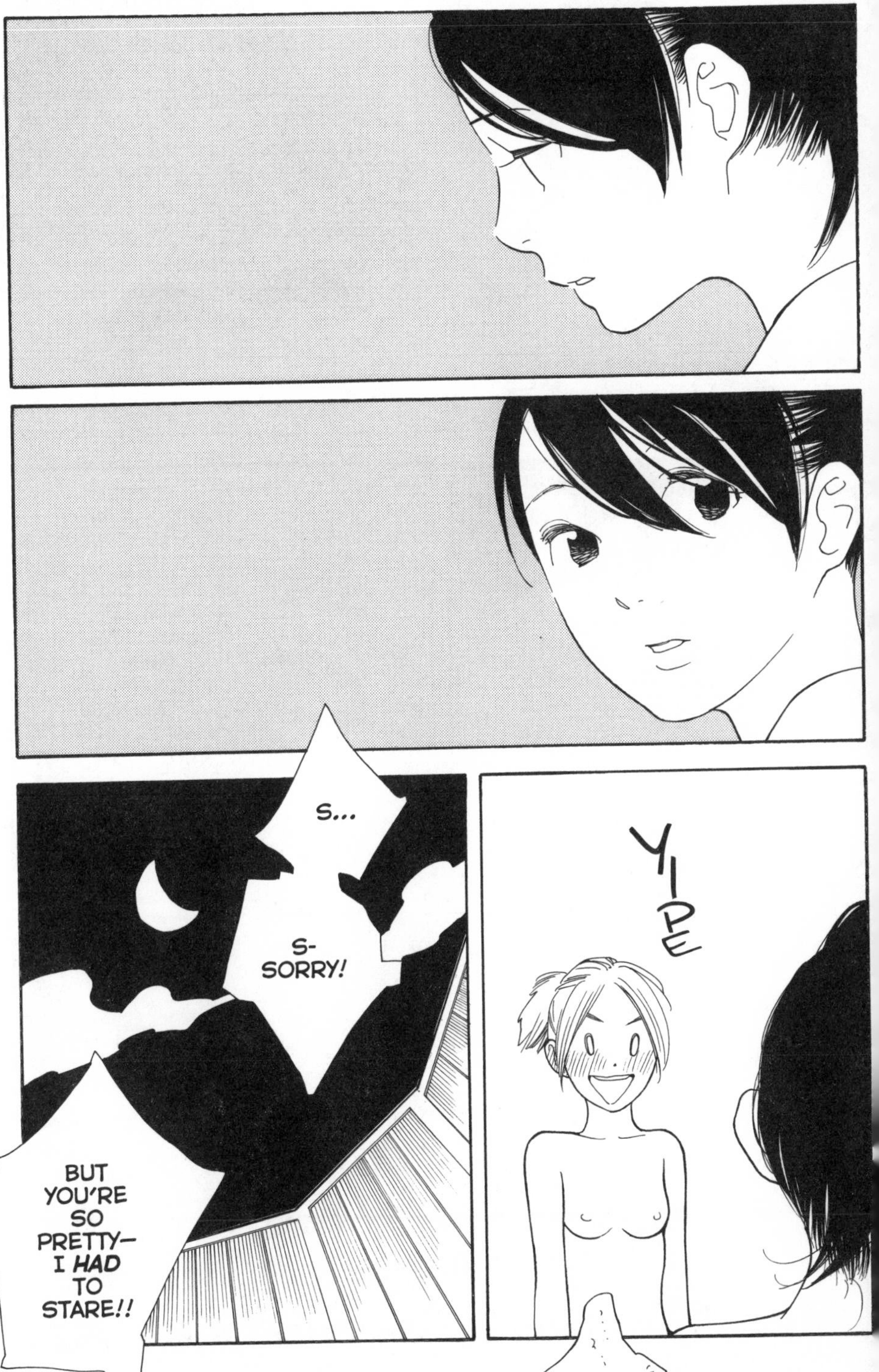
YIPE
S...
S-
SORRY!
BUT YOU'RE SO PRETTY— I *HAD* TO STARE!!

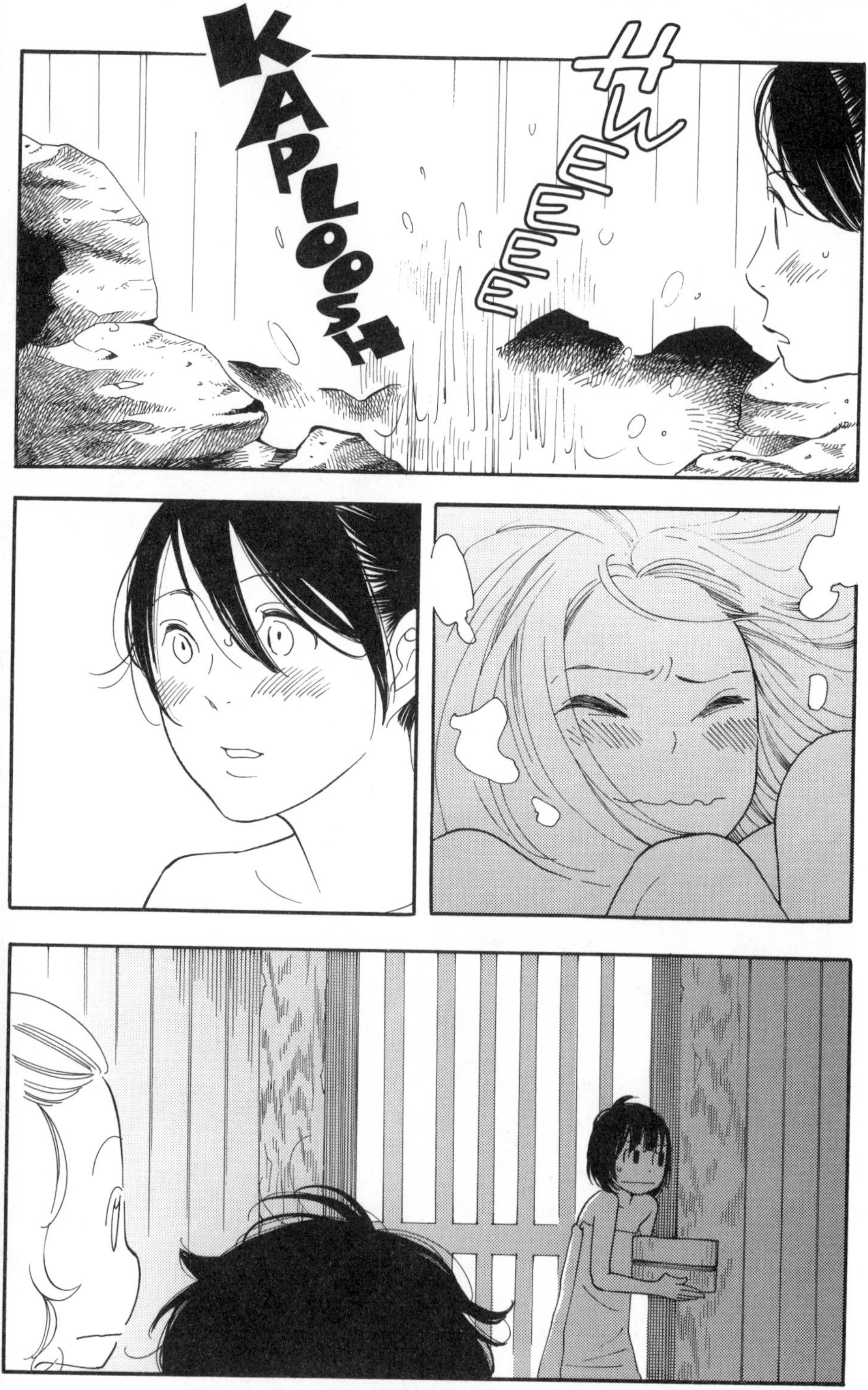
HUEEEEE
KAPLOOSH

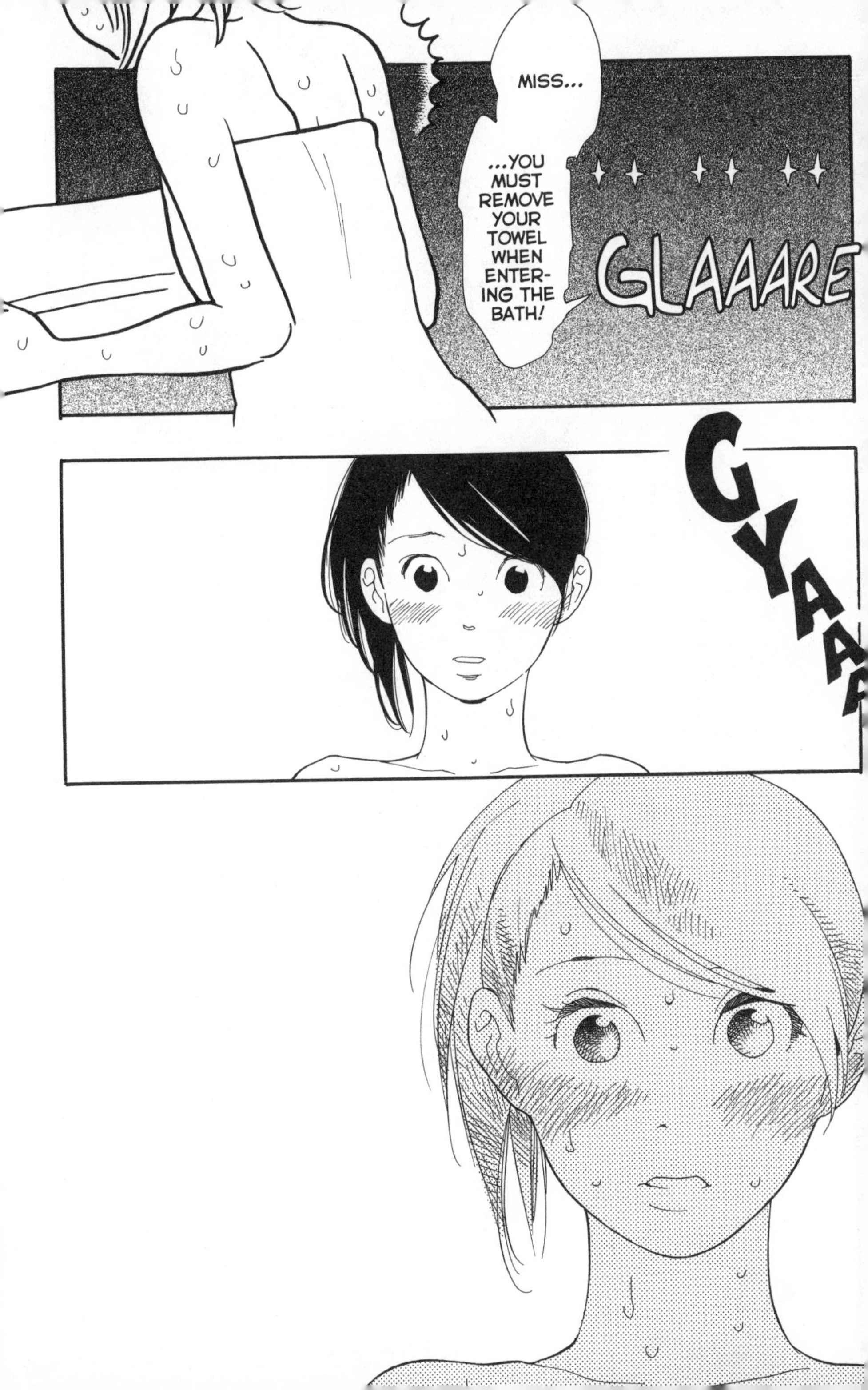
MISS...
...YOU MUST REMOVE YOUR TOWEL WHEN ENTER-ING THE BATH!
GLAAARE
GYAAA

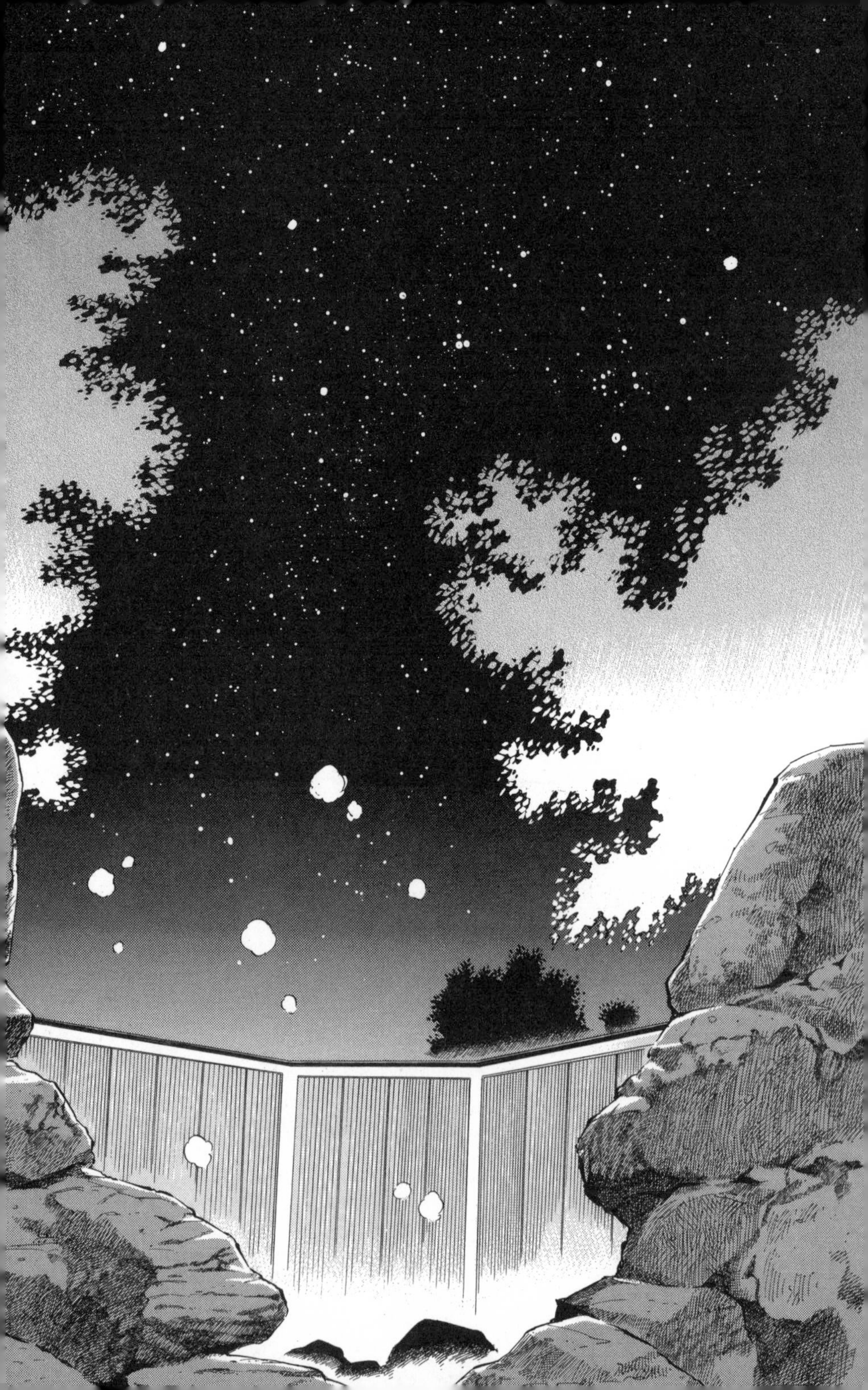

Sweet Blue Flowers

#33 The Door into Summer, Part 3

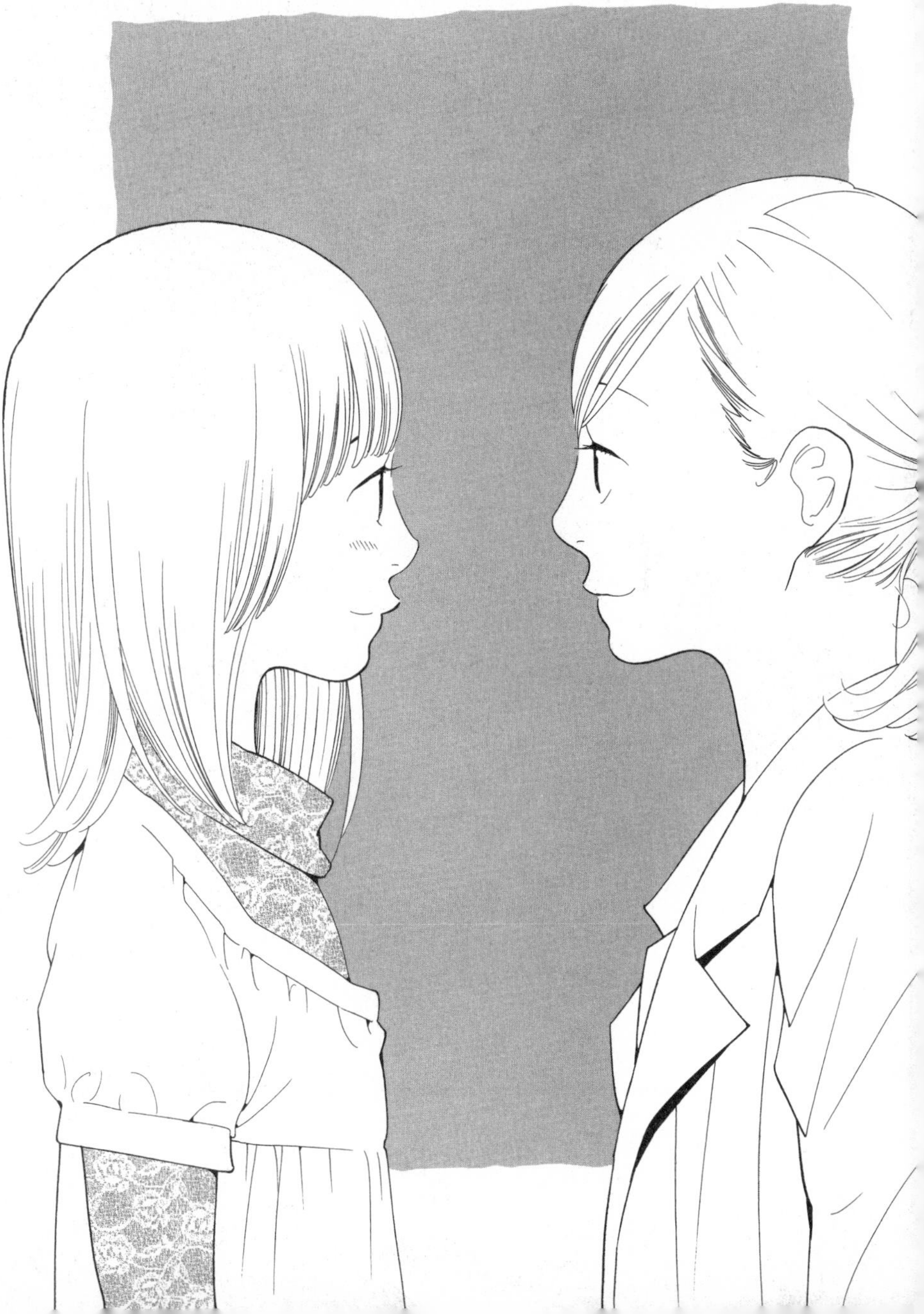

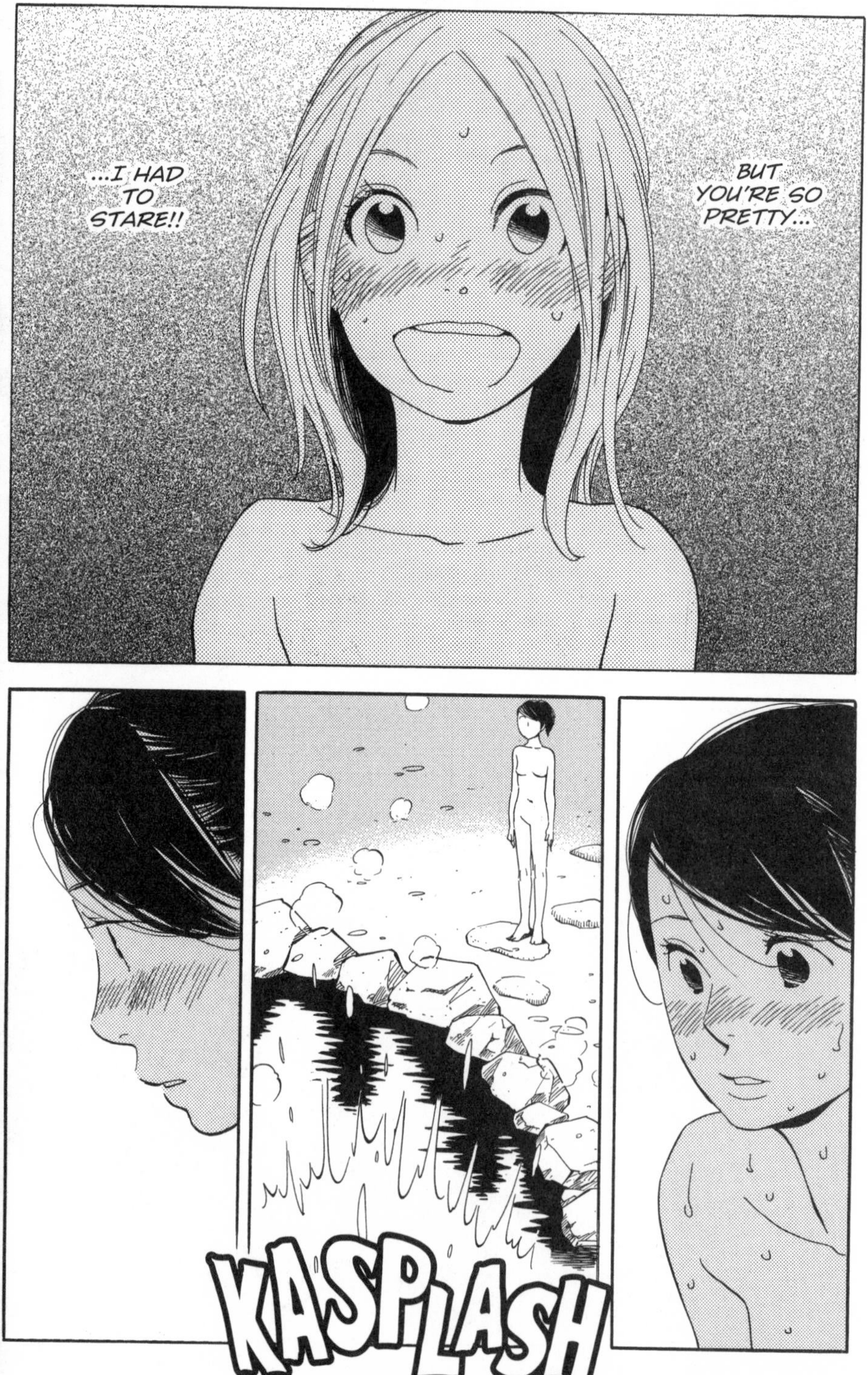
BUT YOU'RE SO PRETTY...
...I HAD TO STARE!!
KASPLASH

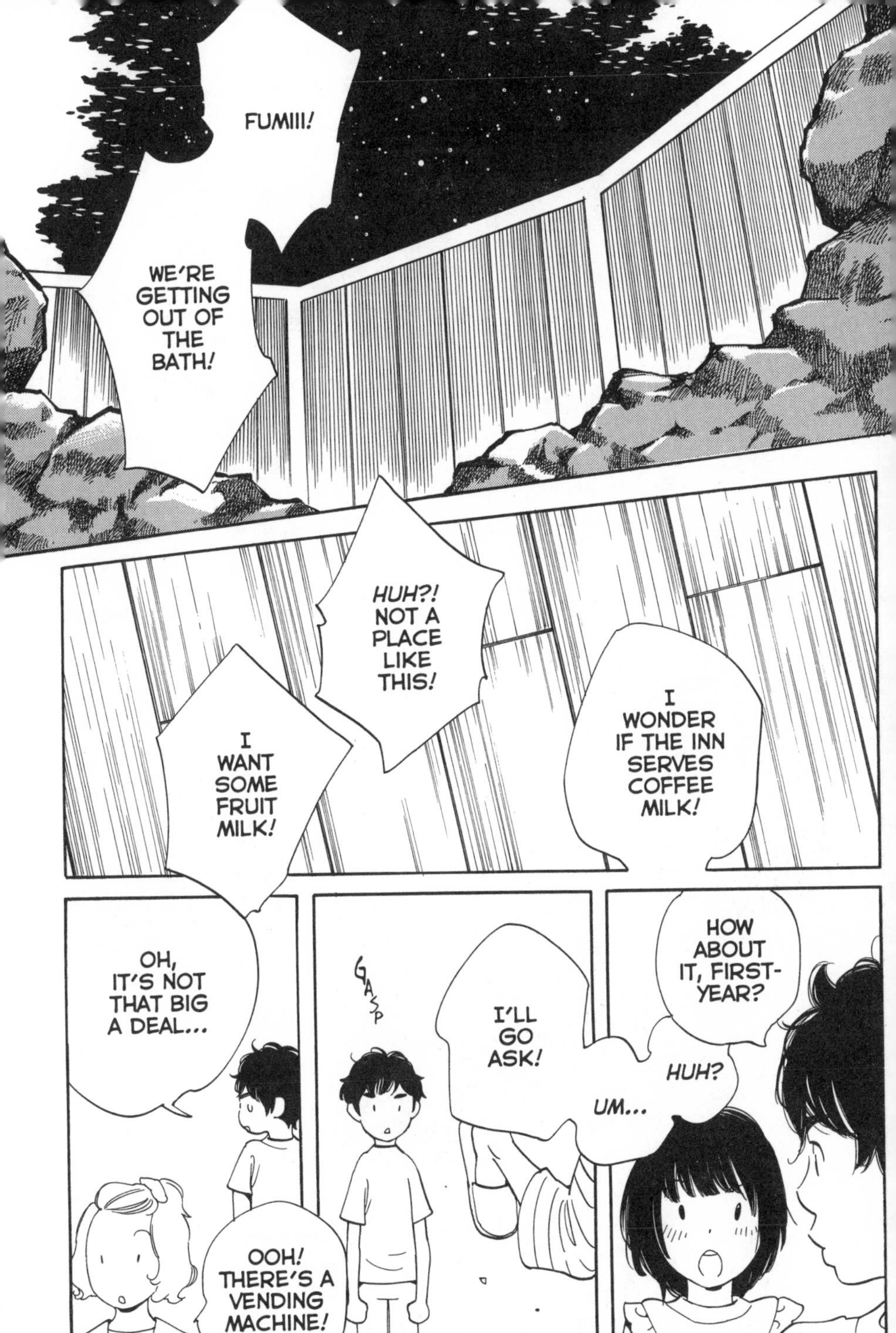
FUMIII!
WE'RE GETTING OUT OF THE BATH!
I WONDER IF THE INN SERVES COFFEE MILK!
HUH?! NOT A PLACE LIKE THIS!
I WANT SOME FRUIT MILK!
HOW ABOUT IT, FIRST-YEAR?
HUH?
UM...
I'LL GO ASK!
GASP
OH, IT'S NOT THAT BIG A DEAL...
OOH! THERE'S A VENDING MACHINE!

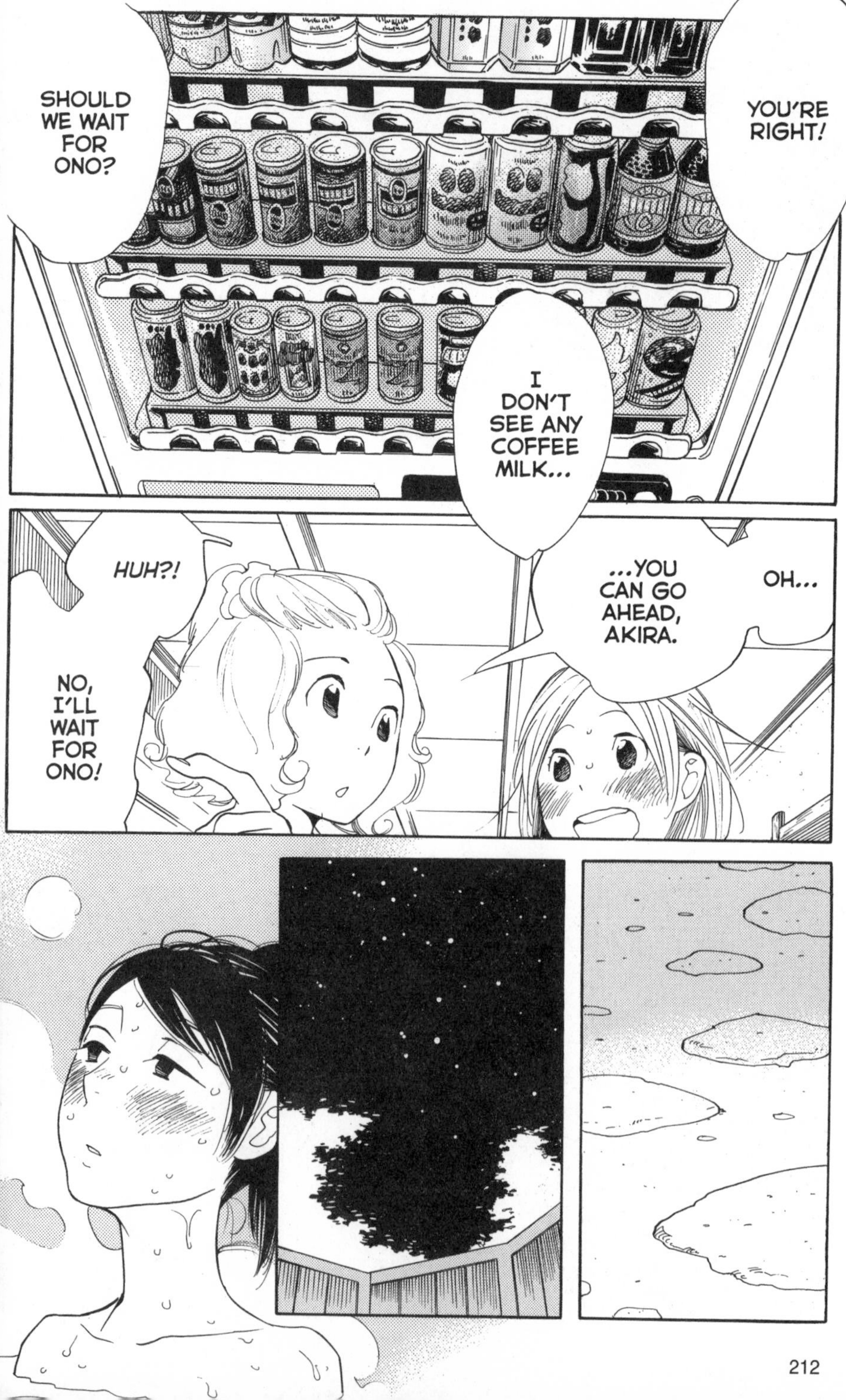
YOU'RE RIGHT!
SHOULD WE WAIT FOR ONO?
I DON'T SEE ANY COFFEE MILK...
OH...
...YOU CAN GO AHEAD, AKIRA.
HUH?!
NO, I'LL WAIT FOR ONO!

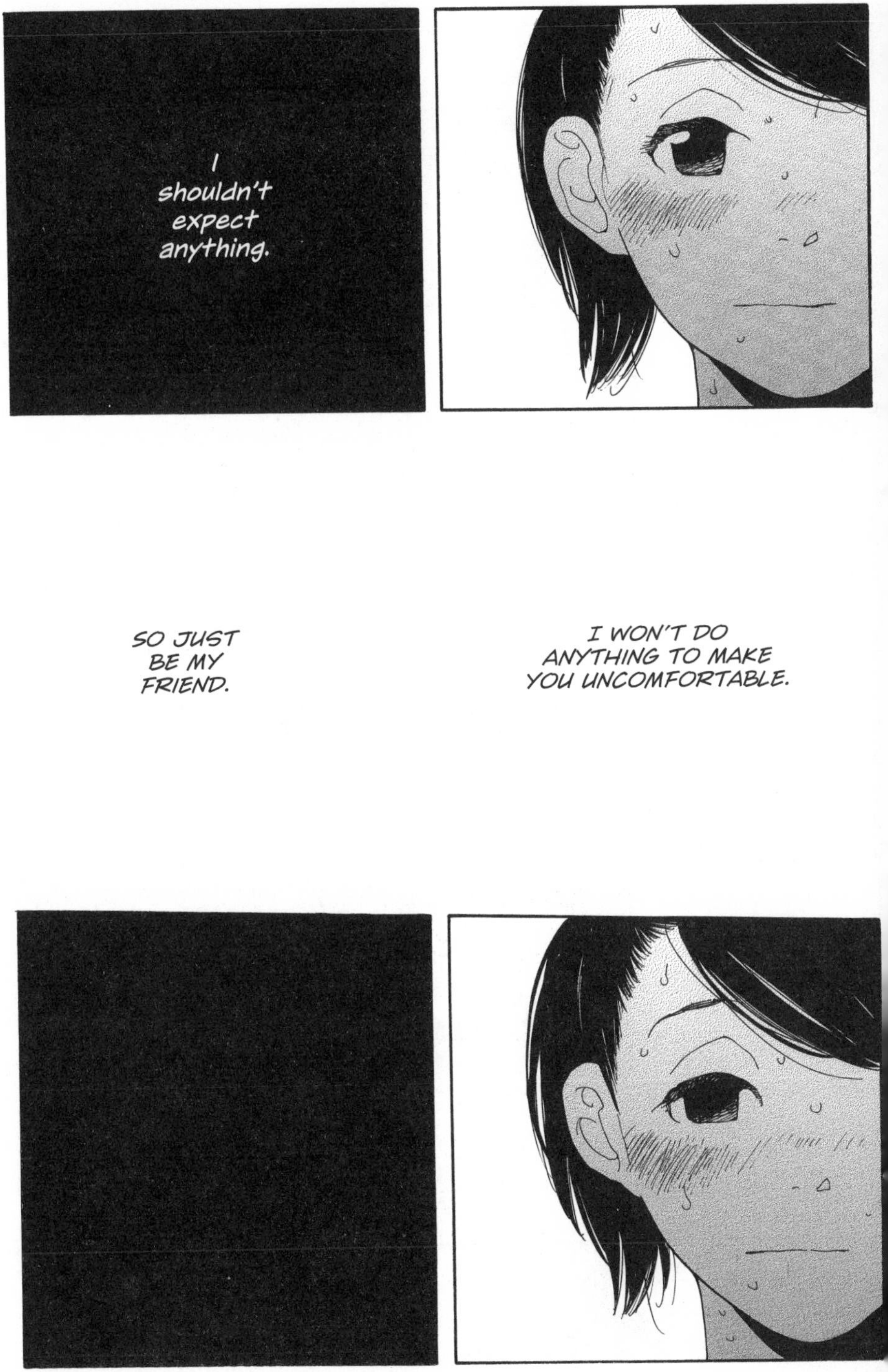
I shouldn't expect anything.
I WON'T DO ANYTHING TO MAKE YOU UNCOMFORTABLE.
SO JUST BE MY FRIEND.

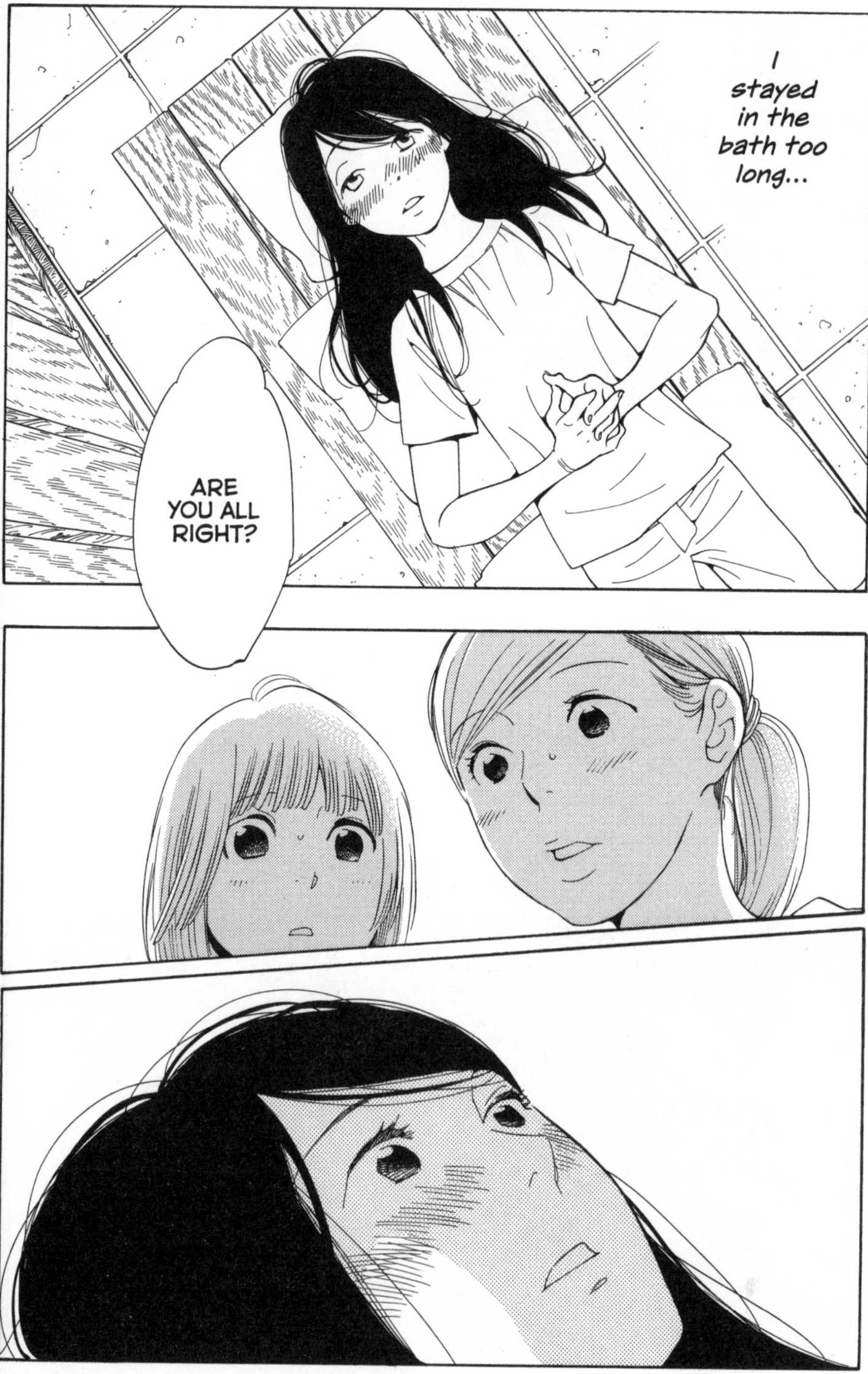
I stayed in the bath too long...
ARE YOU ALL RIGHT?

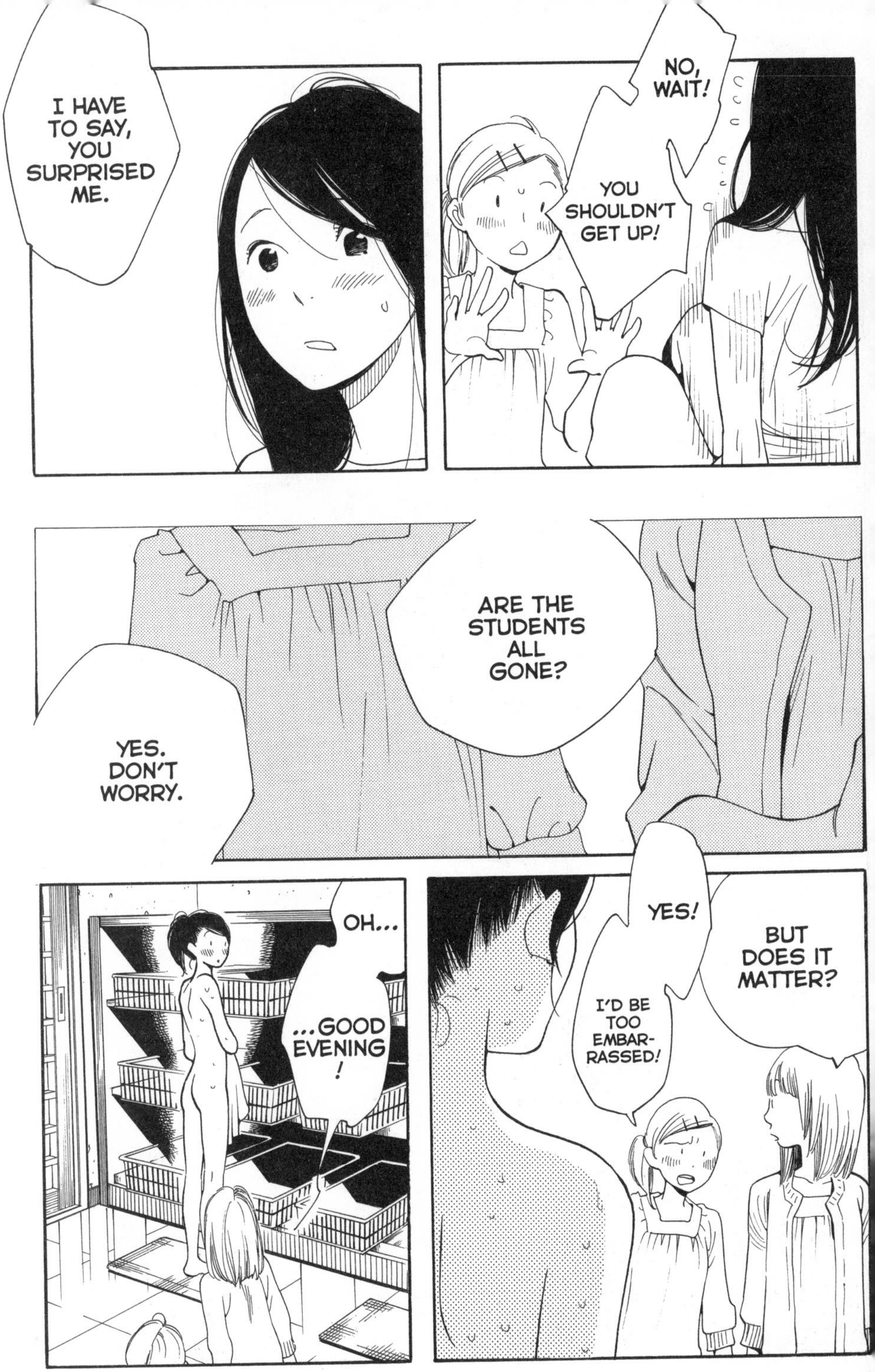
NO, WAIT!
YOU SHOULDN'T GET UP!
I HAVE TO SAY, YOU SURPRISED ME.
ARE THE STUDENTS ALL GONE?
YES. DON'T WORRY.
BUT DOES IT MATTER?
YES!
I'D BE TOO EMBARRASSED!
OH...
...GOOD EVENING!

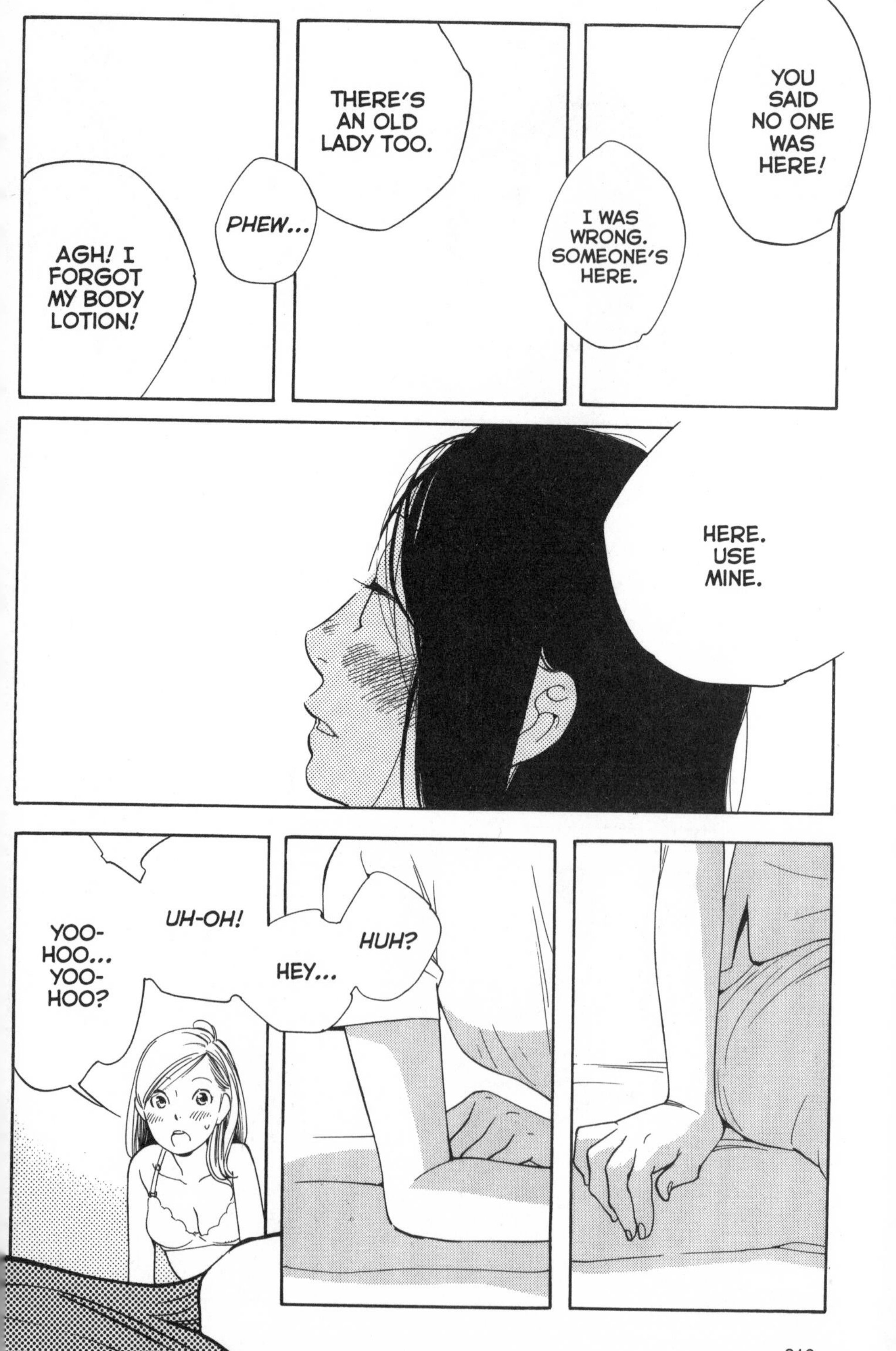
YOU SAID NO ONE WAS HERE!
I WAS WRONG. SOMEONE'S HERE.
THERE'S AN OLD LADY TOO.
PHEW...
AGH! I FORGOT MY BODY LOTION!
HERE. USE MINE.
HUH?
HEY...
UH-OH!
YOO-HOO... YOO-HOO?

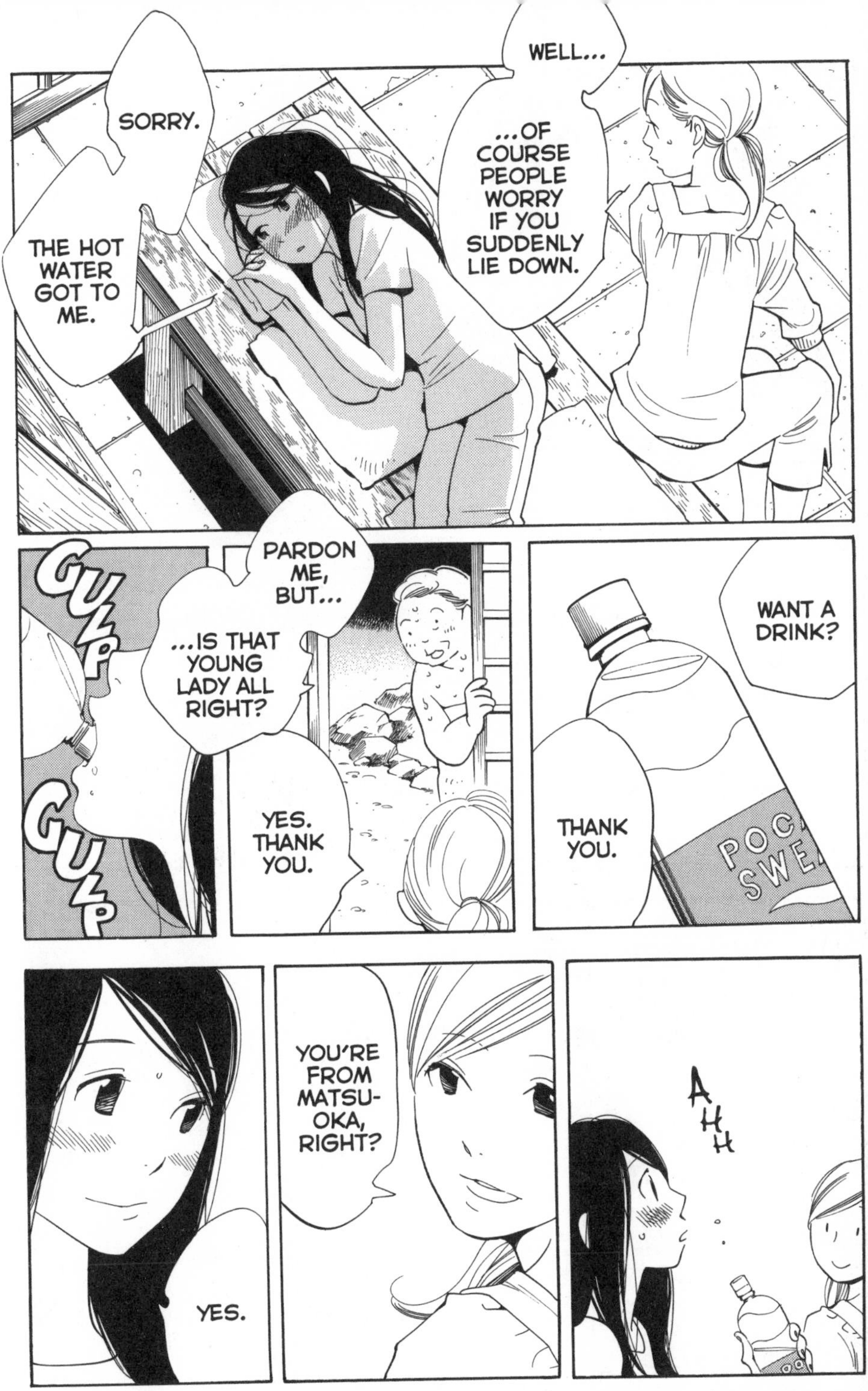
WELL...
...OF COURSE PEOPLE WORRY IF YOU SUDDENLY LIE DOWN.
SORRY.
THE HOT WATER GOT TO ME.
WANT A DRINK?
THANK YOU.
PARDON ME, BUT...
...IS THAT YOUNG LADY ALL RIGHT?
YES. THANK YOU.
GULP
GULP
AHH
YOU'RE FROM MATSU-OKA, RIGHT?
YES.

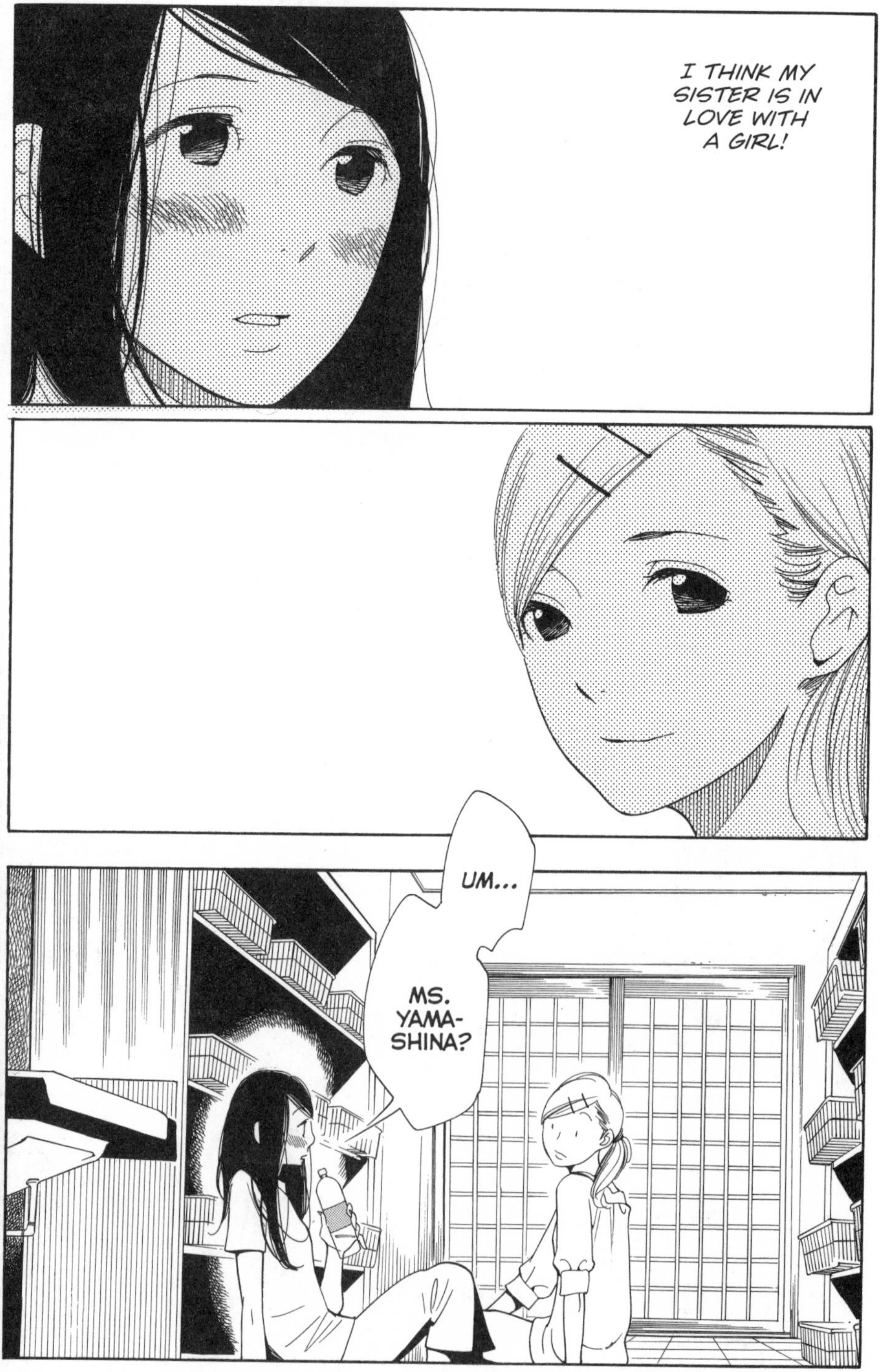
I THINK MY SISTER IS IN LOVE WITH A GIRL!
UM...
MS. YAMA-SHINA?

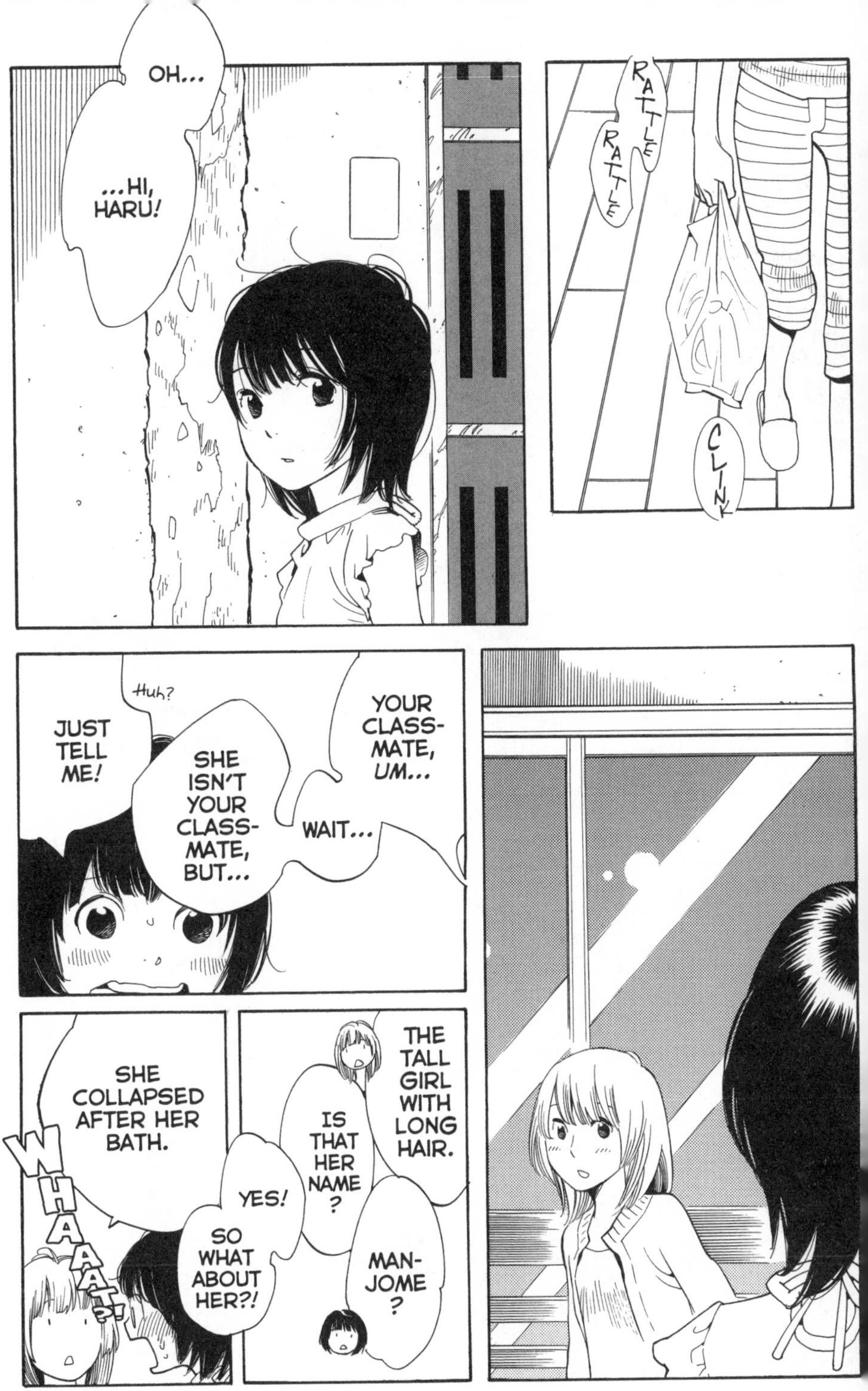
RATTLE
RATTLE
CLINK
OH...
...HI, HARU!
YOUR CLASSMATE, UM...
WAIT...
SHE ISN'T YOUR CLASSMATE, BUT...
Huh?
JUST TELL ME!
THE TALL GIRL WITH LONG HAIR.
IS THAT HER NAME?
MAN-JOME?
YES!
SO WHAT ABOUT HER?!
SHE COLLAPSED AFTER HER BATH.
WHAAAAT?!

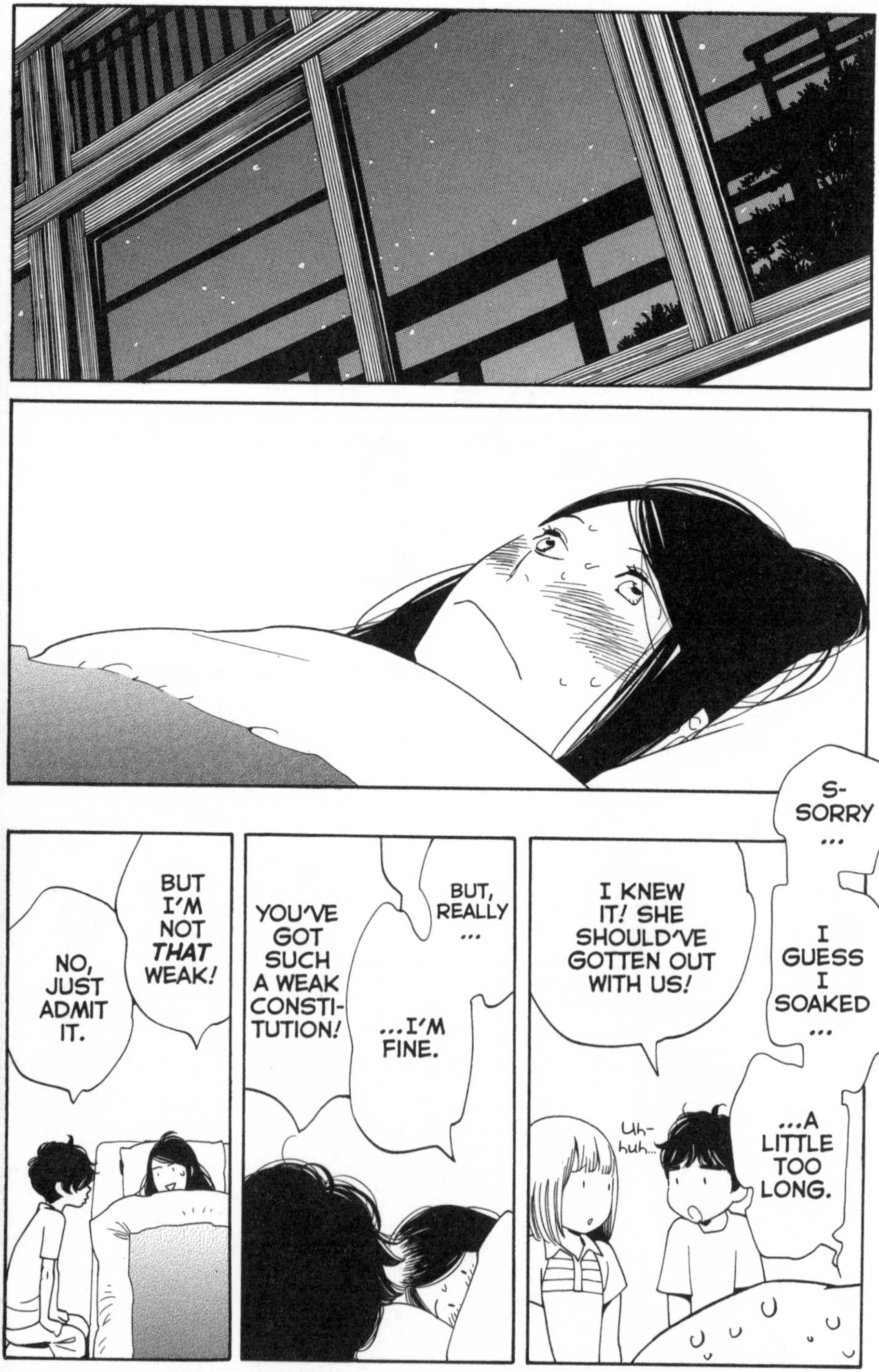
S-SORRY... I GUESS I SOAKED... ...A LITTLE TOO LONG.
I KNEW IT! SHE SHOULD'VE GOTTEN OUT WITH US!
Uh-huh...
BUT, REALLY...
YOU'VE GOT SUCH A WEAK CONSTI-TUTION!
...I'M FINE.
BUT I'M NOT *THAT* WEAK!
NO, JUST ADMIT IT.

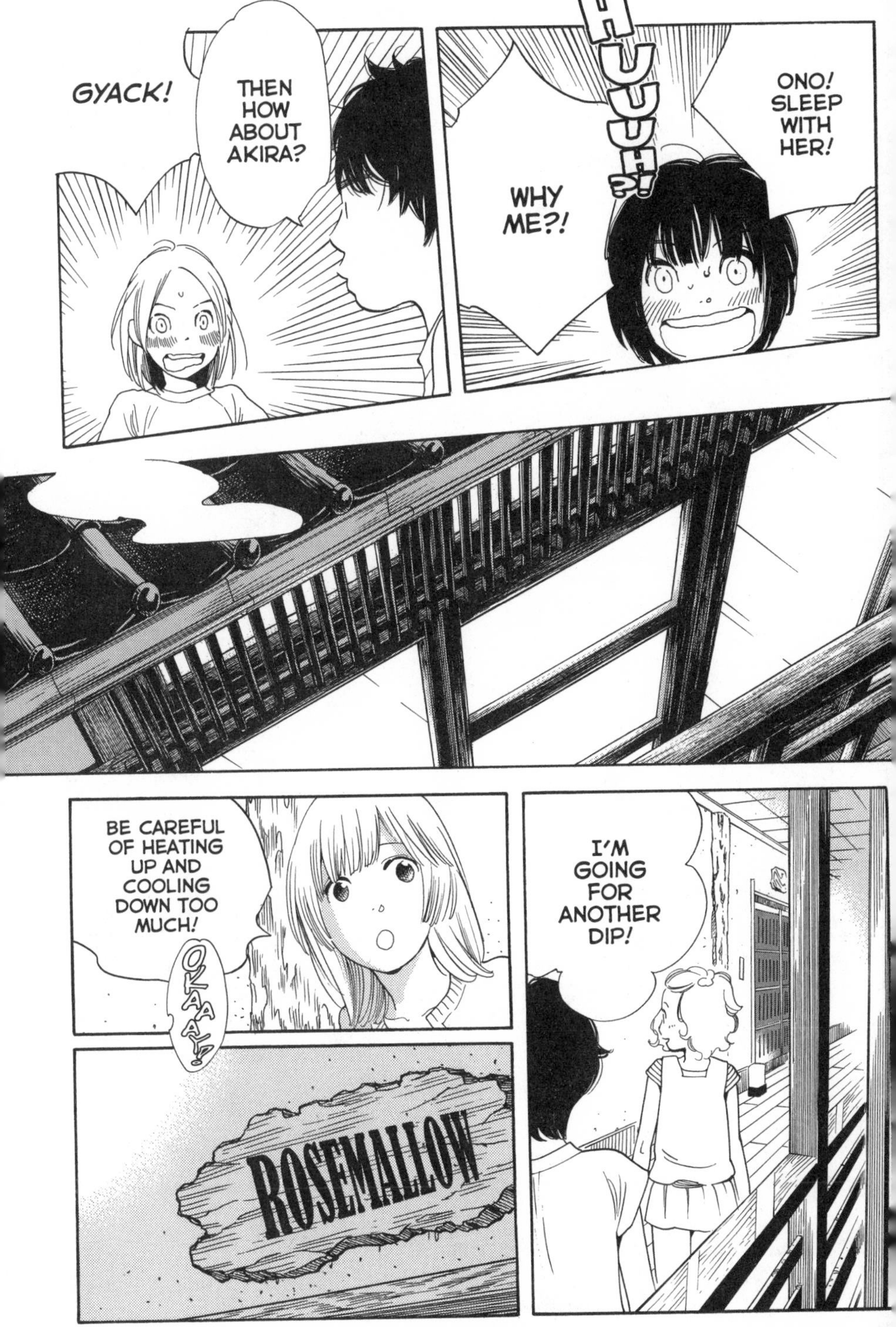
ONO! SLEEP WITH HER!
HUUUH?!
WHY ME?!
THEN HOW ABOUT AKIRA?
GYACK!
I'M GOING FOR ANOTHER DIP!
BE CAREFUL OF HEATING UP AND COOLING DOWN TOO MUCH!
OKAAAY!
ROSEMALLOW

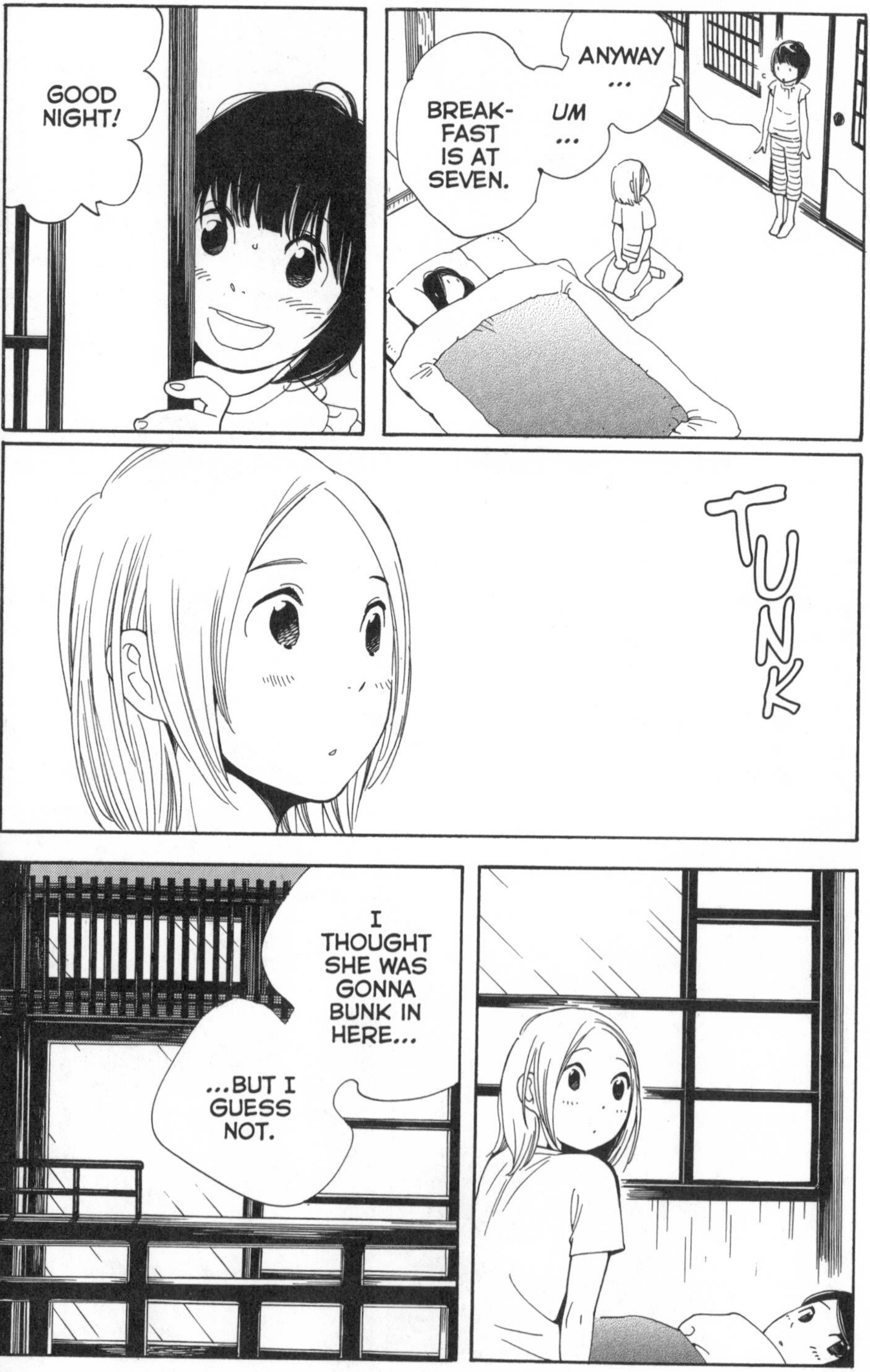
ANYWAY ... UM ... BREAKFAST IS AT SEVEN.
GOOD NIGHT!
TUNK
I THOUGHT SHE WAS GONNA BUNK IN HERE...
...BUT I GUESS NOT.

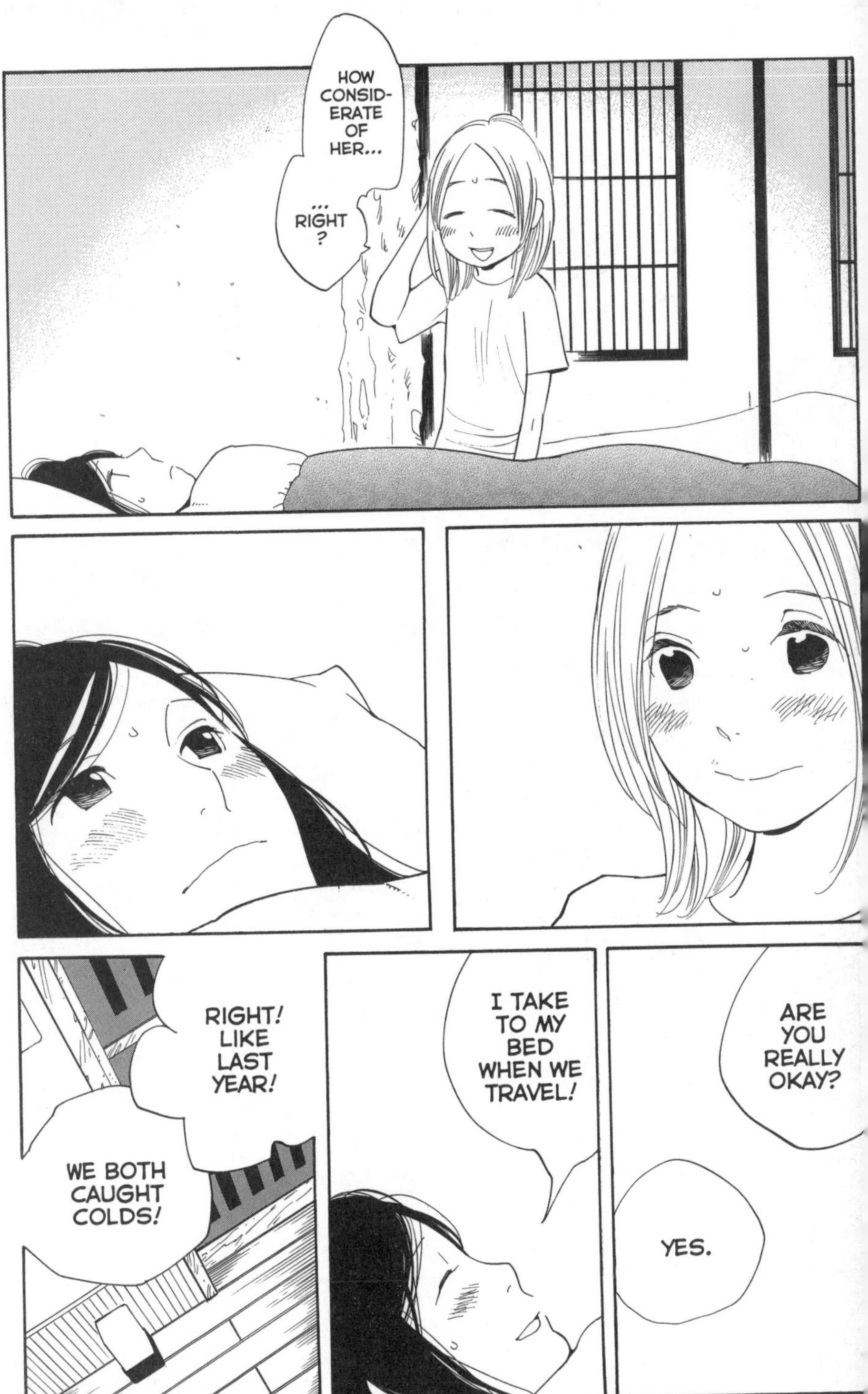
HOW CONSIDERATE OF HER...
...RIGHT?
ARE YOU REALLY OKAY?
YES.
I TAKE TO MY BED WHEN WE TRAVEL!
RIGHT! LIKE LAST YEAR!
WE BOTH CAUGHT COLDS!

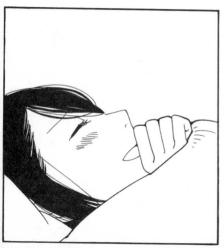

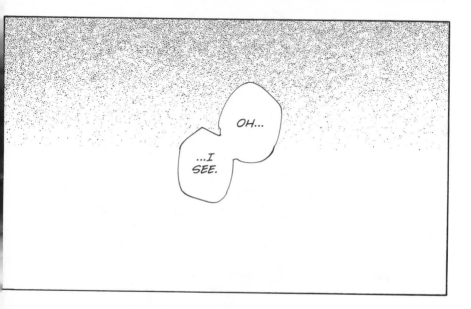

OH...

...I SEE.

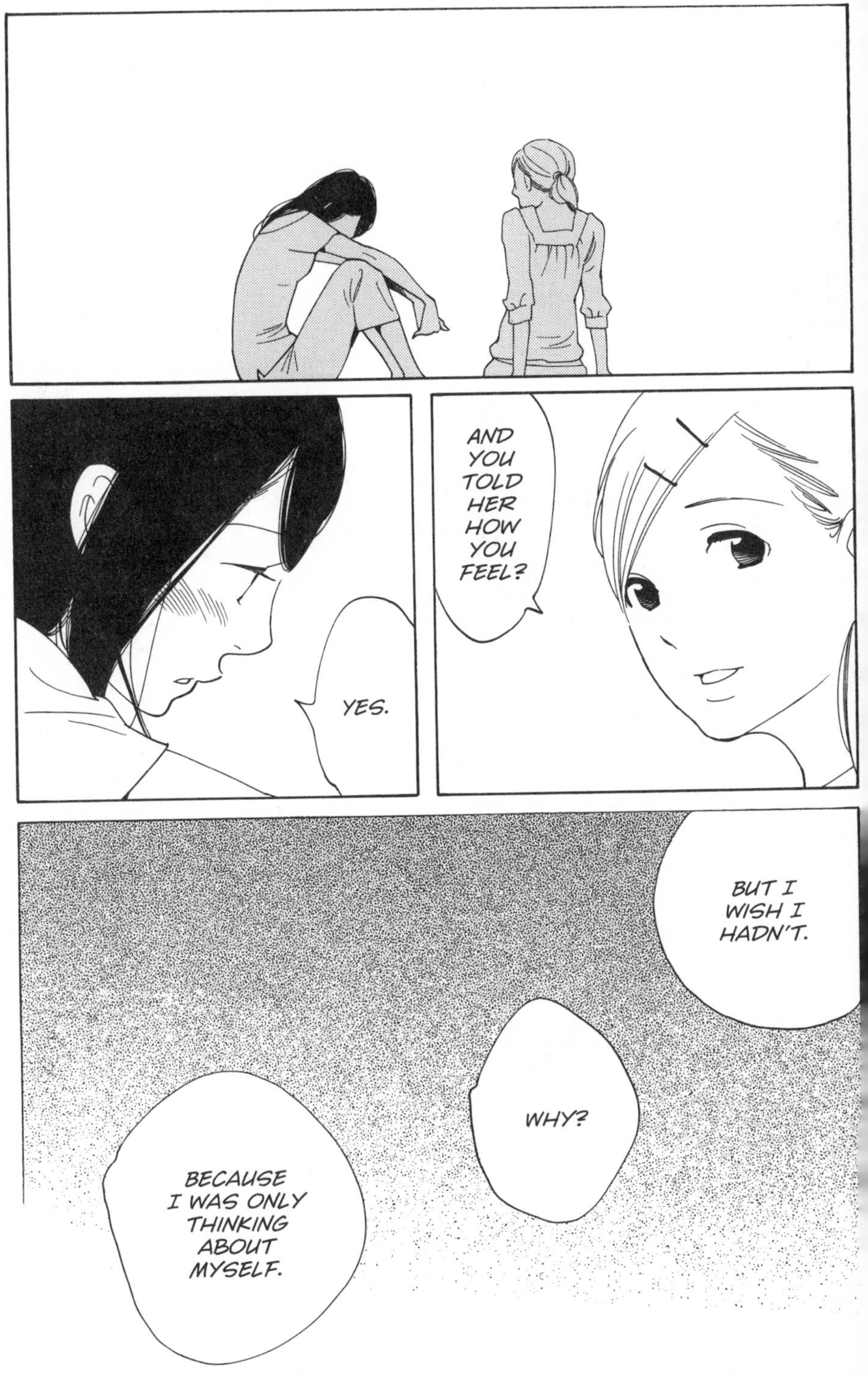
AND YOU TOLD HER HOW YOU FEEL?
YES.
BUT I WISH I HADN'T.
WHY?
BECAUSE I WAS ONLY THINKING ABOUT MYSELF.

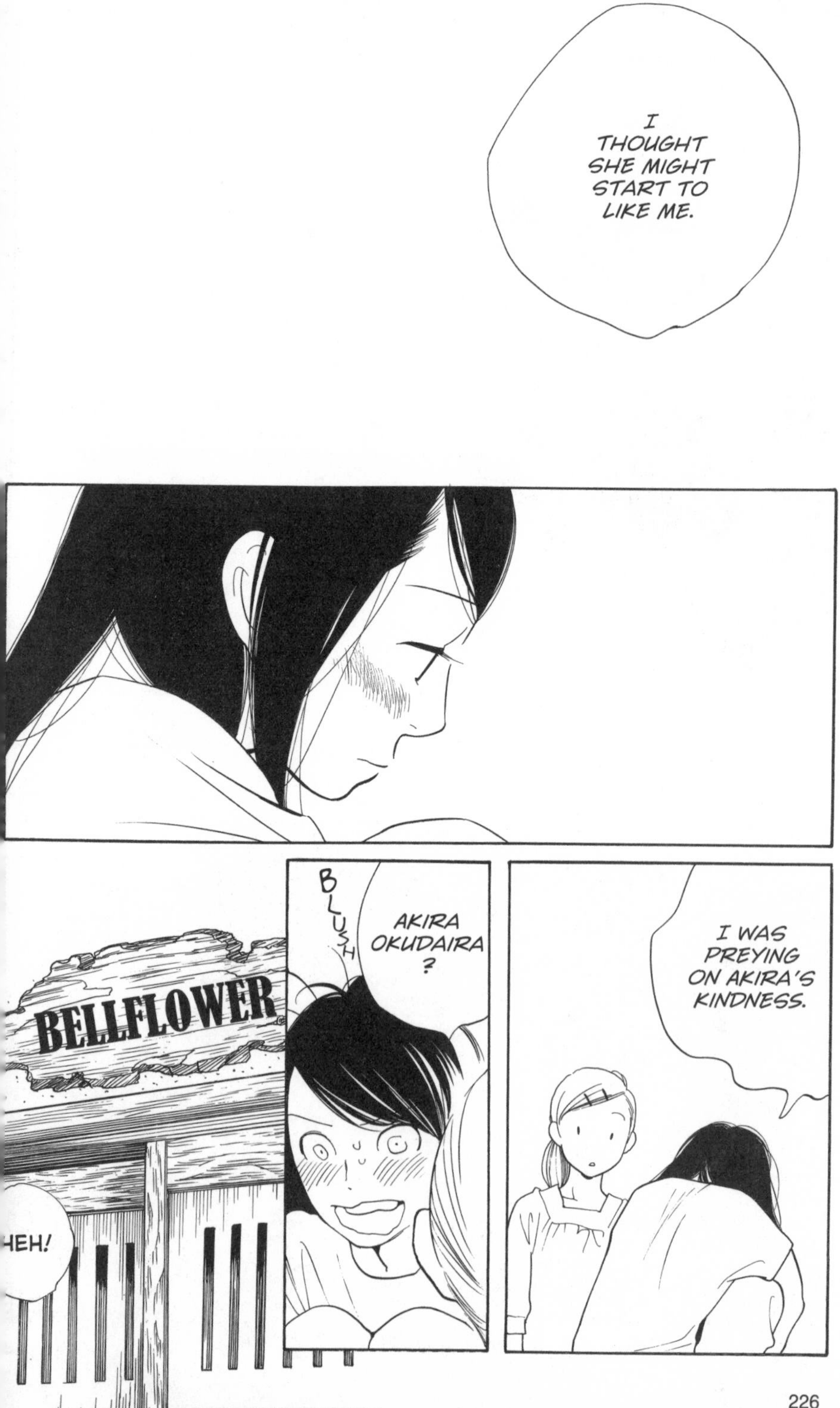
I THOUGHT SHE MIGHT START TO LIKE ME.
I WAS PREYING ON AKIRA'S KINDNESS.
BLUSH
AKIRA OKUDAIRA?
BELLFLOWER
HEH!

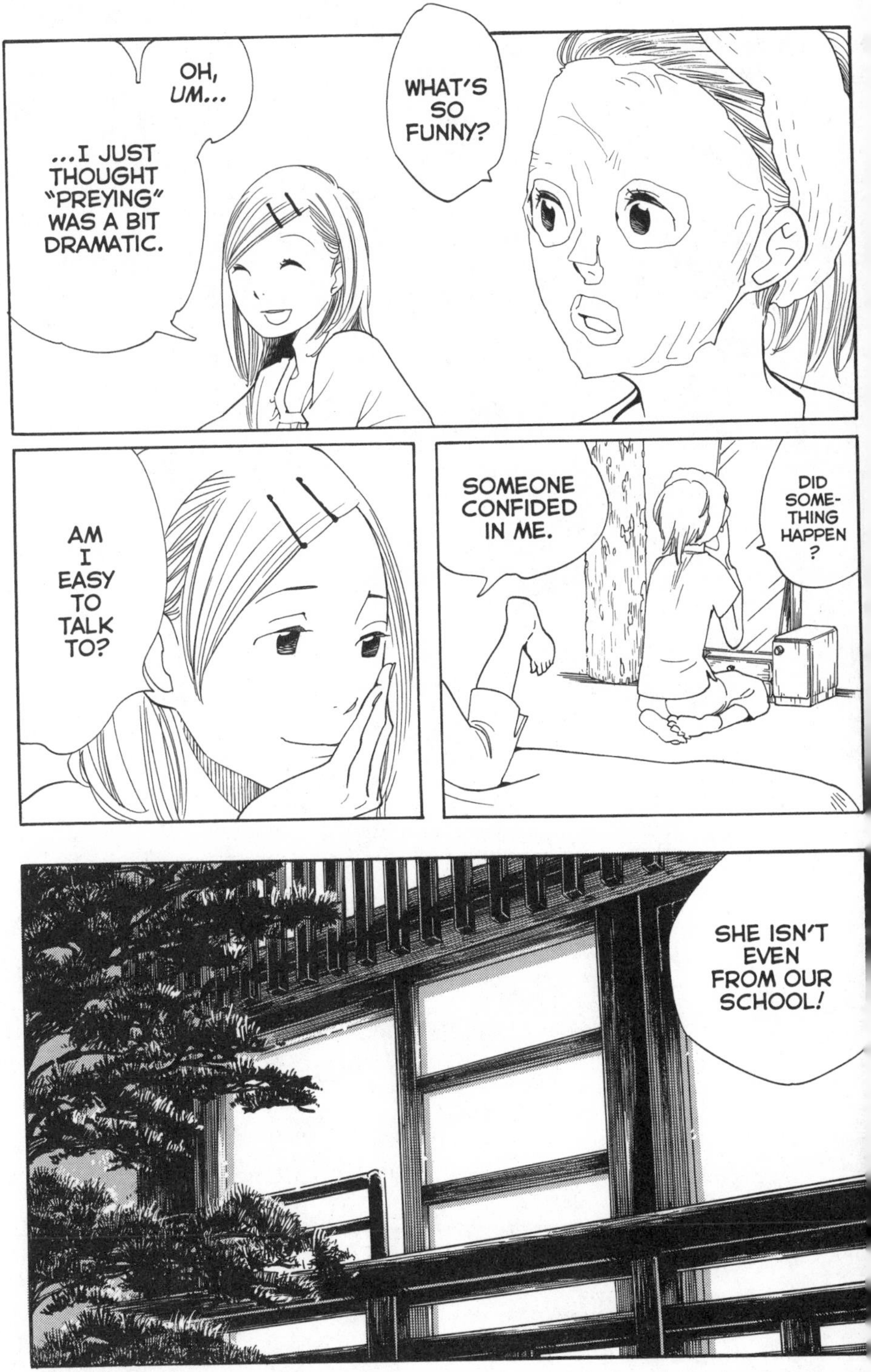
WHAT'S SO FUNNY?
OH, UM...
...I JUST THOUGHT "PREYING" WAS A BIT DRAMATIC.
DID SOMETHING HAPPEN?
SOMEONE CONFIDED IN ME.
AM I EASY TO TALK TO?
SHE ISN'T EVEN FROM OUR SCHOOL!

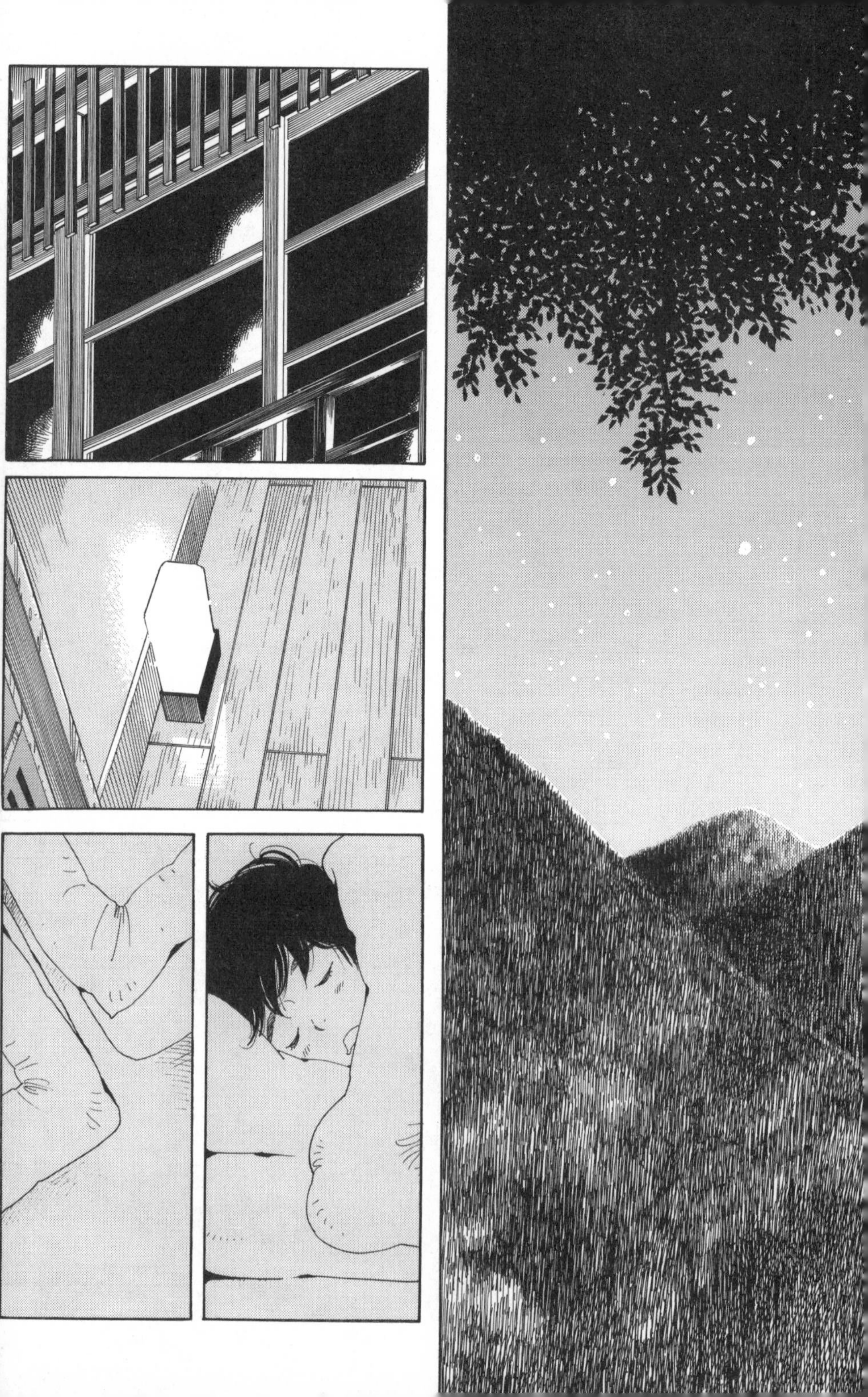

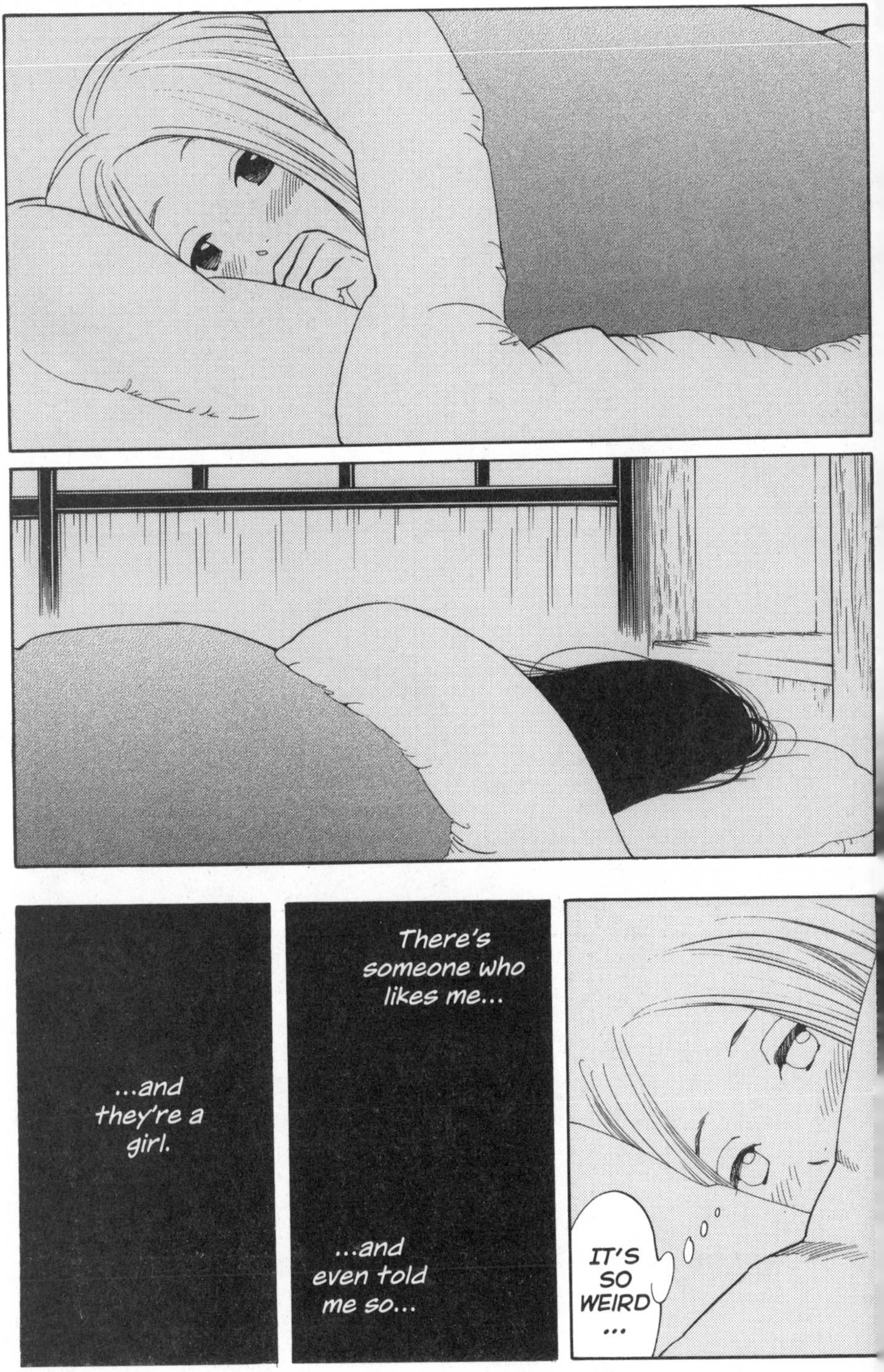
IT'S SO WEIRD ...
There's someone who likes me...
...and even told me so...
...and they're a girl.

MM...

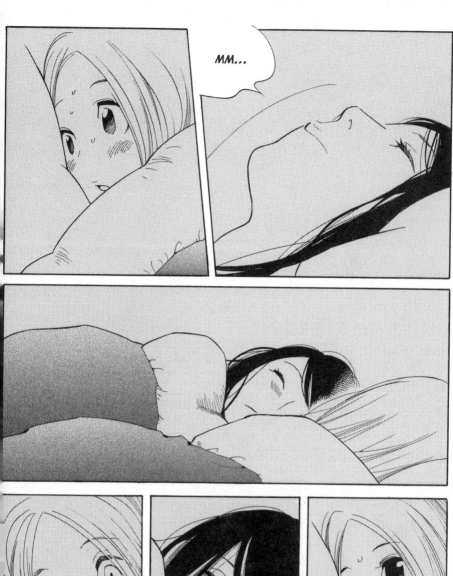

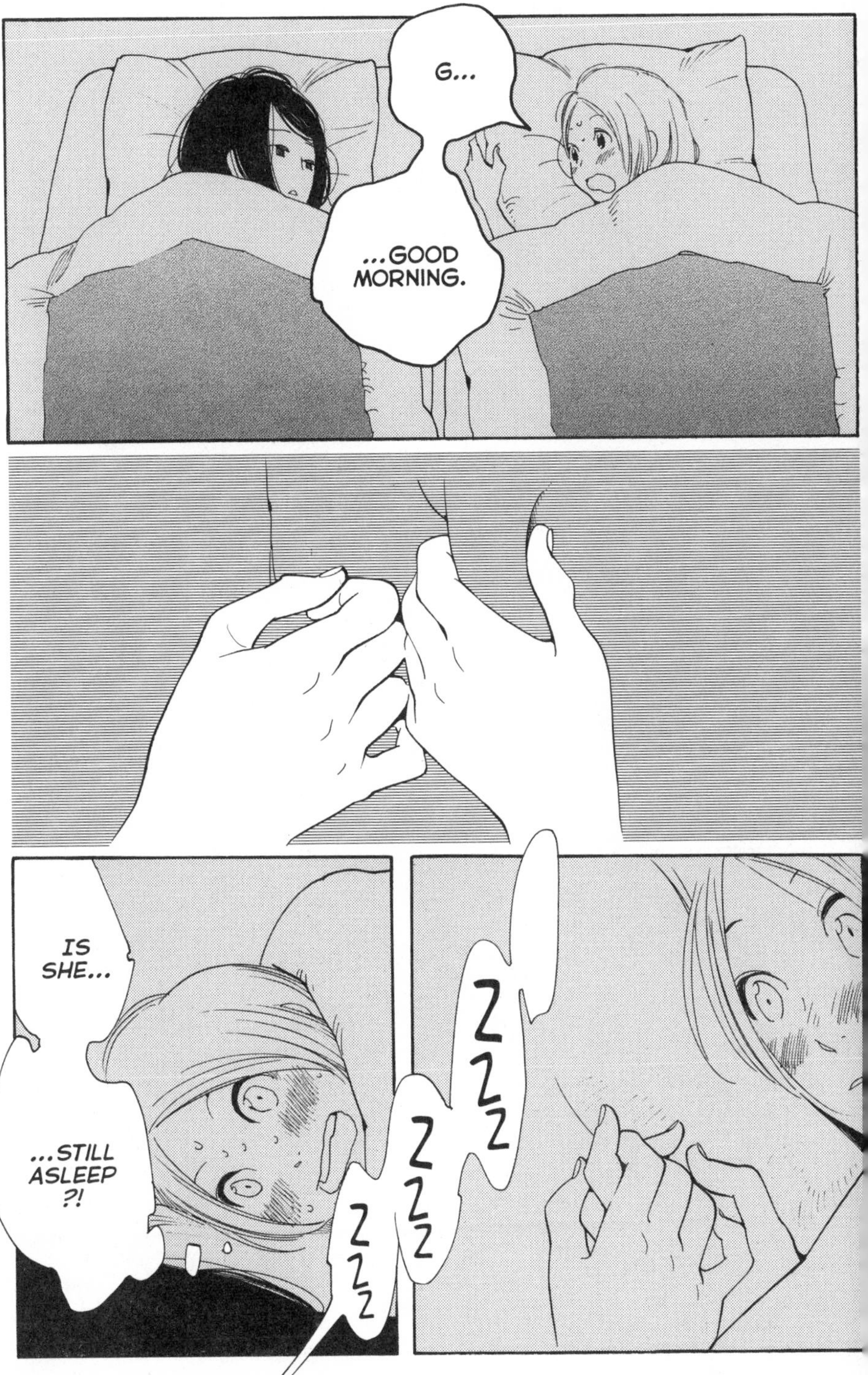
G...
...GOOD MORNING.
IS SHE...
...STILL ASLEEP ?!
ZZZ
ZZZ
ZZZ

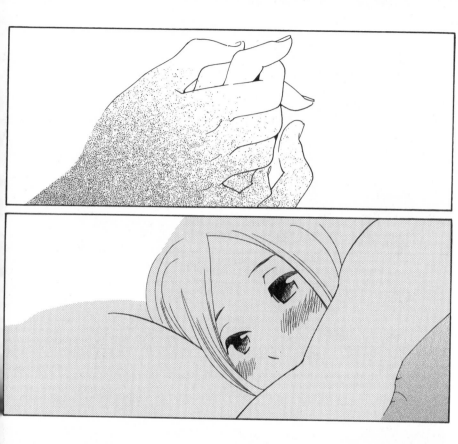

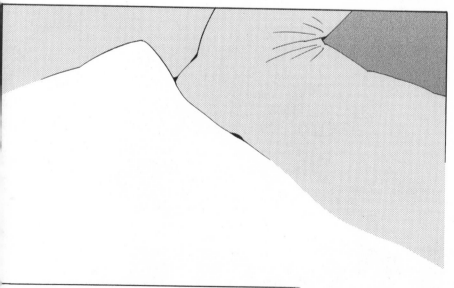

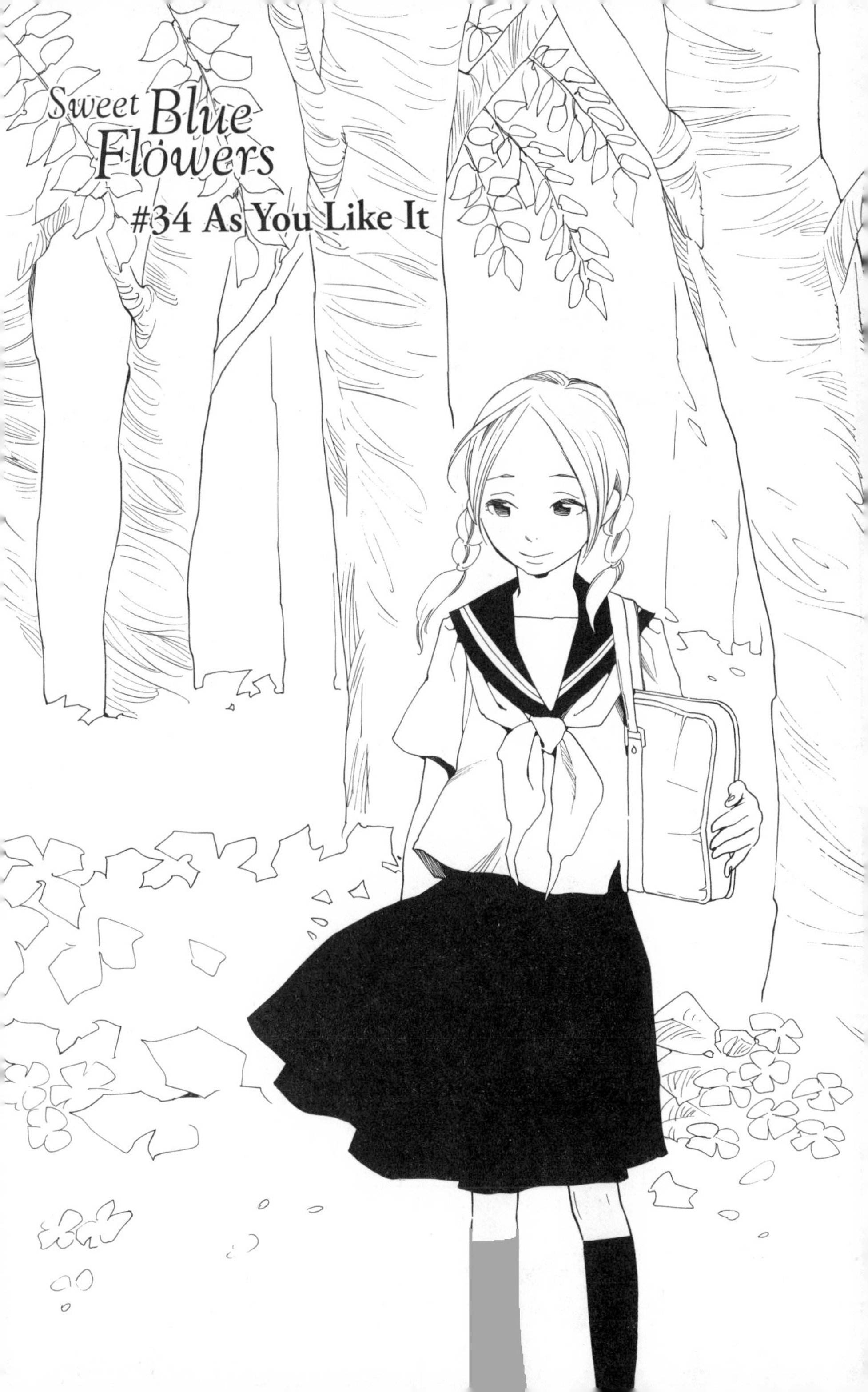
Sweet Blue Flowers
#34 As You Like It

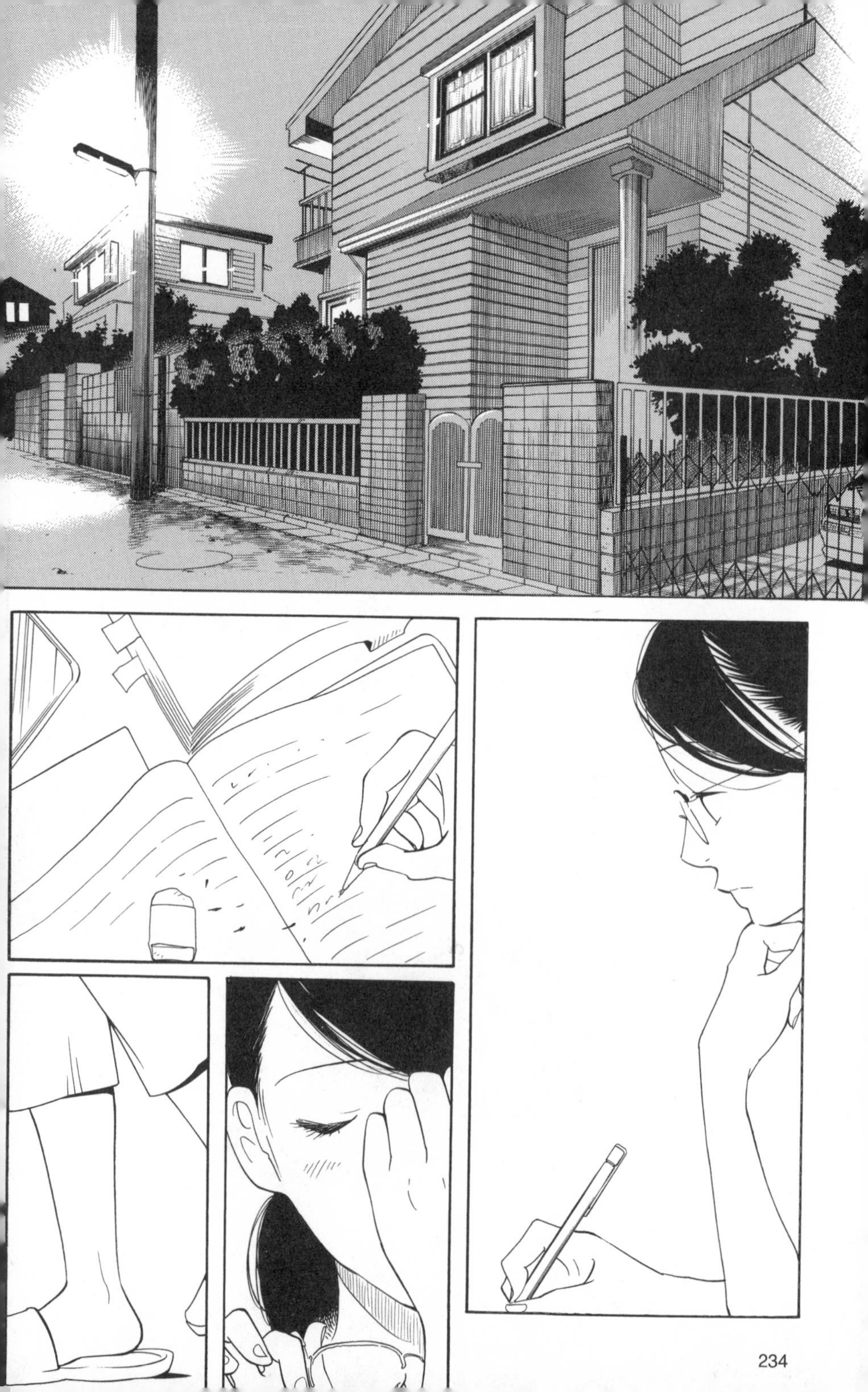

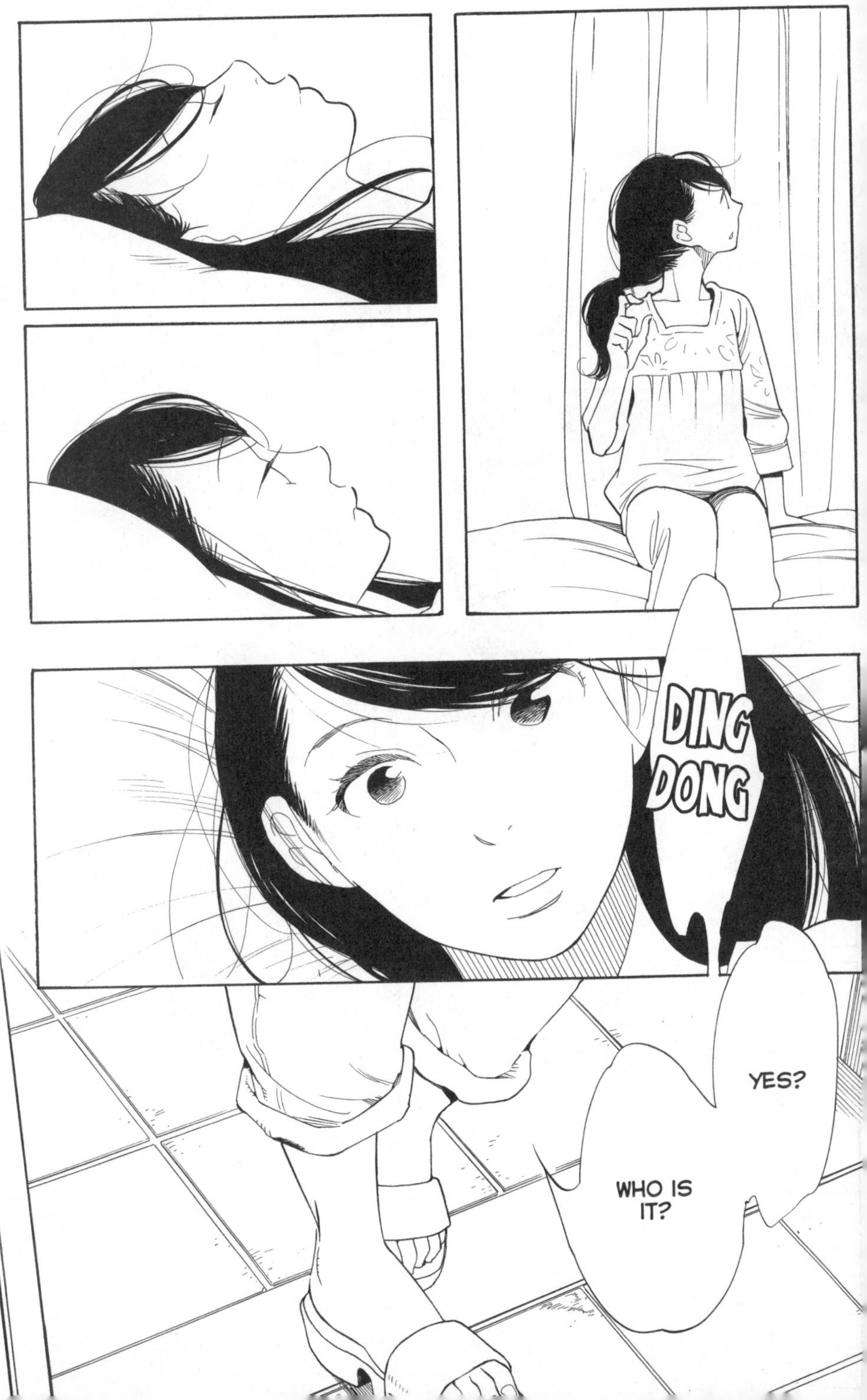
DING DONG
YES?
WHO IS IT?

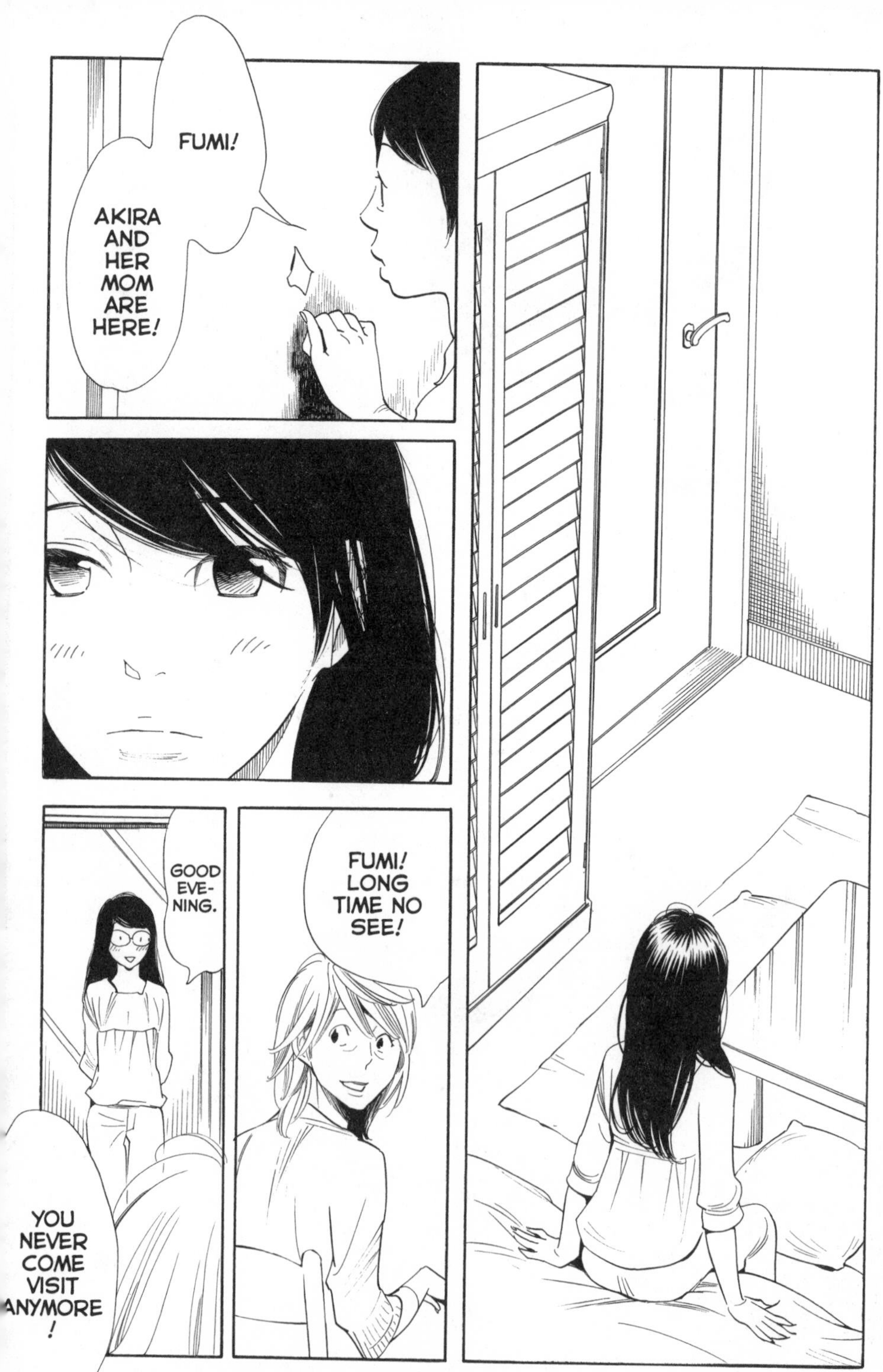
FUMI!
AKIRA AND HER MOM ARE HERE!
FUMI! LONG TIME NO SEE!
GOOD EVE-NING.
YOU NEVER COME VISIT ANYMORE!

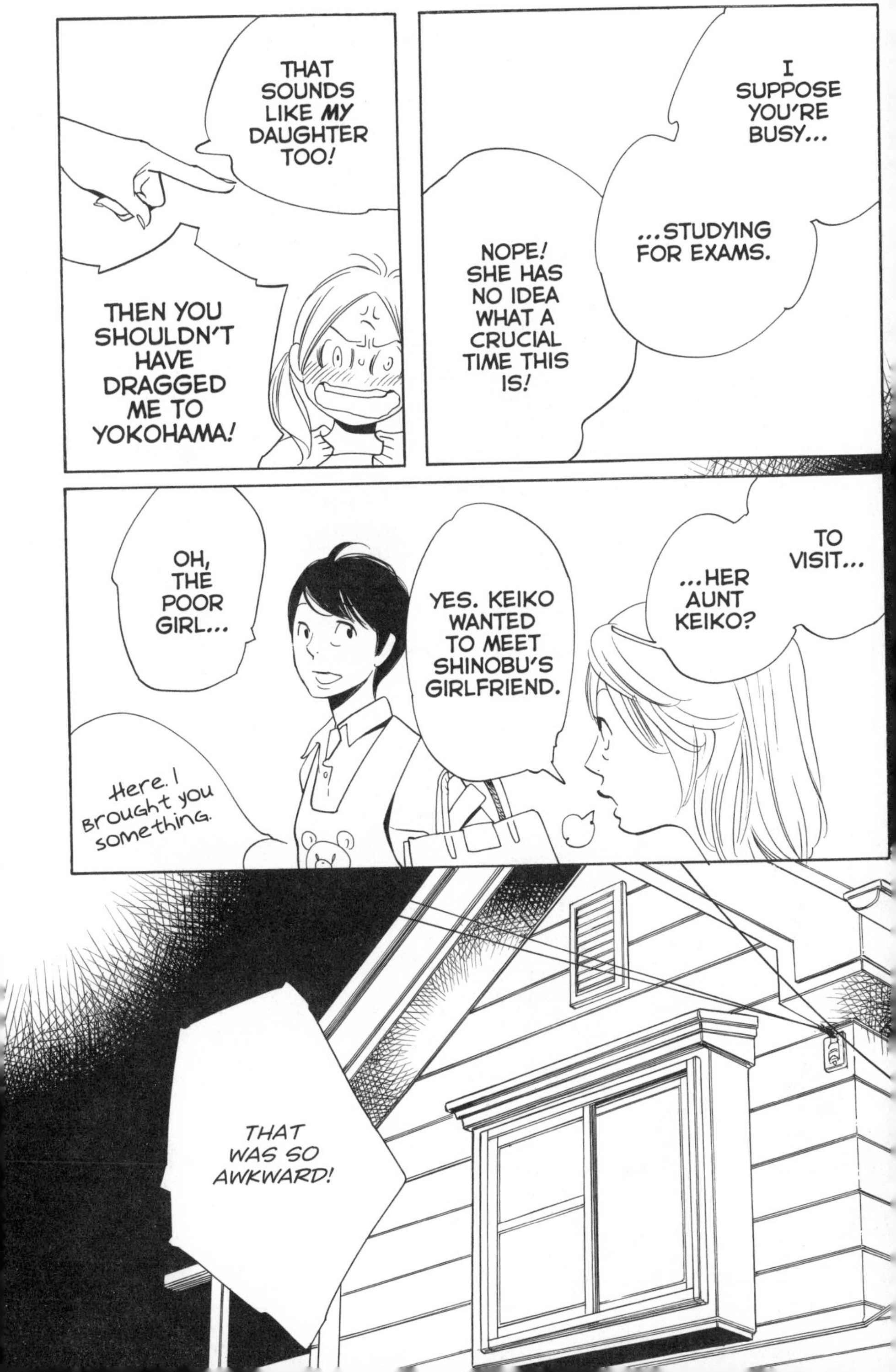
I SUPPOSE YOU'RE BUSY...
...STUDYING FOR EXAMS.
NOPE! SHE HAS NO IDEA WHAT A CRUCIAL TIME THIS IS!
THAT SOUNDS LIKE MY DAUGHTER TOO!
THEN YOU SHOULDN'T HAVE DRAGGED ME TO YOKOHAMA!
TO VISIT...
...HER AUNT KEIKO?
YES. KEIKO WANTED TO MEET SHINOBU'S GIRLFRIEND.
OH, THE POOR GIRL...
Here. I brought you something.
THAT WAS SO AWKWARD!

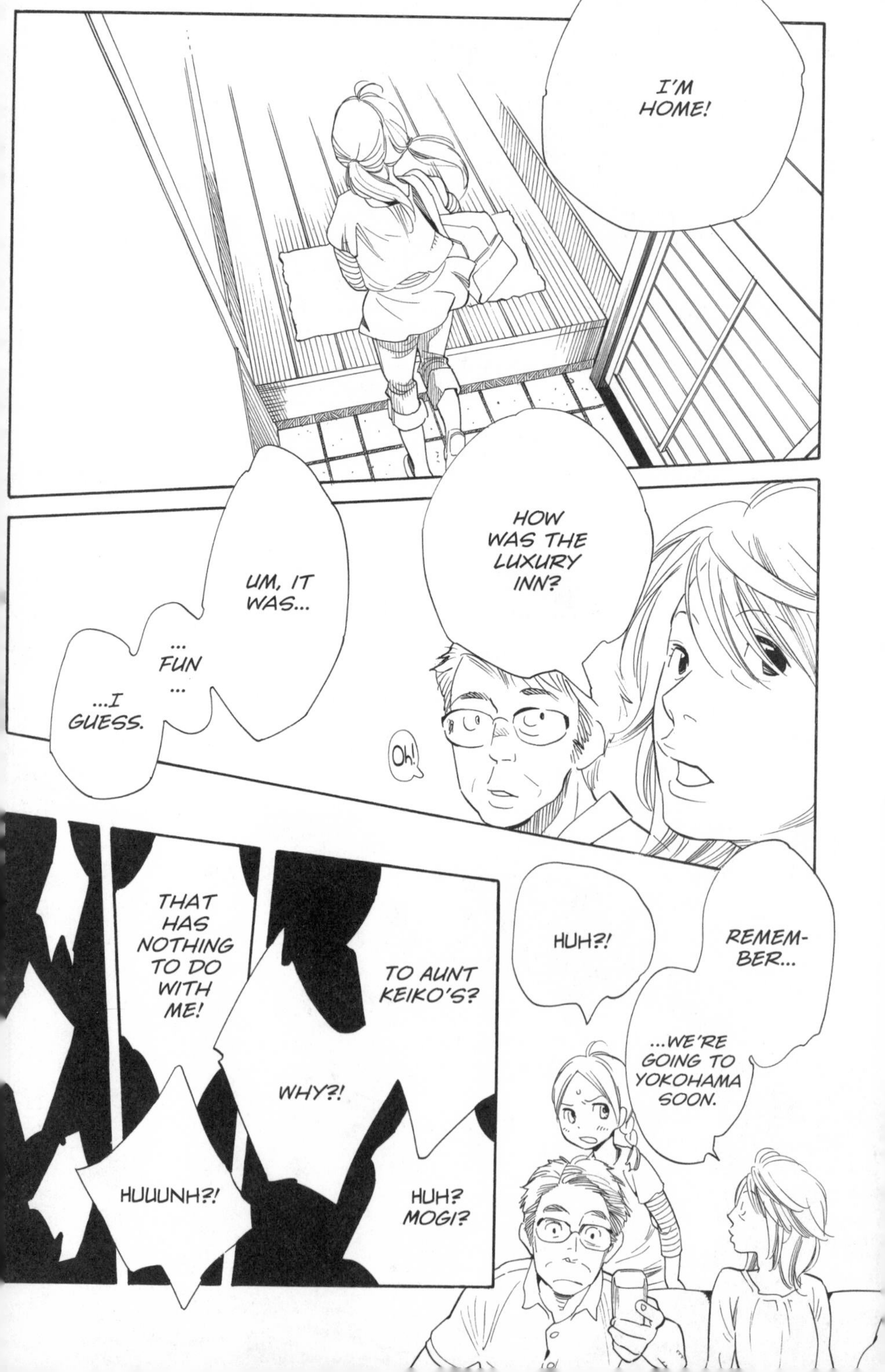
I'M HOME!
HOW WAS THE LUXURY INN?
UM, IT WAS...
... FUN ...
...I GUESS.
Oh!
REMEMBER...
HUH?!
...WE'RE GOING TO YOKOHAMA SOON.
TO AUNT KEIKO'S?
THAT HAS NOTHING TO DO WITH ME!
WHY?!
HUH? MOGI?
HUUUNH?!

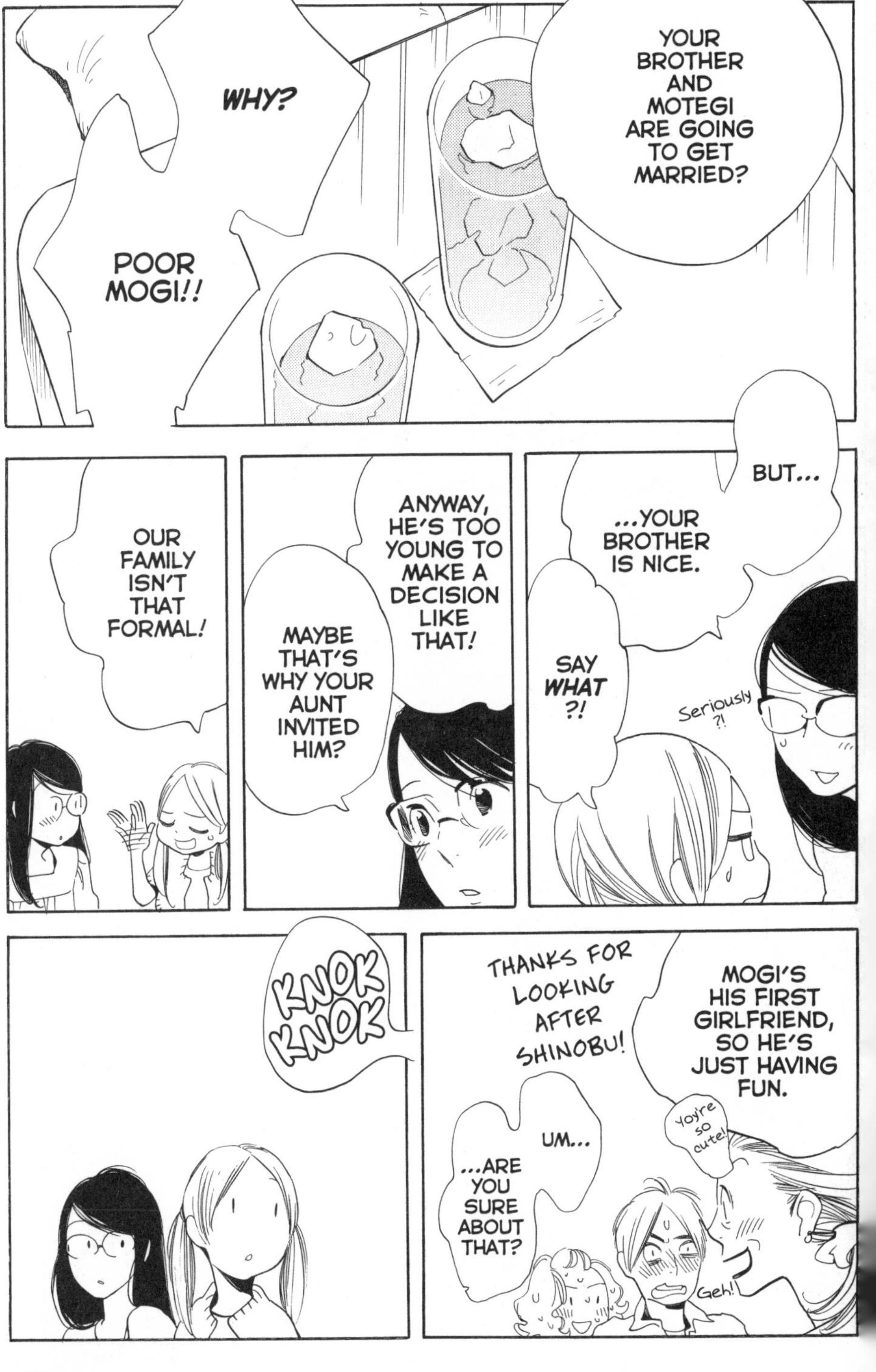
YOUR BROTHER AND MOTEGI ARE GOING TO GET MARRIED?
WHY?
POOR MOGI!!
BUT...
...YOUR BROTHER IS NICE.
Seriously?!
SAY WHAT?!
ANYWAY, HE'S TOO YOUNG TO MAKE A DECISION LIKE THAT!
MAYBE THAT'S WHY YOUR AUNT INVITED HIM?
OUR FAMILY ISN'T THAT FORMAL!
MOGI'S HIS FIRST GIRLFRIEND, SO HE'S JUST HAVING FUN.
THANKS FOR LOOKING AFTER SHINOBU!
You're so cute!
UM...
...ARE YOU SURE ABOUT THAT?
Geh!
KNOK KNOK

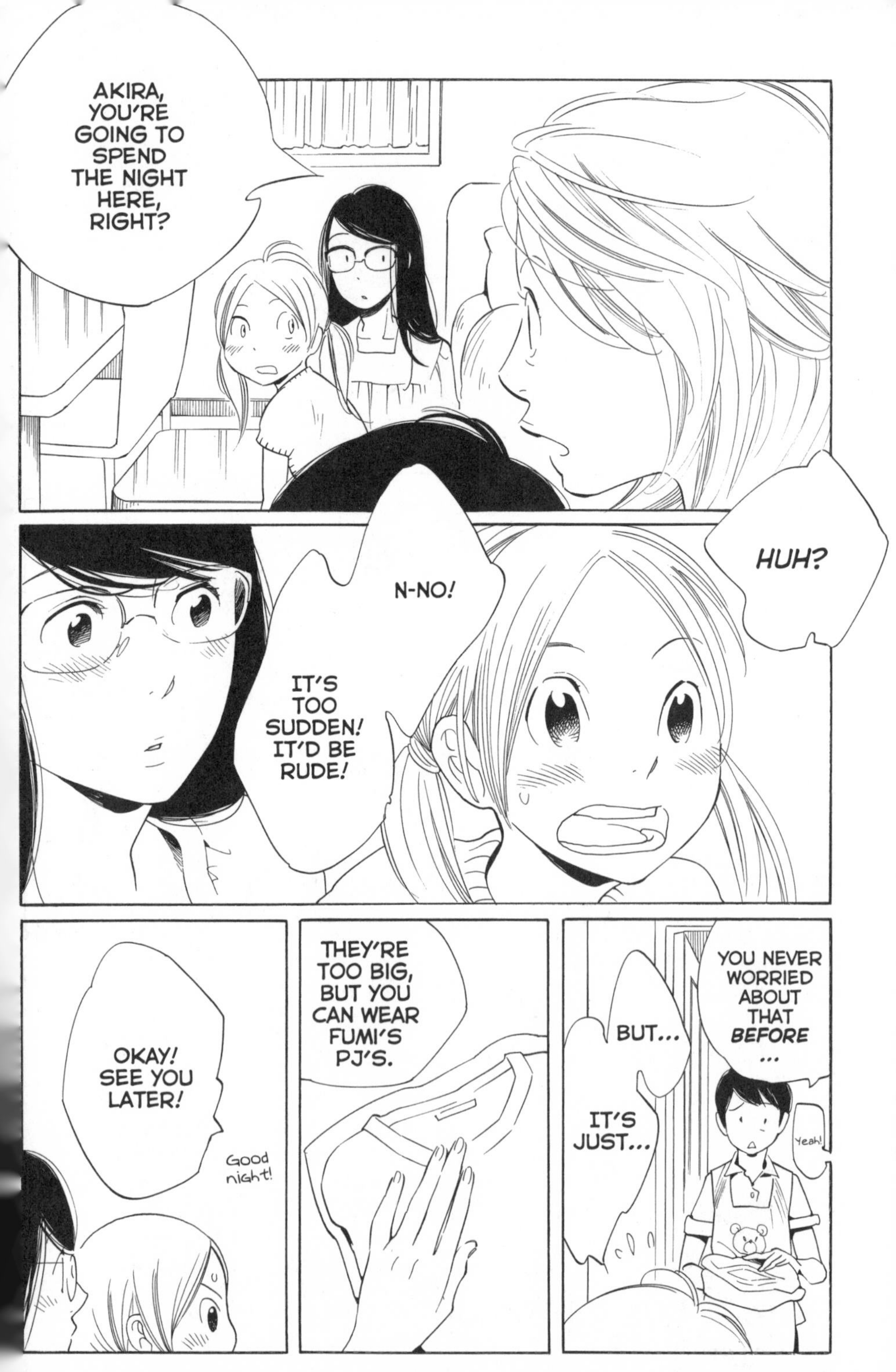
AKIRA, YOU'RE GOING TO SPEND THE NIGHT HERE, RIGHT?
HUH?
N-NO!
IT'S TOO SUDDEN! IT'D BE RUDE!
YOU NEVER WORRIED ABOUT THAT *BEFORE* ...
Yeah!
BUT...
IT'S JUST...
THEY'RE TOO BIG, BUT YOU CAN WEAR FUMI'S PJ'S.
OKAY! SEE YOU LATER!
Good night!

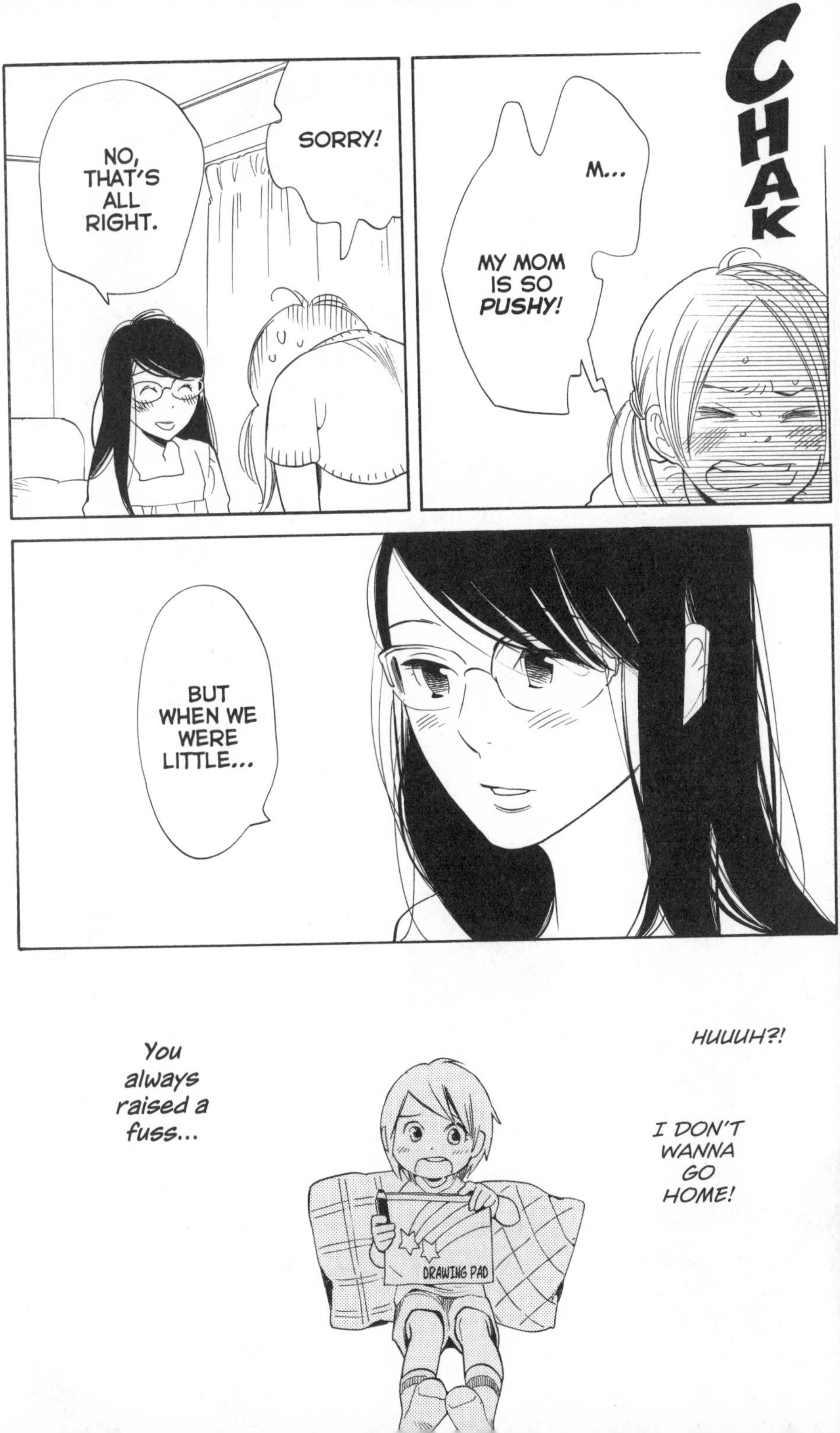
CHAK
M...
MY MOM IS SO PUSHY!
SORRY!
NO, THAT'S ALL RIGHT.
BUT WHEN WE WERE LITTLE...
HUUUH?!
You always raised a fuss...
I DON'T WANNA GO HOME!
DRAWING PAD

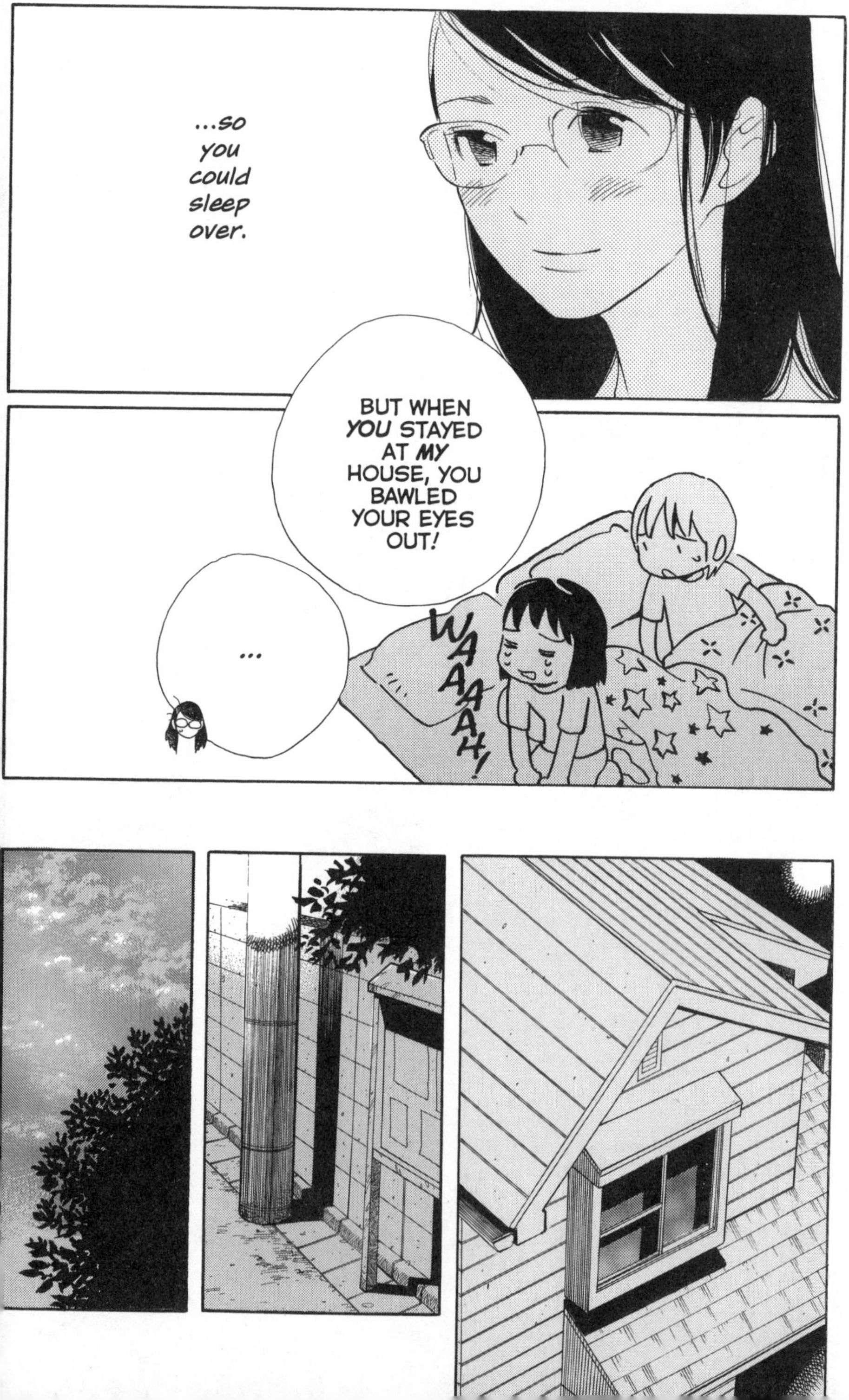
...so you could sleep over.
BUT WHEN *YOU* STAYED AT *MY* HOUSE, YOU BAWLED YOUR EYES OUT!
WAAAAAH!
...

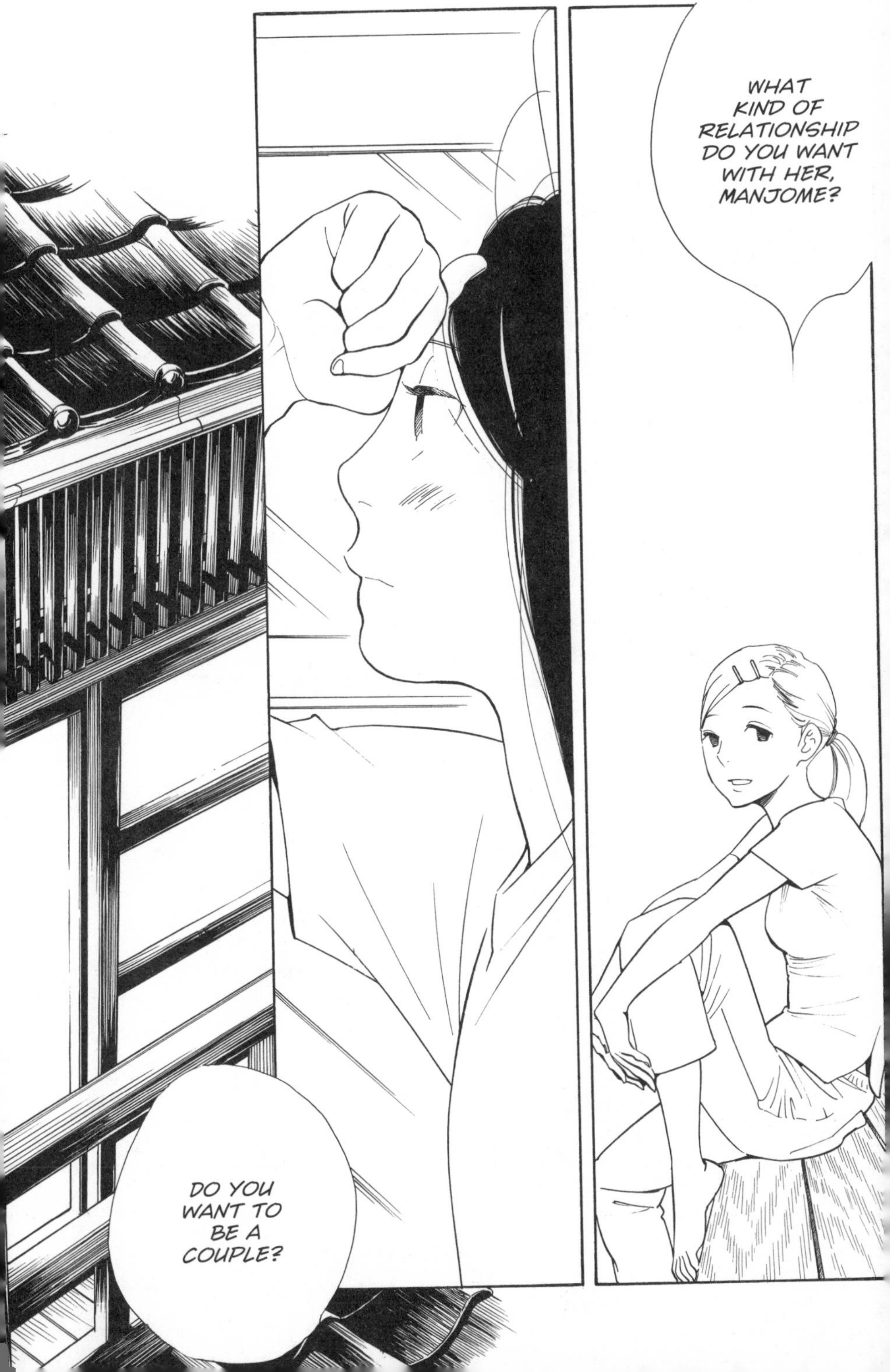
WHAT KIND OF RELATIONSHIP DO YOU WANT WITH HER, MANJOME?
DO YOU WANT TO BE A COUPLE?

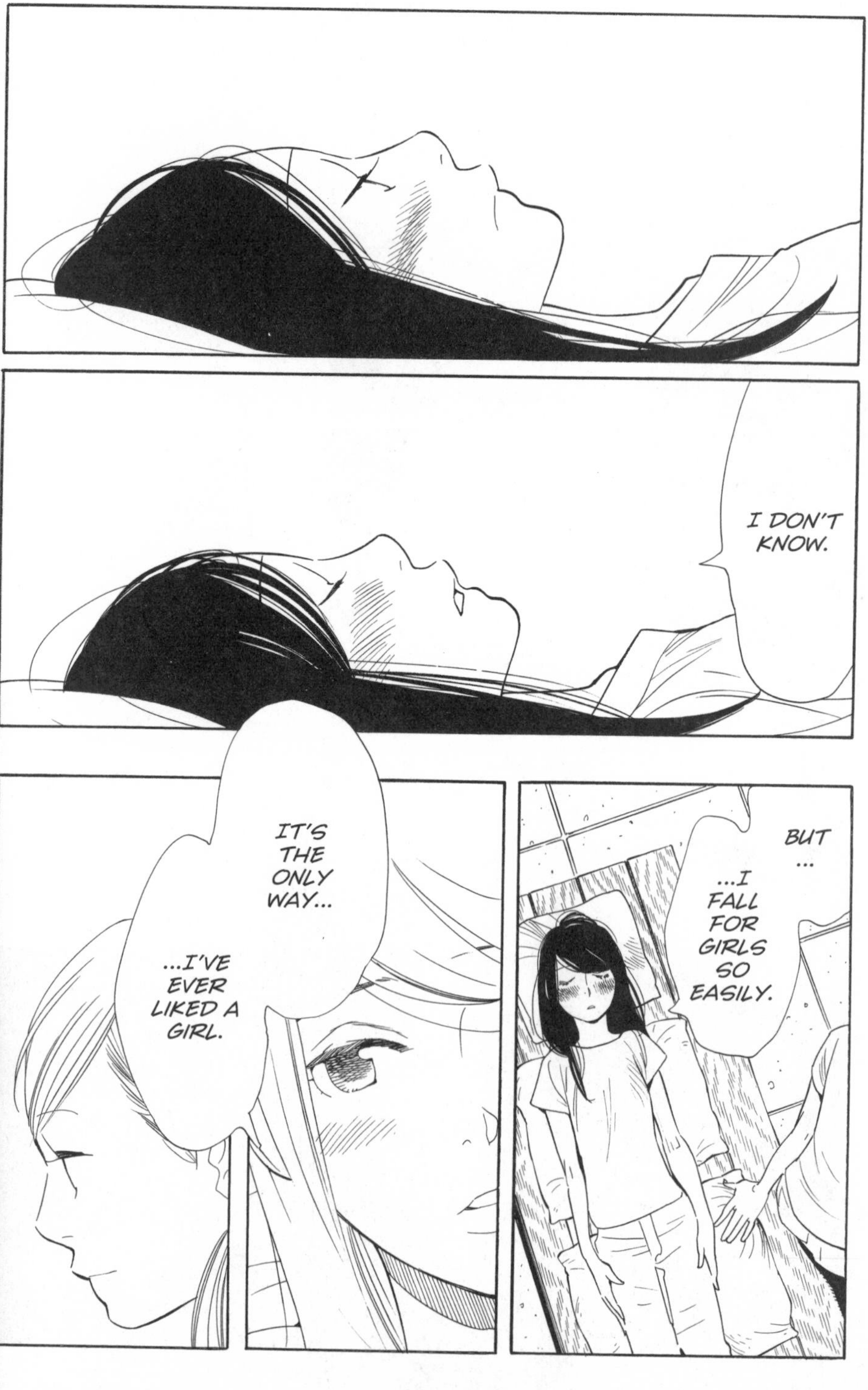
I DON'T KNOW.
BUT ...
...I FALL FOR GIRLS SO EASILY.
IT'S THE ONLY WAY...
...I'VE EVER LIKED A GIRL.

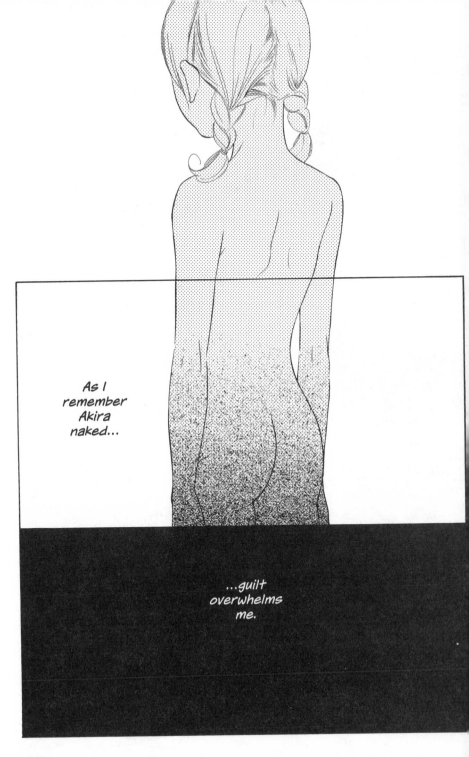

As I remember Akira naked...

...guilt overwhelms me.

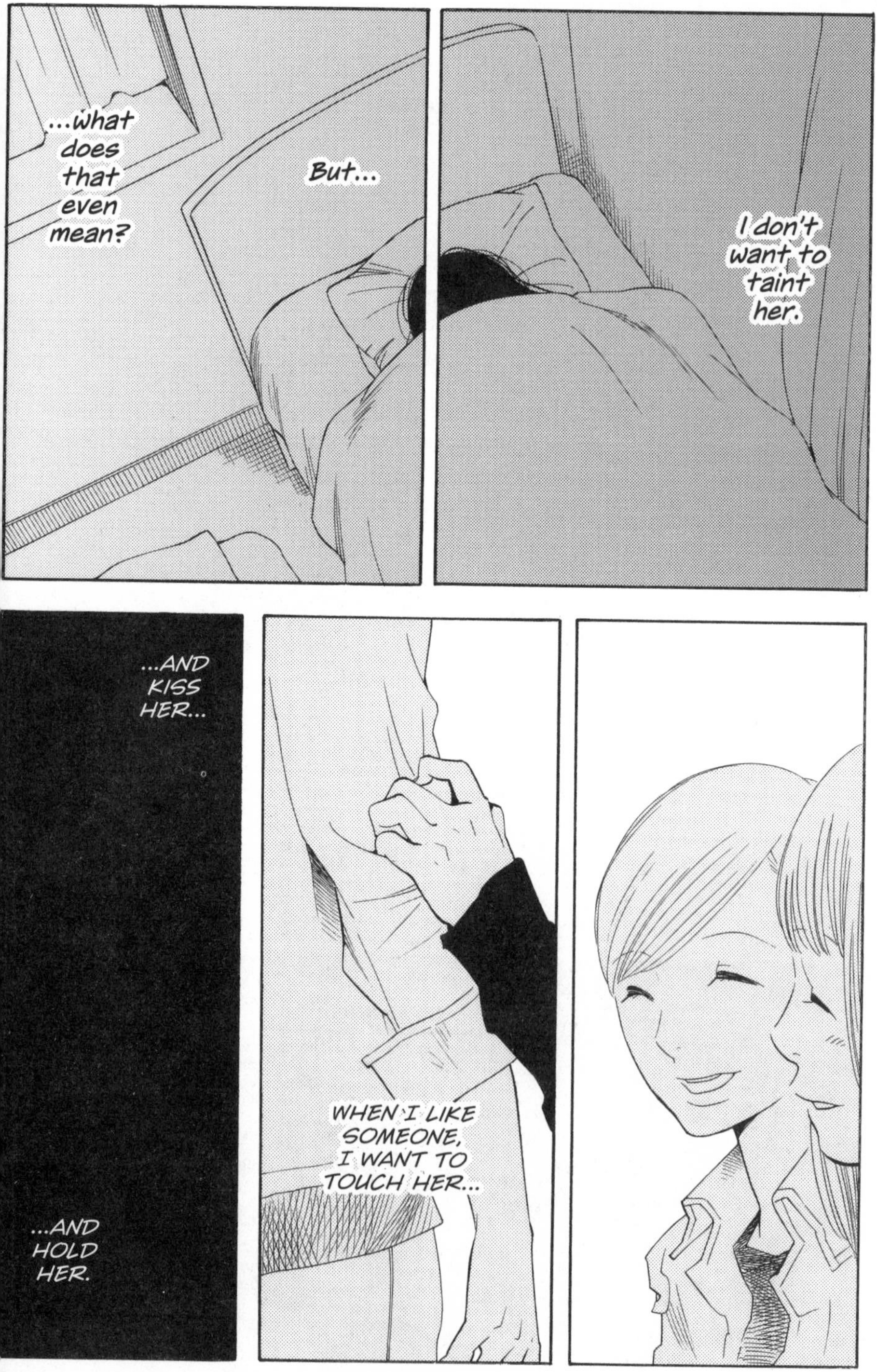
I don't want to taint her.
But...
...what does that even mean?
WHEN I LIKE SOMEONE, I WANT TO TOUCH HER...
...AND KISS HER...
...AND HOLD HER.

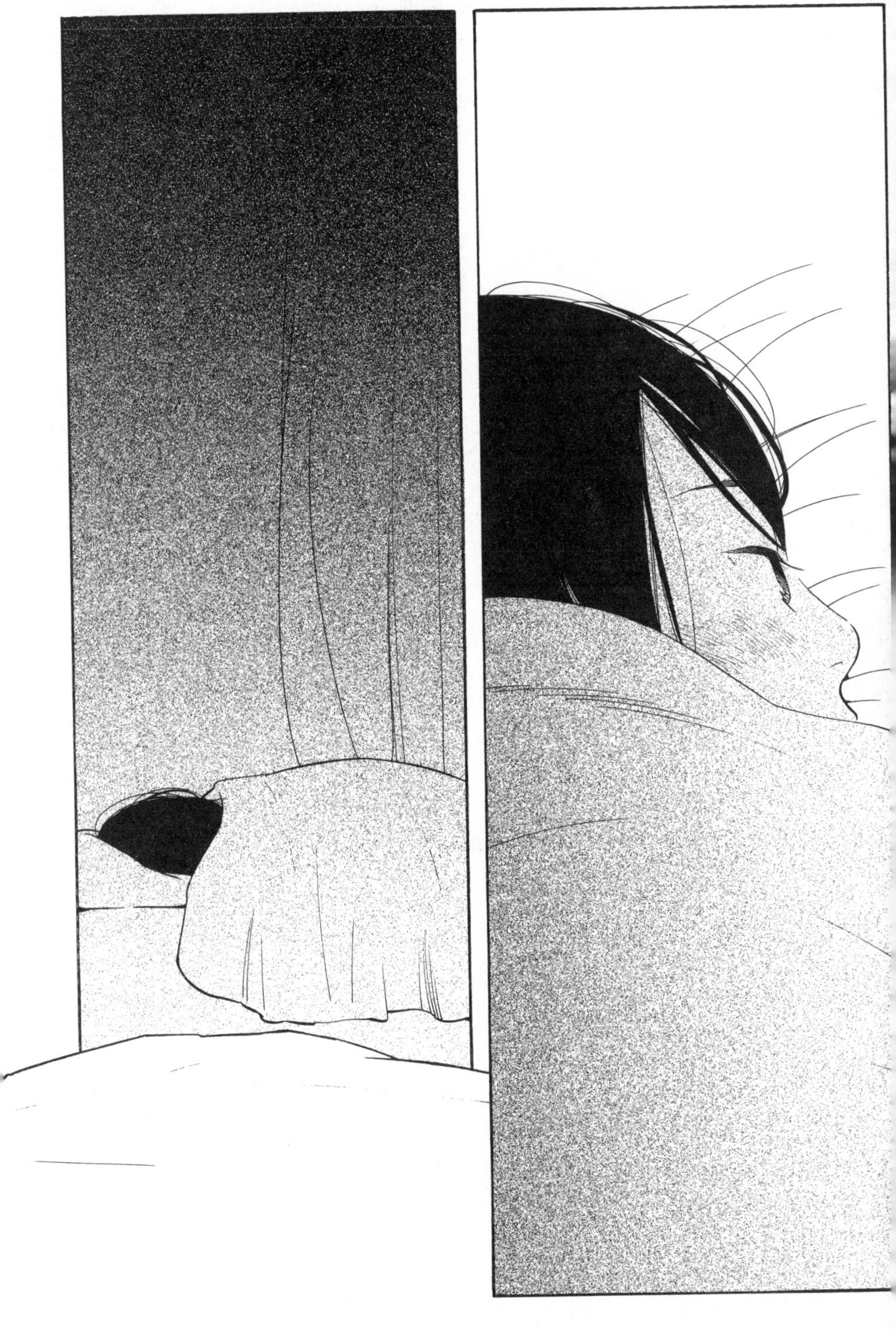

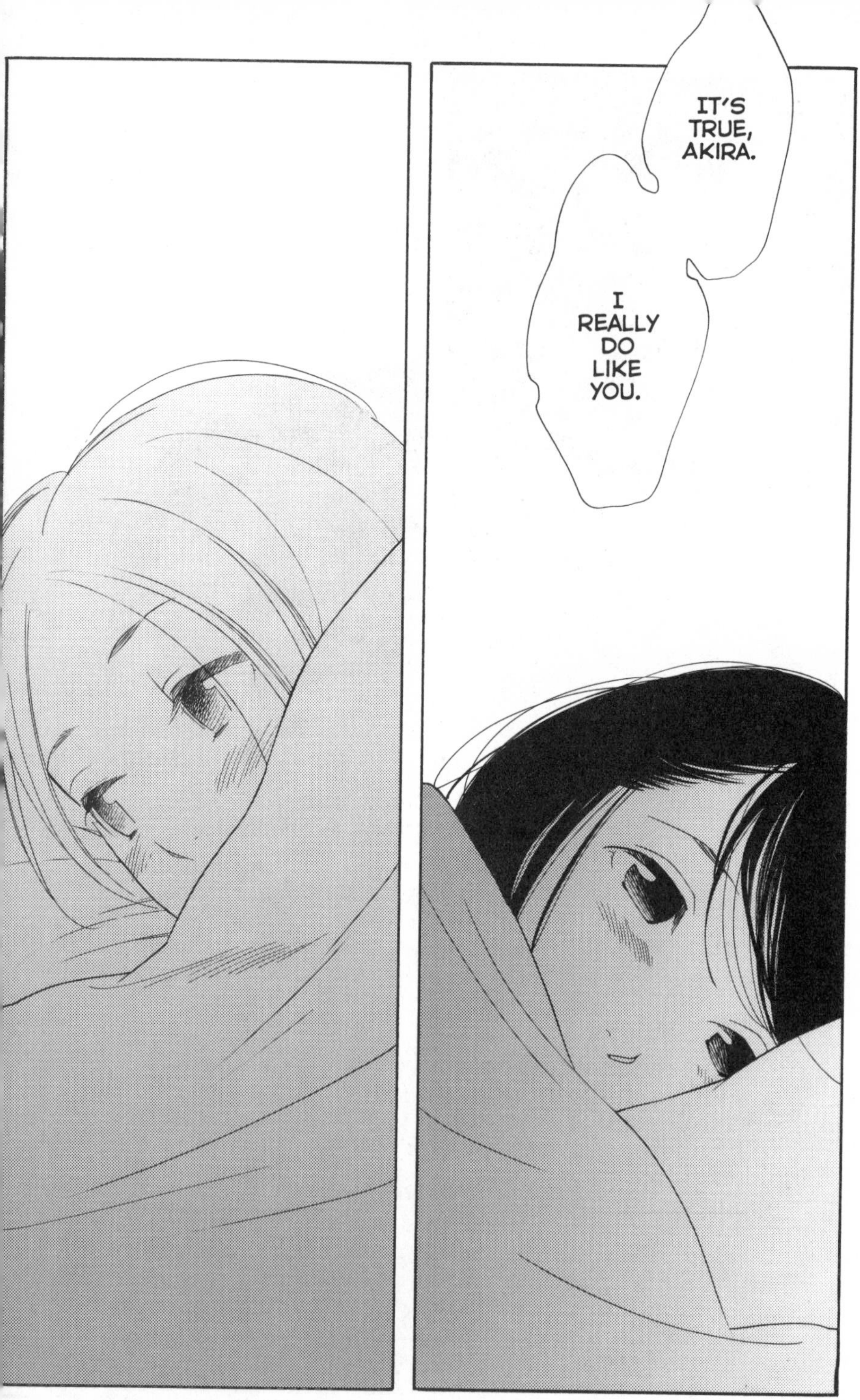
IT'S TRUE, AKIRA.
I REALLY DO LIKE YOU.

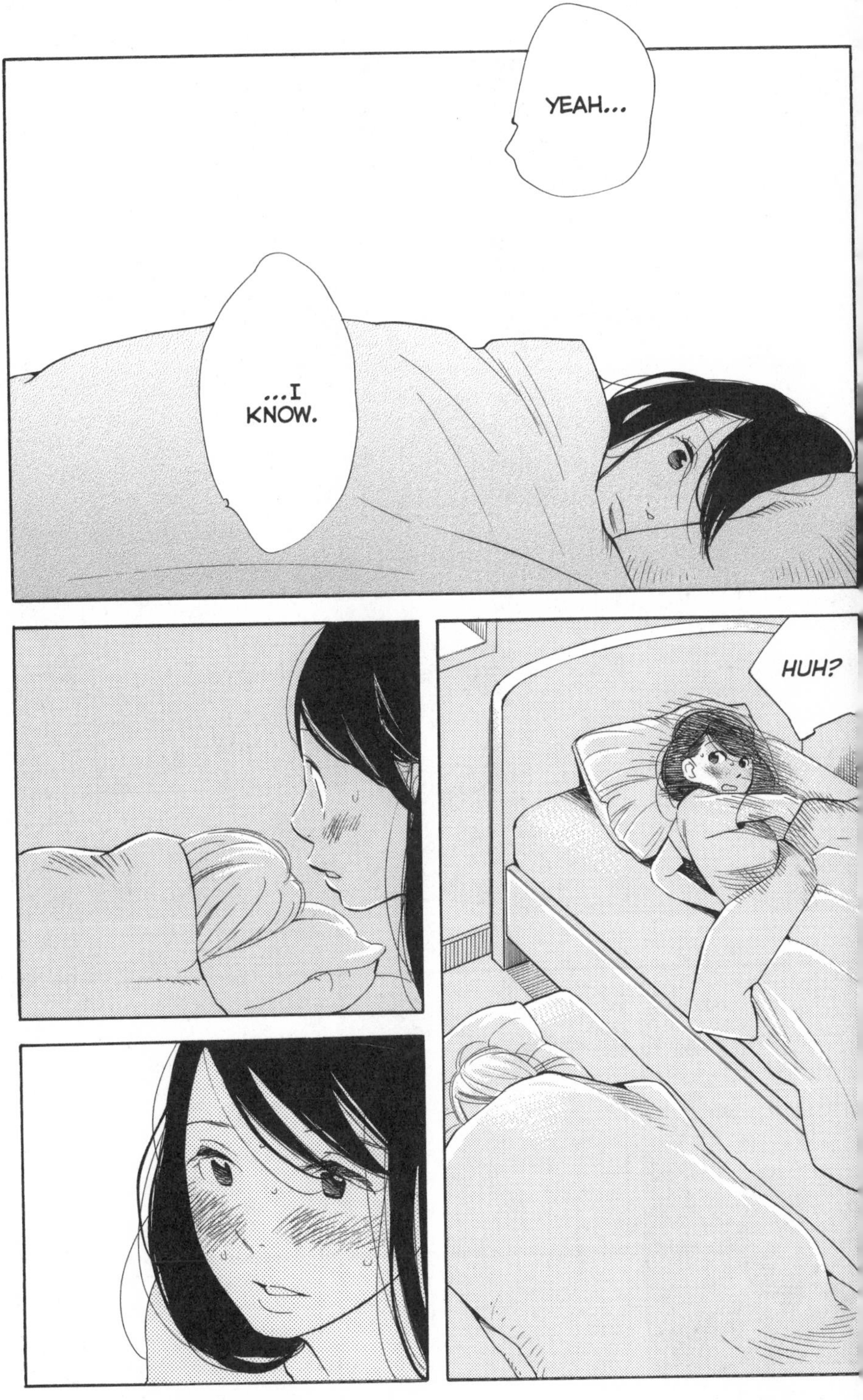
YEAH...
...I KNOW.
HUH?

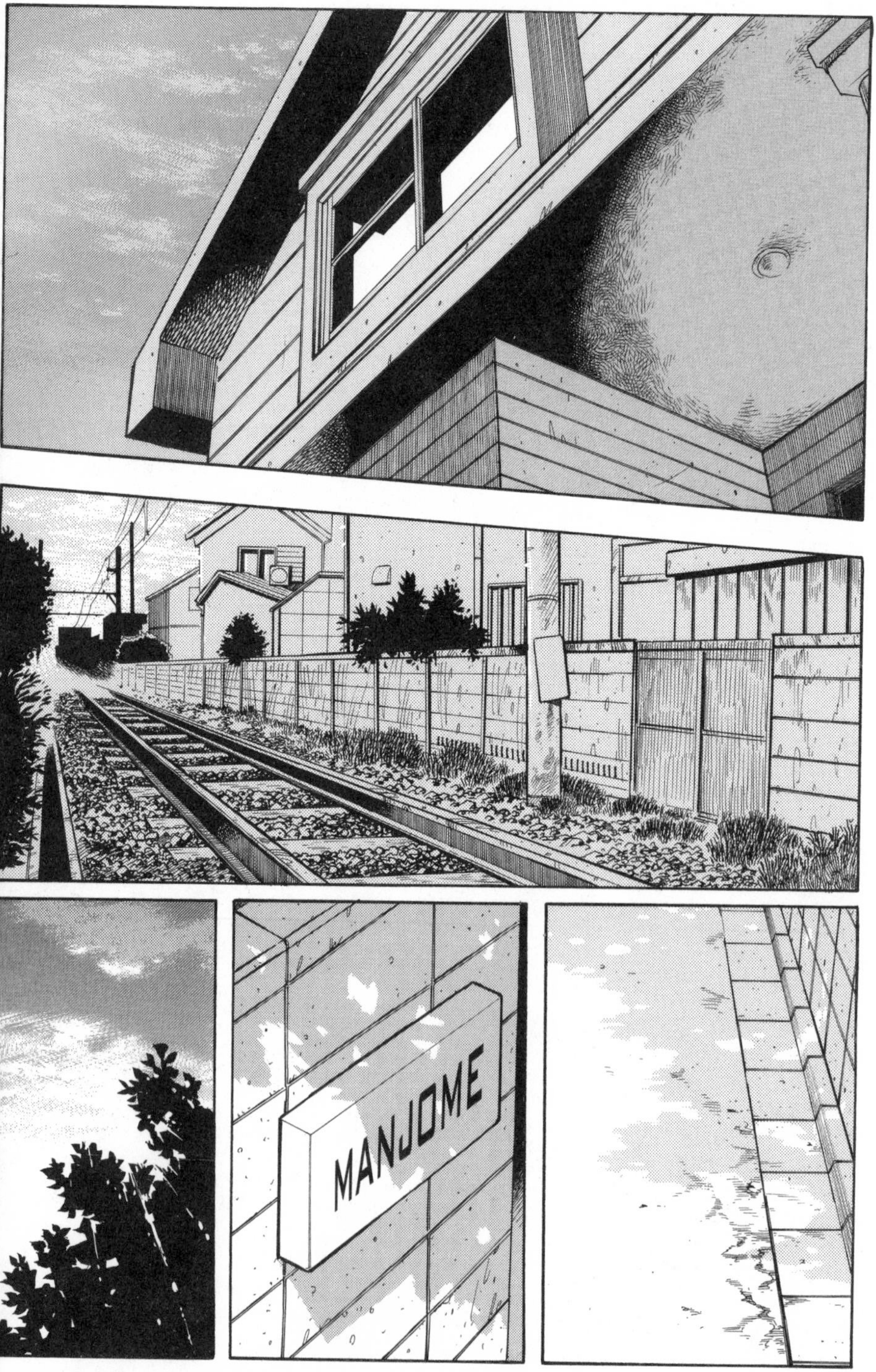
MANJOME

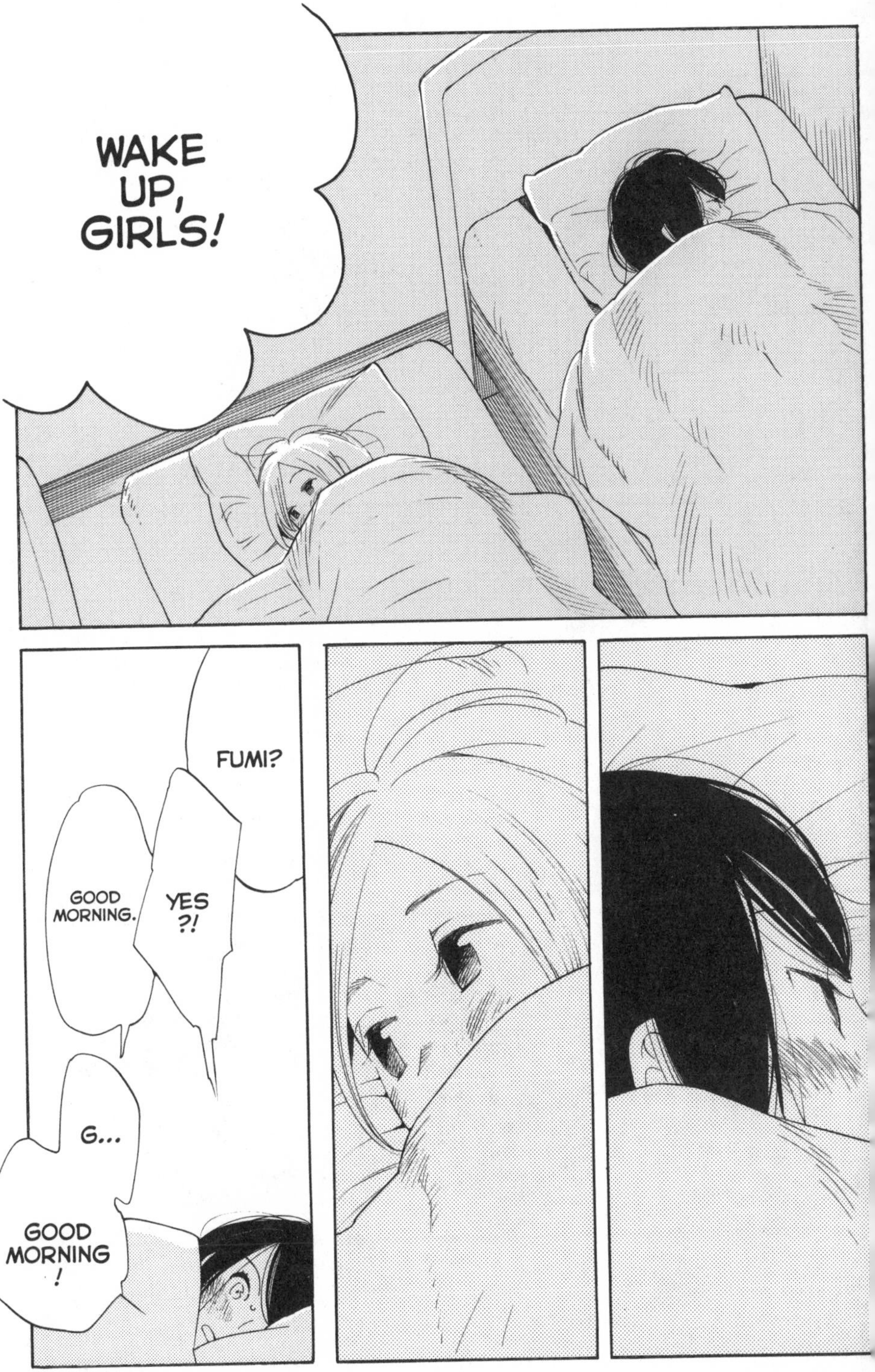
WAKE UP, GIRLS!
FUMI?
YES?!
GOOD MORNING.
G...
GOOD MORNING!

UM...

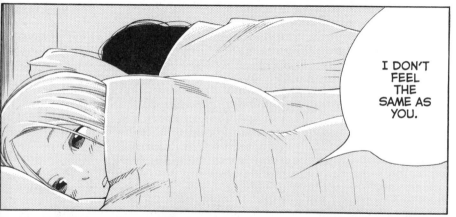

I DON'T FEEL THE SAME AS YOU.

I KNOW.

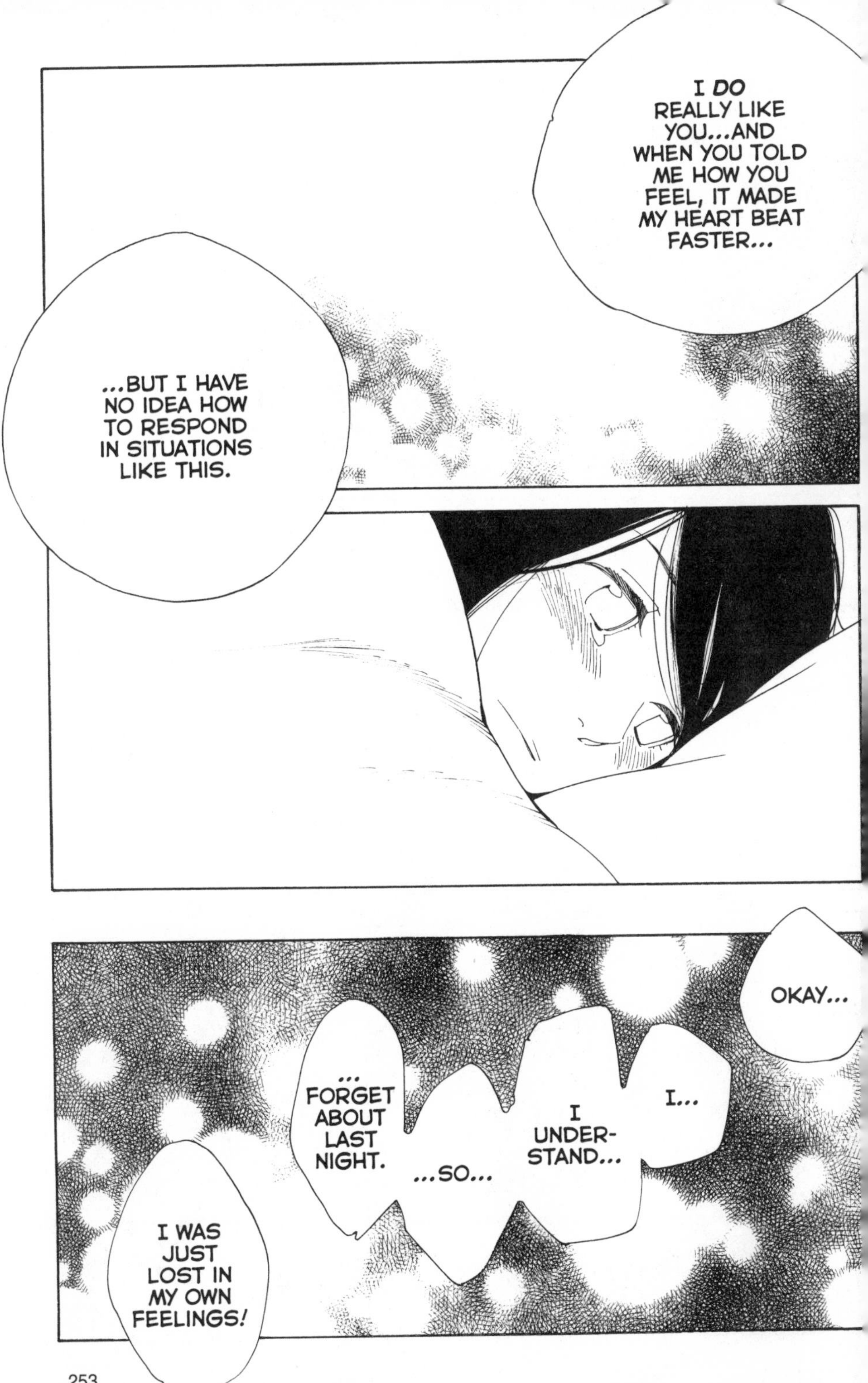
I *DO* REALLY LIKE YOU...AND WHEN YOU TOLD ME HOW YOU FEEL, IT MADE MY HEART BEAT FASTER...
...BUT I HAVE NO IDEA HOW TO RESPOND IN SITUATIONS LIKE THIS.
OKAY...
I...
I UNDER-STAND...
...SO...
...FORGET ABOUT LAST NIGHT.
I WAS JUST LOST IN MY OWN FEELINGS!

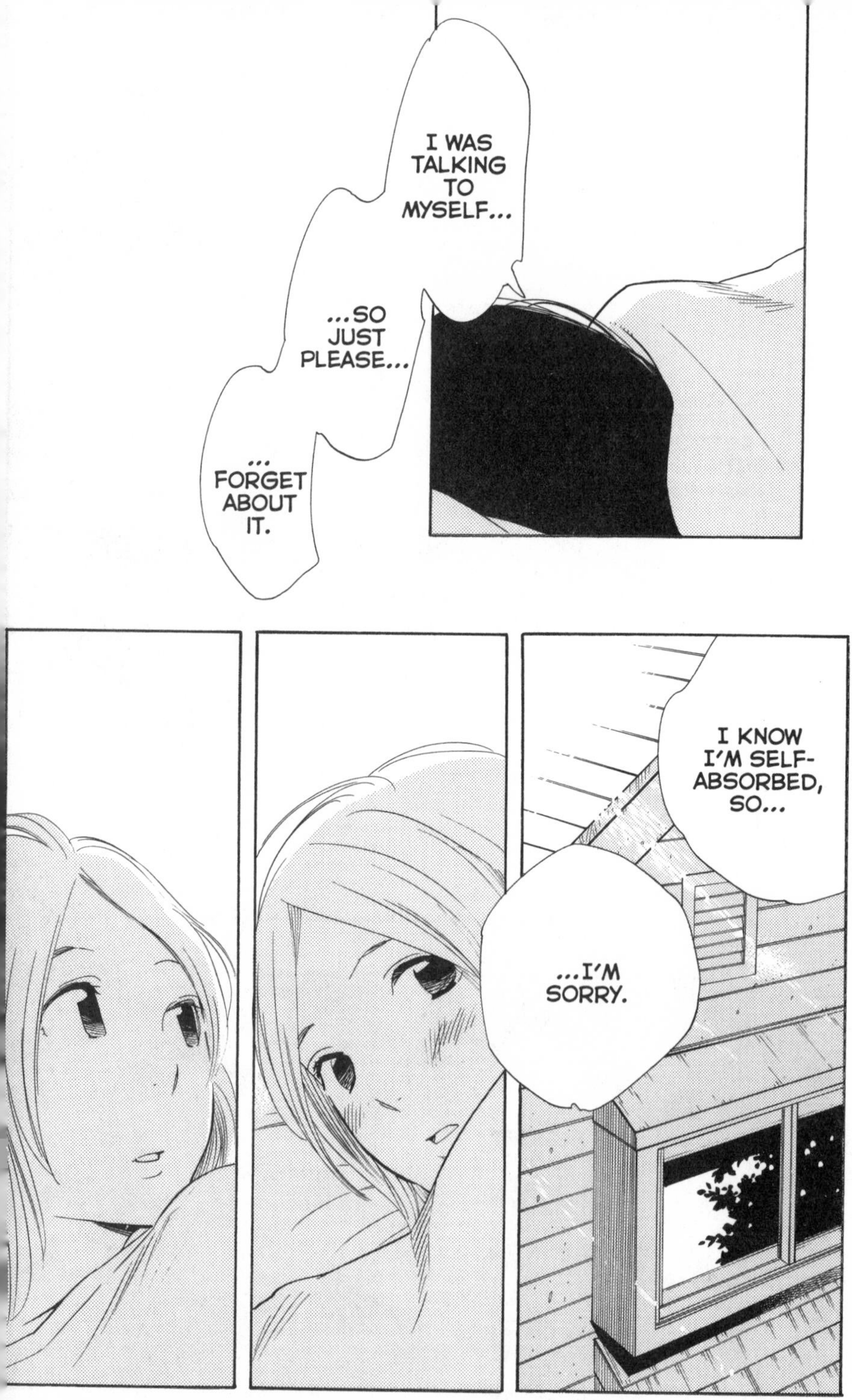
I WAS TALKING TO MYSELF...
...SO JUST PLEASE...
... FORGET ABOUT IT.
I KNOW I'M SELF-ABSORBED, SO...
...I'M SORRY.

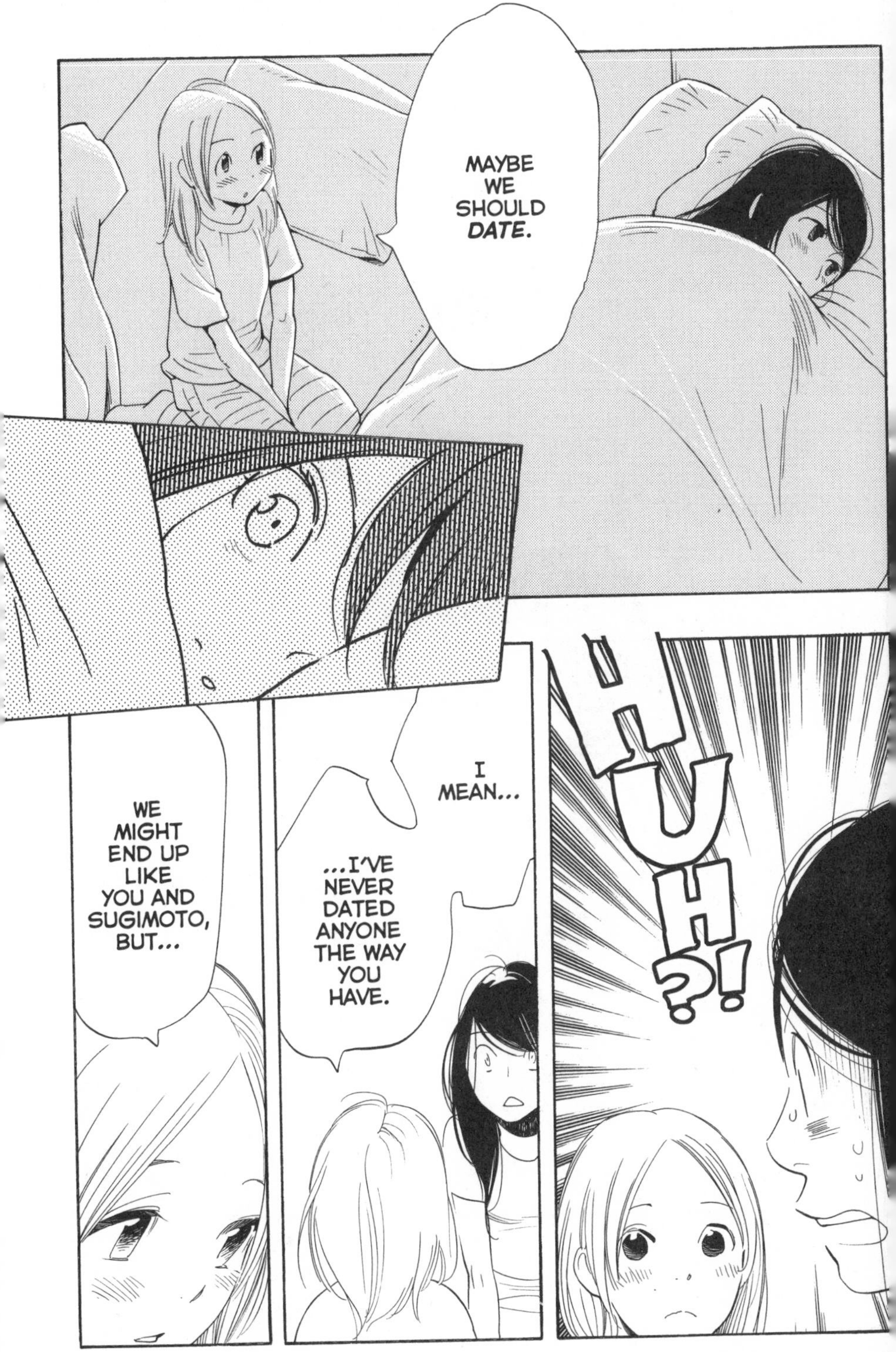
MAYBE WE SHOULD *DATE.*
HUH?!
I MEAN...
...I'VE NEVER DATED ANYONE THE WAY YOU HAVE.
WE MIGHT END UP LIKE YOU AND SUGIMOTO, BUT...

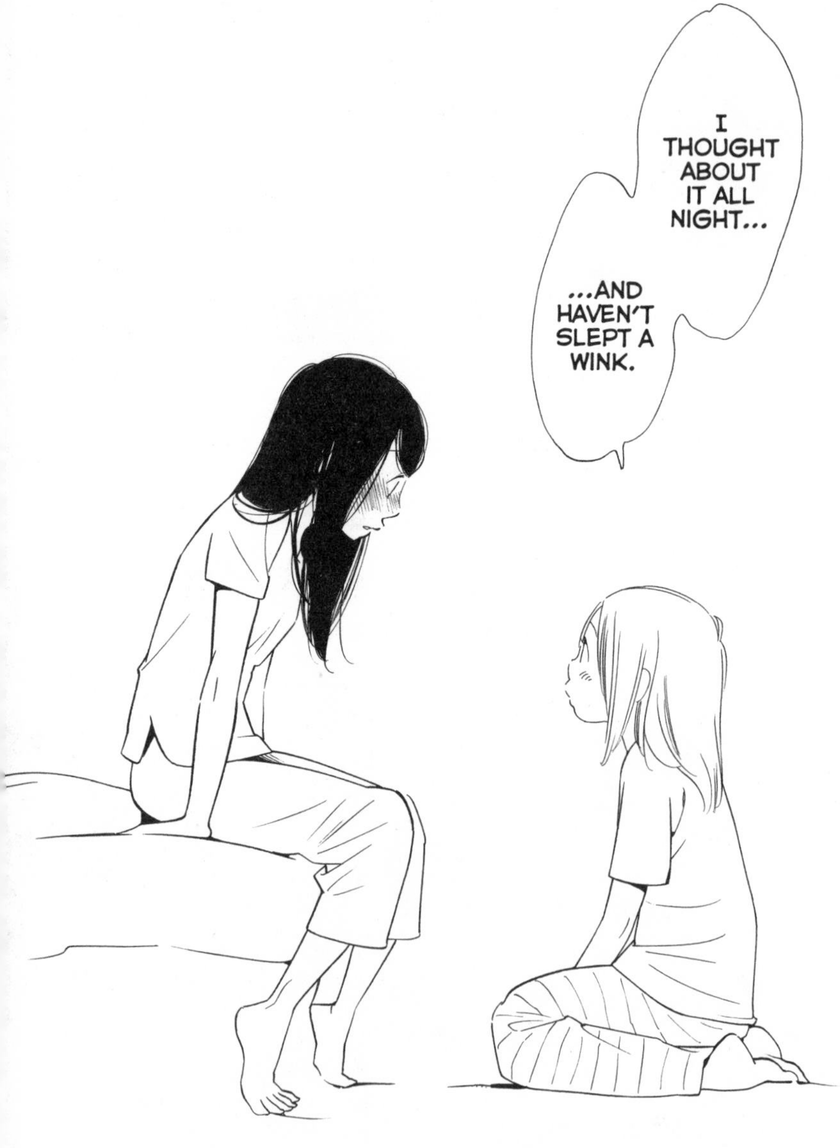
I THOUGHT ABOUT IT ALL NIGHT...
...AND HAVEN'T SLEPT A WINK.

Sweet **Blue**
Flowers

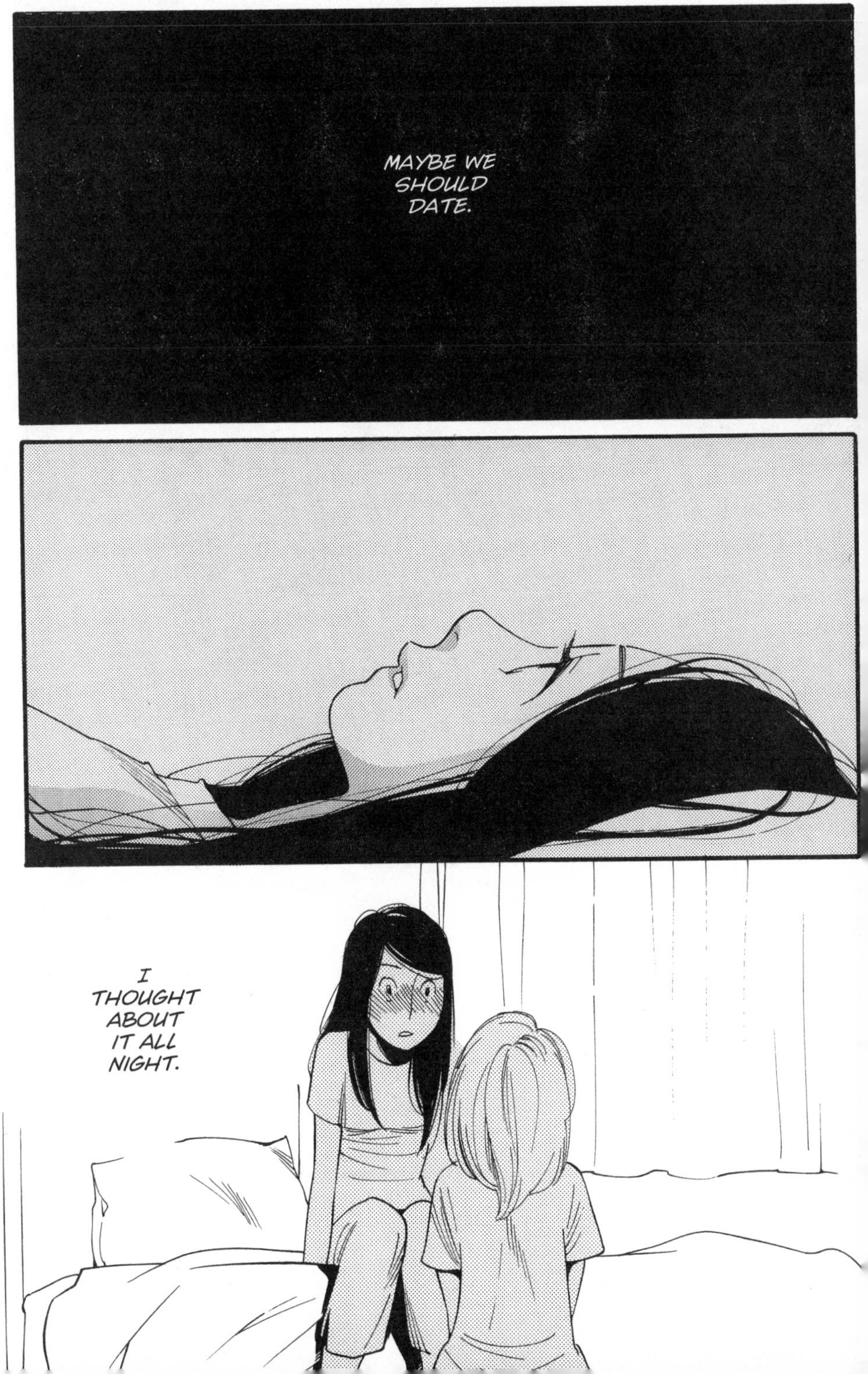
MAYBE WE SHOULD DATE.
I THOUGHT ABOUT IT ALL NIGHT.

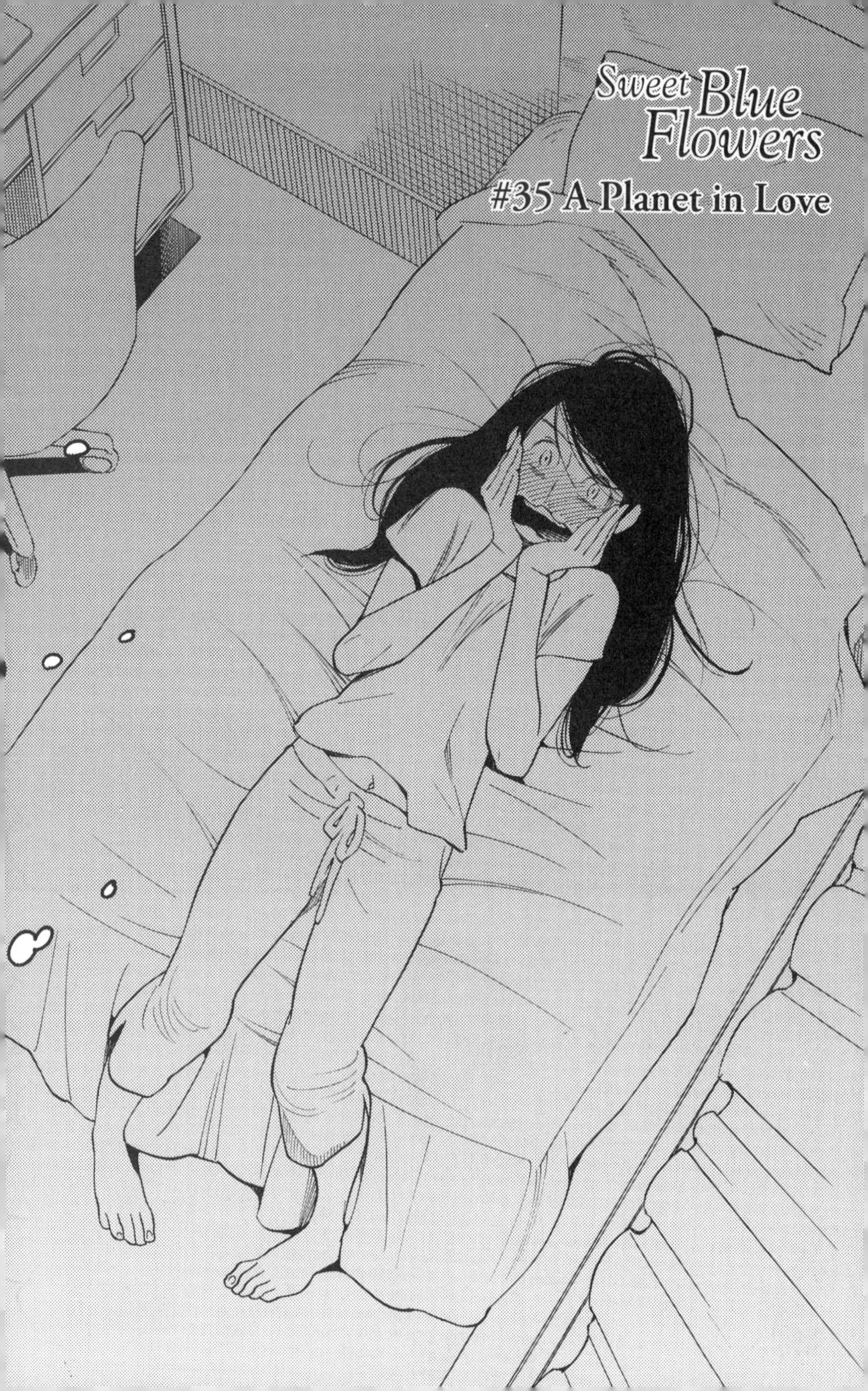
Sweet Blue Flowers
#35 A Planet in Love

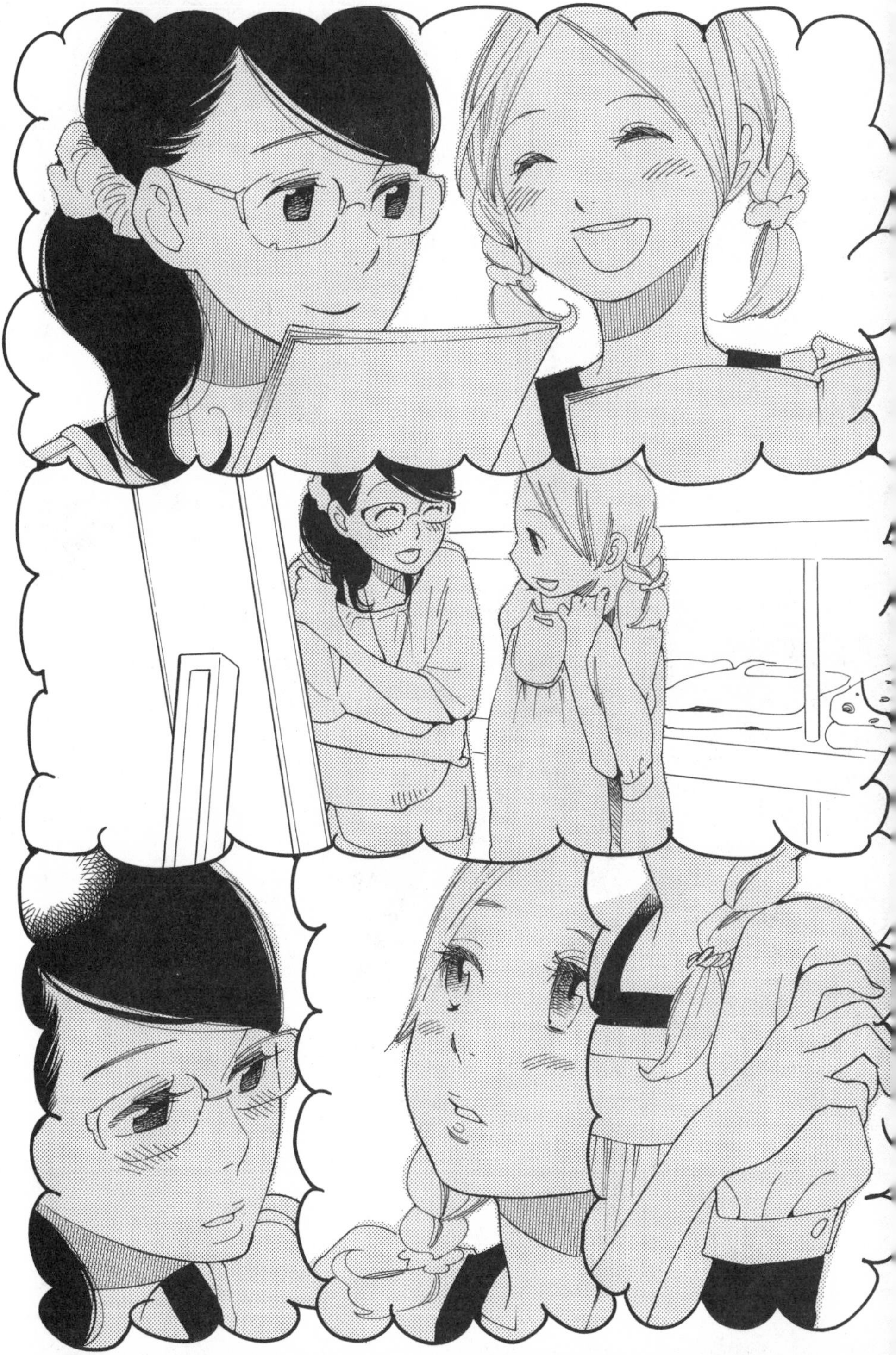

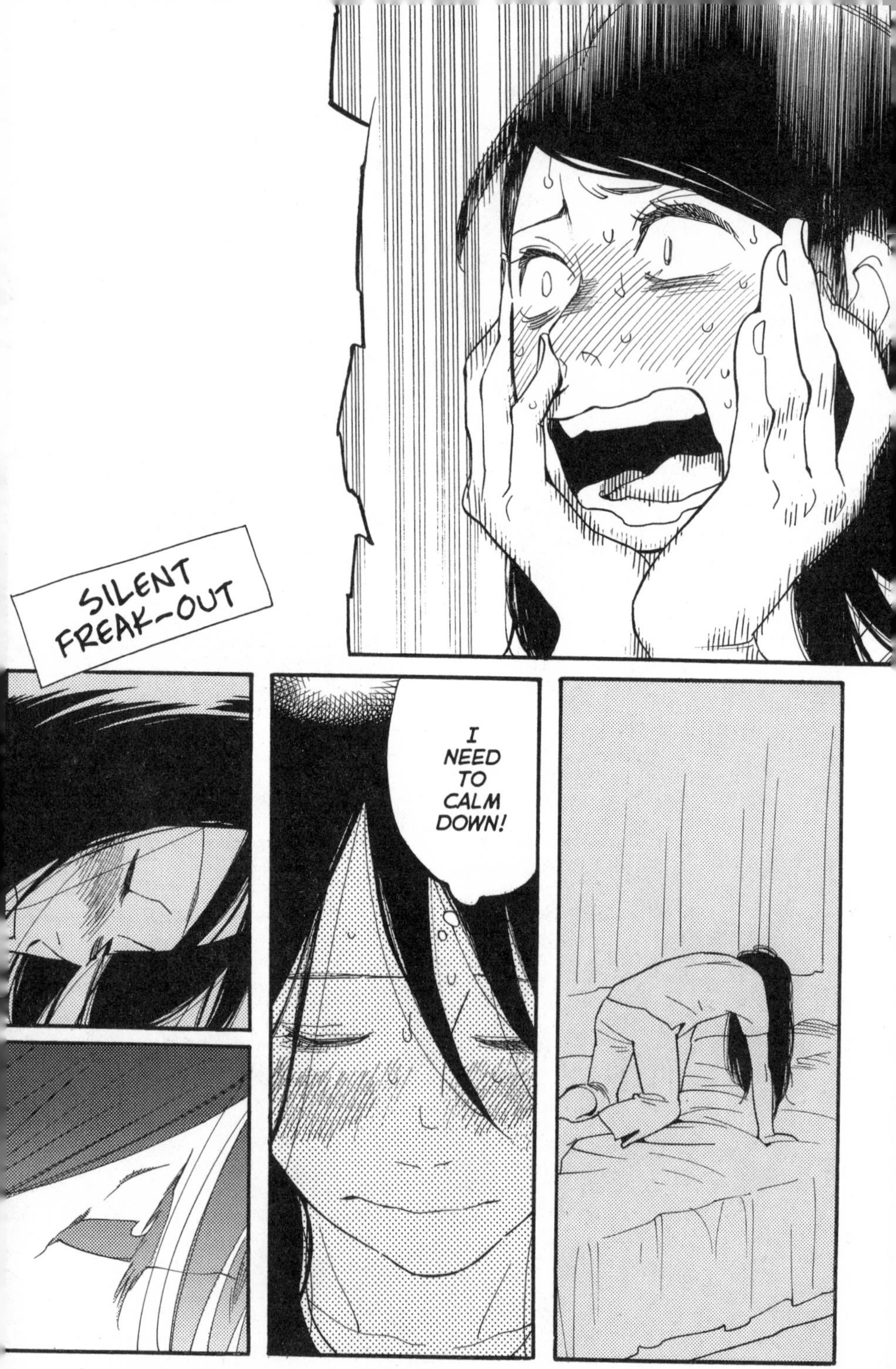
SILENT FREAK-OUT
I NEED TO CALM DOWN!

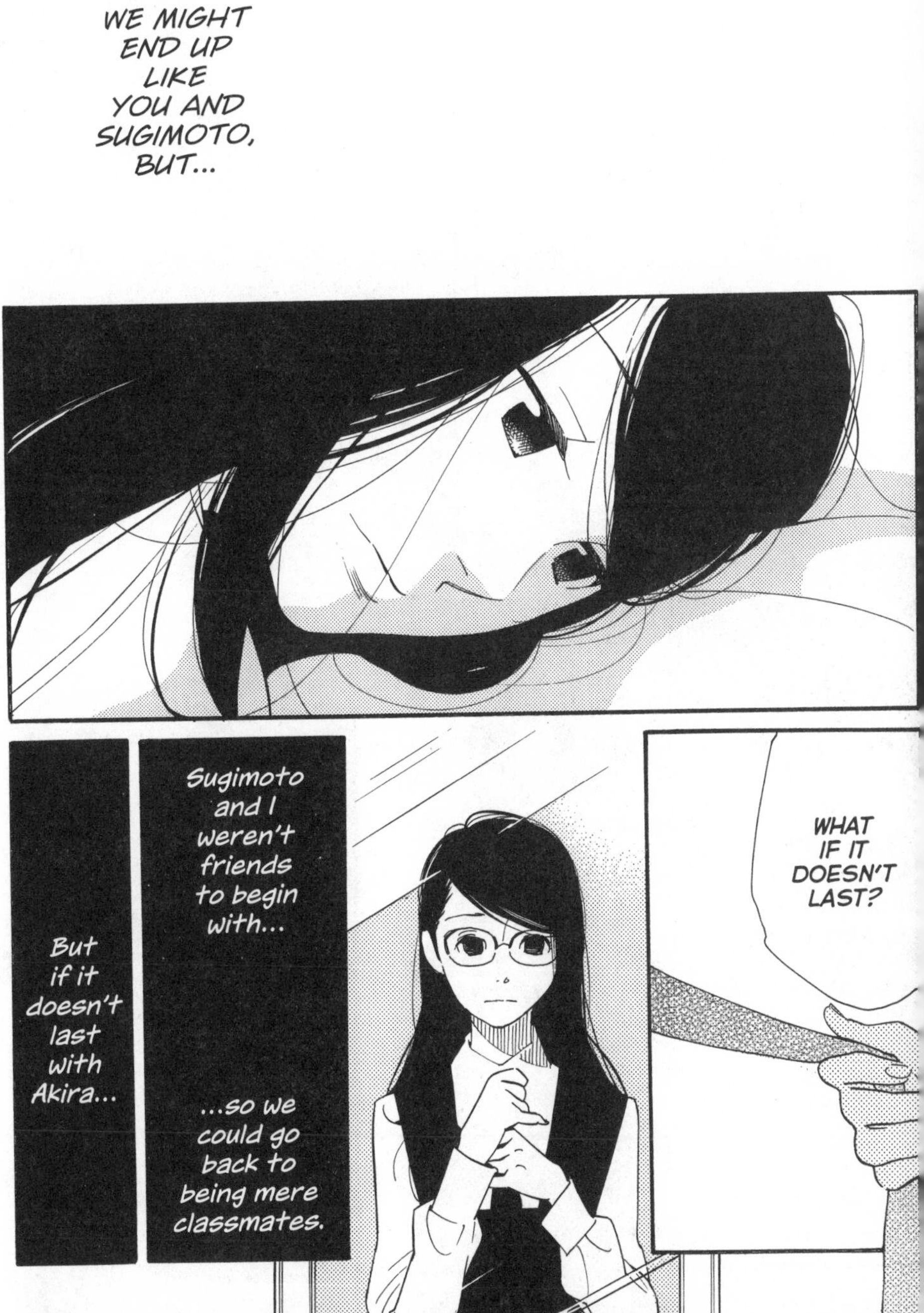
WE MIGHT END UP LIKE YOU AND SUGIMOTO, BUT...
WHAT IF IT DOESN'T LAST?
Sugimoto and I weren't friends to begin with...
...so we could go back to being mere classmates.
But if it doesn't last with Akira...

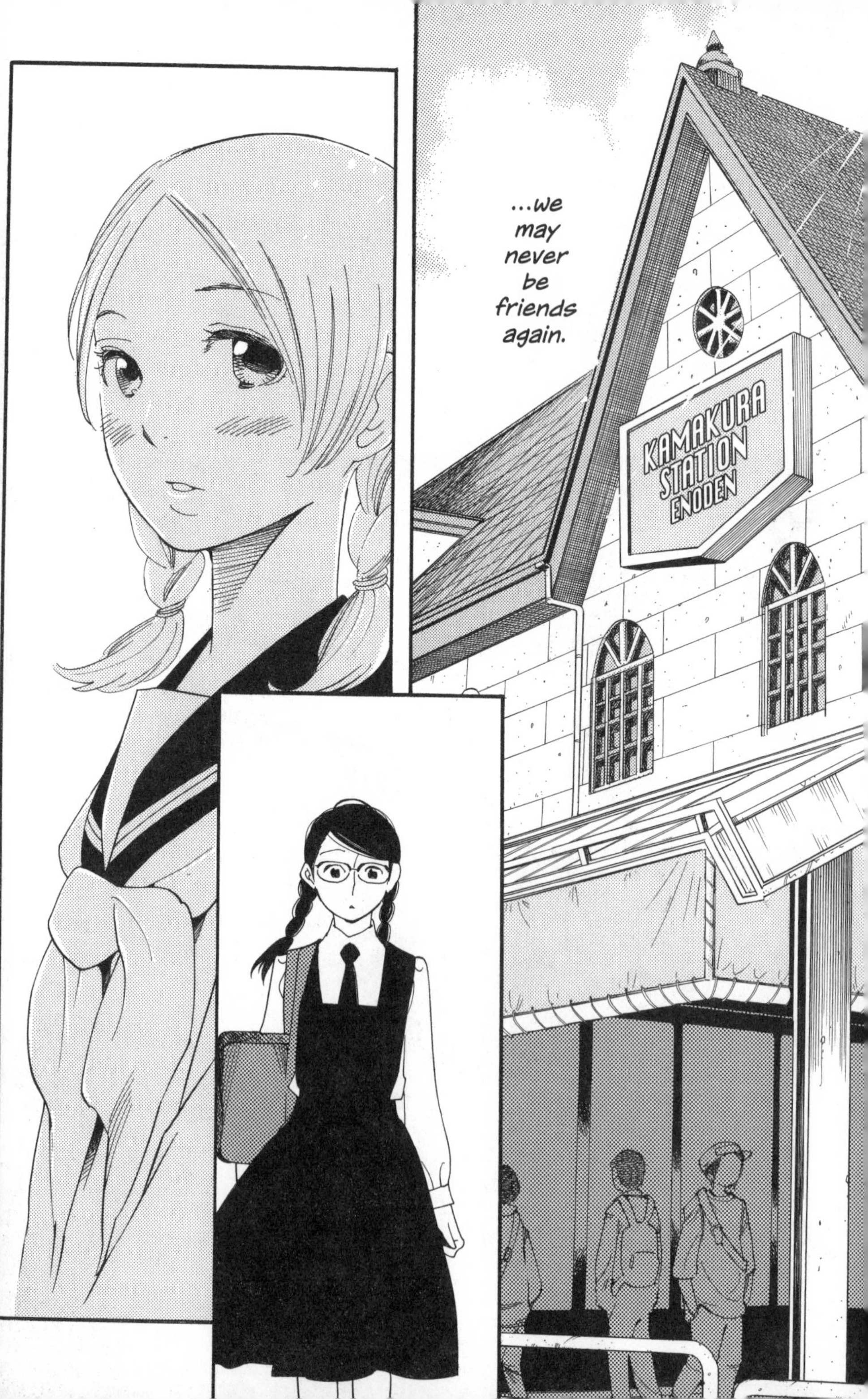
...we may never be friends again.
KAMAKURA STATION ENODEN

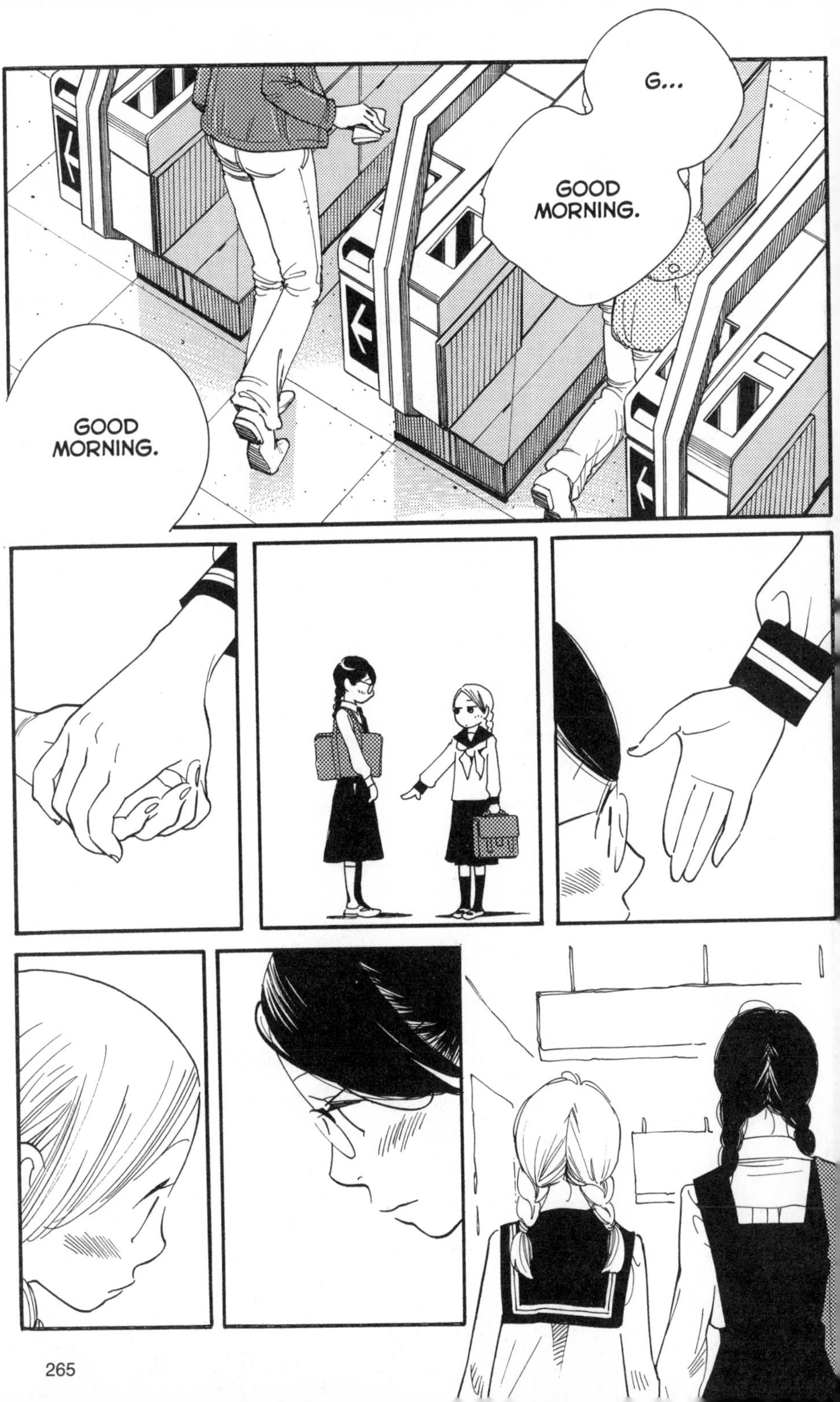
G...
GOOD MORNING.
GOOD MORNING.

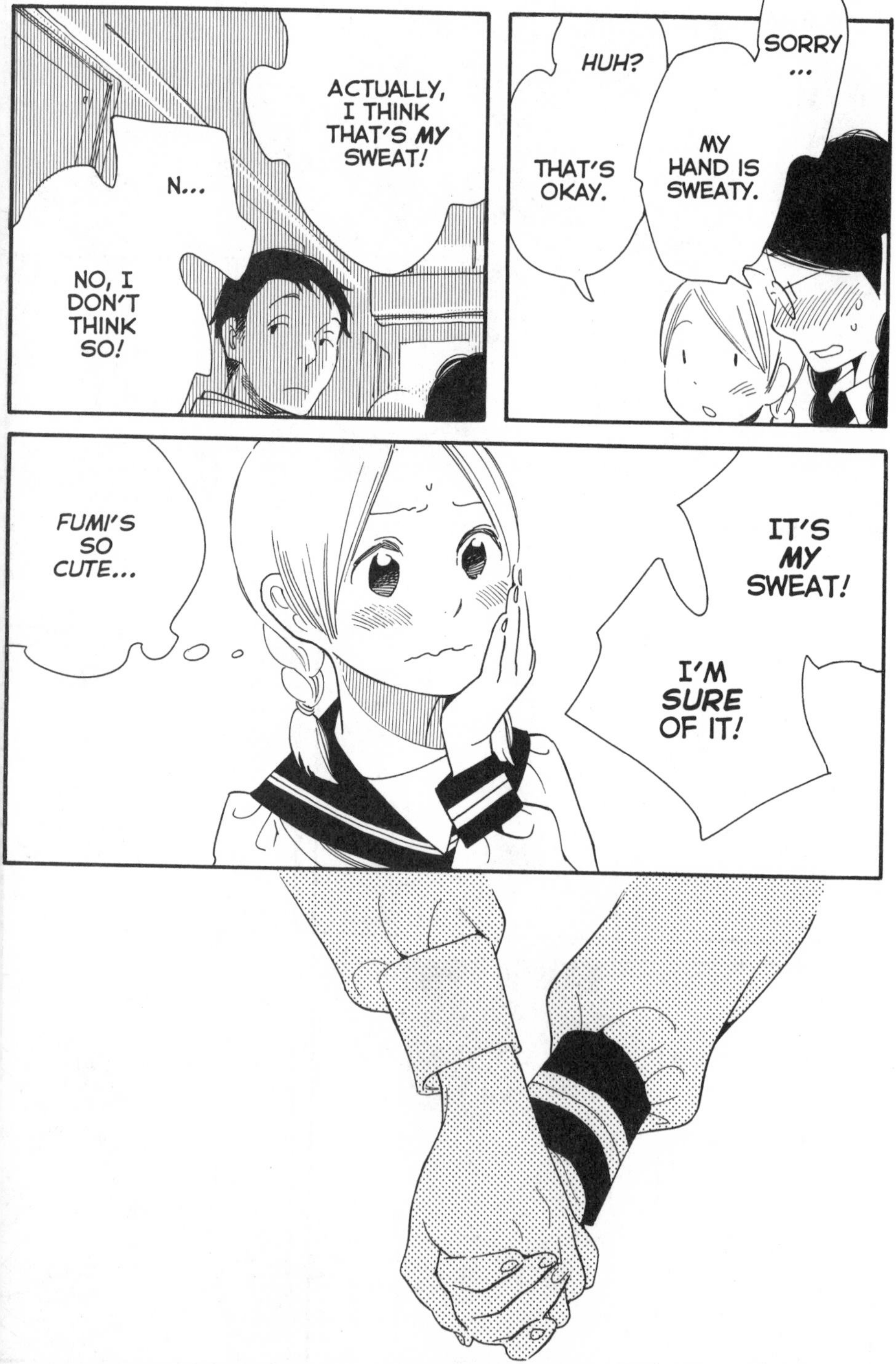
SORRY ...
MY HAND IS SWEATY.
HUH?
THAT'S OKAY.
ACTUALLY, I THINK THAT'S *MY* SWEAT!
N...
NO, I DON'T THINK SO!
IT'S *MY* SWEAT!
I'M *SURE* OF IT!
FUMI'S SO CUTE...

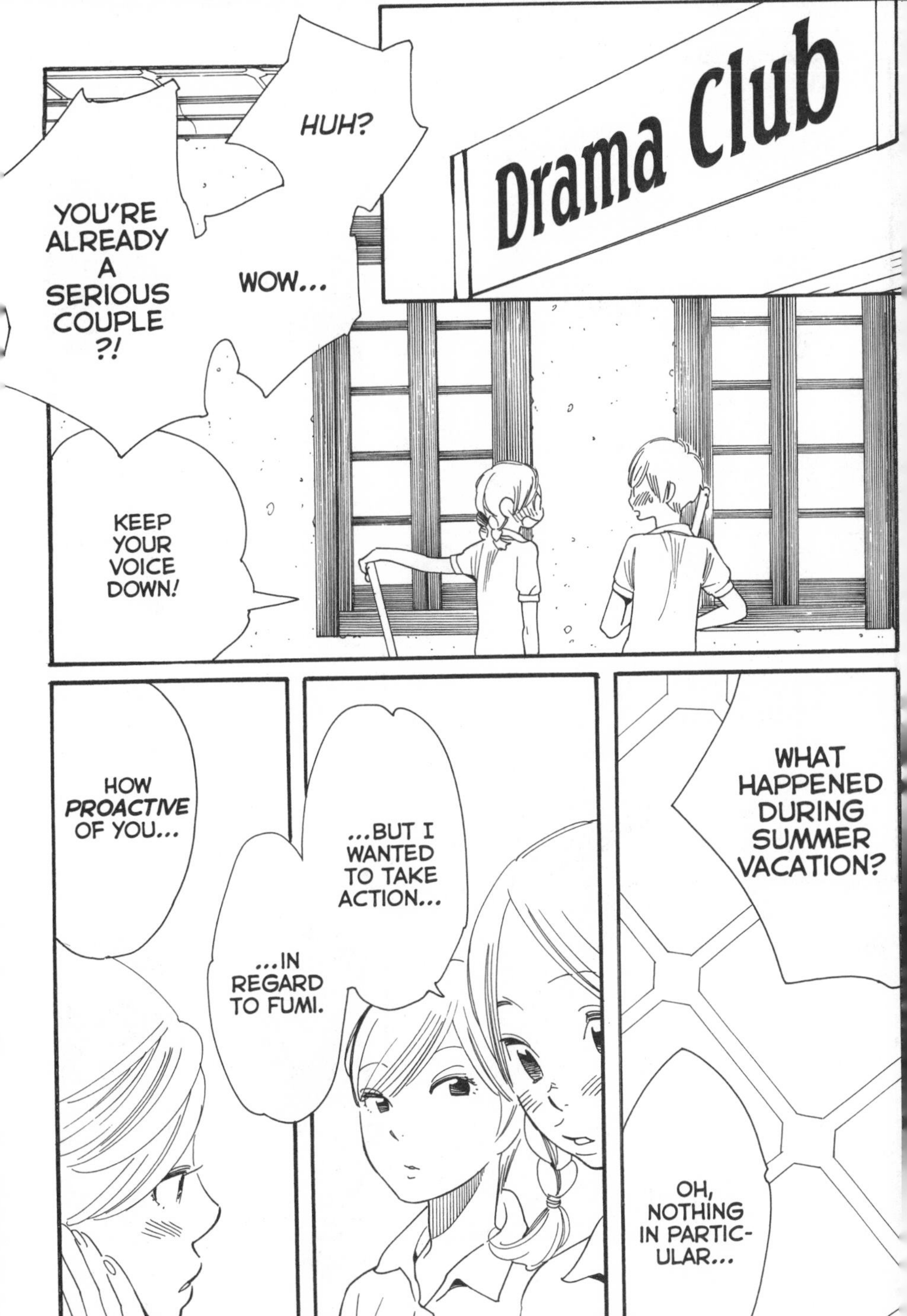
Drama Club
HUH?
WOW...
YOU'RE ALREADY A SERIOUS COUPLE?!
KEEP YOUR VOICE DOWN!
WHAT HAPPENED DURING SUMMER VACATION?
OH, NOTHING IN PARTIC-ULAR...
...BUT I WANTED TO TAKE ACTION...
...IN REGARD TO FUMI.
HOW *PROACTIVE* OF YOU...

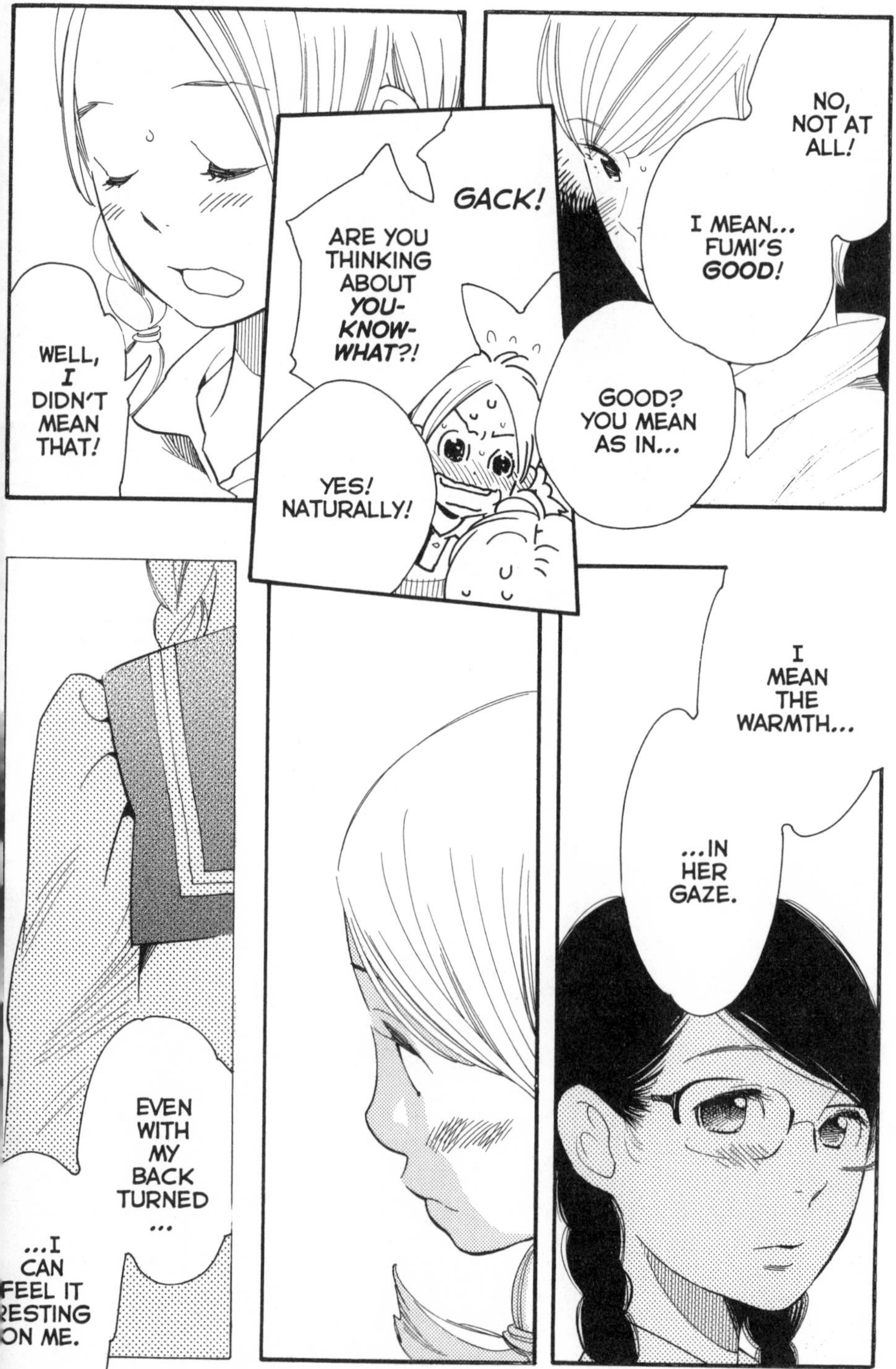
NO, NOT AT ALL!
I MEAN... FUMI'S GOOD!
GOOD? YOU MEAN AS IN...
GACK!
ARE YOU THINKING ABOUT YOU-KNOW-WHAT?!
YES! NATURALLY!
WELL, I DIDN'T MEAN THAT!
I MEAN THE WARMTH...
...IN HER GAZE.
EVEN WITH MY BACK TURNED...
...I CAN FEEL IT RESTING ON ME.

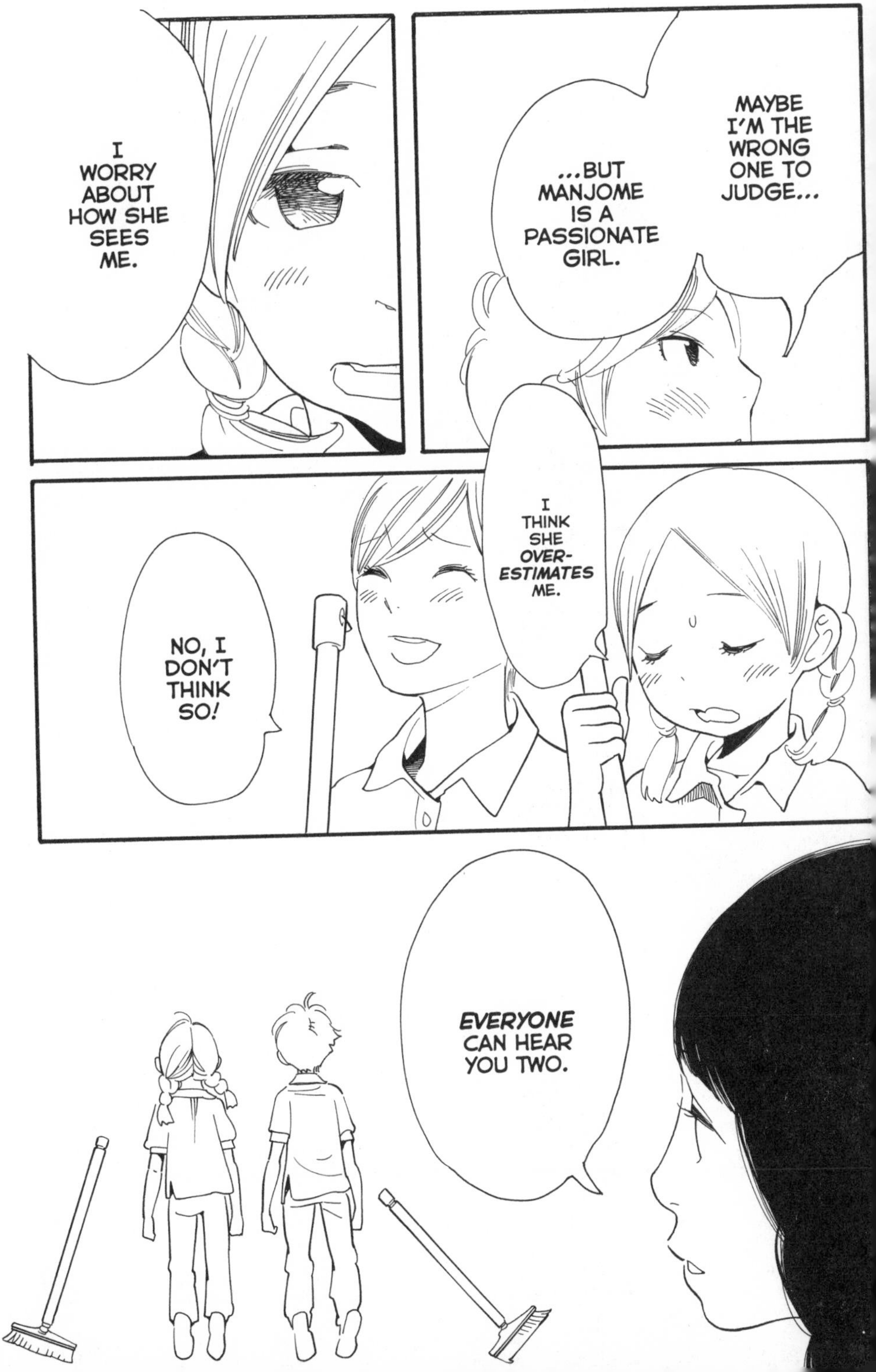
MAYBE I'M THE WRONG ONE TO JUDGE...
...BUT MANJOME IS A PASSIONATE GIRL.
I WORRY ABOUT HOW SHE SEES ME.
I THINK SHE OVER-ESTIMATES ME.
NO, I DON'T THINK SO!
EVERYONE CAN HEAR YOU TWO.

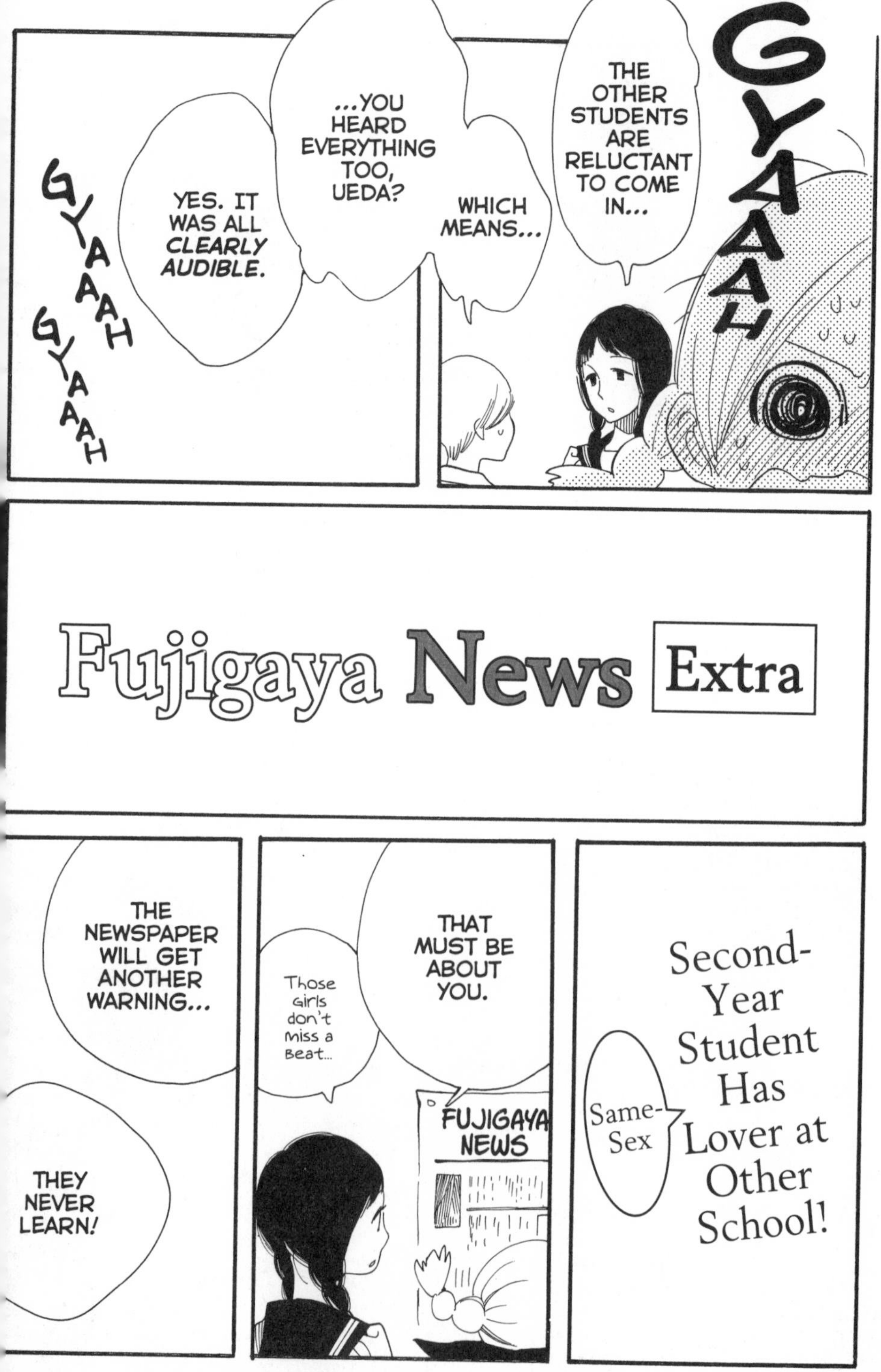
GYAAAH
THE OTHER STUDENTS ARE RELUCTANT TO COME IN...
WHICH MEANS...
...YOU HEARD EVERYTHING TOO, UEDA?
YES. IT WAS ALL *CLEARLY AUDIBLE.*
GYAAAH GYAAAH
Fujigaya News Extra
Second-Year Student Has Lover at Other School!
Same-Sex
THAT MUST BE ABOUT YOU.
Those girls don't miss a beat...
FUJIGAYA NEWS
THE NEWSPAPER WILL GET ANOTHER WARNING...
THEY NEVER LEARN!

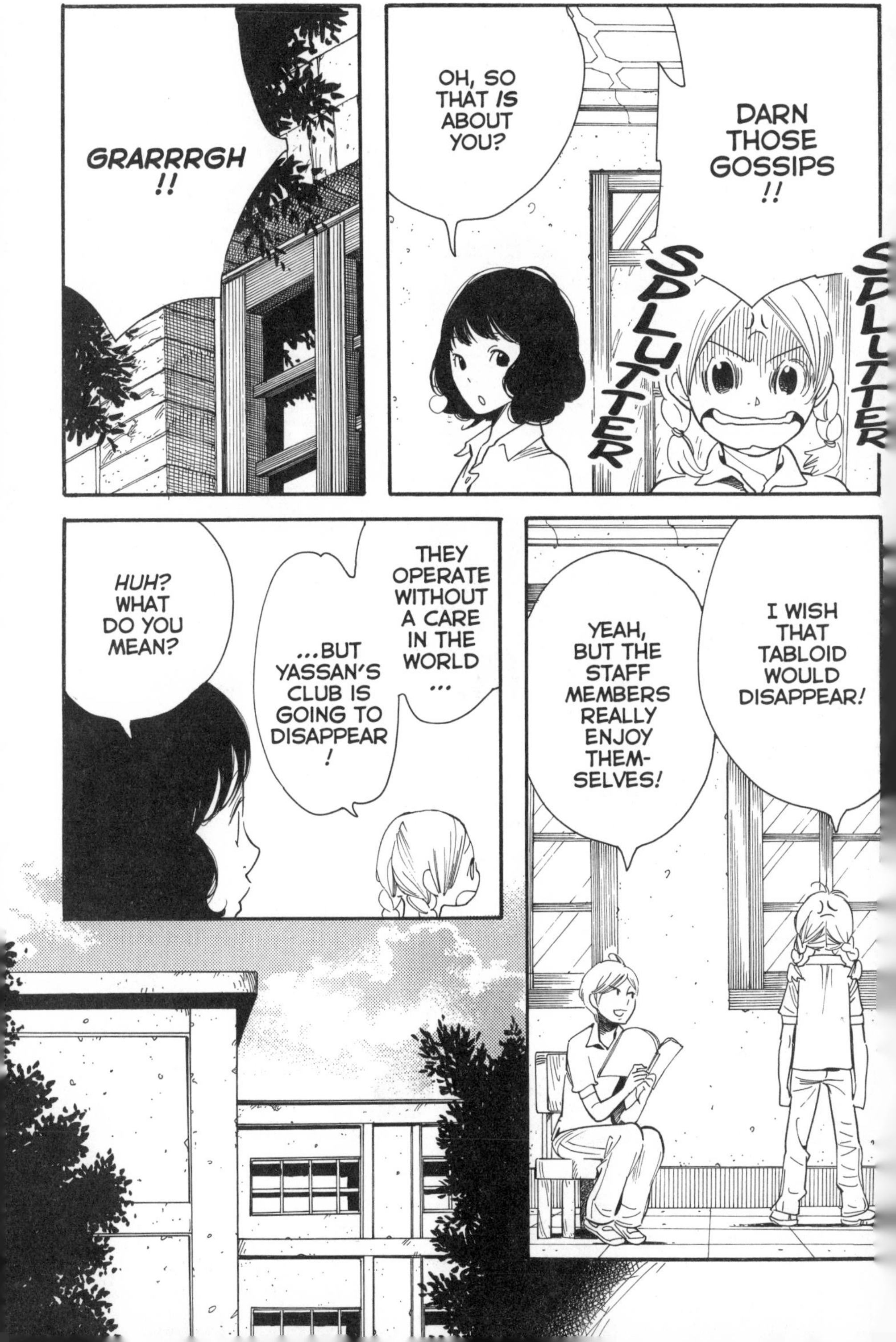
DARN THOSE GOSSIPS!!
SPLITTER
OH, SO THAT IS ABOUT YOU?
SPLUTTER
GRARRRGH!!
I WISH THAT TABLOID WOULD DISAPPEAR!
YEAH, BUT THE STAFF MEMBERS REALLY ENJOY THEM-SELVES!
THEY OPERATE WITHOUT A CARE IN THE WORLD...
...BUT YASSAN'S CLUB IS GOING TO DISAPPEAR!
HUH? WHAT DO YOU MEAN?

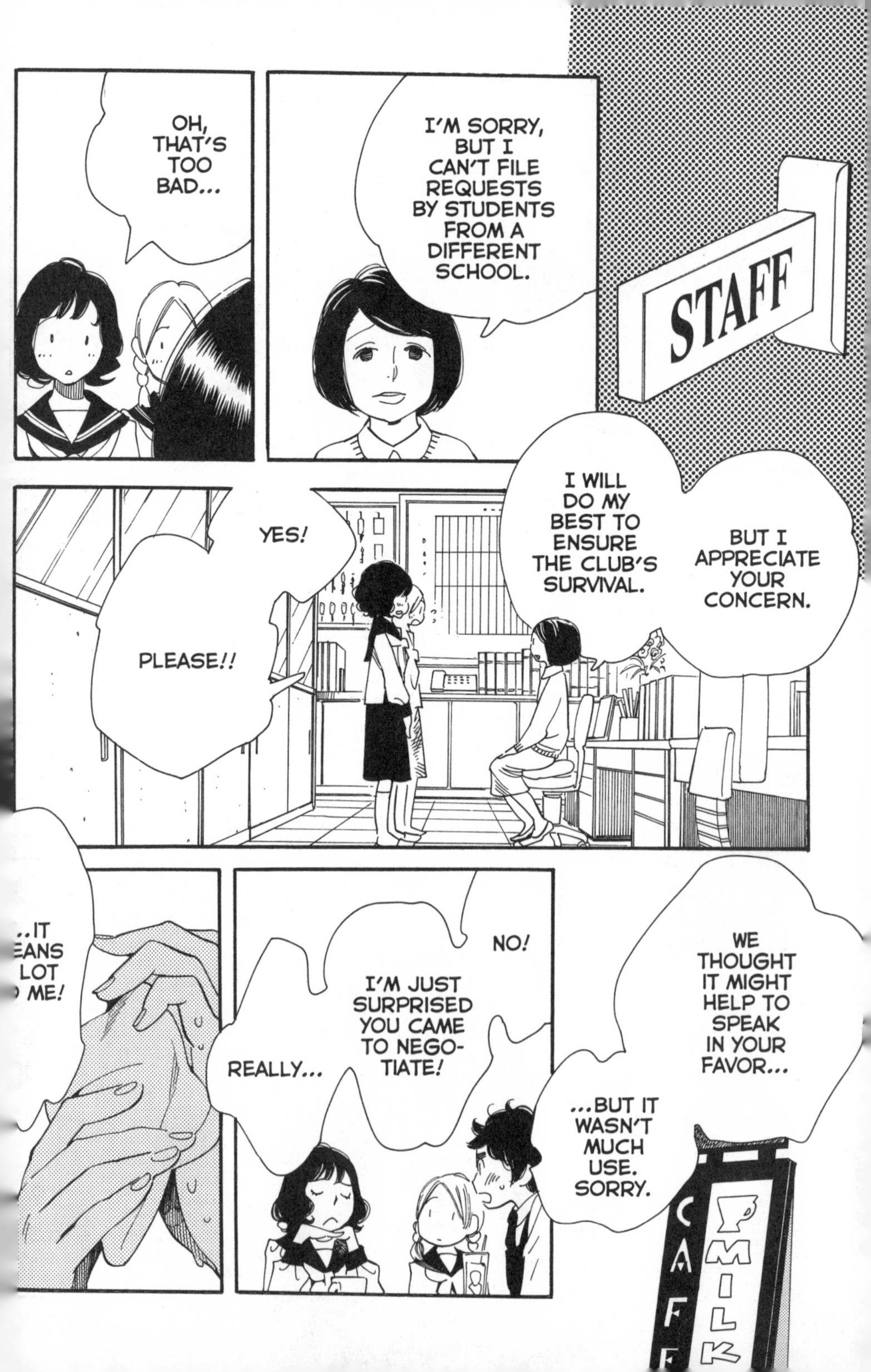
STAFF
I'M SORRY, BUT I CAN'T FILE REQUESTS BY STUDENTS FROM A DIFFERENT SCHOOL.
OH, THAT'S TOO BAD...
BUT I APPRECIATE YOUR CONCERN.
I WILL DO MY BEST TO ENSURE THE CLUB'S SURVIVAL.
YES!
PLEASE!!
CAF
MILK
WE THOUGHT IT MIGHT HELP TO SPEAK IN YOUR FAVOR...
...BUT IT WASN'T MUCH USE. SORRY.
NO!
I'M JUST SURPRISED YOU CAME TO NEGOTIATE!
REALLY...
..IT EANS LOT ME!

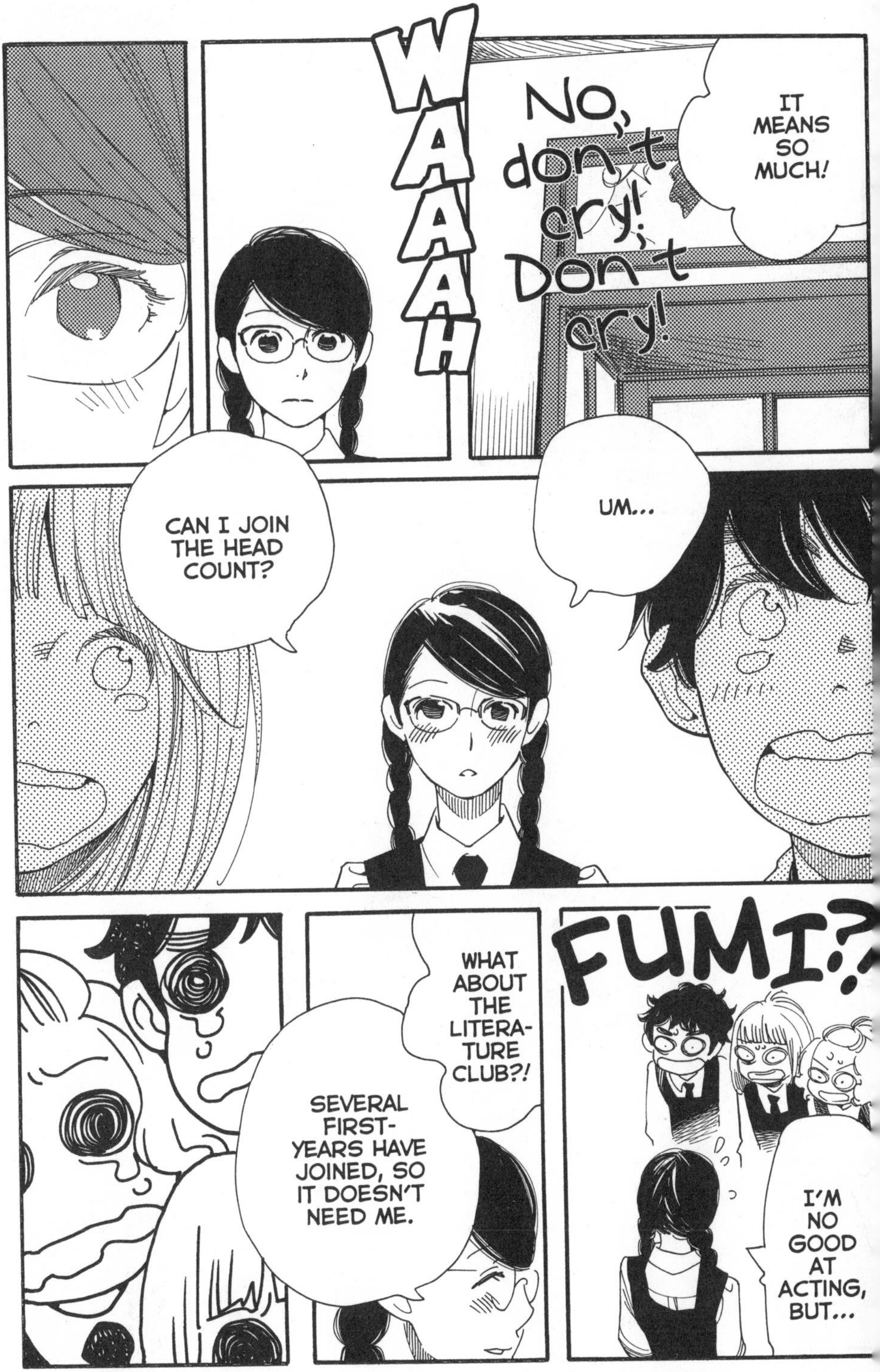
IT MEANS SO MUCH!
No, don't cry! Don't cry!
WAAAAH
UM...
CAN I JOIN THE HEAD COUNT?
FUMI?!
I'M NO GOOD AT ACTING, BUT...
WHAT ABOUT THE LITERATURE CLUB?!
SEVERAL FIRST-YEARS HAVE JOINED, SO IT DOESN'T NEED ME.

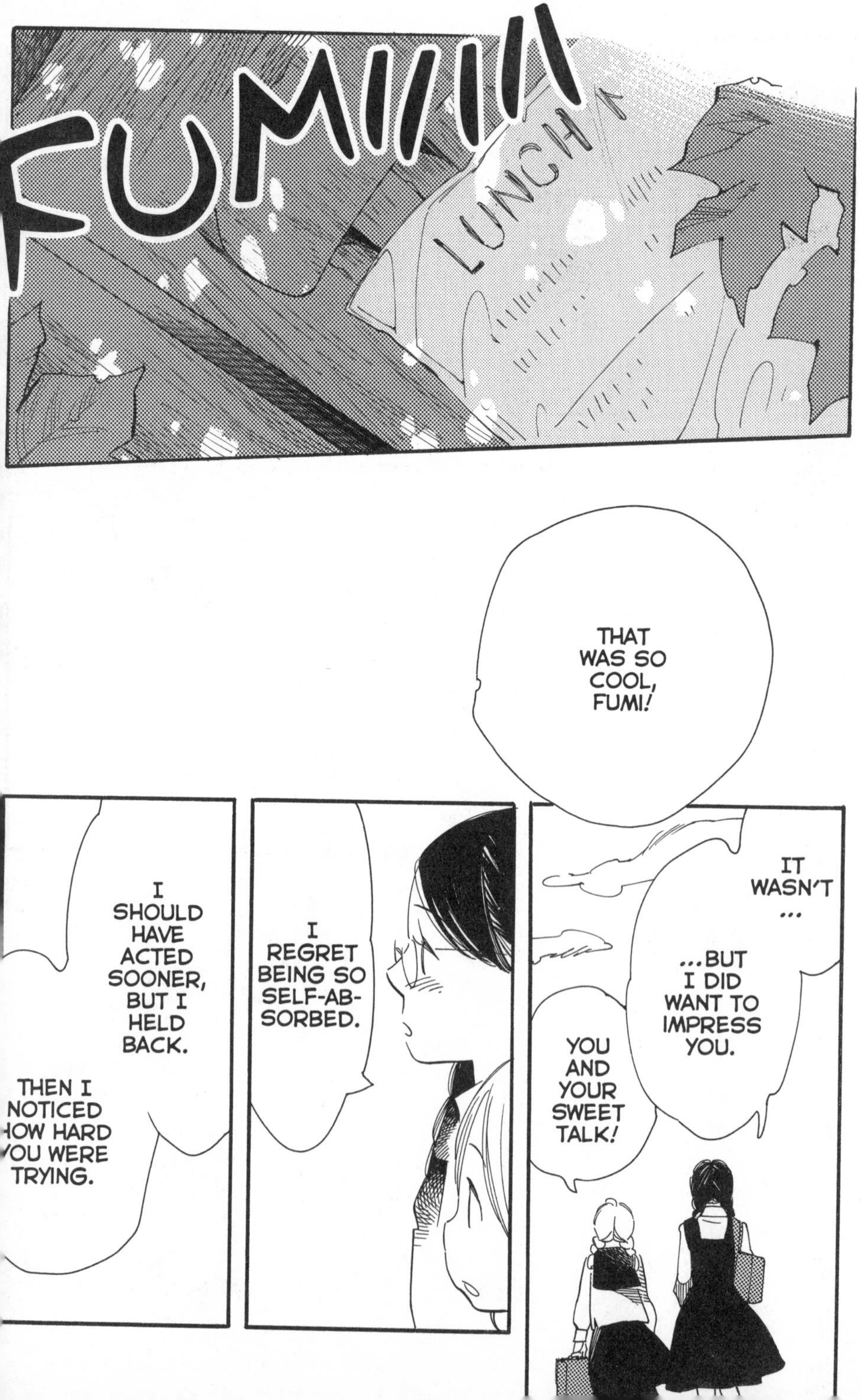
FUMIIII
LUNCH
THAT WAS SO COOL, FUMI!
IT WASN'T...
...BUT I DID WANT TO IMPRESS YOU.
YOU AND YOUR SWEET TALK!
I REGRET BEING SO SELF-ABSORBED.
I SHOULD HAVE ACTED SOONER, BUT I HELD BACK.
THEN I NOTICED HOW HARD YOU WERE TRYING.

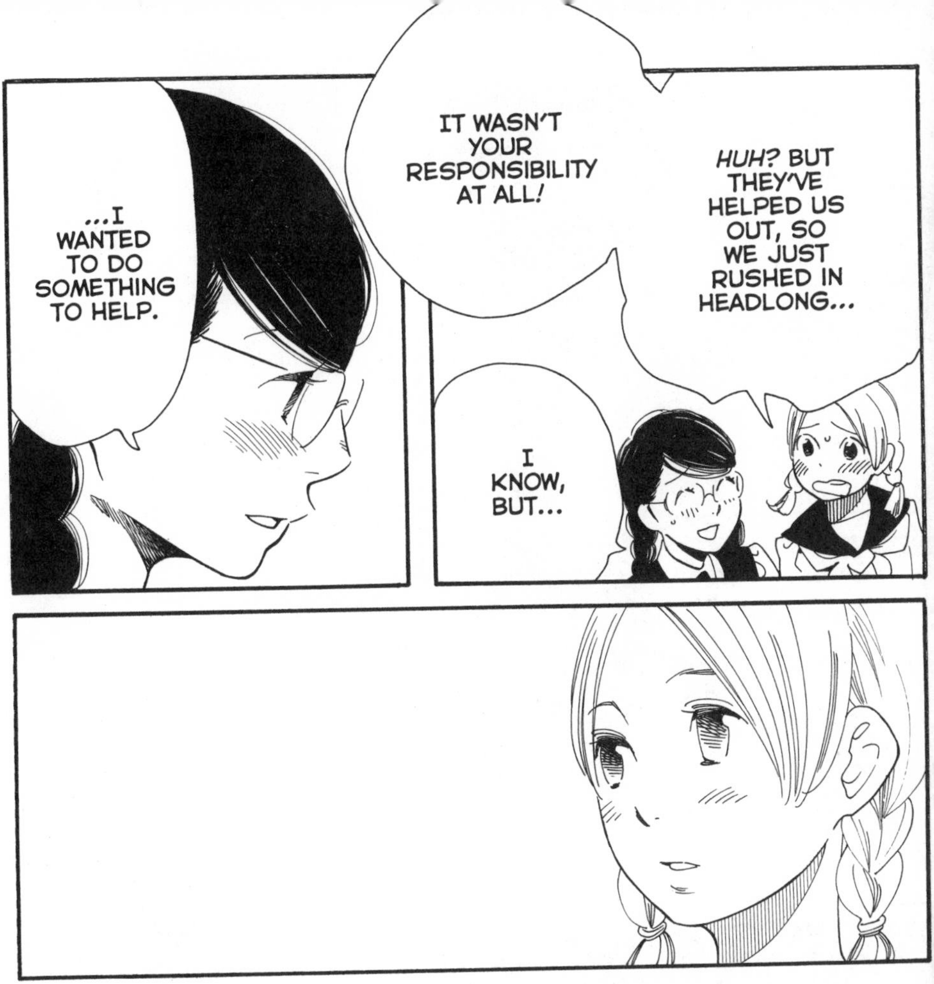
HUH? BUT THEY'VE HELPED US OUT, SO WE JUST RUSHED IN HEADLONG...
I KNOW, BUT...
...I WANTED TO DO SOMETHING TO HELP.
IT WASN'T YOUR RESPONSIBILITY AT ALL!

If this is the power of love...

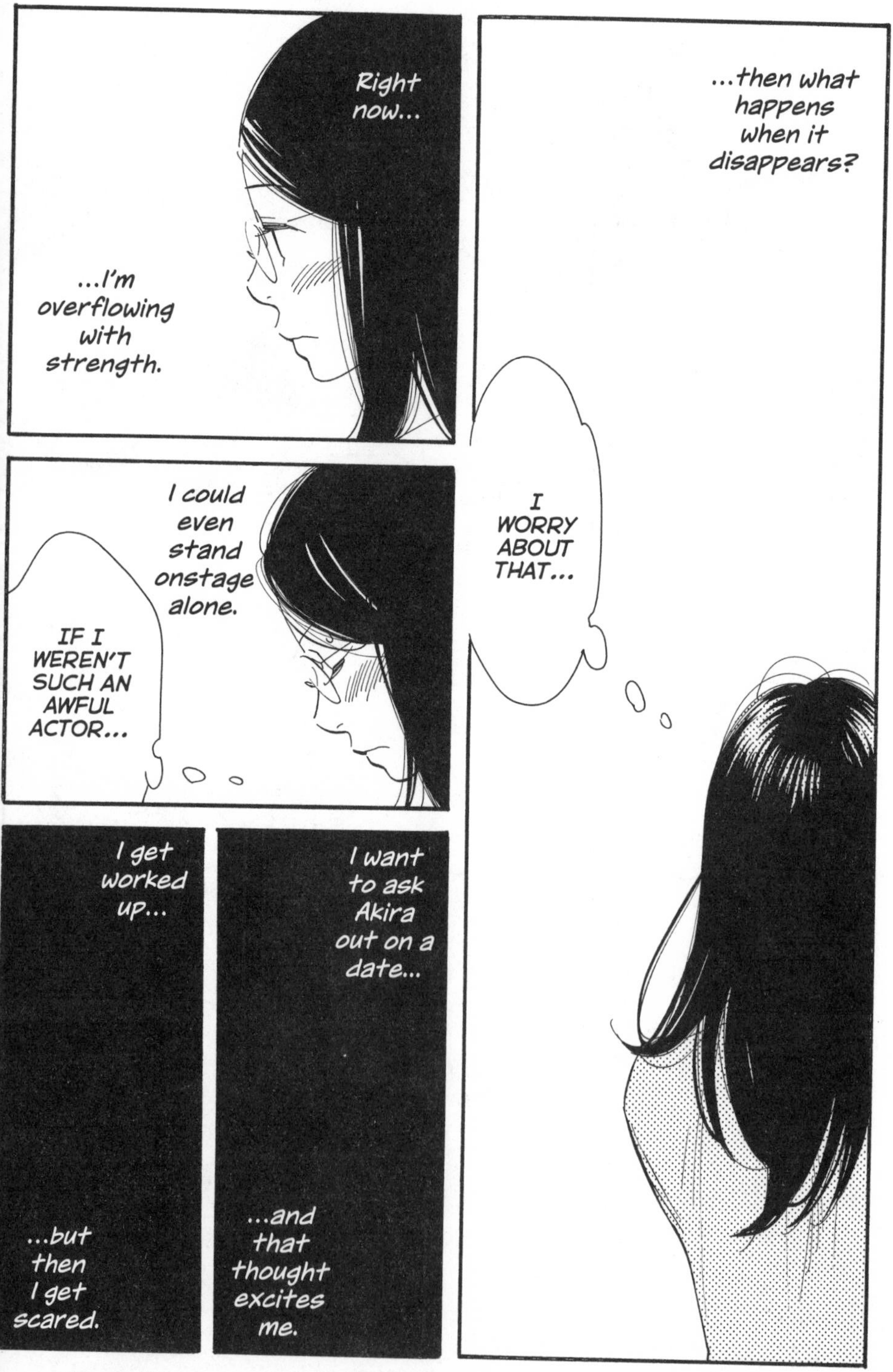

Right now...
...I'm overflowing with strength.
I could even stand onstage alone.
IF I WEREN'T SUCH AN AWFUL ACTOR...
I want to ask Akira out on a date...
...and that thought excites me.
I get worked up...
...but then I get scared.
...then what happens when it disappears?
I WORRY ABOUT THAT...

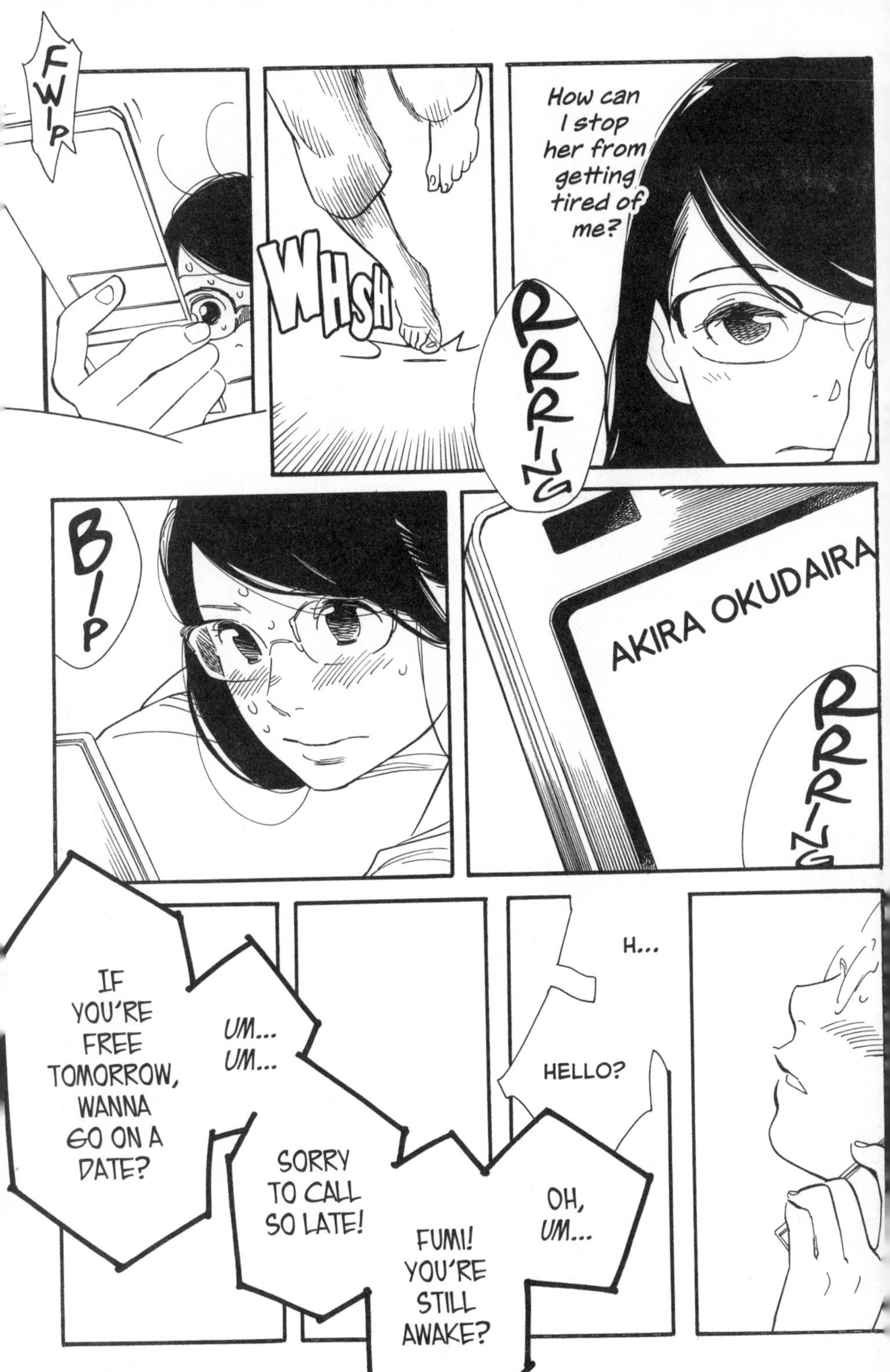
How can I stop her from getting tired of me?
RRRING
WHSH
FWIP
AKIRA OKUDAIRA
RRRING
BIP
H...
HELLO?
OH, UM...
FUMI! YOU'RE STILL AWAKE?
SORRY TO CALL SO LATE!
UM... UM...
IF YOU'RE FREE TOMORROW, WANNA GO ON A DATE?

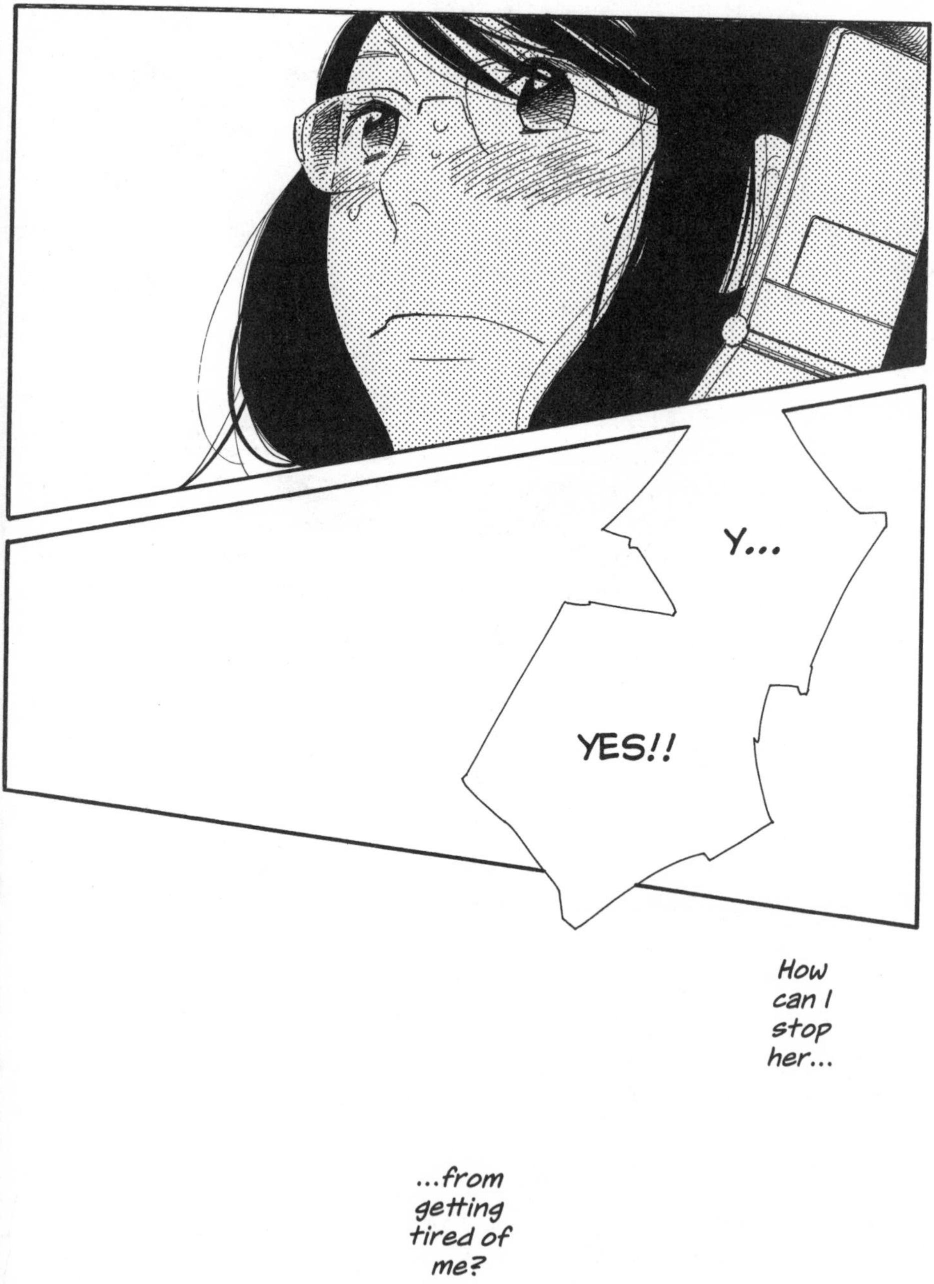
Y...
YES!!
How can I stop her...
...from getting tired of me?

Sweet Blue Flowers

#36 First Love

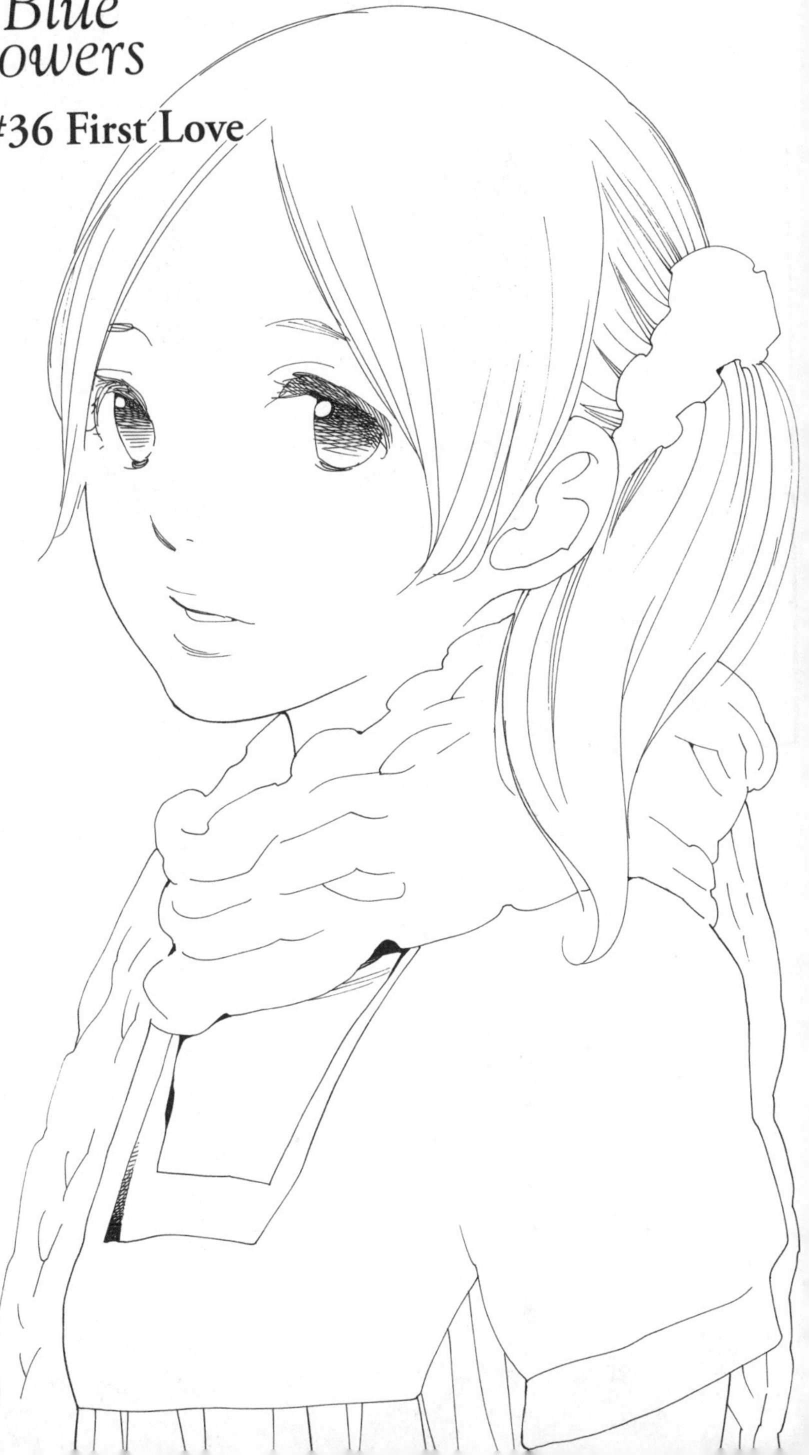

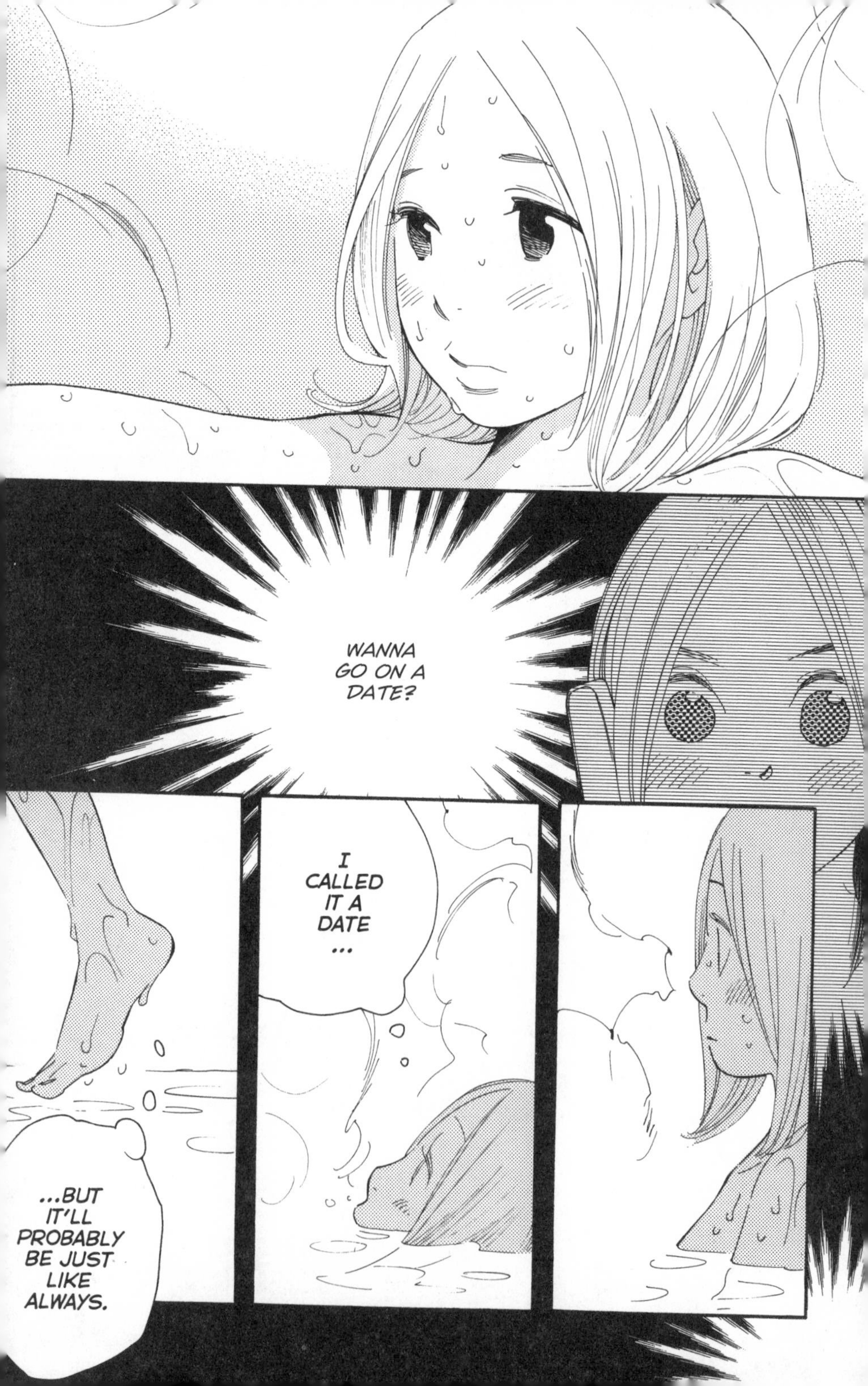
WANNA GO ON A DATE?
I CALLED IT A DATE...
...BUT IT'LL PROBABLY BE JUST LIKE ALWAYS.

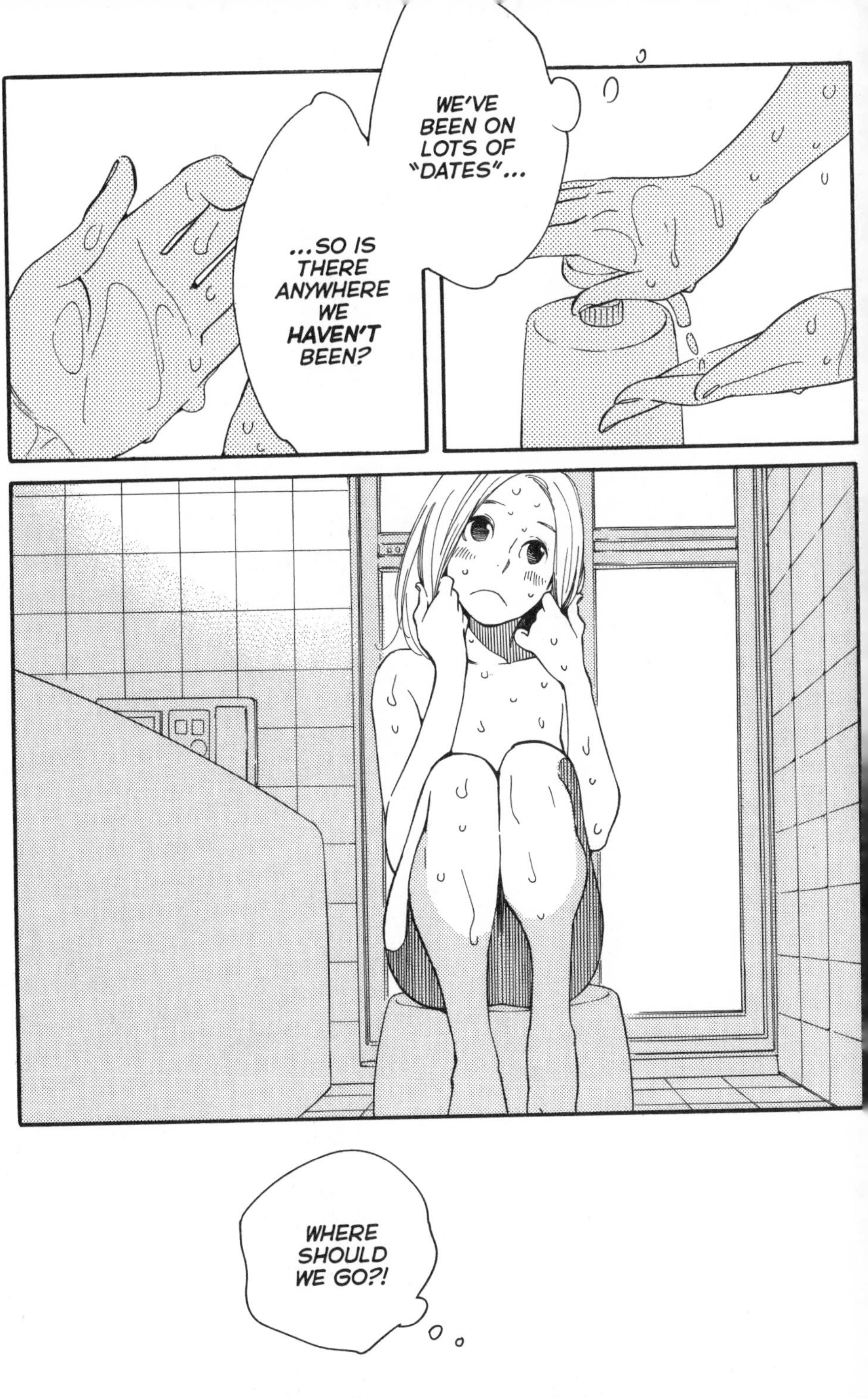
WE'VE BEEN ON LOTS OF "DATES"...
...SO IS THERE ANYWHERE WE HAVEN'T BEEN?
WHERE SHOULD WE GO?!

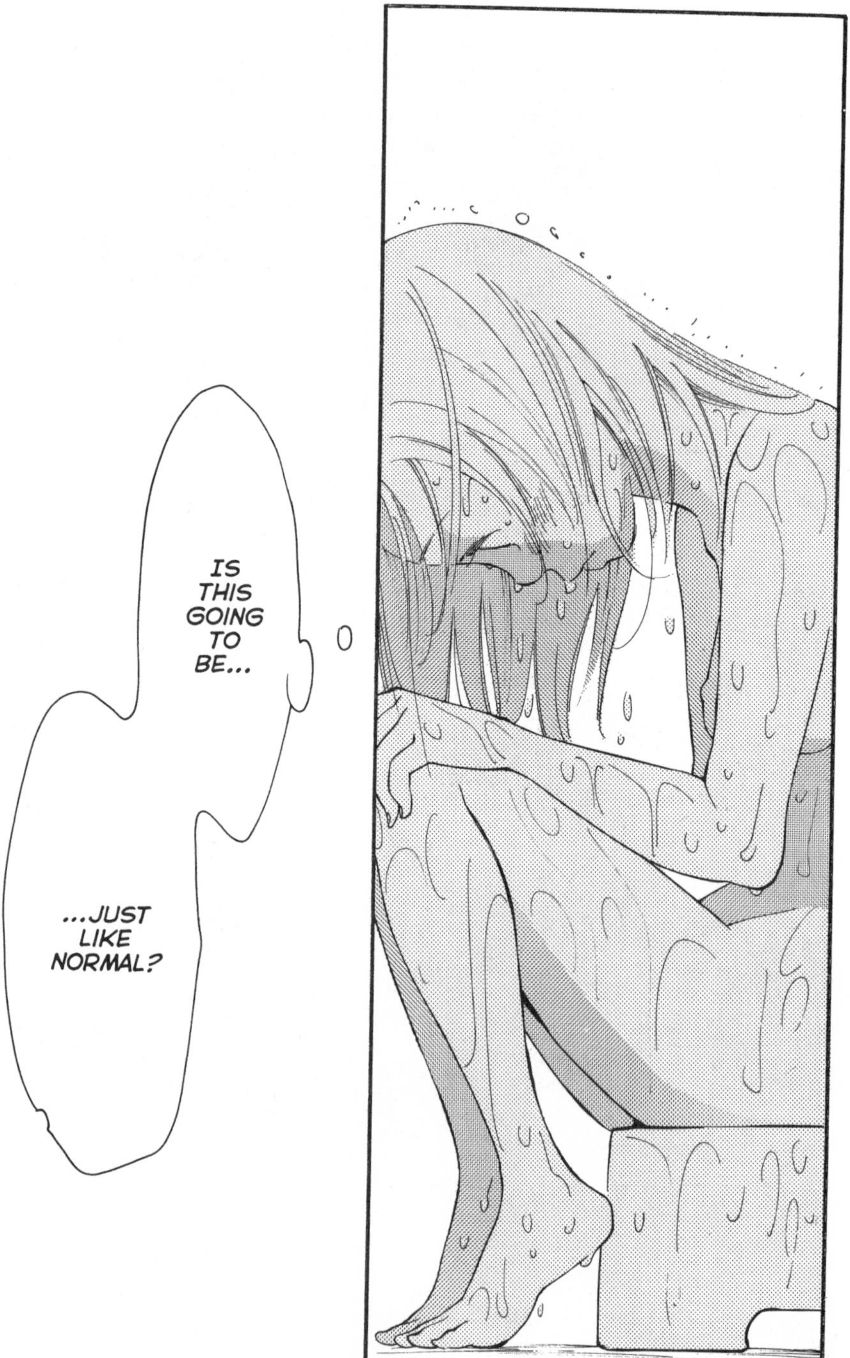
IS THIS GOING TO BE...
...JUST LIKE NORMAL?

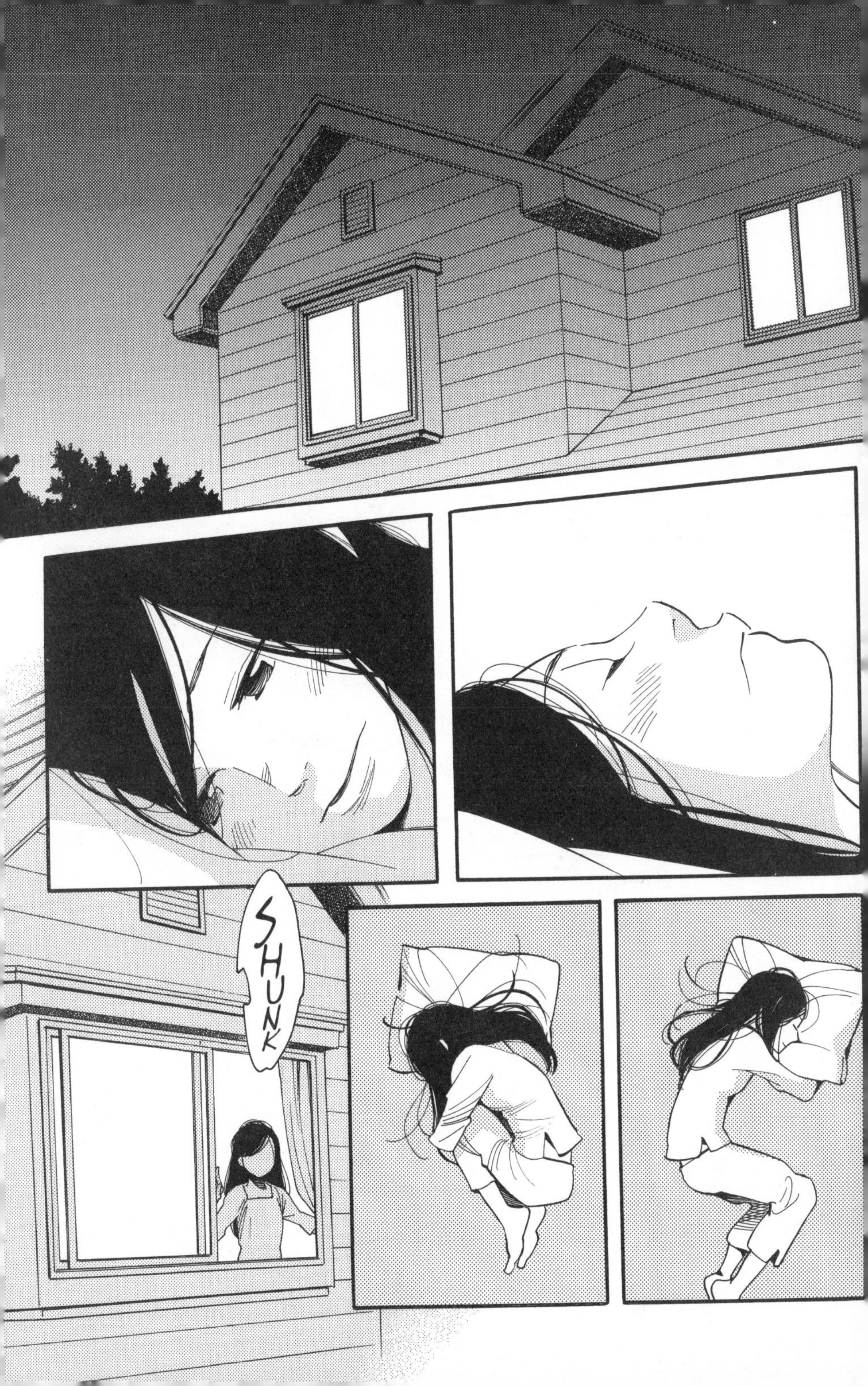
SHUNK

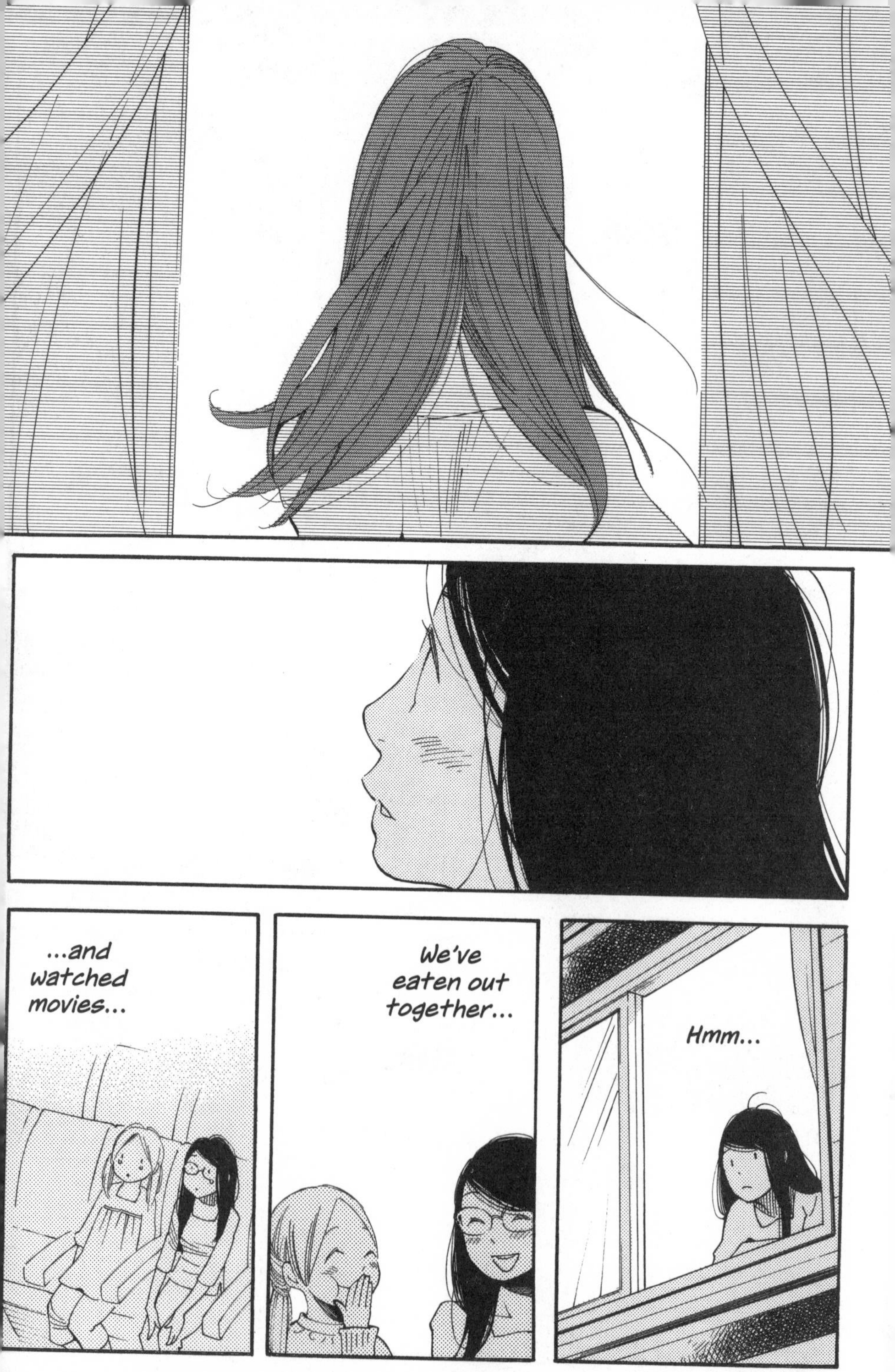
Hmm...
We've eaten out together...
...and watched movies...

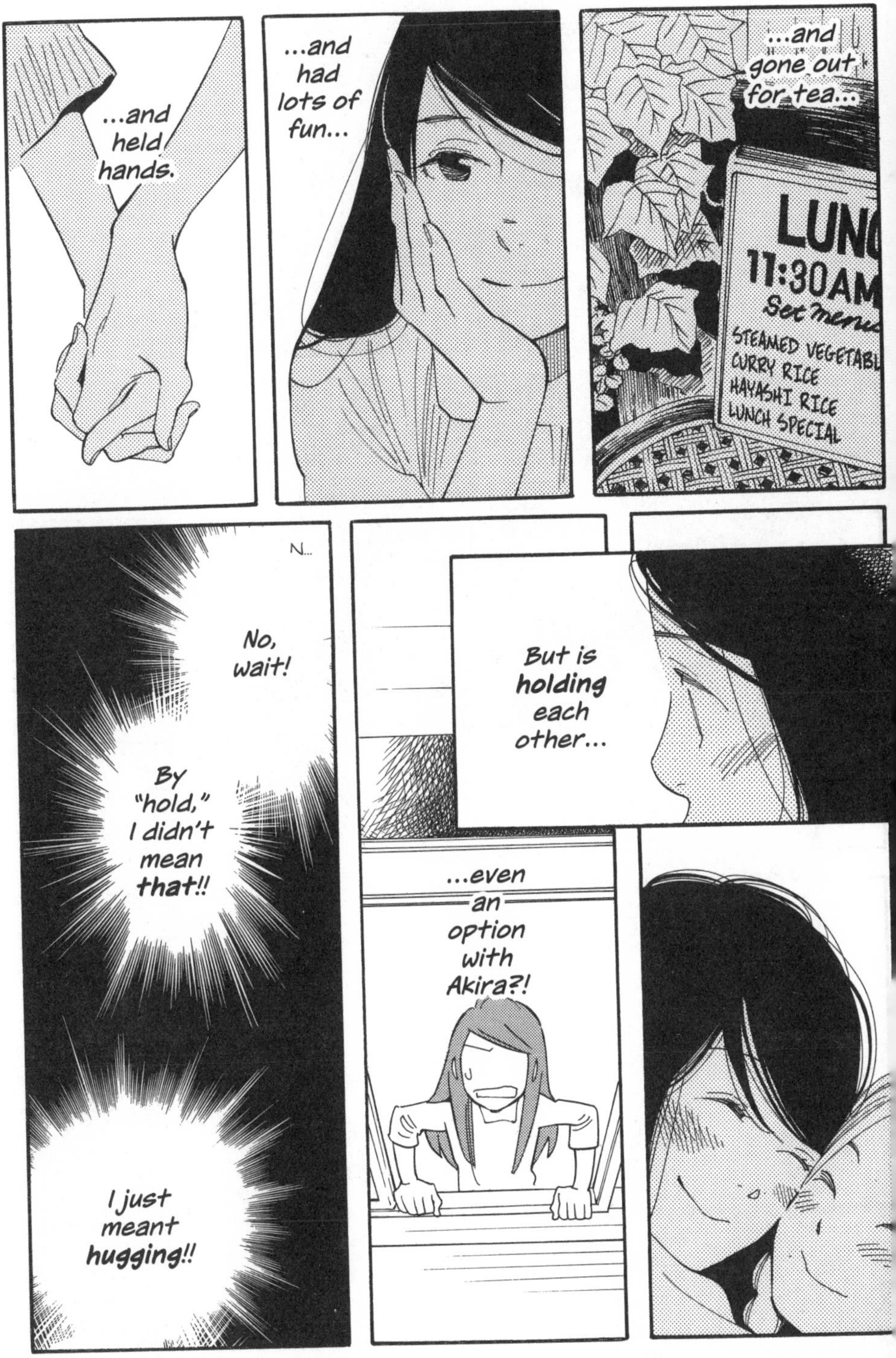
...and gone out for tea...
11:30AM
CURRY RICE
HAYASHI RICE
LUNCH SPECIAL
...and had lots of fun...
...and held hands.
But is **holding** each other...
...even an option with Akira?!
N...
No, wait!
By "hold," I didn't mean **that**!!
I just meant **hugging**!!

Akira might not like that.

She might not want to get cuddly.

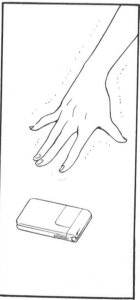

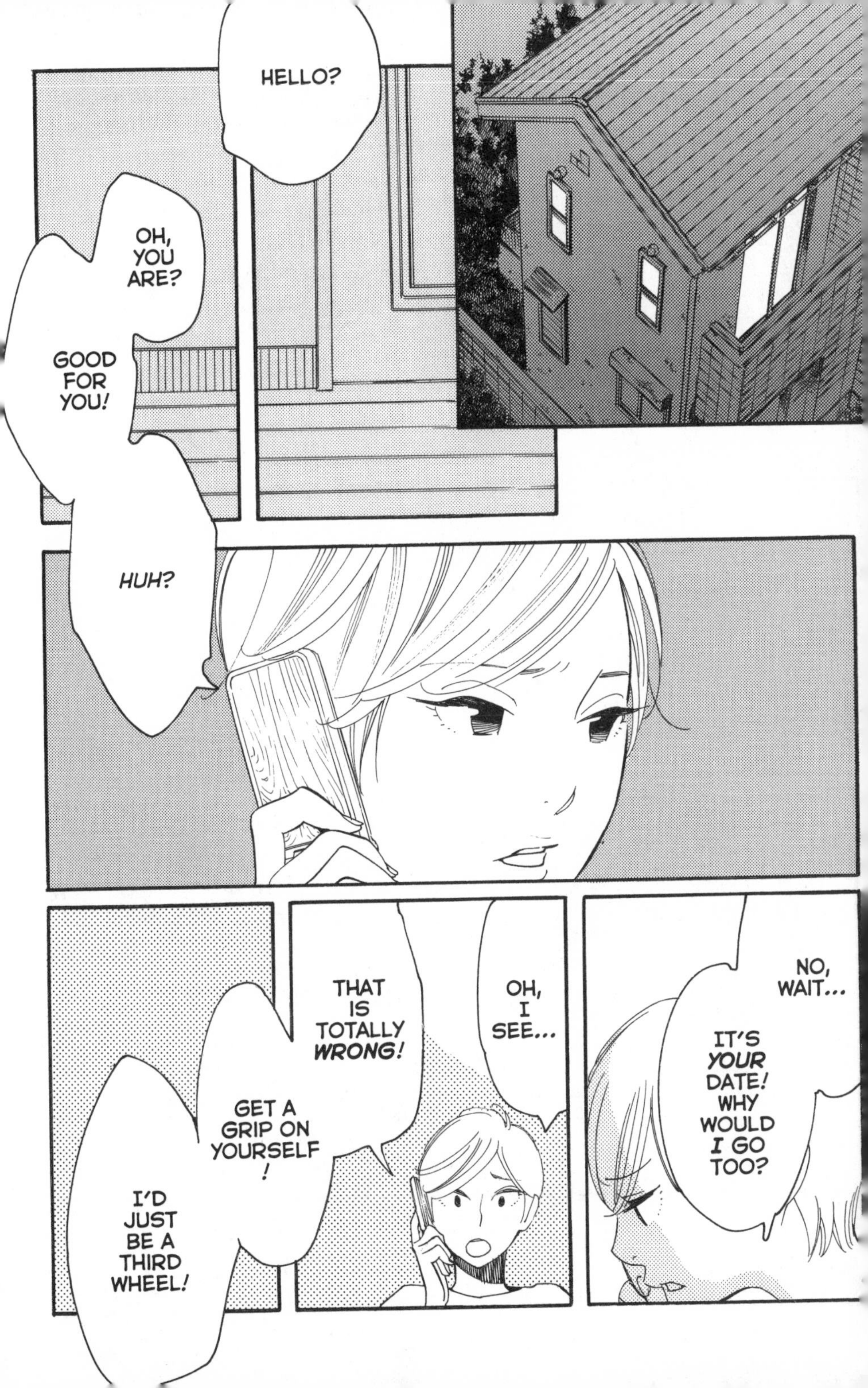
HELLO?
OH, YOU ARE?
GOOD FOR YOU!
HUH?
NO, WAIT...
IT'S ***YOUR*** DATE! WHY WOULD ***I*** GO TOO?
OH, I SEE...
THAT IS TOTALLY ***WRONG!***
GET A GRIP ON YOURSELF!
I'D JUST BE A THIRD WHEEL!

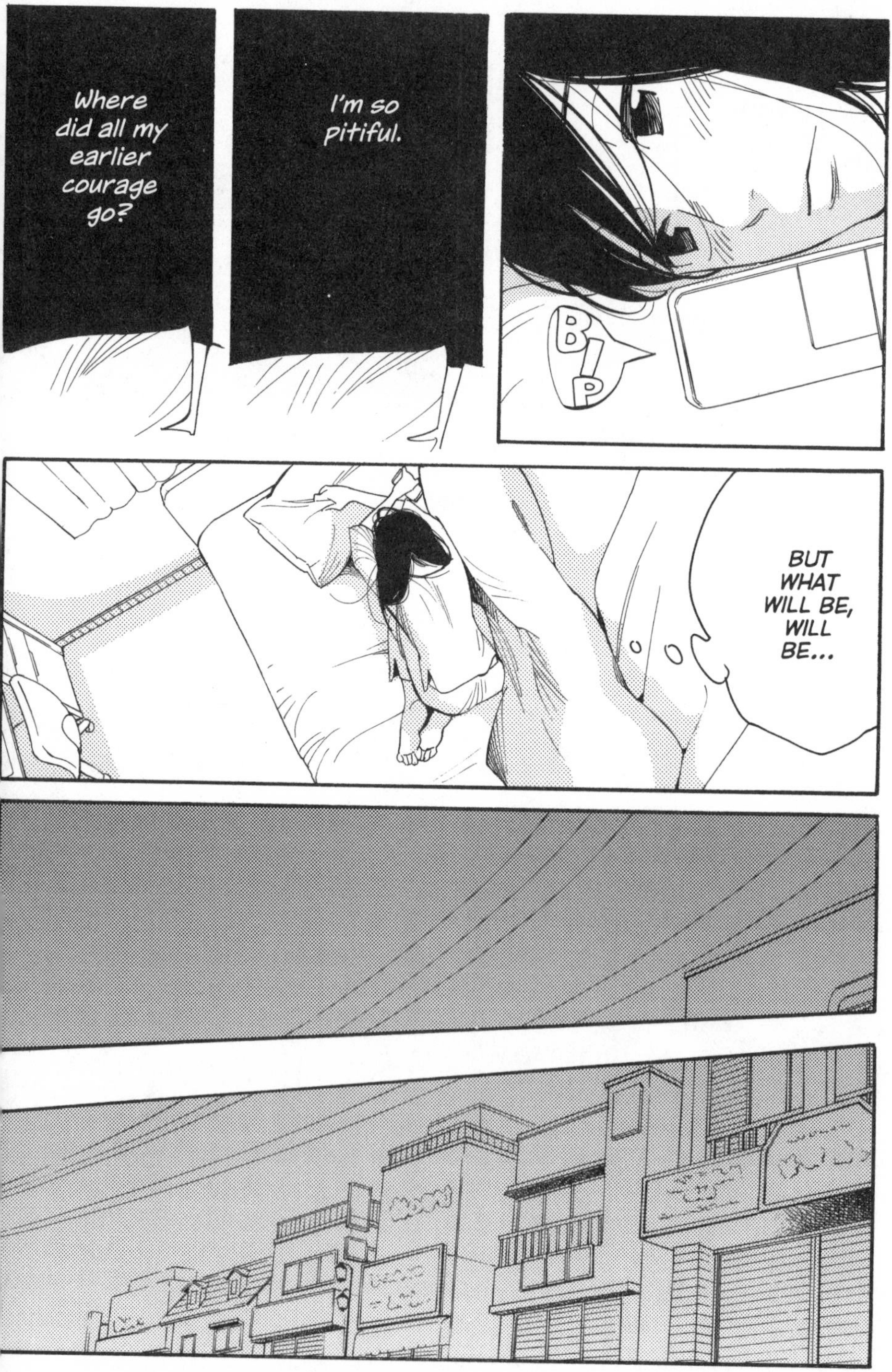
BIP
I'm so pitiful.
Where did all my earlier courage go?
BUT WHAT WILL BE, WILL BE...

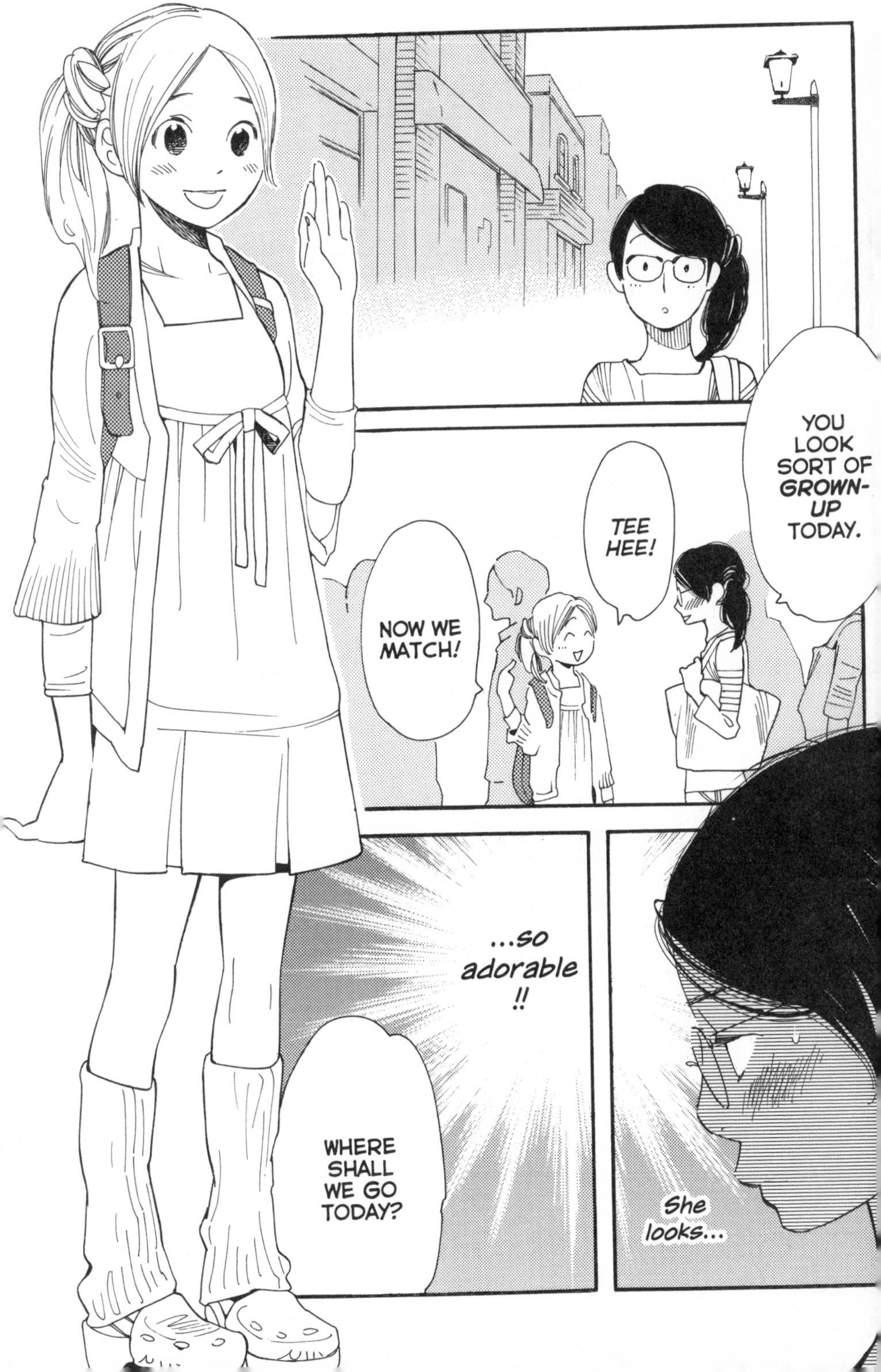
YOU LOOK SORT OF GROWN-UP TODAY.
TEE HEE!
NOW WE MATCH!
She looks...
...so adorable!!
WHERE SHALL WE GO TODAY?

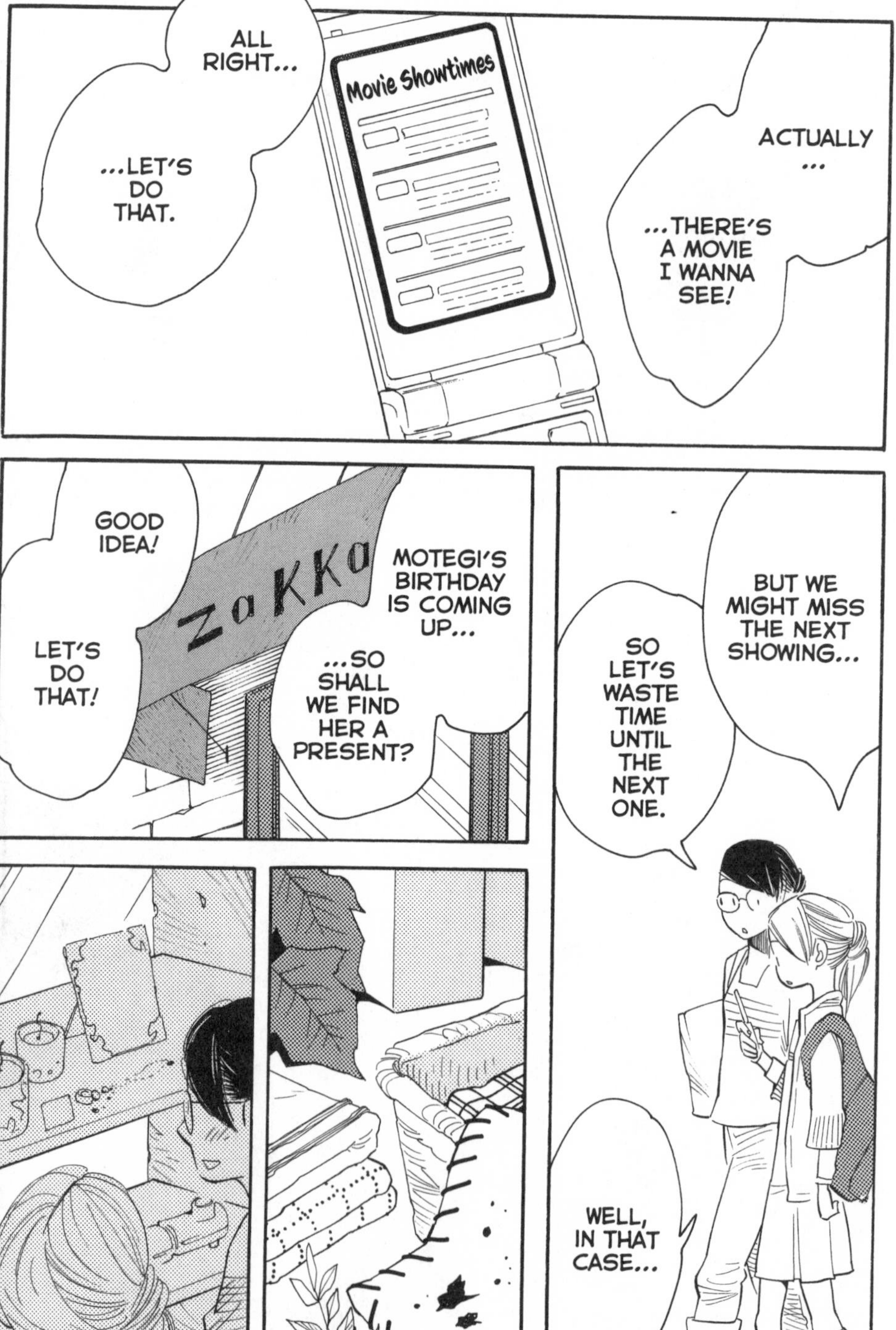

ACTUALLY...
...THERE'S A MOVIE I WANNA SEE!
Movie Showtimes
ALL RIGHT...
...LET'S DO THAT.
BUT WE MIGHT MISS THE NEXT SHOWING...
SO LET'S WASTE TIME UNTIL THE NEXT ONE.
WELL, IN THAT CASE...
MOTEGI'S BIRTHDAY IS COMING UP...
...SO SHALL WE FIND HER A PRESENT?
ZaKKa
GOOD IDEA!
LET'S DO THAT!

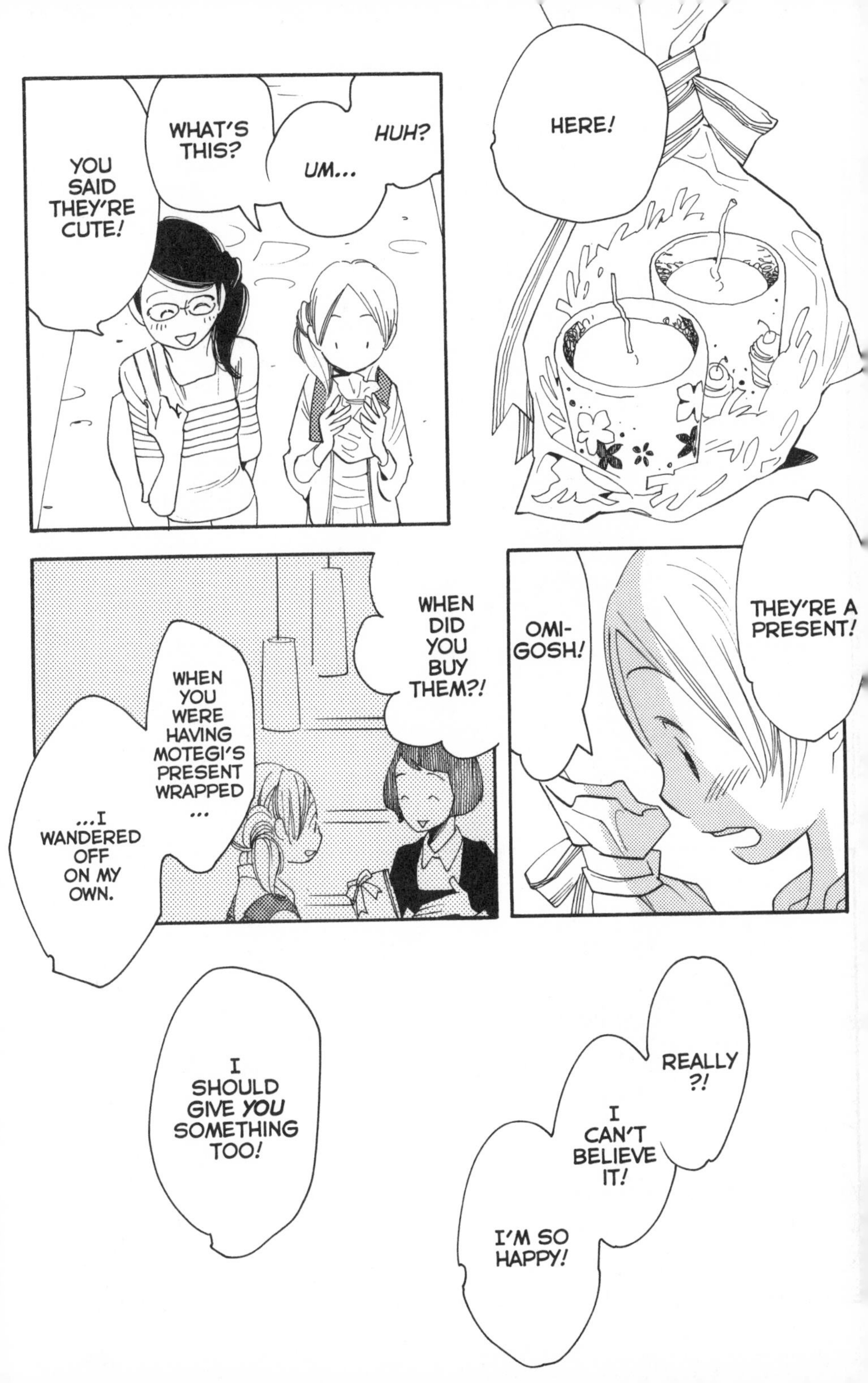
HERE!
HUH? UM...
WHAT'S THIS?
YOU SAID THEY'RE CUTE!
THEY'RE A PRESENT!
OMI-GOSH!
WHEN DID YOU BUY THEM?!
WHEN YOU WERE HAVING MOTEGI'S PRESENT WRAPPED...
...I WANDERED OFF ON MY OWN.
REALLY?!
I CAN'T BELIEVE IT!
I'M SO HAPPY!
I SHOULD GIVE *YOU* SOMETHING TOO!

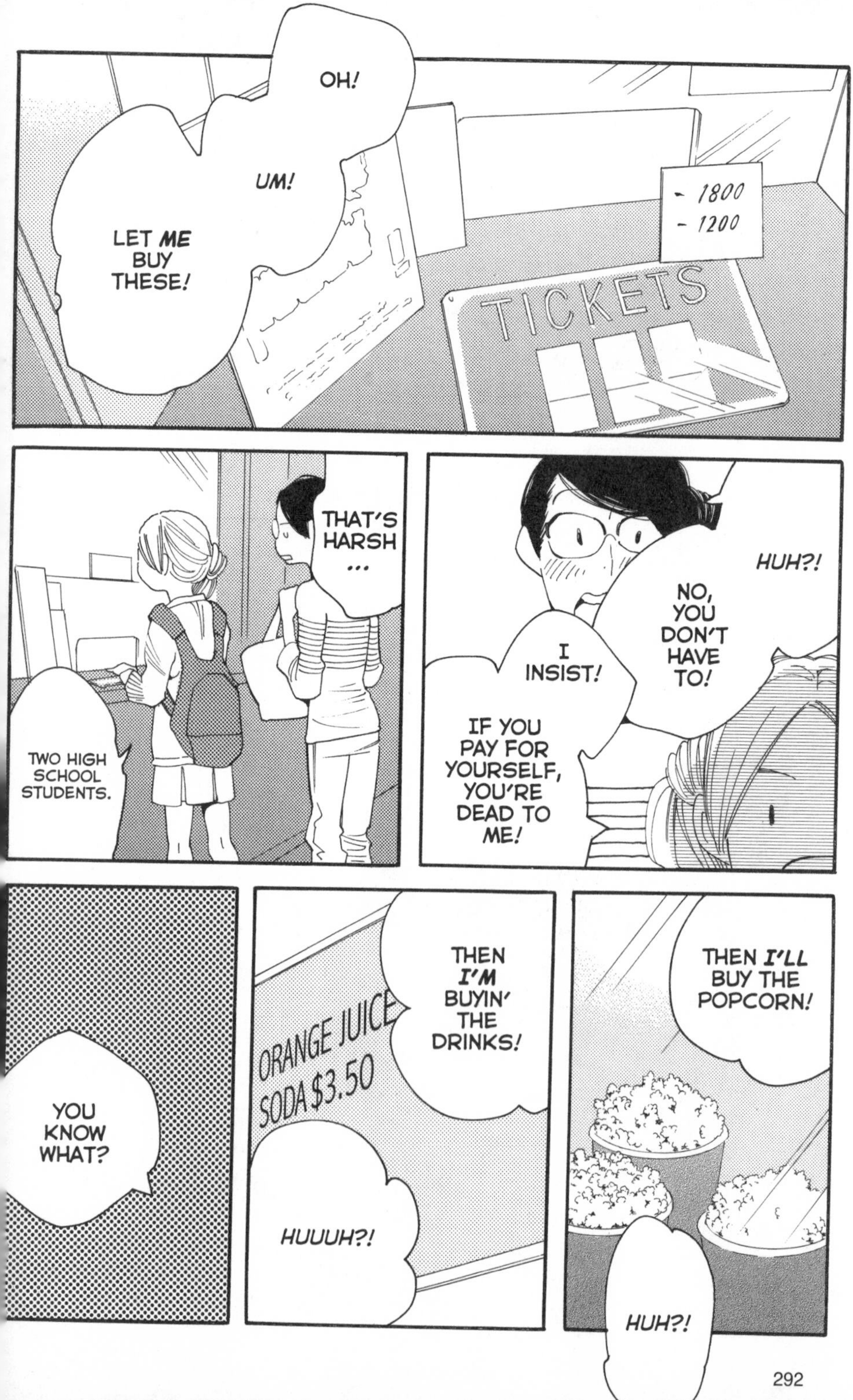
OH!
UM!
LET *ME* BUY THESE!
- 1800
- 1200
TICKETS
HUH?!
NO, YOU DON'T HAVE TO!
I INSIST!
IF YOU PAY FOR YOURSELF, YOU'RE DEAD TO ME!
THAT'S HARSH...
TWO HIGH SCHOOL STUDENTS.
THEN *I'LL* BUY THE POPCORN!
HUH?!
THEN *I'M* BUYIN' THE DRINKS!
ORANGE JUICE
SODA $3.50
HUUUH?!
YOU KNOW WHAT?

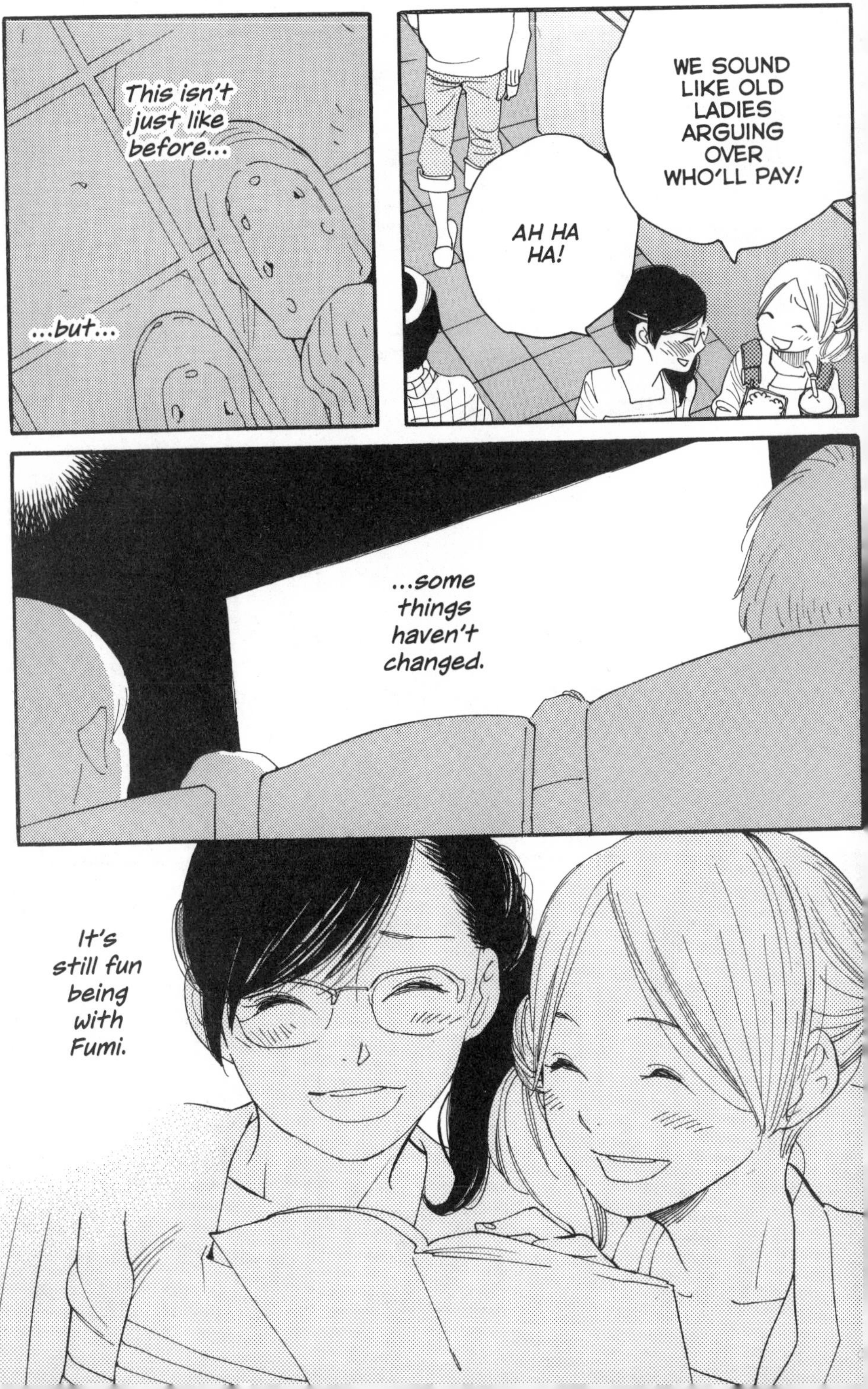
WE SOUND LIKE OLD LADIES ARGUING OVER WHO'LL PAY!
AH HA HA!
This isn't just like before...
...but...
...some things haven't changed.
It's still fun being with Fumi.

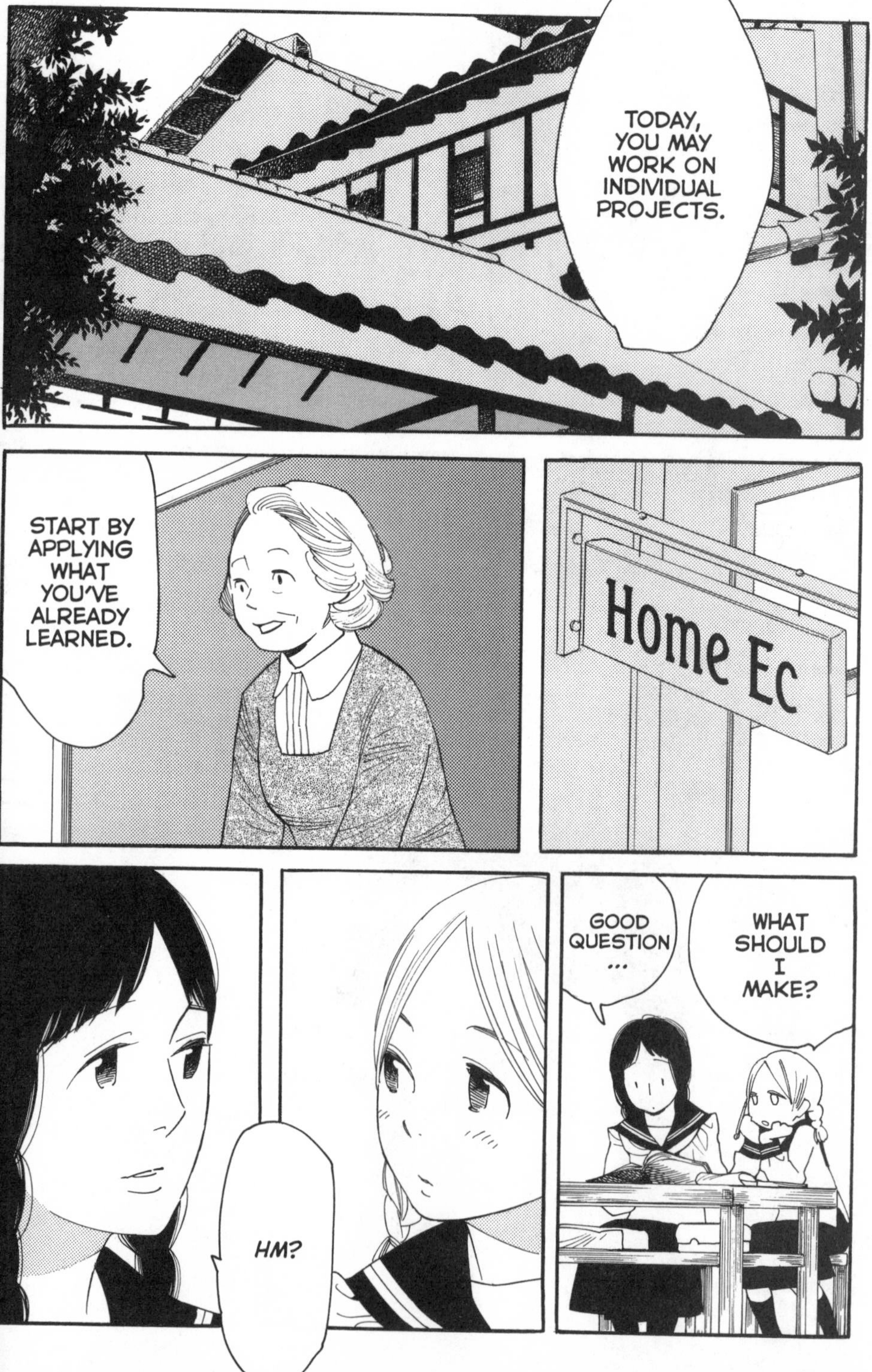
TODAY, YOU MAY WORK ON INDIVIDUAL PROJECTS.
Home Ec
START BY APPLYING WHAT YOU'VE ALREADY LEARNED.
WHAT SHOULD I MAKE?
GOOD QUESTION...
HM?

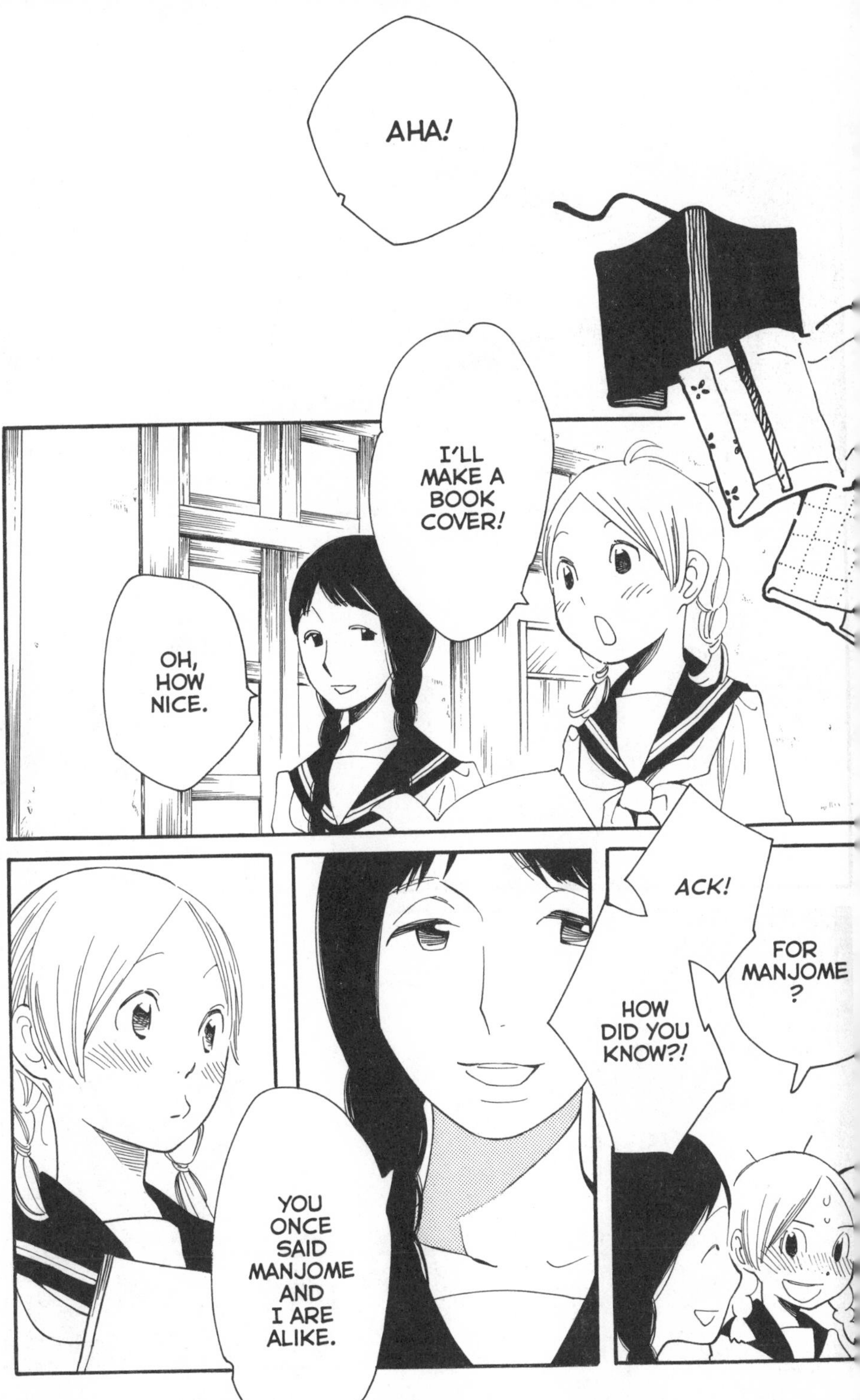
AHA!
I'LL MAKE A BOOK COVER!
OH, HOW NICE.
FOR MANJOME?
ACK!
HOW DID YOU KNOW?!
YOU ONCE SAID MANJOME AND I ARE ALIKE.

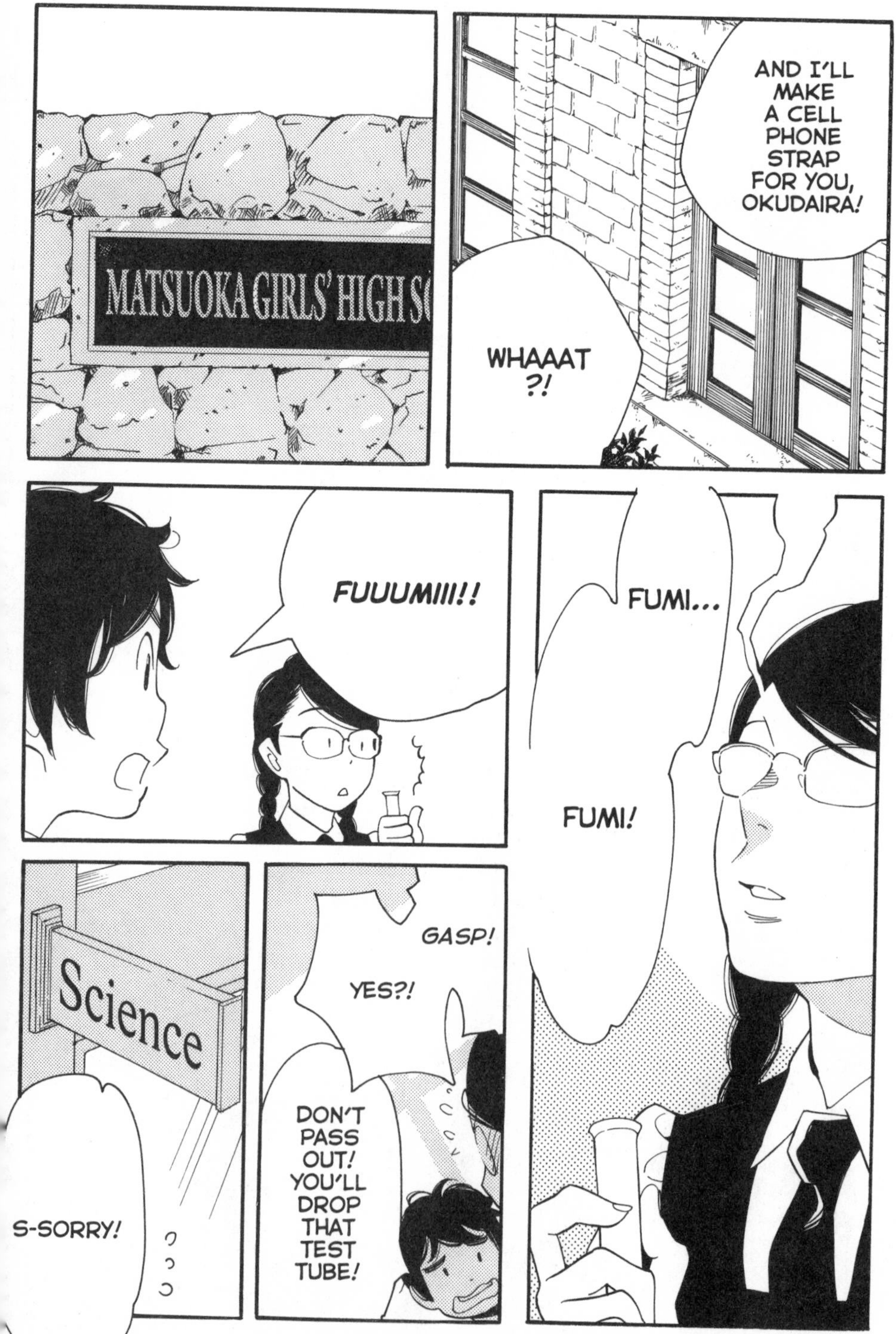
AND I'LL MAKE A CELL PHONE STRAP FOR YOU, OKUDAIRA!
WHAAAT?!
MATSUOKA GIRLS' HIGH SC
FUMI...
FUMI!
FUUUMIII!!
GASP!
YES?!
DON'T PASS OUT! YOU'LL DROP THAT TEST TUBE!
Science
S-SORRY!

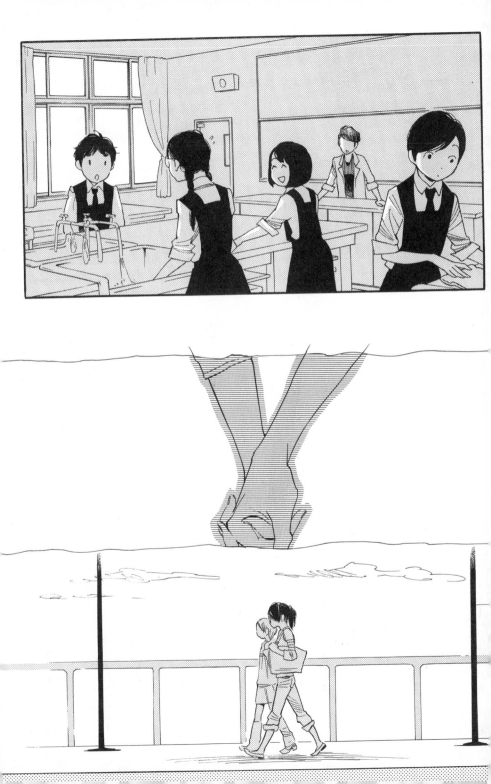

YES?

UM...

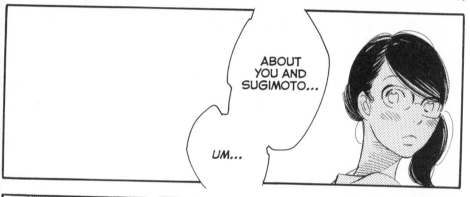

ABOUT YOU AND SUGIMOTO...

UM...

WAH!

UM...

UMMM...

HOW FAR DID WE—

HOW FAR DID YOU GO?

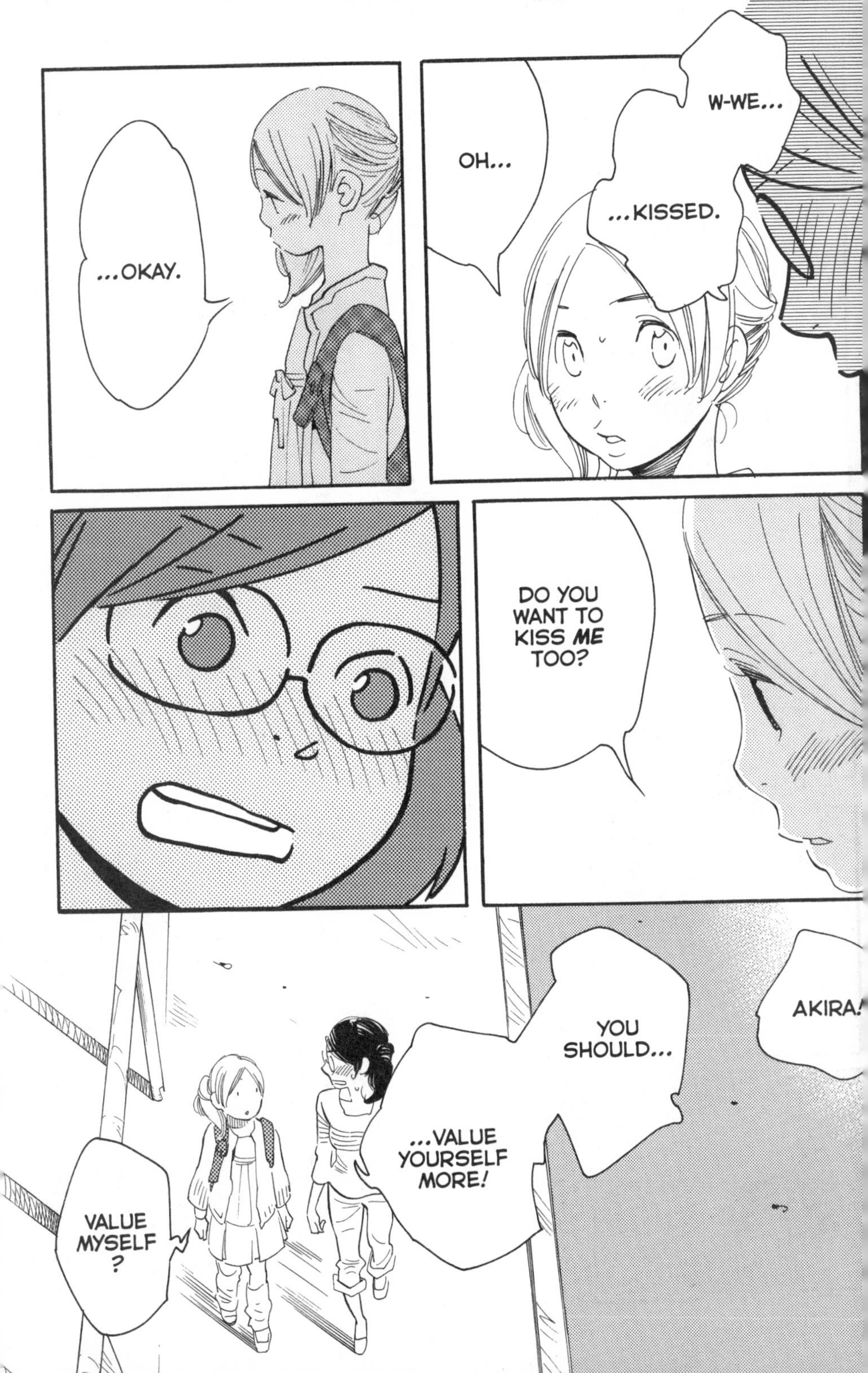
W-WE...
...KISSED.
OH...
...OKAY.
DO YOU WANT TO KISS *ME* TOO?
AKIRA!
YOU SHOULD...
...VALUE YOURSELF MORE!
VALUE MYSELF?

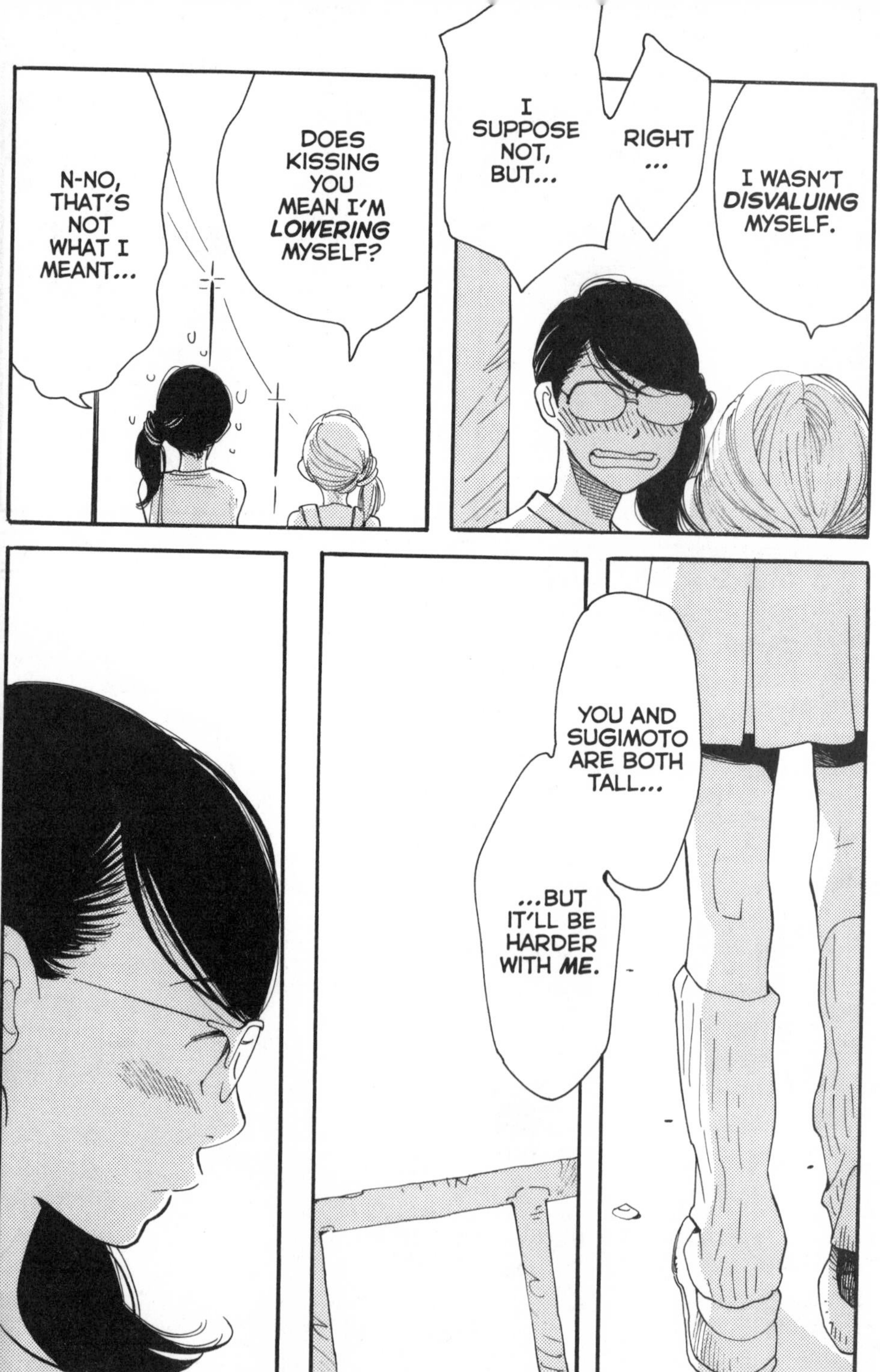
I WASN'T *DISVALUING* MYSELF.
RIGHT...
I SUPPOSE NOT, BUT...
DOES KISSING YOU MEAN I'M *LOWERING* MYSELF?
N-NO, THAT'S NOT WHAT I MEANT...
YOU AND SUGIMOTO ARE BOTH TALL...
...BUT IT'LL BE HARDER WITH *ME*.

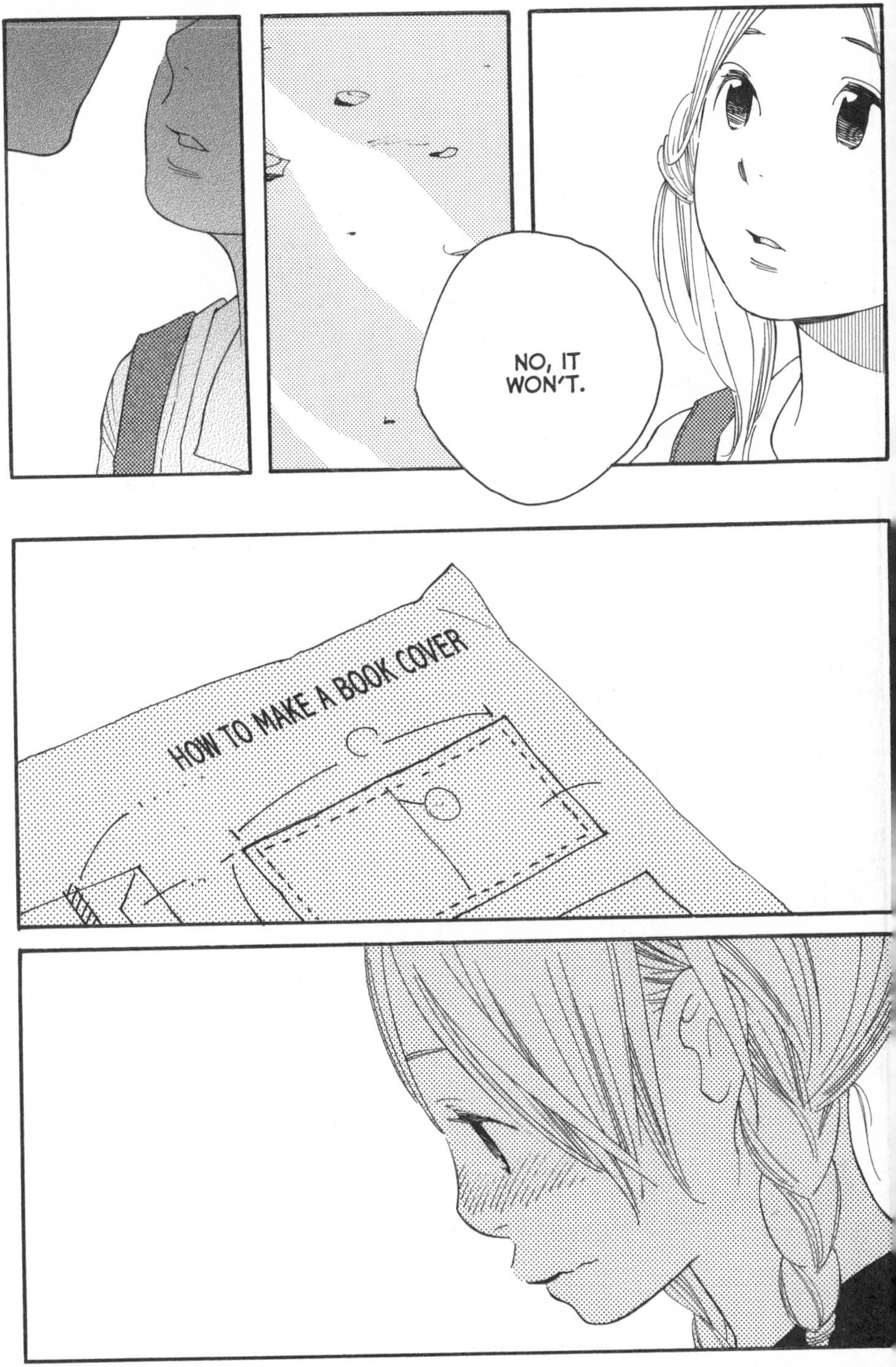
NO, IT WON'T.
HOW TO MAKE A BOOK COVER

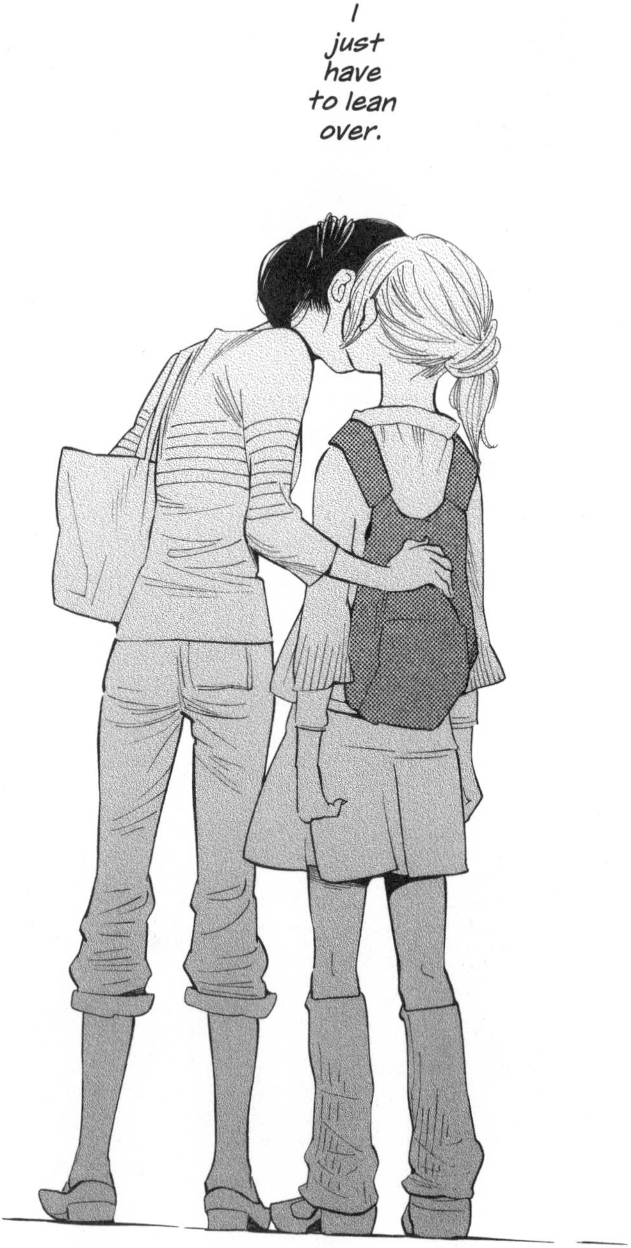
I just have to lean over.

Sweet Blue Flowers

#37 The Lily of the Valley

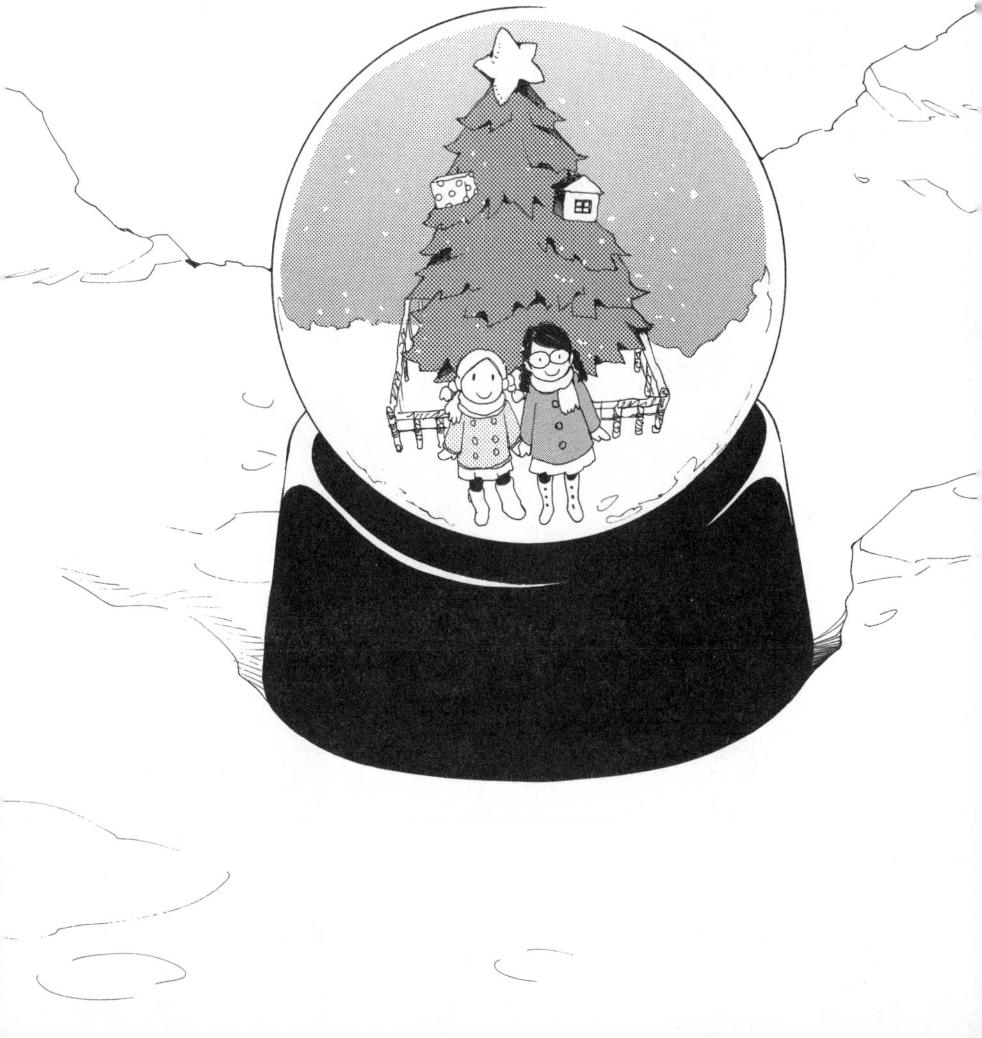

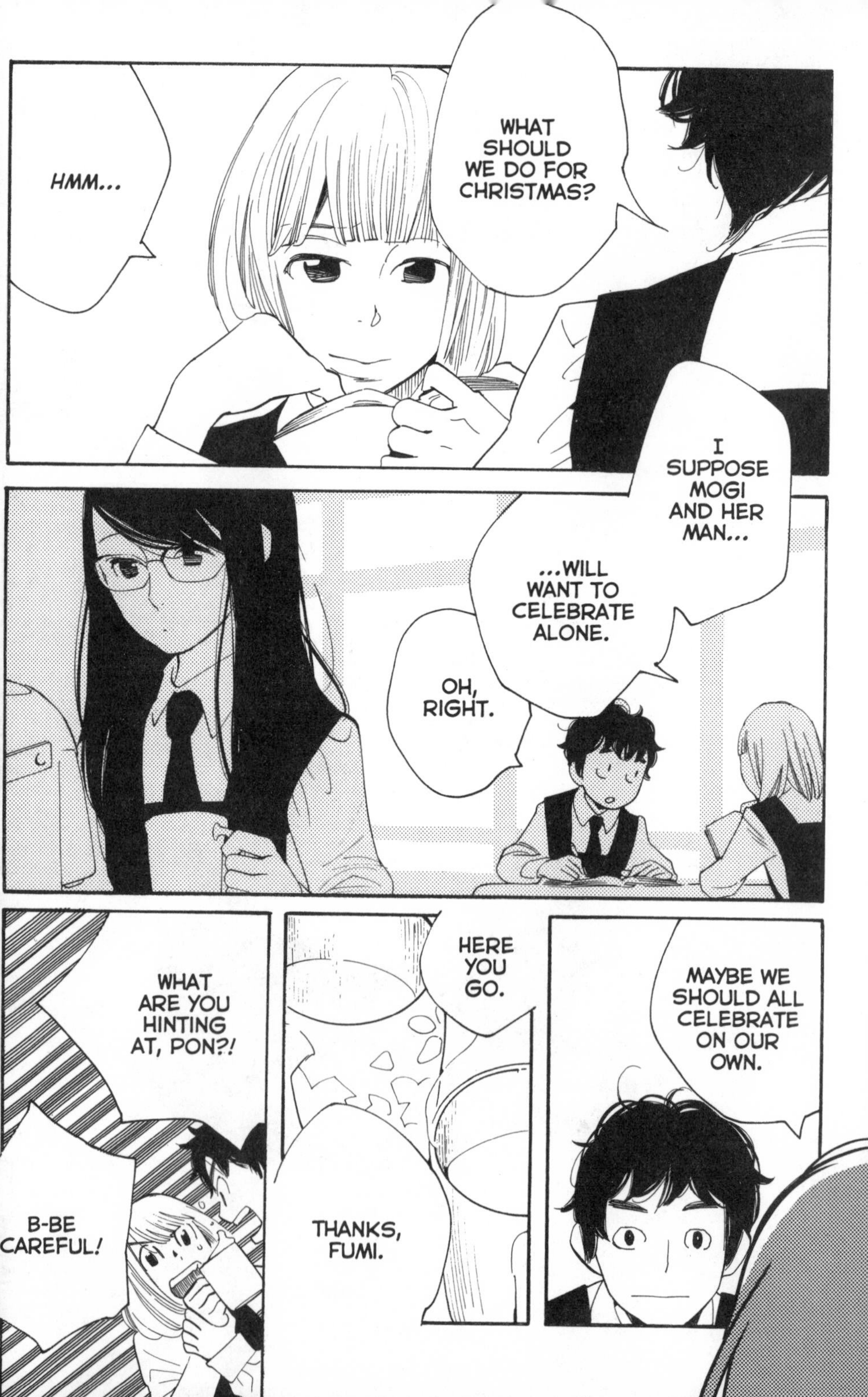
WHAT SHOULD WE DO FOR CHRISTMAS?
HMM...
I SUPPOSE MOGI AND HER MAN...
...WILL WANT TO CELEBRATE ALONE.
OH, RIGHT.
MAYBE WE SHOULD ALL CELEBRATE ON OUR OWN.
HERE YOU GO.
THANKS, FUMI.
WHAT ARE YOU HINTING AT, PON?!
B-BE CAREFUL!

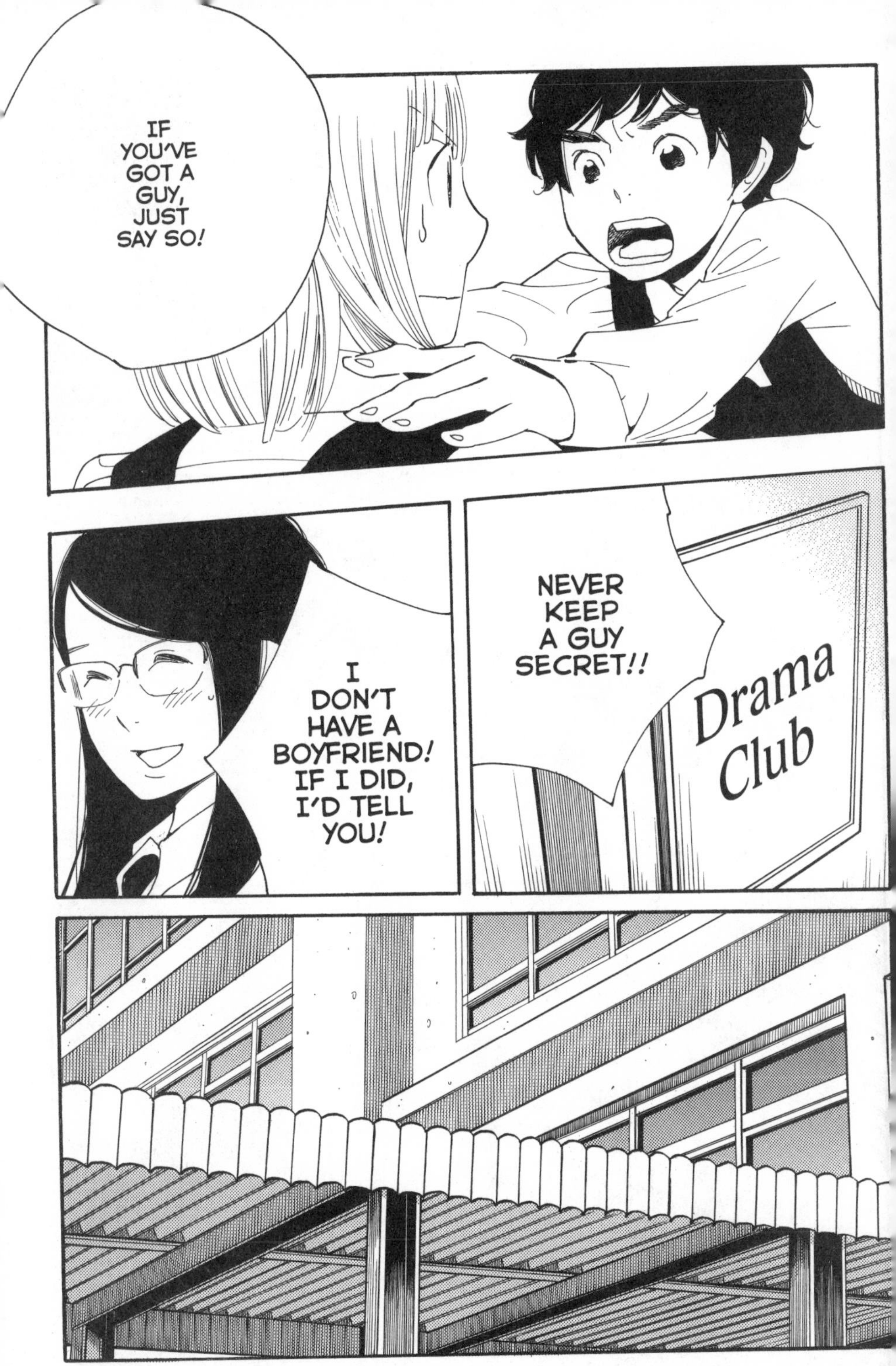
IF YOU'VE GOT A GUY, JUST SAY SO!
NEVER KEEP A GUY SECRET!!
Drama Club
I DON'T HAVE A BOYFRIEND! IF I DID, I'D TELL YOU!

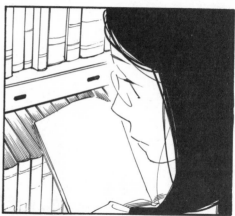

AFTER ALL, I'D DO THE SAME FOR YOU!

WHAT'S GOTTEN INTO YOU?!

DON'T BE WEIRD!!

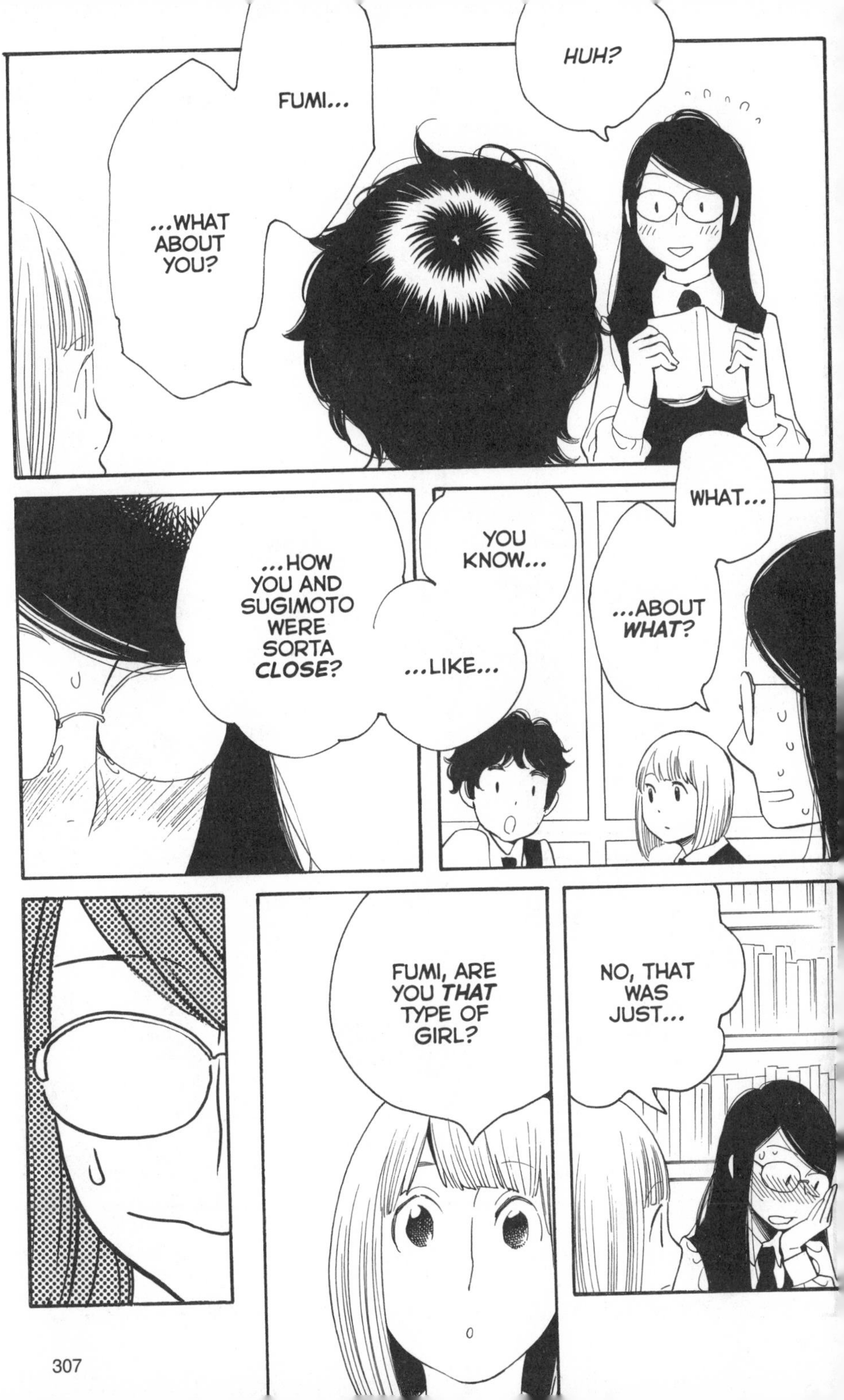
FUMI...
...WHAT ABOUT YOU?
HUH?
WHAT...
...ABOUT *WHAT?*
YOU KNOW...
...LIKE...
...HOW YOU AND SUGIMOTO WERE SORTA *CLOSE?*
NO, THAT WAS JUST...
FUMI, ARE YOU *THAT* TYPE OF GIRL?

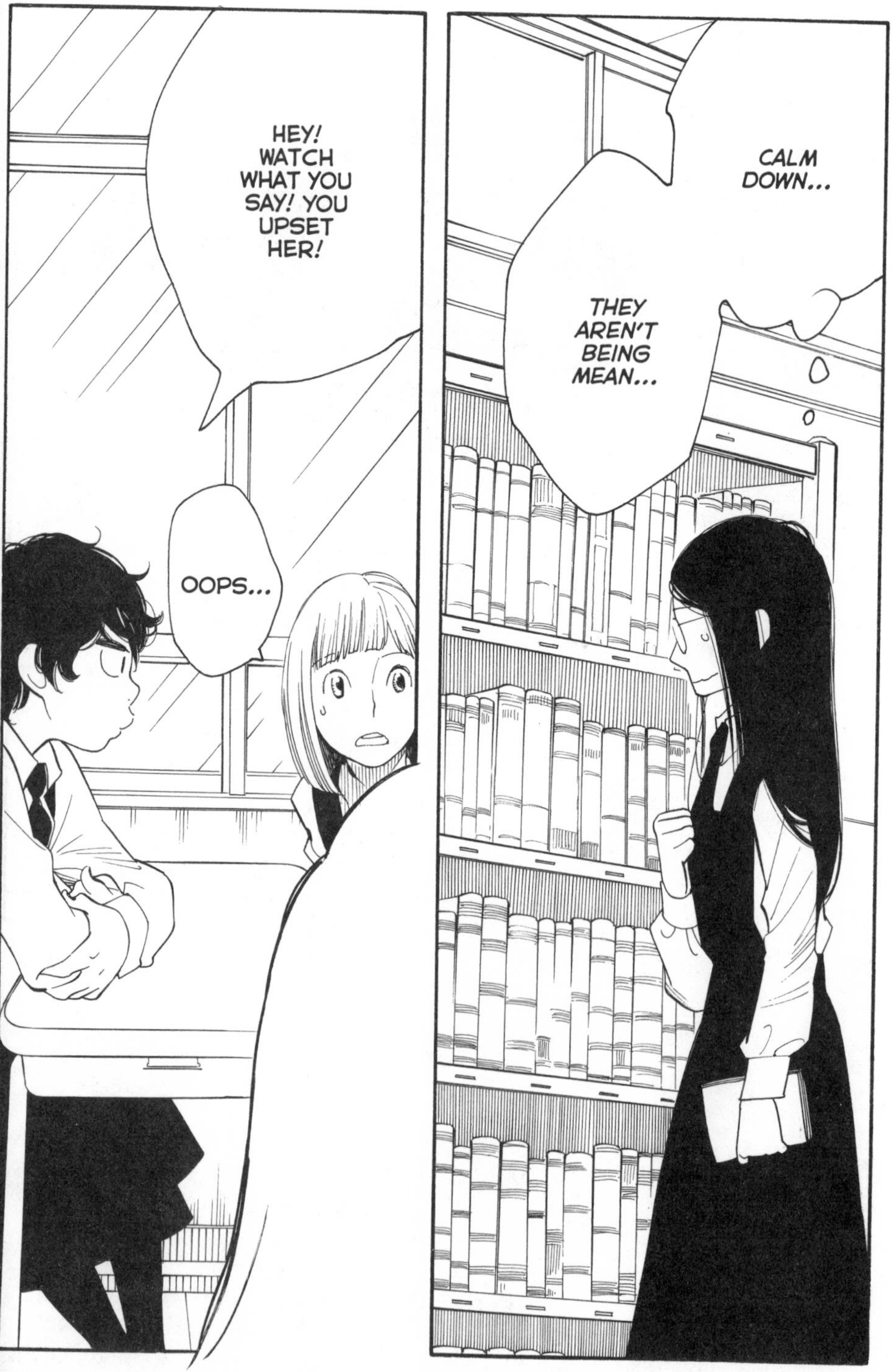
CALM DOWN...
THEY AREN'T BEING MEAN...
HEY! WATCH WHAT YOU SAY! YOU UPSET HER!
OOPS...

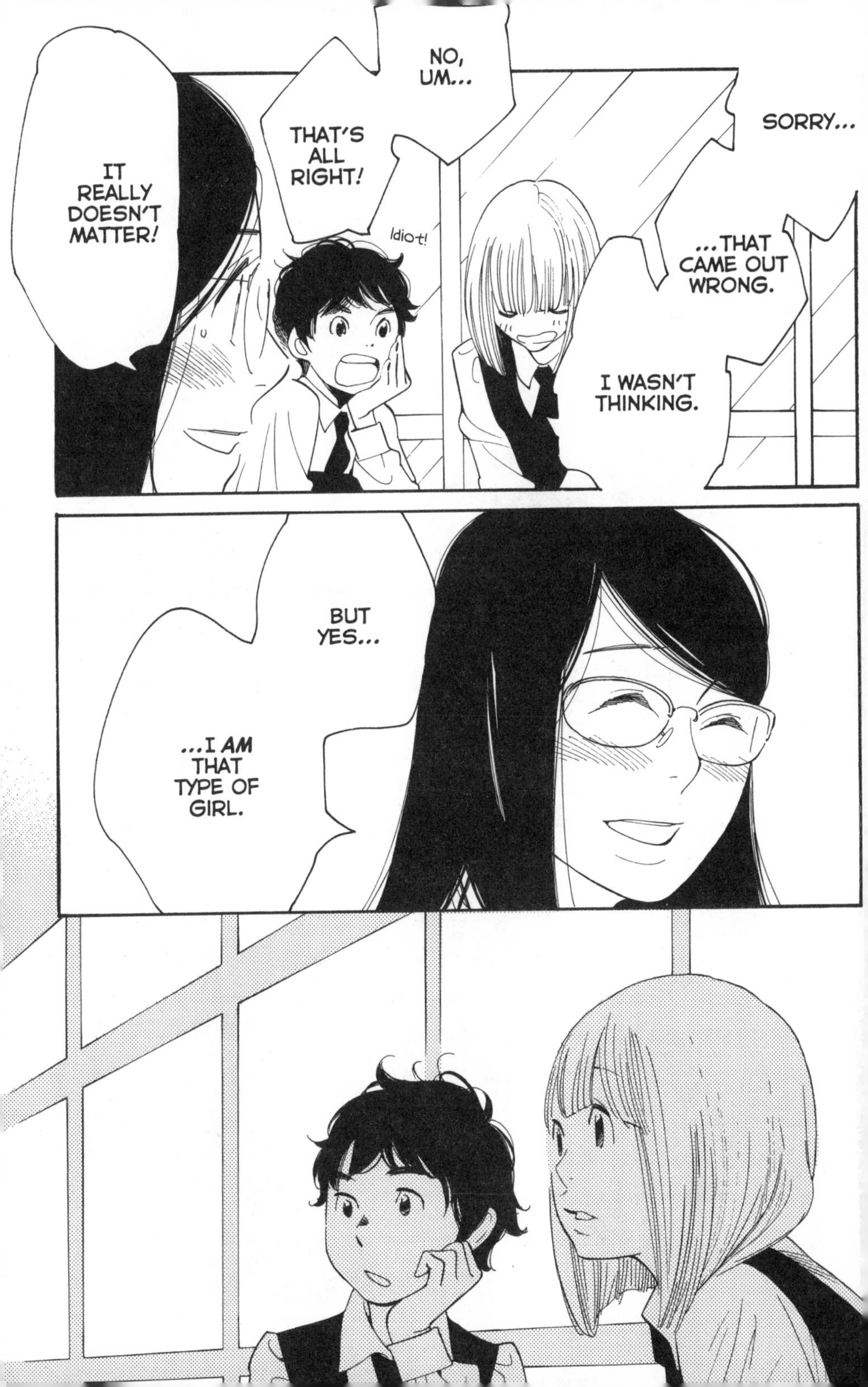
SORRY...
...THAT CAME OUT WRONG.
I WASN'T THINKING.
NO, UM...
THAT'S ALL RIGHT!
Idiot!
IT REALLY DOESN'T MATTER!
BUT YES...
...I *AM* THAT TYPE OF GIRL.

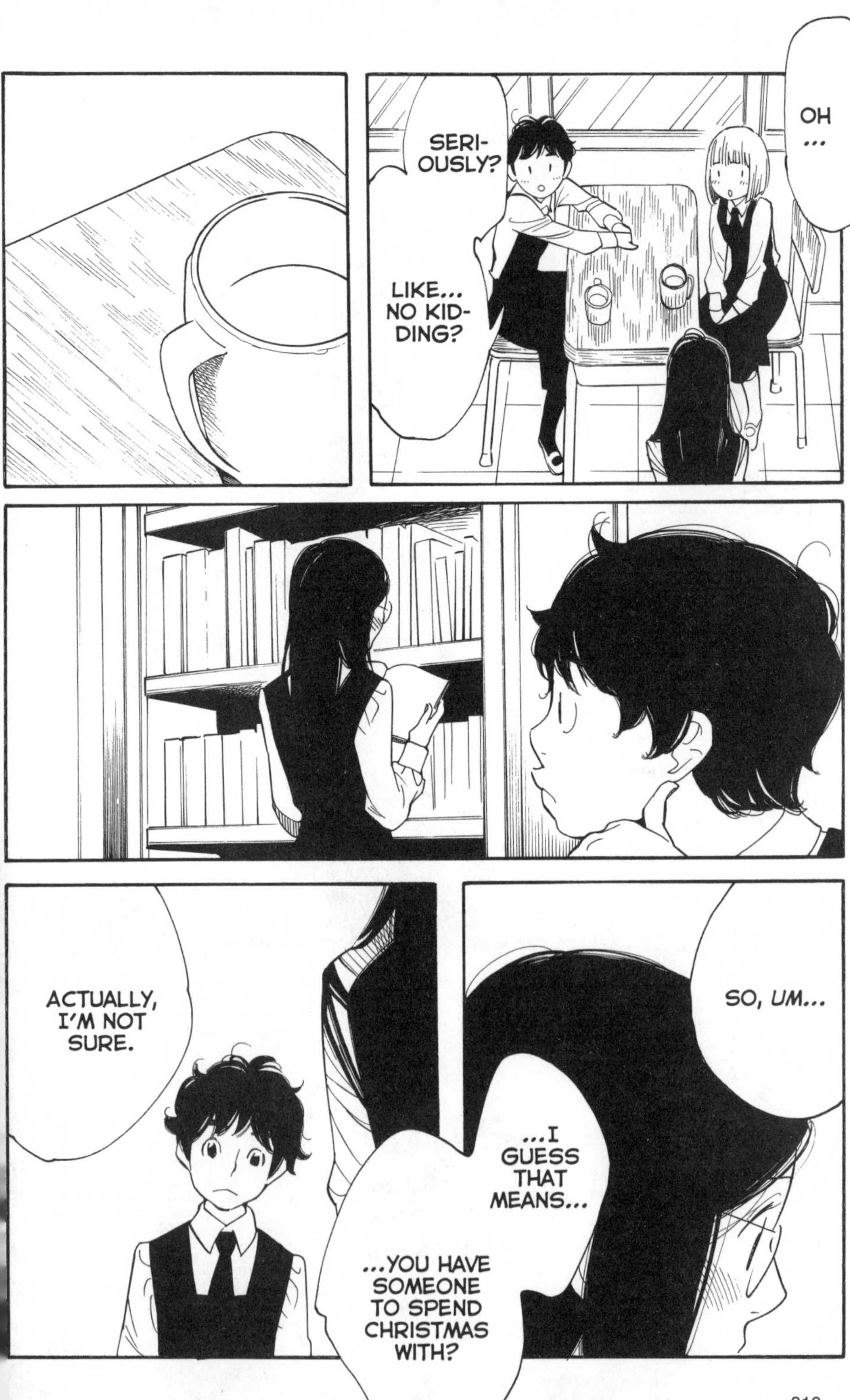
OH ...
SERIOUSLY?
LIKE... NO KIDDING?
SO, *UM*...
...I GUESS THAT MEANS...
...YOU HAVE SOMEONE TO SPEND CHRISTMAS WITH?
ACTUALLY, I'M NOT SURE.

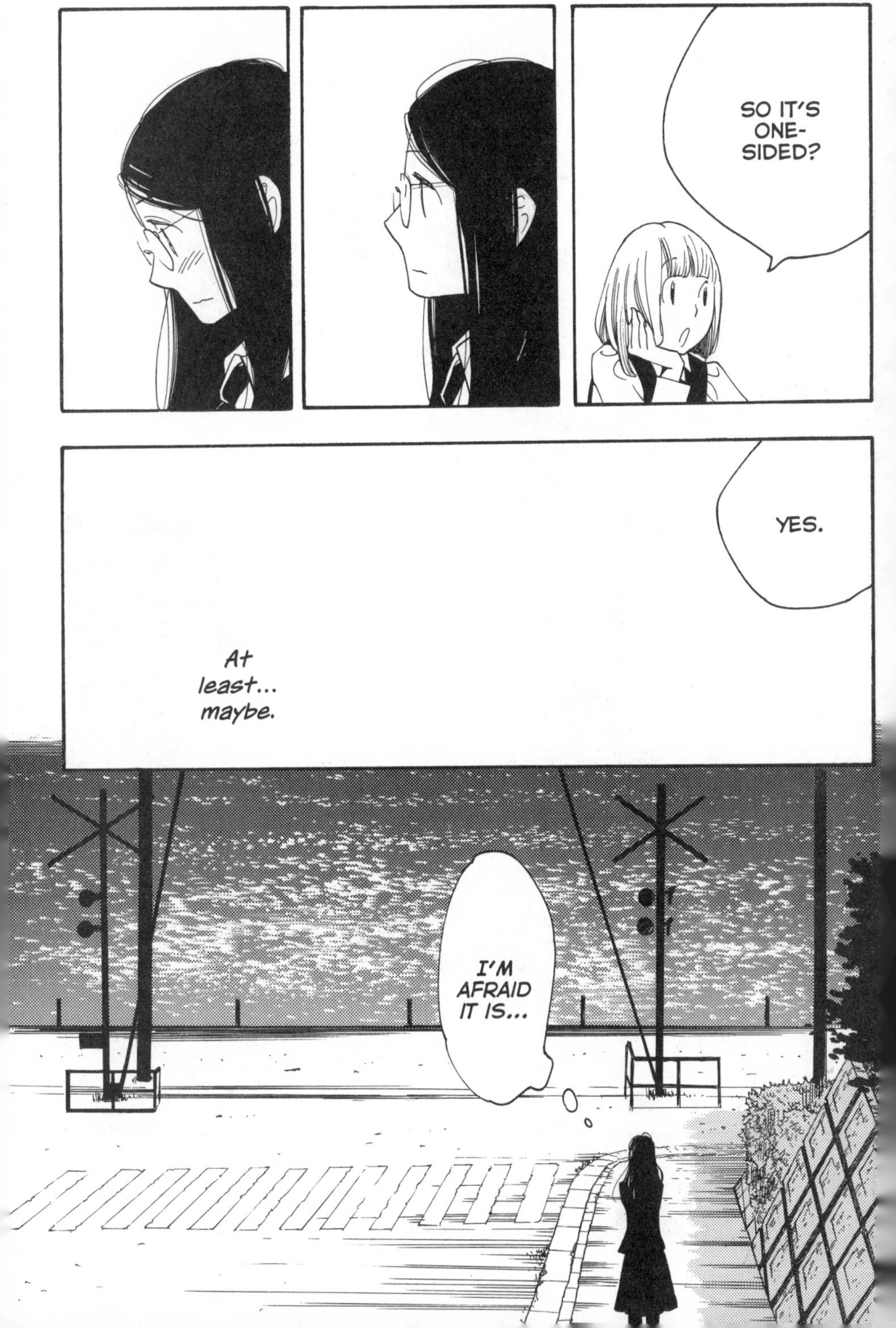
SO IT'S ONE-SIDED?
YES.
At least... maybe.
I'M AFRAID IT IS...

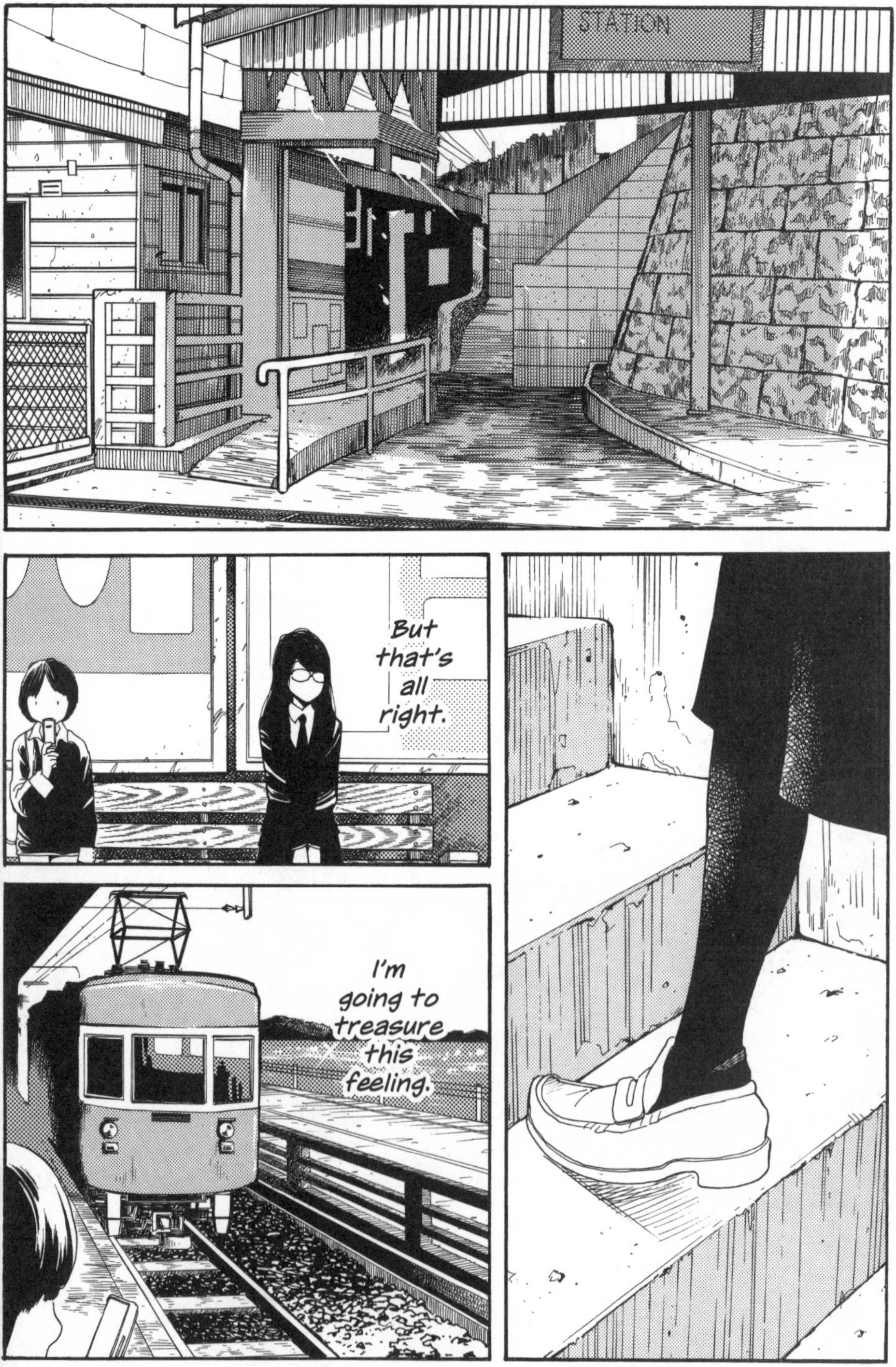
STATION
But that's all right.
I'm going to treasure this feeling.

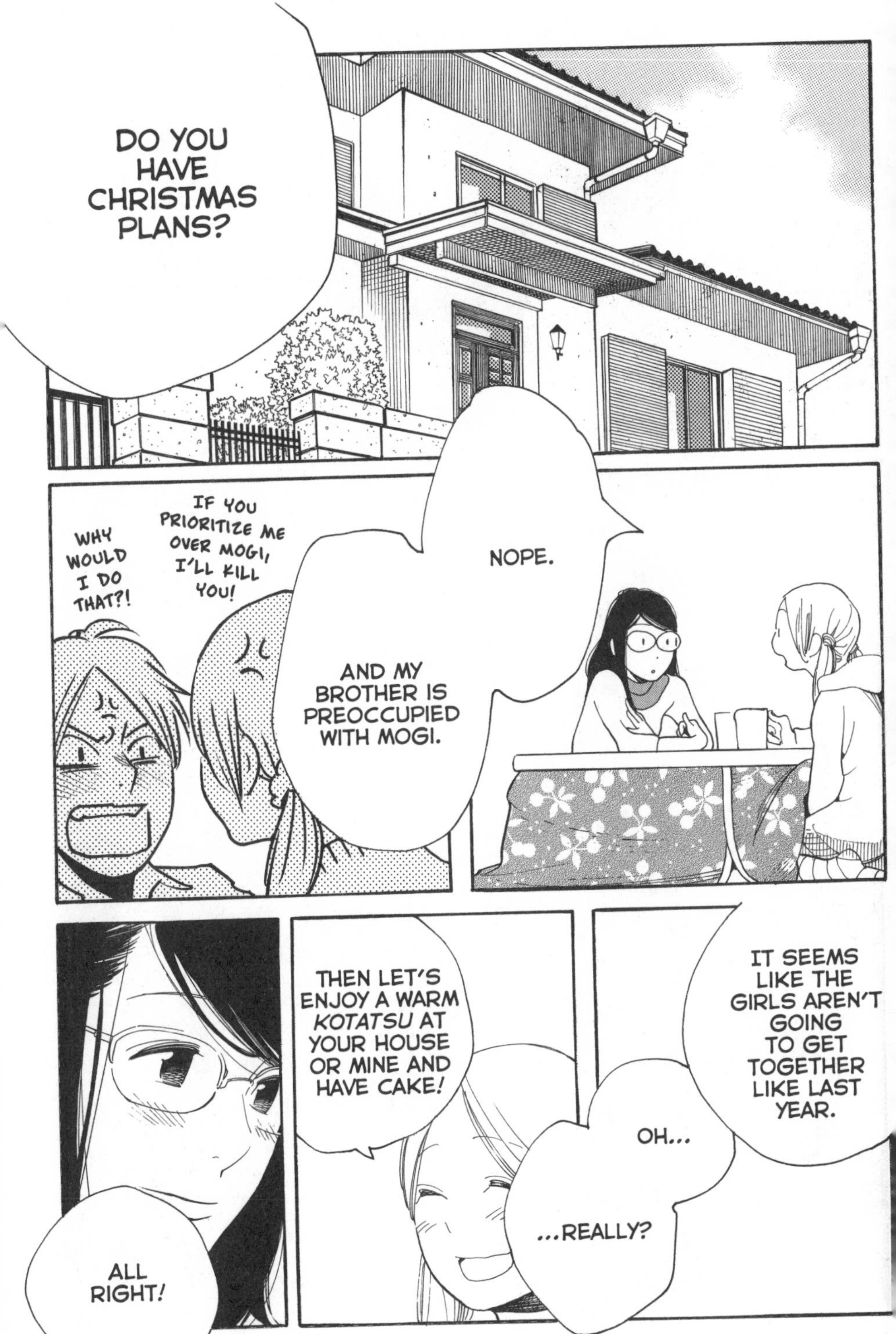
DO YOU HAVE CHRISTMAS PLANS?
NOPE.
AND MY BROTHER IS PREOCCUPIED WITH MOGI.
IF YOU PRIORITIZE ME OVER MOGI, I'LL KILL YOU!
WHY WOULD I DO THAT?!
IT SEEMS LIKE THE GIRLS AREN'T GOING TO GET TOGETHER LIKE LAST YEAR.
OH...
...REALLY?
THEN LET'S ENJOY A WARM *KOTATSU* AT YOUR HOUSE OR MINE AND HAVE CAKE!
ALL RIGHT!

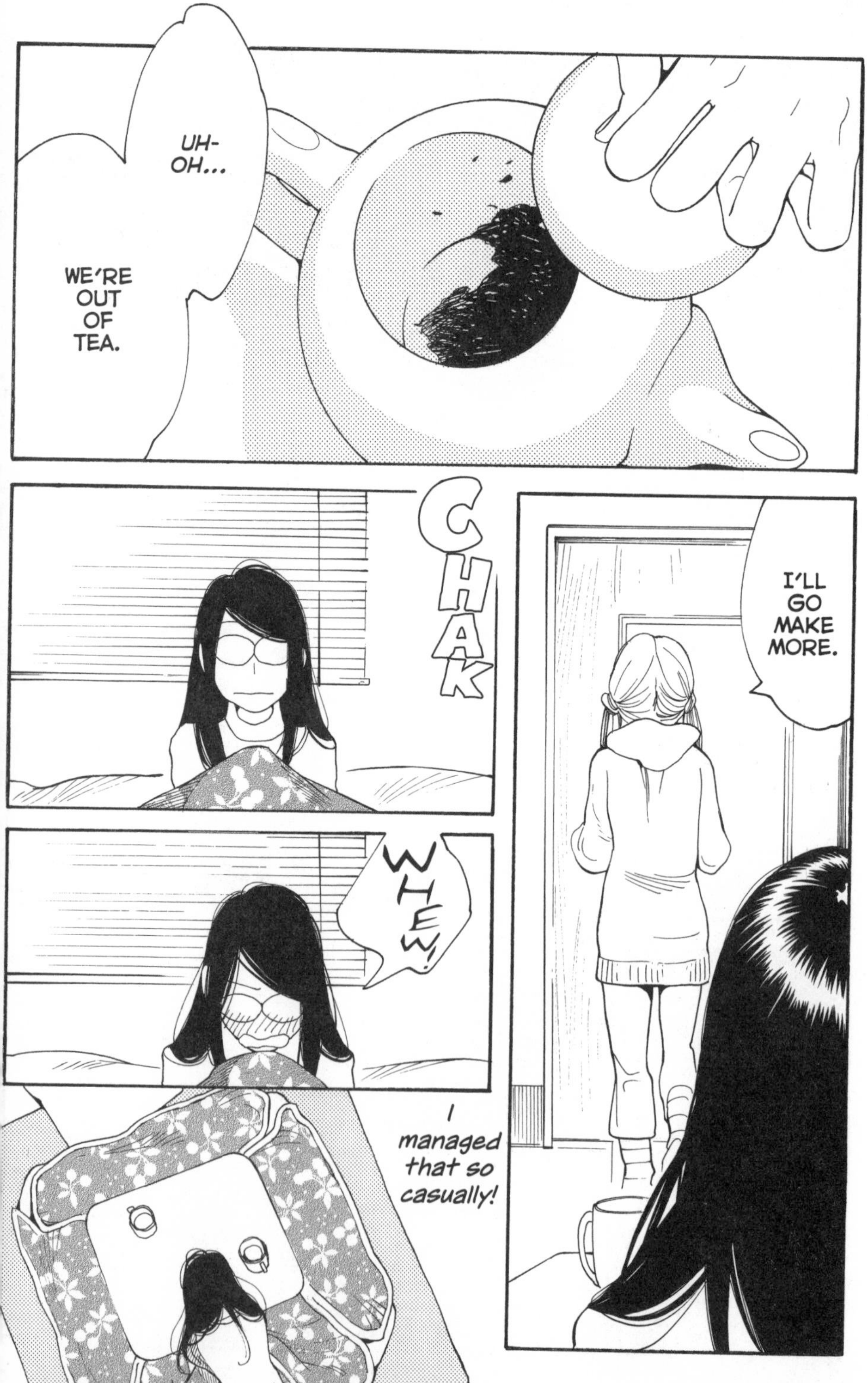
UH-OH...
WE'RE OUT OF TEA.
I'LL GO MAKE MORE.
CHAK
WHEW!
I managed that so casually!

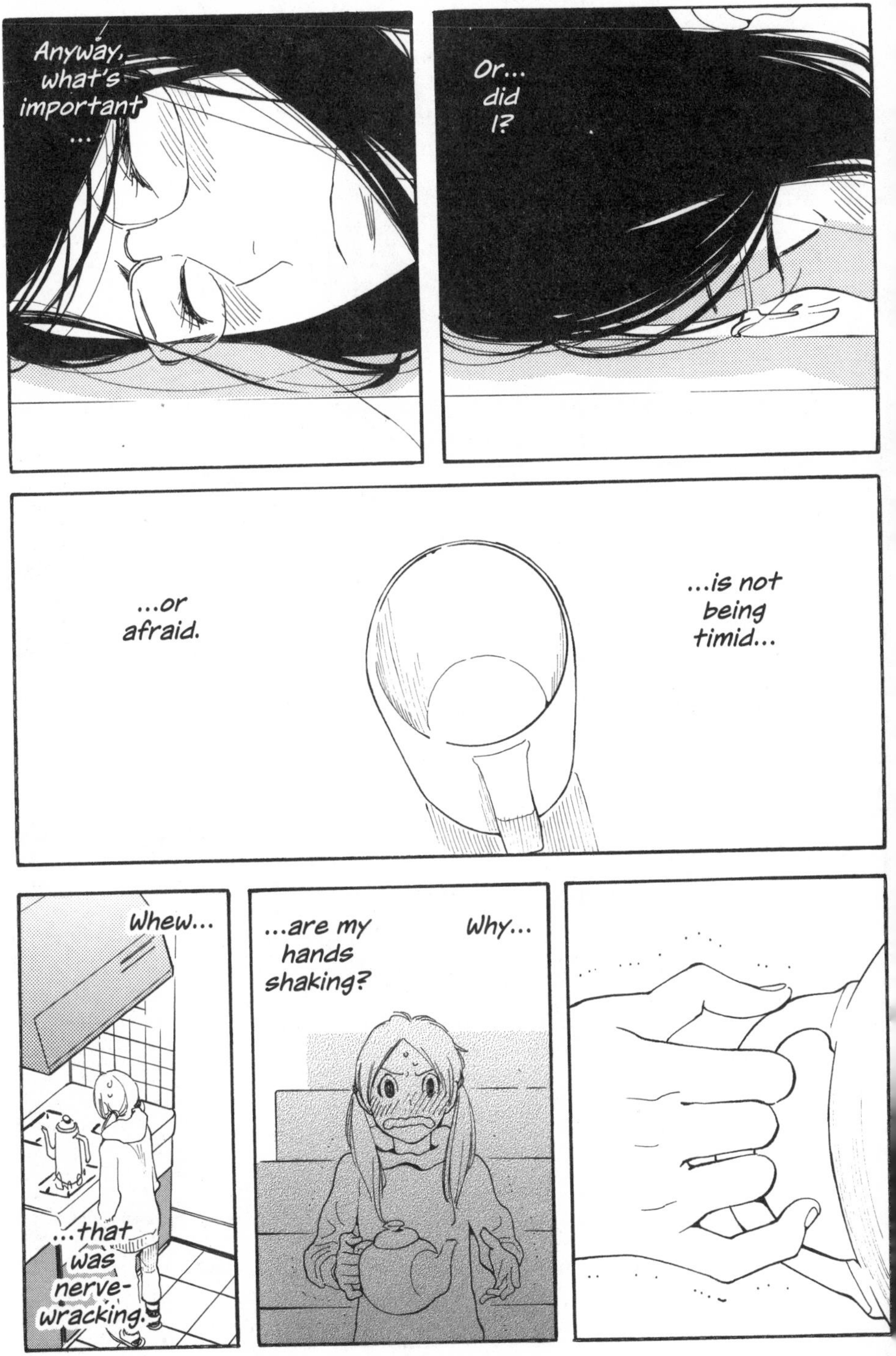
Or... did I?
Anyway, what's important...
...is not being timid...
...or afraid.
Why...
...are my hands shaking?
Whew...
...that was nerve-wracking.

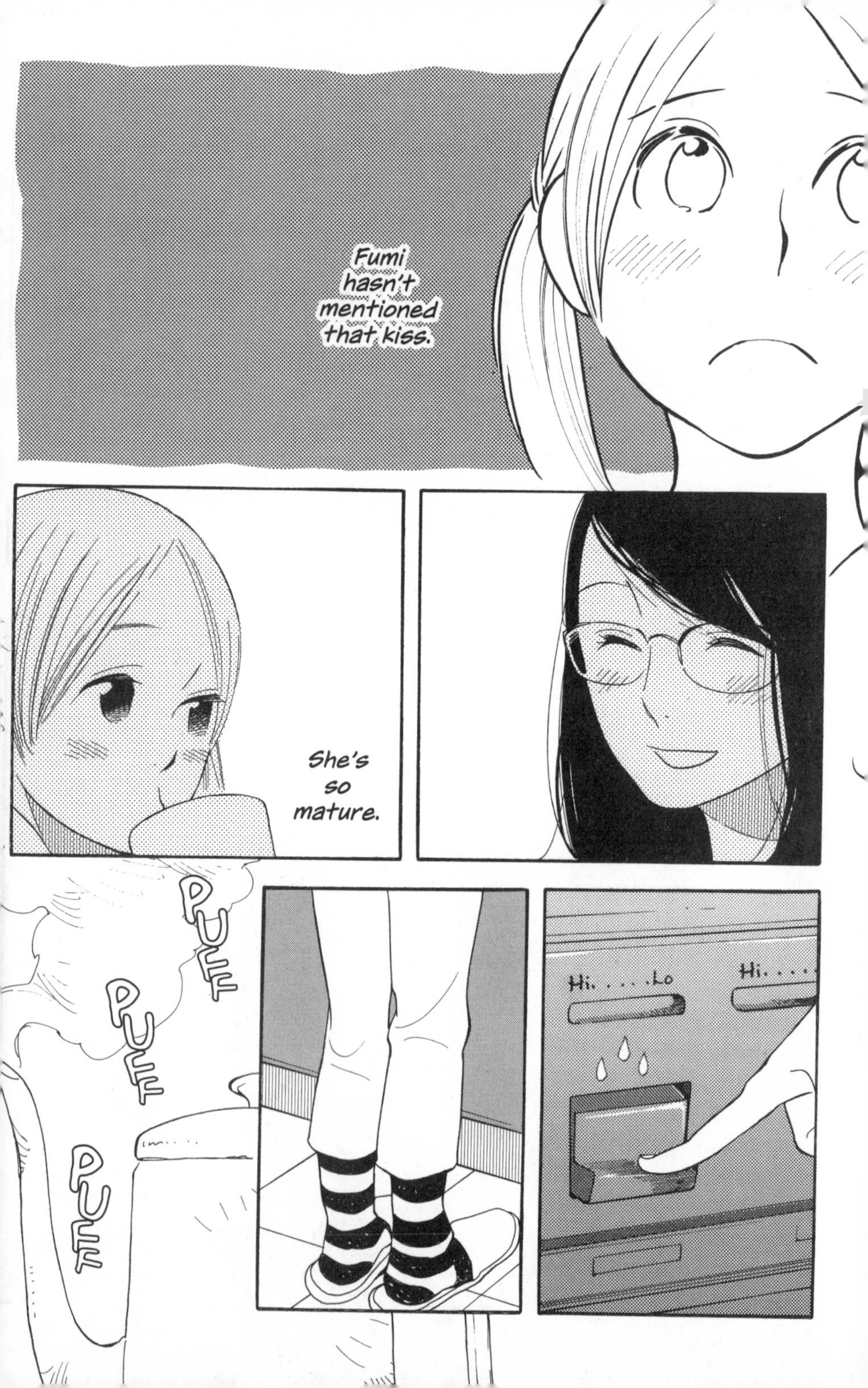
Fumi hasn't mentioned that kiss.
She's so mature.
Hi. . . . Lo
Hi. . . .
PUFF
PUFF
PUFF

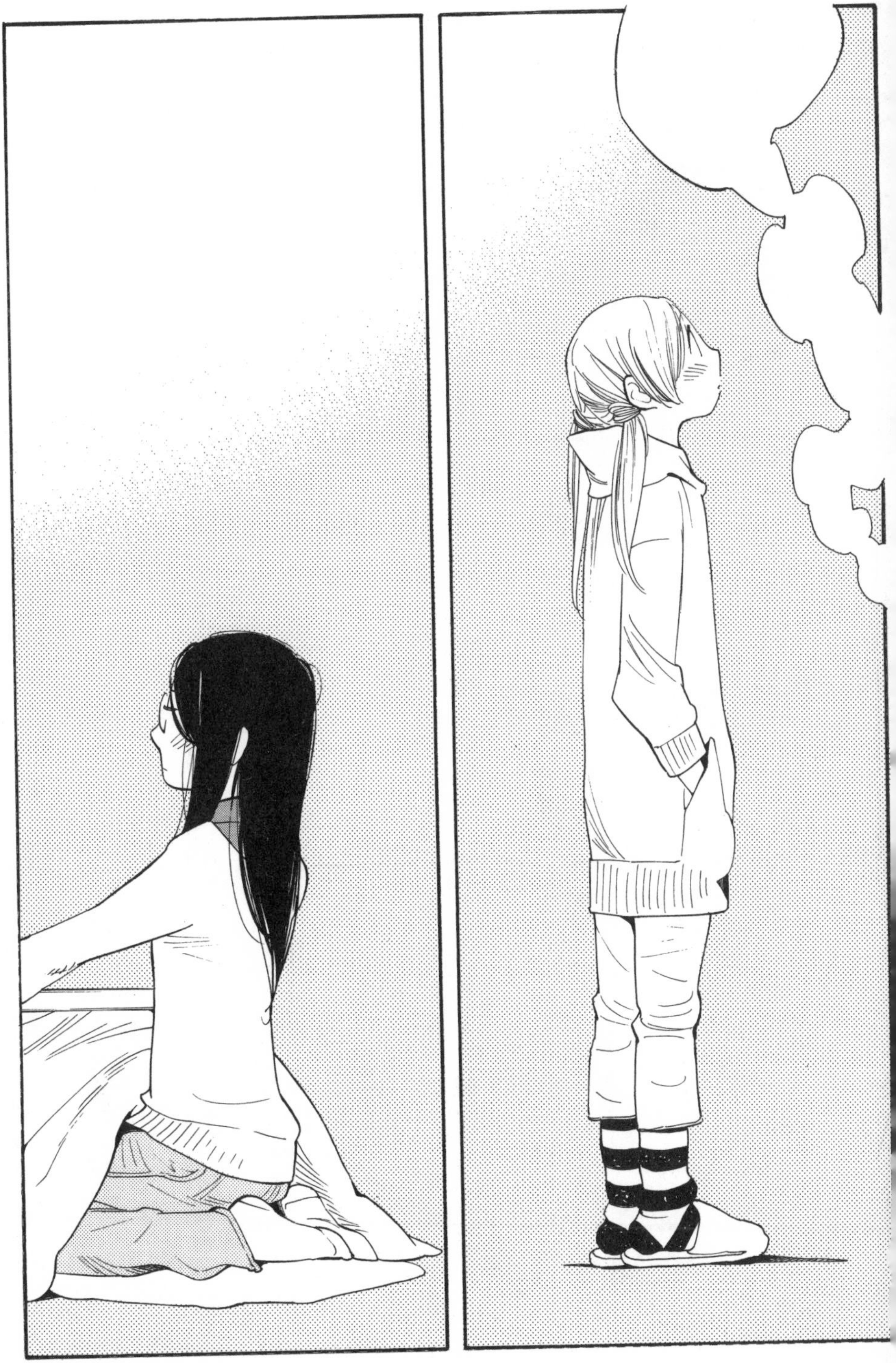

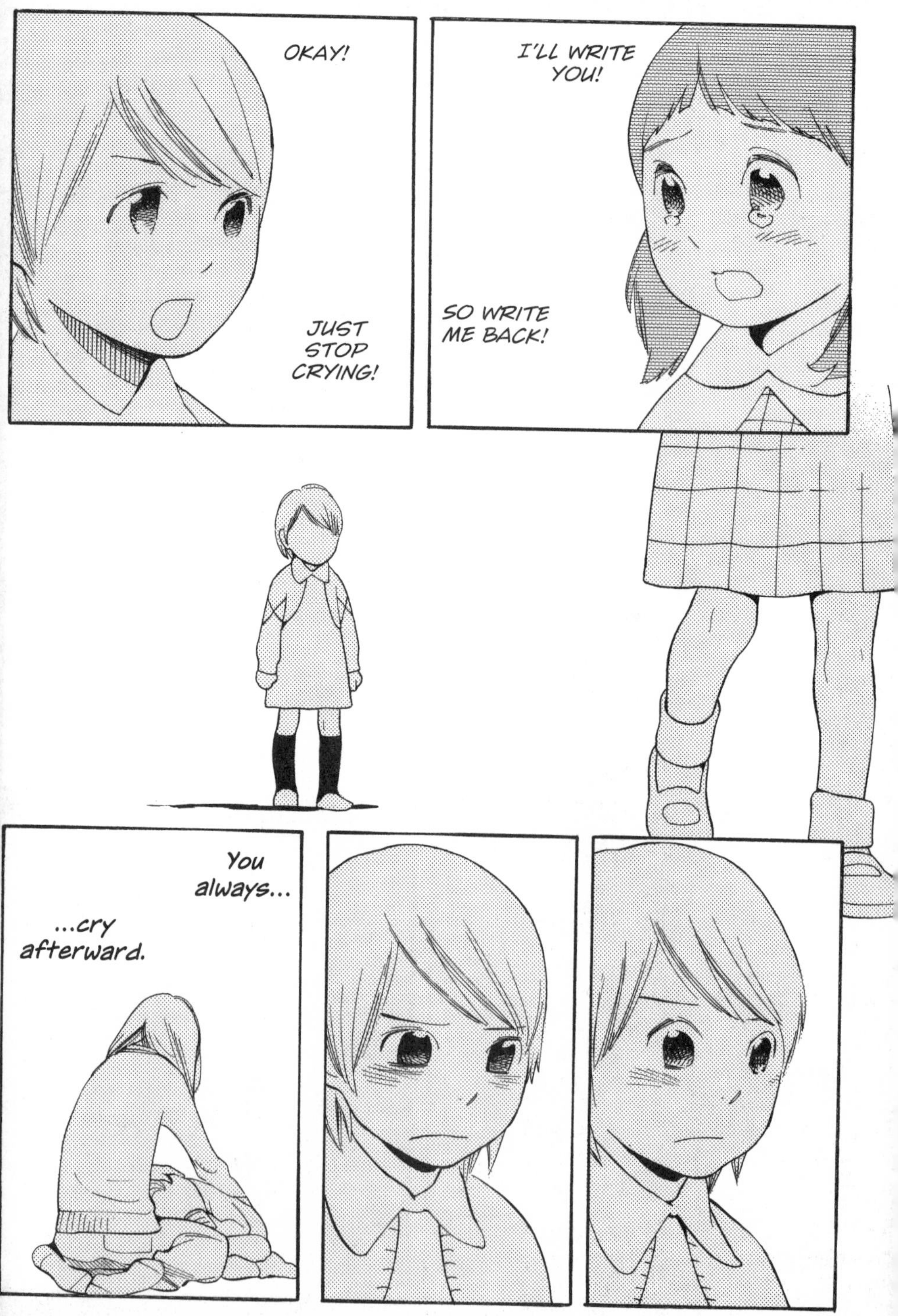
I'LL WRITE YOU!
SO WRITE ME BACK!
OKAY!
JUST STOP CRYING!
You always...
...cry afterward.

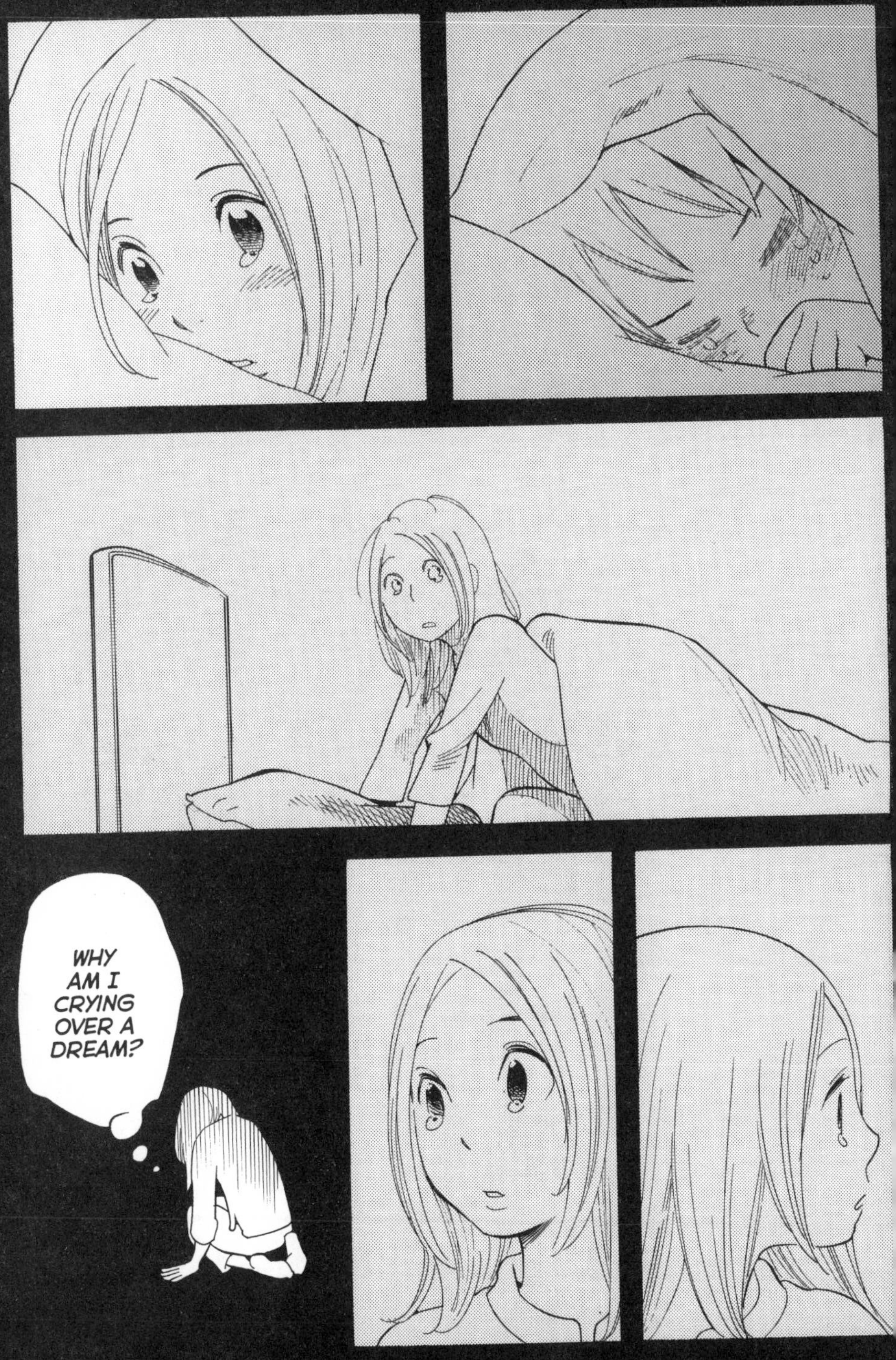
WHY AM I CRYING OVER A DREAM?

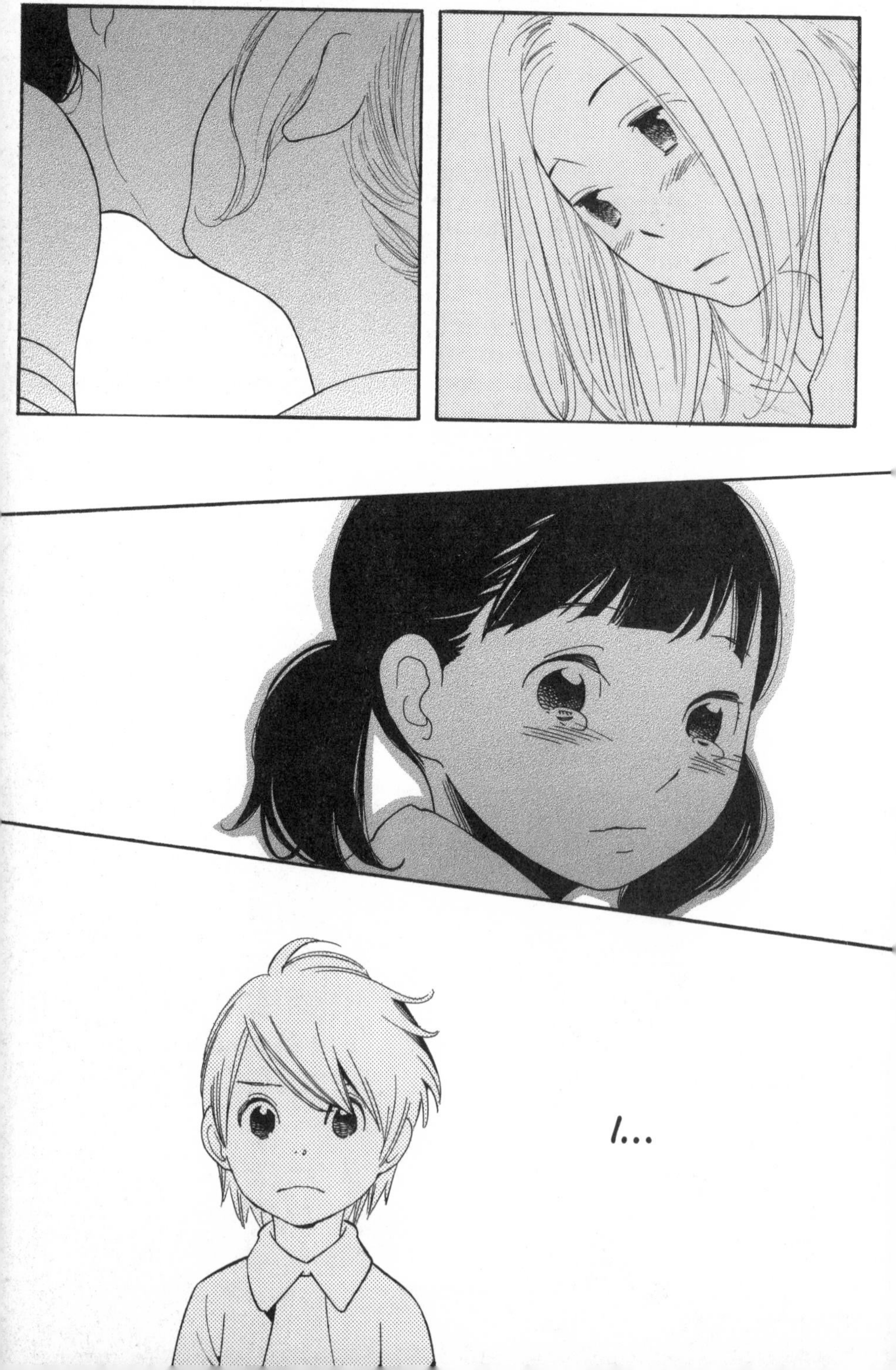
I...

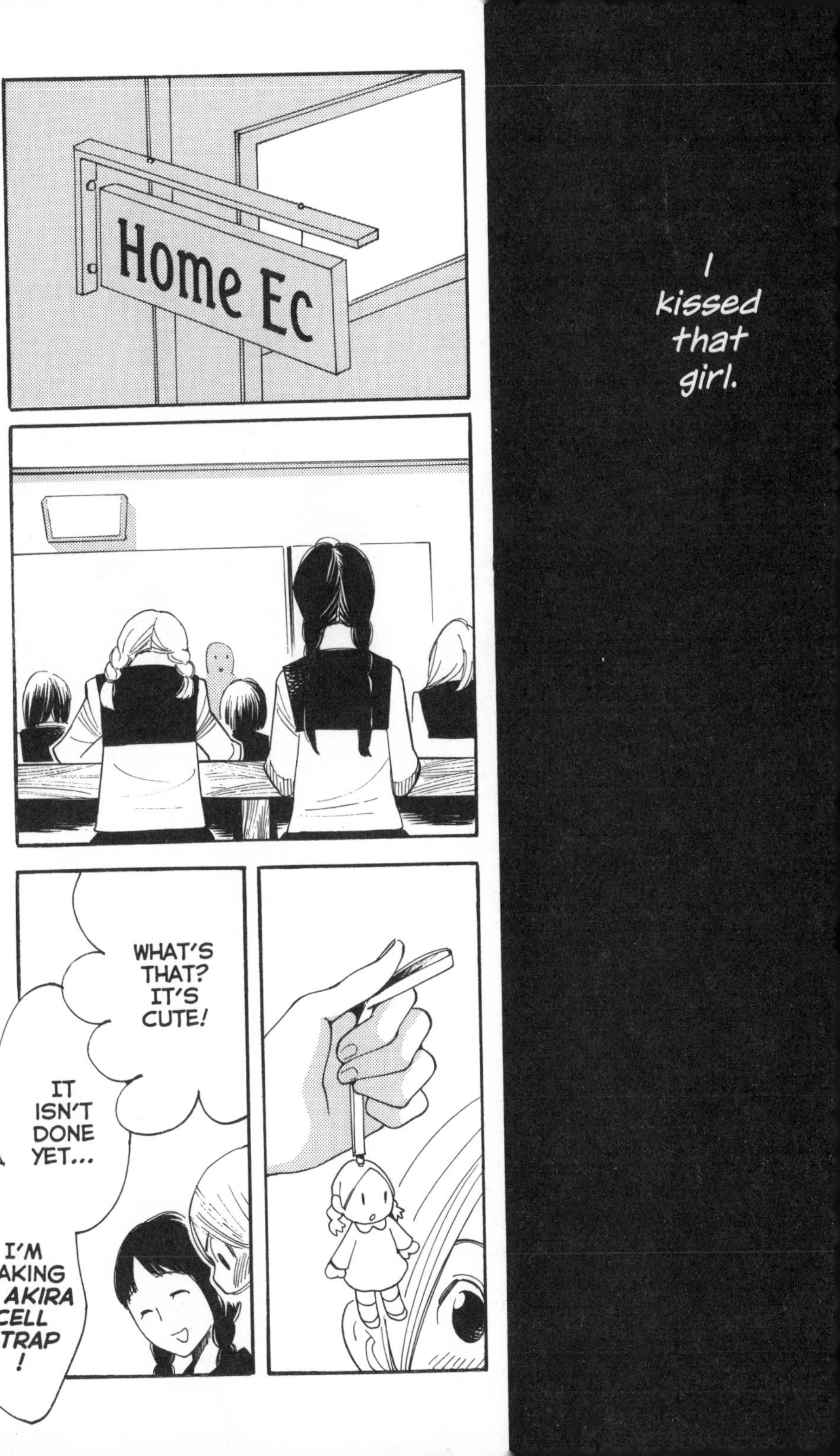
I kissed that girl.
Home Ec
WHAT'S THAT? IT'S CUTE!
IT ISN'T DONE YET...
I'M MAKING AN AKIRA CELL STRAP!

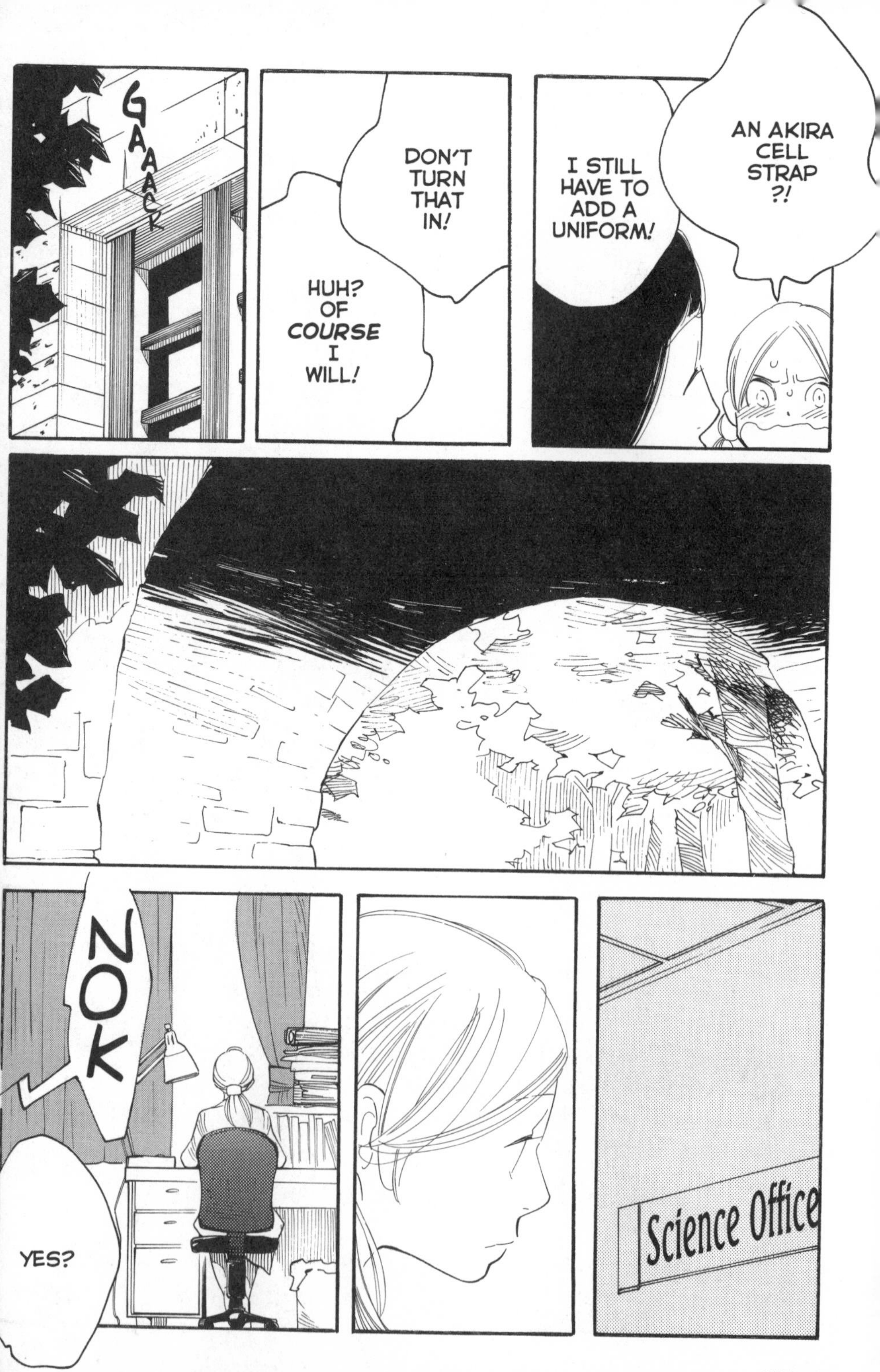
AN AKIRA CELL STRAP ?!
I STILL HAVE TO ADD A UNIFORM!
DON'T TURN THAT IN!
HUH? OF COURSE I WILL!
GAAAACK
Science Office
NOK
YES?

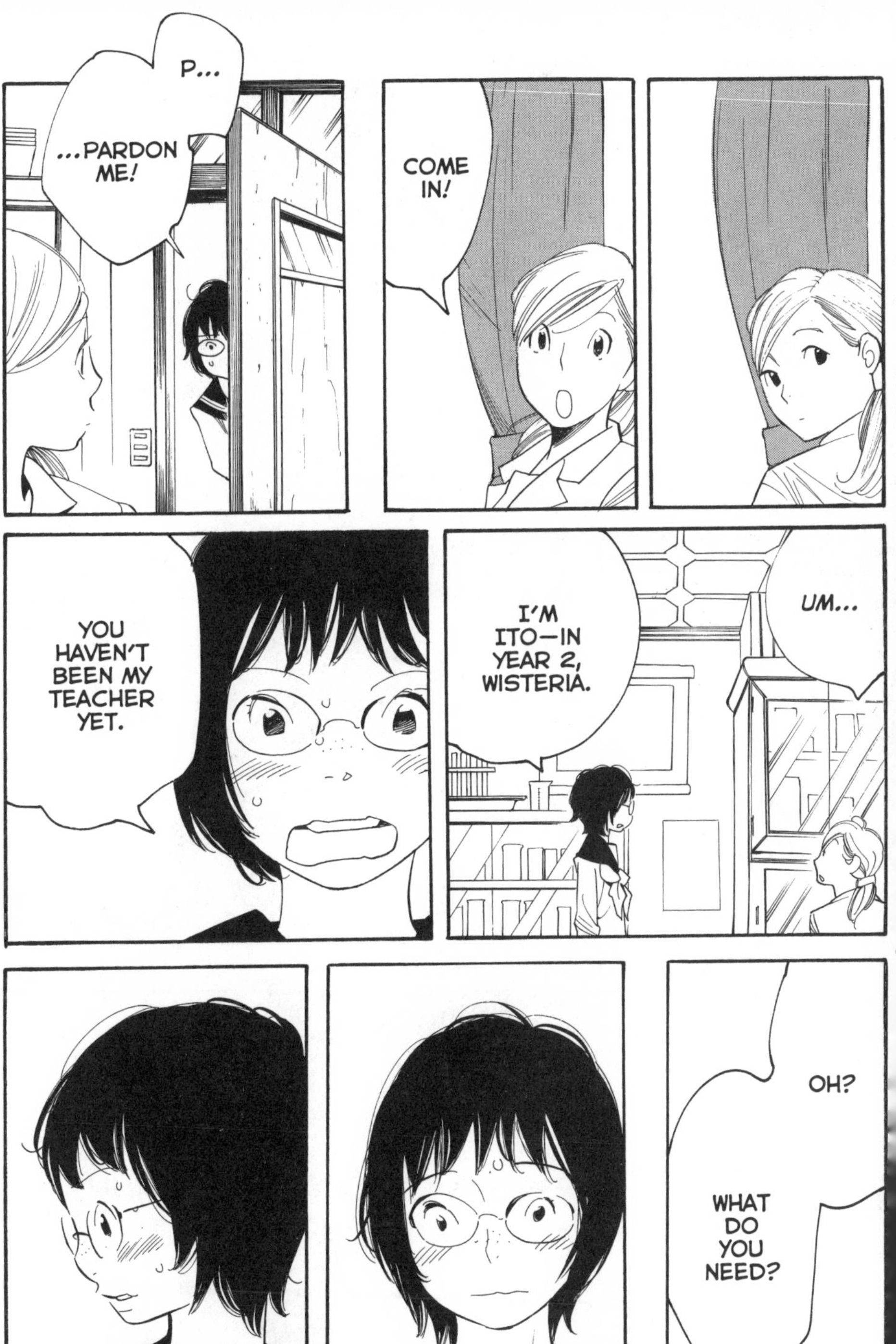
COME IN!
P...
...PARDON ME!
UM...
I'M ITO—IN YEAR 2, WISTERIA.
YOU HAVEN'T BEEN MY TEACHER YET.
OH?
WHAT DO YOU NEED?

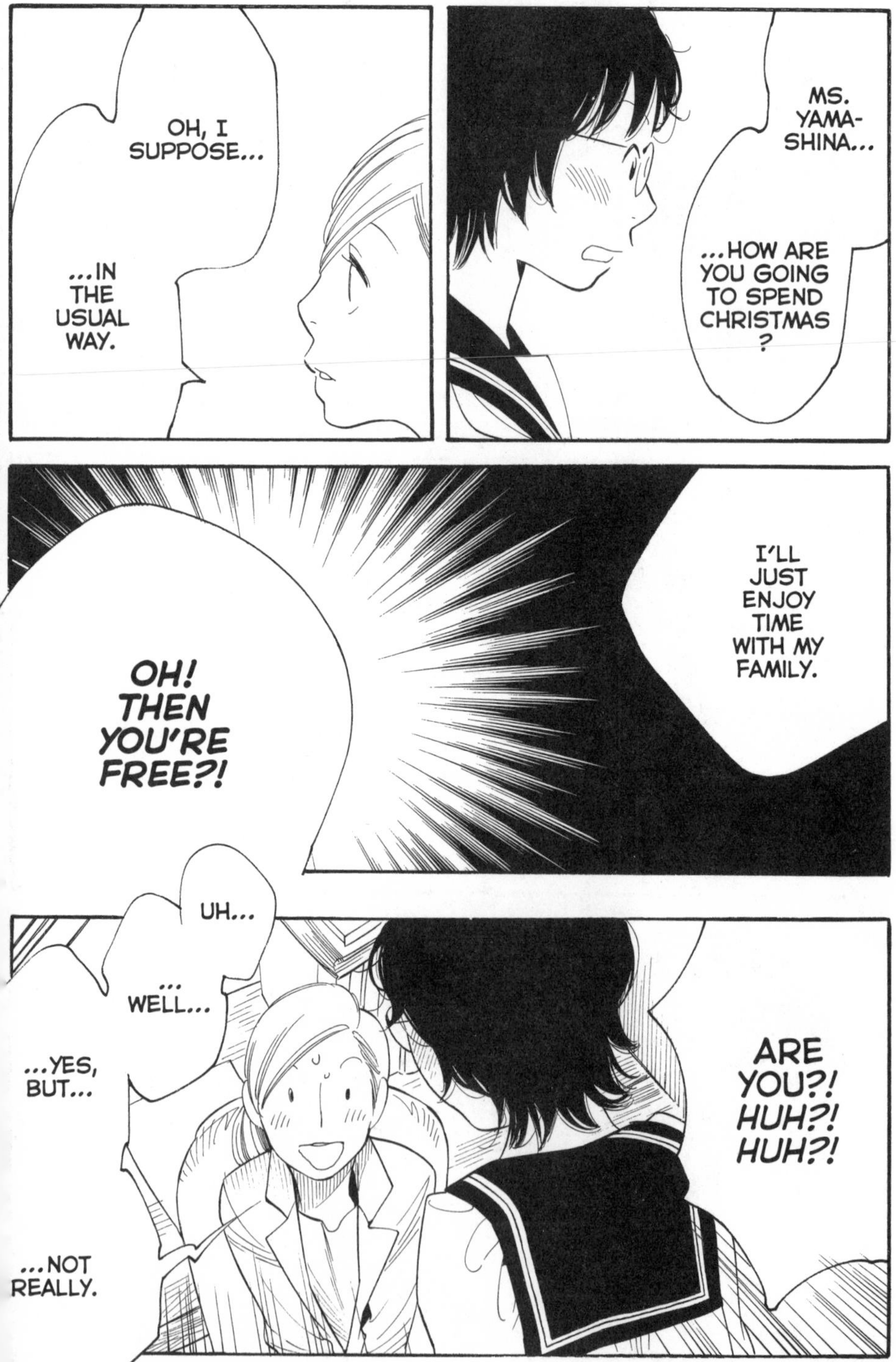
MS. YAMA-SHINA...
...HOW ARE YOU GOING TO SPEND CHRISTMAS?
OH, I SUPPOSE...
...IN THE USUAL WAY.
I'LL JUST ENJOY TIME WITH MY FAMILY.
OH! THEN YOU'RE FREE?!
ARE YOU?! HUH?! HUH?!
UH...
...WELL...
...YES, BUT...
...NOT REALLY.

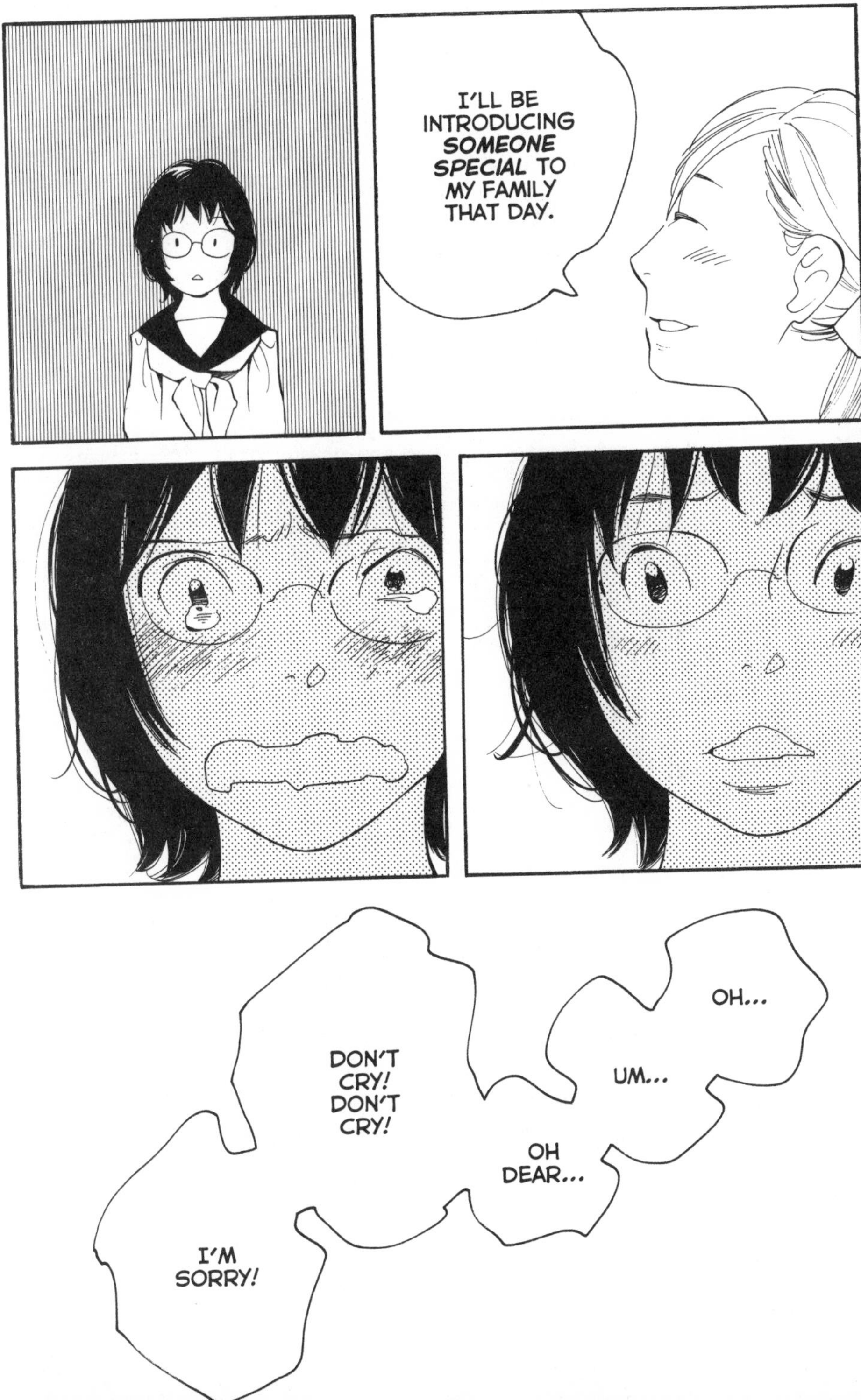
I'LL BE INTRODUCING *SOMEONE SPECIAL* TO MY FAMILY THAT DAY.
OH...
UM...
OH DEAR...
DON'T CRY! DON'T CRY!
I'M SORRY!

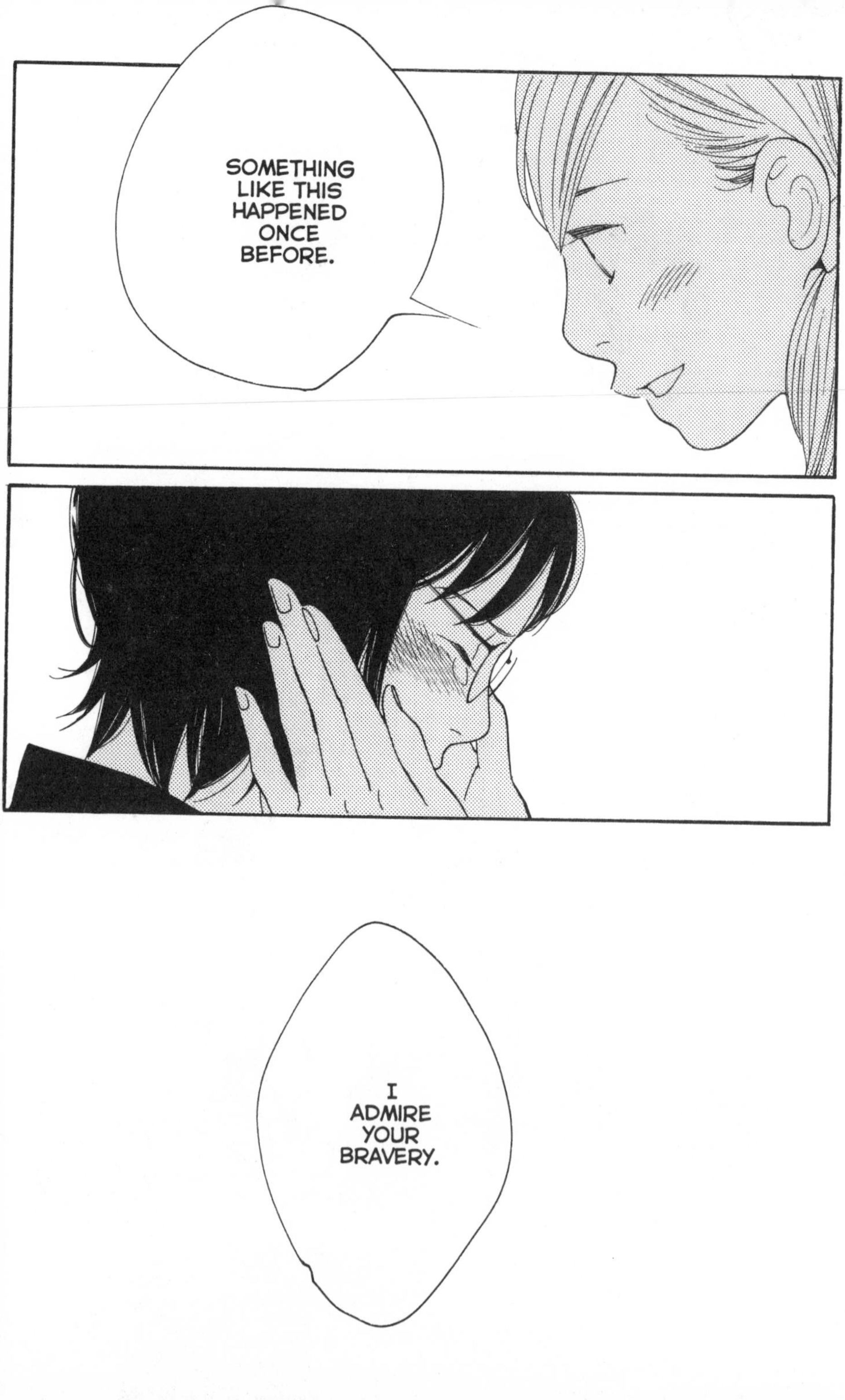
SOMETHING LIKE THIS HAPPENED ONCE BEFORE.
I ADMIRE YOUR BRAVERY.

Sweet Blue Flowers

#38 A Christmas Carol

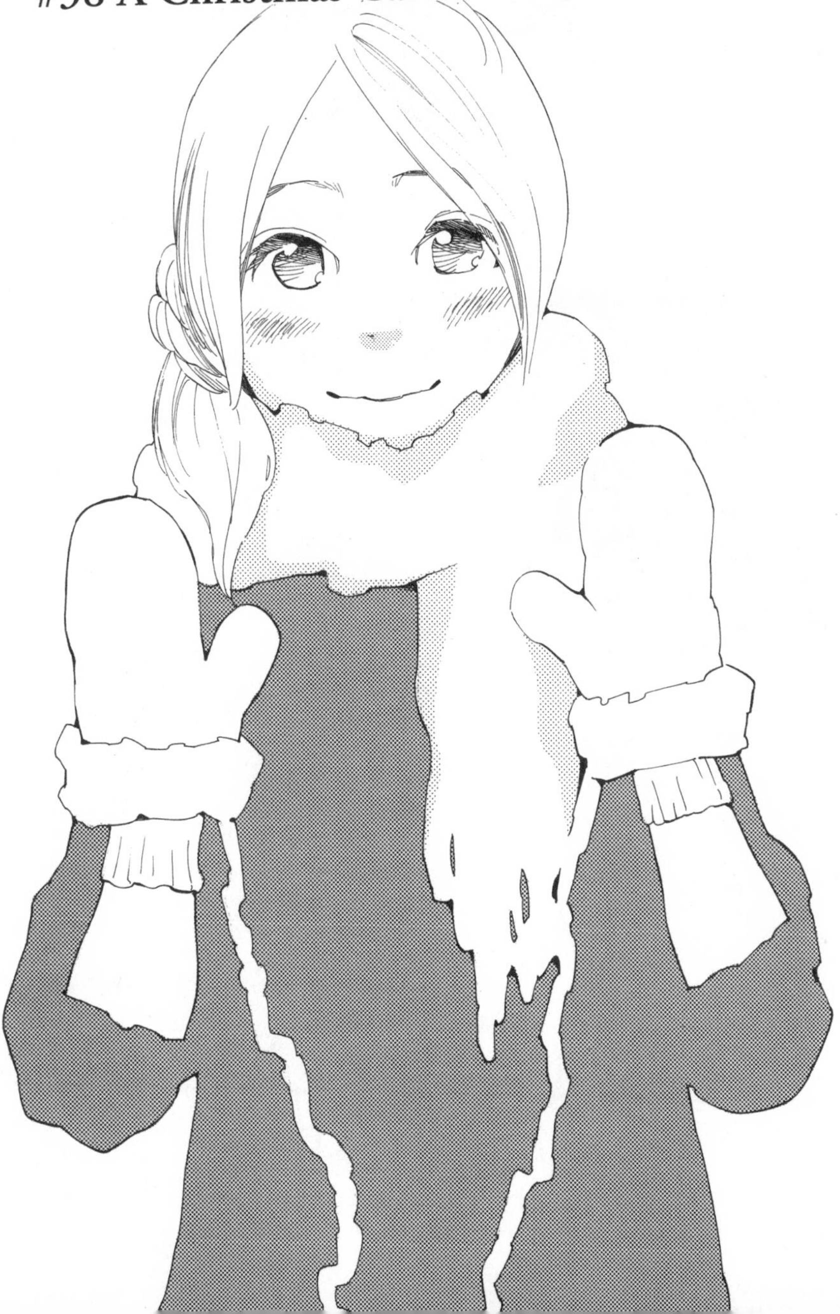

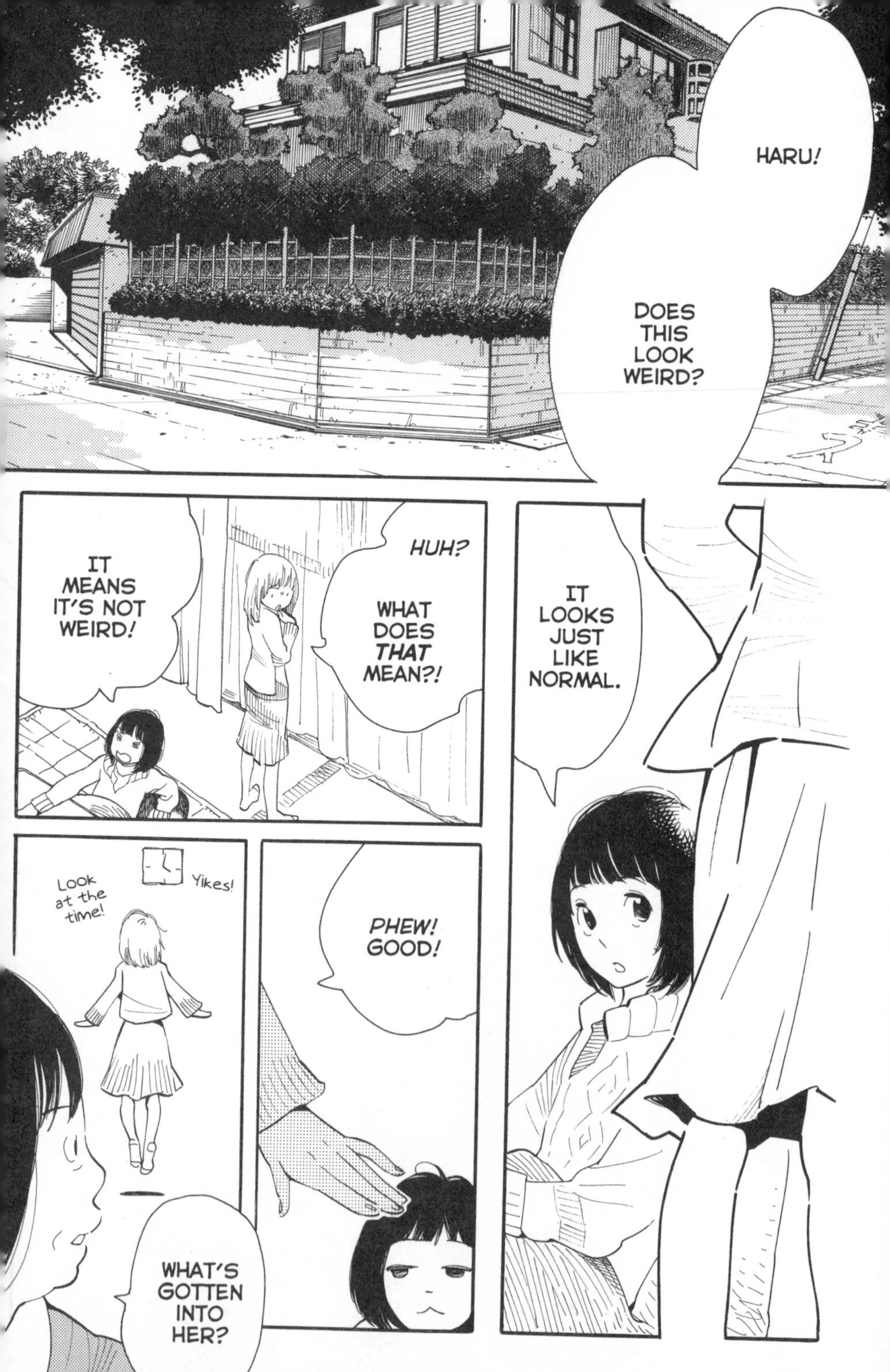
HARU!
DOES THIS LOOK WEIRD?
IT LOOKS JUST LIKE NORMAL.
HUH?
WHAT DOES *THAT* MEAN?!
IT MEANS IT'S NOT WEIRD!
PHEW! GOOD!
Yikes!
Look at the time!
WHAT'S GOTTEN INTO HER?

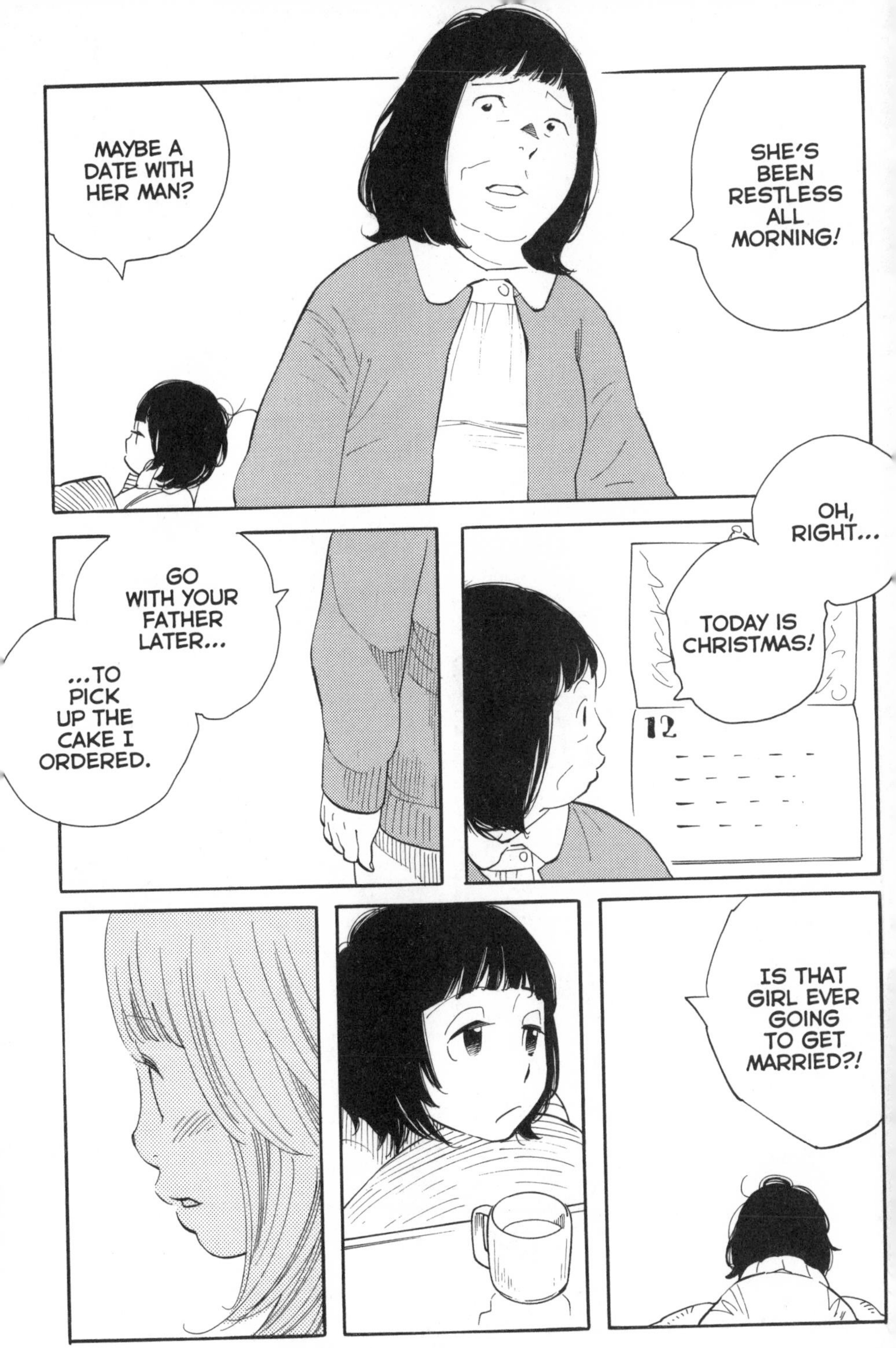
SHE'S BEEN RESTLESS ALL MORNING!
MAYBE A DATE WITH HER MAN?
OH, RIGHT...
TODAY IS CHRISTMAS!
GO WITH YOUR FATHER LATER...
...TO PICK UP THE CAKE I ORDERED.
IS THAT GIRL EVER GOING TO GET MARRIED?!

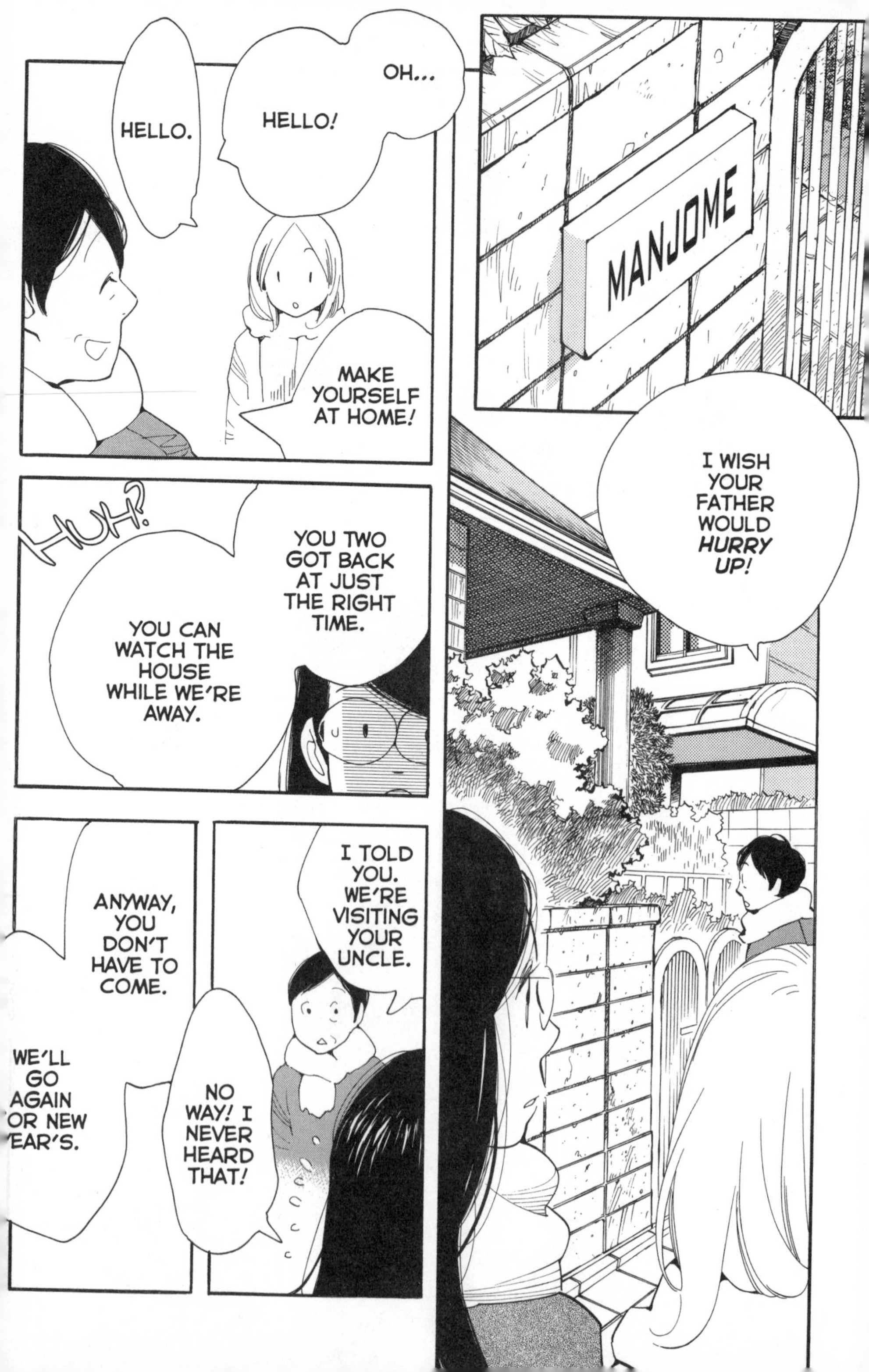
MANJOME
I WISH YOUR FATHER WOULD *HURRY UP!*
OH...
HELLO!
HELLO.
MAKE YOURSELF AT HOME!
HUH?
YOU TWO GOT BACK AT JUST THE RIGHT TIME.
YOU CAN WATCH THE HOUSE WHILE WE'RE AWAY.
I TOLD YOU. WE'RE VISITING YOUR UNCLE.
NO WAY! I NEVER HEARD THAT!
ANYWAY, YOU DON'T HAVE TO COME.
WE'LL GO AGAIN OR NEW EAR'S.

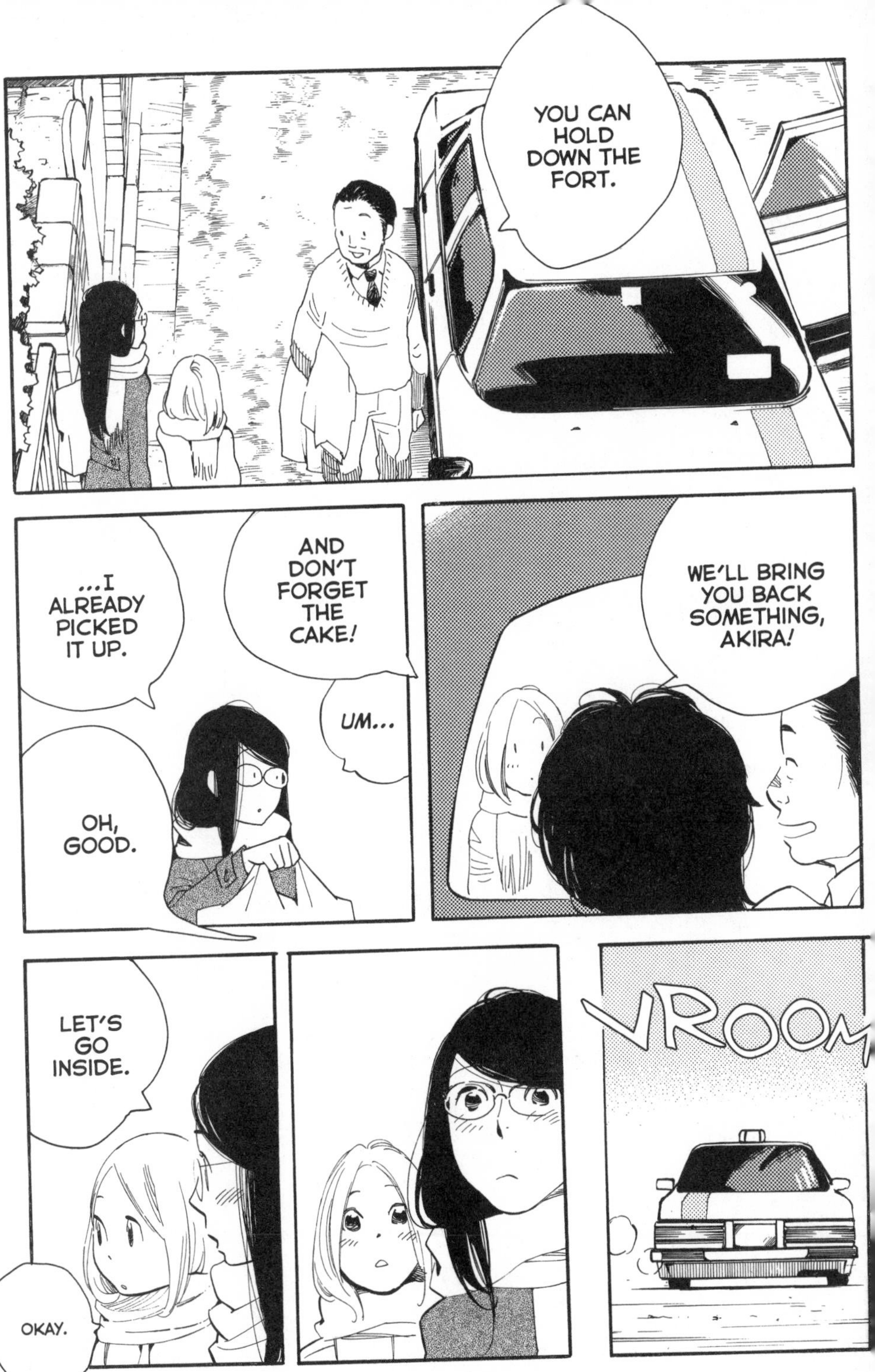
YOU CAN HOLD DOWN THE FORT.
WE'LL BRING YOU BACK SOMETHING, AKIRA!
AND DON'T FORGET THE CAKE!
...I ALREADY PICKED IT UP.
UM...
OH, GOOD.
VROOM
LET'S GO INSIDE.
OKAY.

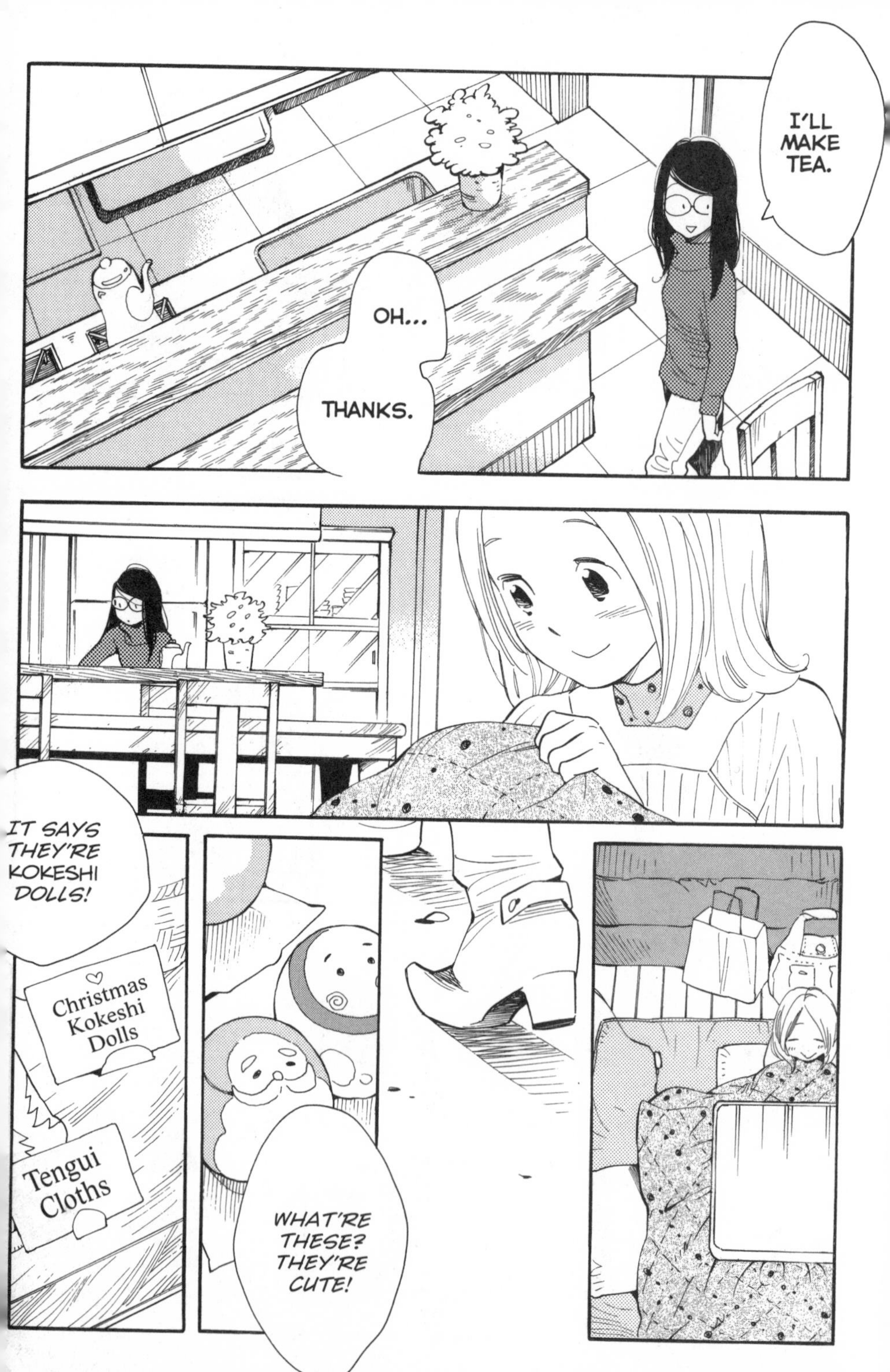
I'LL MAKE TEA.
OH... THANKS.
WHAT'RE THESE? THEY'RE CUTE!
IT SAYS THEY'RE KOKESHI DOLLS!
Christmas Kokeshi Dolls
Tengui Cloths

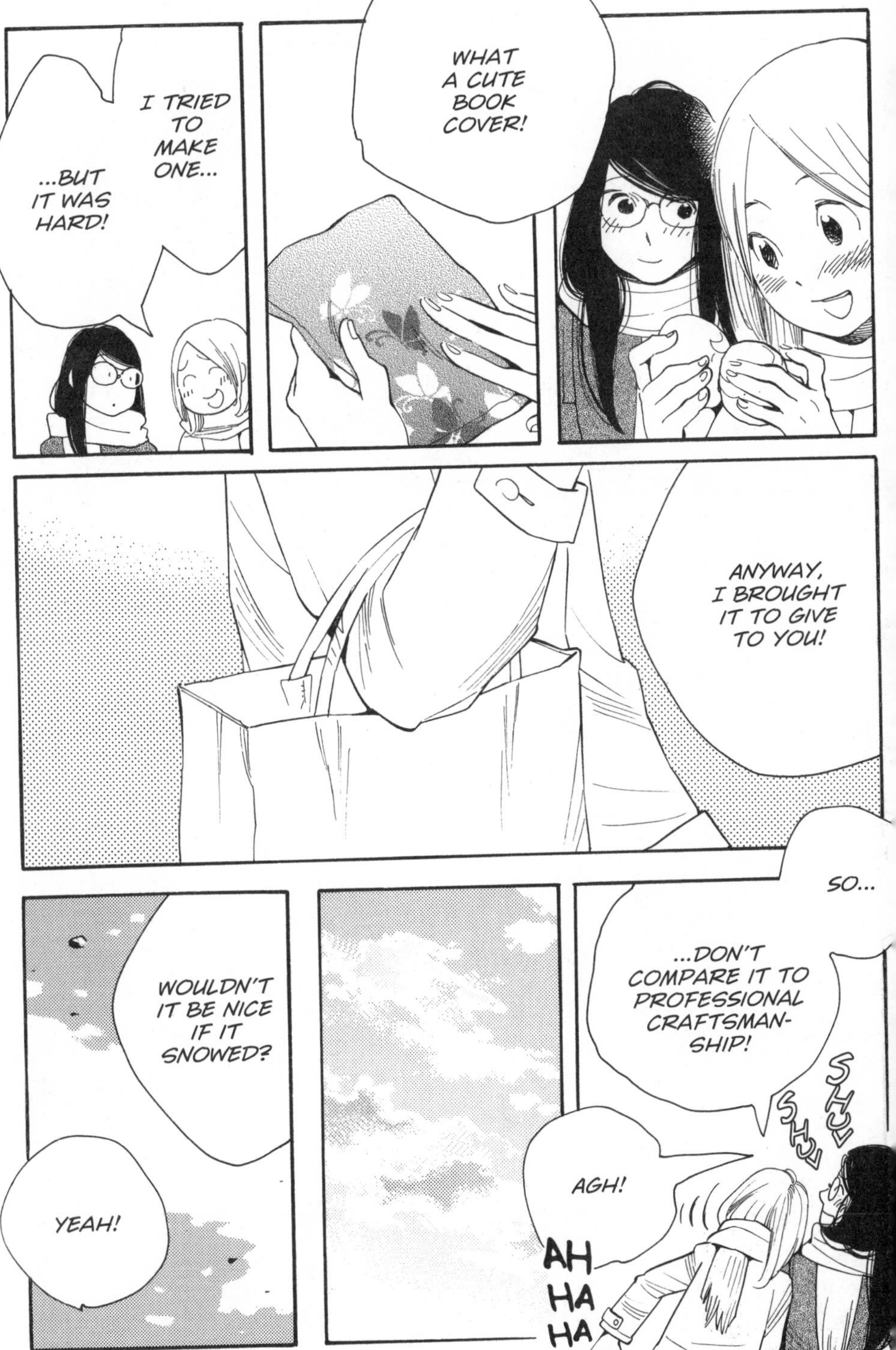
WHAT A CUTE BOOK COVER!
I TRIED TO MAKE ONE...
...BUT IT WAS HARD!
ANYWAY, I BROUGHT IT TO GIVE TO YOU!
SO...
...DON'T COMPARE IT TO PROFESSIONAL CRAFTSMANSHIP!
AGH!
AH HA HA
WOULDN'T IT BE NICE IF IT SNOWED?
YEAH!

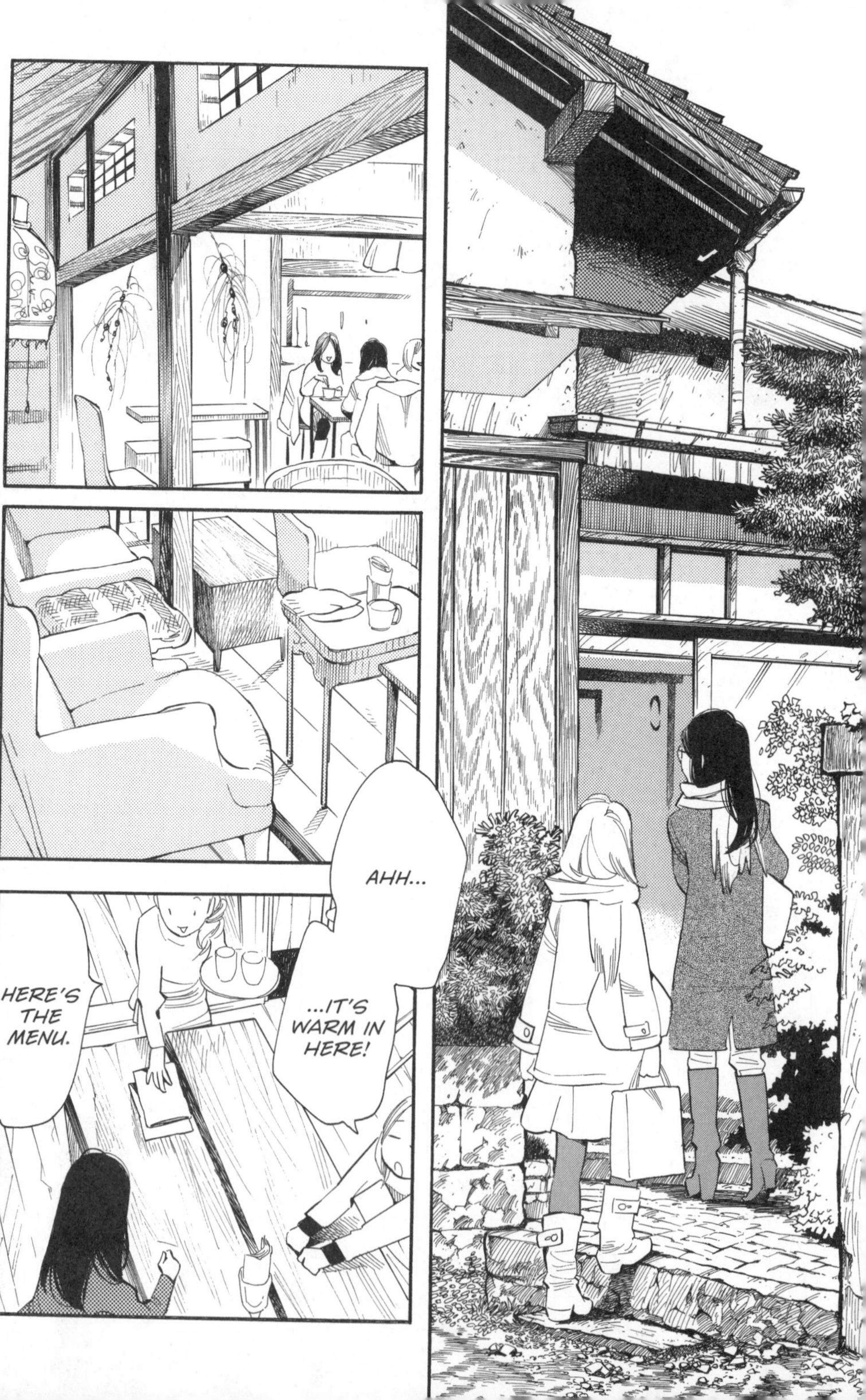
AHH...
...IT'S WARM IN HERE!
HERE'S THE MENU.

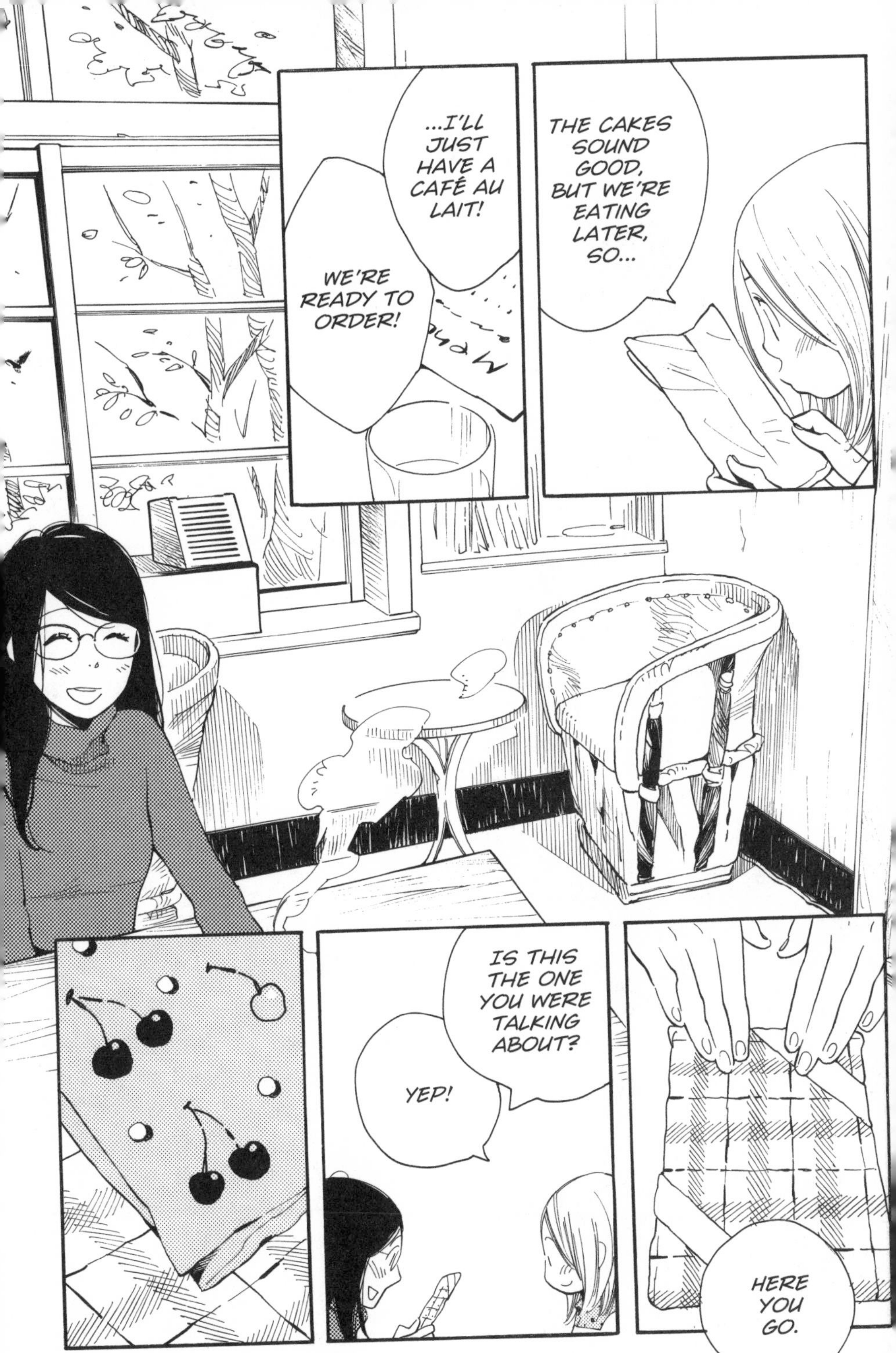
THE CAKES SOUND GOOD, BUT WE'RE EATING LATER, SO...
...I'LL JUST HAVE A CAFÉ AU LAIT!
WE'RE READY TO ORDER!
HERE YOU GO.
IS THIS THE ONE YOU WERE TALKING ABOUT?
YEP!

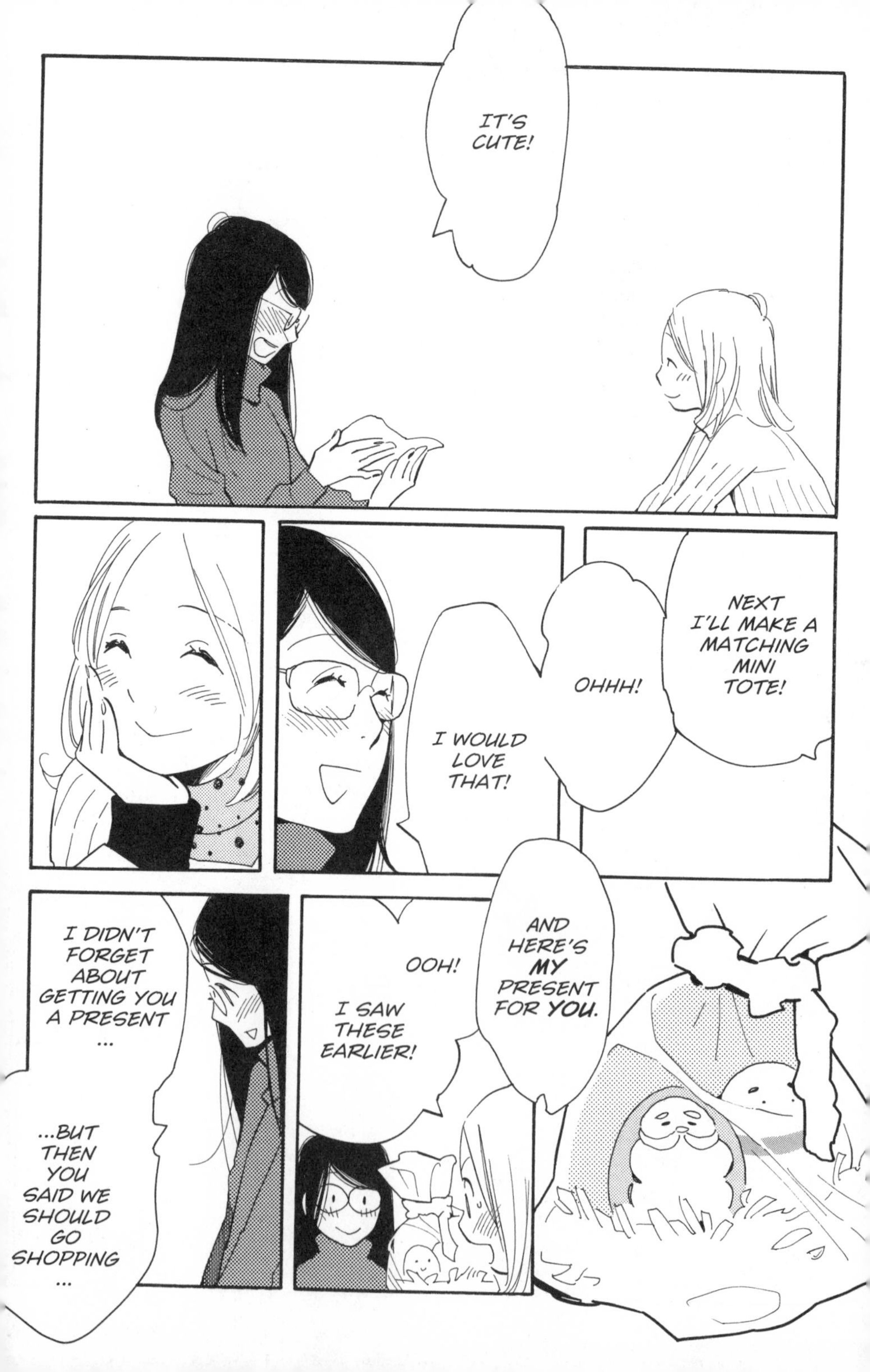
IT'S CUTE!
NEXT I'LL MAKE A MATCHING MINI TOTE!
OHHH!
I WOULD LOVE THAT!
AND HERE'S **MY** PRESENT FOR **YOU**.
OOH!
I SAW THESE EARLIER!
I DIDN'T FORGET ABOUT GETTING YOU A PRESENT ...
...BUT THEN YOU SAID WE SHOULD GO SHOPPING ...

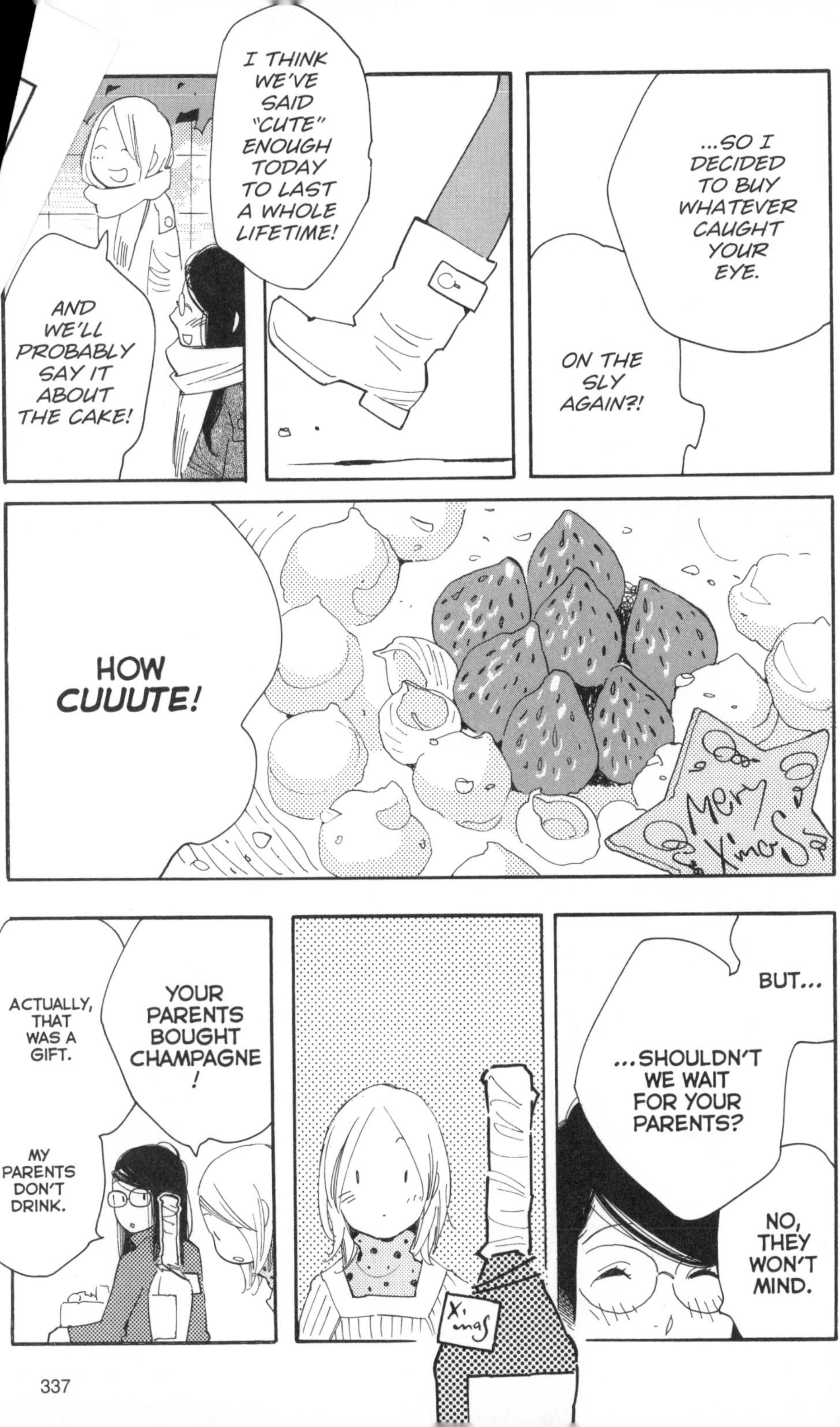
...SO I DECIDED TO BUY WHATEVER CAUGHT YOUR EYE.
ON THE SLY AGAIN?!
I THINK WE'VE SAID "CUTE" ENOUGH TODAY TO LAST A WHOLE LIFETIME!
AND WE'LL PROBABLY SAY IT ABOUT THE CAKE!
HOW CUUUTE!
Merry X'mas
BUT...
...SHOULDN'T WE WAIT FOR YOUR PARENTS?
NO, THEY WON'T MIND.
X'mas
YOUR PARENTS BOUGHT CHAMPAGNE!
ACTUALLY, THAT WAS A GIFT.
MY PARENTS DON'T DRINK.

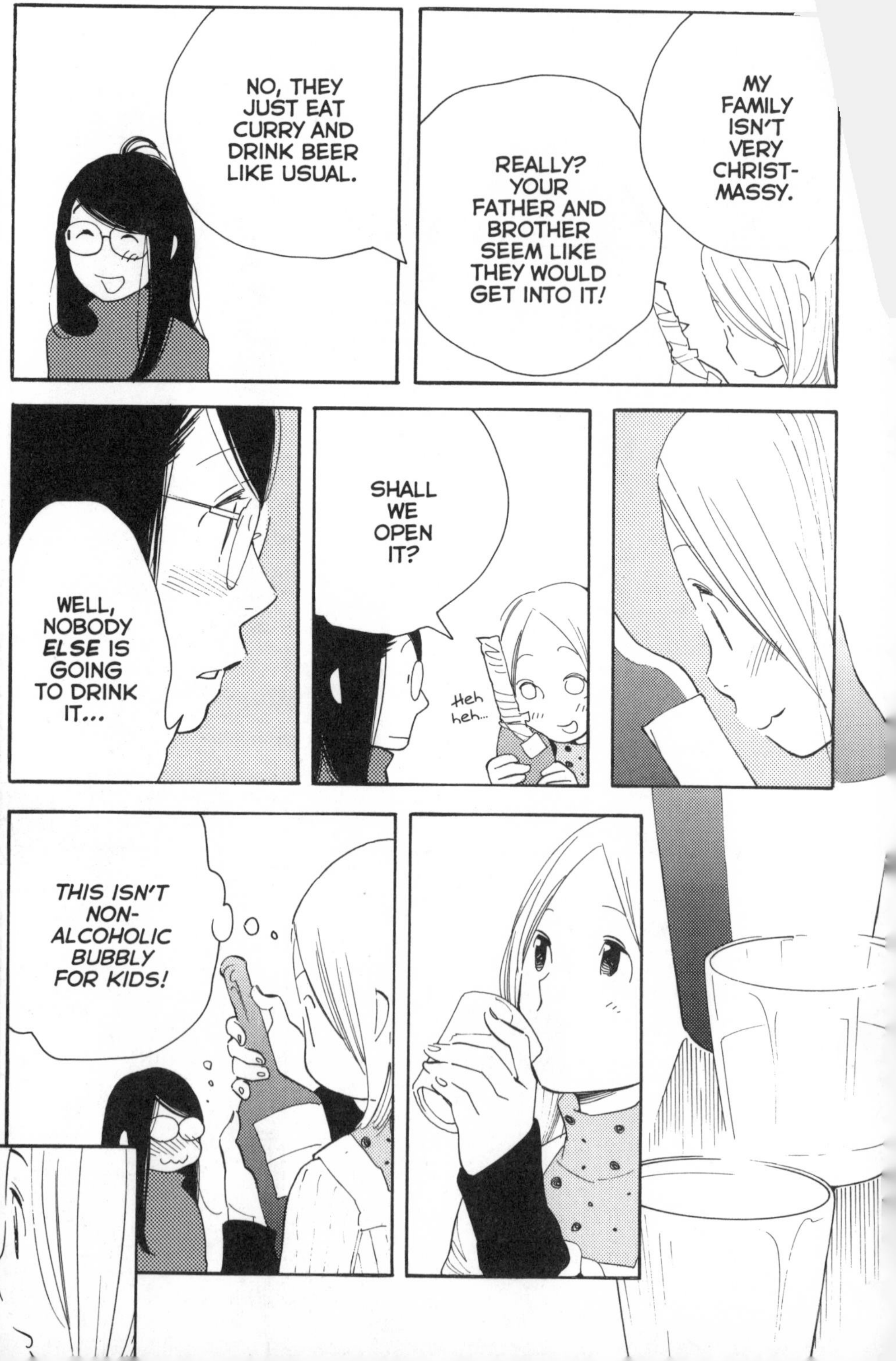
MY FAMILY ISN'T VERY CHRIST-MASSY.
REALLY? YOUR FATHER AND BROTHER SEEM LIKE THEY WOULD GET INTO IT!
NO, THEY JUST EAT CURRY AND DRINK BEER LIKE USUAL.
SHALL WE OPEN IT?
Heh heh...
WELL, NOBODY *ELSE* IS GOING TO DRINK IT...
THIS ISN'T NON-ALCOHOLIC BUBBLY FOR KIDS!

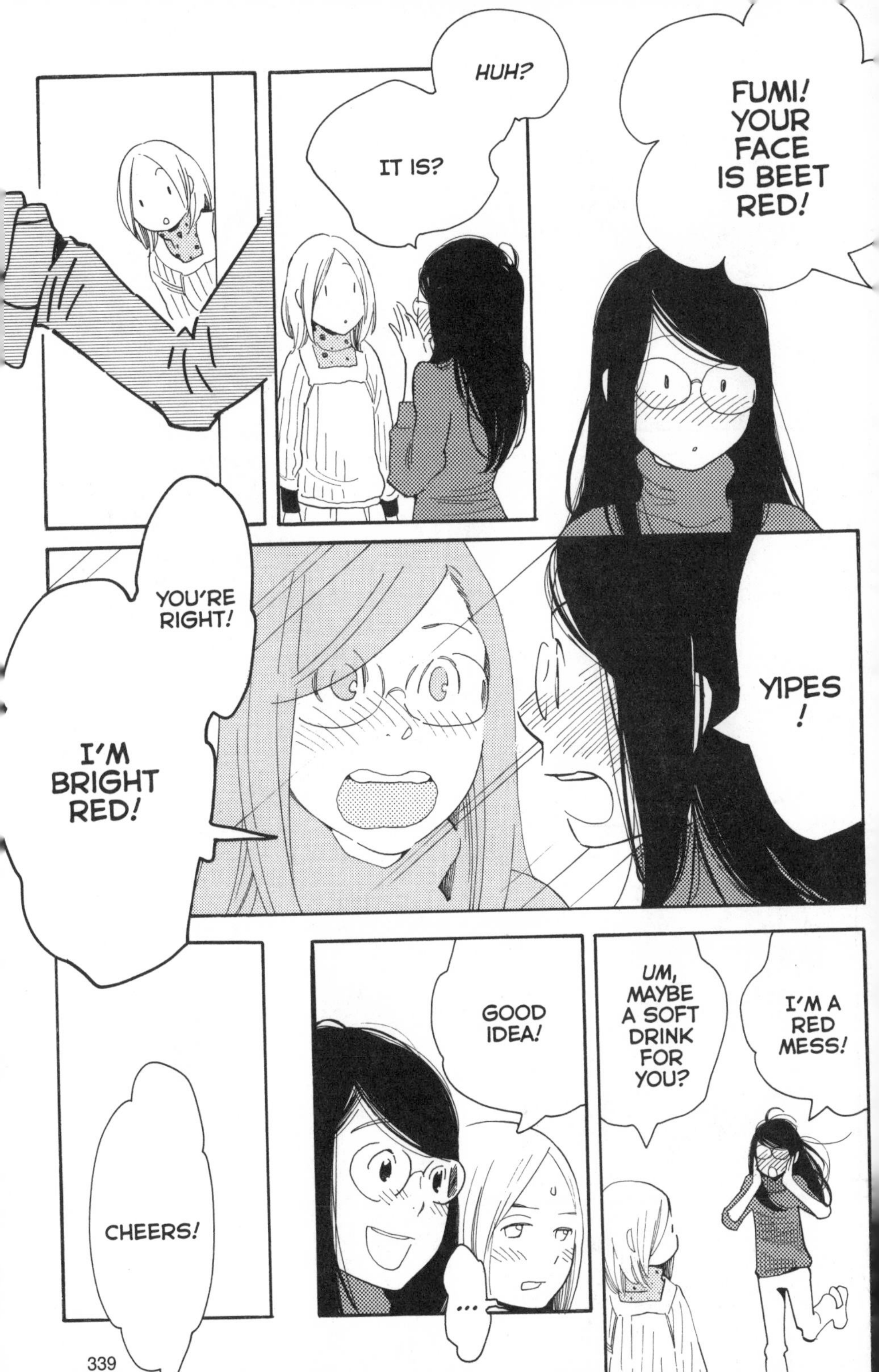
FUMI! YOUR FACE IS BEET RED!
HUH?
IT IS?
YIPES!
YOU'RE RIGHT!
I'M BRIGHT RED!
I'M A RED MESS!
UM, MAYBE A SOFT DRINK FOR YOU?
GOOD IDEA!
...
CHEERS!

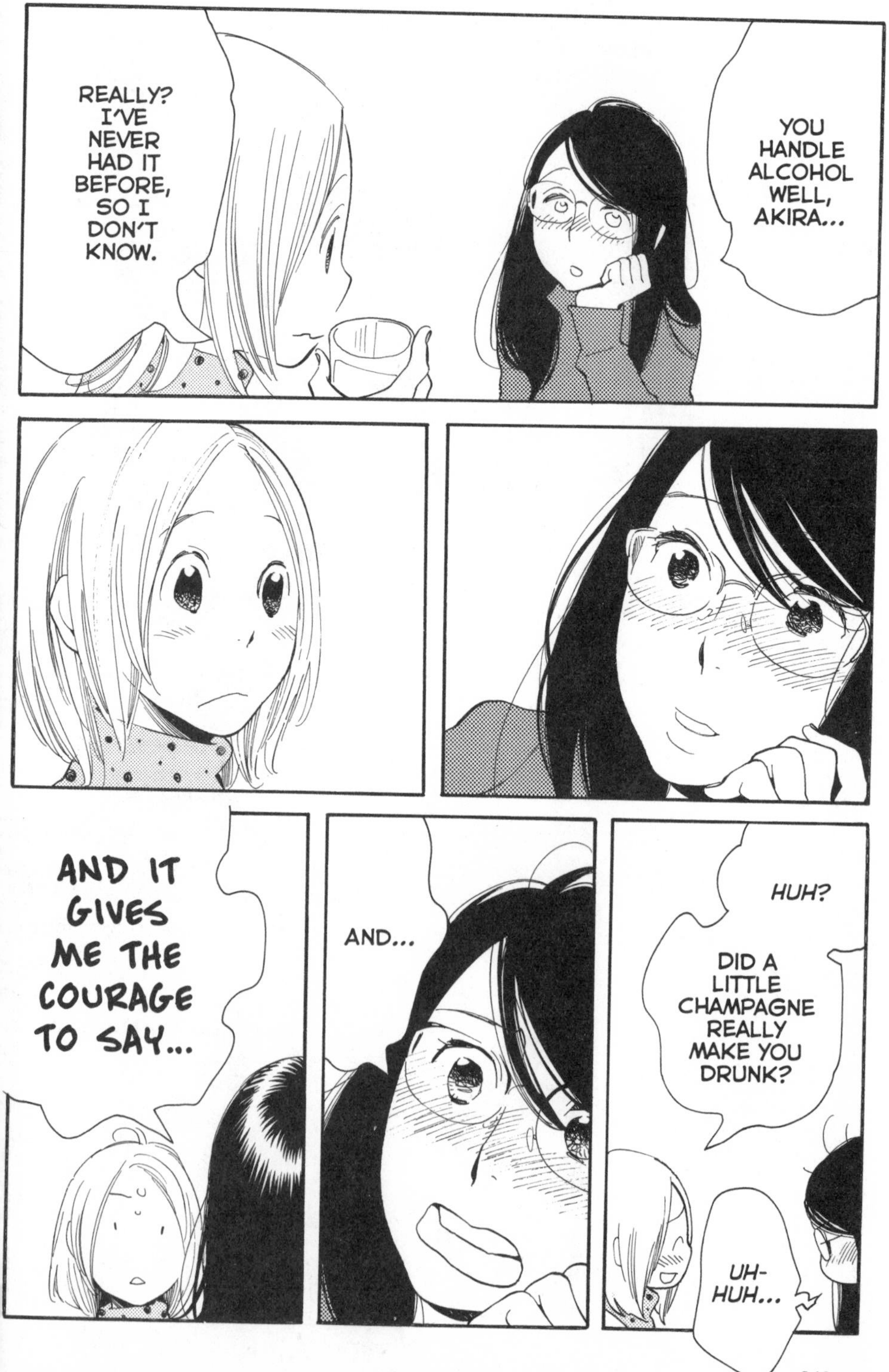
YOU HANDLE ALCOHOL WELL, AKIRA...
REALLY? I'VE NEVER HAD IT BEFORE, SO I DON'T KNOW.
HUH?
DID A LITTLE CHAMPAGNE REALLY MAKE YOU DRUNK?
UH-HUH...
AND...
AND IT GIVES ME THE COURAGE TO SAY...

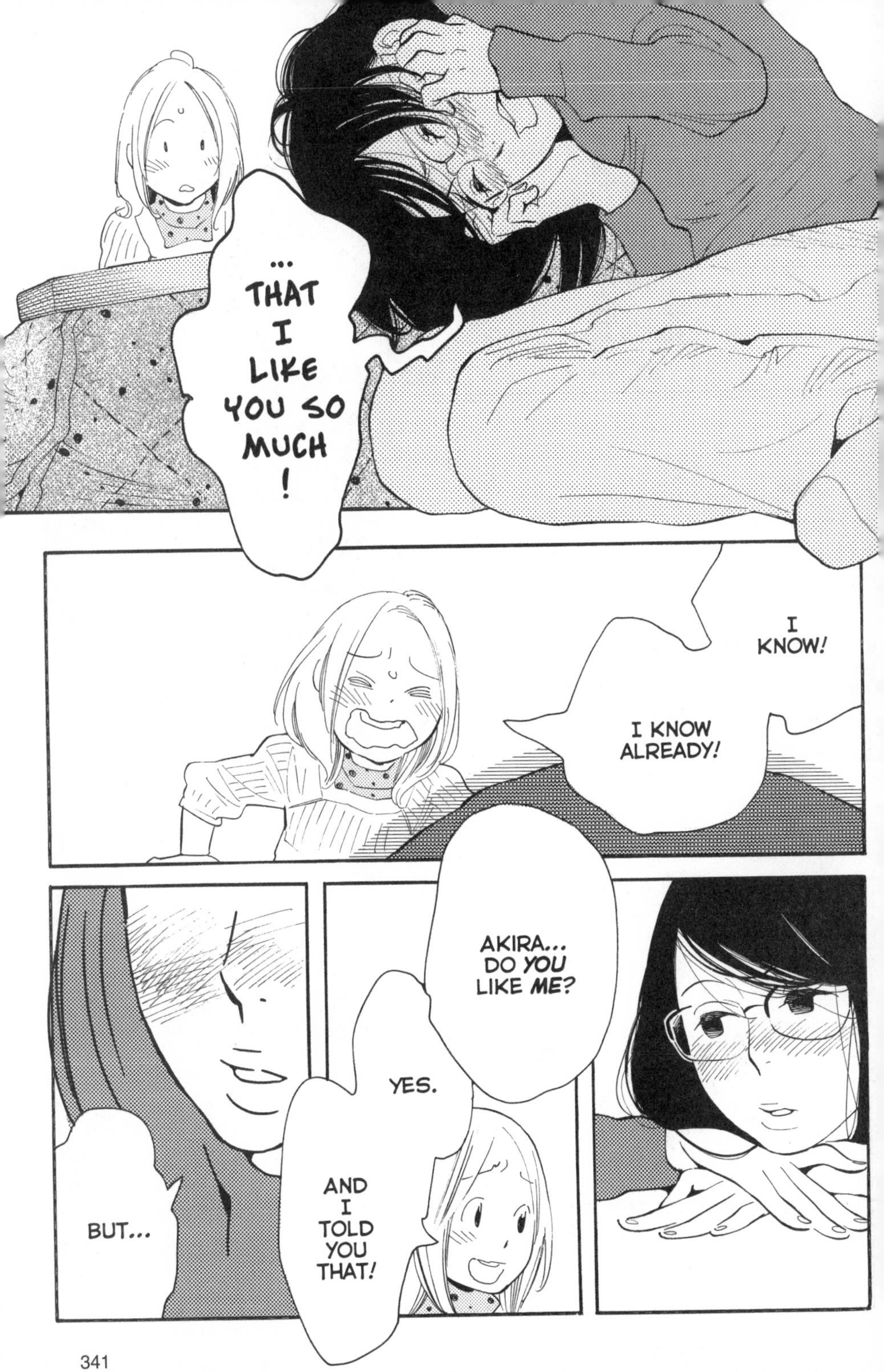
... THAT I LIKE YOU SO MUCH !
I KNOW!
I KNOW ALREADY!
AKIRA... DO *YOU* LIKE *ME*?
YES.
AND I TOLD YOU THAT!
BUT...

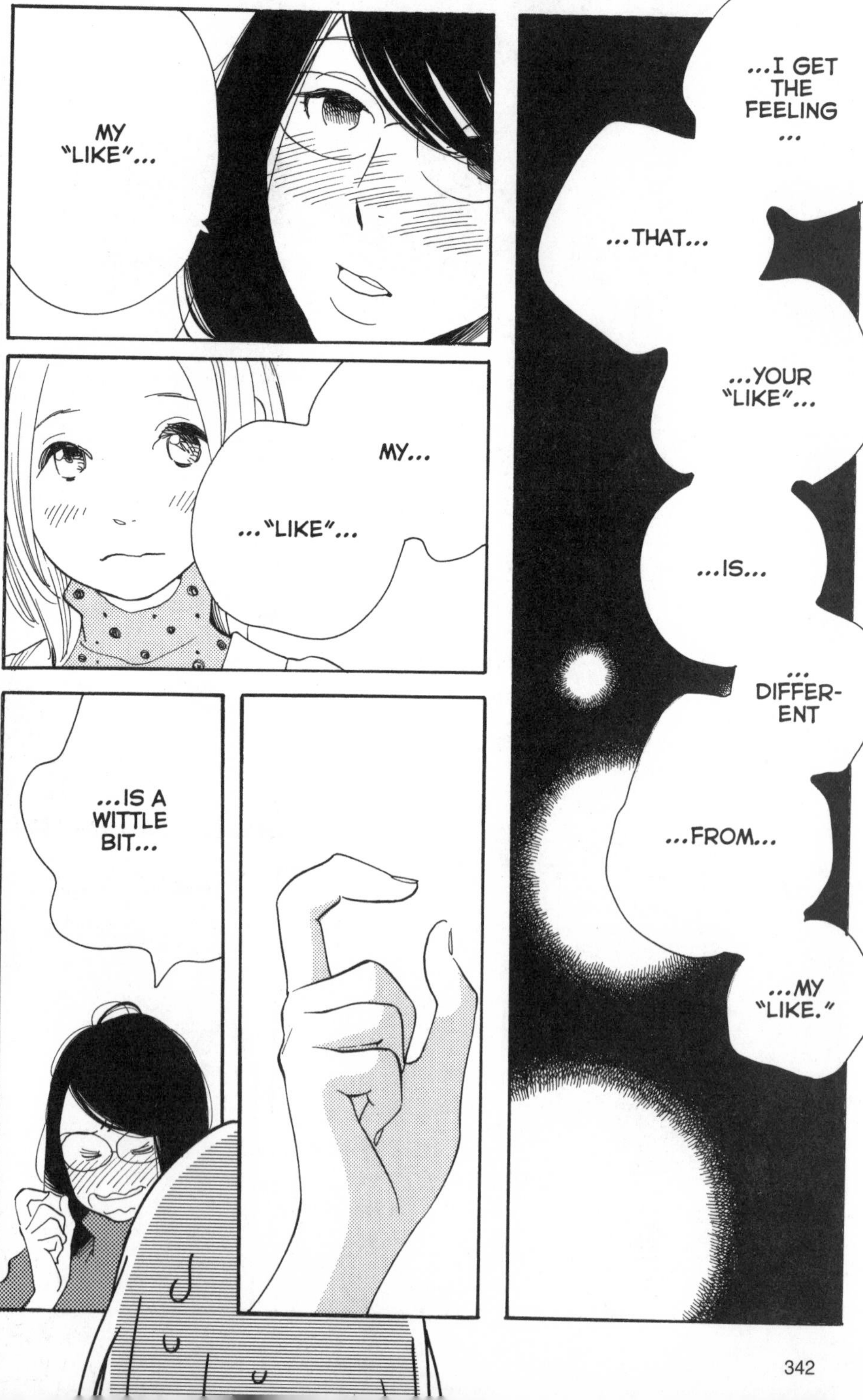
...I GET THE FEELING ...
...THAT...
...YOUR "LIKE"...
...IS...
... DIFFER-ENT
...FROM...
...MY "LIKE."
MY "LIKE"...
MY...
..."LIKE"...
...IS A WITTLE BIT...

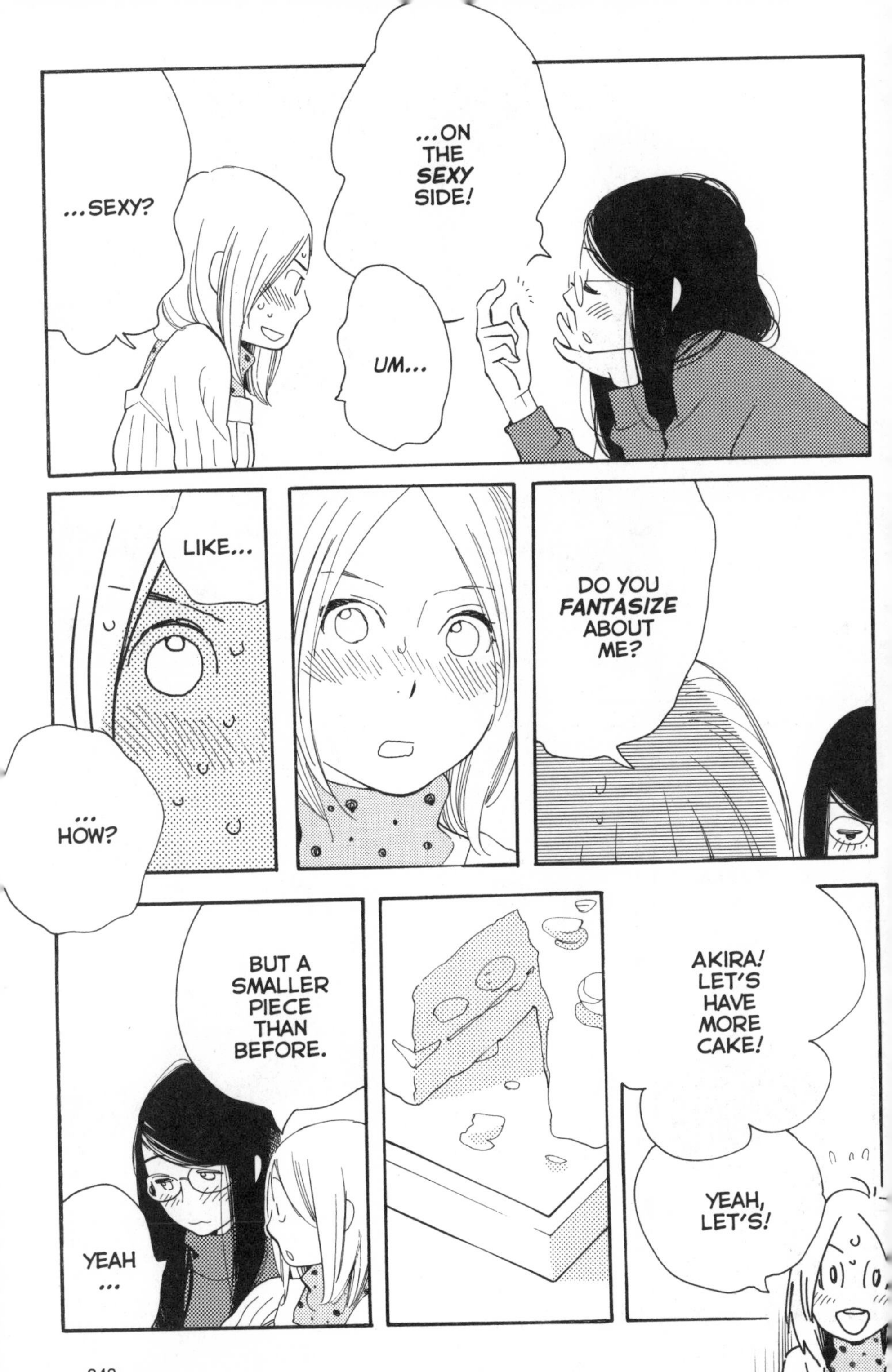
...ON THE SEXY SIDE!
...SEXY?
UM...
DO YOU FANTASIZE ABOUT ME?
LIKE...
...HOW?
AKIRA! LET'S HAVE MORE CAKE!
YEAH, LET'S!
BUT A SMALLER PIECE THAN BEFORE.
YEAH...

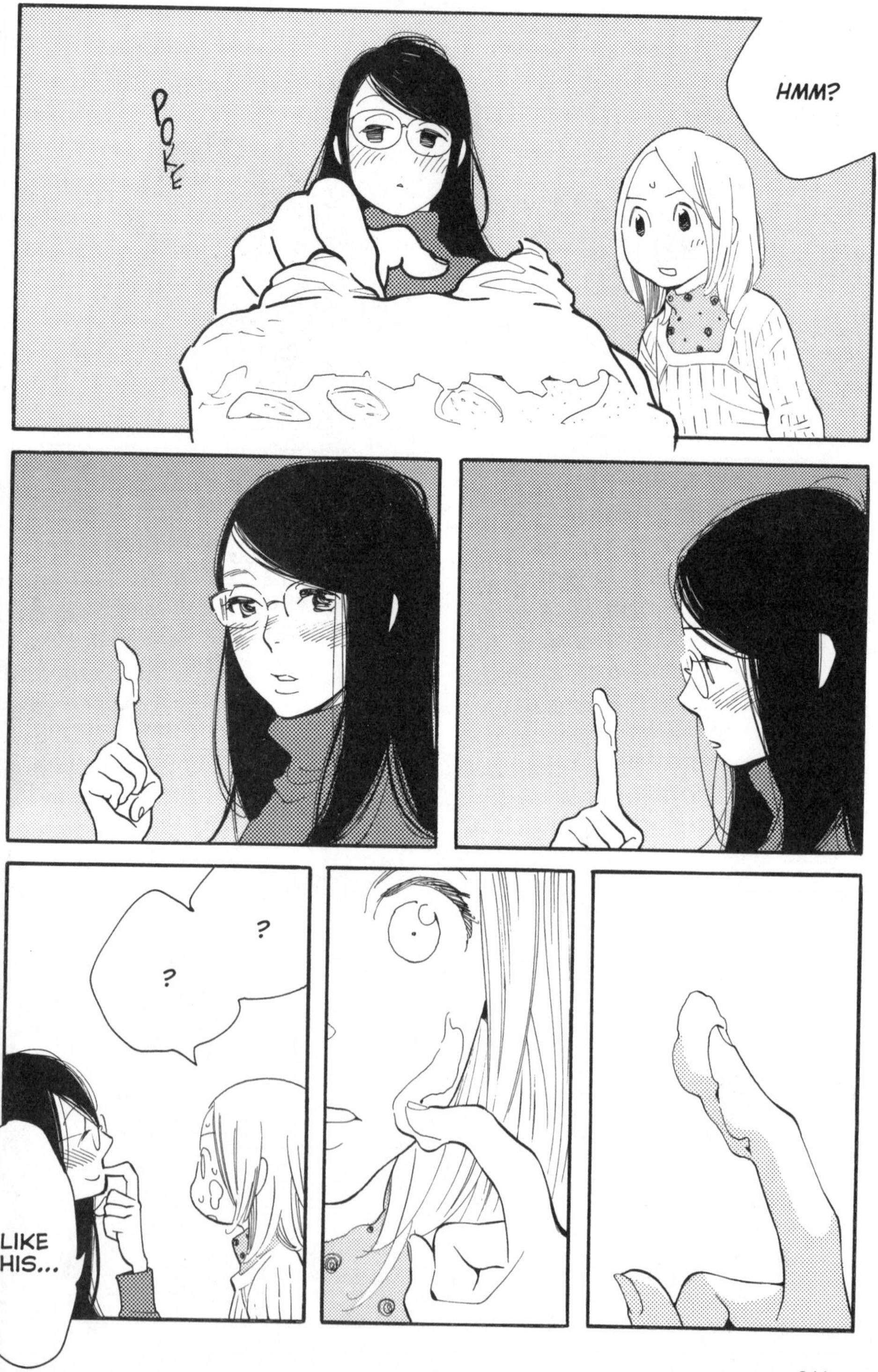
HMM?
POKE
?
?
LIKE THIS...

YOUR "LIKE" MEANS LICKING FROSTING OFF MY FACE?!

NO...

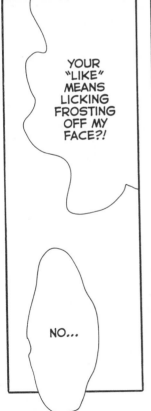

EWWW!

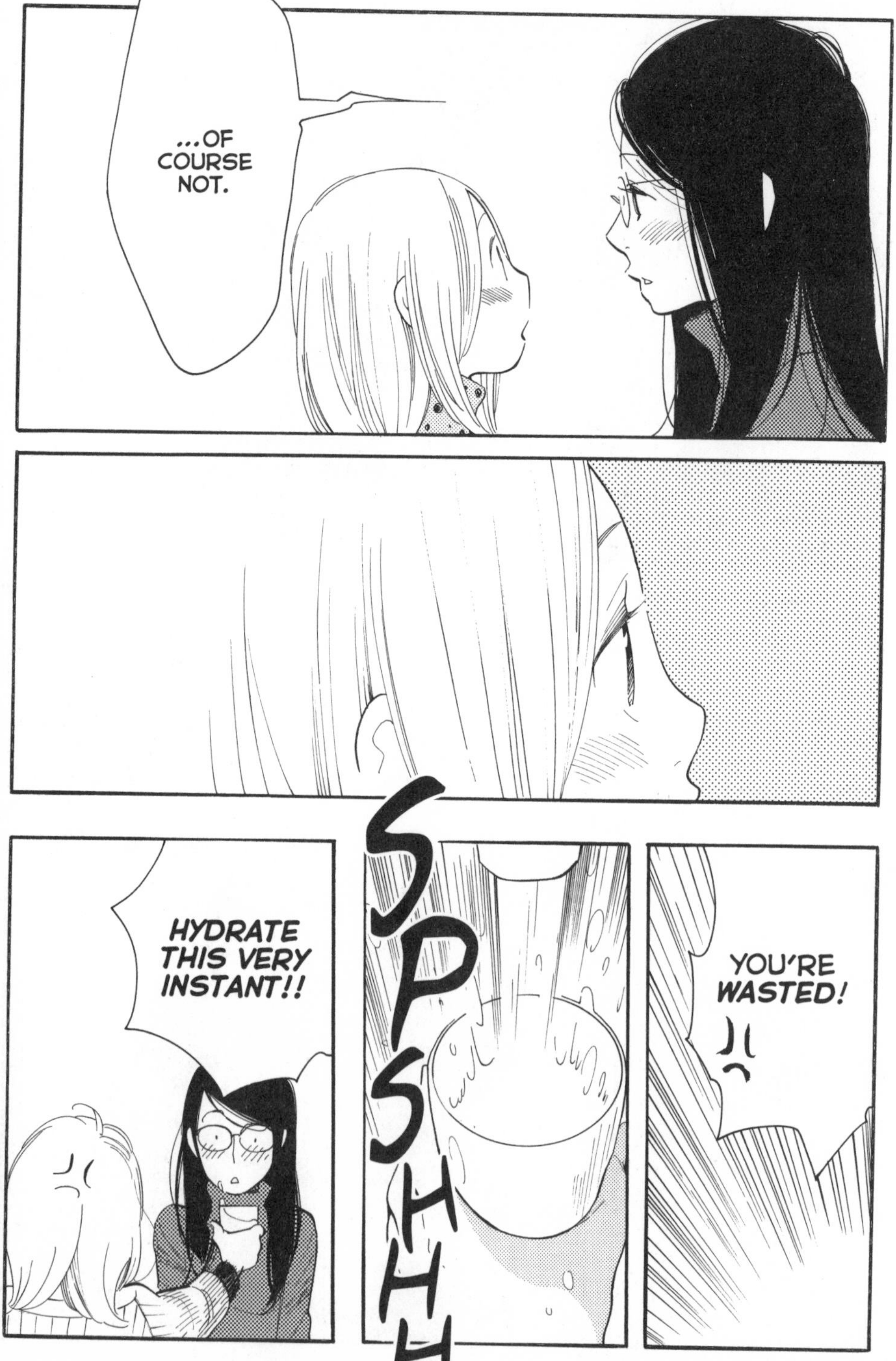
...OF COURSE NOT.
YOU'RE WASTED!
SPSHHHH
HYDRATE THIS VERY INSTANT!!

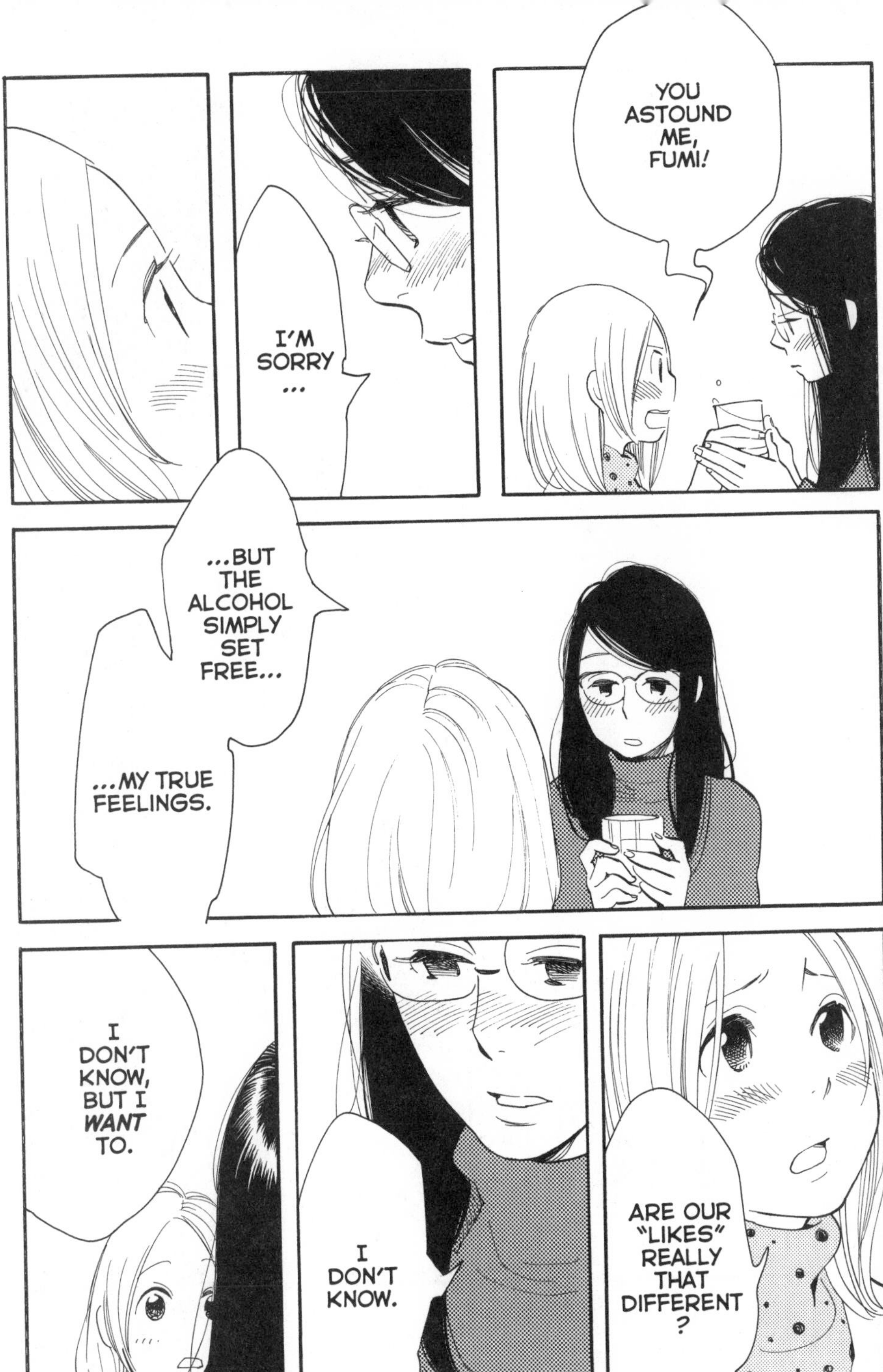
YOU ASTOUND ME, FUMI!
I'M SORRY ...
...BUT THE ALCOHOL SIMPLY SET FREE...
...MY TRUE FEELINGS.
ARE OUR "LIKES" REALLY THAT DIFFERENT?
I DON'T KNOW.
I DON'T KNOW, BUT I *WANT* TO.

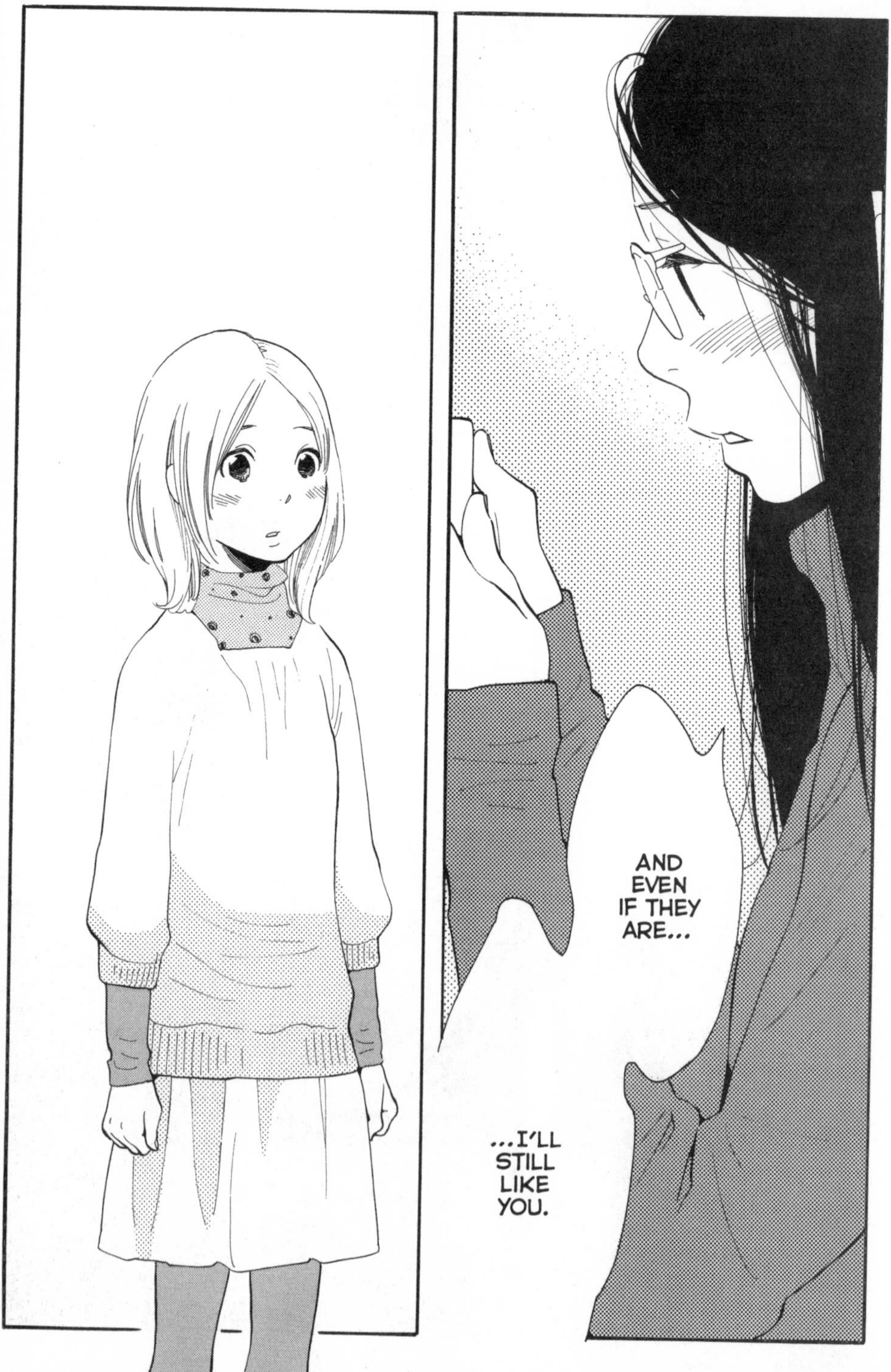
AND EVEN IF THEY ARE...
...I'LL STILL LIKE YOU.

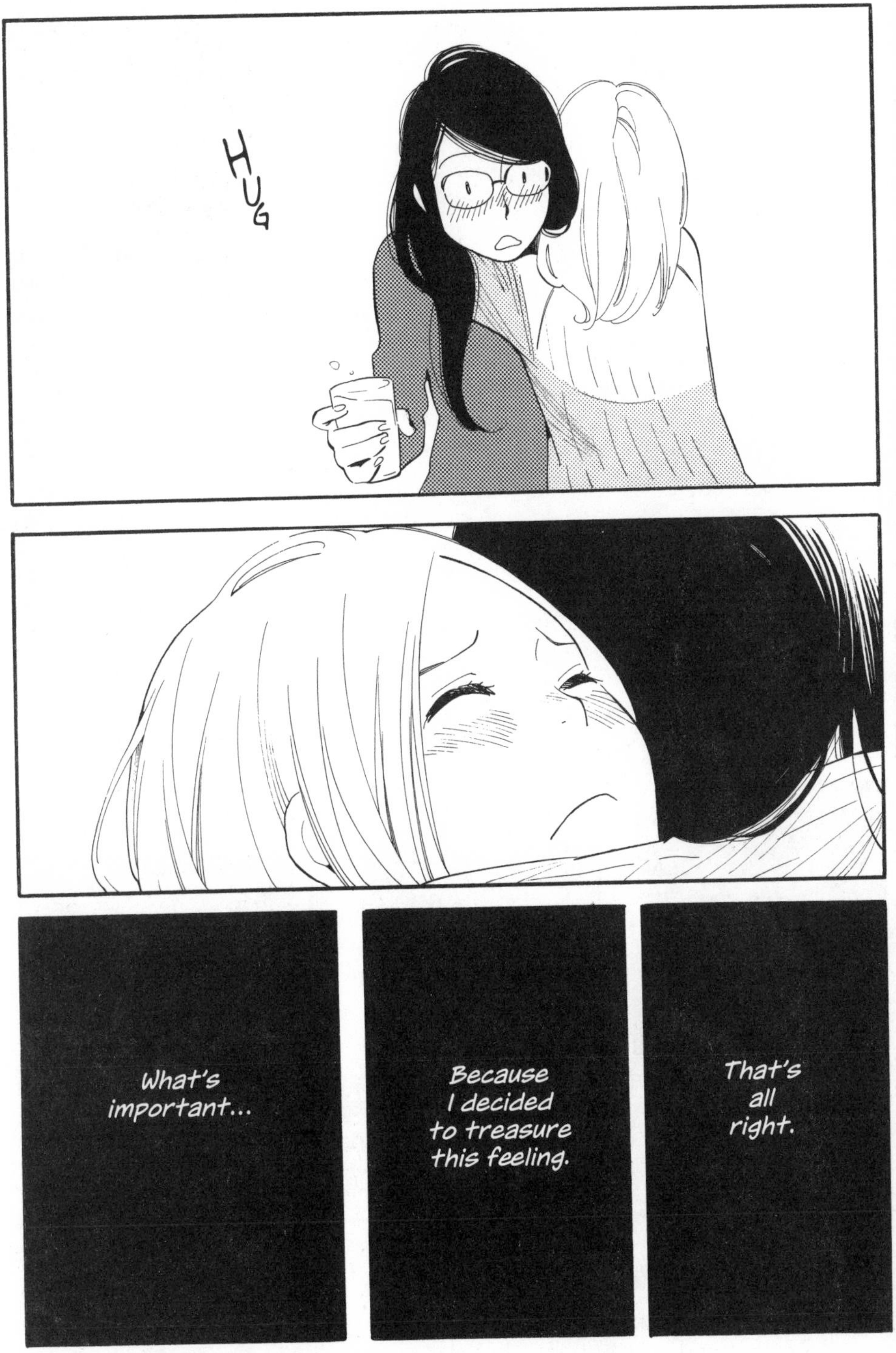
HUG
That's all right.
Because I decided to treasure this feeling.
What's important...

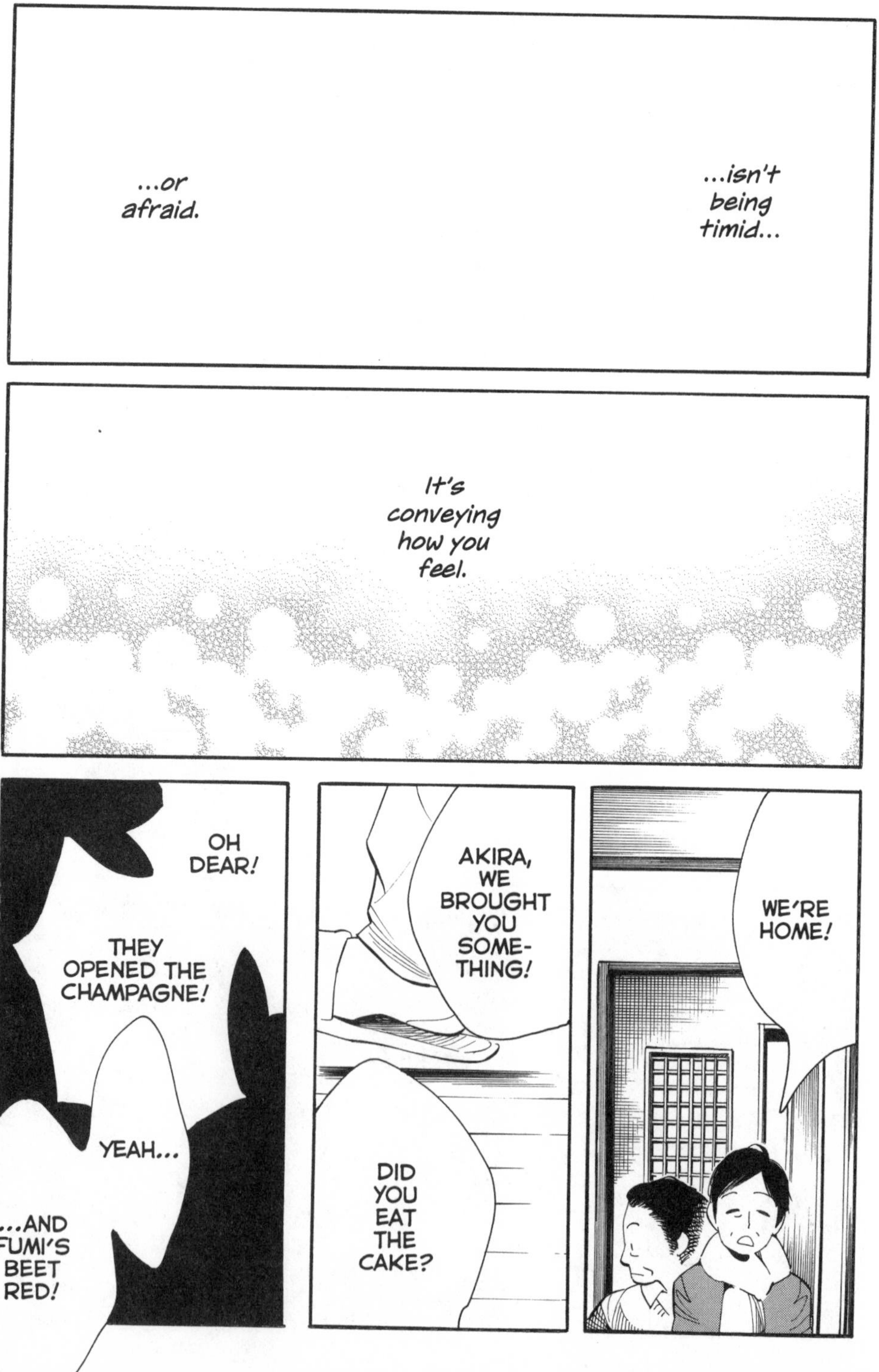
...isn't being timid...
...or afraid.
It's conveying how you feel.
WE'RE HOME!
AKIRA, WE BROUGHT YOU SOME-THING!
DID YOU EAT THE CAKE?
OH DEAR!
THEY OPENED THE CHAMPAGNE!
YEAH...
...AND FUMI'S BEET RED!

Sweet Blue Flowers

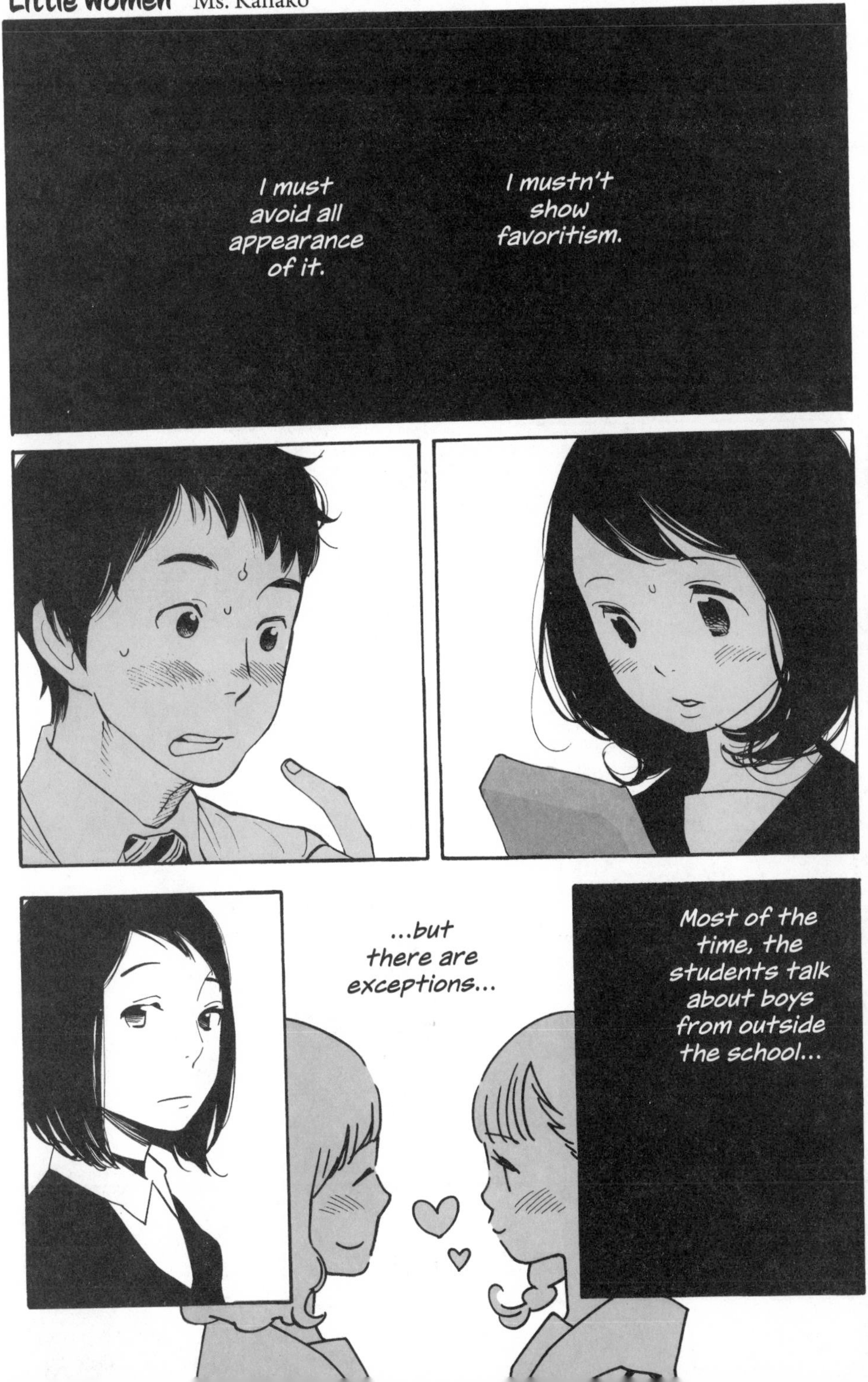
I mustn't show favoritism.
I must avoid all appearance of it.
Most of the time, the students talk about boys from outside the school...
...but there are exceptions...

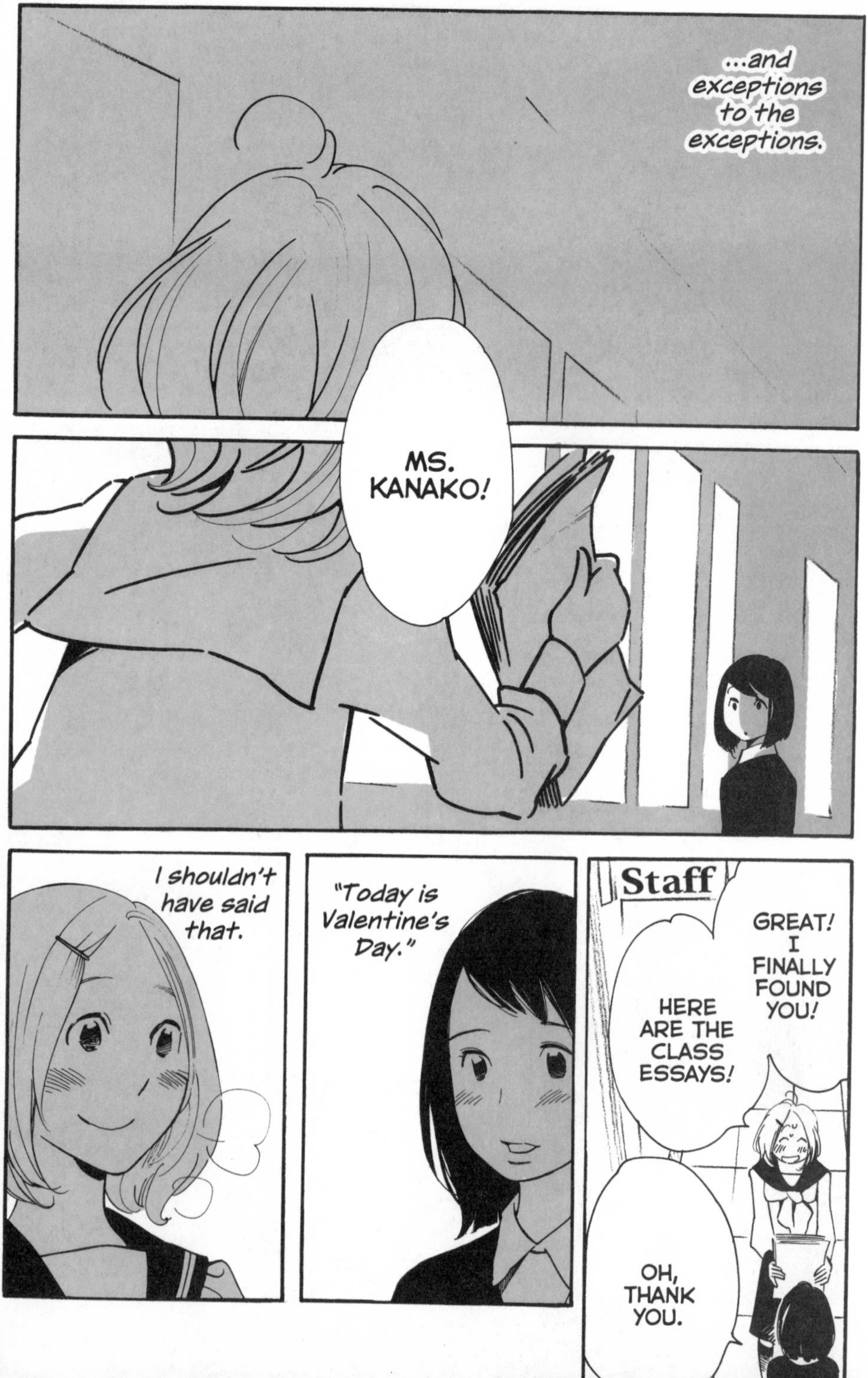
...and exceptions to the exceptions.
MS. KANAKO!
Staff
GREAT! I FINALLY FOUND YOU!
HERE ARE THE CLASS ESSAYS!
OH, THANK YOU.
"Today is Valentine's Day."
I shouldn't have said that.

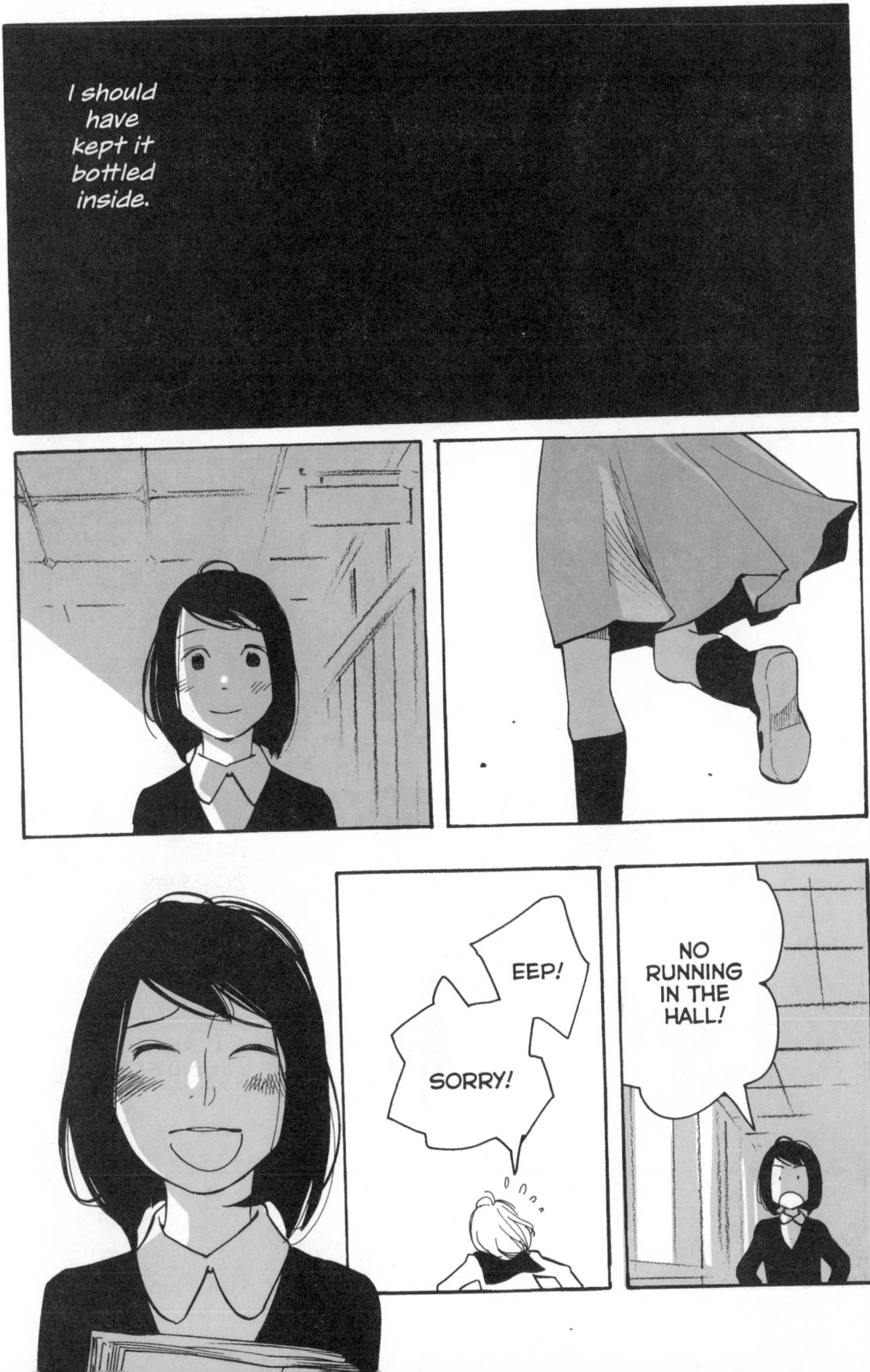
I should have kept it bottled inside.
NO RUNNING IN THE HALL!
EEP!
SORRY!

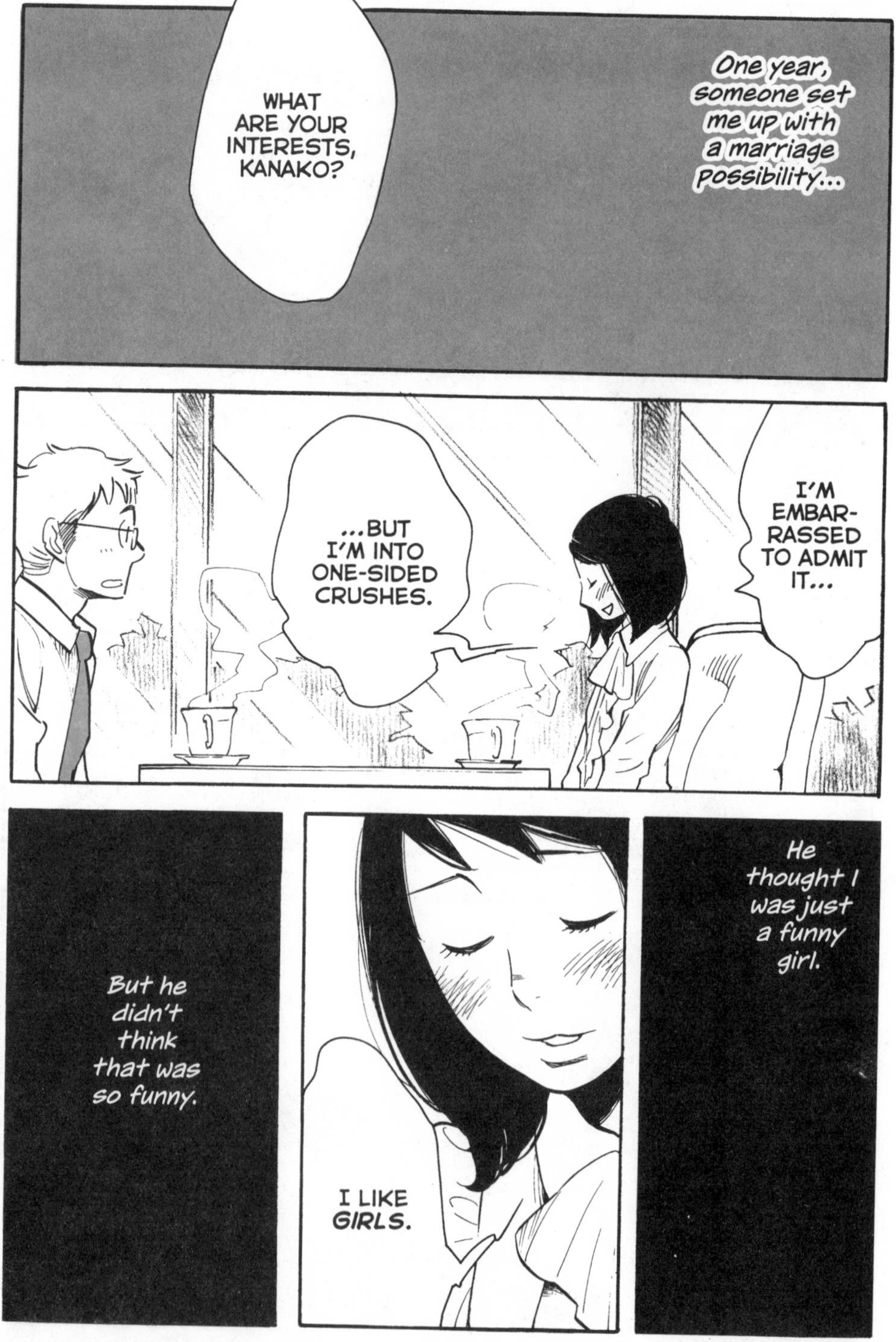
One year, someone set me up with a marriage possibility...
WHAT ARE YOUR INTERESTS, KANAKO?
I'M EMBARRASSED TO ADMIT IT...
...BUT I'M INTO ONE-SIDED CRUSHES.
He thought I was just a funny girl.
I LIKE GIRLS.
But he didn't think that was so funny.

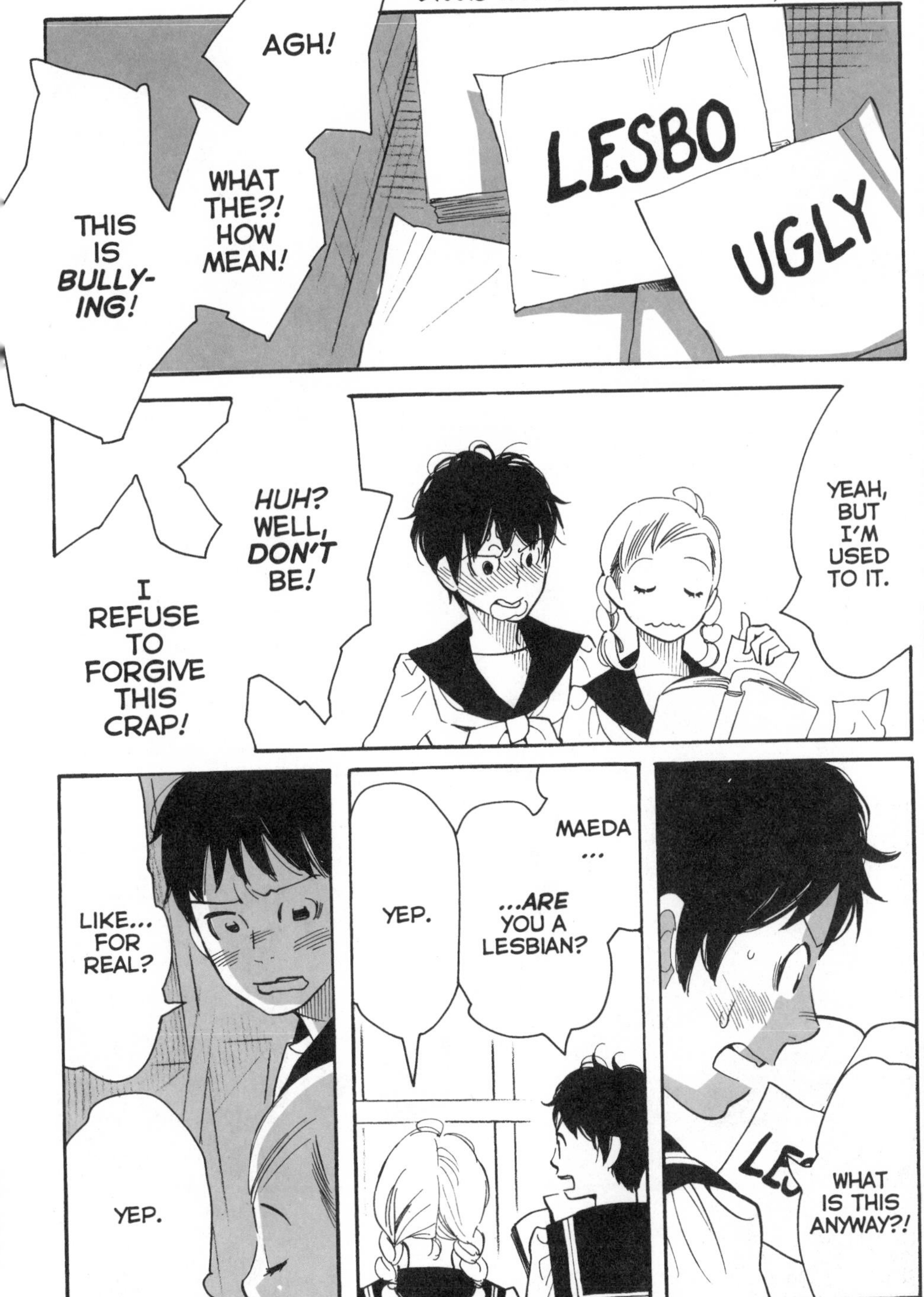
LESBO
UGLY
AGH!
WHAT THE?! HOW MEAN!
THIS IS BULLY-ING!
YEAH, BUT I'M USED TO IT.
HUH? WELL, DON'T BE!
I REFUSE TO FORGIVE THIS CRAP!
WHAT IS THIS ANYWAY?!
MAEDA...
...ARE YOU A LESBIAN?
YEP.
LIKE... FOR REAL?
YEP.

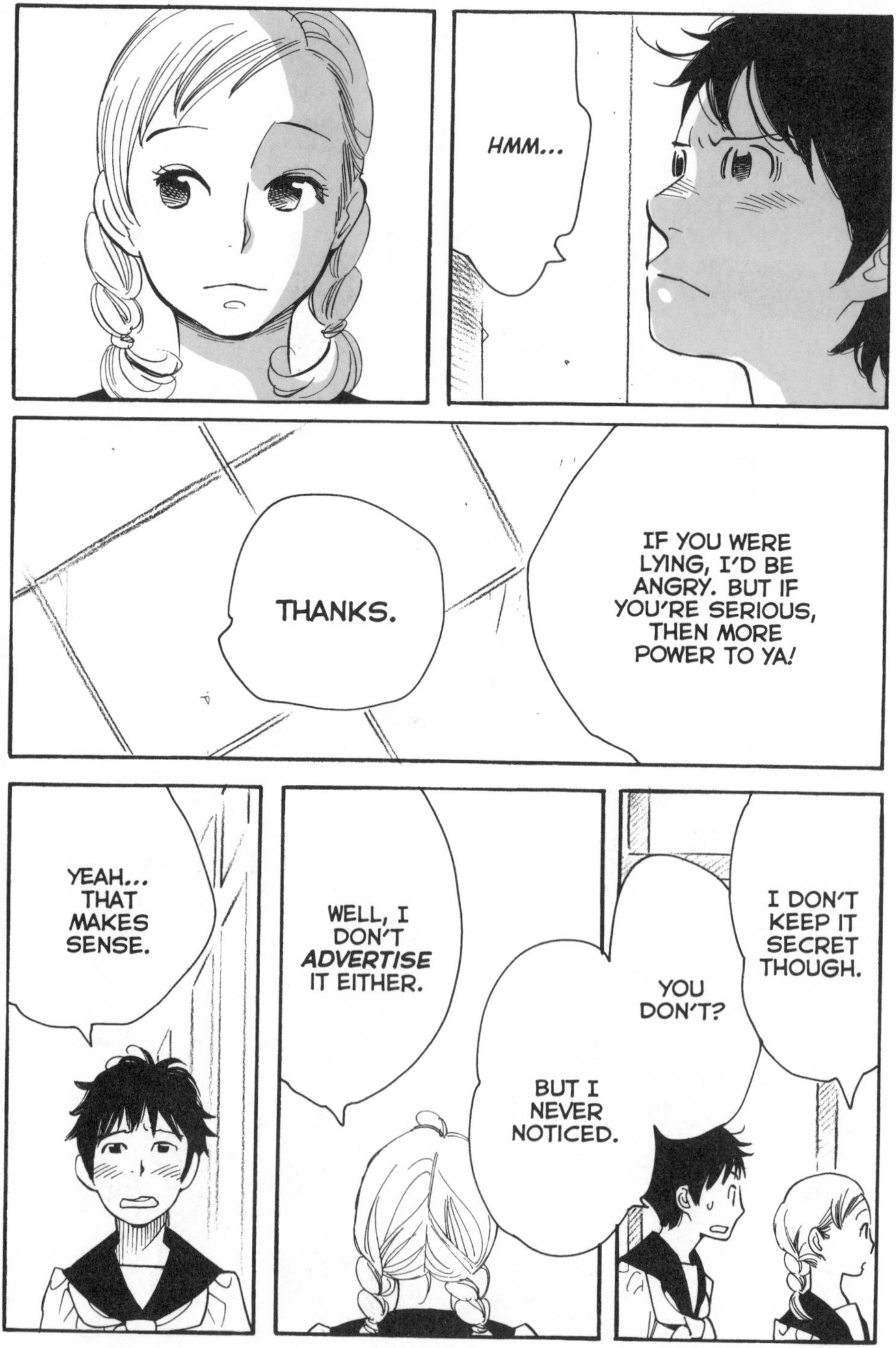
HMM...
IF YOU WERE LYING, I'D BE ANGRY. BUT IF YOU'RE SERIOUS, THEN MORE POWER TO YA!
THANKS.
I DON'T KEEP IT SECRET THOUGH.
YOU DON'T?
BUT I NEVER NOTICED.
WELL, I DON'T *ADVERTISE* IT EITHER.
YEAH... THAT MAKES SENSE.

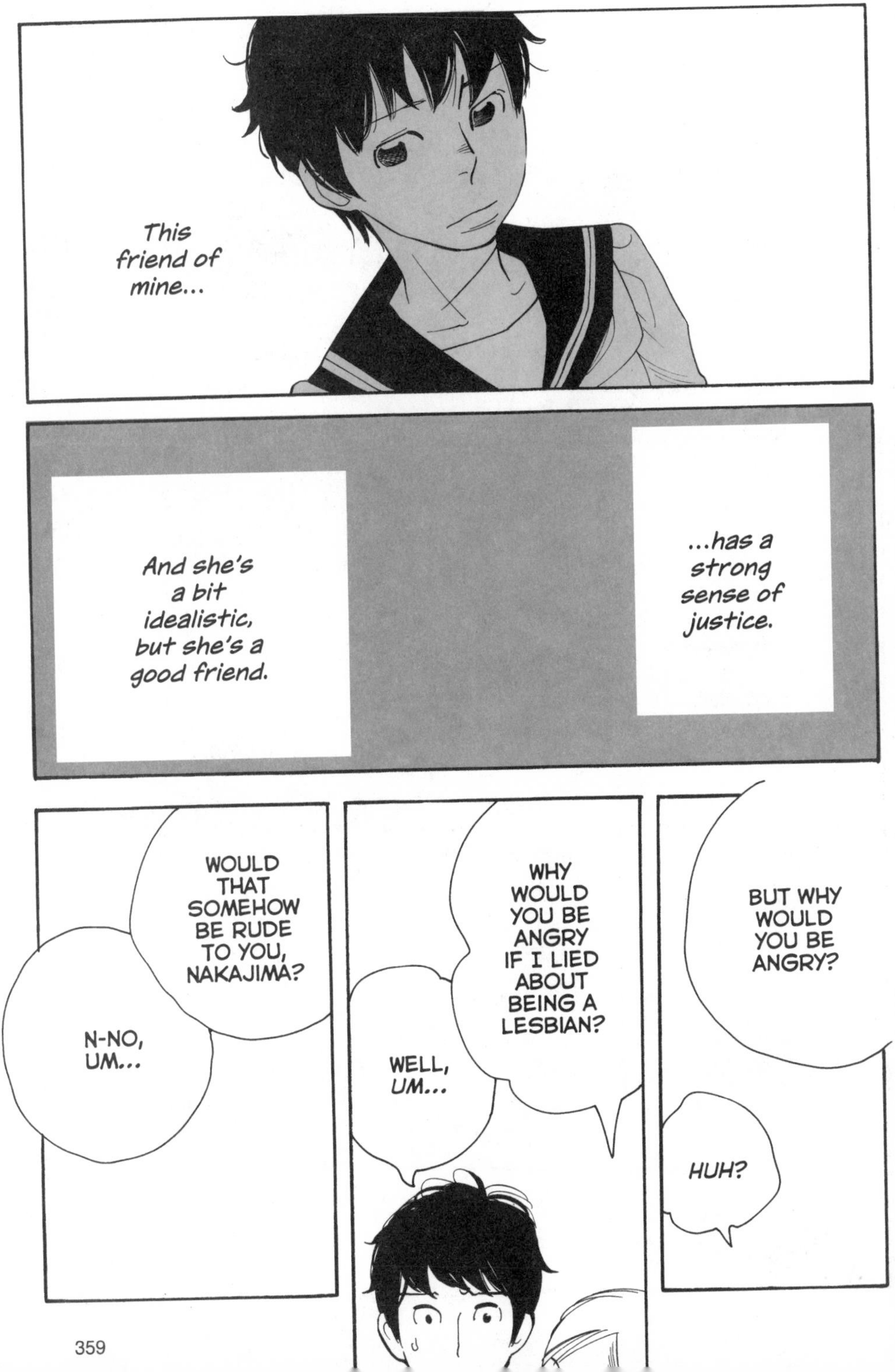
This friend of mine...
...has a strong sense of justice.
And she's a bit idealistic, but she's a good friend.
BUT WHY WOULD YOU BE ANGRY?
HUH?
WHY WOULD YOU BE ANGRY IF I LIED ABOUT BEING A LESBIAN?
WELL, UM...
WOULD THAT SOMEHOW BE RUDE TO YOU, NAKAJIMA?
N-NO, UM...

DON'T WORRY. I'M USED TO DISCRIMINATION.

NO, THAT'S NOT IT!

...THAT ISN'T WHAT I MEANT!

I don't mind at all if I get bullied by people who mean nothing to me...

SORRRY

...and I can't help teasing girls I like.

Sweet Blue
Flowers

End Notes

Page 10, panel 1: The Bamboo Cutter
A Japanese folktale, also known as "The Tale of Princess Kaguya," about an old bamboo cutter who finds a baby moon princess in a glowing bamboo stump.

Page 10, panel 1: The Izu Dancer
A short story about the memory of early love written in 1928 by Nobel Prize-winning Japanese author Yasunari Kawabata.

Page 74, panel 2: Obi
The wide sashes worn as belts around kimono.

Chapter 31: The Door into Summer
The title of a book by Robert Heinlein.

Chapter 35: A Planet in Love
The English translation of the Japanese title of the Wong Kar-wai film *Chungking Express.*

Chapter 37: The Lily of the Valley
A novel by Honoré de Balzac.

Page 196, panel 3: Yosegi
Yosegi-zaiku is a type of traditional Japanese parquetry, or ornate wooden inlay.

Page 313, panel 5: Kotatsu
A low, wooden table frame that houses a heater and is covered by a heavy quilt.

Page 332, panel 6: Kokeshi Dolls
Peg-shaped dolls from northern Japan.

Page 332, panel 6: Tengui Cloths
A thin Japanese hand cloth that can be used for a variety of purposes, including wrapping gifts.